The Cambridge Anthology of British Medieval Latin
Volume II: 1066–1500

This anthology presents in two volumes a series of Latin texts (with English translation) produced in Britain during the period AD 450–1500. Excerpts are taken from Bede and other historians, from the letters of women written from their monasteries, from famous documents such as Domesday Book and Magna Carta, and from accounts and legal documents, all revealing the lives of individuals at home and on their travels across Britain and beyond. It offers an insight into Latin writings on many subjects, showing the important role of Latin in the multilingual society of medieval Britain, in which Latin was the primary language of written communication and record and also developed, particularly after the Norman Conquest, through mutual influence with English and French. The thorough introductions to each volume provide a broad overview of the linguistic and cultural background, while the individual texts are placed in their social, historical and linguistic context.

Carolinne White was a member of the Faculty of Classics at the University of Oxford. She collaborated on the *Dictionary of Medieval Latin from British Sources*, completed in 2013, is the author of *Christian Ideas of Friendship in the Fourth Century* (1992) and has translated *Early Christian Lives* (1997), *The Rule of Benedict* (2007) and *Lives of Roman Christian Women* (2010) for Penguin Classics.

Catherine Conybeare is Leslie Clark Professor in the Humanities at Bryn Mawr College, Pennsylvania. She is an authority on the Latin texts of late antiquity, and is the author of five books, most recently *Augustine the African* (2024). She is also the editor of a new series for Cambridge University Press, Cultures of Latin.

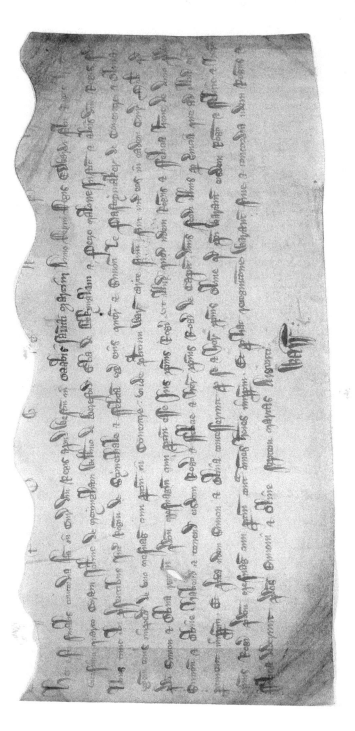

Example from 1296 of the Feet of Fines documents (Pedes finium) used in the conveyancing of property: after the agreement (*finalis concordia*) was recorded in triplicate, the bottom ('foot') of the document was cut off along a wavy line (the origin of the English word 'indenture') through the word CHIROGRAPHUM written across the document. The 'foot' was retained in the treasury, while the two halves of the remaining document were given to each of the parties. In the case of later dispute, the three parts could be aligned to check for forgery. In this example, the names of one of the parties, Simon Le Pasteymaker from Coventry, and his wife Olivia, can be seen in the third line, providing the earliest evidence of the English word 'pasty'. See Sections II.26B and II.28A. TNA: CP25/1/245/35(20). Permission given by the National Archives, London.

THE CAMBRIDGE ANTHOLOGY OF BRITISH MEDIEVAL LATIN
VOLUME II
1066–1500

Carolinne White
University of Oxford

With Foreword by
Catherine Conybeare
Bryn Mawr College, Pennsylvania

Shaftesbury Road, Cambridge CB2 8EA, United Kingdom

One Liberty Plaza, 20th Floor, New York, NY 10006, USA

477 Williamstown Road, Port Melbourne, VIC 3207, Australia

314–321, 3rd Floor, Plot 3, Splendor Forum, Jasola District Centre, New Delhi – 110025, India

103 Penang Road, #05–06/07, Visioncrest Commercial, Singapore 238467

Cambridge University Press is part of Cambridge University Press & Assessment, a department of the University of Cambridge.

We share the University's mission to contribute to society through the pursuit of education, learning and research at the highest international levels of excellence.

www.cambridge.org
Information on this title: www.cambridge.org/9781107186576

DOI: 10.1017/9781316890738

© Cambridge University Press & Assessment 2024

This publication is in copyright. Subject to statutory exception and to the provisions of relevant collective licensing agreements, no reproduction of any part may take place without the written permission of Cambridge University Press & Assessment.

First published 2024

A catalogue record for this publication is available from the British Library

ISBN – 2 Volume Set 978-1-316-63729-6   Hardback
ISBN – Volume I 978-1-107-18651-4   Hardback
ISBN – Volume II 978-1-107-18657-6   Hardback

Cambridge University Press & Assessment has no responsibility for the persistence or accuracy of URLs for external or third-party internet websites referred to in this publication and does not guarantee that any content on such websites is, or will remain, accurate or appropriate.

Contents

List of Maps   x
Foreword   xi
List of Abbreviations   xv

Introduction   1

ELEVENTH CENTURY

II.1   The Battle of Hastings and Its Aftermath   33
A.   The Bayeux Tapestry   33
B.   William of Malmesbury, *A History of the English Kings*   36
C.   Orderic Vitalis, *An Ecclesiastical History*   40

II.2   Two Charters of William the Conqueror   44

II.3   Goscelin of Canterbury, *The Book of Consolation*   48

II.4   The Domesday Book of 1086   55
A.   Henry of Huntingdon, *A History of the English*   56
B.   Richard FitzNigel, *The Dialogue of the Exchequer*   57
C.   The Domesday Book   60

II.5   *The Life of St Swithun*: the Miracle of the Broken Eggs   68
A.   Anonymous I, from the Prose *Life of St Swithun*   68
B.   Anonymous II, *A Poem on the Miracle of the Broken Eggs*   70

II.6   *The Life of St Birinus*   74
A.   Anonymous (Prose)   74
B.   Henry of Avranches (Verse)   78

II.7   St Anselm of Canterbury   83
A.   *Letter* to His Friend Gundulf   83
B.   *Proslogion*   86

TWELFTH CENTURY

II.8   Eadmer, *The Life of Archbishop Anselm*   95

II.9   Sæwulf, *An Account of a Pilgrimage to Jerusalem*   100

II.10   Twelfth-Century Law Codes   106
A.   *Quadripartitus*   107
B.   *The Laws of Henry I*   108

vi Contents

II.11 The Wreck of the White Ship in 1120, as Recorded by Historians of the Twelfth Century 111
A. Eadmer, *A History of Recent Events in England* 113
B. William of Malmesbury, *A History of the English Kings* 115
C. Orderic Vitalis, *An Ecclesiastical History* 120
D. Symeon of Durham, *A History of the English and Danish Kings* 126
E. Hugh the Chanter, *A History of the Church at York* 129
F. Henry of Huntingdon, *Contempt for the World* 130

II.12 Geoffrey of Monmouth, *A History of the Kings of Britain* 134

II.13 Two Twelfth-Century Lives of St Frideswide 142
A. *Vita* A 143
B. *Vita* B 146

II.14 Ælred of Rievaulx, *Letter Regarding the Nun of Watton Priory* 150

II.15 William Fitzstephen, *A Description of London* 164

II.16 Thomas Becket 173
A. Correspondence between Thomas Becket and the Empress Matilda 173
B. The Murder of Becket in Canterbury Cathedral: Two Eyewitness Accounts 179

II.17 Glanvill, *The Laws and Customs of the Kingdom of England* 190

II.18 Richard of Devizes, *Chronicle of the Reign of King Richard I* 197

II.19 Walter Map, *Courtiers' Trifles* 203

II.20 Hugh Nonant, Bishop of Coventry, *Letter* Recounting the Spectacular Downfall of Chancellor William de Longchamp 209

THIRTEENTH CENTURY

II.21 Gerald of Wales 219
A. *An Account of Gerald's Achievements* 220
B. *The Jewel of the Church* 223

II.22 Jocelin of Brakelond, *The Chronicle of the Deeds of Abbot Samson* 228

II.23 Scientific Teaching of the Twelfth Century 235
A. Adelard of Bath, *Questions on Natural Science* 235
B. *The Salernitan Questions* 237

II.24 Matthew Paris, *The Major Chronicles*: King John Offers His Kingdom to the Caliph of Morocco 241

II.25 Magna Carta 247

Contents vii

II.26 Roger de Montbegon: a Life in Administrative Documents 252

II.27 Edmund of Abingdon 261
A. *Speculum religiosorum* (Latin original: thirteenth century); *Mirour de seinte Eglyse* (French translation: thirteenth century); *Speculum Ecclesiae* (translation from French into Latin: fourteenth century); *The Myrrour of seynte Edmonde* (translation from French into English: fourteenth century) 262
B. *Speculum religiosorum* (Latin original: thirteenth century); *Speculum Ecclesie* (French translation: fourteenth century) 265

II.28 The Study of Latin and Other Languages 267
A. John of Garland, *Dictionary* 267
B. Alexander Neckam, *The Priest at the Altar* 273
C. Roger Bacon, *The Usefulness of Studying Languages* 276

II.29 A Miracle Associated with St John of Beverley: a Boy Falls from the Minster Roof 284

II.30 The 1297 Visitation of Chiswick Church by the Authorities of St Paul's Cathedral 289

FOURTEENTH CENTURY

II.31 King Edward I, *Letter* to Pope Boniface VIII on Relations between England and Scotland 295

II.32 The Trial of Alice Kyteler on a Charge of Witchcraft 299

II.33 John of Gaddesden, an Operation to Remove a Cataract, from *Rosa Anglica* 304

II.34 Historians of the Fourteenth Century 309
A. Henry Knighton, *Chronicle* 309
B. Thomas Walsingham, *The Major Chronicles* 312

II.35 Wills of Lay Men and Women 318
A. Three Yorkshire Wills of the Late Fourteenth Century 319
B. A London Will of the Fifteenth Century 321

FIFTEENTH CENTURY

II.36 Duke Humfrey Sets Up Home: the King's Grant of Furniture to His Son 327

II.37 The *Pennal Letter* from Owain Glyndŵr, Prince of Wales, to the King of France 330

viii Contents

II.38 Sermon Writing 335
A. Thomas of Chobham, *Sermon* 23 for Palm Sunday 336
B. A Macaronic Sermon in Latin and English 339
C. A Ghost Story from a Preacher's Commonplace Book 344

II.39 An Heir Proves He Can Inherit: Oral Testimony of Witnesses in Proof of Age Texts 347

II.40 A Woman Is Tried for Heresy at Norwich: a Court Record 352

II.41 Military Historiography 357
A. The Battle of Bannockburn (1314) in the *Chronicle of Lanercost* 357
B. The Siege of Harfleur and the Battle of Agincourt (1415) in *The Deeds of Henry V*; Thomas Elmham's *Metrical Book on Henry V*; Titus Livius, *The Life of Henry V*; Ps.-Elmham, *The Life and Deeds of Henry V* 360
C. The Battle of Bosworth Field (1485) in Polydore Vergil's *English History* 374

II.42 A Miracle Associated with King Henry VI: a Painful Football Injury Is Healed 378

II.43 The Black Death and Its Effects 382
A. Henry Knighton, *Chronicle* 382
B. *The Ordinance of Labourers* of 1349 388

II.44 Forest Documents 392
A. Richard FitzNigel, *The Dialogue of the Exchequer* 393
B. A Letter of Mandate from Waleran de Beaumont, Count of Meulan 394
C. *The Charter of the Forest* 397
D. A Plea of the Forest Regarding the Taking of a Deer 401
E. The King Grants Firewood to His Daughter 404

II.45 Manorial and Agricultural Documents 407
A. The Cartulary of St Peter's, Gloucester 407
B. Estate Management in the Letters of Ralph Neville and Simon of Senliz 409
C. The Custumals of Battle Abbey 413
D. *Fleta* on the Role of the Reeve of the Manor 416
E. Records of Elton Manor: the Reeve's Accounts 420
F. Assessment of the Royal Estates in the Channel Islands 424

II.46 Town Life and Trade: Administrative Documents 427
A. Newcastle upon Tyne: an Early Municipal Charter 427
B. Sourcing Food for the King 431
C. Records of Leicester: a Guild Meeting 432
D. The King Settles the Price of Wine in London 434
E. Imports and Exports: Customs Accounts 435

Contents   ix

II.47 Buildings: Construction and Reparation   439
A.   Gervase of Canterbury on the Destruction by Fire and the Rebuilding of Canterbury Cathedral in 1174   439
B.   Fire Regulations in London after the Great Fire of Southwark, 1212   445
C.   Refurbishment and Repairs at Windsor Castle and at Westminster Abbey   448
D.   Repairing the Clock on the Tower at Westminster Palace   451
E.   Building a Merchant's House in the City of London: the Builder's Contract   454

II.48 Royal and Ecclesiastical Accounts   459
A.   Liberate Roll Payments for the King's Bear at the Tower of London   460
B.   Countess Eleanor's Accounts for the de Montfort Household   461
C.   Accounts of Everyday Expenditure at the Priory of Durham   465
D.   Royal Household Expenditure: the Wardrobe Book of William de Norwell   467
E.   An Account Entry from the Scottish Exchequer Rolls   471

II.49 In the Courts   474
A.   Two Entries from the Curia Regis Rolls: Alice Takes on the Bishop of Lincoln in a Property Dispute; Flemish Merchants Take Two Jewish Men to Court on a Charge of Assault and Robbery   474
B.   Ecclesiastical Suit Rolls: Litigation with Reference to Sex and Marriage   480
C.   Gaol Delivery Rolls   484
D.   The Assize of Bread at the Guildhall   487

II.50 Safeguarding, Accidents and Death   491
A.   The Bishops' Safeguarding Advice for Mothers and Babies: Statutes of Church Councils of the Thirteenth Century   491
B.   Reports of Accidental Deaths in Various Sources: a Miracle Associated with Thomas Becket; Assize Rolls; Curia Regis Rolls; Coroners' Rolls   495

Select Bibliography for Volume II   505

Indexes
  General Index   510
  Index of Passages Cited   516

Map

1 Britain in the later Middle Ages.   xvii

Foreword

No less an authority than the classical philologist Ulrich von Wilamowitz-Moellendorff wrote to his former student Schadewaldt, 'I have never been able to make a start with the word "classic", which is an abomination to me.' The letter was destroyed with the rest of Schadewaldt's books and papers during the Second World War, but it had made such a deep impression on its recipient that he had memorised it.

'Abomination': *ein Greuel*. The word suggests horror or loathing. No wonder Schadewaldt was shocked. He was a classical philologist himself, and had just sent Wilamowitz the offprint of a paper entitled 'Concept and Essence of the Ancient Classic'. In his letter, Wilamowitz seems to be implying that the term 'classic' is vapid and contentless. It has no meaning; there is certainly no 'essence of the classic'.

Some twenty-first-century scholars find the term 'classic' an abomination too, but for the opposite reason: that 'classic' and 'the classics' have accrued an unmerited superfluity of meaning, a hegemonic overload that crushes other histories, other languages, other points of view. Latin and Greek writings and thought and, above all, language were considered to be at their acme in specific times and places – Periclean Athens, late republican and early imperial Rome – and developed a nimbus of superiority that placed them at the heart of the European educational curriculum for centuries. Conversely, Latin and Greek from later periods were dubbed inferior, and most philologists disdained to give them proper attention.

The object of the current critique of 'the classics' is above all the way in which they have been used to support not just a narrative of colonisation, but the violent practice of colonisation itself. The hegemony of European powers and their expansionist ambitions relied on a project of 'civilisation' which necessitated constructing the lands and peoples they wished to appropriate as savage, ignorant and immune to history – in short, 'uncivilised'. The ultimate test of 'civilisation' was knowledge of the classics; its goal was the spread of Christianity. Hegel wrote of Africa that 'it is no historical part of the world; it has no movement or development to exhibit'. His deeper point, which distilled the assumptions of an era well beyond his own, was that Africa by its very nature simply could not have a history in any cognisable sense. On this conclusion lay the justification for the cruel movement of the slave trade. As the principal recipient of the enslaved, the United States was in no way exempt from this harsh logic. Slaveholders used arguments from classics to justify the notion that their human property was, in fact, less than human. If a human was a rational mortal animal, and the rationality of enslaved people was not acknowledged, then they were not human either. In every arena of European expansion – the British incursion into India, for example, that of the Spanish and Portuguese into South America – the cultural tools

xii Foreword

of domination were the classics and the Bible. The present discipline of classics is haunted by its violent and domineering past.

In terms of the longevity of classics, however, this past is a relatively recent one. These volumes remind us that there is a deeper history to classics which is obscured by the long-running fantasy of the classical. Specifically, Latin continued to be written, spoken, loved or loathed long after the 'classical' period; it continued to shape and be shaped by the cultures in which it was used. The fetishisation of a particular period as authentically classical, and the construction of the discipline to celebrate a particular notion of classicism, has destroyed that sense of continuity. This does a radical disservice to the cultural and literary continuities into the Middle Ages and to the copious textual traces that the medieval period has left us. It ensures that medieval writings are repeatedly dismissed as inferior. Some scholars today write of the need to 'decolonise' classics; though that is an urgent impulse, it is only part of the story. The classical has not always been an agent of colonisation. In Winchester in the ninth century, or Paris in the twelfth, or Vercelli in the fourteenth, for example, Latin was above all a language to think with. It was not complicit with empire in the ways we have come to deplore.

The discipline of classics is a significant part of our history – the history of Western Europe, that is, and subsequently of all those parts of the globe that Western Europe touched with intent to colonise and edify. We cannot simply ignore its existence. But we need to analyse and question its nimbus of superiority. And we need to prise classics apart from the narratives of colonisation. One way to do that is to retell that entangled recent history with proper attention to the extraordinary power dynamics involved. But another way is dramatically to rethink the purview of classics. This is the approach essayed by Carolinne White in these two volumes of British medieval Latin. As a technique, it is granular and precise and unspectacular; but the implications of the magnificent whole are far greater than the sum of its parts.

Let me list the ways in which these volumes are revolutionary and show how radically they expand the notion of 'classics'.

First, geography. In some ways, to speak of 'British medieval Latin' is to retroject modern national boundaries artificially into a medieval context. At the same time, Britain, by virtue of its literal insularity, offers a contained unit that enables us to explore a vast range of written culture. Its position on the edge of Europe and its contact – both peaceful and enforced – with Celtic and Breton cultures to the west and south and Nordic ones to the north-east makes its language development excitingly distinctive. After the Norman invasion of 1066, its language patterns change again, dramatically, and this gives an internal logic to the break between these two volumes. Moreover, while at different times there was a vibrant Latin culture and educational structure in Winchester or York or St David's or Canterbury, no one writing or reading or talking in Latin could ever have forgotten that they were geographically on the periphery of a great European tradition. Whether that gave rise to defiance or subservience, vivid invention or an anxious attempt to follow metropolitan trends or even (as with Alcuin) achievement so stellar that Europe itself was forced into imitation, the sense of being on the periphery seems always to have been stimulating and productive. It generated extraordinary works in Latin – and I use the adjective in both its positive and its negative sense.

This speaks to my second point. The works are extraordinary; so is their range, of genre, style, aspiration. The genius of these volumes lies in part in the sheer variety of Latin that they contain. We read excerpts from the textbooks that grounded Latin education for centuries; we read history, theology, hagiography, yes, but also riddles and acrostics and administrative documents. What an inspiration to start the second volume with excerpts from the Latin on the Bayeux Tapestry that told the story of the Norman Conquest. What inspiration to include charters, wills, royal grants, passages from the Domesday Book. Above all, the assortment of letters – abject or hopeful or joyous, learned or stumbling, always in their different ways reaching for connection – brings before our eyes an astonishing range of the aspirations and fears of the men and women who wrote them. We escape from the straitjacket of elite Latinities offered by the classical period, enlivened only occasionally by attention to graffiti or epigraphy. Here we have a vast array of Latinities. It includes elite Latinities, to be sure, but also plenty of non-elite writings. Once we abandon the etiolated logic of classicism, we can enjoy this incredible richness of material.

Third: in tandem with this sampling of multifarious Latinities, we hear a rich array of voices. In the texts of classical antiquity, we hardly ever hear the voices of women. But here, women are living, yearning, passionate writing presences, not just the exemplary or fetishised figures observed by the male writers of classical texts. Even – perhaps especially – in the lives of saints there is a fresh valuation of the personal and the quotidian. We see ordinary people struggling to make sense of their lives, making ad hoc decisions, noticing ordinary things. Sometimes they reach for a grand interpretative framework. Mostly they are just getting by.

There is one final way in which the hegemonic power and notional purity of 'classics' is creatively besmirched by these volumes. All the writings emerge from a context in which Christianity is the dominant religion; many of them deal explicitly with Christian ideas. Most of this is very far, however, from the self-justificatory force of nineteenth-century colonising Christianity. We read, for the most part, something much humbler, a personal and textured Christianity, something that provides basic structures and timetables for life, as well as all levels of education. For some people it is an exalted and exalting focal point. For many, it is just part of the way they manage their daily affairs. Yet again, the particularity of the passages selected here tells the story not of magisterial narratives and rationalisations but of individual struggles and small-scale dispensations.

With these two volumes, Carolinne White takes her place in the remarkable line of distinguished women who, unvalued in the institutional context of classics or simply excited by an oblique and non-traditional line of enquiry, made their

xiv Foreword

names reading and interpreting medieval Latin texts. Eleanor Shipley Duckett, Helen Waddell, Christine Mohrmann, Sister Benedicta Ward: all these and more established in their work a distinctive nexus of sound scholarship and profound engagement. They are rarely recognised as the creative giants that they were. And in these volumes, White restores to us – among other voices – some of the women on whose shoulders they stand.

Catherine Conybeare

Abbreviations

Abbreviations for the titles of texts can also be found in the bibliography to the *Dictionary of Medieval Latin from British Sources*.

ALMA	*Archivum Latinitatis medii aevi (Bulletin du Cange)*
AN	Anglo-Norman
ANTS	Anglo-Norman Text Society
ASChr	*Anglo-Saxon Chronicle*
ASE	*Anglo-Saxon England*
BACS	*British Academy Charter Series*
BBC	British Borough Charters
BHL	*Bibliotheca hagiographica Latina*
BL	British Library
BML	British Medieval Latin
CalPat	*Calendar of Patent Rolls*
CCCM	*Corpus Christianorum continuatio medievalis*
CCSL	*Corpus Christianorum series Latina*
CIPM	*Calendar of Inquisitions post mortem*
CL	Classical Latin
DB	Domesday Book
DMLBS	*Dictionary of Medieval Latin from British Sources*
EETS	Early English Text Society
EHD	*English Historical Documents*
EHR	*English Historical Review*
GCS	*Die griechische christliche Schriftsteller der ersten Jahrhunderte*
JMH	*Journal of Medieval History*
JML	*Journal of Medieval Latin*
JRS	*Journal of Roman Studies*
l.	*lege* (read)
?l.	suggested reading
LL	Late Latin, i.e. from the period between classical and medieval Latin, c.300–600
ME	Middle English, c.1200–1500
MGH	*Monumenta Germaniae Historica*
OE	Old English (used of the language of the Anglo-Saxons)
OED	*Oxford English Dictionary*
OF	Old French
OMT	Oxford Medieval Texts
PL	*Patrologia Latina* (also database)
PMLA	*Publications of the Modern Language Association of America*
RB	*Revue Bénédictine*

xvi List of Abbreviations

RC	Record Commission
RL	*Royal Letters*
RS	*Rolls Series* (also online in Cambridge Library Collection – Rolls)
s.a.	*sub anno* (indicating date in a chronicle)
s.v.	*sub verbo* (indicating lemma in a dictionary)
TNA	The National Archives
TRHS	*Transactions of the Royal Historical Society*
v.l.	*varia lectio* (variant reading)

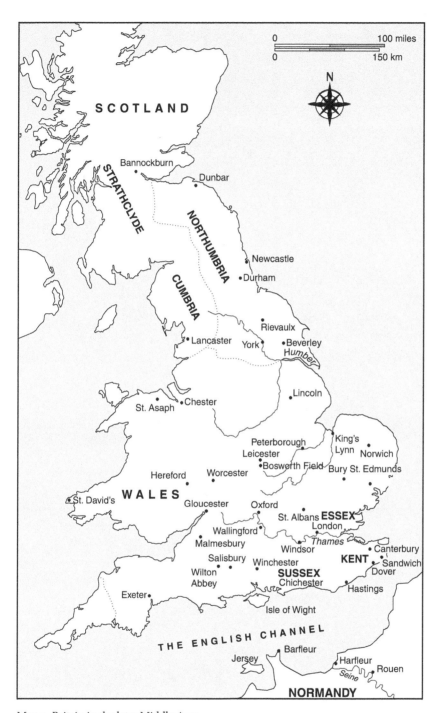

Map 1 Britain in the later Middle Ages.

Introduction

The Aims of This Volume

This volume, the second of the set, contains passages of British Latin writing from the time of the Norman Conquest in 1066 to approximately 1500, a period when Latin was used more widely and when it developed in a more or less distinct manner, depending on the type of text involved.[1] The aim, as in the first volume, is to provide a broad sample of literary (mainly prose but some verse) and documentary texts. These will include excerpts from some of the most famous historical documents, such as the Domesday Book and Magna Carta, from administrative and legal documents underpinning the society of the time, from eyewitness accounts of people and events, and from a variety of literary genres, many of them inherited from Roman and Christian antiquity. The passages are selected to demonstrate the range of social contexts, genres and registers, for the overall aim is to provide an overview of the characteristics of British medieval Latin and a degree of chronological perspective. The passages are presented against the backdrop of the *Dictionary of Medieval Latin from British Sources* (*DMLBS*), whose completion in 2013 opened the door to a more comprehensive and comparative study of the complete lexis of British medieval Latin (BML) than has hitherto been feasible. This connection means that the principal focus in the linguistic analyses of the texts will be on the vocabulary. However, beside the lexis, the syntax and morphology of the Latin can also be studied across the various authors and registers; in many of the passages included here, the reader will be able to appreciate fine sentence structures with sounds and rhythms created out of the words, constructions and clauses the author has selected.

Each year sees the production of new editions of medieval Latin texts, supplemented by handbooks and edited collections of individual essays on particular themes in this area of scholarship. Few of these engage with the nature of the language, apart from some recent editions of Latin texts, e.g. in the Oxford Medieval Texts or *Corpus Christianorum* series, which might include a short section on the style and language of the author. However, scholars such as Jacques Fontaine, Pascale Bourgain and Peter Stotz have realised the need to overturn longstanding departmental barriers, and for historians and philologists to collaborate in engaging with the Latin of medieval texts.[2] There is now the opportunity to do so

---

1 For a caveat about the use of the complex and somewhat fluid terms *Britannia* and *Anglia*, see the Preface to Volume I.

2 *Fontaine (1970); *Bourgain (2005); *Stotz (1996–2004), with a section on England at 1.680–7.

2 Introduction

in the context of British Latin, taken as referring predominantly to the Latin written in England, Wales and Scotland; the *Dictionary of Medieval Latin from Celtic Sources*, being compiled in Dublin, deals mainly with the Latin written in Ireland. The study of BML should prove extremely interesting as part of the history of the Latin language across millennia, and also for the history of Anglo-Norman (the term usually applied to the Norman French dialect in England) and of English, from the first charters after the Conquest, but especially from the Domesday Book of 1086, which contains many new Latin words drawing on French and English.

Close engagement with first-hand evidence from the period allows the reader to perceive rather than preconceive. Many have been daunted by the plethora of Latin sources surviving in post-Conquest Britain and by a belief that the Latin of this period is sub-standard (judged from the viewpoint of the Latin of an earlier age), or unpalatable (as the language of power, used predominantly by a male elite).[3] However, modern bibliographical information makes it much easier to find one's way around the sources, and the sources themselves, in their variety, reveal Latin of many kinds, each suited to its context. There are examples of texts aimed at a wider audience, such as the Magna Carta, historical writings and sermons; there are also the slightly formulaic texts concerned with administration and the law, and there are writings dealing rather with technical or scientific subjects.[4]

And then there are those in which the author has greater freedom of expression and in which questions of personal style, level of education and purpose in writing come into play. An underlying aim in these volumes has been to highlight the more personal texts, and those relating to specific people and places. Although the texts may mostly be the work of male writers, of a small minority within the population as a whole, in many of the passages it is possible to glimpse details of the lives of thousands of men, women and children, often named individuals who were not members of the elite: the world of BML is more open and diverse than it is given credit for. The texts fascinate, too, because of the frequent mention of place names that tie the people and events to specific locations, in town or countryside, from castles to villages, churches and particular features of

---

3 Condemnation through condescension is not limited to medieval Latin; for equivalent comments applied to regional Koine Greek, cf. T. V. Evans (2020) 'Not overstrong in his Greek: modern interpretation of "Egyptian" Greek texts in the Zenon archive' in *Papers in ancient Greek linguistics*, ed. M. Leiwo, M. Vierros and S. Dahlgren, Helsinki.

4 A few passages from such writings have been included in this volume, but the decision has been taken to leave to others the linguistic investigation of works whose subject matter is so specialised that it requires a dense commentary even in English translation, or works in which neither the Latin nor the content is distinguished as peculiarly British. These would include many of the philosophical and theological works written in Britain: readers interested in the works of such writers as Duns Scotus, Ockham and Wyclif, or less well-known ones, are advised to consult the *DMLBS* bibliography or the list of authors in *Sharpe (1997), both of which also include Latin works that are as yet unedited.

the landscape, most of which can be located and explored today. The topographical information can itself be helpful in analysing the language in which it occurs and thereby providing clues as to the inhabitants of a specific place at a particular time.[5]

The Linguistic Background to British Medieval Latin after the Conquest

The Norman Conquest changed the course of British society in many ways as William the Conqueror introduced powerful elements of Norman French culture into a society that had already combined British Celtic, Anglo-Saxon and Norse (Viking) elements.[6] Since the beginning of the seventh century British society had predominantly used Latin (initially the language of the Roman settlers until the Romans departed in the fifth century and then the language of the Roman Church) and the language of the Anglo-Saxons (English) for writing.

Soon after the Conquest comes one of the surprising developments that will be noted during this period. The Normans do not impose their French dialect (which would also have contained elements of other dialects, as well as a few terms from Norse, brought into Normandy by the Vikings when they settled there in the tenth century) on the whole of British society, but it does remain the first language of royalty and aristocracy for about two centuries[7] and is likely to have filtered down into parts of the existing population of Britain as the result of intermarriage.[8] Anglo-Norman is also less common than Latin in written form until the second half of the thirteenth century, when it gradually became instead a non-mother tongue and predominantly a written language in a limited range of (mainly legal, governmental and educational) contexts, while maintaining a

---

5 See M. Gelling (1997) *Signposts to the past: place-names and the history of England*, 3rd ed., Chichester.

6 See *Garnett (2007) for questions of change and continuity in government. Garnett does not discuss the linguistic situation, apart from a reference to the fact that Orderic Vitalis records that King William did attempt to learn English (*HE* 2.256) *ut sine interprete querelam subiectae gentis posset intelligere* ('so that he could understand the complaints of the subject people without an interpreter').

7 Even at the end of the twelfth century the French-born Bishop Hugh of Lincoln (1186–1200) needed an interpreter to understand an English *mulier rusticana* (Adam of Eynsham, *Life of St Hugh* 5.8), possibly because of her dialect; at the same period the Chancellor of England, William de Longchamp, was said to be utterly ignorant of English (see Section II.20).

8 Both the historians William of Malmesbury (*GR* Book 3, pref.) and Orderic Vitalis, for example, had one Norman and one English parent. William believed this gave him a balanced point of view (*temperamentum dicendi*), allowing him to praise William the Conqueror's achievements without suppressing his errors.

4 Introduction

lower academic status than Latin.[9] Meanwhile, English remained the mother tongue among the majority in Britain, alongside Celtic languages such as Welsh (often referred to as *lingua Britannica*, e.g. in Gerald of Wales (*IK* 1.2) with reference to the Welsh word 'aber') in certain regions. These vernaculars do continue as literary languages, but English becomes less prominent as a written language than it had been in the Anglo-Saxon period, until the flowering of English literature in the mid-fourteenth century with the writings of Gower, Chaucer etc. and the gradual increase in the use of English in official documents. It is Latin that becomes the primary written, administrative language soon after the Conquest, while continuing as the language of the Church. In short, from around 1100, Latin, English and French developed over the following centuries not so much side by side as in a complex choreography of linguistic contact, intertwining in close intimacy, as first Latin, then French and finally English assumed the dominant cultural and linguistic role. By the third quarter of the fourteenth century, the author of the *Speculum vitae* could defend his use of English by claiming that only the educated knew Latin, apart from those who might know just a bit, while those who had lived at court might know French, but not Latin: English, however (so he claimed), was understood by all.[10]

The closeness of this contact is clear from the great extent of the borrowings between these languages, as will be explored below.[11] Such borrowings support the suggestion that Latin was a very active language that needed to extend its lexis to deal with changes in society. Certain features link the Latin of Britain to the Latin of the Continent, while others distinguish it. It definitely bears similarities to the Latin of countries where it was learned as a non-mother tongue, as was the case in Germanic regions. However, the fact that after 1066, the French dialect of Anglo-Norman was a key element in the linguistic mix of Britain suggests that BML was in some ways similar to the Latin of countries where the underlying vernacular was a Romance language. One should bear in mind that the Continental regions bordering the English Channel and North Sea were multilingual from an early stage, with strong Germanic influence on the developing Romance language.

The complexity of the linguistic situation in multilingual Britain and the amount of documentary evidence make this an attractive and intriguing period

---

9 On questions relating to Anglo-Norman, see *Ingham (2010) and (2012).

10 *Speculum vitae* (2008) ed. R. Hanna, EETS, Oxford, lines 61–78. Cf. Alfred the Great, who, in his preface to the OE translation of Gregory the Great's *Pastoral Rule*, speaks of English as 'the language we can all understand'.

11 For borrowings into English and the relation between English and Latin, see P. Durkin and S. Schad, 'The *DMLBS* and the *OED*: medieval Latin and the lexicography of English' in *Ashdowne and White (2017); P. Durkin (2020) 'The relationship of borrowing from French and Latin in the Middle English period with the development of the lexicon of Standard English' in *The multilingual origins of Standard English*, ed. L. Wright, Berlin.

for linguistic study, but these factors do mean that one should beware of generalisations, repeated from one generation of scholars to the next without reference to the sources.[12]

The Sources of the Texts

The passages in this volume derive from such sources as administrative documents and from manuscripts preserved mainly in archives and libraries throughout Britain, and occasionally elsewhere in Europe and in the United States. Large numbers of administrative documents were preserved for centuries at Westminster and in the Tower of London and then transferred to the Public Record Office, and in 2004 to the National Archives at Kew in London. Most of these documents can be consulted, and many have been published over the last two hundred years (or at least calendared, i.e. summarised in English, to assist historians), but work continues on making more available in printed and digital form. Meanwhile there remain texts in manuscripts, especially among the philosophical and theological writings of the thirteenth and fourteenth centuries, that await editing and publication, for which library catalogues can be supplemented by *Sharpe (1997), providing basic information about editions, or the lack of them. The majority of the texts in this volume have been selected from printed editions. The accompanying translations are, however, the work of this editor.

Communication and Record

These medieval texts were primarily intended to communicate and to record. Written works were needed to an even greater degree in British society in the post-Conquest period as communication became enormously important, between the king and his officers, between the pope and the members of his Church, between individuals collaborating on some project or seeking to inform others of important events, and of course between instructors and learners. Record became increasingly part of everyday life as the royal administrative machine expanded from the late twelfth century to deal with every walk of life, requiring royal writs and charters, statutes and accounts, as well as a wide range of legal decisions to be recorded, as Michael Clanchy made clear in his book *From Memory to Written Record*. Monastic houses also produced historical works, recording their own history as well as local and national events. The sophistication and effectiveness of these systems, lasting for centuries, indicate that the linguistic skills of those com-

---

12 Cf. Gervase of Canterbury, *Gesta regum* 2.60 and Ralph Higden, *Polychronicon* 2.156–62, for medieval perspectives on the post-Conquest linguistic situation.

6 Introduction

municating and recording were usually of a high order: those writing Latin would hardly have continued to do so in the ways that developed after the Conquest if their Latin had failed in its purpose. Nevertheless, sufficient texts survive to allow us also to perceive misunderstandings which may only be apparent, sometimes occasioned by similarities between different languages or within one language, and this can be of interest in itself. An example of the linguistic complexity is the fact that CL *scamnum*, meaning a bench, also occurs in the sense of 'embankment' (Section II.10): in this case the Latin equivalent for AN 'banc' ('stool' or 'bench') has been given the sense of the English 'bank', both of which had in fact developed from the same early Germanic word.

The Writers of These Texts: Gaining an Education

So who was writing these texts? While Latin may have been learned as a first language by some in Britain during the period of Roman settlement in the first four centuries of the common era, once the Romans withdrew it was largely the Celtic and then Anglo-Saxon vernaculars that remained as the native languages of the inhabitants of Britain. When Latin was in effect reintroduced into England on the arrival of Augustine of Canterbury's mission from Rome in 597, it was now learned as a second language (L2), through the education provided primarily by churches and monasteries, but also in the home and by schoolmasters, often priests, who might teach the children of the parish.[13] In the early Middle Ages the emphasis was on an ability to recite and read the Scriptures, starting with the Psalms. The next stage was to understand the language of the Bible, and to write, using the Bible (rich in stories and as a source of metaphors and allegories) and the writings of the Church Fathers. This education was supplemented by those texts of classical literature that were accepted as part of the curriculum to be grammatical models and sources of a wide vocabulary, but also, at higher levels, to teach rhetorical skills admired by writers of antiquity. By the twelfth century, access to education was increasing at all levels and a more secular syllabus was also available, as outlined in Alexander Neckam's work *The Priest at the Altar* (see Section II.28B).[14] Roger Bacon appears to indicate (*Tert.* 10 p. 34) that many lay people could speak Latin well without the use of grammar books: this no doubt allowed them to understand more than they could compose in written

---

13 Cf. Gilbert of Sempringham, who taught *scolaria rudimenta* and *morales et monasticae disciplinae* ('basic school subjects' and 'moral and monastic teaching') to boys and girls in Lincolnshire (*The Book of St Gilbert* 3); also W. Cant. *Mir. Thom.* 5.30, where a five-year-old girl, whose parents send her to school for a good education, is stabbed with a penknife, but healed by praying to Thomas Becket.

14 Cf. J. Murphy (2005) 'The teaching of Latin as a second language in the twelfth century' in *Latin rhetoric and education in the Middle Ages and Renaissance*, Aldershot.

Latin.[15] After a basic education in literacy, children who had not been entrusted to the monastic life might move to the household of a high-ranking secular or ecclesiastical person to continue their education, learning to use their Latin for administrative purposes to fill the increasing number of posts in this field. It is striking how many of the celebrated writers of the late twelfth and early thirteenth centuries had been educated in this way. As a further step in their education, some, like John of Salisbury and Walter Map in the twelfth century, might go to Paris for a few years, to attend the nascent university there before returning to England: John of Salisbury later took the post of personal secretary of Thomas Becket, while Walter Map worked for King Henry II, while others, especially in the thirteenth century, returned to teach, for example at Oxford University.

Increasingly, no doubt, clerks would be trained by means of an apprenticeship in the Latin skills they needed for a specific task, such as compiling business accounts.[16] It is certainly the case that there existed a range of educational levels, but education always centred on the learning of Latin, albeit for various purposes. An idea of what was regarded as a good education can be gained from the writings of a number of authors, such as John of Salisbury and Gerald of Wales, who sometimes express slight contempt for those who have not benefited from one. In exploring educational levels and varieties of register, the use of *illiteratus* applied to a person, and *communis, popularis, usitatus* and *vulgaris* applied to language, can be significant. However, one needs to be aware of semantic ambiguities in some of these terms, just as one must beware of the imprecision of such English terms as low-register, colloquial, or sub-standard in linguistic discussions. Social distinctions existed as much between ecclesiastical or monastic and lay people as between upper and lower social levels. It is clear that the question of education with regard to social standing and whether one is a cleric or a lay person is a fraught one, particularly in the twelfth century when education was expanding in different directions.

Medieval Literary Tastes: What the Sources Reveal

It is possible to learn about literary standards and tastes from the comments that writers make about other authors, as when William of Malmesbury (*GP* 1.15) says of the challenging tenth-century writer Frithegod that he uses verses *non ita improbandis nisi quod Latinitatem perosus Grecitatem amat, Grecula verba frequentat, ut merito dictis eius aptetur illud Plautinum, 'haec quidem preter Sibyllam leget nemo'* (that are not totally without merit, except that, hating Latin, he loves Greek

---

15 See *Stotz (1996–2004: 1.149–54) on spoken Latin.

16 N. Orme (1989) *Education and society in medieval and Renaissance England*, London; for the later period, see R. Hanna (2011) 'Literacy, schooling, universities' in *The Cambridge companion to medieval English culture*, ed. A. Galloway, Cambridge, 172–94.

8 Introduction

and uses lots of Greek words, so that one might rightly apply to his poetry the words of Plautus, 'No one will read this apart from the Sibyl').[17] A critical view of other writers is also apparent when writers consider it appropriate to produce a revised version of an earlier text they deem insufficiently clear or elegant. In the preface to his *Life of St Ninian*, for example, Ælred of Rievaulx writes with characteristic elegance that he has been asked *ut clarissimi viri* (i.e. of Ninian) *vitam, veraci quidem sed nimis barbarico a prioribus exaratam stilo, a sermone rustico quasi a quibusdam tenebris eruens, in lucem latine locutionis educam* ('to bring the life of a distinguished man, written by earlier writers with an accurate but rather barbarous pen, into the light of Latin locution, pulling it out of its clumsy style as if out of darkness'). Here, too, the reader should beware, for the references to *stilus barbaricus* and *sermo rusticus*, contrasted with *locutio latina*, may mislead, seeing that *barbaricus* and *rusticus* could refer to the vernacular. It is therefore unclear whether Ælred, alongside his use of Bede's account of Ninian, is translating a lost vernacular version of the Life, or upgrading a previous Latin version; both translation and revision were widespread. At other times, when writers quote not only from classical texts and the Bible but from other medieval Latin authors, whether predecessors or contemporaries, this is usually a sign of approval, as well as an interesting indication of what texts were known to them.

Encountering the Medieval Texts in Their Physical Medium

When first encountering the medieval Latin texts produced as the result of such varied educational opportunities, readers may be puzzled by various features, particularly if they have studied the Latin usually labelled 'classical', distilled from the writers of the Roman Republic and early Empire into a somewhat unrealistically homogeneous language, with rules prescribed by late Roman grammarians who did not always follow their own advice. In their original form, in manuscripts and documents, the medieval texts are usually written on parchment, usually by a scribe other than their author. However, occasionally a manuscript contains the autograph version of a text: for example, MS 341 in Corpus Christi College, Cambridge, contains two loose leaves from Eadmer's work *A History of Recent Events in England* and his *Life of Anselm*, written by the author, while the *History of the English Bishops* in a manuscript (MS 172) preserved in Magdalen College, Oxford, is written by its author, William of Malmesbury (for which see the cover to this volume). Many of these manuscripts can now be viewed digitally. The handwriting is often extremely beautiful, in contrast to that written by administrative clerks, which can initially be hard to decipher, particularly at certain

---

17 Here William cites Plautus, *Pseudolus* 25, probably culled from the opening to Jerome's well-known work *Against Jovinianus*, given that Jerome was a rich (and occasionally the only) source of classical quotations.

periods of the later Middle Ages. Abbreviations are common, as is the use of symbols to replace particular words of high frequency. Furthermore, the multiple downward strokes ('minims') of certain letters can be confusing, as Roger Bacon points out (*CSPhil* 479), giving the example of the words *inviolati* and *inmolati* as potentially hard to distinguish *quia tres lineae sunt in m litera sicut in v et i et multi errant ibi* ('because there are three lines (downward strokes) in the letter m as also in v and i, and many people make a mistake here'). The spelling can be confusing (as when *hiems* is spelled *yem-* or even *gem-*, mirroring the pronunciation), particularly for words adopted from the vernacular: in some cases, every surviving instance of the word seems to be spelled in a different way, examples of this being the words for 'sugar' and 'scaffolding', as is evident in the entries for *succarum* and *scaffaldus* in the *DMLBS*. Matters improve once the reader is aware that s and f are easily confused in the script, t is often replaced by c, and that the diphthong ae is very often flattened to e (and even *aequus* turning into *equus* can briefly throw the reader, as Gerald of Wales indicates in his *Gemma ecclesiastica* 2.36). The reverse, termed hypercorrection, when a short e is written as a diphthong, e.g. *aecclesia* for *eccl-*, is also evident, as also in earlier Roman inscriptions. Homonyms are frequent, often the result of the variety of languages on which BML draws, as in the case of *planus*, which can be the CL word meaning 'flat' etc., or can signify 'wandering', derived from Greek, via Latin, or can bear the sense of 'plane tree', springing up in the thirteenth century at about the same time as AN 'plane' (while ME 'plane (tree)' is first attested in the fourteenth century), having come via Latin *platanus* from a Greek word. Further problems may be caused by the fluidity of gender characteristic of later BML, as can be seen from the complexity of homonyms around *polus* and *pola*.

Language Contact

Although one should be wary of imposing too many labels on a language which cannot be divided into strict chronological or social categories, one might broadly say that the language resulting from the combination of classical, Christian and Late Latin, as transmitted in written form, becomes the standard language of the Middle Ages. However, neither in pre- nor post-Conquest Britain did Latin function in a vacuum. It interacted not only with earlier written texts but also with the surrounding vernaculars, as is evident from the texts and from the glossaries compiled throughout the medieval period in Britain and on the Continent. After 1066, this version of Latin as it developed in Britain became a linguistic storehouse, from which the developing vernaculars adopted words over the next centuries, to a greater degree than during the Anglo-Saxon period. At the same time, the Latin storehouse was added to by an increasing number of Latin words formed from the contemporary vernaculars, again to a greater degree than previously. These new words were adopted in the same manner as classical Latin

10 Introduction

had borrowed from Italic languages, from Greek and Gaulish, for example, and in the same way as contact languages all over the world frequently borrow from each other.

Adoption from the vernacular should be seen against the complex background of the relation between the languages on either side of the English Channel from around the fourth century. This background includes Latin and the developing Romance forms, as well as the Germanic languages. In Britain the Germanic language par excellence was of course Old English, which developed from the west Germanic language of the Angle and Saxon immigrants, but Latin was also affected by other Germanic languages such as Continental Frankish, another west Germanic language, and occasionally by Gothic, an east Germanic language, as in the later Latin *tubrucus* for a type of leggings, which existed alongside the earlier, Gaulish-derived CL *bracae* ('breeches').

Investigation of the contacts between these languages can throw light on all of them. At an early stage of contact, it would seem that Germanic languages had adopted some Latin words, such as *caseus*, *vinum* and *cucina*, which were eventually to lead to modern English 'cheese', 'wine' and 'kitchen', and modern German 'Käse', 'Wein' and 'Küche'. In their new Germanic form they are likely to have been already present in OE when the Anglo-Saxons came to Britain. Other words were borrowed on contact with Christian culture, either on the Continent or in Britain: words such as *angelus* and *monasterium*. In reverse, words from the Germanic languages, mainly Frankish, were transmitted into Latin and the developing Romance vernacular (including the Norman dialect) and into English over the centuries. Finally, in the post-Conquest period, Latin also draws from spoken Anglo-Norman and English words which may themselves be derived from Germanic and earlier Latin vocabulary. David Trotter described the 'complex routes of transmission' in terms of 'multiple etymology' to explain how a word like BML *warda* could have different etymologies, associated with its various senses.[18]

A further feature of BML, resulting from the vagaries of language contact and development, is that it often contains doublets (as does English when deriving words such as 'ward' and 'guard' from the different forms in AN and OF). In such instances one form may derive directly from Latin while another has moved from early Latin into Romance to reappear in the Romance form in BML. There is indeed constant movement between French and BML in both directions. For example, there are forms for the word 'drain' that are based on Latin components, e.g. *exaquia* appearing in the twelfth century, but also related forms that have flowed from Latin through Romance to issue in a different Latin form, e.g. (*es-*)*sewera* in the thirteenth century. English 'sewer', however, remains underground until the fifteenth century. Another example of multiple etymological

---

18 D. Trotter, 'Anglo-Norman, medieval Latin and words of Germanic origin' in *Ashdowne and White (2017).

strands is provided by the three related verbs *trahere*, *tractare* and *trainare*: *trahere* is classical Latin, and so is *tractare* except that the latter is not attested in the first nine senses in which it appears in BML (senses which largely overlap with the basic meanings of *trahere*, i.e. 'to drag or draw'), while *trainare* comes through AN trainer, in the sense of 'to drag', but also applied to luring or training (a hawk).

The reader will quickly observe that medieval Latin is even more lexically rich in the extant texts than classical Latin, although the earlier Latin lexis has recently been enriched by such non-literary linguistic discoveries as those at Vindolanda or in curse tablets, for example.[19]

Lexis

In general it is striking how many words found in classical Latin appear in BML. In addition there are numerous words confidently formed from a CL stem, with the addition of productive affixes to create words that may not be attested in the surviving CL literature but will be perfectly comprehensible to a reader of that literature.[20] Then there are those words usually labelled as Late Latin (many of them included in the massive *Thesaurus Linguae Latinae* dictionary being produced in Munich to cover the period down to about AD 600). This does not imply that these words were not used in classical Latin, only that they are unattested there: it should be remembered that a great deal of writing in Latin from the classical period has been lost. Admittedly certain words and senses, in particular those applied to specific Christian concepts, could not have appeared before a certain date. Indeed, the term Late Latin is given to many words first found in the Latin translations of the Bible, words sometimes drawn from Greek which become part of the ever-expanding lexical repository of the Middle Ages.

First in this brief overview of the different kinds of lexical items in BML is the large category of words attested in CL sources, including rare words only attested once or twice in those sources. William of Malmesbury is perhaps the supreme example of a writer familiar with a wide variety of words and a range of senses as used by classical authors, a familiarity no doubt gained from wide reading. For example, he is the only writer of BML to use the CL *tumultuarius* in the sense of 'makeshift' or 'unplanned' (*GR* 3.245). In fact, it is remarkable how many of the writers are aware not only of the vocabulary but of any particular rules that govern a word in its grammatical context. It is not just a question of using the correct case after a preposition (which medieval writers are often said to fail to do), but of knowing how a particular verb behaves in a particular form, as with the deponent

---

19 J. N. Adams (1995) 'The language of the Vindolanda writing tablets: an interim report', *JRS* 85: 86–134.

20 Cf. *Stotz (1996–2004: 2.231–482) on the creation of words without borrowing from other languages.

12 Introduction

mederi with the dative in the *Liber custumarum* listing fire regulations after the London fire of 1212: *civitati mederi volentes* (Section II.47B); or how it behaves in a particular sense, as for example *intendere* ('to apply oneself to') with the dative in the *Life of Frideswide A* (4): *vigiliis et orationibus ... intendens* (Section II.13A); or *obtinere* used absolutely, by Gerald of Wales, in the sense 'to win one's case, prevail' (Section II.21B).

With the classical vocabulary one can include the semantic extensions, as in the early fourteenth-century records of Elton Manor where the fourth declension CL *tractus* is extended to mean the straps on a horse's collar, for which cf. modern English 'traces' (Section II.45E), or in many financial accounts in which CL *onerare* comes to be used to mean 'to charge with, hold accountable for' (e.g. Section II.48E). Semantic extensions can be traced by comparing the *Oxford Latin Dictionary* and the *DMLBS*. Some classical terms are used in a British context with a slightly new sense, especially words relating to appointed officials, e.g. *senator, satrapa* and *fetialis*. Greek words occur, as they had done in classical Latin, sometimes apparently taken directly from Greek, sometimes via Latin, and sometimes as technical terms.

In the text embroidered on the Bayeux Tapestry two words appear that are regarded as characteristic of Late Latin, and indeed spoken Latin: *parabolare* (in the sense 'to converse') and *caballus* ('horse') are both closely associated with modern French ('parler') and Spanish words ('caballo') that developed from these Latin forms. Interestingly, *parabolare* occurs only here in BML, except in Wyclif's treatise on blasphemy where he uses it in the sense 'to tell by means of a comparison or parable': the different Latin senses seem to derive from various words connected to the Greek verb *paraballein*. Christian and biblical vocabulary, mainly deriving from the Late Latin period, is of course woven more or less densely into many texts, particularly such works as the sermons of Thomas of Chobham (e.g. Section II.38A).

The second major feature of post-Conquest BML is the number of neologisms. Many words are created with prefixes and suffixes used in CL and LL according to a recognised semantic system, not unlike the system of derived forms for Arabic verbs or of affixes to the three-letter roots, allowing the language to coin new words without necessarily borrowing foreign words. In Latin this usually involves creating nouns ending, for example, in *-ura* or *-tio* or *-men*, adjectives with productive endings such as *-bilis* or *-osus*, and verbs with different conjugational terminations. Occasionally this can lead to homonyms with opposite meanings, e.g. *inhumatio*, which can mean both burial and non-burial as the result of the different senses inherent in the two CL prefixes *in-* with intensive and negative sense respectively: indeed, even in CL one finds similar ambiguity in the adjective *inauratus*.

Throughout the history of Latin, attitudes to neologisms varied, not only from one period to another, but from one writer to another, and even within the writings of a particular author. The widespread use of neologisms seems often to be regarded as a negative characteristic of medieval Latin. And yet, despite their rejection by the grammarians, writers as respected as Cicero, Jerome and Dante appreciated the need for neologisms: indeed, Dante went as far as believing that neologisms were one of the linguistic tools for transcending the limitations of human language and bridging metaphysical dichotomies.[21]

Loanwords

If the majority of BML words can be labelled as CL or LL – or at least are morphologically connected with such – the next largest group consists of borrowings from the vernacular.[22] As noted in the Introduction to the first volume of this anthology, borrowings from the vernacular were rare in the pre-Conquest period, though there are examples of Latin words probably derived from Irish, Cornish, Frankish, Gothic and English. In the post-Conquest period, on the other hand, loanwords are one of the major distinguishing factors, particularly in certain genres.

Most of these are formed from French (itself very frequently drawing on Latin and Germanic languages) and, increasingly over the period and in certain registers, from English. Sometimes it is unclear whether the source word is French or English because of morphological similarity between the languages at that stage of development. An example is ML *hameletta* from the vernacular 'hamelet', which is the form both in AN and ME, a double diminutive via AN 'hamel', from a Frankish word 'haim' meaning a house or small village, related to modern German 'Heim' and English 'home'. Similarly, one finds the form 'werre' (modern English 'war') in both AN (from around 1120) and early ME (in the *Peterborough Chronicle*), though 'guerre' is the more common form in AN and OF: the word derives from a Germanic form 'werra' and appears in Latin as both *werra* and *guerra* at the same period, with *guerra* already employed by William of Malmesbury. Another example is the common BML word *wikettum*, for a small gate (which gives modern English 'wicket (gate)' and '(cricket) wicket'): appearing at the end of the twelfth century, it is found in the form 'wiket' in both Anglo-Norman (from the late twelfth century) and Middle English (around 1300). This word is likely to be the source also of modern French 'guichet', applied to a small ticket office.

Borrowings occasionally occur in an unassimilated vernacular form within the Latin matrix, either as a gloss on a Latin word, or embedded in a kind of code-switching. Examples of both are found in a building contract from 1405

---

21 *The Dante Encyclopaedia* (2010) ed. R. Lansing, New York, *s.v.* neologisms.

22 Cf. *Stotz (1996–2004: 1.503–723) on medieval Latin borrowings from different languages.

14 Introduction

(Section II.47E): '*duas fenestras ... vocatas* Bay Wyndowes' and '*cum uno* Upright Roof'. This text also provides instances where the Latin word is derived from a vernacular but given a Latin ending, as in the case of the verb *gettare* ('to jut'), cognate with AN 'geter' ('to throw'), ultimately derived from CL *jactare*, and the noun *garita* in the sense of 'garret', though originally it applied to a watchtower, deriving from the Frankish 'warjan', meaning 'to defend'. This is in fact the most common way in which borrowed words appear, for the vernacular word is more likely to take root in the language if it is given a Latin termination. When being made into a verb, vernacular words are usually given a first-conjugation form, but other conjugations are evident, too. Most frequently a noun is accorded a termination of the first or second declension, but sometimes three declension forms are found for a single word, as in the case of *galo, -onis*, which appears in BML at the end of the twelfth century; here the third declension is more common than the forms *galona* or *galonus*. This word, of unknown origin, occurs in AN as 'galun' and other spellings around 1285 and is taken into English by 1300 to become the modern English liquid measure, a gallon.

Vernacular words can also be given CL productive affixes to extend their semantic range, but this is far less common than with CL and LL nouns. One example is AN 'trusse': attested from c.1130, it occurs as a Latin noun (*trussa*) around 1165 and in ME in the *Ancrene Wisse* around 1200, in the sense of 'bundle' or 'parcel', i.e. modern English 'truss'. The Latin word then produces various useful forms over the next couple of centuries through the addition of familiar endings, e.g. *trussare* ('to tie in a bundle'), *trussabilis* and *-tilis* ('suitable for packing', usually applied to a packing chest), *trussatio* ('act of packing') and *trussura* ('act of, or equipment for, packing'), all of which occur in different texts over a period of time. Another example is *daubare*, in the sense of 'to daub or plaster', deriving from French 'dauber', itself a development from CL *dealbare*: the CL suffixes *-arius, -tio, -tor* and *-tura* added to the stem *daub-* also provide related nouns and adjectives in the expected senses. Examples with such affixes are frequently based on an English word connected with domestic activities, sometimes occurring in a single example, e.g. *sincatio* ('sinking of a pit') or *watelatio* ('covering a wall in wattle'), words found in account rolls that list domestic expenses (e.g. Section II.48). A search in *DMLBS* demonstrates that neologisms ending with *-tio* were particularly common in the fourteenth century.

While some neologisms and borrowings are rare, others become key words for aspects of life in medieval Britain. An example of a key word is *saisina* ('seisin', possession of land) which comes into Latin after the Conquest, with AN *saisine, seisine*, probably cognate with Frankish **sakjan* ('to lay claim to') and related to English 'to seize'. In this case, too, related words are formed, e.g. *saisire* ('to put a person in legal possession') as a fourth-conjugation verb, alongside *dissaisire* ('to dispossess') and *resaisire* ('to resume possession'), both formed with CL prefixes.

It is true that the adoption – in other words the intentional borrowing of lexical items from a native language into an L2, i.e. a secondary language – occurs in different ways in different kinds of texts/registers and at different periods. At one end of the scale there are literary and theological works which continue to draw almost wholly on classical and biblical vocabulary in a way that must have been perfectly comprehensible to their readers. Then there are, for example, saints' lives and historical writings, which, from the late eleventh century, incorporate the occasional vernacular-based word which has presumably already become part of the Latin lexicon. Goscelin's *Life of Edith* contains an early example of *perla* ('pearl'), a word of complex origin, probably coming into BML around 1080 from French, here specifically to refer to an English pearl, as opposed to CL *margarita*, taken from Greek. A slightly later example is *herciare* ('to harrow') in Orderic Vitalis' *Ecclesiastical History* (5.20): the Romance form (AN 'hercer') probably developed from the LL noun *herpica*, a version of CL *(h)irpex*. Eadmer (*V. Anselmi* 2.58) uses *strivile* (*equus … hominem tergo dejecit eumque uno pede per strivile pendentem … per terram longius traxit* ('the horse threw the man from his back and dragged him a long way over the ground, hanging from the stirrup with one foot')). This derives from a Germanic word (related to OE 'stigráp', i.e. 'climb-rope', which developed into modern English 'stirrup') but passed through a (now invisible) French form that first becomes visible at the end of twelfth century as AN 'estrivele'. Sometimes an author adds a specific comment to show he is conscious of giving a non-Latin word in a Latin form, as when William of Malmesbury speaks of the tidal bore in the Severn as *higram* (*GP* 4.153) using the feminine accusative singular, from the OE form 'egor'. William comments on *higra: sic enim Anglice vocant* ('for this is what they call it in English'), even though he has used the word in a Latin form. Similarly, Matthew Paris (*Maj.* 5.709) writes *dispersis predonibus quos bedeweros vocant*, and Gervase of Canterbury (*Combust.* 6) *columpnae … ecclesiae quae vulgo pilarii dicuntur*, adding what amounts to a quasi-technical term apparently associated with AN 'piler'.[23]

Some of these words had entered BML soon after the Conquest, and many appear throughout the Domesday Book. Another early source for the study of such words are the Latin translations of Anglo-Saxon and AN law codes, collected in **Die Gesetze der Angelsachsen*. In a document of 1136 King Stephen assures the Church that he will maintain its freedom, using such words as *foresta* and *murdrum* which were to become very common in BML and in current English. Gradually an increasing number of technical terms were required, predominantly drawn from the French vernacular in use at the royal court: words such as

---

23 Cf. the sixteenth-century Scottish historian John Major, discussing oats (*Historia Majoris Britanniae* 1.2), writes of the bannock as *panem … prope cineres coctum, quem* '*bannokam*' (*a vulgari Latinum fingendo) nostri appellitant.* Here the vernacular he refers to may be Gaelic. There is room for further investigation of the widespread use of such comments as *vulgares appellant* or *vulgariter vocatus*.

16 Introduction

escaetum ('escheat') and *essartum* ('assart') which have left their mark on English legal terms and place names. The second half of the twelfth century, especially from the 1180s, when Henry II and his chancellors expanded the role of royal administration, and right through the thirteenth century, is the period when most AN words are adopted into BML. From the mid-thirteenth century an increasing number of agricultural and construction terms for tools, materials and practices, some of them the result of technological advances, turn up in customaries, accounts and manuals, with more adopted from English words in the fourteenth and fifteenth centuries.

A further source of linguistic interest for the relationship between BML and the vernaculars is provided by the bilingual texts, such as glossaries, or some of the sermons of the fourteenth century that use elaborate code-switching. In addition, it should be remembered that contact borrowing comes about not only when people speaking different languages are in prolonged contact, but also when languages meet in written translation, as when Latin borrowed terms from Arabic and Greek scientific texts. Calques, i.e. literal translations, were a useful means of dealing with technical terms found in foreign languages, as an alternative to transliteration of the foreign term.[24] Roger Bacon's theories on translation in the context of scientific and philosophical works are of interest in this context (Section II.28C).

The unusual flexibility and openness of BML after the Conquest has not been fully explained and requires further investigation. Certainly the use of neologisms and borrowings varies according to genre and register, apparently suitable in one context but less so elsewhere. An awareness of such differences is seen in the comment made by Gerald of Wales (*V.Galfridi* 2.9) – a multilingual writer sensitive to delicate nuances of sense and tone as well as being interested in etymology – in his account of the disgrace of the chancellor William de Longchamp (cited with reference to Hugh Nonant's account in Section II.20). Gerald uses the CL word *communio* first to refer to the rights of the governing body, but adds *vel ut Latine minus, vulgariter magis loquamur, communa seu communia eis concessa*, where *communa* and *communia* are both commonly attested forms of a medieval Latin word deriving from the French 'commune'. In general BML offers an unparalleled source for the study of loanwords in various genres, registers and contexts, providing information about semantic and cultural changes in a multilingual society.[25]

---

24 Latin *sinus*, for example, was chosen as the trigonometrical term now referred to in English as 'sine', because it was a loan translation of an Arabic word meaning 'bosom' or 'breast', paralleled in one sense of *sinus*: however, the Arabic word was in fact a misunderstanding, due to a confusion between the similar Sanskrit and Arabic forms, of the correct Sanskrit term 'jya-ardha', meaning 'half-chord'.

25 On loanwords cf. D. Trotter in *Ashdowne and White (2017), and E. Dickey (2018) 'What is a loanword? The case of Latin borrowings and codeswitches in Ancient Greek', *Lingue e linguaggio* 17.1: 7–36.

Morphology and Syntax: the Texture of British Medieval Latin

If post-Conquest BML is striking both for the confidence with which the classical word stock is applied and for the multiplicity of vernacular-based words in certain contexts, one might also claim that it is striking for the general regularity of its morphology and syntax (as is the case also in the pre-Conquest period), while nevertheless characterised by great variety across a broad range of possibilities. This might surprise those who tend to regard medieval Latin merely as a debased form of classical Latin or as valuable only as a source for Romance forms. It is true that there are greater differences in the texture of the Latin between different genres than in the pre-Conquest period, mainly because Latin was used in the post-Conquest period in so many hitherto unattested genres, largely connected with administration at every level of society. One characteristic of the Latin of these genres is that a Latin word, often a neologism or loanword, can be used in any of the three genders, but that is hardly something to worry about. However, in general there is remarkably little deviation from the classical rules of morphology and little evidence of evolution from a synthetic to an analytic language, apart from the very occasional use of prepositions instead of plain cases, where indeed the use of *de* may parallel the development of French 'de'. In general one finds an impressive awareness of the correct forms of irregular declension and conjugation (e.g. the different participles *insertus* and *insitus* for the two CL homonym verbs *inserere*), even in rare words.

With regard to syntax, there is certainly plentiful evidence of usages that have long been stamped as non-classical and non-standard.[26] Some of these usages can indeed unsettle the reader, as with irregular tense sequences or when the reflexive *suus* and the genitive pronoun *eius* are occasionally confused, both of which are easy errors to make in certain complex sentences.[27] However, in recent years the work of, for example, J. N. Adams has demonstrated that many of these features (as for example, occasional interchangeability between active and deponent verbs) in fact occur in the writings of the standard authors of classical antiquity, where there is far more fluidity and continuity in morphological and syntactical usage than the textbooks have hitherto led one to believe. The commonest examples of such variants are the continued use of *quod* or *quia* with the indicative or subjunctive for object clauses after verbs of saying or knowing, as in Orderic

---

26 A summary of some characteristics regarded as typical of the Latin of the medieval period can be found in the chapter on medieval Latin by Greti Dinkova-Bruun in *Clackson (2011). However, many of these are less applicable to BML.

27 That this was a common source of problems is shown by the fact that the arbiter of Renaissance linguistic taste, Lorenzo Valla, in his little book *De reciprocatione sui et suus*, devotes his ninth chapter to explaining why people mistakenly use *eius*, *ipsius* and *illius* for *suus*.

18   Introduction

Vitalis' account of the wreck of the White Ship, in Section II.11C, where he writes *audacter quia omnes qui iam precesserant praeiret spondebat*, where *quia* can be translated 'that'; note, however, that in the following sentence, *quia* is equivalent to 'because', despite the presence of *nesciebant*, which is followed by an indirect question: *laeti quia quid eis ante oculos penderet nesciebant*. The use of *quia* and *quod* to introduce object clauses did allow flexibility but could also be a source of confusion because of the various, very common senses of these words. Another variant usage is the past participle with a perfect, rather than present, form of *esse*, to form the past passive, as when William of Canterbury (*Mir. Thom.* 5.30) writes *postquam hec per interpretem patrem locuta fuerat* ('after she had said these things, with her father acting as translator'). It should, however, be borne in mind that one and the same text often contains examples of various forms of expression, showing that the author was aware of a wide range of lexical and syntactic possibilities.

The texts included in this volume have been selected to highlight this range of possibilities and to demonstrate some aspects of the important role Latin played in the culture of medieval Britain. Latin had long been a language of prestige, admired for the calibre of its ancient literature, just as the Romans had admired Greek literature and language. It was also valued as the primary language of education, necessary for the functioning of the Church and providing access to higher positions within society. It might also be found in the briefest of snippets, as embedded in Chaucer's English, introduced to hint at a veneer of learning. And yet it was by no means merely a language of rhetorical flourishes, literary imitation and quotations from a few authoritative texts, a thin layer floating on the linguistic surface of medieval Britain. It is true that its status as a learned and written language had an inevitable effect on it, what with the continuing pull of *consuetudo* (in the sense of 'existing usage'). In addition, there was the respect for *auctoritas* ('authority') and the tendency of education and records to turn to the models and forms of earlier times. The central position of the Bible in medieval culture might be regarded as also having a somewhat conservative influence on the language, given the common practice of interlacing the text with biblical quotations and allusions. Such forces might be expected to produce a limited and artificial language used within the community of the educated, superficially similar to some aspects of the community created in contemporary society among social media users.

Nevertheless, other aspects of the linguistic situation served to create a greater variety of Latin expression within the generally consistent picture. The widespread use of borrowing from contact languages was probably the most important factor, as mentioned, in giving BML a particular identity as well as a certain flexibility. In the more literary writings it is possible that some authors were influenced by the more relaxed attitude to the grammarians' rules evident in earlier Christian writers, such as the highly educated Augustine of Hippo, whose writings are full of interesting linguistic observations. In the *De doctrina Christiana*

(4.10.24) for example, he points out that clarity and communication are more important than adherence to pedantic rules, particularly when explaining theology to an audience with a more limited education, when he asks pointedly: *quid enim prodest locutionis integritas, quam non sequitur intellectus audientis, cum loquendi omnino nulla sit causa, si quod loquimur non intelligunt propter quos ut intelligant loquimur?* ('What use is correct speech if it does not allow the hearer to understand, since there is absolutely no reason to speak if those for whose understanding we are speaking cannot understand what we are saying?'). Then, as a language of record, Latin was widely used also in mundane contexts, for example in business accounts and legal proceedings necessitating different vocabulary and forms of expression: this would also have affected the Latin in various ways with respect to lexis and syntax.[28] A further contributing factor to the variety of types of Latin was the difference in the provision of education and the amount of contact any individual might have with Latin in their daily lives, which would affect the manner in which they would use Latin.

The Multilingual Context: Latin and the Vernaculars

The use of loanwords alerts the reader to the multilingual context in which BML functions. A consequence of this is that linguistic scholars are in fact dependent on BML for much material relating to the development of the vernaculars, even if few are aware of this. While many scholars mention in passing the trilingual nature of Britain, it is rare for them to delve deeper into the French and Latin of the period. To be sure, the Anglo-Norman scholar William Rothwell wrote widely about the influence of Anglo-Norman, rather than the Continental French which has hitherto been spotlighted in histories of the English language: he not only stressed the way in which AN can help to fill in the gaps in Middle English and Old French, but also the necessity of studying English, Anglo-Norman and Latin together.[29] However, in the context of multilingualism, Latin remains overlooked and undervalued, particularly for the later Middle Ages. The Latin of pre-Conquest Britain, often referred to as Anglo-Latin or Insular Latin, has attracted more scholarly attention, partly as the result of being included in such courses (if not in the title) as that in Anglo-Saxon, Norse and Celtic at the University of Cambridge. And yet the recent publication of such scholarly resources as the *Anglo-Norman Dictionary* (https://anglo-norman.net) and the *Bilingual Thesaurus of Everyday Life in Medieval England*, focusing on Anglo-Norman and Middle

---

28 P. Brand, 'The Latin of the early English common law' in *Ashdowne and White (2017).

29 For example, W. Rothwell (1998) 'Arrivals and departures: the adoption of French terminology into Middle English', *English Studies* 79: 144–65; and 'Aspects of lexical and morpho-syntactical mixing in the languages of medieval England' in *Trotter (2000). For further articles, consult https://anglo-norman.net.

20 Introduction

English, can be more than amply supplemented by the *DMLBS*, also online, for information about the post-Conquest linguistic situation.

An example of the importance of Latin texts for knowledge of the vernaculars and their development is the appearance of Latin forms of vernacular words soon after the Conquest, a feature revealed by the *DMLBS*. This points to a phenomenon that is crucial for the study of all three languages, namely that Latin texts provide evidence of vernacular words that are not documented in vernacular texts until later.[30] With regard to the history of English, during the first century after the Conquest, English was less in evidence as a written language than in the period before 1066, apart from in a few royal writs, in glosses added to scientific works and Psalters (e.g. BL MS Arundel 60) and in the *Peterborough Chronicle*, the one manuscript (Bodleian MS Laud 636) of the *Anglo-Saxon Chronicle* which continues its account in OE into the twelfth century. Around 1200 there appear the (Middle) English *Ancrene Wisse* and Laȝamon's *Brut* (based on Wace's AN epic that itself draws on Geoffrey of Monmouth's Latin *History of the Kings of Britain*).

What is true of English is equally the case for Anglo-Norman. Early written evidence is restricted to the *Leis Willelme* (Laws of William the Conqueror), perhaps dating from the early twelfth century, and then translated into Latin around 1200, and a few AN charters from the same period.[31] The paucity of early AN written texts does explain why contemporary Anglo-Norman scholars focus on the writings of the thirteenth century and beyond. However, they fail to remark on the fact that early attestations of AN words are quite rare, even though Anglo-Norman was spoken in England from the time of the Conquest. Indeed, Norman French had been known to pre-Conquest English kings such as Edward the Confessor, who spent decades in exile in Normandy and may have brought Norman influence to his court in England already in the mid-eleventh century. It is possible that the majority of those who knew Latin also knew Anglo-Norman and could translate between them. More work certainly needs to be done on the question of possible linguistic overlap between the Latin documents of Britain and those of pre-Conquest Normandy, for which one may consult e.g. the *Index rerum* in **Recueil des Actes des ducs de Normandie de 911 à 1066* (1961) and SCRIPTA, the database of Norman documents from the tenth to thirteenth centuries, based at Caen.

---

30 Cf. M. Goyens and W. Verbeke (ed.) (2003) *The dawn of the written vernacular in western Europe*, Louvain; M. Mostert and A. Adamska (ed.) (2014) *Uses of the written word in medieval towns*, Turnhout; and (2022) *Oral and written communication in the medieval countryside*, Turnhout.

31 Cf. Y. Otaka (1993) 'Sur la langue des *Leis Willelme*' in *Anglo-Norman anniversary essays*, ed. I. Short, London, 293–308; *Clanchy (1993: 218–19); and the Early English Laws website, https://earlyenglishlaws.ac.uk/.

On the Continent there is a similar picture with respect to the other French dialects of northern France, the 'langues d'oïl', including what developed into standard French. The earliest extended evidence of written French is in the Strasbourg Oaths of 842, given in a Romance and a Germanic Frankish version.[32] This document is followed by a handful of works, mainly in verse, over the next centuries, culminating in the *Chanson de Roland*, which probably dates from the late eleventh century but is preserved in a single Anglo-Norman copy (Bodleian MS Digby 23) from the mid-twelfth century, the period when French took off as a literary language.[33]

During the two centuries after the Conquest thousands of Latin words are derived from these vernaculars. The fact that the vernacular words are found embedded in Latin texts before they appear in vernacular writings gives BML an ancillary usefulness, making it an important resource for the study of the early development of French and English. These vernacular words presumably existed in a spoken form, but their early existence would be unknown had they not been preserved in Latin. This is the case also with words specific to certain geographical areas, preserved in Latin and giving Latin a perhaps unexpected hint of regionalism even within Britain. *Falla*, as a unit of measure, in northern English 'fall', is attested in Latin in 1211 but not until 1388 in English. Latin *croa* derives from a Scottish word (*OED s.v.* cruive) for a fish trap: it appears in 1157 in a Latin document from Scotland, but not until the fifteenth century in a Scottish document. There is also evidence of a medieval Cornish term, 'motlet', embedded in Latin (*DMLBS s.v. motletum*) and of Manx-specific Latin in church statutes of the thirteenth and fourteenth centuries.[34]

The Question of Spoken Latin in the Context of Written Latin

It is clear from what has been said about BML as a source of knowledge for the history of Latin as well as other languages that the fact that Latin is preserved in writing, in such a wide variety of texts, is of crucial importance. One aspect of our knowledge of the language is the question of whether Latin itself was spoken in medieval Britain. To what extent can this question be answered with reference to written Latin? Latin was undoubtedly spoken in the liturgy in church, where people would have become familiar with the language in a limited way, but as for conversation, scholarly interest has focused primarily on either early BML or on

---

32 See B. Frank-Job, 'A structural comparison between Latin and Romance' in *The Oxford guide to the Romance languages* (2016) on the earliest sources for Romance.

33 Cf. D. Howlett (1996) *The English origins of Old French literature*, Blackrock; and the website for France-Angleterre: manuscrits médiévaux entre 700 et 1200, https://manuscrits-france-angleterre.org.

34 *Councils and Synods* (1964), for the years 1230 and 1292.

22 Introduction

the emaciated Latin resulting from the Italian Renaissance and its tendency to Ciceronianism, rather than on the period in between.[35] However, post-Conquest writers do talk about Latin speech specifically, in certain contexts and within certain communities, whether among monks, school and university students, or educated friends,[36] as well as in less usual circumstances, as between Gerald of Wales and the uneducated Welsh anchorite who could speak Latin using only infinitives instead of inflected verbs, for which see Section II.21A. Some form of Latin is also likely to have been used as a spoken lingua franca by priests, nuns and monks, pilgrims and traders travelling on the Continent, for British travellers could not at that time expect foreigners to speak English. Different standards were perhaps expected when it came to talking to the pope. An instance where a lack of education presented difficulties is found in the *Gesta* (2.113) of St Albans Abbey: in 1308 the abbot Hugh de Eversden is recorded as being second to none in spoken English and French but as having only basic Latin. As a result he dreaded having to visit the pope, but his great munificence to the pope and Curia ensured that he was well treated in Rome.[37]

Written texts not only mention occasions when Latin was used in conversation. Many kinds of texts, such as saints' lives, for example, record what is alleged to be direct speech (as can be seen in a number of the passages selected in these volumes). Although at times the Latin may be a translation of the vernacular speech, the simple, colloquial form in which the conversation is recorded was presumably plausible and comprehensible to the reader. With so many examples there is certainly opportunity for further investigation into the direct speech recorded in BML and its relation to contemporary vernaculars. For example, comparison could be made with direct speech recorded in earlier Latin writings when Latin was a first language.

---

35 On the early period, cf. M. Lapidge, 'Colloquial Latin in the Insular Latin scholastic colloquia?' and M. Winterbottom, 'Conversations in Bede's *Historia Ecclesiastica*' in *Dickey and Chahoud (2010). On the plentiful post-medieval colloquies, such as those of Erasmus, see T. Tunberg (2020) 'Spoken Latin in the Late Middle Ages and Renaissance revisited', *Journal of Classics Teaching* 21: 66–71. For a more general account of the so-called 'Neo-Latin' of the Renaissance and its view of the Latin of the past, see K. Sidwell, 'Classical Latin – Medieval Latin – Neo-Latin' in *The Oxford handbook of Neo-Latin* (2015) and V. Moul (ed.) (2017) *A Guide to Neo-Latin literature*, Cambridge.

36 See for example W. J. Ong (1984) 'Orality, literacy and medieval textualization', *New Literary History* 16: 1–12; J. Barrau (2011) 'Did monks actually speak Latin?' in *Understanding monastic practices of oral communication (Western Europe, tenth–thirteenth centuries)*, ed. S. Vanderputten, Turnhout.

37 Petitions from Hugh de Eversden to King Edward I, in French, survive in the National Archives. For difficulties in communicating with the pope, cf. Willibald of Mainz, *Life of Boniface* (6), cited in the Introduction to Volume I.

Medieval Latin and Modern Sociolinguistic Studies

The question of the spoken language leads to that of whether it is possible to apply to written BML some of the sociolinguistic concepts that have been discussed over the past half-century with regard primarily to spoken vernaculars, particularly English. Terms such as language contact, borrowing and interference, source languages and target or receptor languages, L1 and L2 languages, diglossia, bilingualism and code-switching have all become part of linguistic study. Although the primary emphasis in such language studies has been on speech, the related discipline of historical sociolinguistics allows for the study of language in a written form. Much of the study has hitherto taken the form of theoretical discussions, but it is now possible to test the theories on the primary sources. In the last twenty years a start has been made on treating Latin from a sociolinguistic point of view. J. N. Adams, for example, has examined Latin in a broad survey of bilingual contexts in which Latin encountered other languages, in his 2003 work *Bilingualism and the Latin language*. More recently he has attempted to apply certain aspects of sociolinguistics to the Latin of the post-classical period (long designated by the unfortunate term 'Vulgar Latin'), a type of Latin thought to reflect the (spoken) language of the non-elite and keenly examined as a source of proto-Romance elements.[38] As Adams makes clear, written texts must be treated with care, given their tendency to be conservative, which means that they do not necessarily reflect the spoken Latin of the period when they were written. Another problem is the paucity, indeed the often fragmentary nature, of sources for non-elite Latin in the late Roman period.

There are, however, many interesting differences between the linguistic situation in the late Roman period and that in medieval Britain. For example, in the case of BML, the aim is not to discover Latin texts with apparently anachronistic features, merely in order to pan the written texts for the gold of a spoken language. Written Latin, ranging from the more stylistically and linguistically conservative to that which seems to be responding quickly to developments in the vernacular (as with the abundance of new terms in royal administration at the end of the twelfth century), can be appreciated in its own right, rather than as incomplete evidence for the spoken, and need not be regarded as 'bad data',[39] a label often applied to written evidence by experts in historical linguistics. The scale and range of the extant material, from the mid-seventh century to around 1500, is a further factor which makes BML appropriate for sociolinguistic study. This allows a degree of both diachronic and synchronic study, to examine the variety of register at any one time, and any changes visible over time. The fact

---

38 See the first two chapters of *The Oxford guide to the Romance languages* (2016). For various ways in which this phrase has been interpreted, see *Adams (2013: 7–27).

39 W. Labov (1994) *Principles of linguistic change*, Oxford, 1.11.

24 Introduction

that after the Conquest, Latin was used in a wider range of types of writing than before 1066 invites investigation of what kind of Latin was appropriate for each and reveals an awareness on the part of its users as to what was suitable for the particular material as well as for the context.

Another difference is that since BML is a written L2 language, the label 'non-educated' is less likely to be applicable to the language, since anyone who knew Latin in anything but the most passive manner is likely to have had some education. Indeed, there is a need to review the accepted forms of classification and labelling, with regard to such terms as colloquial, literary, and high or low register, evident in sociolinguistic discussions.[40] Certainly a discussion of the Latin of this later period must take into account legal, administrative and business language as well as the literary. There is no justification for limiting the study of Latin to what are regarded as high registers. It may be easy to recognise formality in Becket's attempt at diplomacy, for example, in his letter to the Empress Matilda (Becket, *Ep.* 40), in contrast to a more direct, if not exactly colloquial tone in Grosseteste's personal letter to his sister Juetta, a nun, in response to her request for a report on his health (Gros. *Ep.* 8). However, different terms may be needed for the royal business letters in the Close Rolls, for the vivid summaries of crimes brought to court, for building contracts, wills or accounts. Are these high-register because they are official and formal? Are contracts and accounts low-register as being non-literary, even if they can hardly be termed colloquial? British Latin of the medieval period will certainly not slip easily into the existing scholarly pigeonholes, without further discussion. Such questions must be examined, too, in relation to the concept of diglossia, as discussed below.

Levels of Education and Varieties of Register

With regard to the knowledge required by the medieval writer to select the appropriate register, it is true that the term *literatus* might be applied to anyone with enough learning to use Latin effectively. It was a word that could be used in the comparative or superlative, as when Peter of Blois, in the letter in which he defends King Henry II against the charge of murdering Thomas Becket, writes that the king of England is *longe litteratior* than the king of Sicily, both of whom he has tutored (P. Blois, *Ep.* 66). It is not sufficient to talk in terms of an elite who had gained an education, as opposed to the masses who were illiterate and could only speak a vernacular language. It was not only the wealthy and powerful who gained an education. As in the case of the poet Horace, even those of a humbler background were able to do so, given ambitious parents and good fortune: Robert Grosseteste, for example, the future Bishop of Lincoln, born in poverty, was given

---

40 For a discussion of registers in Latin writing, see *Dickey and Chahoud (2010).

an education by the mayor of Lincoln and eventually described by Matthew Paris as *vir quidem nimis literatus* (*Chr. Maj.* 3.306). In this way, education, though not available to all, did allow a degree of social mobility, even if the areas in which that education could be used were quite specialised.[41] As Latin came to be used also for types of writing such as business accounts, training could be provided for specific purposes involving the ability to write and the use of a particular jargon. Even such everyday uses of Latin display evidence of a knowledge of grammar and cannot be labelled as sub-standard. Furthermore, it should be remembered that the ability to write Latin lay at the top of a range of familiarity with the language. Throughout British society, contact with Latin would occur in different forms: at one end of the spectrum people might listen to the liturgy in church and recite prayers and sing hymns in Latin, and grow to understand this Latin by means of the priest's explanations. At school or at home they might learn the Latin alphabet and be able to read aloud and copy words in Latin and other languages. As a further stage they would read Latin with a view to increasing their understanding of the language, and finally acquire the linguistic confidence to compose in Latin. That readers or listeners had various levels of Latin understanding is clear from many texts. In the introduction to his work *The Conquest of Ireland*, for example, Gerald of Wales claims to be writing in an unadorned and easy style (*plano facilique stilo*) because he is writing for lay people and for the *parum litterati principes*, i.e. the aristocracy, only able to read Latin if it is not too complex and abstruse.[42] Characteristically, Gerald also mentions the importance of an elegant style, even when adjusting the words to the understanding of his readers, but he does at least recognise in theory the importance of clarity, quoting the phrase *satius ... est mutum esse quam quod nemo intelligat palam proferre* ('it is better to remain silent than to say publicly something that no one is going to understand') from Cicero's *Philippics* (3.9.22), though he attributes the words to Seneca. This passage of *The Conquest of Ireland* is of great interest: it includes Gerald's assertion that he has chosen to use words that are *popularia*, rejecting the *durum et austerum* style of some ancient writers and agreeing with the philosophical advice to imitate the way of life of the older generation, but to adopt the speech of the younger generation.

In short, it is important to realise that each individual would be different, with his or her own level of (multi-linguistic) expertise, as is the case in any society.

---

41 Cf. Walter Map (*De nugis curialium* 1.10), who takes a dim view of the ambitions of the lower classes (*servi*) for their children's education, playing on the words *liber, liberi, libertas* and *liberales artes*.

42 Cf. the preface to Anselm's *Monologion*, in which he uses the phrase *plano stilo* in response to his students' request for a clear exposition of his views on the essence of God. For a seventeenth-century British Neo-Latin revision of a passage of Gerald's work *The Conquest of Ireland*, see J. Barry (2004) 'Richard Stanihurst's *De rebus in Hibernia gestis*', *Renaissance Studies* 18: 1–18; for another Neo-Latin revision, see Section II.33.

26   Introduction

However, in multilingual societies like that in which BML had such an important role to play, there is not always an overlap in people's knowledge of the different languages, which is why translators and interpreters are needed, and this was certainly the case in medieval Britain, where texts can reveal scenes of mutual incomprehension. For example, Gerald of Wales (*Expugnatio Hibernica* 1.40) tells of an encounter between a man who addresses King Henry II *Teutonice*, i.e. in English ('God holde thee, cuning') and the king who speaks French and cannot understand the man: a knight accompanying the king is able to speak both French and English and can interpret for them, and the incident is then recorded by Gerald in Latin.

Diglossia and Code-Switching

Even if one accepts that there were individual differences in Latin competence across society, it is still true that Latin's particular role as the dominant written language of Britain over roughly a millennium sparks the question of whether the term diglossia, current in sociolinguistic discussions, can be applied to post-Conquest Britain. This would mean that Latin acted as the high-register form, with French and English acting as lower registers within the linguistic context of Britain.[43] Diglossia was originally applied to varieties within a single language, as with standard and colloquial or regional Arabic, or Katharevousa and demotic Greek, but it was extended to apply also to different languages used for different functions within a single community.[44] Peter of Blois appears to provide an example of Latin as the high-register language when he writes to a friend (*Serm.* 65), *petis ... ut habitum sermonem ad populum ... tibi communicem et quae laicis satis crude et insipide (sicut eorum capacitatis erat) proposui, in Latinum sermonem studeam transferre* ('You ask that I impart to you a sermon given to the people, and that I attempt to translate into Latin what I presented to the laity in a very rough and watered-down style (in accordance with their ability to comprehend)'). Here it seems that a sermon given in an unsophisticated form to a lay audience is now being turned into a more elegant (with quotations from Juvenal and from Ovid's *Fasti*), expansive (as demanded by *Latini eloquii dignitas*) and more effective Latin version. It is possible that the original sermon was communicated in a vernacular rather than in colloquial Latin, but the semantic ambiguities of such words as *idioma*, *quotidianus*, *sermo* and *transferre* make certainty impossible.

Code-switching, when the speaker or writer switches between languages, has already received attention with regard to its use in Latin and in the

---

43 *Garrison et al. (2013). On functional diglossia in BML, cf. *Ashdowne and White (2017: 22–6).

44 C. Ferguson (1959) *Diglossia*, repr. in T. Huebner (ed.) (1996) *Sociolinguistic perspectives*, Oxford.

multilingual context of medieval Britain, but much remains to be done.[45] It is a phenomenon found in many different kinds of texts in BML, usually with French and/or English words, sometimes flagged by the French definite article 'le' or 'les', embedded in a Latin (or occasionally Anglo-Norman) matrix. Laura Wright has demonstrated in a number of articles the linguistic competence and subtlety of the code-switching between Latin, French and English in late medieval business accounts.[46] Sermons are another type of text in which code-switching occurs (Section II.38). However, the reasons for code-switching in a Latin matrix are not always clear and merit further examination within a wider context. Certainly the corpus of BML texts includes many multilingual texts (as for example the Account Rolls of Durham Priory (Section II.48C) and the Fabric Rolls of York Minster) that offer an opportunity for the study of code-switching and such concepts as bilingual teaching, functional bilingualism and coordinate bilinguals.

However, the most marked feature of BML after the Conquest that appears to make it fertile ground for sociolinguistic discussion is, as mentioned, the explosion of borrowings from the vernaculars and its inventive use of neologisms. Readers of BML need to adopt a more open attitude to the Latin in front of them, bearing in mind that borrowings and neologisms are accepted elements in both colloquial and literary languages, as a natural consequence of language contact.[47]

An investigation into how such sociolinguistic terms might apply to BML is likely to reveal hitherto unappreciated features of the Latin of post-Conquest Britain. Indeed, if BML is considered on its own terms, it should gain a more equal status alongside other languages of the period than it has had hitherto. Further research may well challenge existing sociolinguistic theories to explain how the Latin of the Middle Ages perhaps accords with certain theories but not with others. There are certainly a number of rather paradoxical features of the Latin of medieval Britain. It is a regional version of a more universal language, which, like Modern English outside Britain, produces a confident literature of its own among those who have learned it as an L2. Despite being a regional version, BML can in some respects be described as a standard language, and yet it avoids

---

45 *Adams (2003); H. Schendl and L. Wright (ed.) (2011) *Code-switching in Early English*, Berlin; H. Schendl, 'Multilingualism, code-switching, and language contact in historical sociolinguistics' in *The Handbook of historical sociolinguistics* (2012).

46 See e.g. L. Wright, 'Non-integrated vocabulary in the mixed-language accounts of St. Paul's Cathedral, 1315–1405' in *Ashdowne and White (2017: 273–98).

47 Modern Swedish, for example, adopted many everyday words from French in around 1800, partly as a consequence of having imported a Frenchman as the Swedish king, producing e.g. 'pjäs' for a theatre play from the French 'pièce', retaining the French pronunciation but altering the orthography. This continues with such recent colloquial borrowings as 'hajpa', from the English 'to hype' (apparently an abbreviation of 'hypodermic'), with the Swedish verb-ending -a added to the English word in a spelling conforming to Swedish principles.

28 Introduction

the lack of variation usually associated with this term. In fact it provides further evidence in support of Adams' discovery that linguistic innovation is possible at higher educational levels. However, in the case of BML the innovation comes not only from within but also from the adoption of elements from the spoken vernaculars, which arguably make this written language more colloquial than one might expect. To what extent such changes over time amount to a development in the language remains to be evaluated: for this, the evidence of the BML of the late fourteenth and the fifteenth centuries needs to be measured against that of the earlier post-Conquest period.

Conclusion

There is, then, much more to the study of medieval Latin than quick glances and broad generalisations. There is a need for close consideration of the evidence in the light of recent research and with the assistance of the many new editions and reference works that have appeared in the last half-century, as well as the increasing number of digital resources, allowing analysis of the language. For such study, the national medieval Latin dictionaries already produced or currently in production in Europe, based on the extant sources of each country, as well as the dictionaries of Old and Middle English, the *Oxford English Dictionary* and the *Anglo-Norman Dictionary*, are indispensable, enabling the student and scholar to explore both the lexical and semantic history of each word now stored in the *Dictionary of Medieval Latin from British Sources*. A huge amount of exciting work remains to be done: in fact, in many areas the linguistic study of BML and its impact on British and Continental European culture has scarcely begun. As the European medieval Latin dictionaries gradually reach completion, comparisons between regional variations in different areas and the relation of Latin to the local vernaculars become increasingly possible.[48] The Anglo-Norman and various English dictionaries will enable the reader to trace the way the three main languages of medieval Britain interacted over the centuries, developing different forms and senses and passing them to each other. This may provide answers as to the broader question of what effect BML had on the linguistic situation one finds in the extant texts of the three main languages. How does this situation differ from that which might have developed if Anglo-Norman had been used instead of Latin, or had become the dominant vernacular instead of English, or if English had continued to develop its strong role, as a written as well as a vernacular language, after the Conquest?

---

48 Cf. *Adams (2007); A. Adamska, 'Latin and three vernaculars in East Central Europe from the point of view of the history of social communication' in *Garrison et al. (2013).

However, the primary aim of these volumes is to encourage and assist engagement with the literary and documentary sources from medieval Britain, in which one witnesses a language of enormous cultural richness being transposed into a new context, engaging with society on every level to produce a body of writings of interest in its own right. Detailed exploration across the range of BML texts will allow readers to appreciate these writings more profoundly. If readers can approach them with a sense of perspective, aware that there are complexities and gradations in the language and its usage, they will be better able to understand the texts within their social and linguistic context. To be sure, different texts may initially attract different readers. For example, readers who are engaging with medieval Latin for the first time may find the saints' lives and letters of the early period an attractive place to start. Classicists may principally be interested by the large number of classical words, and by examples of semantic extension as well as evidence of etymological senses not attested in surviving CL, as with senses 1–2 of *stipulari* (from which the English verb 'to stipulate' is derived) relating to *stipula* ('stubble') which are recorded in *DMLBS* from the thirteenth century. For students of Latin literature, the period has much to offer, down to the renewed classicism of the fifteenth century, as in the Abbot of St Albans' epic-style description of his sea crossing in 1423 (John Amundesham, *Annals* 1.126–7). Historians will find much of interest in the historiography and in the administrative texts providing information on a national and local level. Throughout there are observations about human life. There is satire and black humour, for example in the chronicle of Meaux Abbey in Yorkshire, whose author comments (*RS* 43.3: 45) that after the naval battle of Sluys in 1340, the fish had eaten so many dead Frenchmen that if God had given fish the ability to talk, they would have spoken French. And everywhere there are records of human tragedy, often in unexpected places, as in the royal household accounts where an early indication of the death of Henry, the six-year-old son of King Edward I, in 1274 is given by the simple mention of eight pounds of wool purchased to line his bier at Westminster.[49]

It is hoped that from an engagement with the particular, with Latin itself, will develop the desire to explore more widely and deeply, as well as a familiarity with the language, allowing the reader to deal with texts and linguistic corpora that have not yet been translated or analysed. However, stepping back from the particular, one might venture to claim that as a written language, engaging with many aspects of contemporary society but also expecting to be preserved, it was a language of the long term, looking both to the past and the future. The Latin of medieval Britain provided important linguistic continuity in a multilingual society, offering a framework within which the vernaculars could develop until Latin was gradually superseded by English in almost all its roles, as by other

---

49 H. Johnstone (1922) 'The wardrobe and household of Henry, son of Edward I', *Bulletin of the John Rylands Library* 7: 384–420.

30 Introduction

vernaculars in other countries at that period. By 1500 Latin across Europe had been reduced to a largely rigid and artificial language: as such it was to continue in a restricted role as a literary plaything, a language of record for certain types of documents and as an academic language, occasionally of international use into modern times,[50] to which it has bequeathed a vast amount of information about life throughout the thousand years of medieval Britain.

------

50 D. Verbeke, 'Neo-Latin's interplay with other languages' in *The Oxford handbook of Neo-Latin* (2015).

ELEVENTH CENTURY

Section II.1

The Battle of Hastings and Its Aftermath
A: The Bayeux Tapestry (excerpts: sections 34–5, 37–61, 63–73)
B: William of Malmesbury, *A History of the English Kings* (*Gesta regum Anglorum*) (excerpt: 3.241–2)
C: Orderic Vitalis, *An Ecclesiastical History* (*Historia ecclesiastica*) (excerpt: 2.230–2)

For more-or-less contemporary accounts of the Battle of Hastings, compare *ASChr s.a.* 1066 (OE); Guy of Amiens, *Carmen de Hastingae proelio*, also referred to as *Carmen Widonis* (verse, c.1067/8, which has been likened to the OE poem *The Battle of Maldon*); William of Jumièges, *Gesta Normannorum ducum* (c.1070); William of Poitiers, *Gesta Guillelmi ducis Normannorum et regis Anglorum* (c.1075); and in the twelfth century: William of Malmesbury, *A History of the English Kings*; Orderic Vitalis, *An Ecclesiastical History*; Gaimar, *L'Estoire des Englais* (AN, 1139); Wace, *Roman de Rou* (AN, 1160).

Further Reading

Brown, R. Allen (1981) 'The Battle of Hastings', *Anglo-Norman Studies* 3: 1–21.
Gransden, A. (1974) 'Historians of the Norman Conquest' in *Gransden (1974).

A: The Bayeux Tapestry (excerpts: sections 34–5, 37–61, 63–73)

Date: ?before 1080.

Work: The Bayeux Tapestry, one of the most well-known cultural artefacts in Britain, is an embroidered linen strip about 68 m in length and 50 cm in height, probably made before 1080 for Odo of Bayeux, the half-brother of William the Conqueror. Although it has been preserved for many centuries in Bayeux in Normandy, it is likely to have been made in England, as English needlework was renowned already at this time: William of Poitiers in the *Gesta Guillelmi* (2.42) writes, *Anglicae nationis feminae multum acu et auri textura egregie* ('the English women were outstanding at needlework and weaving with gold'). However, there is no contemporary mention of this masterpiece. It is of interest not only as an exquisite work of art but also as a historical source, with both images and words, to set beside the relevant writings of contemporary authors. The 'tapestry' gives

34 Eleventh Century

a pictorial account, in scenes like those in a comic strip, with brief explanatory captions added above and around the pictures, of the relations between Harold of England and William of Normandy, culminating in the Battle of Hastings on 14 October 1066, which William of Malmesbury describes succinctly as *dies fatalis Angliae ... pro novorum dominorum commutatione* ('a fatal day for England ... as the country exchanged its old masters for new ones') (*GR* 3.245).

Linguistic points: The text uses both present and perfect tense. It contains non-classical forms such as *caballus* and *parabolare*, Latin words that underlie Romance forms such as 'cheval' and 'parler'. There are also examples of unusual semantics or syntax, e.g. *fodere* as 'to build by digging', *alloqui* with accusative or dative, and possible occasional confusion of active and passive forms of the verb, as with *dux iussit naves edificare* and *ut cibum raperentur*. While *narrare* does exist with the sense 'to inform', it is rare to find it taking a direct object of the person informed, as here. As often in ML the spelling is not always consistent. The names are mostly uninflected. Some names occur in an OE form, as in Pevenesae, Gyrð and Hestenga, but the influence of French vernacular may be detectable, as in the form Edward for Eadward. The words *at* and *ceastra* are definitely OE: the latter may be a suffix to 'Hestenga' or may stand alone, as a label for the castle in the picture. The nature of the Latin used on the tapestry has attracted little attention, apart from the discussion by Ian Short from the viewpoint of an AN specialist, as to whether the 'author' was a native English- or French-speaker: Short claims that the choice of Latin words, and even the syntax, indicate that French is the underlying vernacular. Note that the Normans are referred to as *Franci* on the Bayeux Tapestry, rather than *Normanni*. The *DMLBS* shows how both these terms had a range of meanings which could be confusing: *Francus* could mean Frankish, French or Norman, while *Nor(th)mannus* could apply to Scandinavians or Normans.

TEXT II.1A

[34–5] HIC WILLELM DUX IUSSIT NAVES EDIFICARE.
[37] HIC TRAHUNT^{ur} NAVES AD MARE.
[38–9] ISTI PORTANT ARMAS AD NAVES ET HIC TRAHUNT CARRUM CUM VINO ET ARMIS.
[39–42] HIC WILLELM DUX IN MAGNO NAVIGIO MARE TRANSIVIT ET VENIT AD PEVENESÆ.
[43–4] HIC EXEUNT CABALLI DE NAVIBUS
[44–5] ET HIC MILITES FESTINAVERUNT HESTINGA UT CIBUM RAPERENTUR (...)
[46–8] HIC EST WADARD: HIC COQUITUR CARO ET HIC MINISTRAVERUNT MINISTRI. HIC FECERUNT PRANDIUM ET HIC EPISCOPUS CIBUM ET POTUM BENEDICIT. ODO EP[ISCOPU]S, ROTBERT, WILLELM.

II.1 | The Battle of Hastings and Its Aftermath 35

[49] ISTE IUSSIT UT FODERETUR CASTELLUM¹ AT HESTENGA CEAS-TRA.²

[50–1] HIC NUNCIATUM EST WILLELMᴼ DE HAROLD[O]. HIC DOMUS INCENDITUR.

[51–2] HIC MILITES EXIERUNT DE HESTENGA

[52–4] ET VENERUNT AD PRELIUM CONTRA HAROLDUM REGE[M].

[54–5] HIC WILLELM DUX INTERROGAT VITAL SI VIDISSET EXER-CITU[M] HAROLDI.

[56–7] ISTE NUNTIAT HAROLDUM REGE[M] DE EXERCITU WILELMI DUCIS.

[57–61] HIC WILLELM DUX ALLOQUITUR SUIS MILITIBUS UT PREPARA-RENT SE VIRILITER ET SAPIENTER AD PRELIUM CONTRA ANGLORUM EXERCITU[M].

[63–5] HIC CECIDERUNT LEWINE ET GYRÐ FRATRES HAROLDI REGIS.

[65–6] HIC CECIDERUNT SIMUL ANGLI ET FRANCI IN PRELIO.

[67–8] HIC ODO EP[ISCOPU]S BACULU[M] TENENS CONFORTAT PUER-OS (…)

[68–70] HIC FRANCI PUGNANT ET CECIDERUNT QUI ERANT CUM HAROLDO.³

[71] HIC HAROLD REX INTERFECTUS EST

[72–3] ET FUGA VERTERUNT ANGLI.

Translation (of the above inscriptions)

Here Duke William ordered (them) to build ships. Here ships are hauled to the sea. These men are carrying arms to the ships and here they pull a wagon with wine and arms. Here Duke William crossed the sea in a large ship and came to Peven-sey. Here the horses leave the ships and here the soldiers have hurried to Hastings to seize food. (…) This man has given orders that a fortification be thrown up at Hastings. The castle. Here a report is given to William about Harold. Here a house is burned. Here the soldiers left Hastings and came to the battle against King Harold. Here Duke William asks Vital whether he has seen Harold's army. This man tells King Harold about Duke William's army. Here Duke William addresses his soldiers, so that they might prepare themselves bravely and wisely for the battle against the

---

1 This castle with motte, the fifth to be depicted on the Tapestry, is one that still exists, in a ruined state, at Hastings; note the variant spelling Hestenga.

2 This could be part of the place name of Hastings, or a label for the castle, as with the word *Ecclesia* on the scene with Bosham church.

3 Cf. *DB* f. 50a with the reference to two people at Tytherley, Hants.: *duo ex his qui tenu-erunt occisi fuerunt in Bello de Hastinges*: 'two of those who held, were killed in the Battle of Hastings.

36 Eleventh Century

army of the English. Here were killed Lewine and Gyrth, King Harold's brothers. Here the English and French fell at the same time in battle. Here Bishop Odo holding a staff encourages the young men. (…) Here the French fight and those who were with Harold have fallen. Here King Harold has been killed and the English have turned in flight.

Primary Sources

Wilson, D. M. (1985) *The Bayeux Tapestry*, London. With colour plates of the complete tapestry and, on pp. 172–3, the Latin inscriptions, numbered 1–73 (as followed in the excerpt above).

Further Reading

Bouet, P., Levy, B. and Neveux, F. (ed.) (2004) *La Tapisserie de Bayeux: l'art de broder l'histoire*, Caen.

Brilliant, R. (1991) 'A stripped narrative for their eyes and ears', *Word and Image: A Journal of Verbal/Visual Imagery* 7.2: 98–126.

Carson Pastan, E. and White, S. (2015) *The Bayeux Tapestry and its contexts: a reassessment*, Woodbridge.

Owen-Crocker, G. R. (2006) 'The embroidered word: text in the Bayeux Tapestry' in **Medieval clothing and textiles* (2005–), vol. 2.

Short, Ian (2001) 'The language of the Bayeux Tapestry inscription' in *Anglo-Norman studies XXIII: proceedings of the Battle conference*, ed. J. Gillingham, Woodbridge, 267–80, including complete text of inscriptions.

B: William of Malmesbury, *A History of the English Kings* (*Gesta regum Anglorum*) (excerpt: 3.241–2)

Date: 1125–35.

The OMT edition lists the many MSS, grouped into four versions of the text. The number witnesses to William's immediate popularity and influence.

Author: William (c.1090–c.1142) was a monk at Malmesbury who wrote a number of historical works, drawing on Norman and English historiography and biography. His major works were *A History of the English Kings* (*GR*), dealing with British history from the coming of the Saxons to 1120, and *A History of the English Bishops* (*GP*) – referred to by Antonia Gransden as 'a guidebook for pilgrims' – from 597–1125, both of which were influenced by Bede's *Ecclesiastical History*.

II.1 | The Battle of Hastings and Its Aftermath 37

William's writings display his phenomenally wide-ranging familiarity with earlier Latin literature, including many writings from the classical period, both prose and verse, as is clear from the list compiled by R. M. Thomson, cited below. He can be regarded as one of the greatest writers of Latin from any period: not because he slavishly follows classical models but because he confidently employs his vast vocabulary, including multiple senses of the same word, and his stylistic acumen to produce a text that is imaginative, concise and clear. William makes use of topography, charters, manuscripts, monuments (as in his work on the antiquity of the church at Glastonbury) and oral accounts as sources, while writing in an engaging and readable manner. He also wrote a commentary on the Old Testament book Lamentations, and Lives of English and Irish saints.

Work: In the *GR* William rejected the annalistic form of history used by the *Anglo-Saxon Chronicle* and instead wrote a continuous narrative, seeking to edify as well as please while he filled in the historiographical gap between Bede and his own day with anecdotes and descriptions of individuals and national characteristics. In its treatment of the English and Normans William is quite even-handed, reflecting his mixed Norman and English parentage, but he does display admiration for the Normans' military skill in his description of the battle of Hastings when he blames the English defeat on their characteristically rash behaviour (3.245). William's account of the battle shows that he knew William of Poitiers' version, and it is possible he had seen the Bayeux Tapestry in Normandy. The excerpt below includes the earliest mention of the medieval French epic *La Chanson de Roland*, the oldest copy of which survives in the twelfth-century part of MS Digby 23, in the Bodleian Library, Oxford.

Linguistic points: William was not only a skilful historian but a writer of Latin that is usually pellucid. He has a very extensive classical vocabulary, and is particularly notable for his ability to use a range of senses of classical words, some very rare. He avoids Grecisms or neologisms, and only rarely does he use a post-classical word deriving from Germanic, as for example *tunna* (*GR* 4.373). It is, however, interesting to note that he does use the word *werra* for 'war', which only entered BML in the late eleventh century via French (and entered English, in the form *werre*, in the twelfth century): in *GR* 4.310 he writes *belle scis actitare guerram, qui hostibus prebes aquae copiam* ('that's a fine way to wage war, to give your enemy plenty of water'), where he may be playing on the assonance with the usual phrase for 'to wage war' – *bellum gerere*. His many classical and occasional patristic allusions are elegantly embedded in the text. William's aim was to make the information accessible to many (*ut quod a multis scribitur a multis legatur*, *GR* Book 4, pref.) and variations of style were a conscious means to achieve the necessary readability. The phrase *levi negotio* is a favourite of this author. The spelling used here is that of the OMT text, which follows the orthography of William himself in the holograph MS of the *GP*, Oxford MS Magdalen

38 Eleventh Century

College lat. 172, dated no later than 1125, where t replaces c before i followed by a vowel, as in *fatiunt* below.

TEXT II.1B

The battle of Hastings

[3.241] ita utrimque animosi duces disponunt acies, patrio quisque ritu. Angli, ut accepimus, totam noctem insomnem cantibus potibusque[4] ducentes, mane incunctanter in hostem procedunt; pedites omnes cum bipennibus, conserta ante se scutorum testudine, impenetrabilem cuneum fatiunt; quod profecto illis ea die saluti fuissent, nisi Normanni simulata fuga more suo confertos manipulos laxassent. rex ipse pedes iuxta vexillum stabat cum fratribus ut, in commune periculo aequato, nemo de fuga cogitaret. vexillum illud post victoriam papae misit Willelmus, quod erat in hominis pugnantis figura, auro et lapidibus arte sumptuosa intextum.

[3.242] contra Normanni, nocte tota confessioni peccatorum vacantes, mane Dominico corpori communicarent. pedites cum arcubus et sagittis primam frontem muniunt, equites retro divisis alis consistunt. comes vultu serenus et clara voce suae parti utpote iustiori Deum affuturum pronuntians, arma poposcit; moxque ministrorum tumultu loricam inversam indutus, casum risu correxit, 'Vertetur', inquiens, 'fortitudo comitatus mei in regnum.' tunc cantilena Rollandi inchoata, ut martium viri exemplum pugnaturos accenderet, inclamatoque Dei auxilio prelium consertum bellatumque acriter, neutris in multam diei horam cedentibus. quo comperto, Willelmus innuit suis ut ficta fuga campo se subtraherent. hoc commento Anglorum cuneus solutus, quasi palantes hostes a tergo cesurus, exitium sibi maturavit; Normanni enim, conversis ordinibus reversi, dispersos adoriuntur et in fugam cogunt. ita ingenio circumventi pulchram mortem pro patriae ultione meruere nec tamen ultioni suae defuere, quin crebro consistentes de insequentibus insignes cladis acervos facerent. nam occupato tumulo Normannos, calore successus acriter ad superiora nitentes, in vallem deiciunt, levique negotio in subiectos tela torquentes, lapides rotantes, omnes ad unum fundunt. item fossatum quoddam preruptum compendiario et noto sibi transitu evadentes, tot ibi inimicorum conculcavere ut cumulo cadaverum planitiem campi aequarent. valuit haec vicissitudo, modo illis modo istis vincentibus, quantum Haroldi vita moram fecit; at ubi iactu sagittae violato cerebro procubuit, fuga Anglorum perhennis in noctem fuit.

---

4 Wace in his Anglo-Norman *Roman de Rou* mentions the English drinking on the night before the battle, and the English toasts 'weisseil' and 'drincheheil', for which cf. Geoffrey of Monmouth, *HRB* 100 (Section II.12).

Translation: William of Malmesbury, *A History of the English Kings*

[3.241] *And so the spirited leaders on both sides drew up their forces, each according to his own country's practice. The English, as we have learned, spent the whole night singing and drinking, getting no sleep at all, and in the morning they marched on the enemy without hesitation. All the foot soldiers with their battle axes formed an impenetrable wedge formation, holding their shields in front of them in a closely fitted screen; this would have saved them that day if the Normans had not pretended to retreat and managed to loosen the serried unit in their customary manner. King Harold, on foot, stood next to the banner beside his brother soldiers so that if they all shared the same danger no one would consider fleeing. After the victory William sent that banner to the pope: it had a picture of a warrior on it and was richly woven with gold and jewels.*

[3.242] *Opposite them, the Normans, after spending the whole night confessing their sins, in the morning took part in the Eucharist. Their foot soldiers, with bows and arrows, protected the front line, while horsemen took their stand behind them, formed into units on each flank. The duke (of Normandy), with a calm expression and a clear voice, announced that God would be on his side because it was more just. He then called for his weapons; when he put on his chain mail the wrong way round, because his squires got muddled, he put it right with a laugh, saying, 'Let's hope the strength of my dukedom is turned into a kingdom!' Then William began to sing the Song of Roland so that the example of a heroic warrior might fire them as they went into battle; calling on God's help, they joined battle and fought fiercely, and for much of the day neither side would give way. When William learned of this he indicated to his men that they should pretend to flee and withdraw from the battlefield. As a result of this deception, the English soldiers, who had broken up their wedge formation so that they could cut the scattering enemy down from behind, hastened their own destruction; for the Normans, turning their lines round and retreating, attacked the English as they scattered, forcing them to flee. The English were thus deceived by this cunning trick and earned a noble death for avenging their country, and yet they also managed to avenge themselves, for by repeatedly making a stand, they made great piles of dead bodies out of those who were pursuing them. By occupying the hill they drove back into the valley the Normans who were fiercely pushing up to higher ground, driven on by the heat of success. Discharging their weapons against those below with minimum effort, and hurling rocks, they all streamed together. Then escaping from a steep trench by means of a short passage known to them, they trampled upon so many of the enemy there that the piles of corpses created a level field. This back and forth, with one side winning one moment, the other the next minute, lasted as long as Harold's life; but when an arrow pierced his brain and he fell forward, the flight of the English lasted long into the night.*

Primary Source

William of Malmesbury, *Gesta regum Anglorum*, vol. 1 (text) and vol. 2 (introduction and commentary), ed. R. M. Thomson and M. Winterbottom, OMT, Oxford, 1998–9.

Further Reading

Momma, H. (2013) 'Narrating the battle of Hastings: multilingual Britain and the monolingualism of William of Malmesbury' in *Jefferson and Putter (2013).

Thomson, R. (1987) *William of Malmesbury*, Woodbridge. Includes a list of Latin writings known to William of Malmesbury at first hand.

Winterbottom, M. (1995) 'The *Gesta regum* of William of Malmesbury', *JML* 5: 158–73.

—— (2003) 'The language of William of Malmesbury' in *Rhetoric and renewal in the Latin West, 1100–1540*, ed. C. Mews, C. Nederman and R. Thomson, Turnhout.

—— (2017) 'Words, words, words' in *Discovering William of Malmesbury*, ed. R. Thomson, E. Dolmans and E. Winkler, Woodbridge.

—— (2019) 'Beginning a history: studies in William of Malmesbury's *Gesta regum Anglorum*, Book One', *JML* 29: 101–21.

C: Orderic Vitalis, *An Ecclesiastical History* (*Historia ecclesiastica*) (excerpt: 2.230–2, cited by volume and page of OMT edition)

Date: 1114–41.

Orderic's *Ecclesiastical History* survives in thirteen books, most of them in autograph MSS; this passage is taken from one of these (Paris MS BN lat. 5506). Books 7 and 8, however, are preserved in Vatican MS Reginensis latina 703B.

Author: Orderic (1075–c.1142) was born of a Norman father and English mother in England. Educated by an English priest in Shrewsbury until the age of 10, he was then sent to the monastery of Saint-Evroul in Normandy for further studies, and there he lived as a monk for the rest of his life. Apart from compiling his *Ecclesiastical History* (for which he writes an autobiographical epilogue in 1141: 6.550ff.), he edited and copied the work of William of Jumièges and made a copy of Bede's *Ecclesiastical History of the English People*.

Work: Orderic's work is an account of his own monastery from its refoundation in 1050, within the wider history of Normandy down to 1141, moving in and out of ecclesiastical and political matters in England and Normandy, while Book 7 introduces the perspective of a universal history onto the world beyond Normandy. In general Orderic cites documents often, but he also invents speeches and dialogues. He often makes authorial comments, as in the following excerpt, where his compassion is evident. In his account of William the Conqueror he largely relies on the account of William of Poitiers, though he cuts down the classical references and gives a more critical account of William, as in the passage below where he stresses William's brutality in the northern campaign of 1069–70 when William was working to put down the rebellions of the English from Cornwall up to Durham. The English were supported along the east coast by an army of Danes, with the help of troops from Poland, Frisia and Saxony. William arrives at York to find that the Danes have fled; he fortifies York and sets up protection against the Danes.

Linguistic points: Orderic, like William of Malmesbury, has a wide vocabulary, but his prose is distinguished by more words influenced by (Norman) French: not only does *werra* (*gue-*) regularly appear, but also such words as *calfagium* ('heating'), *canardus* (a type of boat), *dangio* ('dungeon') and *fustanium* ('fustian cloth'). Traces of his childhood in England have been perceived in the forms of English place names he uses.[5] There is also the influence of Scripture and of patristic and early medieval sources. Here a factual section with short sentences and asyndeton moves into a section that relates the terrible effects of William's violence, and the author's anger, as expressed in the tricolon of verbs in -*eo* and, in the following sentence, of the nouns *iudex*, *vindex* and *lex*, culminating in the certainty of God's vengeance, a powerful theme throughout Orderic's work.

TEXT II.1C

The aftermath of the Conquest: the harrying of the north 1069–70
[2.230–2 Chibnall] ipse vero in saltuosa quaedam et difficillime accessibilia loca contendit, et abditos illic hostes persequi summopere studuit. spacio centum miliariorum castra eius diffunduntur. plerosque gladio vindice ferit, aliorum latebras evertit, terras devastat, et domos cum rebus omnibus concremat. nusquam tanta crudelitate usus est Guillelmus. hic turpiter vitio succubuit, dum iram suam regere contempsit, et reos innocuosque pari animadversione peremit. iussit enim ira stimulante segetibus et pecoribus cum vasis et omni genere alimentorum

---

5 M. Faulkner (2019) 'Orderic and English' in *Orderic Vitalis: life, works and interpretations*, ed. C. Crozier, G. Gasper, D. Roach and E. van Houts, Woodbridge.

42 Eleventh Century

repleri, et igne iniecto penitus omnia simul comburi, et sic omnem alimoniam per totam regionem Transhumbranam pariter devastari. unde sequenti tempore tam gravis in Anglia late sevit penuria, et inermem ac simplicem populum tanta famis involuit miseria, ut Christianae gentis utriusque sexus et omnis aetatis homines perirent plus quam centum milia. in multis Guillelmum nostra libenter extulit relatio, sed in hoc quod una iustum et impium tabidae famis lancea aeque transfixit laudare non audeo. nam dum innocuos infantes iuvenesque vernantes et floridos canicie senes fame periclitari video, misericordia motus miserabilis populi meroribus et anxietatibus magis condoleo, quam tantae cedis reo frivolis adulationibus favere inutiliter studeo. praeterea indubitanter assero, quod impune non remittetur tam feralis occisio. summos enim et imos intuetur omnipotens iudex, et aeque omnium facta discutiet ac puniet iustissimus vindex, ut palam omnibus enodat Dei perpetua lex.

Translation: Orderic Vitalis, *An Ecclesiastical History*

William marched into densely wooded areas that were extremely difficult to reach, putting all his efforts into pursuing the enemy hiding there. His castles were spread over an area of a hundred miles. With his sword he took revenge on large numbers, destroyed the hiding places of others, laid waste to their land, burning down their homes and all their possessions. Nowhere else did William behave with such cruelty. Here he shamefully succumbed to vice, when he disdained to control his anger and killed both innocent and guilty, punishing them equally. Goaded by anger he ordered the area to be filled with crops and animals together with vessels and every kind of food and then fire was to be thrown in and everything totally destroyed: in this way all the food throughout the whole region north of the Humber was equally devastated. In the following period such serious poverty raged far and wide in England and such hunger oppressed the unarmed and simple people with misery that more than 100,000 Christians of both sexes and from every age group died. On many subjects our account has been happy to praise William but in this matter I do not venture to praise him because with the single lance of wasting hunger he pierced the just person and the wicked equally. When I see innocent babies and blossoming young people and the elderly, grey-haired but vigorous, dying of hunger, I am moved by pity and sympathise with the sorrows and worries of these poor people, rather than uselessly attempting to favour with false flattery a person who is guilty of so much slaughter. Moreover I assert without hesitation that such savage killing will not go unpunished. For the omnipotent judge looks down upon the high and the low and the most just avenger will put on trial and punish the deeds of all equally, as God's everlasting law explains clearly to all.

Primary Sources and Related Texts

Orderic Vitalis, *Historia Ecclesiastica*, ed. M. Chibnall, 6 vols, OMT, Oxford, 1969–80.

William of Malmesbury, *GR* 3.249, gives a poignant but less harrowing summary of the harrying of the north, the effects of which he claims are visible half a century later. William concludes with a description reminiscent of Gildas' description of Britain in the sixth century (*EB* 3, for which see Section I.2): *urbes olim preclaras, turres proceritate sua in caelum minantes, agros laetos pascuis irriguos fluviis, si quis modo videt peregrinus, ingemit; si quis superest vetus incola, non agnoscit* ('Those cities, formerly so beautiful, the towers so tall they threatened the sky, the fields of fertile pasture irrigated by rivers: if a traveller from abroad were to see them he would sigh; if a former inhabitant were to see them, he would not recognise them'). Certainly the drop in population and lack of economic resources were noticeable in 1087, when the Domesday Book records that many places in Yorkshire were 'waste', probably implying that they had been devastated.

Thomas Walsingham, *Ypodigma Neustriae*, for a history of England, with a partial focus on Normandy between 911 and 1419.

Further Reading

Orderic Vitalis, *Historia Ecclesiastica*, vol. 1: *General introduction*, including pp. 100–10 on Orderic's style and language.

Bates, D. (2018) *William the Conqueror*, New Haven, CT.

Crozier, C., Gasper, G., Roach, D. and Van Houts, E. (ed.) (2019) *Orderic Vitalis: life, works and interpretations*, Woodbridge.

Palmer, J. (1998) 'War and Domesday waste' in *Armies, chivalry and warfare in medieval Britain and France*, ed. M. Strickland, Stamford.

Section II.2

Two Charters of William the Conqueror (excerpts: nos 31 and 185)

Dates: Late 1060s and early 1070s.

Author: During his reign as William I of England, William the Conqueror produced hundreds of charters recording grants he made to many different beneficiaries in Normandy and England, primarily donating land to abbeys and churches. Of those made for English beneficiaries, about seventy-eight are authentic Latin documents. Initially OE continued to be used in writs and charters after the Conquest, but this practice was soon abandoned in favour first of bilingual documents for a short time, and then Latin ones, accompanied by a change of form in these documents. It is possible that this linguistic change led to the destruction of many pre-Conquest royal documents.

Work: The first charter selected here is no. 31 in Bates' edition. It dates from just after the Conquest: it is a rare example of one written in OE (preserved in later copies in TNA), for which a later (probably twelfth-century) Latin translation, found in a separate MS, is appended here. William informs his French and English thegns in Yorkshire that he has granted land to the church in Beverley. Aldred (or Ealdred) was Archbishop of York from 1060–9, at the time of this charter. He had led a colourful life, travelled to Jerusalem on a pilgrimage in 1058 and was closely involved in ecclesiastical and secular politics; after crowning William the Conqueror, he supported the king, even during the harrying of the north in 1069 (for which, see Section II.1C).

The second example is no. 185, dating from the 1070s and unique in combining Latin and OE in the same document. It is preserved in later copies in TNA and in St Paul's DC Muniments. In this charter William informs his faithful French and English men that he has granted land and rights to St Paul's, London. Lanfranc, the first Norman Archbishop of Canterbury (1070–89), is one of the witnesses.

Linguistic points: In no. 31 *baro* shows an early use of this term, not attested from pre-1066 extant texts, apart from in a curse tablet from Uley, Gloucestershire probably from the late Roman period, where it means 'man' as opposed to 'woman'.[1] Here *baro* refers to a royal vassal, as in the English equivalent 'baron'. *syrie* is the genitive of *scira*, the Latin form of the OE word for 'shire', which only appears

---

1 Cf. *Adams (2016: 415–16).

II.2 | Two Charters of William the Conqueror 45

in Latin after the Conquest.[2] The more technical OE terms *witword* and *caupland* are not rendered in a Latin form but rather glossed as *testatio morientium* and *emptio*, i.e. '(by) the witness statement of the dying' and '(by) purchase'. *disfacere* is a calque on the OE 'undo' with the Latin prefix *dis-*, for which see *OED s.v.* dis- as a prefix, with the complex history of this Latin prefix in English and French.

No. 185 contains an early example of the phrase *sciatis quod ego concedo*, which will become, in varying forms, a formula of medieval charters. The author mentions the Anglo-Saxon privilege of sake and soke in their integrated Latin form, but from *tol et theam* he continues in OE with the formulaic list of Anglo-Saxon privileges granted to landowners. Cf. *Fleta* 1.45 for a list of such terms with Latin definitions.

TEXT II.2A

King William confirms the lands belonging to the Church of St John at Beverley

[31] (1066–9)
Old English original
Willelm cynge gret alle mine þegenas on Eoferwicscire frencisce et englisce freon- dlice. et ic cyðe eow þæt ich hæbbe gegyfen sce (St) Johanne æt Beuerlic sac et socna ofer eallum þam landum þe wæron gyfene on Ædwærdes dæg cynges innto sce Jo- hannes mynstre et eac ofer þæm landum þe Ealdred ærcebiscop hæfð siðþan begitan on minan dagan þider inn on witword oðð on caupland. beo hit all freo wið me et wið æghwilcum men butan ðam biscope et ðam mynster preosten. et ne beo nan man swa deort þe hit undo þæt ic hebbe gecyðet Criste and sce Johanne. et ic wylle þæt ðær beo æfre mynsterlif et canonica samnung ða hwile þe ænig man leofað. Godes bletsunge beo mid eallum cristenum mannum ðe filstað to þæs halgan we- ordscipe. Amen.

Twelfth-century Latin translation of eleventh-century OE original
Willelmus rex omnibus baronibus suis Eboraci syrie francis et anglis salutem. no- tifico quod ego dedi sancto Johanni de Beverlaco sacam et socam[3] super omnes illas terras que fuerunt date ecclesie sancti Johannis in diebus Edwardi regis. si- militer et super illas terras quas Aldredus archiepiscopus postea illuc perquisivit in diebus meis aut testatione morientium aut emptione. sit illa libera adversum me et adversum omnes homines preter archiepiscopum et presbiteros ipsius ec- clesie. et nemo sit tam audax ut hoc disfaciat quod ego concessi Christo et sancto

---

2 Cf. *syra vero Anglice, Latine dicitur provincia*, H. Hunt, *HA* 1.5. See also Section II.4.

3 This term 'sake and soke' for an Anglo-Saxon grant of jurisdiction survived after the Conquest for a while, with the OE terms being used in a Latin matrix or, as here, Latinised.

46 Eleventh Century

Johanni. et volo ut ibi sit semper vita ecclesiastica et canonicorum congregatio quamdiu aliquis vixerit. benedictio Dei sit cum omnibus Christianis qui auxilium fecerint ad ipsius sancti honorem. Amen.

Translation: Latin Writ

King William sends greetings to all his barons in Yorkshire, both French and English. I make known that I have given sake and soke to St John of Beverley over all those lands which were given to the Church of St John in the days of King Edward. Similarly also over those lands which Archbishop Ealdred afterwards acquired there during my time either by the bequest of the dying or by purchase. May this land be free from my control and that of all men apart from the archbishop and priests of this church. And may no one be so bold as to undo this which I have granted to Christ and to St John. And I wish that the ecclesiastical life and the assembly of the canons should always be there as long as anyone lives. May God's blessing be with all Christians who have given assistance to the honour of this saint. Amen.

TEXT II.2B

King William confirms the lands belonging to St Paul's Church in London
[185] (1073–8) Willelmus gratia Dei rex Anglorum omnibus fidelibus suis francis et anglis salutem. sciatis quod ego concedo Deo et ecclesie sancti Pauli de Lundonia et rectoribus et servitoribus eius in omnibus terris quas ipsa ecclesia habet vel habebit infra burgum et extra, sacam et socnam et *thol et theam et infeageneþeof et griþbrice et alle frioscipes bi strande et bi lande, on tide et of tide et ealle þa gerithte þe into þam cristendome gebyrað, on morðspraeche et on unricht haemed et on unricht weorc, ofaer eall þe bisceoprice on mine lande et on oelce oðres mannes lande.* quia volo ut ipsa ecclesia ita sit libera in omnibus sicut volo esse animam meam in Die Iudicii. t(estibus) Osmundo cancellario, et Lanfranco archiepiscopo Cantuar' et Toma Eboracensi archiepiscopo (1070–1100) et Rogero comite de Seropesbiria et Alano comite et Gaufrido de Magnavilla et Ranulfo Peverel.

Translation: Latin Writ

William by the grace of God king of the English sends greetings to all his faithful, both French and English. You should know that I grant to God and to the Church of St Paul in London and to its rectors and servants in all the lands which this church has or will have within the borough and outside it, sake and soke and (the rest in OE) etc. because I wish that this church should be as free in all things as I wish my

soul to be on the Day of Judgement. As witnesses, Osmund the chancellor and Lan-
franc Archbishop of Canterbury and Thomas Archbishop of York and Roger Earl of
Shrewsbury and Earl Alan and Geoffrey de Magnavilla and Ralph Peverel.

Primary Sources and Related Texts

Bates, D. (ed.) (1998) *Regesta regum Anglo-Normannorum: the Acta of William I
(1066–1087)*, Oxford. With *Index verborum*.
*Recueil des Actes des ducs de Normandie de 911 à 1066 (1961).
Cf. earlier Latin charters, from the Anglo-Saxon period, in Sections I.3, 22, 31
and 33.

Further Reading

BACS 10 (St Paul's, London), ed. S. E. Kelly, Oxford, 2004. Contains Anglo-
Saxon charters of grants to St Paul's, with introduction on early history of
London and St Paul's.
Broun, Dauvit (ed.) (2011) *The reality behind charter diplomatic in Anglo-
Norman Britain*. Glasgow.
Royal writs from the Conquest to Glanvill, Selden Society 77 (1959).
Sharpe, R. (2013) 'Addressing different language groups: charters from the
eleventh and twelfth centuries' in *Jefferson and Putter (2013).

Section II.3

Goscelin of Canterbury (or Saint-Bertin), *The Book of Consolation* (*Liber confortatorius*) (excerpts: Book 1, pp. 27 and 41 (ed. Talbot))

Date: c.1080.

BL MS Sloane 3103, of the twelfth century, is the unique extant witness.

Author: Goscelin (c.1035–c.1107) was born in Flanders and entered the Benedictine monastery of Saint-Bertin, at Saint-Omer, a centre for literary production with links to England. He moved from Saint-Bertin in about 1060 to work with Bishop Herman of Ramsbury and later Sherborne (between 1045 and 1078). He acted as chaplain to the nuns at Wilton near Salisbury, one of the most powerful nunneries in medieval England. After leaving Wilton in about 1080 Goscelin spent the rest of his life at various monasteries in England, writing many saints' Lives, particularly of earlier Anglo-Saxon women, and liturgical works. William of Malmesbury (*GR* 4.342) praises him as second only to Bede for his literary works and to Osbern of Canterbury for his musical talents.

Work: The *Book of Consolation*, divided into four short books, is an intensely private work addressed to Eva, a young English girl of Danish and Lotharingian parents who had come to Wilton to be educated. When her friendship with Goscelin became too intense, she moved to a convent at Angers in France to become a recluse and Goscelin never saw her again: in this, their story resembles that of Abelard and Heloise in the following century, and indeed the way Goscelin speaks of spiritual love, with frequent use of antithesis, also looks forward to the letters of those more famous lovers. The work praises Eva's virtues, depicts the development of their spiritual love, encourages her in her devotion to asceticism, and meditates on human life, in a text threaded with quotations from Scripture and early Christian classics (including works by the Greek Father Gregory of Nazianzus), and references to past saints, as well as to classical and medieval Latin literature and liturgical works. Below are selected the opening section which follows the prologue addressed 'to one shut in from one shut out' and a section from later in Book 1, where Goscelin muses imaginatively, and with characteristic empathy, on the things that endure and those that pass away as part of his advice to Eva to steer clear of the snares of this world. Notable is his compassion for the fate of princesses who are sent abroad to live their whole lives in a foreign culture, far from their families, though they do so for love of their husbands, as the human soul must also move to a new land for the sake of its salvation. Cf. Æthelweard's allusion, in the prefatory letter to his *Chronicle*, to the Anglo-Saxon princesses in his family who were sent to the Continent to be married (Section I.36).

Linguistic points: The opening of the work, though addressed to Eva rather than to God, bears certain similarities to the opening of Augustine's *Confessions*, with the direct address, series of antitheses, citation from the Psalms, and emotional tone. Goscelin displays a liking for wordplay and assonance, e.g. *conjungi/sejungi*, *natalis/mortalis*, often playing with antitheses that are central to Christian theology. *repraesentare* is used in its literal sense of 'to make present', when he alludes to the topos of absent friends being reunited by letters. *resolidare* is a favourite of Goscelin's, here used of two souls. *series* probably means 'narrative' here, as in Orderic's account of the White Ship disaster in Section II.11C (*seriem tristis eventus ... enucleavit*).

TEXT II.3

Goscelin's spiritual love for Eva
[Book 1, p. 27 Talbot] O luce dilectior anima, adest tibi Goscelinus tuus, inseparabili anime presentia; adest meliori parte, ea qua te diligere potuit, individua, qua nulla excludant terrarum interstitia; salutat te in Christo salute sempiterna. ecce tetigit nos manu sua, illa omnia discernens et dispensans sapientia, et ad tempus separans docuit altiora consilia, ut scilicet in illa patria anhelemus et festinemus coniungi, ubi numquam perpetuo possimus seiungi. quo autem longius corpore removit, eo inseparabilius unicam aliquando duorum animam resolidabit. sic quondam ipse fons dilectionis discipulorum affectus corporali absentia quo acrius vulneravit, eo sublimius in spirituali caritate conflagravit. unde, quia nec potuit nec meruit unanimis tuus te accessibus visitare corporeis, querit nunc anxiis litteris et longis querelis. paravit nobis hanc consolationem provida miseratio Domini ut, locis elongati, fide et scriptis possimus representari. et que meis debebantur sceleribus, hec separationis tormenta, alligare et refovere nos poterit intercurrens epistola. loquetur etiam edificatius tenax pagina quam fluxa lingua; poterit et tua dilectio videre lectione quem reliquit facie, et vocem et verba nostra suspiriosa oculis pro auribus haurire. ne ergo me putes abscisum a te, quotiens, in Christo nostri memor, dignaberis hec nostra monimenta respicere, estimato me tecum Wiltonie coram sancta domina nostra Eadgyda[1] aut etiam in hac pudica serie residere, te alloqui, te exhortari, te consolari, anhelantibus vulnerose caritatis affectibus Christum tuo infundere pectori.

---

1 Eadgyda is the OE form of St Edith (961–84), the daughter of King Edgar (for whom see Section I.40C) and of a young woman he had taken from Wilton.

50 Eleventh Century

sed ecce, dum scribo, grassans dolor non potuit dissimulari, cecidere manus et usus scriptorii; rugitus et eiulatus invasit me; corrui coram altari tui Laurentii, ut sedebam in eius ecclesia remotiori, clamabam frequens in diluvio lacrimarum quasi inter ictus et verbera Domini: Domine, miserere, Domine, miserere. rapui

Ps. 50:3 psalmum, 'Miserere mei Deus', et cum eiulatu illum intonui, 'et cor contritum et
Ps. 50:19 humiliatum' atque in alio psalmo tibi competentes versiculos: 'similis factus sum
Ps. 101:7 pelicano solitudinis', et 'Dominus de celo in terram aspexit, ut audiret gemitum
Ps. 101:20-1 compeditorum.' magnis clamoribus infremui: sancta Maria, succurre miseris, iuva pusillanimes.[2] repetens ergo interruptam interrumpente luctu loquelam, quotiens, inquam, hic dignaberis nostram devotionem recolere, consolationem quasi presentis, si qua pietas diligentis movet, accipe. (…)

Translation: Goscelin, *The Book of Consolation*

O soul dearer than light, your Goscelin is with you, in an inseparable spiritual presence; he is with you in the best part of him, the part with which he could love you, undivided, from which no distance between our countries separates us; he greets you in Christ with eternal salvation. Look how He has touched us with His hand, deciding and managing everything with His wisdom; although He has separated us for a time He has taught us His higher plans so that we might hasten, breathless, to be joined in that land where we can never ever be separated. For the greater the physical distance He puts between us, the more inseparable He will make us one day, when He firmly reunites the two of us into a single soul. In the same way, the more painfully that fountain of love wounded His disciples' feelings long ago by His physical absence, the more sublimely He fired them with spiritual love. And so, because your companion, who shares one soul with you, could not and did not deserve to approach you physically to visit you, he seeks you now with anxious letters and long complaints. The Lord's provident compassion has prepared this consolation for us, so that although we are separated from each other by long distance, we might be present through our faith and writings. And the letter that runs between us will be able to bind up these torments of separation caused by my sins and can revive us. The retentive page, too, will speak more edifyingly than the fluid tongue; and by reading, your love will be able to see the person whose face it has left behind, and your eyes soak up our sighing words better than your ears. In case you should think that I have been cut off from you, whenever you are kind enough to look at these memorials of ours and to remember me in Christ, imagine that I am sitting with you at Wilton in the presence of our holy lady Edith or even in this chaste narrative, that I am talking to you, consoling you and pouring Christ into your breast with feelings of longing and wounded love.

---

2   Cf. the eighth-century prayer to the Virgin Mary in Section I.25.

But see now! while I was writing, my grief increased and could no longer be disguised; my hands fell to my side and my pen would not write. I am filled with howls and laments; I collapsed before the altar of your Laurence as I was sitting in a remote part of his church. I shouted repeatedly in floods of tears, as if I was suffering the blows and beatings of the Lord, 'Lord, have mercy, Lord have mercy.' I grasped at the psalm, 'Have mercy on me, O God', and as I cried out, I sang this verse, too, 'And a contrite and humiliated heart'; I chanted the verses that in another psalm I felt applied to you, 'I have become like a pelican in the wilderness', and 'The Lord looked down from heaven upon the earth to hear the groans of the chained.' I roared loudly: 'Holy Mary, help the wretched, assist the faint-hearted.' To resume what I was saying when grief interrupted it: whenever, I say, you are kind enough to remember our loyal affection, take consolation from me as if I were with you, if you are moved by the devotion of the one who loves you. (…)

Things that endure and things that pass away

[Book 1, p. 41 Talbot] an vero ad eterne claritatis patriam tendentem, patria non tam natalis quam mortalis sollicitat? filie regum et principum in deliciis a lacte nutrite, nichil scientes preter gloriam et felicitatem natalitie terre, nubunt in exteras nationes et aliena regna, barbaros mores et ignotas linguas disciture, sevisque dominis ac repugnantibus a naturali usu legibus serviture, sicut nuper filia marchisi Flandrensium nupsit Cunuto regi Danorum.[3] tales semel valedixere parentibus et natalibus patrie, ultra non valentes aut nolentes patriam respicere, maritali affectu plus omnibus valente. quanto magis anima Christum tota mente ac perpetua caritate secuta debet oblivisci populum suum et domum patris sui ut concupiscat rex decorem que induet sibi mater dilectionis pulchre, de Christi **Ps. 44:11–12** scilicet dilectionis pulchritudine. quam multi ob terrena lucra in longinquos fines cognationes mutant et genituram, de Gallia in Galatiam, in Hispaniam, de Anglia in Apuliam, in Greciam, pro perituris rebus ponentes animam suam, et nos dissimulamus migrare ad beatitudinem sempiternam? transferuntur denique gentes et regna, ut Israel in Egiptum, de Egipto in Chananeam, de Chananea in Assirios et Babilonem, sic Cuthite in Samariam, Troiani in Italiam et Romam, hodieque Normanni in Angliam, Britanniam, in qua te quoque cum Anglica gente constat fuisse advenam: sed et patre Dano et matre Lotaringa a claris natalibus filiam emersisse Anglicam. non solum autem homines sed et ipsa permutantur sola ac maria ut ubi quondam populorum et urbium floruerant insignia, iam vasta et profundissima regnent equora cunctaque se protestantur tam fluxa et caduca quam instabilia ac mutabilia. sic omnia disponuntur et ordinantur ab eterno consilio maiestatis Dei et prudentia, tam paganos quam Christianos, tam incredulos quam fideles, dispensante lance moderantissima, simulque docente rerum mutatione nos hic manentem civitatem non habere sed futuram inquirere

---

3   Adela, daughter of Robert of Flanders, married (St) Cnut IV, king of Denmark 1080–6.

52 Eleventh Century

oportere. sol unicus omnibus lucet, celum unicum omnibus patet, unum gremium orbis terrarum omnes fovet. et Andecavis et Anglis eadem sidera fulgent, flumina, prata, nemora, eademque rerum oblectamenta tam hic quam ibi reflorent. si qua desunt pro his que tua tellus minus habuit, alia assunt. hinc Prosper, 'non timeo exilium, mundus domus omnibus una est.'[4] ubique mixta bonis mala, ubique vepres et spine, ubique rose Christi sunt. soli ether et infernus norunt partes suas, soli dividunt hereditatem, unde nos assumat in sua idem redemptor et iudex seculorum.

Translation: Goscelin, *The Book of Consolation*

Or when one is heading towards the homeland of everlasting brightness, is one concerned with the country not so much of birth but of death? The daughters of kings and princes are brought up from babyhood amid luxury, and know only splendour and happiness in their home country, but they marry into foreign peoples and alien kingdoms. They will have to learn barbarous customs and unknown languages and be subservient to savage lords and laws that are inconsistent with natural practices, as for example the daughter of the Count of Flanders who recently married Cnut, the king of the Danes. These people say goodbye once and for all to their parents and their origins in their homeland, unable or unwilling to look upon their country again, for love of one's spouse is stronger than anything else. How much more ought the soul that follows Christ with its whole mind and with everlasting love to forget its people and its father's home so that the king may desire her beauty in which she will be clothed by the mother of beautiful love, beautiful, that is, from the beauty of the love of Christ? How many for the sake of worldly profit transfer their relatives and children to distant lands, from Gaul to Galatia, to Spain, from England to Apulia, to Greece, laying down their soul for perishable things, while we neglect to travel towards eternal blessedness? And then peoples and kingdoms also migrate from one place to another, like Israel to Egypt, from Egypt to Canaan, from Canaan to the Assyrians and Babylon, like the Cuthites to Samaria, the Trojans to Italy and Rome and in our time the Normans to England, to Britain, where it is known that you too were a stranger among the English people: but with your Danish father and Lotharingian mother from illustrious origins you emerged as an English daughter. Not only people but also lands and seas change places so that where once famous peoples and cities flourished, now vast and deep seas rule the waves and everything is shown to be fluid and transitory, unstable and changeable. This is how all things are managed and ordained by the eternal judgement and wisdom of God's

---

4   This hexameter line (*PL* 51.614B) is from a poem from a husband to his wife, where Goscelin's version replaces *metuo* with *timeo*.

majesty, with His scales that regulate most carefully both pagans and Christians, both non-believers and the faithful. At the same time the changes in things teach us that we do not have a lasting city here but must seek one in the life to come. A single sun shines upon all, a single sky is spread above us, the world's single embrace cherishes us all. The same stars shine for the Angevins and the English, the same rivers, fields, woods, the same delights flourish here as there. If your country lacks some things, it has other things instead which they do not have. And so Prosper writes, 'I do not fear exile, for the world is one home for all people.' Everywhere good and bad are mixed up, everywhere there are thorns and brambles, everywhere there are the roses of Christ. Only heaven and hell have their own regions and they alone divide up the inheritance; and so may the same redeemer and judge of the world take us up to His home.

Primary Sources and Related Texts

Talbot, C. (ed.) (1955) 'The *Liber Confortatorius* of Goscelin of Saint Bertin', *Analecta Monastica* 3 (Studia Anselmiana 37): 1–117 (Latin text).

Otter, M. (ed. and transl.) (2004) *Goscelin of Saint-Bertin: the Book of Encouragement and Consolation*, Cambridge. (Latin and English).

Goscelin of Saint-Bertin, *The hagiography of the female saints of Ely*, ed. R. Love, OMT, Oxford, 2004.

Muriel, poet of Wilton: poems addressed to her by Hildebert of Lavardin, Baudri of Bourgueil and Serlo of Bayeux.

The letter collection of Peter Abelard and Heloise, ed. D. Luscombe and transl. B. Radice, OMT, Oxford, 2013.

The Life of Christina of Markyate, transl. and ed. C. Talbot, S. Fanous and H. Leyser, Oxford, 2008.

Further Reading

Bugyis, K. (2016) 'Recovering the histories of women religious in England in the central Middle Ages: Wilton Abbey and Goscelin of Saint-Bertin', *JMH* 42.3: 1–19.

Canatella, H. (2010) 'Long-distance love: the ideology of male–female spiritual friendship in Goscelin of Saint-Bertin's *Liber confortatorius*', *Journal of the History of Sexuality* 19.1: 35–53.

Green, D. (2007) *Women readers in the Middle Ages*, Cambridge.

Hollis, S. (ed.) (2004) *Writing the Wilton Women: Goscelin's Life of Edith and Liber confortatorius*, Turnhout. With translation by W. Barnes and R. Hayward. Note that some secondary literature refers to the *Liber confortatorius* according to Hollis' page numbers, rather than Talbot's, which Hollis retains in bold within text of translation.

O'Brien O'Keeffe, K. (2012) 'The silence of Eve' in *Stealing obedience: narratives of agency and identity in late Anglo-Saxon England*, Toronto.

Watt, D. (ed.) (2020) *Women, writing and religion in England and beyond, 650–1100*, London.

Section II.4

The Domesday Book of 1086
A: Henry of Huntingdon, *A History of the English* (*Historia Anglorum*) (excerpt: 6.36)
B: Richard FitzNigel, *The Dialogue of the Exchequer* (*Dialogus de Scaccario*) (excerpt: 1.15–16, OMT pp. 96–8)
C: The Domesday Book (excerpts)

The work now known as the Domesday Book is in fact a two-volume work in Latin, comprising a survey of land, owners, tenants and taxes: the first volume covers most of the shires of Norman England apart from the northern counties, and the second volume covers the three counties of East Anglia, namely Suffolk, Norfolk and Essex. It is now preserved in the National Archives at Kew in London. In 1085 William the Conqueror ordered a nationwide inquest to provide him with information that would then be written up by a single scribe at Winchester. Richard FitzNigel informs us that by the twelfth century it was referred to by the vernacular term *Domesdei*, apparently because the assessor's reckonings, like those of the Last Judgement, were unalterable. In the Latin documents of the following centuries it is known as *Liber de Wintonia, Liber censualis/judiciarius, Liber/Rotulus regis*. In documents composed by the king it may be referred to as *Liber noster*, which is useful to know if one is searching in the archives for medieval references to it. The volumes contain an enormous amount of information, mostly about places and individuals, usually in formulaic phrases with frequent abbreviations. It also contains tiny details pertaining to well-known elements of national history, e.g. the Vikings (f. 40c), the battle of Hastings (f. 50a), as well as to events in individuals' lives, to the climate etc., as these affected the lives of ordinary people. In addition to the two volumes of Great Domesday and Little Domesday, there is also the Exeter Domesday (covering the south-west). London and Winchester were not covered. As a national tax and land tenure survey the Domesday Book found successors in the class of document known as the *Inquisitions post mortem*, which provide information on demographic trends; also in the Hundred Rolls of 1279, in the *Taxatio* of 1291, in the so-called Lay Subsidies of 1327 and following, in the tax accounts of TNA: E179, and in the so-called Nonae Rolls for 1340–1.

Further Reading

EHD 2.858–62 on the making of the Domesday Book.
Gullick, M. (1987) 'The Great and Little Domesday manuscripts' in *Domesday Book Studies*, Alecto Historical Editions, London.

56 Eleventh Century

A: Henry of Huntingdon, *A History of the English* (*Historia Anglorum*) (excerpt: 6.36)

Date: c.1130–54.

This work is preserved in a large number of MSS, listed in the OMT edition.

Author: Like Orderic Vitalis, Henry (c.1088–c.1157) was the son of a Norman clerk and an English woman, but unlike Orderic, Henry did not enter a monastery but became Archdeacon of Huntingdon. In his youth he studied grammar, rhetoric and verse composition in Lincoln, in the household of Robert Bloet, Bishop of Lincoln.

Work: The ten books of the *History of the English* cover the period from Julius Caesar's arrival in Britain to the coronation of Henry II in 1154. The material is structured around the five invasions of Britain, by Romans, Picts and Scots, Anglo-Saxons, Danes and Normans, and contains moral stories that have become part of popular history, such as Cnut's clash with the tide (6.17) and Henry I's death from a surfeit of lampreys (7.43). Henry's primary sources were Bede's historical writings, the eighth-century *Historia Romana* of Paul the Deacon, versions of the *ASChr* and OE poetry which Henry translated and adapted.

Linguistic points: Note that *scyra*, the post-Conquest Latin form of the OE word, is used for 'shire', but the need is felt to gloss it with *id est provincia*; this is also the case with *hida*, glossed with the CL *iugera*.

TEXT II.4A

William gives orders for the compilation of the Domesday Book in 1085
[6.36] misit autem dehinc rex potentissimus iusticiarios suos per unamquamque scyram, id est provinciam, Anglie, et inquirere fecit per iusiurandum quot hide, id est iugera uni aratro sufficientia per annum, essent in unaquaque villa, et quot animalia. fecit etiam inquiri quid unaquaque urbs, castellum, vicus, villa, flumen, palus, silva, redderet per annum. hec autem omnia, in cartis scripta, delata sunt ad regem et inter thesauros reposita usque hodie servantur.

Translation: Henry of Huntingdon, *A History of the English*

[6.36] *Then the very powerful king (William) sent his justiciars throughout each shire of England and made them ask on oath how many hides, i.e. tracts of land sufficient for one plough for a year, there were on each estate, and how many animals. He also had enquiry made as to what each city, castle, settlement, estate, river, marsh, and wood rendered each year. All these facts, written down in documents, were brought to the king and deposited in the treasuries where they are preserved to this day.*

Primary Source

Henry of Huntingdon, *Historia Anglorum*, ed. D. Greenway, OMT, Oxford, 1996.

Further Reading

Rigg, A. G. (1991) 'Henry of Huntingdon's metrical experiments', *JML* 1: 60–72.

B: Richard FitzNigel, *The Dialogue of the Exchequer* (*Dialogus de Scaccario*) (excerpt: 1.15–16, OMT pp. 96–8)

Date: c.1178 with later additions.

The text is derived from three copies from the thirteenth century, in the British Library and the National Archives in London.

Author: Although this work is attributed in the MSS to Gervase of Tilbury, in the thirteenth century an attribution was made to Richard FitzNigel (Fitzneal) (1130–98), Lord Treasurer and Bishop of London (1189–98), who was involved in both ecclesiastical and secular politics, including the affair of William de Longchamp, whose power Richard helped to crush (cf. Section II.20).

Work: As Lord Treasurer to Henry II, Richard was well placed to write a work describing the financial administration of the royal household, focused on the department known as the Exchequer, named after the chessboard-like table on which the accounts were calculated. In the preface Richard states that he will use *rusticano sermone* and *communibus ... verbis* to write about these useful matters, rather than the *verba incognita* used by writers in the liberal arts to make themselves seem more knowledgeable: his interlocutor agrees, adding that it is also acceptable to invent new terms. The exact sense of these terms is disputed, but it is interesting to note that he uses the phrase *communia verba* to apply also to the linguistic register of the Domesday Book. This passage is also the first to record the term *Domesdei*.

58 Eleventh Century

Linguistic points: The term *Scaccarium* is referred to by William Fitzstephen in his *Life of St Thomas* (ch. 39; cf. Sections II.15 and 16) in the early 1170s as a new term, almost a sort of nickname, when he writes *ad quadrangulam tabulam, quae dicitur Calculis bicoloribus, vulgo 'Scaccarium'; potius autem est regis tabula nummis albicoloribus, ubi etiam placita corona tractantur* ('at the square table which is commonly called the "chequer board" from its black and white counters; but it is rather the king's table for silver coins, where pleas of the crown are also dealt with'). Anglo-Norman French, as the language of the royal court, formed the linguistic base for the Latin of this text, particularly for the administrative terms necessitated by developments in England since the Norman Conquest, with words such as *escaeta, baillia, talea, essaium*. The passage here cited is followed by explanations of the terms *hida, centuriata* and *comitatus. comitatus* is a CL word meaning 'company', but extends its sense to various more technical terms in BML, signifying either 'earldom' or 'county/shire': it acts as an alternative to the OE-derived *scira* (for which see Section II.2). *centuriata* (or *centuria*) seems to be a post-Conquest neologism, a Latin calque on the English word 'hundred' (cf. Section II.4B) as a subdivision of a county, perhaps of one hundred hides. In the north of England the equivalent of *centuriata/hundredum* was *wapentacum*, also derived from OE. *hida* is the OE 'hid' with a Latin feminine termination, for an area of land: this form does not occur in pre-Conquest BML, where the OE word is replaced by such Latin words as *mansa* or *casata* or (in Bede) *familia*. It is in fact in the Domesday Book that the BML *hida* is first attested. The phrase *tenent in capite* refers to those who hold land directly from the king, i.e. his so-called tenants in chief: in the Domesday Book their holdings are listed first in the account of each county. *infatuare* here has the sense 'to render ineffective', which is a semantic development of the CL. Note that FitzNigel uses the term Neustria to refer to Normandy, as is common in BML, though the word was originally a Merovingian and Carolingian designation for a larger region, forming the western part of the Frankish kingdom.

TEXT II.4B

Description of the Domesday Book
[1.15, OMT p. 96] porro liber ille de quo queris sigilli regii comes est individuus in thesauro. huius institutionis causam ab Henrico quondam Wintoniensi episcopo sic accepi.
[1.16] cum insignis ille subactor Anglie, rex Willelmus eiusdem pontificis sanguine propinquus, ulteriores insule fines suo subiugasset imperio et rebellium mentes terribilibus perdomuisset exemplis, ne libera de cetero daretur erroris facultas, decrevit subiectum sibi populum iuri scripto legibusque subicere. propositis igitur legibus Anglicanis secundum tripartitam earum distinctionem, hoc est *Merchenelage, Danelage, Westsexenelage*, quasdam reprobavit, quasdam

autem approbans illis transmarinas Neustrie leges, que ad regni pacem tuendam efficacissime videbantur, adiecit. demum ne quid deesse videretur, ad omnem totius providentie summam, communicato consilio, discretissimos a latere suo destinavit viros per regnum in circuitu. ab his itaque totius terre descriptio diligens facta est, tam in nemoribus quam pascuis et pratis nec non et agriculturis, et verbis communibus annotata in librum redacta est, ut videlicet quilibet iure suo contentus alienum non usurpet impune. fit autem descriptio per comitatus, per centuriatas et hidas, prenotato in ipso capite regis nomine, ac deinde seriatim aliorum procerum nominibus appositis secundum status sui dignitatem, qui videlicet de rege tenent in capite. apponuntur autem singulis numeri secundum ordinem sic dispositis, per quos inferius in ipsa libri serie que ad eos pertinent facilius occurrunt. hic liber ab indigenis *Domesdei* nuncupatur, id est dies iudicii per metaphoram. sicut enim districti et terribilis examinis illius novissimi sententia nulla tergiversationis arte valet eludi, [p. 98] cum orta fuerit in regno contentio de his rebus que illic annotantur, cum ventum fuerit ad librum, sententia eius infatuari non posset vel impune declinari. ob hoc nos eundem librum 'iudiciarium' nominavimus, non quod in eo de propositis aliquibus dubiis feratur sententia, set quod ab eo, sicut a predicto iudicio, non licet ulla ratione discedere.

Translation: *The Dialogue of the Exchequer*

[1.15] *Furthermore that book you are asking about is the inseparable companion of the royal seal in the treasury. I received the reason for its institution from Henry (of Blois), one-time Bishop of Winchester.*

[1.16] *When that conqueror of England, King William, a close relative of this bishop, had subjugated the furthest territories of the island to his rule and had subdued the minds of the rebels by terrible examples, so that there would be no clear opportunity for error in future, he decided to make his subject people submit to written justice and laws. And so, after setting out the English laws according to a threefold distinction, i.e. Mercian law, Danelaw and West Saxon law, he criticised some of them but approved others which he added to the overseas laws of Neustria, because these seemed the most effective for keeping the peace in his kingdom. Finally, in case anything should seem to be missing for the total amount of the whole province, he sent the most discerning men from his party on a round tour of the kingdom and they made a detailed survey of the whole country, in woodland and meadows and fields and also agricultural land, and this was written up in a book, recorded in ordinary language, so that each person would be content with their own rights and not appropriate those of others with impunity. The description was made by counties, hundreds and hides, with the king's name written at the head of each chapter, and then the names of other noblemen were added in order according to their rank, namely those who were the king's tenants in chief. Numbers were also given to each*

60 Eleventh Century

of them set out in this way, to make it easier for those looking down the list record-ed in the book to encounter the information relevant to them. This book is known metaphorically by English people as Domesdei, i.e. the Day of Judgement. For just as it is impossible to escape the sentence of that strict and terrible last judgement by means of any attempt to postpone it, whenever a dispute should arise in the kingdom regarding the things noted there, if one turned to this book, its sentence could not be rendered ineffective or denied without punishment. For this reason we have called this the judgement book, not because in it a sentence is given regarding any doubtful arguments, but because it is not permissible to depart from it by any means, just as with the aforesaid judgement.

Primary Sources and Related Texts

Richard Fitzneale, *Dialogus de Scaccario*, ed. E. Amt and S. Church, OMT, Oxford, 2007.

Further Reading

*Clanchy (1993).
Jones, M. (2008) 'The *Dialogus de Scaccario* (c.1179): the first Western book on accounting?', *Abacus* 44.4: 443–74.

C: The Domesday Book (excerpts: references by folio of the 1783 edition of A. Farley)

Date: 1086.

MSS: The Domesday Book exists in several volumes, namely Great Domesday and Little Domesday (both in the National Archives at Kew), and Exeter Domesday (in Exeter Cathedral Library).

Linguistic points: Apart from the articles by Thorn and Baxter cited below, little work has been done on the Latin in which the Domesday Book was written. There is ambiguity in the term *verbis communibus* used in the *Dialogus de Scaccario* to apply to the text, but it seems clear that there is a sharp contrast between the official Latin of pre-Conquest documents and that of Domesday and charters after the Conquest. Domesday, as is clear from many lemmata in *DMLBS*, often contains the earliest use of particular Latin words, and many of these are in fact vernacular words (English, French or Old Norse) with a Latin termination. In a number of cases, as with *hida* or *scira*, the concept existed in British culture before the Conquest, but the Latin terms used for these were usually semantic extensions of classical words such as *familia* (for 'hide', as a measure of land) or *provincia* or *comitatus* (for 'shire'). The vernacular words occur occasionally in a non-integrated form, e.g. *huscarl* or *danegeld* (from English and Old Norse) or *gorz* (from French, though ultimately from CL *gurges*). 'Hundrez' occurs in its non-integrated Latin form, rather than the Latin form *hundredum* that was to become more common.[1] However, more frequent are those vernacular words with a Latin termination, such as *geldum* from English, and *baconus* from French. Such vernacular forms often occur alongside the more classical terms, e.g. *census*, which, like *gelda*, means a tax paid to the king. That the officials recording the local information on property needed to translate between Latin and the vernacular is indicated by the evidence of the words *interpres* and *latimarius*, the latter also used as a surname. Further investigation is needed as to whether it is possible to distinguish between the use of French and English words in different regions and on the possible linguistic continuity between the language of the charters of Normandy and England immediately before and after the Conquest, influencing the terminology of Domesday.

In the excerpts below, one can see many words which are unattested in pre-Conquest BML or are making their first appearance, words which were to have a great future in BML, such as *forisfactura*. This does occur in a pre-Conquest Norman charter of William, as no. 131 in *Recueil des Actes des ducs de Normandie de 911 à 1066* (1961), related to modern English 'forfeit'. Other examples are *burgensis* (a resident in a borough), *tainus*, one of many variant spellings of *thegnus*, an integrated form of OE 'þegn', *foresta* (a borrowing from Norman charters, here in the sense of land subject to forest law), *braciare* (here in the spelling *braz-*) from OF *bracier*, meaning 'to brew (ale)', and *forgea* (immediately from OF 'forge' but ultimately from CL *fabrica*). *masura* (in *DMLBS s.v. maisura*), 'tenement', derives from Latin *mansura* via the French form *masure*. It is interesting that *manerium* does not seem to occur in pre-Conquest Norman documents: its presence in a charter of William, as no. 224 in *Recueil des Actes des ducs de Normandie de 911 à 1066* (1961), most of which dates from 1063, is accounted for by the fact that it actually occurs in a post-Conquest addendum to this charter, relating to property in south-west England.

---

1 Cf. W. Malm. *GR* 2.122, where he writes that King Alfred introduced *centurias quas dicunt hundrez et decimas quas tithingas vocant.* Note William's use of two CL words, applied to land measurements, and then their vernacular-based equivalents, *hundrez* being a French form of an English word, without Latin termination, and *tithingas* an English word assimilated into Latin.

62 Eleventh Century

There are also rare words such as *ineuuardos*, i.e. *inwardus* ('watchman'), which only occurs in Domesday, but in several different places and with variant spellings: it is formed from the prefix *in-* and the English word 'weard/ward'.[2]

TEXT II.4C

The Survey of Hereford and its surroundings: owners and property in 1086
[179a] in Hereford civitate tempore regis Edwardi erant c et iii homines commanentes intus et extra murum. et habebant has subterscriptas consuetudines.

siquis eorum voluisset recedere de civitate poterat concessu praepositi domum suam vendere alteri homini servitium debitum inde facere volenti et habebat praepositus tercium denarium hujus venditionis. quod siquis paupertate sua non potuisset servitium facere relinquebat sine precio domum suam praeposito qui providebat ne domus vacua remaneret et ne rex careret servitio. intra murum civitatis unaquaque integra masura reddebat vij den. et obolum et iiij denar' ad locandos caballos[3] et iij diebus in Augusto secabat ad Maurdine et una die ad fenum congregandum erat ubi vicecomes volebat. qui equum habebat ter in anno pergebat cum vicecomite ad placita et ad hundrez ad Vrmelauia. quando rex venatui instabat de una quaque domo per consuetudinem ibat unus homo ad stabilitionem in silva. alii homines non habentes integras masuras inveniebant ineuuardos ad aulam quando rex erat in civitate.

burgensis cum caballo serviens cum moriebatur habebat rex equum et arma ejus. de eo qui equum non habebat si moreretur habebat rex aut x solid' aut terram ejus cum domibus. siquis morte praeventus non divisisset quae sua erant, rex habebat omnem ejus pecuniam. has consuetudines habebant in civitate habitantes et alii similiter extra murum manentes, nisi tantum quod integra masura foris murum non dabat nisi iij denar' et obolum. aliae consuetudines erant communes. cujuscunque uxor braziabat intus et extra civitatem dabat x denarios per consuetudinem. sex fabri erant in civitate. quisque eorum de sua forgia reddidit unum denar' et quisque eorum faciebat cxx ferra de ferro regis et unicuique eorum dabantur iij denarii [inde] per consuetudinem. et isti fabri ab omni servitio erant quieti. septem monetarii erant ibi. unus ex his erat monetarius episcopi. quando moneta renovatur, dabat quisque eorum xviij solid' pro cuneis recipiendis et ex eo die quo redibant usque ad unum mensem dabat quisque eorum regi xx solid' et similiter habebat episcopus de suo monetario xx solid'. quando veniebat rex in civitatem quantum volebat denar' faciebant ei monetarii de argento scilicet regis. et hi vij habebant sacam et socham suam. moriente aliquo regis monetario

---

2 Cf. the forms 'weard' (West Saxon) and 'vard' (Northumbrian) in the first line of Caedmon's OE hymn (Bede, *HE* 4.24(22)), for which see Section I.17.

3 On the problem of determining the precise tone of *caballus* as opposed to *equus*, see *Adams (2016: 553–4); cf. Section II.1 for *caballus* on the Bayeux Tapestry.

II.4 | The Domesday Book of 1086   63

habebat rex xx sol' de relevamento. quod si moreretur non diviso censu suo, rex habebat omnem censum. si vicecomes iret in Wales cum exercitu, ibant hi homines cum eo. quod siquis ire jussus non iret, emendabat regi xl solid'.

in ipsa civitate habebat Heraldus ^{comes 4} xxvij burgenses easdem consuetudines habentes quas et alii burgenses. de hac civitate reddebat praepositus xij lib' regi ^{E.} et vj lib. comiti ^{Heraldo}. et habebat in suo censu supradictas omnes consuetudines. rex vero habebat in suo dominio tres forisfacturas, hoc est pacem suam infractam et heinfaram et forestellum. quicunque horum unum fecisset emendabat c sol' regi cujuscunque hoc fuisset. modo habet rex civitatem Hereford in dominio⁵ et anglici burgenses ibi manentes habent suas priores consuetudines. francigeni vero burgenses habent quietas per xij denar' omnes forisfacturas suas praeter tres supradictas. hec civitas reddidit regi lx lib' ad numerum de candidis denariis. inter civitatem et xviii maneria qui in Hereford reddunt firmas⁶ suas computantur cccxxxv lib' et xviii sol' exceptis placitis de hund' et de comitatu.

[179b] In Arcenefelde habet rex tres aecclesias. presbiteri harum aecclesiarum ferunt legationes regis in Wales et quisque eorum cantat pro rege ij missas una quaque ebdomada. siquis eorum moritur rex habet de eo xx sol' per consuetudinem. siquis Walensium furatur hominem aut feminam equum bovem vel vaccam convictus inde redd' prius furtum et dat xx solid' pro forisfactura. de ove vero furata vel fasciculo manipulorum emendat ij sol'. siquis occidit hominem regis et facit heinfaram dat regi xx sol' de solutione hominis et de forisfactura c sol'. si alicujus taini hominem occiderit, dat x sol' domino hominis mortui. quod si Walensis Walensem occiderit congregantur parentes occisi et praedantur eum qui occidit ejusque propinquos et comburunt domos eorum donec in crastinum circa meridiem corpus mortui sepeliatur. de hac praeda habet rex terciam partem. illi vero totum aliud habent quietum. aliter autem qui domum incenderit et inde accusatus fuerit, per xl homines de defendit. quod si non potuerit xx solid'   **MS: se defendit** regi emendabit. siquis de consuetudine sextarium mellis celaverit probatur inde pro uno sextario reddit quinque, si tantum terrae tenet ut debeat dare. si vicecomes evocat eos ad siremot' meliores ex eis vj aut vij vadunt cum eo. qui vocatus non vadit dat ij sol' aut unum bovem regi et qui de hundret remanet tantundem persolvit. similiter emendat qui jussus a vicecomite secum ire in Walis non pergit. nam si vicecomes non vadit nemo eorum ibit. cum exercitus in hostem pergit ipsi per consuetudinem faciunt auantwarde et in reversione redrewarde. hae consuetudines erant Walensium TRE in Arcenefelde. Riset de Wales reddit regi W. xl lib. de terra Calcebuef; habet rex x sol' extra firmam.

---

4   This is a reference to Earl Harold, king of England for a few months in 1066.

5   In the specific sense of land for the king's use, the English word 'demesne', deriving from *dominium* via the OF form *demeine*, is used.

6   Cf. *DMLBS s.v.* 2 *firma* from OF 'ferme' and also *OED s.v.* farm n. 2; the similarities of sense between 1 *firma* and 2 *firma* and between 2 *firmare* and 3 *firmare*, none of them CL, sometimes lead to confusion.

64 Eleventh Century

[179c] Terra regis. In Bromesais hundred'
rex W. tenet Lintune. Rex Edwardus tenuit. ibi erant v hidae et reddebant quartam partem firmae unius noctis. modo est valde imminutum. ibi sunt in dominio iij car' et x vill' et v bord' cum xij car'. ibi vj servi et molinum de viij denar'. ibi i francigena tenet dimid' hidam quae reddebat iiij sol' TRE. hoc manerium sicut est modo reddit x lib' de albis denariis. de hoc manerio tenet S. Maria de Cormeliis aecclesiam et presbiterum cum sua terra et totam decimam et unum villanum cum una virga terra. de ipso manerio tenet Ansfridus de Cormeliis ij hid' et ix vill' et ix car' et Willelmus filius Baderon tenet unam virgam terrae quae ibi jacuit TRE. Ilbertus vicecomes habet ad firmam suam de Arcenefeld consuetudines omnes mellis et ovium quae huic manerio pertinebat TRE. Willelmus filius Normanni habet inde vj sextaria mellis et vj oves cum agnis et xij denarios. (…)
[179d–180a] In Bremesse hundred
Rex tenet Clive. Heraldus ^{comes} tenuit. ibi xiiij hidae et dimid' cum berewicha nomine Wiltone. in dominio sunt iiij car' et xx villani et praepositus et xj bord' cum xvj car'. ibi vij servi et v ancillae et unus bovarius. ibi ij molini de vj solid' et piscaria nil reddit. ad hoc manerium pertinet tot Walenses qui habent viij car' et reddunt x sext' mellis et dimid' et vj sol' et v den'. hujus manerii aecclesiam presbiterum et decimam cum j villano tenet S. Maria de Cormeliis. de hoc manerio est in foresta regis W. tantum terrae quae TRE reddebat vj sextar' mellis et vj oves cum agnis. de isto manerio tenet Willelmus Baderon i hid' et iij virg'. et Godefridus tenet j virg'. Rogerus de Laci tenet dimid' piscariam quae pertinebat huic manerio tempore RE et tunc pertinebat ibidem xxv mittae[7] salis de Wich et ipso tempore erant in ipso manerio duae hidae una virga minus quae sunt in Ascis. Alured de Merleberge tenet modo. Heraldus tenebat quando mortuus fuit et scira dicit quod de hoc manerio sunt. hoc manerium reddit ix lib' et x solid' denariorum candidorum.

Translation: Domesday Book

[179a] *In the city of Hereford in the time of King Edward there were 103 men dwelling within and outside the wall and they had the following customs: if any of them wished to withdraw from the city he could with the consent of the reeve sell his house to another man who was willing to do the service due from it, and the reeve had the third penny of this sale. But if anyone due to poverty could not perform his service, he surrendered his house without payment to the reeve, who saw that the house did not remain empty and that the king did not lack his service. Within the wall of the city each whole messuage rendered 7½d. and 4d. for*

---

7   This word for a measure of salt or grout derives from the OE 'mitta', but has, like other technical terms such as *hida*, *saca* and *soca*, been integrated into Latin as a feminine noun; cf. *OED s.v.* mit.

the hire of horses and 3 days reaping in August at Marden, and one day gathering the hay wherever the sheriff wanted. Anyone who had a horse went 3 times a year with the sheriff to the pleas and to the hundred (courts) at Wormelow. When the king was engaged in hunting, one man from each house by custom went to head off game in the wood.

Other men who did not have whole messuages provided watchmen for the hall when the king was in the city. When a burgess serving with a horse died, the king had his horse and weapons. If someone without a horse died, the king had from him either 10s. or his land with the houses on it. If anyone died intestate the king had all his goods. Those living in the city, and others likewise dwelling outside the wall, observed these customs except only that a whole messuage outside the wall only gave 3½d. The other customs were common to both. Anyone whose wife brewed within or outside the city gave 10d. according to custom. There were 6 smiths in the city; each of them paid 1d. from his forge and each of them made 120 shoes of the king's iron and to each one of them was given 3d. on that account according to custom, and those smiths were exempt from every other service. There were 7 moneyers there. One of these was the bishop's moneyer. When the coinage was renewed each of them gave 18s. for receiving the dies, and within 1 month of the day on which they returned, each of them gave the king 20s., and likewise the bishop had from his moneyer 20s. When the king came into the city the moneyers coined pennies for him, as many as he wanted, that is of the king's silver. And these 7 had their sake and soke. On the death of any of the king's moneyers, the king had 20s. for relief. But if he died without having divided up his wealth, the king had all his money. If the sheriff went into Wales with the army these men went with him. But if anyone ordered to go did not go, he paid 40s. fine to the king.

In the city itself Earl Harold had 27 burgesses having the same customs as the other burgesses. From this city the reeve paid £12 to King Edward and £6 to Earl Harold and he had in his farm all the aforesaid customs. The king, however, had in his demesne the 3 forfeitures, namely breaking his peace, housebreaking and highway robbery. Anyone who committed one of these paid 100s. to the king, no matter whose man he was. Now the king has the city of Hereford in his demesne and the English burgesses dwelling there have their former customs but the French burgesses are exempt for 12d. from all their forfeitures, except the 3 already mentioned. This city renders to the king £60 by tale of blanched pennies. Between them the city and 18 manors which render their farms in Hereford account of £335 18s., beside the pleas in the hundred and shire courts.

[179b] In Archenfield the king has 3 churches. The priests of these churches undertake the king's embassies into Wales and each of them sings 2 masses every week for the king. If one of them dies the king has 20s. from him as a customary due. If one of the Welshmen steals a man or woman, horse, ox or cow, upon conviction for it he first restores the stolen goods and then gives 20s. as a forfeiture. For a stolen sheep, however, or a bundle of sheaves, he pays 2s. fine. If anyone kills one of the king's men and commits housebreaking, he gives the king 20s. in payment for the man and as

a forfeiture, 100s. If he kills a thegn's man he gives 10s. to the dead man's lord. But if a Welshman kills a Welshman, the relatives of the slain meet together and plunder the slayer and his kin and burn their houses until at about noon the next day the corpse of the dead man is buried. Of this plunder the king has the third part but all the rest they hold is exempt. Otherwise, he who sets a house on fire and is accused of it, defends himself by 40 men. But if he is unable to do so, he pays 20s. fine to the king. If anyone conceals a sester of honey due by custom, upon proof of it he renders for 1 sester 5, if he holds as much land as he should give for it. If the sheriff calls them out to the shiremoot, 6 or 7 of the better of them go with him. Anyone who does not go when summoned gives 2s. or an ox to the king and he who stays away from the hundred (court) pays the same. He who does not go forth when ordered by the sheriff to go with him into Wales pays a similar fine. But if the sheriff does not go, none of them goes. When the army goes forth against the enemy these men, according to custom, make up the vanguard and on the return the rear guard. These were the customs of the Welsh TRE in Archenfield. Rhys of Wales renders to King William £40. From the land of 'Calcebuef' the king has 10s. over and above the farm (i.e. in addition to the revenue).

[179c] The king's land in Bromsash Hundred

King William holds Linton. King Edward held it. There were 5 hides there and they paid the fourth part of one night's revenue. Now it is extremely reduced. There are in demesne there 3 ploughs and 10 villans and 5 bordars with 12 ploughs. There are 6 slaves and a mill rendering 8d. There 1 Frenchman holds half a hide which rendered 4s. TRE. This manor as it is now renders £10 of blanched pennies. Of this manor Sainte-Marie de Cormeilles holds the church and its priest with its land and all the tithes and 1 villan with 1 virgate of land. Of this manor Ansfrid de Cormeilles holds 2 hides and 9 villans and 9 ploughs and William fitzBaderon holds 1 virgate of land which belonged there TRE. Ilbert the sheriff has as his farm (in his revenue) from Archenfield all the customs of honey and sheep which belonged to the manor TRE. William fitzNorman has from this 6 sesters of honey and 6 sheep with lambs and 12d. (…)

[179d–180a] In Bromsash Hundred

The King holds Cleeve. Earl Harold held it. There are 14½ hides there with an outlier called Wilton. In demesne 4 ploughs; and 20 villans and a reeve and 11 bordars with 16 ploughs. Nine slaves there and 5 female slaves and 1 oxman. Two mills there rendering 6s. and a fishpond rendering nothing. To this manor belong as many Welshmen as have 8 ploughs and render 10½ sesters of honey and 6s. 5d. Of this manor Sainte-Marie de Cormeilles holds the church, a priest and the tithes, with 1 villan. Of this manor there is in the forest of King William as much land as rendered TRE 6 sesters of honey and 6 sheep with their lambs. Of this manor William Baderon holds 1 hide and 3 virgates; Godfrey holds 1 virgate. Roger de Lacy holds half a fishery which belonged to this manor in the time of King Edward; and then 25 mits of salt from Droitwich belonged there and at that time there were in that manor 2 hides less 1 virgate which are in Ashe (Ingen). Alfred of Marlborough holds them now. Harold was holding them when he died and the shire says that they are part of this manor. This manor renders £9 10s. of blanched pennies.

Primary Sources and Related Texts

Domesday Book (by county), ed. John Morris, Chichester, 1975–92, with Latin text and folio numbers of A. Farley (1783), and modern English translation.
Municipal charter for Newcastle (twelfth century), for which see Section II.46A.

Further Reading

Baxter, S. (2011) 'The making of Domesday Book and the languages of lordship in conquered England' in *Tyler (2011).
Dalton, P. (2021) 'The *Acta* of William the Conqueror, Domesday Book, the Oath of Salisbury and the legitimacy and stability of the Norman regime in England', *Journal of British Studies* 60: 29–65.
Holt, J. C. (ed.) (1987) *Domesday Studies*, Woodbridge.
Roffe, D. (2015) *Decoding Domesday*, Woodbridge.
Thorn, F. (2016) '*Non pascua sed pastura*: the changing choice of terms in Domesday' in *Domesday now: new approaches to the inquest and the book*, ed. D. Roffe and K. Keats-Rohan, Woodbridge.

Section II.5

The Life of St Swithun: the Miracle of the Broken Eggs
A: Anonymous I, from the Prose *Life of St Swithun* (*Vita S. Swithuni*) (excerpt: chapter 6)
B: Anonymous II, *A Poem on the Miracle of the Broken Eggs*

A: Anonymous I, *The Life of St Swithun* (*Vita S. Swithuni*) (excerpt: chapter 6)

Date: c.1080.

There are ten surviving MSS of this text in England and on the Continent.

Author and subject: Various possible authors have been suggested for this short anonymous work: Lapidge considers it unlikely that it is by Goscelin of Canterbury, but it may be by the same (anonymous) author as the *Life of St Birinus* (Section II.6A). The author may also have composed the longer work, the *Miracles of St Swithun* (partly based on Wulfstan's verse narrative, for which cf. Section I.35B). Swithun was a Bishop of Winchester (852–63) whom Dunstan and Æthelwold chose as the patron of the cathedral a century later because of the many miracles associated with him after his death. His shrine was destroyed at the Reformation, and has now been replaced by a modern representation.

Work: This biography of Swithun has been said to have more historical veracity than the prose and verse biographies of Lantfred and Wulfstan of Winchester in the tenth century (for which see Section I.35). Here is presented the story of the mending of the broken eggs, one of the most popular of St Swithun's miracles, which is depicted in a wall painting in the Saxon church at Corhampton in Hampshire, but is not used by Lantfred or Wulfstan. It is set against the background of Swithun's civic works, particularly the building of a vaulted stone bridge as early as 852–63, on the site of the modern City Bridge over the river Itchen.

Linguistic points: The author's literary style appears unlike that of Goscelin, though they are likely to have been contemporaries; nevertheless, it displays rhetorical care and syntactical confidence while avoiding flamboyance. The description of Swithun's virtues is suitably grand, while the account of the miracle is brief but vivid and compassionate. Note the wordplay between *liberaliter* and *libere* and the balanced sentences with occasional antithesis, as well as the author's penchant for a series of infinitives either attached to a single finite verb or as historical infinitives, and the series of tricola with which the account of the miracle culminates.

TEXT II.5A

The miracle of the broken eggs
[6] huius (i.e. Swithuni) oratione et exhortatione clementissimus et serenissimus iam dictus rex Athulfus ecclesiis Dei universam decimam terre regni sui munificentissima donatione donavit; et quod liberaliter dedit, libere possidere concessit. speculationi vero et contemplationi divine interno dilectionis ardore cum assidue et intense inhiaret, active tamen discipline operibus non minus insudabat: pro opportunitate rei et temporis utriusque exercitii opera variatione decentissima commutabat. unde factum est ut, necessitate exigente, de spiritualibus ad forinseca exiens, utilitati communi civium sicut semper et aliquando provideret, pontemque ad orientalem portam civitatis arcubus lapideis opere non leviter ruituro construeret. huic ergo operi cum sollicite et laboriose operam daret et incepto difficili consummationis finem addere festinaret, contigit – residente illo ad opus – quadam die pauperculam mulierem usque ad locum operis venire, ova venalia in vase deferre, ab operariis lascivientibus et ludentibus miseram apprehendi, ova universa non eripi sed confringi. que cum ab eis qui sanioris intelligentie erant flens et eiulans pro dampno et illata sibi iniuria in presentiam domini episcopi sisteretur, motus pietate et misericordia, beatus antistes vas in quo erant ova reposita sumit; dexteram levans, signum crucis super ova componit; signando celeri redintegratione incorrupta restituit. mirari omnes qui aderant pro virtute; pauper illa recuperato quod perdiderat vehementer gaudere; qui autem dampnum intulerant resipiscere et stupere.

Translation: *Life of St Swithun*

[6] *As the result of Swithun's prayer and encouragement, the very compassionate and gentle king Æthelwulf (king of Wessex 839–58) gave a most generous donation to the churches of God, a universal tenth of the land in his kingdom; and he granted that they could possess freely what he gave generously. While Swithun focused with constancy and concentration on the investigation and contemplation of God with the inner passion of love, he put just as much effort into works of active discipline; he used to alternate between the two tasks, varying them as was most appropriate according to the situation and the time. And so it was that, when necessity demanded, he left the spiritual and turned to external matters, and saw to the common good of the citizens, as always and at any time. He constructed a bridge with stone arches at the east gate of the city, employing techniques which would prevent it easily collapsing.*

70 Eleventh Century

While he was concentrating on this project, working hard and with great care, and hurrying to put the finishing touches to the challenging project, it happened, while he remained at work, that one day a poor woman came to the work site carrying some eggs for sale in a container, and the wretched woman was grabbed by some workmen who were fooling around and joking and all the eggs were smashed though the men did not take them. The woman wept and wailed at her loss, and because of the offence done to her she was taken to the lord bishop by some people who were more sensible. She stood before the bishop and he was moved by love and compassion. The saintly bishop took the container in which the eggs were placed and raising his right hand he made the sign of the cross over the eggs; and by this sign he quickly restored them to their former wholeness. Everyone who was there marvelled at this miracle; the poor woman was very pleased to have regained what she had lost, while those who had caused the damage were dumbfounded and regretted their action.

Primary Sources and Related Texts

Vita S. Swithuni (prose; c.1090) in *Lapidge (2003: 630–9).
Miracula S. Swithuni, *Lapidge (2003: 648–97).
ASChr s.a. 855 for King Æthelwulf's grant of land to the Church.
Section I.35.

Further Reading

Introduction to *Vita S. Swithuni* in *Lapidge (2003: 611–28).

B: Anonymous II, *A Poem on the Miracle of the Broken Eggs*

Date: c.1080.

The poem survives in two MSS, BL MS Royal 15.C.vii (also containing the works on Swithun by Lantfred and Wulfstan of Winchester: cf. Section I.35) and Bodleian MS Auct. F.2.14.

Work: This complete, thirty-six-line rhythmic poem is formed of trochaic lines of fifteen syllables, with a caesura (break) after the eighth syllable: the first half therefore ends with an unstressed syllable, the second half with a stressed; it is sometimes referred to in the form 8p+7pp, i.e. eight syllables with stress on the penultimate (paroxytone), followed by seven syllables with stress on the syllable before the penultimate (proparoxytone). This is the same form as the famous sixth-century hymn of Venantius Fortunatus: *pange lingua gloriosi proelium* *certaminis*, to which the anonymous author of these verses on Swithun is likely to be alluding, with the use of *gloriosi* in the first line. This rhythmic verse form is related to the classical metre known as the trochaic septenarius. The whole poem focuses simply on the popular story of Swithun's mending of the smashed eggs, which forms one chapter (6) in the prose *Life* (cf. Section II.5A): this forms the first half of the poem and is followed by an exhortation to worship Swithun as the special saint of Winchester.

Linguistic points: Whoever wrote these verses did so with clarity, precision and lightness of touch, using standard Latin. However, the specific senses of the CL words *antistes*, *pontifex* and *pastor* in their application to Swithun as bishop, and *signum* in the sense of 'miracle' are, as so often, indications that the text is Christian.

TEXT II.5B

The miracle of the broken eggs
inter signa gloriosi Suuithuni antistitis
que per eum rex caelestis hac in vita edidit,
hoc ex multis unum refert prisca fama populi
conditoris quod in laude paucis libet promere.
idem namque pastor almus et provisor strenuus   [5]
forte pontem extruebat geminasque ianuas
per quas urbis Winthonie adeuntur moenia.
artifices congregati huic instabant operi.
forum petens casu venit illuc muliercula
ova ferens unde vite mercetur subsidia.   [10]
que ludendo operantum confregit stultitia
atque victum miserande ademit paupercule.
illa pium atque mitem requirit pontificem
et plorando illi suum exponit dispendium.
cui cultor pietatis benignus et dapsilis   [15]
percunctatus, mox ovorum duplum reddit precium.
post hec ille Deo plenus, caritate profluus,
puras celo manus librat, effundens oramina,
et creantis nutu cuncta mox ova redintegrat.
gaudens illa sic discessit; Deo laudes reddidit.   [20]
Deus suis qui in sanctis semper est mirabilis
tunc a plebe infinitis effertur preconiis,
qui in parvis et in magnis exaudit quos diligit
nec cunctatur dare sui quicquid poscunt famuli.
illum toto diligamus corde sed et opere,   [25]

72 Eleventh Century

> et in eius sacra lege meditemur sedule,
> qui beatum hunc Suuithunum terris fecit inclitum
> et in celis gloriosum ut solem clarissimum.
> gratuletur et exultet felix urbs Wintonia,
> [30] que virtute tanti patris meritisque rutilat,
> cuius sacra fovet ossa, sentit et miracula:
> incessanter illi plaudat odas cum letitia!
> quantis namque apud Deum meritis emineat,
> quo splendore, quo decore niteat in gloria,
> [35] clamant istic manifesta signorum indicia
> et ad sui cultum corda excitant fidelia.

Translation: *Poem on the Miracle of the Broken Eggs*

Among the miracles of the glorious bishop Swithun, which the heavenly king performed in this life through him, this is one of many reported by people from the rumours of old which I would like to make known in a few words in praise of the Creator. For this loving shepherd and hard-working bishop happened to be building a bridge and twin gates through which one entered Winchester's city walls. Skilled workmen had gathered to work on this job. A poor woman came there by chance on her way to the marketplace, carrying eggs from which she could earn a living. The stupid workmen were fooling around and smashed the eggs, depriving the poor old woman of her source of income. She sought out the pious and gentle bishop, and in tears explained to him her loss. In reply to her request, this kind and generous man, who practised goodness, immediately repaid her twice the value of her eggs. For then this man filled with God, flowing with love, held his pure hands up to heaven, pouring forth prayers, and mended all the eggs at the Creator's behest. The woman was overjoyed and departed, praising God. God, who is always wonderful in His saints, was then extolled by the people with infinite proclamations of praise, God, who listens to those He loves, in minor matters and in important ones, and does not hesitate to grant whatever His servants ask for. Let us love Him with all our heart but also in deed, and let us meditate earnestly on His sacred law, He who made this man, the blessed Swithun, famous and glorious in heaven, like the brightest sun. The blessed city of Winchester should give thanks and rejoice because it gleams with the virtue and merits of such a great father whose sacred bones it cares for and whose miracles it experiences: may it joyfully sing hymns of praise to him without cease! For the clear signs of these miracles here proclaim with what great merits he will excel before God, with what splendour, with what beauty he will shine in glory, and they rouse faithful hearts to his cult.

Primary Sources and Related Texts

*Lapidge (2003: 795).

Further Reading

Norberg, D. and Ziolkowski, J. (ed.) (2004) *An introduction to the study of medieval Latin versification*, Washington, DC.

Section II.6

The Life of St Birinus
A: Anonymous (Prose) (*Vita S. Birini*) (excerpts: from chapters 6–9)
B: Henry of Avranches (Verse) (excerpts: from lines 282–354)

A: Anonymous (Prose) (*Vita S. Birini*) (excerpts: from chapters 6–9)

Date: c.1080.

The *Life of St Birinus* survives complete in five MSS among collections of saints' Lives, four MSS in England and also among the British saints' Lives in Gotha MS Forschungsbibliothek I.81, ff. 113r–118v.

Author and subject: The author is unknown: the OMT editor discusses the suggestion that he was Goscelin of Canterbury but concludes that the linguistic and stylistic evidence is not convincing. Birinus was sent from the Continent with instructions from Pope Honorius (625–38) to convert any pagan Anglo-Saxons he encountered, which he did among the Gewisse in the Thames valley area, until he died in about 650. He was buried in Dorchester, where a minster had been founded for him by King Cynegisl in 630 on the site of a former Roman settlement, but his body was twice translated, once to Winchester by Bishop Hædde (for whom see Section I.4B) and then in 980 to the New Minster by Æthelwold, who revived his cult.

Work: This *Life of St Birinus* was written at a period when the writing of hagiographies of early Anglo-Saxon saints was very popular. However, many of these saints had already been given mini-biographies in Bede's *Ecclesiastical History*, and this is true of Birinus, whose life was outlined in *HE* 3.7. The chapters excerpted here tell of Birinus' setting off from Rome on his mission to Britain and his terrifying crossing of the Channel by ship. At the end of chapter 7 and in chapter 8 the author offers a series of comparisons between Julius Caesar and Birinus, stressing Birinus' superior success in conquering Britain.

Linguistic points: While the vocabulary is on the whole classical, the text is unusually full of rhetorical devices. In this excerpt the author plays on the assonances between *exultare* and *exulare* and between *reicere* and *recipere*, and there is also grammatical wordplay with *venire* and *vincere* in the context of Caesar's arrival in Britain. There is anaphora in the repetition of *exultat*, as well as antithesis and highly rhetorical apostrophe, addressing Britain at some length in chapter 7. Some may find the author's style excessively verbose, as in the description of rocks and monsters in the English Channel, but at times he is extremely brief, as at the end of chapter 9, with the triple asyndeton of the nouns in *illum vultu manu sermone requirunt, periculum dampnum mortem se declinare contendunt*. There are in fact tricola in abundance, and in general the author is attracted to any rhetorical device that involves more rather than less (for which tendency one might compare Aldhelm, in Section I.6). The author's learning is evident from the numerous scriptural allusions, but also the references to classical literature, as here to Horace, Virgil and Lucan in the description of the storm in the English Channel. At several points in the work the author quotes sections of Leo the Great's *Sermon* 82, as at the beginning of chapter 7.

TEXT II.6A

Birinus leaves Rome for Britain

[6] beatus vero Birinus quia sciebat ex precepto apostoli omnem animam potestatibus sullimioribus esse subdendam, et quia qui potestati resistit Dei ordinationi resistit, profitetur obedientiam, suscipit iussionem, opus iniunctum libenter inire promittit. benedictione denique suscepta, parato comitatu, sumptis viaticis, quod sibi mandatum est, confisus de misericordia Dei, implere festinat. Romanus civis Roma egreditur, patriam parentesque dum relinquit, exultat. exultat, inquam, dum egreditur, dum exulat gaudet, dum se egenum facit, exultat. nec de civium affinitate relicta merebat qui Deum inhabitantem in civitate mentis habebat. nec de civitate multitudinis exiens turbabatur qui de unius Dei inhabitatione interius letabatur. quam pulchrum quamque Deo dignum commercium, distracta multitudine unitatem adquiri! in multitudine enim confunderis, in unitate firmaris. (...) **Rom. 13:1–2**

[7] iste est beatissimus vir ille per quem tibi evangelium Christi, Britannia, resplendeat (...). iam iam respexit te oriens ex alto stella matutina de celo. ecce aurora tibi orta est, que fugatis tenebris diem adesse denuntiet. iam iam lucifer oritur tibi qui noctem ignorat, qui nescit occasum, lucifer ille qui ascendit super occasum et Dominus nomen est illi. ecce sol iustitie illuxit tibi et radium sue illustrationis tibi luminosum aperuit. de occulto celorum tibi cometa dirigitur, que interitum imperii tui et commutationem fideliter preconetur. Aquilonaris enim rex qui frigidus est et frigidos facit, rex venti et turbinis qui habet potestatem aerem commovendi, dominabatur tibi a principio, dum serviebas idolis, dum demonum famulabaris imperio. et ecce iste fortis armatus predicante Birino **Luke 1:78/Rev. 2:28 Cant. 6:9 2 Pet. 1:19 Ps. 67:5/Mal. 4:2**

76 Eleventh Century

debellabitur. rex autem ille qui calore spiritus sancti gelu peccatorum evacuat regnaturus inducitur. venit ecce adversum te – immo pro te – miles fortissimus, non armis quidem sed precibus pugnaturus. procedit in pugnam non manu non hasta, sed lingua et fide bellaturus. ecce sacerdotalis debellat humilitas, quam nec Romanorum potentia prevaluit, nec cesariana vesania. plus valuit lingua sacerdotis, quam manus exerta imperatoris. tela militaria omnis armorum apparatus milia populorum non valuerunt efficere quod devotio, quod caritas mentis in uno potuit sacerdote perficere.

Birinus and Caesar compared
[8] mira res, Cesar reicitur, et sacerdos recipitur. venit Romanus imperator, vincitur et fugatur; venit sacerdos humilis, vincit et honoratur. revertitur denuo collecto exercitu Cesar et vincit, sed quod a Deo non habebat, diu habere non potuit. venit semel humilis presbiter, vicit predicando et quia non sibi sed Deo vicit, possidet eam in perpetuum, immo Deus in sacerdote suo possidet eam in eternum. Cesar de morte sua illam perdidit, Birinus de morte vivens melius eam habere iam cepit. moritur moriente Cesare, Roma, imperium tuum in Britannia, sed quod in eo amittis, in sacerdote recuperas. (…)

Birinus prepares to sail across the English Channel in the face of a storm
[9] decursis igitur multis diversarum terrarum spatiis pervenit beatus Birinus ad mare, quo transacto fines debeat intrare Britannie. opponit sibi mare natura; situs loci ne intret mari interiecto repugnat. pugnat mare pro terra, evomit terra mare, ut in venientem deseviat. offert mare fluctus marinos, sales equoreos, representat scopulos infames, animalia predicat monstruosa. hostes marini ad mentem occurrunt, sed vincuntur hec omnia, dum a transitu mari sacerdotem Dei deturbare contendunt. periculum timor non dissuasit, quod caritas vehemens in cordis aure persuasit. neque poterant eum a transeundo divertere, quem gentis asperitas, barbara lingua,[1] mores inversi, ritus inordinatus non prevalebant a predicando repellere. iam in se quidem furor maris populi furorem figurabat, sed miles Dei prepotens tam de maris quam de gentis subiectione gloriam sibi a Deo humiliter expectabat. interea navim ascensurus gloriosus antistes divina celebrat misteria, sibi suisque viaticum parans; offert Deo hostie salutaris pia libamina. quibus rite peractis, urgente et instante navigationis articulo ad navim festine deducitur, quo ascendente tolluntur armamenta, naturam arte oppugnant, nauticus clamor in immensum porrigitur. flat aura, ventus insurgit, desevit mare, navis unda tumultuante succutitur. insistunt naute remigio, portus in voto est, illum vultu manu sermone requirunt, periculum dampnum mortem se declinare contendunt.

---

1   Cf. Augustine of Canterbury (Bede *HE* 1.23) and Lanfranc (*Ep.* 1), who both expressed nervousness at the prospect of dealing with the English and their strange language; it should be remembered that the many English people who travelled on the Continent and to the Holy Land would have had similar problems. For the idea of a lingua franca used by travellers, see Section II.21A.

Translation: Anonymous, *Life of St Birinus*

[6] *Because the blessed Birinus knew from the Apostle's command that every soul must be subject to higher powers and because anyone who resists God's power resists God's plans, he professes obedience, accepts the command, promises willingly to undertake the task he has been given. Then, receiving a blessing, his companions ready, provisions packed, Birinus hastens to carry out the orders he has been given, confident of God's mercy. The Roman citizen departs from Rome and, leaving behind his home and his parents, he exults. He exults, I say, when he departs, and rejoices as he goes into exile, and as he adopts a life of poverty, he exults. He does not grieve at leaving his friends in the city, he who has God living in the city of his mind. Nor is he upset as he leaves the city's crowds, he who rejoices that the one God lives within him. How beautiful, how worthy of God is the exchange that involves losing the many to find the one! For in the multitude you are confused, in the one you are strengthened.* (…)

[7] *This is that most blessed man who made it possible for the Gospel of Christ to shine forth for you, Britain,* (…). *At this very moment the morning star, rising from the deep, has looked down on you from heaven. Look, dawn has broken for you, driving away the darkness and announcing that day is here. At this very moment Lucifer is rising for you, he who knows not the night, he who does not set, the Lucifer who rises above the setting and his name is the Lord. Look! the sun of justice has shone for you and extended the luminous rays of his illumination. From the hidden parts of the heavens a comet is sent to you, reliably foretelling the destruction of your empire and a reversal. For the king of the north is cold and makes people cold, the king of the wind and the whirlwind who has power to set the air in motion ruled over you from the beginning while you were enslaved to idols, while you served the demons' empire. And look! this one who is armed and strong will be defeated as the result of Birinus' preaching. That king who by means of the heat of the Holy Spirit removes the ice of sins is brought in to reign. Look, here he comes towards you, or rather for you, the bravest soldier, who will fight with prayers rather than with weapons. He moves forward into battle, not planning to wage war with his hand or lance but with his tongue and with faith. Look! the priestly humility is fighting which neither the power of the Romans nor Caesar's rage can overcome. The priest's tongue is more powerful than the emperor's extended hand. Military weapons and all the paraphernalia of arms and thousands of people cannot accomplish what devotion, what love in one's heart could achieve in a single priest.*

[8] *How remarkable! Caesar is rejected and a priest is welcomed. A Roman emperor comes, is overcome and put to flight; a humble priest comes, overcomes and is honoured. Caesar assembles an army once more and returns and overcomes, but he could not keep for long what he did not possess from God. The humble priest came once, overcame by preaching, and because he overcame not for himself but for God, he possesses it for ever, or rather God, in his priest, possesses it in eternity. Caesar lost it at his death, Birinus, living by his death, now begins to possess it more fully. Rome, when Caesar dies, your empire in Britain dies, but what you lose in him, you recover in the priest.* (…)

78 Eleventh Century

[9] *And so after travelling great distances through so many different countries, the saintly Birinus reaches the sea, which he had to cross to enter the borders of Britain. The sea is naturally in his way, its location drives him back so that he cannot get onto the sea which stands in his way. The sea fights to protect the land, the land spews out the sea, so that it rages against anyone who comes. The sea offers the waves of the sea, the salt of the sea, it makes manifest the notorious rocks and it tells of monstrous animals. Dangerous marine creatures spring to mind, but all these things are overcome while they strive to put the priest off crossing the sea. Fear did not dissuade him from the danger which strong love was persuading him in the ear of his heart to undertake. They were unable to deflect him from crossing, he whom the savageness of the race, the barbarous language, the perverted customs, the disordered rites did not have the power to repel from preaching. Now the raging of the sea was a figure of the people's rage against him, but the soldier of God was strong and humbly awaited glory from God as a result of both overcoming the sea and the people. Meanwhile, just as he is about to board a ship the glorious bishop celebrates the divine mysteries, preparing the meal for himself and his companions; he offers to God the pious offering of the salvific host, and when this is done according to the rite, he rushes hurriedly down to the ship just as it is about to sail. He goes on board and they pull up the anchor, setting skill against nature, and the sailors' shouts reach up into the sky. The breeze blows, the wind rises, the sea rages, the ship is shaken by the tumultuous waves. The sailors pull hard on the oars, they long to reach the harbour; their faces, hands and words express this desire while they strive to avoid danger, loss and death.*

Primary Sources and Related Texts

Three eleventh-century Anglo-Latin saints' Lives, ed. R. Love, OMT, Oxford, 1996.
Goscelin of Saint-Bertin: the hagiography of the female saints of Ely, ed. R. Love,
  OMT, Oxford, 2004.

Further Reading

Zimmerman, H. C. (2012) 'Comparing conquests: the *Life of St. Birinus* and the
  Norman invasion of England', *Studies in Philology* 109.3: 153–72.

B: Henry of Avranches (Verse) (excerpts: from lines 282–354)

Date: c.1225.

The text survives in two thirteenth-century MSS, Cambridge University Library
MS Dd.11.78 and Bodleian MS 40, ff. 43v–52v.

Author: Henry (died c.1263) was a Norman by birth, but spent the beginning and end of his career in England in the service of Henry III. He was well known as a poet: he is referred to by John of Garland (cf. Section II.28A) as *regius vates* ('royal poet'). From about 1228–43 he lived in Italy, Germany and France. He wrote in a variety of genres, mainly in hexameters and elegiac couplets.

Work: This hexameter poem of 678 lines was written in praise of St Birinus of Dorchester, possibly at the time when Dorchester and Winchester were squabbling over Birinus' relics. Like many of Henry's poems, it is a verse version of a prose text (just as Wulfstan's poem on Swithun is a version of Lantfred's prose *Life*, for which see Section I.35). It is loosely based on the eleventh-century prose *Life* (Section II.6A); equally original and audacious, it is more controlled and elegant. In the section below, Birinus realises, midway between France and England, that he has left behind in France an essential gift from the pope, and is stricken with anxiety as to how to retrieve it. Both the prose and the verse versions provide an interesting psychological depiction of his deliberations, with the verse version including a simile. Miraculously, Birinus' faith then allows him to walk back to France over the waves, and then return to the ship, to the crew's amazement.

Linguistic points: Note the elegant antitheses, e.g. *opus/actor* etc., and the word-play, as well as the echoing assonance of *reliqu-* and of *sinu/sine*. With *qua pro-scribente timorem* Henry paraphrases the scriptural saying (1 John 4:18): *perfecta caritas foras mittit timorem*. The phrase *vult duo, vult neutrum* nicely sums up the agony of choice. While the sea voyage has an epic quality, the deliberations are reminiscent of Ovid's love poems.

The verses excerpted below, in TEXT II.6B(b), from the poem of Henry of Avranches, are based on the following passage from chapters 10 and 11 of the Anonymous prose *Life of St Birinus*.

B(a): Anonymous, *Vita S. Birini* (excerpt: 10–11)

TEXT II.6B(a)

Birinus realises he has lost a precious gift
[10] dum autem navis illa multo labore multoque sudore nautarum alta sulcar-et pelagi, reminiscitur beatus Birinus se quod carius quod pretiosius sibi erat amisisse seque a negotio navigationis correptum et nautis urgentibus conclaman-tibusque prepeditum in littore unde ascenderat reliquisse. (…)
[11] cepit (coep-) interea beatus antistes contristari et dolere, attendit, observat si quod amisit aliqua posset ratione recipere. cupit reverti, sed virtus nature non temeranda resistit. consulit nautas, artem remigandi rimatur, multa promit-tit, plurima pollicetur. denegatur sibi omne humanum auxilium, timet experiri

80 Eleventh Century

divinum. (…) quid multa? fide armatus in mare descendit, naturam terre experitur in mari. prestat mare soliditatis obsequium quem fidei soliditas vehebat ad Dominum. (…) ecce quod olim operabatur Dominus in Petro, operatur modo in Petri vicario. quod olim exhibuit in magistro, iterare voluit in discipulo. Petrus fidei petra firmatus pedibus super mare pervenit ad petram, ad eum qui participium nominis sui contulerat ei, quia super eum edificaturus erat ecclesiam.

Translation: Anonymous, *Life of St Birinus*

[10] *While that ship is ploughing a furrow through the ocean's depths by means of the sailors' great effort and sweat, the saintly Birinus remembers that, distracted by the business of embarking and hindered by the sailors' urgent shouts, he has left behind on the shore where he boarded the ship something that was rather dear and precious to him, and has lost it. (…)*

[11] *The bishop becomes sad and sorrowful; he considers a while to see if there is any way he can retrieve what he has lost. He wants to go back but the inviolable power of nature resists. He consults the sailors, enquires about the technique of rowing, promises many things, will promise even more. All human help is denied him and he is afraid to ask for divine help. (…) What more is there to say? Armed with faith he climbs down onto the sea, and senses that the sea has the characteristics of land. The sea offers solid assistance to the one whose solid faith carried him to the Lord. (…) Look! The Lord achieves in Peter's deputy what He long ago achieved in Peter; what He long ago displayed in the master, He wished to repeat in the disciple. Peter, strengthened by the rock of faith, walked over the water to the rock, to the one who had conferred on him a share in His name, because upon him would He build His Church.*

B(b): Henry of Avranches, *Life of St Birinus* (excerpts: from lines 282–354)

TEXT II.6B(b)

Birinus agonises over whether to return to France to find the gift he lost

[282] o quotiens nocuit mala festinatio, qua sic
       precipitatur opus ut non deliberet actor!
       magna feret nocumenta more qui parva recusat:
       sanctus in exemplo Birinus, qui celebratis
       rite mynisteriis ad navem dum properaret
       curas postposuit reliquas pallamque reliquit
       quam discessuro donarat Honorius ille,
       in qua corpus habens Christi consuevit amicum
[290] circumferre sinu, sine quo non vinceret hostem.
       tam gravis oblitum thesauri se reminiscens

intercisa trahit mesto suspiria corde.
poscit opem, promittit opes; suffragia naute
implorata negant. quid tandem restat agendum?
nescit an expediat procedere sive reverti:
nam si procedat perdet post terga relictum
pignus et incurret irrestaurabile dampnum;
si redeat per diluvium sine nave redibit,
eius enim voto communia vota repugnant.
vult duo, vult neutrum; pavor est utrobique molestus. (…)
mensque licet, raro dubios experta tumultus,   [306]
ex gravitate sui soleat consistere firma,
instar habet summo pendentis in aere nubis
quam flatus eque fortes Aquilonis et Austri
concutiunt, donec in componentia molis   [310]
prima liquefacte vapor eliciatur et humor.
haut aliter sacrum pectus, rationibus eque
fortibus innitens, amor et timor ad dubitandum
impellunt, amor ex Austro, timor ex Aquilone,
donec ad extremum vapor exit amoris et humor
exprimitur fidei; qua proscribente timorem
ingreditur pro nave fidem comitesque relinquit
presul, et intrepidus tumidas maris insilit undas. (…)
o petra Petre super quam stat stabitque per evum   [351]
ecclesie fundata fides! si dicere fas est,
pace tua dicam, tuus iste vicarius (i.e. Birinus) audet
per mare de titulo fidei contendere tecum. (…)

Translation: Henry of Avranches, *Life of St Birinus*

How often has unfortunate haste caused harm,   [282]
when a hurried deed means the doer fails to consider.
Avoiding the minor problems of delay will cause major ones.
An example is St Birinus: having duly celebrated
the offices and while hastening to the ship,
he neglected his other cares and left behind the pallium
granted to him by Pope Honorius on the point of departure.
In this he kept the Body of Christ, carrying his friend around
in his bosom – without it he would not overcome his enemy.   [290]
Remembering that he had forgotten such an important treasure,
he sobbed and sighed from his grief-stricken heart.
He begged for help, he promised wealth; but the sailors refused
the assistance he sought. In the end what remained to be done?

82 Eleventh Century

He was unsure whether it was best to go on or turn back:
if he went on he would lose the pledge he had left behind
and would incur an irretrievable loss.
If he went back over the sea he would return without a ship,
for the general wishes clashed with his own desire.
He wants both; he wants neither. Both possibilities fill him with fear. (…)

[306] *Although his mind, rarely experiencing turbulent doubts,*
usually stands firm as the result of its own gravity,
it is like a cloud hanging high in the sky,
shaken by the equally strong blasts of winds from north and south,

[310] *until vapour and moisture are drawn out*
into the primary components of the liquefied mass.
In just the same way love and fear drive the saint's thoughts
to hesitate as they struggle with arguments that are equally strong,
love from the south and fear from the north,
until finally the vapour of love emerges and the moisture of faith
is expelled; as faith drives out fear
the bishop enters faith instead of a ship, leaving his companions,
and fearless he leaps over the swelling waves of the sea. (…)

[351] *O Peter, the rock on which the faith of the Church is founded*
and stands and will for ever stand! If I may say so, with all due respect,
when it comes to crossing the sea this deputy of yours
ventures to compete with you for the title of faith. (…)

Primary Sources and Related Texts

Townsend, D. (1994) 'The *Vita sancti Birini* of Henry of Avranches (BHL 1364)',
   Analecta Bollandiana 112: 309–38.
—— (2014) *Saints' Lives: Henry of Avranches*, Dumbarton Oaks Medieval
   Library 30, Cambridge, MA.

Further Reading

Russell, J. and Heironimus, J. P. (ed.) (1935) *The shorter Latin poems of Master
   Henry of Avranches relating to England*, Cambridge, MA.

Section II.7

St Anselm of Canterbury
A: *Letter* to His Friend Gundulf (1.33)
B: *Proslogion* (excerpts: chapter 1 (part); chapter 2)

Author: Anselm (c.1033–1109), from Aosta in Italy, became a monk and abbot at Bec in Normandy, before coming to England in 1093 to become, against his will, Archbishop of Canterbury as successor to his mentor, Lanfranc. He was one of the greatest theologians and philosophers of the Middle Ages, the author of a number of works, such as the *Monologion, Proslogion* and the *Cur Deus Homo* as well as prayers, meditations and many letters. These excerpts from two different genres, his letters and the *Proslogion*, were written before his move to England but are included here as exquisite examples of the intensely pure but highly wrought style he adopted on occasion.

Further Reading

Southern, R. (1990) *Saint Anselm: a portrait in a landscape*, Cambridge.
Vaughn, S. (2012) *Archbishop Anselm 1093–1109: Bec missionary, Canterbury
   primate, patriarch of another world*, Farnham, 2012. With illustrative sources
   in Latin, and English translation.

A: *Letter* to His Friend Gundulf (1.33)

Date: ?c.1074.

This letter appears in a number of the base MSS of Anselm's work. It occurs in two versions, with slightly different forms of the address.

Addressee: Gundulf (c.1023–1108) was born in Normandy and came to Bec in 1057 after an eventful pilgrimage to Jerusalem; at Bec he became a close friend of Anselm, who had arrived at nearly the same time. In the 1070s Gundulf accompanied Lanfranc to England and was made Bishop of Rochester in 1077. For nearly twenty years Gundulf and Anselm were separated, until Anselm came to England, and the two were bishops in adjacent dioceses until their deaths in consecutive years. In the *Textus Roffensis* (ed. T. Hearne, London, 1720: 146), a twelfth-century collection of documents relating to Rochester, Gundulf is described as skilled in

84 Eleventh Century

building in stone (*in opere caementarii plurimum sciens et efficax*), and in this capacity he assisted William the Conqueror in the construction of the White Tower at the Tower of London, worked for Archbishop Lanfranc to rebuild Rochester Cathedral and later helped King William Rufus with Rochester Castle.

Work: This letter is one of several from Anselm to Gundulf. It may date from the period when Gundulf was in England but not yet a bishop, while Anselm was still prior at Bec, probably around 1073, some seven years before Anselm even visited England and twenty years before he succeeded Lanfranc as Archbishop of Canterbury in 1093. The letter is included here as an early example of the beautiful writing style of someone who was to become one of the greatest writers and ecclesiastical figures in British history. Unfortunately, no letters from Gundulf to Anselm survive. The anonymous *Life of Gundulf*, which survives only in one British Library MS, includes several of Anselm's letters. Here the perfection of the product reflects the perfection of the spiritual relationship in God between the friends, as Anselm perceives it. In describing his friendship, he wittily and profoundly concludes that there is actually no need for a letter: all he needs to do is ask God to do what God knows is best for his friend.

Linguistic points: Anselm constructs this brief letter on a number of contrasting concepts, such as body and soul, absence and presence, parchment and the (figurative) repository of the heart. Against the background of such tensions, the two friends' perfect unity in God stands in strong relief. This unity is reflected in the syntax Anselm uses: he employs the singular *est* when speaking of the two of them. Note the repetition of sounds, as in *absentes* and *praesentes*, in the first two syllables of each of the adjacent words *invicem indicemus*, and in *noti* and *nota*. There is frequent wordplay, as with the use of *indigemus* and *indicemus* in the same sentence: this only works because Anselm has constructed the sentence to demand a subjunctive of the first conjugation verb *indicare* to match the second-conjugation verb *indigere*.

TEXT II.7A

A letter of friendship in God
[address] suo suus, amico amicus, fratri frater, Gundulfo Anselmus, pro amore felicitatis perseverantiam in sanctitate, pro praemio sanctitatis aeternitatem in felicitate.
et meus Gundulfus et tuus Anselmus est testis quia ego et tu nequaquam indigemus ut mutuos nostros affectus per epistolas nobis invicem indicemus. quoniam enim anima tua et anima mea sese <ab> invicem nequaquam esse patiuntur absentes, sed sunt indesinenter se mutuo amplectentes, nichil nobis invicem

deest de nobis, nisi quia corpore non sumus nobis praesentes. cur autem tibi dilectionem meam describam in carta, cum eius veram imaginem assidue serves in cordis tui archa? quid enim aliud est dilectio tua erga me quam imago dilectionis meae erga te? invitat igitur me nota michi tua voluntas ut propter corporalem nostram absentiam aliquid tibi scribam. sed quia nobis noti sumus per animarum praesentiam, nescio quid tibi dicam, nisi Deus tibi faciat quod ipse scit sibi placere et tibi expedire. Vale.

Translation: Anselm's Letter to Gundulf

His own to his own, a friend to a friend, a brother to a brother, Anselm (wishes) for Gundulf perseverance in holiness, for the sake of the love of bliss, and as a reward for holiness, eternity in bliss.

My Gundulf and your Anselm is witness that I and you in no way need to indicate to each other by letter our mutual feelings. For since your soul and my soul in no way allow themselves to be absent from each other, but are in an everlasting mutual embrace, we lack nothing of each other, except for the fact that we are not physically present to each other. Why should I describe my love for you on parchment, when you preserve a true copy of it in the strongbox of your heart? For what is your love for me but an image of my love for you? And so your wishes, known to me, invite me to write something to you on account of our physical absence; but because we are known to each other by the presence of our souls, I do not know what to say to you, except that I wish God to do for you what he knows pleases him and benefits you. Farewell.

Primary Sources and Related Texts

Epistolae Anselmi Cantuarensis Archiepiscopi/Letters of Anselm, Archbishop of Canterbury, vol. 1: *The Bec Letters*, ed. S. Niskanen, OMT, Oxford, 2019.

Further Reading

Aird, W. M. (2011) 'The tears of Bishop Gundulf: gender, religion and emotion in the late eleventh century' in *Intersections of gender, religion and ethnicity in the Middle Ages*, ed. C. Beattie and K. Fenton, Basingstoke.

Smith, R. A. L. (1943) 'The place of Gundulf in the Anglo-Norman Church', *EHR* 58: 257–72.

Vaughn, S. (2002) *St Anselm and the handmaidens of God: a study of Anselm's correspondence with women*, Turnhout.

86 Eleventh Century

B: *Proslogion* (excerpts: chapter 1 (part); chapter 2)

Date: 1077–8.

This work survives in numerous MSS. See the six-volume edition of the *Opera omnia* of Anselm, ed. F. Schmitt, Edinburgh, 1938–61.

Work: This work was written after the *Monologion*, which had taken the form of a soliloquy. Anselm invented the title *Proslogion* to convey the fact that this work is an address to God. It is widely known for what is supposed to be its formulation of a proof for the existence of God, *credimus te esse aliquid quo nihil maius cogitari possit* (which translates less elegantly as 'we believe you are something than which nothing greater can be conceived'), often referred to as the ontological argument. However, Anselm's distinctive work opens with a passionate exploration of the nature of God and his relation to each human individual, akin to much of Augustine's *Confessions*, which also addresses God directly. It begins with an invitation to detach oneself from the world around, to withdraw into one's mental space in order to seek God. As Anselm stresses at the end of the first chapter, he is not looking for a rational proof of God's existence to convince him to believe, but (as he memorably puts it, echoing several passages in Augustine), *credo ut intelligam* ('I believe so that I might understand'); in other words, faith precedes understanding. Most readers study the work from a philosophical or theological viewpoint; however, study from a literary viewpoint is also important, as the work bears similarities to a prayer.

Linguistic points: The *Proslogion* is highly wrought and at the same time lucid, conveying a tense balance between the exhilaration of man's closeness to God and a devastating awareness of the distance between them, the result of man's *durus et dirus casus* ('hard and harsh fall'). The text is interlaced with biblical references, especially from the Psalms, which were generally taken as relevant to many aspects of the human condition. Anselm constantly uses rhetorical devices such as similes, antitheses, assonance and wordplay, as in *ne desperem suspirando, sed respirem sperando* with its clever choice of verbs, making the two phrases mirror each other, sharply contrasted in sense but echoing each other in sound. The rhetoric is used not only to delight the reader but more importantly to represent the truth Anselm is attempting to convey, a truth which involves both similarities and contrasts between God and man.

Apart from Anselm's own coinage of the title *Proslogion*, and the use of *indulcare* ('to sweeten', not attested earlier than LL) in a figurative sense, the vocabulary in this excerpt derives largely from the writings of the Church Fathers and from the Bible, without being particularly technical. When quoting from the Psalms Anselm uses Jerome's translation from the Greek Septuagint, rather than from the Hebrew original.

TEXT II.7B

Anselm addresses his fellow human beings, and asks God to explain His nature

[1] eia nunc, homuncio, fuge paululum occupationes tuas, absconde te modicum a tumultuosis cogitationibus tuis. abice nunc onerosas curas, et postpone laboriosas distentiones tuas. vaca aliquantulum Deo, et requiesce aliquantulum in eo. intra in cubiculum mentis tuae, exclude omnia praeter Deum et quae te iuvent **Matt. 6:6** ad quaerendum eum, et clauso ostio quaere eum. dic nunc, totum cor meum, dic nunc Deo: quaero vultum tuum; vultum tuum, Domine, requiro. **Ps. 26:8**

eia nunc ergo tu, Domine Deus meus, doce cor meum ubi et quomodo te quaerat, ubi et quomodo te inveniat. Domine, si hic non es, ubi te quaeram absentem? si autem ubique es, cur non video praesentem? sed certe habitas lucem inaccessibilem. et ubi est lux inaccessibilis? aut quomodo accedam ad lucem **1 Tim. 6:16** inaccessibilem? aut quis me ducet et inducet in illam, ut videam te in illa? deinde quibus signis, qua facie te quaeram? numquam te vidi, Domine Deus meus, non novi faciem tuam. quid faciet, altissime Domine, quid faciet iste tuus longinquus exsul? quid faciet servus tuus anxius amore tui et longe proiectus a facie tua? **Ps. 50:13** anhelat videre te, et nimis abest illi facies tua. accedere ad te desiderat, et inaccessibilis est habitatio tua. invenire te cupit, et nescit locum tuum. quaerere te affectat, et ignorat vultum tuum. Domine, Deus meus es, et Dominus meus es et numquam te vidi. tu me fecisti et refecisti et omnia mea bona tu mihi contulisti, et nondum novi te. denique ad te videndum factus sum, et nondum feci propter quod factus sum.

o misera sors hominis, cum hoc perdidit ad quod factus est. o durus et dirus casus ille! heu, quid perdidit et quid invenit, quid abscessit et quid remansit! perdidit beatitudinem ad quam factus est, et invenit miseriam propter quam factus non est. abscessit sine quo nihil felix est, et remansit quod per se nonnisi miserum est. manducabat tunc homo panem angelorum, quem nunc esurit, manducat **Ps. 77:25** nunc panem dolorum, quem tunc nesciebat. heu publicus luctus hominum, uni- **Ps. 126:2** versalis planctus filiorum Adae! ille ructabat saturitate, nos suspiramus esurie. ille abundabat, nos mendicamus. ille feliciter tenebat et misere deseruit, nos infeliciter egemus et miserabiliter desideramus, et heu, vacui remanemus. cur non nobis custodivit cum facile posset, quo tam graviter careremus? quare sic nobis obseravit lucem, et obduxit nos tenebris? ut quid nobis abstulit vitam et inflixit mortem? aerumnosi, unde sumus expulsi, quo sumus impulsi! unde praecipitati, quo obruti! a patria in exsilium, a visione Dei in caecitatem nostram. a iucunditate immortalitatis in amaritudinem et horrorem mortis. misera mutatio! de quanto bono in quantum malum! grave damnum, gravis dolor, grave totum. (...) obsecro, Domine, ne desperem suspirando, sed respirem. obsecro, Domine, amaricatum est cor meum sua desolatione, indulca illud tua consolatione. obsecro, Domine, esuriens incepi quaerere te, ne desinam ieiunus de te. famelicus accessi, ne recedam impastus. pauper veni ad divitem, miser ad misericordem; ne redeam vacuus et contemptus. et si antequam comedam suspiro, da vel post suspiria quod **Job 3:24**

88 Eleventh Century

comedam. Domine, incurvatus non possum nisi deorsum aspicere, erige me ut possim sursum intendere. iniquitates meae supergressae caput meum obvolvunt me, et sicut onus grave gravant me. evolve me, exonera me, ne urgeat puteus earum os suum super me. liceat mihi suspicere lucem tuam, vel de longe, vel de profundo. doce me quaerere te, et ostende te quaerenti; quia nec quaerere te possum nisi tu doceas, nec invenire nisi te ostendas. quaeram te desiderando, desiderem quaerendo. inveniam amando, amem inveniendo.

fateor, Domine, et gratias ago, quia creasti in me hanc imaginem tuam, ut tui memor te cogitem, te amem. sed sic est abolita attritione vitiorum, sic est offuscata fumo peccatorum, ut non possit facere ad quod facta est, nisi tu renoves et reformes eam. non tento, Domine, penetrare altitudinem tuam, quia nullatenus comparo illi intellectum meum; sed desidero aliquatenus intelligere veritatem tuam, quam credit et amat cor meum. neque enim quaero intelligere ut credam, sed credo ut intelligam. nam et hoc credo: quia nisi credidero, non intelligam.

Ps. 37:5
Ps. 68:16

Gen. 1:27

Translation: Anselm, *Proslogion*

[1] *Come now, you poor creature, turn away for a little while from everything that occupies you, hide a while from your tumultuous thoughts. Throw away now the worries that weigh you down and set aside your troublesome distractions. Just focus on God for a moment and rest in him for a while. Enter into the chamber of your mind, shut out everything except God and what will help you to seek him, and once you have closed the door, seek him. Say now, my whole heart, say now to God, I seek your face; your face, Lord, I look for.*

Come now, then, Lord my God, teach my heart where and how it should seek you, where and how it might find you. Lord, if you are not here, where should I see you when you are absent? But if you are everywhere, why do I not see you when you are present? But it is certain that you live in light inaccessible. And where is light inaccessible? Or how might I approach the light inaccessible? Or who will lead me and bring me into it, so that I may see you in it? Then by what signs, what appearance should I seek you? I have never seen you, Lord my God, I do not know what you look like. What should this distant exile, what, highest Lord, should he do? What should your anxious servant do, flung far away as he is from your love and your face. He longs to see you, and your face is too far from him. He desires to approach you, and your dwelling is inaccessible. He wishes to find you, and he does not know your place. He tries to seek you, and he does not know your face. Lord, you are my God and you are my Lord and I have never seen you. You have made me and remade me and you have granted to me all the good things that are mine and I have not yet known you. Finally, I was made in order to see you and I have not yet accomplished that for which I was made.

O wretched is man's lot, for he has lost that for which he was made. O hard and harsh is his fall! Alas, what has he lost and what has he found, what has disappeared and what remains? He has lost the blessedness for which he was made and he has found the misery for which he was not made. That without which nothing is blessed has disappeared, and what remains can by itself only be wretched. At that time man used to eat the bread of angels which he now hungers after, now he eats the bread of sorrow which he did not know at that time. Alas for the human sorrow that affects all, the universal lament of the sons of Adam! He belched because he was full, we sigh because we are hungry. He had plenty, we go begging. He possessed in blessedness and abandoned miserably, we are wretchedly in need and desire pitiably, and alas we remain empty. Why did he not keep it for us when he could easily have arranged that we would not be in such serious need? Why did he block the light out for us and wrap us in darkness? Why did he rob us of life and inflict death? Wretched people, from what have we been driven out, where have we been driven? From what have we been hurled, by what have we been crushed? From our homeland into exile, from a vision of God into blindness. From the joyfulness of immortality to the bitterness and horror of death. Wretched exchange! From what good to what evil! Heavy loss, heavy sorrow, everything heavy. (…) I beg you, Lord, that I should not lose hope in sighing but should breathe by hoping. I beg you, Lord, sweeten with your consolation my heart which is embittered in its desolation. I beg you, Lord, I who began to seek you while I was hungry, may I not cease from you while fasting. Hungry I approached you; may I not return unfed. Poor I came to one who is rich, miserable to one who is merciful; do not let me go home empty and scorned. And if I sigh before I eat, give me something to eat at least after my sighs. Lord, I am bent over and can only look down; raise me up so that I can turn my gaze upwards. My iniquities have gone over my head and envelop me, and like a heavy load they crush me. Release me, relieve me so that the pit of my iniquities does not press its mouth over me. Allow me to look upon your light, even from afar, even from the depths. Teach me to seek you and show yourself to me when I seek; for I cannot see you unless you teach me and cannot find you unless you show yourself. May I see you by desiring, may I desire you by seeking. May I find you by loving, may I love you by finding. I confess, Lord, and I give thanks because you have created in me this image of yourself so that remembering you I may think of you and I may love you. But it has been effaced by the attrition of my faults, and blackened by the smoke of my sins so that it cannot do what it was made for, unless you restore it and renew it. I am not attempting, Lord, to penetrate your heights, because I can to no extent compare my intellect to it; but I desire to some degree to understand your truth which my heart believes and loves. For I do not seek to understand so that I may believe, but I believe so that I may understand. For I believe this, too: that if I did not believe, I would not understand.

[2] ergo, Domine, qui das fidei intellectum, da mihi, ut quantum scis expedire intelligam, quia es sicut credimus, et hoc es quod credimus. et quidem credimus te esse aliquid quo nihil maius cogitari possit. an ergo non est aliqua talis natura, quia dixit insipiens in corde suo: non est Deus? sed certe ipse idem insipiens, **Ps. 13:1, 52:1** cum audit hoc ipsum quod dico: aliquid quo maius nihil cogitari potest, intelligit

90 Eleventh Century

quod audit; et quod intelligit in intellectu eius est, etiam si non intelligat illud esse. aliud enim est rem esse in intellectu, aliud intelligere rem esse. nam cum pictor praecogitat quae facturus est, habet quidem in intellectu, sed nondum intelligit esse quod nondum fecit. cum vero iam pinxit, et habet in intellectu et intelligit esse quod iam fecit. convincitur ergo etiam insipiens esse vel in intellectu aliquid quo nihil maius cogitari potest, quia hoc cum audit intelligit, et quidquid intelligitur in intellectu est. et certe id quo maius cogitari nequit, non potest esse in solo intellectu. si enim vel in solo intellectu est, potest cogitari esse et in re, quod maius est. si ergo id quo maius cogitari non potest, est in solo intellectu: id ipsum quo maius cogitari non potest, est quo maius cogitari potest. sed certe hoc esse non potest. existit ergo procul dubio aliquid quo maius cogitari non valet, et in intellectu et in re.

Translation: Anselm, *Proslogion*

[2] *And so, Lord, you who give understanding to faith, grant to me that I might understand as much as you know is beneficial, because you are just as we believe and you are what we believe. And indeed we believe that you are something than which nothing greater can be conceived. Or is there then nothing of this kind by nature, because the fool has said in his heart, there is no God? But undoubtedly this fool, when he hears what I am saying, 'something than which nothing greater can be conceived', understands what he hears; and what he understands is in his intellect, even if he does not understand that it exists. For it is one thing for something to be in the intellect, another to understand that this thing exists. For when a painter plans what he is going to do, he has it in his intellect but he does not yet understand what he has not yet made. But when he has painted it, he both has it in his intellect and understands that what he has now made exists. So even the fool is convinced that there can be, even in the intellect, a thing than which nothing greater can be conceived, because when he hears this he understands it, and whatever is understood is in the intellect. And that than which it is impossible to think of anything greater, definitely cannot exist just in the intellect. For if it is only in the intellect, then something greater can be conceived as being also in reality. Consequently, if that than which nothing greater can be conceived is only in the intellect, then that thing than which nothing greater can be conceived is something than which something greater can be conceived. But this is definitely impossible. So without doubt there exists something than which nothing greater can be conceived, both in intellect and in reality.*

Primary Sources and Related Texts

St Anselm's Proslogion, transl. and introd. M. J. Charlesworth, London, 1979. With Latin text from *Anselmi opera omnia*, vol. 1, ed. F. S. Schmitt, Edinburgh, 1940. Also in online *Library of Latin texts*, via www.brepols.net.

St Anselm, *Monologion*.
Eadmer, *Vita Anselmi* 1.19 (on Anselm's writing of the *Proslogion*).
Augustine, *Soliloquies* and *Confessions*.

Further Reading

Ortlund, G. (2020) *Anselm's pursuit of joy: a commentary on the Proslogion*,
    Washington, DC.
Sharpe, R. (2009) 'Anselm as author: publishing in the late eleventh century',
    JML 19: 1–87.

TWELFTH
CENTURY

Section II.8

Eadmer, *The Life of Archbishop Anselm* (*Vita Anselmi archiepiscopi*) (excerpt: 1.22)

Date: c.1100.

Cambridge MS CCC 371 is an autograph containing the *Life of Archbishop Anselm* (ff. 147r–188v) as written by Eadmer himself.

Author: Eadmer (c.1060–c.1126) was a Benedictine monk whom Anselm, arriving in England in 1093, chose as a member of his household. Eadmer was Anselm's devoted friend. He accompanied Anselm into exile in France and Italy and was a staunch supporter of the Church at Canterbury. He wrote the *History of Recent Events in England*, focusing on Anselm's career against the background of the contemporary investiture dispute between Church and state, as well as the *Life of Archbishop Anselm* and accounts of the lives and miracles of such Anglo-Saxon saints and bishops as Wilfrid, Dunstan and Oswald (cf. Sections I.15 and I.40).

Work: This work is an intimate biography of Anselm which complements the picture of the archbishop in the *History of Recent Events in England*. It includes public and private aspects of its subject as well as miracles associated with him. It is notable for the amount of conversation and direct speech Eadmer records to convey Anselm's character, ideas, expressions and wit. In 1100 Anselm found out that Eadmer was working on a biography of him and asked him to burn it: Eadmer obeyed but kept a copy of his notes from which he reconstructed it after Anselm's death. However, when it came to the submission of a dossier to the pope in 1162 in a bid to have Anselm canonised, it was the *Life of Archbishop Anselm* by John of Salisbury, written for the occasion, that was included, rather than Eadmer's.

This passage is selected as displaying Eadmer's style, including his use of conversation, and through this, Anselm's general manner of expression (including his habit of using carefully developed similes). In this passage the context is of one of Anselm's main concerns, the education of the young. Here he demonstrates his liking for extended metaphors for the purpose of teaching, as well as his compassion. In mentioning turning the other cheek and praying for our enemies, Anselm is alluding to Christ's Sermon on the Mount in Matthew 5.

Linguistic points: Eadmer's Latin is clear and balanced, embracing a wide but not abstruse vocabulary; his prose is melodious and his style characteristic of monastic writers. In the *Life of Archbishop Anselm* he uses the occasional word

96 Twelfth Century

derived from vernaculars, e.g. *schilla* (*scella*), a Germanic word for 'bell', found in the AN form 'eschelle'; *strivile* (*strevile*), an otherwise unattested form related to *streva* and *strepa* for 'stirrup'; and *sturio*, a word deriving from a Germanic form that passes into English as 'sturgeon'. For the phrase *piae discretionis et discretae pietatis*, compare Aldhelm's phrase in his prose work *On Virginity*: *verbosa garrulitas aut garrula verbositas* (Section I.6A). Eadmer's spelling is retained in Southern's edition: this shows orthographical consistency even if on occasion the spelling might ruffle a classicist. Eadmer also distinguished between e and the diphthong ae. For further discussion of Eadmer's language see Southern's edition of the Life of Anselm, pp. xxv–xxxiv.

TEXT II.8

Anselm discusses the education of children with an overly strict abbot
[1.22] De discretione quam docuit quendam abbatem exercere erga pueros in scola nutritos.
quodam igitur tempore cum quidam abbas qui admodum religiosus habebatur secum de iis quae monasticae religionis erant loqueretur, ac inter alia de pueris in claustro nutritis verba consereret, adjecit, 'Quid, obsecro, fiet de istis? perversi sunt, et incorrigibiles. die et nocte non cessamus eos verberantes, et semper fiunt sibi ipsis deteriores.' ad quae miratus Anselmus. 'Non cessatis', inquit, 'eos verberare? et cum adulti sunt quales sunt?' 'Hebetes', inquit, 'et bestiales.' at ille, 'Quam bono omine nutrimentum vestrum expendistis; de hominibus bestias nutrivistis.' 'Et nos', ait, 'quid possumus inde? modis omnibus constringimus eos ut proficiant, et nihil proficimus.' 'Constringitis? dic quaeso michi domine abba, si plantam arboris in horto tuo plantares, et mox illam omni ex parte ita concluderes ut ramos suos nullatenus extendere posset, cum eam post annos excluderes, qualis arbor inde prodiret?' 'Profecto inutilis, incurvis ramis et perplexis.' 'Et hoc ex cujus culpa procederet nisi tua, qui eam immoderate conclusisti? certe hoc facitis de pueris vestris. plantati sunt per oblationem in horto ecclesiae, ut crescant et fructificent Deo. vos autem in tantum terroribus, minis et verberibus undique illos coarctatis, ut nulla penitus sibi liceat libertate potiri. itaque indiscrete oppressi, pravas et spinarum more perplexas infra se cogitationes congerunt, fovent, nutriunt; tantasque eas vi nutriendo suffulciunt, ut omnia quae illarum correctioni possent adminiculari obstinata mente subterfugiant. unde fit, ut quia nichil amoris, nichil boni postea fidem habeant, sed omnia vestra ex odio et invidia contra se procedere credant. contingitque modo miserabili, ut sicut deinceps corpore crescunt, sic in eis odium et suspicio pietatis, nihil benivolentiae sive dulcedinis circa se in vobis sentiunt, nec illi alicujus in vobis omnis mali crescat, semper proni et incurvi ad vitia. cunque ad nullum in vera fuerint caritate nutriti, nullum nisi depressis superciliis, oculove obliquo valent intueri. sed propter Deum vellem michi diceretis, quid causae sit quod eis tantum infesti estis. nonne

II.8 | Eadmer, *The Life of Archbishop Anselm*

homines, nonne ejusdem sunt naturae cujus vos estis? velletisve vobis fieri quod illis facitis, siquidem quod sunt vos essetis? sed esto. solis eos percussionibus et flagellis ad mores bonos vultis informare. vidistis unquam aurificem ex lammina auri vel argenti solis percussionibus imaginem speciosam formasse? non puto. quid tunc? quatinus aptam formam ex lammina formet, nunc eam suo instrumento leniter premit et percutit, nunc discreto levamine lenius levat et format. sic et vos si pueros vestros cupitis ornatis moribus esse, necesse est ut cum depressionibus verberum, impendatis eis paternae pietatis et mansuetudinis levamen atque subsidium.' ad haec abbas, 'Quod levamen, quod subsidium? ad graves et maturos mores illos constringere laboramus.' cui ille, 'Bene quidem. et panis et quisque solidus cibus utilis et bonus est eo uti valenti. verum subtracto lacte ciba inde lactentem infantem, et videbis eum ex hoc magis strangulari quam recreari. cur hoc dicere nolo, quoniam claret. attamen hoc tenete, quia sicut fragile et forte corpus pro sua qualitate habet cibum suum, ita fragilis et fortis anima habet pro sui mensura victum suum. fortis anima delectatur et pascitur solido cibo, patientia scilicet in tribulationibus, non concupiscere aliena, percutienti unam maxillam praebere alteram, orare pro inimicis, odientes diligere, et multa in hunc modum. fragilis autem, et adhuc in Dei servitio tenera, lacte indiget, mansuetudine videlicet aliorum, benignitate, misericordia, hilari advocatione, caritativa supportatione, et pluribus hujusmodi. si taliter vestris et fortibus et infirmis vos coaptatis per Dei gratiam omnes quantum vestra refert Deo adquiretis.' his abbas auditis ingemuit dicens, 'Vere erravimus a veritate et lux discretionis non luxit nobis.' et cadens in terram ante pedes ejus, se peccasse, se reum esse confessus est; veniamque de praeteritis petiit, et emendationem de futuris repromisit.

haec iccirco dicimus, quatinus per haec quam piae discretionis et discretae pietatis in omnes fuerit, agnoscamus. talibus studiis intendebat, in istis Deo serviebat, per haec bonis omnibus valde placebat. unde bona fama ejus non modo Normannia tota est respersa, verum etiam Francia tota, Flandria tota, contiguaeque his terrae omnes. quin et mare transiit, Angliamque replevit. exciti sunt quaque gentium multi nobiles, prudentes clerici, strenui milites, atque ad eum confluxere, seque et sua in ipsum monasterium Dei servitio tradidere. crescit coenobium illud intus et extra. intus in sancta religione, extra in multimoda possessione.

Translation: Eadmer, *Life of Archbishop Anselm*

[1.22] *And so at one time when an abbot who was regarded as quite a religious man was talking to him about matters concerning the monastic community and amongst other things was discussing boys brought up in the cloister, he added, 'What, I ask, is to be done with them? They are perverse and incorrigible; day and night we do not cease to beat them, and they just become even worse.' Anselm was amazed at this and said, 'You don't cease to beat them? And what are they like when they are*

98 Twelfth Century

grown up?' 'Dull', he answered, 'and brutish.' Then Anselm said, 'You have really used up your food for a good purpose! From humans you have produced beasts.' 'What can we do?' he said. 'We discipline them in every way to get them to improve, but we have no success.' 'You discipline them? Tell me, please, father abbot, if you were to plant a sapling in your garden and then enclosed it on every side in such a way that it could not stretch out its branches at all, when you release it years later, what kind of tree would come of it?' 'A totally useless one, with branches bent and all entangled.' 'And whose fault would this be except yours, since it was you who enclosed it too tightly? Undoubtedly this is what you are doing with your boys. They have been planted by oblation in the garden of the church, so that they might grow and bring forth fruit for God. But you coerce them with such terrors, threats and beatings on every side, that they are completely deprived of freedom. And as a result of your reckless treatment, they feel overwhelmed, and they pile up wicked thoughts inside themselves, encouraging and nourishing these thoughts that are twisted like thorn branches. The boys prop up these thoughts to such an extent by feeding them that the boys stubbornly avoid everything that could help to correct these thoughts. And so it happens that, because they feel no love, no tenderness, no benevolence or kindness towards them from you, they have no confidence in anything good in you afterwards, but they believe that everything that comes from you proceeds from hatred and envy towards them. The tragic outcome is that as they later grow physically, so also there grows within them hatred and a mistrust of kindness. They are always bent over, prone to vices, and since they were brought up without any real love, they cannot look at anyone except with a frown, unable to look one in the eye. But I would like you to tell me, for God's sake, what your reason is for being so aggressive towards them. Surely they are human beings, surely they share the same nature as you? Would you want to be treated as you treat them, if you were them? But so be it. You wish to train them in good behaviour just by beating and whipping them. Have you ever seen a goldsmith give shape to a beautiful image out of gold or silver leaf just by beating it? I do not think so. What then does he do? So as to give the leaf the right shape, he will alternately press and beat it with his tool, then gently raise it and by raising it skilfully, shape it. So if you, too, wish your boys to have attractive characters, it is necessary for you, along with the oppression caused by the beatings, to bestow on them the relief and support that come from fatherly tenderness and kindness.' The abbot replied, 'What relief? What support? We work hard to discipline them so that their behaviour will be serious and mature.' Anselm said to him, 'All right. Bread and any solid food are useful, and it is good to use them for someone who is strong. But if you wean a baby and feed it with such food, you will see that you are causing it to choke rather than making it stronger. I hardly need to explain this, as it is obvious. But bear this in mind, because just as a body has its own food depending on whether it is fragile or strong, so also a fragile or strong soul has its own nourishment according to its own capacity. A strong soul enjoys and eats solid food, namely endurance in tribulation, not desiring what belongs to others, offering the other cheek to anyone who strikes him, praying for his enemies, loving those who hate him, and many similar things. But the fragile soul and the one that is still delicate in God's service needs milk, namely the gentleness, kindness and mercy of others, it needs cheerful encouragement, loving support and many things of this kind. If in this way you adapt your treatment to your boys, both the strong and the weak ones, you will, by God's grace, win them all for God, as far as it depends on you.' When the abbot heard these words he sighed and said, 'We have indeed wandered away from the truth, and the light of discernment has not shone on us.' And falling to the ground in front of Anselm, he confessed that he had sinned and that he was guilty; he asked for mercy for his past deeds and promised to correct his future deeds.

We recount this episode so that we might recognise with what tender discretion and discreet tenderness Anselm behaved towards everyone. He would strive with efforts like these; in this way he would serve God and greatly please all good people. As a result his good reputation spread not only throughout Normandy but also throughout France and Flanders and all the neighbouring countries. In fact, it also crossed the sea and spread throughout England. Many noblemen, wise clerics, vigorous soldiers from every nation were roused and came flooding to him, and surrendered themselves and their wealth to the service of God in that monastery. That monastic community grew inwardly and outwardly, inwardly in holy religion, outwardly in possessions of many different kinds.

Primary Sources and Related Texts

Eadmeri Vita Sancti Anselmi/The Life of St Anselm, ed. R. Southern, OMT, Oxford, 1972.

Eadmer, *Lives and Miracles of Saints Oda, Dunstan and Oswald*, ed. A. Turner and B. Muir, OMT, Oxford, 2006: xxxi–xxxii on Eadmer's style.

John of Salisbury, *Anselm and Becket: two Canterbury saints' Lives*, ed. and transl. R. Pepin, Toronto, 2009.

On the education of children, cf. Jerome, *Letter* 107 to Laeta, in *Lives of Roman Christian women*, transl. C. White, Harmondsworth, 2010.

Further Reading

Southern, R. (1963) *Saint Anselm and his biographer: a study of monastic life and thought 1059–c.1130*, Cambridge.

—— (1990) *Saint Anselm: a portrait in a landscape*, Cambridge.

Staunton, M. (1997) 'Eadmer's *Vita Anselmi*: a reinterpretation', *JMH* 23.1: 1–14.

Winstead, K. (ed.) (2018) *The Oxford history of life-writing*, vol. 1: *The Middle Ages*, Oxford.

Section II.9

Sæwulf, *An Account of a Pilgrimage to Jerusalem* (*Relatio de peregrinatione ad Hierosolymam*) (excerpts: lines 96–169 and 425–46)

Date: after 1103.

This text appears to survive only in a twelfth-century copy contained in Cambridge MS CCC 111.

Author: Nothing is known of the author apart from what we learn from this work, the account of part of his pilgrimage to Jerusalem around 1102–3, though his commitment to the spiritual benefits of pilgrimage and the interest in trade shown in his account might support the suggestion that he is the merchant Sæwulf whom William of Malmesbury records (*GP* 4.146) as having entered a monastery in old age, on the advice of Wulfstan, Bishop of Worcester (1062–95).

Work: The *Account of a Pilgrimage to Jerusalem* gives a first-person account of Sæwulf's journey, from his departure from the coast of Apulia until it breaks off on the return journey with his arrival in Raclea (now Marmara Ereğlisi, whence Helen was taken by Paris to Troy, as Sæwulf points out). It can be compared with similar pilgrimage accounts to the Holy Land and indeed also with the Mediterranean sea voyage and adventures depicted in Homer's *Odyssey*. Sæwulf is informative about travel and trade of the time, as well as giving a picture of Jerusalem, linked to scriptural references, shortly after the Crusaders had regained it from the Saracens in 1099. In the first passage here Sæwulf relates the effects of the storm outside Jaffa (for the account of the shipwreck, cf. the wreck of the White Ship, in Section II.11), and the dangerous journey from Jaffa to Jerusalem; in the second he describes Bethlehem as he saw it (cf. Section I.5 for a seventh-century view of Bethlehem). Sæwulf's account of his journey may be compared with the beautiful pictorial itinerary from London to Jerusalem (via Apulia) created by Matthew Paris to accompany his *Chronicles* (cf. Section II.24) in about 1250. This takes the form of a diagram of the places and stopping points recommended for a thirteenth-century traveller, resembling the seventeenth-century strip maps of Britain by John Ogilby; Matthew's itinerary is preserved in BL MS Royal 14.C.vii, ff. 4r–5r.

Linguistic points: Sæwulf provides a vivid and literary travelogue. At lines 141 and 569 he mentions ships loaded with *palmarii* and cargo: the fact that at line 116 he had used the term *peregrinis* in the same context shows that *palmarius* is an early example of what would become the English word 'palmer' for a pilgrim. Note also the interesting use of the word *idiota* in a slightly different sense from the primary senses of 'an ordinary person or layman' and 'an uneducated person', recorded in *DMLBS*. Here the word apparently means someone who behaves foolishly, perhaps due to ignorance. In these excerpts he also gives the names of different kinds of ships: *ex navibus triginta maximis, quarum quaedam 'dromundi', quaedam vero 'gulafri', quaedam autem 'catti' vulgariter vocantur.* Gerald of Wales mentions the *dromundus* of Saladin (*De principis instructione*, ed. Bartlett, p. 602), suggesting that it was a local type of vessel. *cattus* is usually applied to a kind of siege engine.

TEXT II.9

Witnessing the ships wrecked by a storm outside Jaffa

[96–169] arrigite aures, karissimi, et audite misericordiam quam divina clementia michi, licet ultimo servo suo, meisque exhibuit. nam eadem die qua appulimus quidam dixit michi, ut credo deifice: 'Domine, hodie litus ascende, ne forte, hac nocte vel diluculo tempestate superveniente, cras ascendere non possis.' quod dum audivi, statim captus desiderio ascendendi, naviculam conduxi et cum omnibus meis ascendi. me autem ascendente mare turbatur, crevit commotio et facta est tempestas valida, sed ad litus divina gratia favente perveni illesus. quid plura? civitatem hospitandi causa intravimus et longo labore victi atque lassati refecti pausavimus. mane vero, dum ab aecclesia venimus, sonitum maris audivimus, clamorem populi omnesque concurrentes atque mirantes de talibus prius inauditis, nos autem timentes currendo simul cum aliis venimus ad litus. dum enim illuc pervenimus, vidimus tempestatem altitudinem superexcellere montium, corpora quidem innumerabilia hominum utriusque sexus summersorum in litore miserrime iacentia aspeximus, naves minutatim fractas iuxta volutantes simul vidimus. sed quis preter rugitum maris et fragorem navium quicquam audire potuit? clamorem etenim populi sonitumque omnium tubarum excessit. navis **?l. turbarum** nostra, maxima atque fortissima, aliaeque multae frumento aliisque mercimoniis atque peregrinis venientibus atque redeuntibus oneratae, anchoris funibusque adhuc in profundo utcunque detentae, quomodo fluctibus iactabantur, quomodo mali metu incidebantur, quomodo mercimonia abiciebantur, qualis oculus intuentium tam durus atque lapideus a fletu se posset retinere? non diu illud aspeximus antequam violentia undarum vel fluctuum anchorae lapserunt, funes vero rumpebantur, naves autem, severitate undarum laxatae, omni spe evadendi erepta nunc in altum elevatae, nunc in ima detrusae paulatim de profunditate tandem in arenam vel in scopulos proiciebantur; ibi vero de latere in latus miserrime collidebantur, ibi minutatim a tempestate dilacerabantur, neque ferocitas ventorum in profundum reverti integras neque altitudo arenae sinebat eas ad litus pervenire illesas. sed quid attinet dicere quam flebiliter nautae et peregrini quidam

102 Twelfth Century

navibus, quidam vero malis, quidam antemnis, quidam autem transtris, omni spe evadendi privati, adheserunt? quid plura dicam? quidam stupore consumpti ibidem dimersi sunt, quidem a lignis, propriae navi, quod incredibile multis videtur, adherentes, me vidente ibidem sunt obtruncati, quidam autem a tabulis navi evulsis iterum in profundam deportabantur, quidam autem natare scientes sponte se fluctibus commiserunt, et ita quamplures perierunt, perpauci quippe, propria virtute confidentes, ad litus illesi pervenerunt. igitur ex navibus triginta maximis, quarum quaedam dromundi, quaedam vero gulafri, quaedam autem catti vulgariter vocantur, omnibus oneratis palmariis vel mercimoniis, antequam a litore discessissem vix septem illesae permanserunt, homines vero diversi sexus plusquam mille die illa perierunt. maiorem etenim miseriam una die nullus vidit oculus, sed ab his omnibus sui gratia eripuit me Dominus, cui honor et gloria per infinita saecula. Amen.

The dangerous route from Jaffa to Jerusalem: Saracen bandits
ascendimus quidem de Ioppen in civitatem Ierusalem, iter duorum dierum per viam montuosam, asperrimam et periculosissimam, quia Sarraceni, insidias Christianis semper tendentes, absconditi latent in cavernis montium et in speluncis rupium die noctuque pervigiles, semper perscrutantes si quos invadere possint vel penuria comitatus vel lassitudine post comitatum remissos: modo ubique in circumitu videntur, statim nusquam apparent. quod quislibet illud iter agens videre potest, qualiter humana corpora et in via et iuxta viam innumerabilia a feris iacent omnino dilacerata. miratur fortasse aliquis Christianorum corpora ibi iacere inhumata, sed non est mirandum, quia ibi minime est humus et rupes non leviter se prebet fodere. quod si ibi humus esset, quis adeo esset idiota ut comitatum suum relinqueret et quasi solus socio sepulchrum foderet? siquis hoc faceret, sibimet potius quam socio sepulchrum pararet. in illa equidem via non solum pauperes et debiles, immo divites periclitantur et fortes: multi a Sarracenis perimuntur, plures vero calore et siti, multi penuria potus, plures vero nimis potando pereunt. nos autem cum omni comitatu ad desiderata pervenimus illesi. Benedictus Dominus, qui non amovit deprecationem meam et misericordiam a me. Amen.

Ps. 65:19–20

A description of Bethlehem
[425–46] Bethleem civitas in Iudea sex milibus distat a Ierosolimis in australem plagam. ibi nichil a Sarracenis est remissum habitabile, sed omnia devastata sicut in aliis omnibus sanctis locis extra murum civitatis Jerusalem, preter monasterium Beatae Virginis Mariae matris Domini nostri, quod est magnum atque preclarum. in eadem aecclesia est quaedam cripta sub choro, quasi in medio, in qua conspicitur ipse locus nativitatis dominicae quasi ad levam; ad dexteram vero, paulo inferius, iuxta locum nativitatis Domini est presepe ubi bos et asynus stabant imposito dominico infante coram eis in presepio. lapis autem unde caput Salvatoris nostri in sepulchro supportabatur, a sancto Ieronimo presbitero

II.9 | Sæwulf, *A Pilgrimage to Jerusalem* 103

illuc Ierosolimis delatus in presepio sepius videri potest. ipse vero sanctus Iero-
nimus sub altare aquilonis in eadem aecclesia requiescit, Innocentes quidem, qui
infantes pro Christo infante ibidem ab Herode trucidati sunt, in australi parte
aecclesiae sub altare requiescunt, duae etiam sacratissimae mulieres Paula et filia
eius Eustochium virgo[1] similiter ibi requiescunt. ibi est mensa marmorea, supra
quam comedit beata virgo Maria cum tribus magis, muneribus suis oblatis, ibi est
cisterna in aecclesia iuxta criptam dominicae nativitatis, in quam stella dicitur
dilapsa, ibi etiam dicitur esse balneatorium beatae virginis Mariae.[2]

Translation: Sæwulf, *An Account of a Pilgrimage to Jerusalem*

[96–169] *Listen carefully, dear friends, and hear about the mercy which God's clem-
ency showed to me, although I am the lowest of his servants, and to my companions.
For on the same day that we came to shore, someone was prompted by God, it would
seem, to say to me, 'My lord, get onto shore today in case it happens that when the
storm comes tonight or early tomorrow morning, you are unable to do so.' As soon as
I heard this I was immediately seized by a desire to disembark, and I hired a small
boat and disembarked with all my companions. While I was getting ashore the sea
became turbulent and increasingly agitated as the storm intensified, but with the
help of God's grace I reached the shore safely. What more is there to say? We entered
the city to find somewhere to stay: overcome and exhausted by our long travail we
rested and were restored. In the morning while we were returning from church, we
heard the sound of the sea and the shouts of the people and everyone running to
join the crowd, shocked by things that were hitherto unheard of, while we, in fear,
ran down to the shore together with the others. When we got there we saw that
the storm was whipping up the waves higher than mountains and we gazed at the
innumerable bodies of people of both sexes who had drowned and were lying on the
shore in a most pitiable way and at the same time we saw boats smashed to pieces
and rolling around next to each other. But who could hear anything apart from the
roar of the sea and the crashing of the ships? It was indeed louder than the people's
shouts and the sound of all the warning horns. Who had such an unflinching and
stony gaze that they could restrain themselves from tears when they saw how our
ship, a very large and strong one, and many others loaded with grain and other
kinds of merchandise and with travellers arriving and departing, still somehow held*

---

1   Paula and Eustochium moved from Rome to Bethlehem with St Jerome in 386; their
    letter to Marcella, on visiting Jerusalem, is preserved among Jerome's correspondence
    (*Ep.* 46): *Lives of Roman Christian women*, transl. C. White, Harmondsworth, 2010.

2   A version of the *Life of Willibald*, later than that of Hugeburc (Section I.24), states that
    there was an image of the star in a well at Bethlehem, *MGH* XV.1, p. 98, line 2; cf. J.
    Murphy O'Connor (1986) *The Holy Land: an archaeological guide from earliest times to
    1700*, Oxford.

104 Twelfth Century

fast by their anchors and ropes in the deep, were tossed by the waves, how the masts were cut down out of fear, how their cargo was thrown overboard? We had not stood watching this for long before the violence of the waves loosened the anchors, the ropes were broken and the ships, released by the punishing waves, with all hope of escape torn away, were raised high up one moment, the next were driven down to the bottom of the sea and slowly brought out of the depths and finally thrown onto the sand or onto the rocks; there they lay smashed, side by side, in a most pitiable way, there they were shattered into small pieces by the storm. The ferocity of the winds did not allow them to return undamaged to the deep, nor did the height of the sand allow them to reach the shore unharmed. But what is the point of describing how wretchedly the sailors and travellers clung, some to the ships, some to the masts, some to the ropes, some to the rowers' seats, with no hope of escape? What more can I say? Some, exhausted and numb, drowned there; some who clung to their own ship (many may not believe this but I myself saw it) were cut in half by the planks; some were carried back into the deep by the planks torn from the ships; some who could swim chose to entrust themselves to the waves voluntarily, and in this way a large number perished, while a very few, trusting to their own strength, reached the shore safely. And so out of thirty large ships, some of which were 'dromonds', some 'gulafri', some commonly known as 'catti', all laden with pilgrims or merchandise, scarcely seven remained undamaged by the time I left the shore, while on that day more than a thousand people of both sexes died. No eye has witnessed a greater disaster on a single day, but out of all these the Lord snatched me by his grace, to whom be honour and glory for infinite ages. Amen.

We went up from Jaffa to the city of Jerusalem, a two-day journey by a mountainous route, very rugged and dangerous, because the Saracens, who are always planning attacks on Christians, were lying hidden in the mountain hollows and in the rocky caves, keeping watch night and day, always looking carefully to see if there were lone travellers or exhausted stragglers they could attack; one moment they are visible everywhere around, then they suddenly disappear. Anyone who makes this journey can see how human bodies lie both on the path and next to the path completely torn apart by wild animals. It might surprise some that the corpses of Christians lie there unburied, but it is not surprising, because there is very little soil there and it is hard to dig in the rock. If there were soil there, who would be such a fool as to leave his companions and to dig a grave for his friend on his own? If anyone were to do this, he would be preparing a grave for himself rather than for his friend. On that path it is not only the poor and weak but also the rich and strong who are at risk: many are killed by the Saracens and many perish as a result of the heat and thirst, many through a lack of drink, while many die by drinking too much. We, however, reached our destination safely with our whole group: blessed is the Lord who did not reject my prayer and his mercy from me. Amen.

[425–46] Bethlehem is a city in Judaea, six miles from Jerusalem, on the southern side. The Saracens have left nothing habitable there, but everything has been destroyed just as in all the other holy places outside the walls of the city of Jerusalem,

apart from the monastery of the Blessed Virgin Mary, the mother of our Lord, which is large and very impressive. In this same church there is a crypt beneath the choir, more or less in the centre, in which one can see the place where the Lord was born, on the left; while on the right, a bit further down, beside the place of the Lord's nativity, is the manger where the ox and ass were standing when the infant Lord was laid in the manger in front of them. The stone which supported our Saviour's head in the tomb and which was brought there from Jerusalem by St Jerome the priest can be regularly viewed in the manger. St Jerome himself rests in that church beneath the altar on the north side, and the Innocents, who were the babies massacred there by Herod instead of the infant Christ, rest beneath the altar on the south side of the church, while those two most holy women, Paula and her daughter Eustochium, the virgin, likewise rest there. There is the marble table on which the Blessed Virgin Mary ate with the three magi, after they had presented their gifts; there is the cistern in the church next to the crypt of the Lord's nativity, into which the star is said to have fallen, and there, too, is said to be the bathing place of the Blessed Virgin Mary.

Primary Sources and Related Texts

Peregrinationes tres: Sæwulf, John of Würzburg, Theodoricus, ed. R. Huygens, CCCM 139, Turnhout, 1994. With essay on 'The voyages of Sæwulf' by J. Pryor.

Translated as 'The pilgrimage of Sæwulf to Jerusalem' in *The library of the Palestine Pilgrims' Text Society*, vol. 4, London, 1896, repr. New York, 1971.

For earlier accounts of pilgrimages, compare the accounts of Aetheria (Egeria), Adomnán, who reports Arculf's account (Section I.5A), and Hugeburc of Heidenheim, who reports Willibald's account (Section I.24).

Further Reading

The encyclopaedia of medieval pilgrimage: electronic resource, Leiden, 2010.

**The new Oxford history of England* (2000) 1: 472–6.

Pelteret, D. (2011) 'Travel between England and Italy' in *Anglo-Saxon England and the Continent*, ed. H. Sauer and J. Story, Tempe, AZ.

Section II.10

Twelfth-Century Law Codes
A: *Quadripartitus* (excerpt: **Die Gesetze der Angelsachsen* 1.316–17)
B: *The Laws of Henry I* (*Leges Henrici Primi*) (excerpt: 10.1–3)

Date: *Quadripartitus*, c.1100; *The Laws of Henry I*: before 1118.

The *Laws of Henry I* survives in six medieval MSS, for which see Downer's edition.

Work: Both these works are attributed to the same author, and both are thought to have been composed in the first twenty years of the twelfth century. The *Quadripartitus* is a compendium, conceived as a work of four parts (of which only the first two were completed), of Anglo-Saxon laws from the seventh to the eleventh centuries, translated into Latin from OE. The complex textual tradition presents challenges, and work remains to be done on the relation between the original and its various translations, which shed light on the state of Latin and OE at the time. In the *Laws of Henry I* the unknown author drew on his *Quadripartitus* and other sources to produce a collection of Latin laws relevant to the early twelfth century, focusing firstly on the rights of the king, as in the section below, but also giving much information about feudal law. Already at this period the influence of Roman and canon law on English common law was being felt. Both these Latin versions can be compared with the OE versions of Cnut (dating from c.1030), an excerpt from one of which is given below.

Linguistic points: Downer, in his edition of the *Laws of Henry I*, compares the Latin translations of the two works, demonstrating the various relations between Latin forms of OE words (e.g. Latin literal renderings or calques or paraphrases of the OE originals), which are of great interest for the development of Latin and its handling of the vernacular. The Latin of both works has been criticised for its lack of clarity, and it has been argued, from the preponderance of Gallicisms, the rarity of newly introduced English words, and confusion as to the sense of the English text, that the author was a French-speaker, though one who regarded England as his home. Certainly the texts contained in **Die Gesetze der Angelsachsen* present a range of new Latin words based on French and Germanic vernacular terms.

In the *Quadripartitus*, one finds *utlagius* (from OE 'utlaga') and *forsbannitum* (AN 'forsbanir'), a portmanteau word from *foris* and Germanic 'banna' ('to banish'), coming through French 'banir'. *firmatio*, with the sense of 'supporting' or 'abetting', appears only in these legal texts. There are also OE technical terms, as when *terra testamentalis* is glossed by the OE technical term 'bocland', i.e. land held or granted in hereditary possession by means of a charter. *allegiare* could be a form of CL *allegare* ('to plead') followed by an accusative and infinitive or a *quod* clause, i.e. 'to plead that ...' However, the fact that it is given as the equivalent of OE 'geladian' followed by 'þaet' (which can admittedly have several senses, including both 'that' and 'because'), and is here reflexive, makes it more likely that it is a Latin equivalent of OF 'alegier', which may itself ultimately derive from a Latin form *exlitigare*, i.e. 'unless he clears himself because he was unaware that the person was a fugitive'. *breve* occurs only post-Conquest in the sense of 'writ', a form of sealed letter with instructions from the king.

In the *Laws of Henry I*, *iura* is one of the translations of the OE 'gerihta', others being *consuetudines* and *rectitudines*. Also in this text are the Latin forms *qualstowum*, formed from the ME 'qualstow' (cf. OE 'cwealmstowe'), which is glossed as *occidendorum loca*; and *herestreta*, the Latin form of OE 'herestræt': both occur only in this text. *castellatio* ('fortification'), too, occurs only here. *scamnum*, on the other hand, is CL and has a basic meaning of 'bench' but here is used to mean an embankment, probably as the result of a certain overlap between the English and French words for 'bank' and 'bench': such confusion is not uncommon, an interesting by-product of the close connections between the three dominant languages. *murdrum* appears in BML soon after the Conquest, deriving from a Germanic word that also finds its way into French and English. In its sense of 'murder' it occurs first in these legal texts, as does another crime, *roberia*, earlier than attestations of these words in the vernaculars. For a definition of *murdrum*, cf. *Dialogue of the Exchequer* 1.10.

A: *Quadripartitus* (excerpt: *Die Gesetze der Angelsachsen* 1.316–17)

TEXT II.10A

Old English text
Ðis syndon ða gerihta, ðe se cyning ah ofer ealle menn on Westseaxan: þeat is mundbrice ond hamsocne, forstal ond fyrdwite, buton hwaene he furðor gemaeðian wylle.

se ðe utlages weorc gewyrce, wealde se cyng ðaes friðes. ond gyf he bocland habbe, sy þaet forwoht ðam cynge to hande, sy ðaes mannes man, ðe he sy. ond lochwa ðone fleman fede oððe feormie, gylde fif pund ðam cynge, butan he hine geladige, þaet he hine flema nyste.

Twelfth-century Latin translation of OE
hec sunt iura, que rex habet super omnes homines in Westsexa: *mundbrece* (id est infractionem pacis), hamsocnam (id est invasionem mansionis) *foresteal*

108 Twelfth Century

(id est prohibitionem itineris) et *fyrdung* (id est expeditionem) nisi aliquem amplius honorare velit. et qui opus utlagii fecerit, eius revocatio sit in misericordia regis. et si terram testamentalem habeat (que Anglice dicitur *bocland*) ipsa in manum regis transeat, sit eius homo cuius sit. qui forsbannitum pauerit vel ei firmationem aliquam exhibuerit, emendet regi v libras, nisi se adlegiet, quod infugatum eum nesciebat.

Translation from Latin into modern English

These are the rights that the king has over all the men in Wessex, i.e. breach of the social order, housebreaking, preventing someone from travelling and (fine for non-performance of) military service, unless he wishes to honour someone more. And when someone does the work of an outlaw, then his recall is in the king's mercy. And if he has land that is governed by a charter (which is called 'bocland' in English), it should pass into the king's hand, whoever the man may be. And whoever feeds or offers support to one who has been banished should pay the king five pounds unless he clears himself by oath on the grounds that he was unaware that the person was a fugitive.

B: *The Laws of Henry I (Leges Henrici Primi)* (excerpt: 10.1–3)

TEXT II.10B

The king's rights

[10.1] hec sunt iura que rex Anglie solus et super omnes homines habet in terra sua commoda pacis et securitatis institutione retenta: infractio pacis regie per manum vel breve date; Denagildum;[1] placitum brevium vel preceptorum eius contemptorum; de famulis suis ubicumque occisis vel iniuriatis; infidelitas et proditio; quicumque despectus vel maliloquium de eo; castellatio trium scannorum; utlagaria; furtum morte inpunitum; murdrum; falsaria monete sue; incendium; *hamsocna; foretal; fyrdinga; flemenfyrme*; premeditatus assultus; robaria; *stretbreche*; presumptio terre vel peccunie regis; thesaurus inventus; naufragium; maris laganum; violentus concubinatus; raptus; foreste; relevationes baronum suorum; qui in domo vel familia regis pugnabit; qui in hostico pacem

---

1 Although tribute had been paid to the Danes from the ninth century, the term 'Danegeld' was not used until the eleventh century. Cf. *Dialogue of the Exchequer* 1.11 for a twelfth-century account of Danegeld. For an example of a payment paid to the Danes, see the treaty between Æthelred the Unready and the Viking leader Olaf Tryggvason (Section I.37).

fregerit; qui *burgbotam* vel *brigbotam* vel *firdfare* supersederit; qui excommunicatum vel utlagam habet et tenet; *borchbrege*; qui in bello campali vel navali fugerit; iniustum iudicium; defectus iustitie; prevaricatio legis regie.

[10.2] omnes herestrete omnino regis sunt et omnia qualstowa, id est occidendorum loca, totaliter regis sunt in soca sua.

[10.3] et omnibus ordinatis et alienigenis et pauperibus et abiectis debet esse rex pro cognatione et advocato, si penitus alium non habent.

Translation: *The Laws of Henry I*

[10.1] These are the legal rights which the king of England alone has over all men in his land, reserved by means of a proper ordering of peace and security: breach of the king's peace given by hand or writ; Danegeld; the plea of the contempt of his writs or commands; the killing or injuring of his servants anywhere; breach of loyalty and treason; any contempt or slander of him; fortification consisting of three banks of earth; outlawry; theft unpunished by death; murder; counterfeiting of his coinage; arson; 'hamsocn'; 'forestel'; 'fyrding'; 'flymenfyrm'; premeditated assault; robbery; 'stretbreche'; unlawful appropriation of the king's land or money; treasure-trove; wreck of the sea; things thrown up by the sea; domestic abuse; abduction; forests; the reliefs of his barons; fighting in the king's home or household; breach of the peace in the king's troop; failure to perform 'burgbot' or 'brigbot' or 'firdfare'; receiving and keeping someone who has been excommunicated or outlawed; 'borchbrege'; anyone who flees in a field or naval battle; unjust judgement; failure of justice; violation of the king's law.

[10.2] All highways are the complete responsibility of the king, and all qualstows, that is, places of execution, are wholly within the king's own jurisdiction.

[10.3] The king must act as a relative and protector to all those in holy orders, strangers, poor people and those who have been cast out, if they have no one else at all to take care of them.

Primary Sources and Related Texts

Quadripartitus in **Die Gesetze der Angelsachsen* 1.316–17.

Leges Henrici Primi, ed. L. Downer, Oxford, 1972.

Expositiones vocabulorum, an OE–AN glossary of OE terms found in charters of the post-Conquest period, in *The Red Book of the Exchequer*, vol. 3, *1032–1039*, London, 1896.

Rectitudines singularum personarum, an OE–Latin thesaurus of technical terms regarding rights, in **Die Gesetze der Angelsachsen* 1.444–53.

EHD 2.491–5: *Laws of King Henry I.*

Further Reading

Karn, N. (2010) 'Rethinking the *Leges Henrici Primi*' in *English law before Magna Carta: Felix Liebermann and Die Gesetze der Angelsachsen*, ed. S. Jurasinski, L. Oliver and A. Rabin, Leiden.

Liebermann, F. (1892) *Quadripartitus, ein englisches Rechtsbuch von 1114*, Halle.

Oliver, L. (2012) 'Legal documentation and the practice of the law' in *The Cambridge history of early medieval English literature*, ed. C. Lees, Cambridge.

Wormald, P. (1994) 'Quadripartitus' (with appendix by R. Sharpe) in *Law and government in medieval England and Normandy*, ed. G. Garnett and J. Hudson, Cambridge.

——(1999) *The making of English law: King Alfred to the twelfth century*, Oxford.

Section II.11

The Wreck of the White Ship in 1120, as Recorded by Historians of the Twelfth Century
A: Eadmer, *A History of Recent Events in England* (*Historia novorum in Anglia*) (excerpt: pp. 288–9)
B: William of Malmesbury, *A History of the English Kings* (*Gesta regum Anglorum*) (excerpt: 5.419)
C: Orderic Vitalis, *An Ecclesiastical History* (*Historia ecclesiastica*) (excerpts: vol. 6, pp. 294–306)
D: Symeon of Durham, *A History of the English and Danish Kings* (*Historia regum Anglorum et Dacorum*) (excerpt: chapter 199, *RS* 75.2 (1885) 258–9)
E: Hugh the Chanter (Hugo Cantor), *A History of the Church at York* (excerpt: OMT p. 164)
F: Henry of Huntingdon, *Contempt for the World* (*De contemptu mundi*) (excerpt: chapter 5)

In the prologue to his *Chronicle*, Gervase of Canterbury (*RS* 73.1 (1879) 87–8) distinguishes between writers of chronicles and writers of history: although both have the same aim, namely to report the truth, and use the same material, they deal with the material in different ways. Quoting from Horace and Virgil, Gervase characterises historians as writing grandiloquently and elegantly, depicting lives and behaviour. Chroniclers, on the other hand, work through the material year by year, employing a humble style to catalogue important events, portents and miracles, not for entertainment but to serve the communal memory. Having discussed the author's aim and style, he alludes to the question of a work's audience, when he says that although his own work follows the annalistic form, he denies he is a chronicler because he does not write for a wider readership but only for his *familiola paupercula* ('his humble little community') in his own monastery.

In this section (II.11) are included six accounts, of varying style and length, of the wreck of the White Ship on 25 November 1120. The aim in including so many versions is to illustrate various ways in which twelfth-century historians recorded the same event. Comparison of these will reveal variety not only in factual detail, but also in imagination, expression, style and length, ranging between the literary, the journalistic and the annalistic. Although it would seem that these twelfth-century monastic historians often circulated their work-in-progress and drew on each other's work, it should be clear from the versions cited below that these authors are not merely copying one another or stringing together classical

Twelfth Century

quotations. These versions are a rich source, not only for technical terms for different kinds of boats, for example, but also for a wide range of synonyms.

The wreck of the White Ship took place when King Henry I was returning to England after having fought various opponents, including his eldest brother Robert Curthose, for domination over Normandy and having finally secured the right of his only legitimate son, Prince William, to succeed him in both England and Normandy. William's mother was Matilda, the daughter of Malcolm III and St Margaret of Scotland;[1] she did not live to suffer the death of her only son in this shipwreck in which many other young people from royal and noble families also drowned. The calamitous death of King Henry's heir in particular had major political consequences, not least the struggle for the succession between rival claimants to the English throne (the period referred to as 'the Anarchy', for which see *Gesta Stephani*).

As a background to the Latin accounts one may compare the English of *ASChr* for 1120, preserved in the *Peterborough Chronicle* (here in a modern English translation):

> Before Advent (King Henry) came here to England. And on that journey the king's two sons, William and Richard, were drowned, and also Richard Earl of Chester, and Ottuel his brother and very many of the king's court – stewards and chamberlains and cup-bearers and various other officers and a countless number of very fine people with them. Their death was a double grief to their friends: first, that they were so suddenly deprived of this life; second, that few of their bodies were later found anywhere.[2]

Further Reading

Cleaver, L. and Worm, A. (ed.) (2018) *Writing history in the Anglo-Norman world: manuscripts, makers and readers c.1066–c.1250*, Woodbridge.

Given-Wilson, C. (2007) *Chronicles: the writing of history in medieval England*, London.

Gransden (1974) 'Historians of the Norman Conquest' in *Gransden (1974).

---

1 On Matilda see Eadmer, *HN* p. 122 and the preface to Turgot's *Life of St Margaret of Scotland*, where the biographer addresses her (using a play on words that had been popular since the seventh century) as *rege Angelorum constituta regina Anglorum*. Matilda is also addressed in the second proem to the *Leges Henrici Primi* (cf. Section II.10B), a fact which helps to date the work. She was also the mother of Empress Matilda (cf. Section II.16A).

2 For the OE original of this passage, see *The Peterborough Chronicle*, ed. and transl. B. Muir and N. Sparks, 2 vols, London, 2023.

Spencer, C. (2020) *The White Ship: conquest, anarchy and the wrecking of Henry I's dream*, London.

A: Eadmer, *A History of Recent Events in England* (*Historia novorum in Anglia*) (excerpt: pp. 288–9)

Date: c.1093–1120s.

This work is preserved in BL MS Cotton Titus A.ix and Cambridge MS CCC 452.

Author: On Eadmer (c.1060–c.1126) see above, with reference to his *Life of Archbishop Anselm* (Section II.8). The allusion at the beginning of this passage to a monk of Canterbury refers to Eadmer himself and the dispute concerning his nomination, earlier in 1120, to the see of St Andrews. King Alexander of Scotland, with whom Eadmer corresponded (as seen from the letters he includes in the *HN*), refused to accept the authority of the archdiocese of Canterbury, and so Eadmer was never able to take up his appointment.

Work: The *History of Recent Events in England* originally comprised four books (*RS* 81 (1884) 1–216), finishing with the death of Anselm in 1109, whose time as archbishop in England was the professed focus of the work, as Eadmer states in his preface. There he also informs the reader that he is writing to provide an account of the events *quae sub oculis vidi vel audivi* (which he has seen or heard about) for the benefit of future generations, for he has noticed that his contemporaries have experienced a dearth of writings in their attempts to find out about their past. Eadmer uses his discretion in choosing which documents to include in his history (e.g. *HN* p. 276). Later he added Books 5 and 6, so that the complete work, after a brief summary of the period 960–1066, extends from the reign of William the Conqueror and Lanfranc's accession as archbishop down to 1122. Book 5 finishes with the paragraph quoted below. Eadmer's work was used as a source by John of Worcester and is likely to have influenced William of Malmesbury's historical writing, in particular William's *Historia novella* (*The Contemporary History*) covering the years 1125–42.

Linguistic points: This concise report of the accident contains few details of the event, apart from the mention of the sole survivor, whose name, according to what Eadmer has heard, has not been considered worthy of record, perhaps because he was not one of the aristocratic or royal passengers. Instead he concentrates on the observation that the general shock was calmed by the king's brave acceptance that the tragedy was the result of God's justice. Despite the straightforward style, Eadmer does allow the wordplay *freti freto*, playing with the adjective *freti* and the noun *fretum*; in this sentence the *RS* edition prefers *illapsi* as the *lectio difficilior*

114   Twelfth Century

with the dative *freto*, rather than the reading of MS A, *elapsi*, which would take *freto* as ablative.[3]

TEXT II.11A

The wreck of the White Ship

[p. 288] sed dum talia circa monachum Cantuariensem geruntur in Scotia, quiddam nostris saeculis inauditum contigit in Anglia. Willelmus enim filius regis Henrici cujus in superioribus hujus operis nonnullis meminimus, patrem suum a Normannia in Angliam regressum sequi gestiens, navem ingreditur, copiosa nobilium, militum, puerorum ac feminarum multitudine comitatus. qui mox

MS: elapsi   portum maris evecti miraque aeris serenitate freti freto illapsi, in modico [p. 289] navis qua vehebantur rupem incurrens eversa est et omnes qui in ea residebant, excepto rustico uno et ipso, ut ferebatur, nec nomine digno, qui mira Dei gratia vivus evasit, marinis fluctibus sunt absorpti. que res multorum mentes exterruit atque turbavit, et de occultis justi Dei judiciis in admirationem concussit. eo tamen citius sedata est in plurimorum animis hujus turbationis immanitas, quia animum regis, quem maxime hoc infortunium respiciebat, videbant virili animo se agentem, et equitati judiciorum Dei, cui nemo resistere potest, haec summisso gestu et voce attribuentem. in his namque se consolans humili spiritu et ore dixit quod omnibus Christianis in cunctis eventibus suis dicendum fore intellexit, videlicet 'Sit nomen Domini benedictum in secula. Amen.'[4]

Translation: Eadmer, *A History of Recent Events in England*

But while such things were happening in Scotland with regard to the monk from Canterbury, something unheard of in our time occurred in England. William, the son of King Henry, whom we mentioned in some earlier passages of this work, excited to be following his father, who was returning from Normandy to England, boarded a ship, accompanied by a large number of nobles, knights, and young men and women. Sailing out of the harbour into the sea and confident of marvellously calm weather, they glided into a narrow channel, but shortly afterwards the ship in which they were travelling hit a rock and capsized and all who were on board (apart from one peasant who, it is said, was not even important enough to be named, but who escaped alive through the amazing grace of God) were drowned in the waves of the sea. This event terrified the minds of many, throwing them into confusion.

---

3   For a thirteenth-century version of this wordplay cf. *puppis ... licet omni | freta favore freti ventoque potita secundo | naviget'*, Henry of Avranches, *Vita Sancti Birini* 364–6.

4   These words form part of the episcopal blessing in the Roman Missal.

They were stunned at the hidden judgements of the just God. However, the great turmoil caused by this tragedy settled down more quickly because they saw that the king was dealing with it bravely even though this misfortune had affected him most of all: behaving and speaking with humility, he attributed it to the justice of God's judgements which no one can resist. Consoling himself in these circumstances with a humble spirit and words, he said what he knew all Christians had to say in similar circumstances, namely, 'Blessed be the name of the Lord, for ever and ever. Amen.'

Primary Sources and Related Texts

Eadmeri Historia novorum in Anglia, ed. M. Rule, *RS* 81 (1884). Also Cambridge Library Collection – Rolls, Cambridge, 2012.
Bosanquet, G. (1964) *Eadmer's History of Recent Events in England*, London. With English translation of Books 1–4.

Further Reading

Pohl, B. (2019) 'The (un)making of a history book: revisiting the earliest MSS of Eadmer of Canterbury's *Historia novorum*', *The Library* 20.3: 340–70.
Rozier, C. (2019) 'Between history and hagiography: Eadmer of Canterbury's vision of the *Historia novorum in Anglia*', *JMH* 45.1: 1–19.

B: William of Malmesbury, *A History of the English Kings* (*Gesta regum Anglorum*) (excerpt: 5.419)

For date, MSS and author, see Section II.1B.

Work: At this point in his great historical work covering the years 449–1127, William is writing about the death of a young man of 17, an event that occurred when the author was himself only in his early 20s. The passage follows a section in praise of Queen Matilda, the mother of the young prince who drowned in this episode.

Linguistic points: This passage reveals certain general characteristics of William's writing: his ability to create an imaginative scene, describing the actions and feelings of individuals while seeing the scene in broader terms, as part of a tragic drama or epic (supported by his characteristic allusions to classical epic texts), with Fortune involved in the events. There is an ominous note present in the build-up to that night's events, in the phrase *tam omnium spes in speculam erectas confudit humanae sortis varietas* ('the changeability of human fate smashed everyone's

116 Twelfth Century

high hopes'), and an awareness of the huge impact of this episode, in the phrase *res mirum in modum mutatae*. One striking feature of William's Latin is exemplified by the verb *impingere* here, which he applies to a ship running aground: it is one of the many CL words, often verbs, whose semantic and syntactic potential is exploited more by William than by any other BML writer.

TEXT II.11B

The wreck of the White Ship

[5.419] filium habuit rex Henricus ex Mathilde nomine Willelmum, dulci spe et ingenti cura in successionem educatum et provectum; nam et ei, vix dum duodecim annorum esset, omnes liberi homines Angliae et Normanniae cuiuscumque ordinis et dignitatis, cuiuscumque domini fideles, manibus et sacramento se dedere coacti sunt. filiam quoque Fulconis comitis Andegavensis vix nubilem ipse etiam impubis despondit et accepit, dato sibi a socero comitatu Cinomannico pro munere sponsalitio; quin et Ierosolimam Fulco ire contendens comitatum commendavit regi suum si viveret, futurum profecto generi si non rediret. plures ergo provintiae spectabant nutum pueri, putabaturque regis Eduardi vaticinium in eo complendum; ferebaturque spes Angliae, modo arboris succisa, in illo iuvenculo iterum floribus pubescere, fructus protrudere, et ideo finem malorum

Virg. *Aen.* 2.428 sperari posse. Deo aliter visum, huiuscemodi enim opinionem tulerunt aurae, quod eum proxima dies urgebat fato satisfacere. enimvero socero tunc annitente simulque Thetbaldo filio Stephani et Adalae amitae, Ludovicus rex Frantiae Normanniam concessit puero, ut facto sibi hominio possideret eam iure legitimo. ordinabat haec et effitiebat prudentissimi patris prudentia, ut hominium, quod ipse pro culmine imperii fastidiret facere, filius delicatus et qui putabatur viam seculi

v.l. placida ingressurus non recusaret. his agitandis et placita concordia componendis quattuor annorum tempus rex impendit, in Normannia toto hoc tempore moratus. veruntamen tam splendidae et excogitatae pacis serenum, tam omnium spes in speculam erectas confudit humanae sortis varietas. namque indicto in Angliam reditu, rex sub ipso crepusculo septimo kalendas Decembris apud Barbeflet naves solvit, eumque qui impleverat carbasa ventus feliciter regno et amplae fortunae invexit. at vero adolescentulus, iam septemdecim annorum et paulo plus, cui nichil delitiarum preter nomen regis pro paterna indulgentia deesset, aliam sibi navem parari precepit, omnibus pene adolescentulis procerum filiis quasi pro colludio aetatis puerilis eo accurrentibus. quin et remiges, immodice mero ingurgitati, voluptate nautica quam potus ministrabat, mature illos qui precesserant post tergum relinquendos clamitabant; erat enim navis optima, tabulatis novis et clavis recenter compacta. itaque ceca iam nocte, iuventus sapientiae indiga simulque potu obruta navem a littore impellunt. volat illa pennata pernitior harundine et crispantia maris terga radens imprudentia ebriorum impegit in scopulum, non longe a littore supra pelagus extantem. consurgunt ergo miseri et magno

clamore ferratos contos expediunt, diu certantes ut navem a rupe propellerent; **Virg. *Aen*. 5.207–9**
sed obsistebat Fortuna, omnes eorum conatus in irritum deducens. itaque et
remi in saxum obnixi crepuere concussaque prora pependit. iamque alios undis **Virg. *Aen*. 5.205–6**
exponebat, alios ingressa per rimas aqua enecabat, cum eiecta scafa filius regis
excipitur; salvarique potuisset ad litus regressus, nisi soror eius notha, comitissa
Perticae,[5] in maiori nave cum morte luctans femineo ululatu fratris opem implo-
rasset, ne tam impie se relinqueret. ille misericordia infractus lembum carinae
applicari iussit, ut sororem exciperet, mortem misellus pro clementiae teneritu-
dine indeptus; continuo enim multitudine insilientium scafa victa subsedit, omnesque pariter fundo involvit. evasit unus, et ille agrestis, qui tota nocte malo
supernatans mane totius tragediae actum expressit.

nulla umquam fuit navis Angliae tantae miseriae, nulla toti orbi tam patulae
famae. periit ibi cum Willelmo alter filius regis Ricardus, quem ante regnum ex
provintiali femina susceperat, iuvenis magnanimus et patri pro obsequio acceptus; Ricardus comes Cestrae, et frater eius Otuelus, nutritius et magister filii regis;
filia regis, comitissa Perticae, et neptis eius, soror Thetbaldi, comitissa Cestrae;
preterea quisquis erat in curia lectissimus miles vel capellanus, et optimatum filii ad militiam provehendi. accurrerunt enim undique, ut dixi, non leve gloriae
suae numeraturi commodum si filio regis vel deferrent ludicrum vel conferrent
obsequium; accumulavitque calamitatem difficultas inveniendorum cadaverum,
quia dispersis per littora quesitoribus nullum facile repertum est, sed ierunt tam
delicata corpora 'equoreis crudelia pabula monstris'. iuvenculi ergo morte cognita **Statius, *Theb*. 9.300**
res mirum in modum mutatae. parens enim celibatui renuntiavit, cui post mor-
tem Mathildis studuerat, futuros heredes ex nova coniuge iamiamque operiens.
socer, ex Ierosolimis domum reversus, partibus Willelmi (i.e. William Clito, son
of Robert Curthose) filii Rotberti Normanni comitis improbus astitit, tradens ei
alteram filiam nuptum et Cinomannicum comitatum; irarum stimulos in regem
acuebat dos filiae, post mortem filii in Anglia retenta.

Translation: William of Malmesbury, *A History of the English Kings*

[5.419] *King Henry had a son by Matilda, called William, brought up in delightful
expectation and with great care and advanced so that he might succeed him; for
when William was scarcely twelve years old, all the free men of England and Normandy of whatever rank or office, the loyal subjects of whatever lord, were forced
to submit to him with hands and by oath. Also before he reached adulthood he was
betrothed to, and accepted, the daughter of Fulk, Count of Anjou, although she had*

---

5   The reference is to Matilda Fitzroy, illegitimate daughter of Henry I, wife of Rotrou III
    of Perches.

scarcely reached marriageable age, and he was given the dukedom of Maine as a betrothal gift by his father-in-law; indeed, when Fulk was planning to go to Jerusalem he entrusted his dukedom to the king, if he lived, and if he did not return it would of course pass to his son-in-law. Many provinces, therefore, respected the boy's authority and it was thought that he would fulfil the prophecy of King Edward; the saying was that England's hope, recently cut from the tree, would in this young man again grow to maturity with blossoms and give forth fruit and that an end to the troubles could be hoped for. But God had other ideas: for the breezes carried off any idea of this kind, because the next day drove him to make payment to fate. Indeed, with his father-in-law's assent and that of Theobald, son of Stephen and William's aunt Adela, Louis king of France granted Normandy to the boy, so that when he had paid homage to him he would possess it with legal rights. The very sensible father arranged these matters and brought it about out of good sense, so that his young son who was thought to be about to enter upon the path of secular life could not refuse the homage which he himself would disdain on account of his high office. The king spent four years pursuing and arranging these things after agreeing on peace, staying for this whole period in Normandy. However, the changeability of human fate destroyed the serenity of such a fine and carefully devised peace, and smashed everyone's high hopes. After giving notice of his return to England, the king cast off from Barfleur just before dusk on 25 November and the wind filling the sails carried him tranquilly to his kingdom and his substantial fortune. But the young man, who was now seventeen years old and a bit, who lacked nothing in the way of pleasures, in which his father indulged him, apart from the title of king, gave orders for another ship to be prepared for him and for almost all the young people who were the children of the nobles and who were keen to accompany him, as if it were a childish amusement. What is more, the oarsmen were extremely drunk with wine, and with the excitement of sailing induced by alcohol, they were shouting that they must quickly overtake those who had gone ahead. For it was a very good ship, recently built with new planking and nails. And so, in the black of night, the young people, who lacked experience and who were also overwhelmed by drink, pushed the ship from the shore. It flew faster than a feathered arrow, skimming the rippling surface of the sea, but due to the folly of those who were drunk it hit a rock sticking out above the sea not far from the shore. The wretched people rushed up and with loud shouts they got hold of the poles fitted with metal, and for a long time they struggled to push the ship off the rock. But Fortune stood in their way, frustrating all their attempts. And so the oars cracked as they came up against the rock, and the prow hung there, smashed to pieces. Fortune exposed some to the waves, some she killed when the water came in through the cracks, while the king's son was taken on board the lifeboat which was thrown out; he could have returned to shore and been saved if his illegitimate sister, the Countess of Perche, struggling against death in the larger ship, had not with a woman's screams of distress begged her brother to help her, and not to abandon her so disloyally. He was overcome by compassion and ordered the boat to lie alongside the hull so that it could take his sister on board. As a result of his tenderness and compassion, that poor young man would meet his death. For the lifeboat was immediately overwhelmed by the large number of people jumping in and sank, taking everyone to the bottom at the same time. One man escaped, and he a peasant, who floated all night on the ship's mast and the following morning described the whole tragedy.

Never was there such a wretched ship in England, never one so famous in all the world. Together with William there died there the other son of the king, Richard (of Lincoln), whom he had had with a provincial woman before he became king, a generous young man, dear to his father because of his service; Richard, Earl of Chester, and his brother Ottuel, the guardian and teacher of the king's son; the king's daughter, the Countess of Perche, and her niece, the Countess of Chester, the sister of Theobald; and in addition all the choicest knights and chaplains in the court and the sons of the nobles who were being trained as knights. They had all rushed forward, as I said, from all sides, thinking of the considerable advantage to their reputation if they could contribute to entertaining or offering service to the king's son. The disaster was greater due to the difficulty of finding the corpses: those who had spread out along the shores to search for them had not had an easy time, because these tender bodies had cruelly ended up as food for sea creatures. When news of the young man's death reached them, the situation changed in an extraordinary way. For his father renounced the celibacy to which he had devoted himself after the death of Matilda, hoping that he would very soon get heirs from a new wife. The father-in-law (i.e. Fulk), returning home from Jerusalem, unfairly took the side of William, son of Robert of Normandy, handing over to him his other daughter as a wife and also the dukedom of Maine; his daughter's dowry, which had been retained in England after his son's death, sharpened the goads of his anger against the king.

Primary Source

William of Malmesbury, *Gesta regum Anglorum*, vol. 1 (text) and vol. 2 (introduction and commentary), ed. R. M. Thomson and M. Winterbottom, OMT, Oxford, 1998–9.

Further Reading

Gillingham, J. (2012) 'A historian of the twelfth-century Renaissance and the transformation of English society 1066–c.1200' in *European transformations: the long twelfth century*, ed. T. Noble and J. Van Engen, Notre Dame, IN.

Thompson, R. M., Dolmans, E. and Winkler, E. (ed.) (2017) *Discovering William of Malmesbury*, Woodbridge.

120 Twelfth Century

Winterbottom, M. (2003) 'The language of William of Malmesbury' in *Rhetoric and renewal in the Latin West 1100–1540*, ed. C. Mews, C. Nederman and R. Thomson, Turnhout.

—— (2019) 'Beginning a history: studies in William of Malmesbury, *Gesta regum Anglorum*, Book One', *JML* 29: 101–21.

Wright, N. (1993) '*Industriae testimonium*: William of Malmesbury and Latin poetry revisited', *RB* 103: 482–531.

C: Orderic Vitalis, *An Ecclesiastical History* (*Historia ecclesiastica*) (excerpts: vol. 6, pp. 294–306; references given by page of OMT edition)

For date, MSS and author, see Section II.1C.

Work: Orderic's account of this event is the longest of all extant versions, offering a detailed account that reveals his ability to get inside people's minds, as shown in the focus on specific individuals; the Anglo-Norman Wace is the only other writer to give the sole survivor a name. In a rare instance of direct speech the ship's captain, whose father had accompanied William the Conqueror across the Channel before the battle of Hastings, addresses the king. Later, when shipwrecked, the same captain cries out to ask what has happened to the prince. Overall Orderic's account is a masterpiece of drama, but a drama shot through with the author's compassion for the shock and grief felt by all, from the king to the common people. He adds a certain epic feel with, e.g., rumour flying, but the tone is more Christian and biblical than classical, with the Old Testament allusions to the grief of Jacob for Joseph and David for his sons: in this he offers a contrast to William of Malmesbury.

Linguistic points: Orderic maintains his characteristic rhythmic and rhyming style, using it to bring out the human tragedy during that night in 1120, as in *heu quamplures illorum mentes pia devotione erga Deum habebant vacuas, qui maris immodicas moderatur et aeris iras*, the second half of which forms a hexameter. Orderic uses OE-derived words, like *schippa* (cf. *DMLBS s.v. shiprus* and *OED s.v.* skipper n. 2) and *athelingus* (as well as an otherwise unknown synonym of this, *albeolus*). He also uses the occasional Greek word (e.g. *soma*, applied specifically to a dead body) or a Greek word that has passed into Latin, as with *epibata*, which first appears in BML, in the sense of 'passenger', in the eighth century, in Willibald's *Life of St Boniface* (4); for an excerpt from this work, see Section I.23. *Athelingus* (i.e. OE 'æþeling') is applied to Henry's heir, William; however, it was William's cousin who was in fact named William Clito, using the Latin equivalent of 'æþeling', because he had been a rival heir to King Henry, being the son of Henry's older brother, Robert Curthose, Duke of Normandy. *Feudum*

II.11 | The Wreck of the White Ship   121

(*feod-*) was originally a Frankish word (the equivalent of CL *pecus*), that came to have a wide range of technical meanings relating to feudal society: it only entered BML in post-Conquest documents. The type of light boat Orderic terms *faselus* recalls the *phaselus ille* of Catullus' fourth poem. For *reno* as a waterproof fur coat, cf. the synonym *repte* (Section I.21D and Isid. *Etym.* 19.23.4). Orderic uses CL *adulari* with the dative, which is the normal post-Ciceronian usage according to Quintilian (*Inst.* 9.3.1).

TEXT II.11C

The wreck of the White Ship
[p. 294 Chibnall] Henricus rex in Normannia rebus post multos labores optime dispositis decrevit transfretare, et tironibus ac precipuis militibus qui laboriose fideliterque militaverant larga stipendia erogare, et quosdam amplis honoribus datis in Anglia sullimare. unde classem continuo iussit preparari et copiosam omnis dignitatis militiam secum comitari. (...)

ingente classe in portu qui Barbaflot dicitur preparata, et nobili legione in comitatu regis austro flante aggregata, vii kalendas Decembris prima statione noctis rex et comites eius naves intraverunt, et carbasa sursum levata ventis in pelago [p. 296] commiserunt, et mane Angliam quibus a Deo concessum fuit amplexati sunt. in illa navigatione triste infortunium contigit, quod multos luctus et innumerabiles lacrimas elicuit. Tomas filius Stephani regem adiit, eique marcum auri offerens ait, 'Stephanus Airardi filius[6] genitor meus fuit, et ipse in omni vita sua patri tuo in mari servivit. nam illum in sua puppe vectum in Angliam conduxit, quando contra Haraldum pugnaturus in Angliam perrexit. huiusmodi autem officio usque ad mortem famulando ei placuit, et ab eo multis honoratus exeniis inter contribules suos magnifice floruit. hoc feudum domine rex a te requiro, et vas quod Candida Navis appellatur merito ad regalem famulatum optime instructum habeo.' cui rex ait, 'Gratum habeo quod petis. michi quidem aptam navim elegi quam non mutabo, sed filios meos Guillelmum et Ricardum quos sicut me diligo, cum multa regni mei nobilitate nunc tibi commendo.' his auditis nautae gavisi sunt, filioque regis adulantes vinum ab eo ad bibendum postulaverunt. at ille tres vini modios ipsis dari precepit. quibus acceptis biberunt, sociisque abundanter propinaverunt, nimiumque potantes inebriati sunt. iussu regis multi barones cum filiis suis puppim ascenderunt, et fere trecenti ut opinor in infausta nave fuerunt. duo siquidem monachi Tironis et Stephanus comes[7]

---

6   It is likely that this refers to the man of the same name (Stephen FitzErhard) who was William the Conqueror's tenant in chief, mentioned as owning land in the Domesday Book for Berkshire (f.63c).

7   The reference here is to Stephen of Blois, who, by leaving the ship before it sailed, survived to become King Stephen of England 1135–54.

122 Twelfth Century

cum duobus militibus, Guillelmus quoque de Rolmara et Rabellus camerarius, Eduardus de Salesburia et alii plures inde exierunt, quia nimiam multitudinem lascivae et pompaticae iuventutis inesse conspicati sunt. periti enim remiges quinquaginta ibi erant, et feroces epibatae qui iam in navi sedes nacti turgebant et suimet prae ebrietate immemores vix aliquem reverenter agnoscebant. heu quamplures illorum mentes pia devotione erga Deum habebant vacuas, qui maris immodicas moderatur et aeris iras. unde sacerdotes qui ad benedicendos illos illuc accesserant aliosque ministros qui aquam benedictam deferebant cum dedecore et cachinnis subsannantes abigerunt, sed paulo post derisionis suae ultionem receperunt. soli homines cum thesauro regis et vasis merum ferentibus Thomae carinam implebant, ipsumque ut regiam classem quae iam aequora sulcabat summopere prosequeretur commonebant. ipse vero quia ebrietate desipiebat, in virtute [p. 298] sua satellitumque suorum confidebat, et audacter quia omnes qui iam precesserant praeiret spondebat. tandem navigandi signum dedit. porro schippae remos haud segniter arripuerunt, et alia laeti quia quid eis ante oculos penderet nesciebant armamenta coaptaverunt, navemque cum impetu magno per pontum currere fecerunt. cumque remiges ebrii totis navigarent conatibus, et infelix gubernio male intenderet cursui dirigendo per pelagus, ingenti saxo quod cotidie fluctu recedente detegitur, et rursus accessu maris cooperitur, sinistrum latus Candidae Navis vehementer illisum est, confractisque duabus tabulis ex insperato navis proh dolor subversa est. omnes igitur in tanto discrimine simul exclamaverunt, sed aqua mox implente ora pariter perierunt. duo soli virgae qua velum pendebat manus iniecerunt, et magna noctis parte pendentes auxilium quodlibet prestolati sunt. unus erat Rotomagensis carnifex nomine Beroldus, et alter generosus puer nomine Goisfredus Gisleberti de Aquila filius.

tunc luna in signo Tauri nona decima fuit, et fere ix horis radiis suis mundum illustravit, et navigantibus mare lucidum reddidit. Thomas nauclerus post primam summersionem vires resumpsit, suique memor super undas caput extulit, et videns capita eorum qui ligno utcumque inherebant interrogavit, 'Filius regis quid devenit?' cumque naufragi respondissent illum cum omnibus collegis suis deperisse, 'Miserum', inquit, 'est amodo meum vivere.' hoc dicto male desperans maluit illic occumbere, quam furore irati regis pro pernicie prolis oppetere, seu longas in vinculis poenas luere. in aquis penduli Deum invocabant, et mutua sese cohortatione animabant, et finem sibi a Deo dispositum tremuli expectabant.

[p. 300] frigida gelu nox illa fuit, unde tener albeolus post longam tolerantiam frigore vires amisit, sociumque suum Deo commendans relapsus in pontum obiit nec ulterius usquam comparuit. Beroldus autem qui pauperior erat omnibus, renone amictus ex arietinis pellibus, de tanto solus consortio diem vidit, et mane a ternis piscatoribus faselo receptus terram solus attigit. deinde aliquantulum refocilatus seriem tristis eventus curiose sciscitantibus enucleavit, et postea fere xx annis cum alacritate vixit. Rogerius Constantiensis episcopus (…) aliique multi

II.11 | The Wreck of the White Ship   123

qui adhuc simul in littore stabant, et rex sociique eius qui iam in freto elongati fuerant, terribilem vociferationem periclitantium audierunt, sed causam usque in crastinum ignorantes mirati sunt et inde mutuo indagantes tractaverunt. lugubris rumor per ora vulgi cito volitans in maritimis littoribus perstrepit, ac ad noticiam Tedbaldi comitis aliorumque procerum aulicorum pervenit, sed in illa die sollicito regi multumque percunctanti nunciare nemo presumpsit. optimates vero seorsum ubertim plorabant, karos parentes et amicos inconsolabiliter lugebant, sed ante regem ne doloris causa proderetur vix lacrimas cohibebant. tandem sequenti die sollertia Tedbaldi comitis puer flens ad pedes regis corruit, a quo rex naufragium Candidae Navis causam esse luctus edidicit. qui nimia mox animi angustia correptus ad terram cecidit, sed ab amicis sullevatus et in conclavim ductus amaros planctus edidit. non Jacob de amissione Joseph tristior extitit, nec David pro interfectione Amon vel Absalon acerbiores questus depromsit. tanto itaque patrono plorante omnibus regni filiis palam flere licuit, et huiusmodi luctus multis diebus perduravit. Guillelmum adelingum quem Anglici regni legitimum heredem arbitrati sunt, tam subito lapsum cum flore specialis nobilitatis omnes generaliter plangunt. (…) [p. 302] dum enim prestolatur longevitatem, beatitudinem et sullimitatem, subito incurrit citam perniciem, miseriam et deiectionem, ut in cotidianis eventibus ab inicio mundi usque in hodiernum diem, tam modernis quam antiquis approbationibus manifestam liquido advertere possumus ostensionem. (…) [p. 306] incolae maritimi ut certitudinem infortunii compererunt, fractam navem cum toto regis thesauro ad littus pertraxerunt, et omnia quae ibidem erant praeter homines salva prorsus reperta sunt. deinde pernices viri viiᵒ kalendas Decembris dum Christiana plebs solennia sanctae celebrat Caterinae virginis et martiris, querentes somata perditorum avide discurrunt per littora maris, sed non invenientes muneribus fraudabantur peroptatis. opulenti magnates nandi gnaros et famosos mersores obnixe querebant, et magnos census eis spondebant, si karorum suorum cadavera sibi redderent, ut ea dignae sepulturae traderent.

Translation: Orderic Vitalis, *An Ecclesiastical History*

When King Henry, after many problems in Normandy, had arranged matters in an excellent manner, he decided to cross the sea and to pay generous stipends to his recruits and the leading knights who had fought loyally and with much effort, and to raise some of them in England to higher positions, granting them ample honours. And so he ordered a fleet to be prepared immediately and a large group of soldiers of every rank to accompany him. (…)

When a huge fleet had been made ready in the port called Barfleur, and a noble group of soldiers had gathered to accompany the king, and a southerly wind was blowing, on the seventh day before the Kalends of December (25 November), at the first watch of the night, the king and his companions boarded the ships. Hoisting the sails they entrusted them to the winds on the sea, and the next morning those to whom God granted it embraced England. While they were sailing, a sad misfortune occurred which caused much grief and innumerable tears. Thomas son of Stephen had approached the king and, offering him a gold mark, said, 'My father was Stephen son of Airard and throughout his whole life he served your father on the sea. For he accompanied him when he was transported in his boat to England, when he travelled to England to fight against Harold. In this role he pleased the king in lifelong service, and honoured by him with many gifts, my father flourished magnificently among his fellow vassals. This is the feudal relationship, lord king, that I ask of you, and I have prepared the vessel called the White Ship in the best manner, as befits the royal household.' The king replied, 'I approve your request. For myself I have chosen a suitable ship which I will not change, but I now entrust to you my sons William and Richard, whom I love as myself, with many of my kingdom's nobles.' When they heard this the sailors were overjoyed, and fawning on the king's son, they asked him for wine to drink. William gave orders that they should be given three barrels of wine. On receiving this they drank and poured out large amounts for their companions, and boozing excessively they became inebriated. At the king's command many barons boarded the ship with his sons, and there were, I believe, about three hundred in the doomed ship. In fact, two monks of the Tironensian Order, together with Earl Stephen, and two knights, also William de Rolmara and Rabellus the Chamberlain, Edward of Salisbury and several others left the ship because they realised that there were too many rowdy and arrogant young people on board. For there were fifty experienced rowers there and fierce ship-guards who had already taken their seats on the ship. They were swollen with pride, and because they were drunk, they were not in their right minds and could hardly acknowledge anyone with due respect. Alas, how many of them had forgotten all their pious devotion towards God, He who controls the immoderate anger of sea and air. And so they drove away the priests who had gone there to bless them and the other servants who were bringing the holy water, shouting abuse and laughing loudly at them with insults, but a little later they were punished for this scornful treatment. Only the men with the king's treasure and with vessels carrying wine filled Thomas' ship, and they ordered him to follow with the utmost effort the king's fleet, which was already cutting a furrow through the seas. But Thomas, being befuddled by drink, trusted in his own strength and that of his companions and recklessly promised to overtake all those who had already gone ahead. At last he gave the signal to sail. The sailors then enthusiastically grabbed the oars, while others, who were happy because they were unaware of what was looming before their eyes, fitted all the sailing equipment, and propelling the ship with great force they caused it to speed on its way across the sea. While the drunken oarsmen were concentrating on rowing the ship with all their strength and the unfortunate helmsman was not properly paying attention as he steered the ship across the sea, the left-hand side of the White Ship smashed violently against a huge rock which was uncovered every day at low tide and then covered over again as the tide came in: two wooden panels were unexpectedly smashed to pieces and the ship capsized – what a disaster! Everyone shouted out at once at this great crisis, but soon the water filled their mouths and they perished together. Only two people grabbed hold of a pole on which the sail was hanging and for most of the night they clung to it, waiting for some form of help. One was a butcher from Rouen called Berold and the other a noble-born lad called Geoffrey, son of Gilbert of L'Aigle.

At the time the moon was in the nineteenth night of its cycle in the sign of Taurus and for about nine hours it illuminated the world with its rays and made the sea bright for the sailors. Thomas the sailor regained his strength after the first sinking and, now conscious, he lifted his head above the waves. Seeing the heads of those who were somehow clinging to the wood, he asked them, 'What has happened to the king's son?' When those who had been shipwrecked answered that he had perished together with all his friends, he said, 'My life is now nothing but sorrow.' With these words he lost hope and preferred to die there than to encounter the fury of the king, who would be angry at his son's death, or to serve a lengthy punishment in chains. Those who were suspended on the water called upon God and kept each other alive with mutual encouragement; shivering with fear they awaited the end that God had arranged for them.

That night was freezing cold, and so after the young lord (Geoffrey) had endured for a long time, his strength ebbed away as a result of the cold, and commending his companion to God he fell back into the sea and died, disappearing completely forever. But Berold, who was poorer than everyone, clad in a waterproof coat of sheepskin, alone of all this company saw daybreak. The following morning he was lifted by three fishermen into their fishing boat and was the only one to reach land. Then, after he had rested a bit, he was able to give a narrative of the tragic events to those who were curious to hear. Afterwards he lived for about twenty years in good health. Roger Bishop of Coutances (...) and many others who were still standing on the shore together, as well as the king and his companions who were already far out to sea, heard the terrible cries of the people in danger, but not knowing the cause until the following day, they wondered at it and asked each other what it could mean. The tragic news spread quickly by word of mouth along the seashores and came to the notice of Count Theobald and the other noblemen of the court, but on that day no one dared to give the news to the king, who was worried and asking many questions. The nobles were weeping abundantly in private and grieved inconsolably for their beloved relatives and friends, but they made an effort to restrain their tears in front of the king so as not to betray the reason for their sorrow. Finally, on the following day, thanks to the ingenuity of Theobald, a weeping boy fell down before the king, and it was from him that the king learned that the reason for their grief was the wreck of the White Ship. He was immediately overwhelmed by mental anguish and collapsed but was raised up by his friends and taken to his private chamber, where

126 Twelfth Century

he burst into bitter laments. Jacob was not more grief-stricken at the loss of Joseph, nor did David express more bitter laments at the murder of Ammon or Absalom. And so, when their great patron wept, all the sons of the kingdom were permitted to weep openly, and this expression of grief continued for many days. William Atheling was universally mourned, he whom they considered to be the legitimate heir to the kingdom of England, and who had died so suddenly together with the flower of the dearly loved nobility. (…) For while we expect a long life, happiness and high status, suddenly we encounter swift ruin, misery and downfall, as we can clearly demonstrate by evident proof in everyday events from the beginning of the world down to the present day, both from ancient and modern authorities. (…) The people who lived by the sea, when they learned of the certainty of the disaster, dragged the smashed ship with all the king's treasure to the shore and everything that had been in it was found safe apart from the human cargo. Then, on the seventh day before the Kalends of December (25 November), while Christians were celebrating the feast of St Catherine, virgin and martyr, swift men ran about on the seashores eagerly looking for the bodies of the dead, but they were unable to find them, and so they did not get the reward they had hoped for. Rich magnates were strenuously looking for people who could swim and well-known divers, promising them large sums of money if they could return to them the corpses of their loved ones so that they could give them a decent burial.

Primary Source

Orderic Vitalis, *Historia ecclesiastica*, ed. M. Chibnall, 6 vols, OMT, Oxford, 1969–80.

D: Symeon of Durham, *A History of the English and Danish Kings* (*Historia regum Anglorum et Dacorum*) (excerpt: chapter 199, *RS* 75.2 (1885) 258–9)

Date: c.1129.

The sole MS of this work is the twelfth-century Cambridge MS CCC 139, which mentions Symeon as the author/compiler.

Author: Symeon (died c.1129) is a shadowy figure who seems to have arrived in Durham soon after the foundation, in 1083, of a priory there, where he spent the rest of his life as a scribe and historian. Many manuscripts from the priory survived the dissolution of the monasteries and are currently being digitised by the Durham Library project.

II.11 | The Wreck of the White Ship

Work: Symeon's name is associated with two works. The first is the history of the church at Durham, from its foundation by St Aidan as the bishopric of Lindisfarne in 635 down to the end of the eleventh century (a work variously and confusedly known both as *Libellus de exordio atque procursu istius, hoc est Dunhelmensis, ecclesiae* (e.g. in the early MS in the Durham University Library, MS Cosin V.ii.6), and the *Historia Dunhelmensis ecclesie*, as in *RS* 75.1 (1882). An excerpt from this work is included in Section I.28B on the destruction of Lindisfarne in 793. The second work is the *History of the English and Danish Kings*; Symeon's role in its creation has been controversial. It has been suggested by David Rollason, for example, that much of the text was actually compiled by Byrhtferth of Ramsey around the year 1000, basing his work on Bede's *Ecclesiastical History* (Section I.17), the Northern Annals and Asser's biography of Alfred (Section I.32).

This passage, with its factual account of the shipwreck resembling a modern newspaper report, interlaced with hints of tragedy, comes from the section of the *Historia regum* that provides a chronicle of the years 1119–29. It is probably one of the few sections of which Symeon himself is the author.

Linguistic points: *repacificare*, a compound of the CL prefix *re-* and *pacificare*, appears first in BML in Florence of Worcester, who is one of Symeon's sources. Symeon hints at the tragedy to come in the phrase *nulla (navis) in tota classe videbatur melior, sed, ut eventus ostendit, nulla infelicior*; and he indicates the sorrow awaiting King Henry, still hoping that there is a rational explanation for his beloved son's disappearance, with the phrase laden with dramatic irony, *Angliam attingens, alium portum intrasse putabat filium.*

TEXT II.11D

The wreck of the White Ship

[199, *RS* p. 258] itaque rex, omnibus qui contra se insurrexerant vel devictis vel repacificatis, cunctisque ad votum prospere peractis, quinto profectionis suae anno necdum completo, laetior solito, in Angliam multo navigio revehitur. delegaverat autem filio cunctoque illius comitatui navem qua nulla in tota classe videbatur melior, sed, ut eventus ostendit, nulla infelicior. patre namque praeeunte, paulo tardius sed infelicius sequebatur filius. [p. 259] nave quippe, non longe a terra, in ipso velificationis impetu super scopulos in ipso exitu delata ac dissoluta, filius regis cum omnibus qui secum erant interiit, vi kal. Decembris, feria v, noctis initio, apud Barbafflot. mane facto, thesaurus regis qui in navi fuerat invenitur per arenas, corpora vero pereuntium nulla. perierunt cum filio regis frater suus Ricardus nothus comes, cum filia regis quae fuerat uxor Rotronis, et Ricardus comes Cestrensis cum uxore sua nepte regis, sorore Theobaldi comitis nepotis regis. periit et Othoel magister filii regis, et Goffridus Ridel, et Rodbertus Malduit,

128 Twelfth Century

et Willelmus Bigot, multique alii principales viri; nobiles quoque feminae quamplures, cum regiis pueris non paucis, militaris numeri cxl et nautarum l, cum tribus gubernatoribus navis. solus quidam macellarius tabula naufragii[8] pendens evasit. rex vero prospero cursu Angliam attingens, alium portum intrasse putabat filium, sed die tertio de illius interitu tristi perturbatur nuntio. et quidem primo subito casu veluti pusillanimis deficiebat; sed mox, dissimulato dolore, regios animos ex contemptu resumpsit fortunae. illum quippe solum ex legitimo conjugio susceptum regni post se haeredem constituerat.

Translation: Symeon of Durham, *A History of the English and Danish Kings*

[199] *And so the king, once he had either subdued or reconciled all those who had rebelled against him and all his plans had been successfully carried out, before five years had passed since he set off, more cheerful than normal, he sailed back to England in a large ship. However, he had selected for his son and the son's whole entourage a ship which seemed the best in his whole fleet, but as later events showed, was in fact the most unfortunate. For while his father went on ahead, the son followed a bit later but with greater misfortune. The ship, as the sails pushed it forward and while it was still not far from land, was driven onto the rocks and broken into pieces, and the king's son died with all his companions, on Thursday, the sixth day before the Kalends of December (26 November), at nightfall, near Barfleur. When morning came, the king's treasure which had been in the ship was found on the sands, but not the bodies of the dead. With the king's son there died also his illegitimate brother Earl Richard (of Lincoln), together with the king's daughter who was the wife of Rotrou (of Perche), and Richard Earl of Chester with his wife, the king's niece, the sister of Count Theobald, the king's nephew. Ottuel, the tutor of the king's son, died too, as well as Geoffrey Ridel and Robert Malduit and William Bigot and many other leading men; also many noble women, with several royal children, 140 soldiers and 50 sailors, together with the three helmsmen of the ship. The only one to escape was a butcher who clung to the planks of the wrecked ship. When the king reached England after a fair crossing, he kept thinking that his son had landed at a different port, but on the third day he was devastated by the tragic news of his death. At first he collapsed at the sudden misfortune, as if he lacked courage, but soon he managed to conceal his grief and regained his royal strength of mind, scorning what fortune had done. For indeed he had made William, the only male child born in lawful wedlock, the heir of his kingdom to succeed him.*

---

8 For a figurative use of this phrase, with penance regarded as a raft providing safety after the shipwreck of sin, see Section II.50A.

Primary Source

Symeon of Durham, *Historia regum Anglorum et Dacorum, RS* 75.2 (1885) chapter 199.

Further Reading

Lapidge, M. (1981) 'Byrhtferth of Ramsey and the early sections of the *Historia regum* attributed to Symeon of Durham', *ASE* 10: 97–122.

Rollason, D. (1998) *Symeon of Durham: historian of Durham and the north,* Stamford.

—— (2016) 'Symeon of Durham's *Historia de regibus Anglorum et Dacorum*' in *The long twelfth-century view of the Anglo-Saxon past,* ed. M. Brett and D. Woodman, London.

E: Hugh the Chanter, *A History of the Church at York* (excerpt: OMT p. 164)

Date: after 1127.

The sole copy of this work is preserved in the early fourteenth-century York Minster Library MS L2/1, from which the OMT edition adopts the medieval spellings, unlike the *RS* edition.

Author: Hugh (died c.1140), also known as Hugo Sottovagina, was a canon at York Cathedral. He seems to have written some moral precepts in verse and a poem on the Battle of the Standard (1138) at Northallerton, an event recorded also by Ælred of Rievaulx.

Work: Hugh's history of the church at York covers the years 1066–1127, focusing particularly on the question of the relations between the archdioceses of Canterbury and York. It is likely that Hugh knew Eadmer's *History of Recent Events in England,* and that he was putting the York point of view in contrast to Eadmer's support for Canterbury. The White Ship disaster is described briefly as it affected King Henry I and Archbishop Thurstan of York (1114-40), two of the main protagonists in his account.

Linguistic points: The work consists largely of brief accounts of journeys, messages and discussions, with some direct speech. Hugh does quote from a few classical authors, such as Lucan, Sallust and Persius. It may have been in Isidore's *Etymologies* that he encountered the fragment attributed to Ennius that he cites.

130 Twelfth Century

In this excerpt the use of the pronouns (*eo*, *eius* and *eum*) in the first sentence can cause confusion, with the first two referring to King Henry I, and the last to Archbishop Thurstan.

TEXT II.11E

The wreck of the White Ship
[OMT p. 164] eo discedente filius eius, rex et dux iam designatus, naufragio perierat, et universi qui nave eadem vehebantur, quod eum vehementer contristavit. nam praeter domini sui regis filium et dominum futurum multos amicos amiserat. rex autem nimirum gravi et inmoderato dolore percussus, tandem per se, sicut sapiens homo, et per comitem Teobaldum, qui cum eo venerat, et per alios consolatus est.

Translation: Hugh the Chanter, *A History of the Church at York*

After Henry's departure, his son, who had already been designated king and duke, had died in a shipwreck, together with all those who were travelling in the same ship, which caused the archbishop great distress. For apart from the son of the lord king, the future lord, he had lost many friends. The king was obviously stricken with profound and overwhelming grief, but at last he found consolation, drawing on his own resources as a wise man, and from Count Theobald who had accompanied him, and from others.

Primary Source

Hugh the Chanter: The History of the Church at York (1066–1127), ed. M. Brett, C. Brooke and M. Winterbottom, OMT, rev. ed., Oxford, 1990.

F: Henry of Huntingdon, *Contempt for the World* (*De contemptu mundi*) (excerpt: chapter 5)

Date: 1135.

The earliest text of this letter is found in BL MS Cotton Domitian A.viii, ff. 111r–119r.

Author: On Henry of Huntingdon, see Section II.4A.

Work: Henry's *Contempt for the World* is printed as part of the *History of the English* (Book 8): it takes the form of a letter to his friend Walter, Archdeacon of Leicester, one of three letters in this section. In this context it is less concerned with the facts of the White Ship disaster than with the moral that can be drawn from it: the author stresses it as a punishment for the pride and self-indulgence he had noticed prior to the event. Biblical references add moral weight, and black humour is in evidence. Henry refers to the fact that he and one of those who died, Richard, the illegitimate son of Henry I, were brought up in the same establishment at Lincoln. Henry also deals with this event, more briefly and with the addition of four elegiac couplets on the subject, in *Historia Anglorum* 7.32. Another more famous work *On Contempt for the World* (*De contemptu mundi*) is that of Bernard of Chartres, dating from about 1140.

Linguistic points: Henry displays the effects of his rhetorical education in such features as the tricolon of *indutum, consertum, coruscantem*, or of *scinderetur, volutaretur* and *sepeliretur*, and the antithesis between father and son. *angaria* occurs in BML post-Conquest, adopted from LL, which borrowed it from Greek, in the sense of a kind of compulsory service.[9] Compare the verb *angariare*: these words occur in Continental medieval Latin too. However, Henry of Huntingdon uses both these words with the sense of 'distress', probably influenced by CL *angere*. CL *consul* is used here as synonymous with 'earl', but as a quasi-technical term it can take on different contemporary senses at different times and in different contexts.

TEXT II.11F

The wreck of the White Ship
[5] secundum capitulum ad contemptum mundi est de his quos, in summis deliciis educatos, vidimus summis miseriis tandem deletos. ideo autem per capitula tibi scribo, ut quia diversorum nomina et gesta ubique dispersa intermiscentur hinc apertior et dilucidior fiat tractatus. vidimus igitur Willelmum filium regis, vestibus sericis et auro consutis indutum, famulorum et custodum turba consertum, gloria quasi celesti choruscantem. ipse unicus erat regis et regine filius, nec dubitabat se diademate sublimandum. enimvero nescio quid magis afferebat, ei certa spes in futurum regnandi, quam patri suo ipsa essentia regni, quia patri magnum regnandi spacium iam preterierat, filio vero totum adhuc reservabatur. pater etiam iam de amissione cum mentis angaria cogitabat; filius vero tantum ad habendum cum gaudio totus inhiabat. displicebat autem michi, et in animo meo

---

9   Cf. Neckam, *Sacerdos ad altare* 8, where it is defined as *servitus personalis*; for this text see Section II.28B.

132 Twelfth Century

Isa. 9:5 cladem futuram portendebat, nimius circa eum cultus et nimius in ipso fastus, et dicebat animus meus, 'Hic adeo delicatus nutritur in cibum ignis.' ille autem semper de regno futuro, de fastigio superbo tumidus, cogitabat. Deus autem dicebat, **Ps. 1:4** 'Non sic impii, non sic.' contigit igitur ei quod pro corona auri rupibus marinis capite scinderetur, pro vestibus deauratis nudus in mari volutaretur, pro celsitudine regni maris in fundo piscium ventribus sepeliretur. hec fuit mutatio dextere **Ps. 76:11** excelsi! Ricardus etiam consul Cestrensis, filius unicus Hugonis consulis, summo splendore nutritus, summa expectatione patris heres eximius, adhuc inberbis in eadem nave deperiit et eandem sepulturam habuit. Ricardus quoque, filius regis nothus, ab episcopo nostro Roberto festive nutritus, et in eadem qua degebam familia a me et aliis celebriter honoratus,[10] cuius indolem mirabamur et magna quaeque expectabamus, in eadem navi cautibus illisa, cum mare ventis careret, subita morte raptus est et a mari voratus est.

Translation: Henry of Huntingdon, *Contempt for the World*

[5] *The second chapter on contempt for the world concerns those whom we see brought up amidst the greatest luxuries and then brought down amidst the greatest misfortunes. I am writing to you in chapters so that my treatise may be clearer and more lucid because the names of various people and events scattered all over the place are mixed up in it. We saw William, the king's son, dressed in silk robes embroidered with gold, surrounded by an entourage of servants and bodyguards, glittering with what looked like heavenly glory. He was the only son of the king and queen and had no doubt that he would be exalted with a crown. Indeed, I am not sure what was greater, the young man's firm hope of future rule, or his father's actual rule, because his father's reign was largely in the past, while the whole reign still awaited the son. Moreover, the father was already anxious at the thought of losing his kingdom, but the son was excited by his desire for it. But I did not approve of the excessive cult around him and his excessive pride: in my opinion it portended a future disaster, and I said to myself, 'This person has been so spoiled that he is fuel for the fire.' He spent his whole time thinking about his future royal power, swelling with arrogance. But God was saying, 'Not so the wicked, not so.' And so it happened that instead of wearing a gold crown, his head was cut open by the rocks in the sea, instead of golden robes he was tossed naked in the sea, instead of the heights of royal power he was buried in the stomach of fishes, at the bottom of the sea. Such was the change of the right hand of the Most High! Richard, Earl of Chester, too, the only son of Earl Hugh, brought up in extreme splendour, his father's outstanding heir, with the highest expectations, still a beardless young man, died in the same ship and was*

---

10 I.e. Robert Bloet, Bishop of Lincoln 1093–1123; Henry refers to him as *nostro* because he had lived in Robert's household in Lincoln as a boy, alongside Richard of Lincoln, the king's illegitimate son.

buried in the same manner. Richard, too, the king's illegitimate son, fittingly raised by our Bishop Robert and solemnly honoured by me and others in the same household where I lived, and whose talent we admired and from whom we awaited great things, was carried off by a sudden death and devoured by the sea in this same ship when it smashed on the rocks, even though the sea was calm.

Primary Source

Henry of Huntingdon, *De contemptu mundi*, Book 8 of *Historia Anglorum*, ed. D. Greenway, OMT, Oxford, 1996: 584–618.

Further Reading

Plassmann, A. (2018) 'Bede's legacy in William of Malmesbury and Henry of Huntingdon' in *Bates, D'Angelo and Van Houts (2018).

Sharpe, R. (2017) 'Official and unofficial Latin words in eleventh- and twelfth-century England' in *Ashdowne and White (2017).

Section II.12

Geoffrey of Monmouth, *A History of the Kings of Britain* (*Historia regum Britanniae*) (excerpts: 100, 145–7)

Date: before 1139.

The more than two hundred surviving medieval MSS bear witness to the popularity of Geoffrey's work, but the variety of readings presents textual problems for modern editors. Here the text is taken from the Bern Burgerbibliothek MS 568 of the twelfth century, edited by N. Wright in the first volume of a series of single-manuscript editions. It was while visiting Robert of Torigni at Bec in Normandy in 1139 that Henry of Huntingdon saw a copy of one of the earliest versions of Geoffrey's text.

Author: Little is known of Geoffrey's birth and background, but it seems likely he was of Celtic origin, from the Welsh border area. It is notable that he dedicated the *History of the Kings of Britain* to two lords from this area, namely Robert of Gloucester, an illegitimate son of Henry I, and Waleran of Meulan (for whom, cf. Section II.44B). He may have been a secular canon in Oxford, and by 1151 had been elected Bishop of St Asaph in Wales, though he never took up his post. As well as the *History of the Kings of Britain*, he wrote the *Prophetie Merlini* and a *Vita Merlini* in hexameter verse. Geoffrey died in about 1155.

Work: The work usually referred to as *Historia regum Britanniae* (the title extrapolated from its opening section) was also known as the *Gesta Britonum* (cf. *Vita Merlini* line 1529). It covers the period from Aeneas' flight from Troy and the founding of the kingdom of Britain by Brutus, peaks with the reign of Arthur and traces the country's post-Arthurian downfall as far as the seventh century with the increasing dominance of English culture over the British. Geoffrey claims his work is a translation of an ancient book in the British language, but modern scholars are sceptical of this claim. It seems rather that he weaves a story from various elements taken from Celtic legend and local lore, and from Latin writers. His aim is to fill in areas of British history not covered by Gildas or Bede, and to do so he often uses non-historical accounts within a historical framework. At the end he says he will leave later history to his contemporaries: the history of the Welsh to Caradoc of Llancarfan, of the English to William of Malmesbury and Henry of Huntingdon. The *History of the Kings of Britain* was an immediate success, despite the criticism of William of Newburgh, in

II.12 | Geoffrey of Monmouth, *The Kings of Britain* 135

the preface to the *Historia rerum Anglicarum*, who accuses Geoffrey of cobbling together the account of Arthur from scraps of old British tales (*fabulas de Arturo, ex priscis Britonum figmentis sumptas*), of adding his own fictions and then disguising it as history by presenting it as a Latin narrative. It was also hugely influential throughout the Middle Ages, in works in both prose and verse and in a number of vernacular versions. Although Geoffrey is most famous for the Arthurian section, he was also the source of the story of King Lear, which then appears in the ME version of Laȝamon's *Brut* and later in a simplified Latin version in an English MS of the *Gesta Romanorum*, the popular collection of moralistic tales. This was a source used by such later writers as Chaucer, Boccaccio and Shakespeare. And yet the *History of the Kings of Britain* remains a book of some mystery and controversy as far as the intentions of its author and the veracity of its 'history' are concerned.

The first excerpt here (100) tells of the Saxon Hengist's invitation to the British king Vortigern to visit his new house, a story Geoffrey found in the *History of the Britons* (37) (for which, see Section I.30). Hengist's daughter Renwein presents a cup of wine and greets the king (whom she later betrays) in English. Vortigern asks a translator (from Saxon to a British Celtic language) to help, and is then able to respond correctly to the girl's greeting. Geoffrey informs the reader that this custom still pertains in Britain. Sections 145–7 are taken from the account of Arthur's reign and tell of events leading up to the crucial battle of Badon Hill, where Arthur, with his sword Caliburn, triumphed, and after which the Saxons fled to the Isle of Thanet, where they were forced to surrender.

Linguistic points: The work's popularity was no doubt largely due to the subject matter, but may have been assisted by its unusually simple syntax, the predominantly paratactic nature of its sentences, with the minimum of hyperbaton, and its classically attested vocabulary, which make it more accessible to readers who may be in the early stages of their Latin training. The section on Arthur's battles includes the speech of Bishop Dubricius, aimed at rousing the troops. The fact that the work is primarily a secular history means that it contains very few ecclesiastical words. Geoffrey uses a few words that are classically constructed, if not attested, like *congluttire* and *inequitatio*; he takes on board the OE-derived word for 'boat', *cyula*, first used by Gildas. He also includes an English greeting in the section below which is the earliest evidence for the words used as a drinking formula, namely 'Wassail' and 'Drink-hail'. Geoffrey's use of them in a fifth-century context is one of the anachronisms to be found in this work; the earliest attestation of these words in an English context is in Laȝamon's translation, around 1200, of Wace's *Brut*, the AN verse reworking of Geoffrey's *History*. At the end of the twelfth century these terms appear in Nigel of Canterbury's *Speculum stultorum* (line 1521) as characteristic of English students in Paris, and Gerald of Wales discusses these terms in his

136   Twelfth Century

Speculum ecclesiae 3.13 in his report on the excessive drinking of the Cistercians. Virgilian influence is apparent in the early sections, with their Trojan subject matter.

TEXT II.12

Hengist's daughter teaches Vortigern to toast a drinking companion in English
[100] interea vero reversi sunt nuntii ex Germania conduxerantque x et viii naves electis militibus plenas. conduxerunt etiam filiam Hengisti vocabulo Renwein cuius pulcritudo nulli secunda videbatur. postquam autem venerunt, invitavit Hengistus Vortegirnum regem in domum suam ut novum edificium et novos milites qui applicuerant videret. venit ilico rex privatim et laudavit tam subitum opus et milites invitatos retinuit. ut ergo regiis epulis refectus fuit, egressa est puella de thalamo aurum ciphum plenum vino ferens. accedens deinde propius regi flexis genibus dixit, '*Lauerd king, Waesseil!*' at ille, visa facie puelle, ammiratus est tantum eius decorem et incaluit. denique interrogavit interpretem suum quid dixerat puella et quid ei respondere debeat. cui interpres dixit, 'Vocavit te dominum regem et vocabulo salutationis honoravit. quod autem respondere debes, est "*Drincheil*". respondens igitur Vortegirnus '*Drincheil*' iussit puellam potare cepitque ciphum de manu ipsius et osculatus est eam et potavit. ab illo die usque in hodiernum mansit consuetudo illa in Britannia quia in conviviis qui potat ad alium dicit '*Waesseil*'. qui vero post illum recipit potum, respondet '*Drincheil*'.

Translation: Geoffrey of Monmouth, *A History of the Kings of Britain*

[100] *Meanwhile the envoys returned from Germany bringing with them eighteen ships filled with an elite army. They also brought Hengist's daughter, Renwein, whose beauty was regarded as second to none. After their arrival Hengist invited King Vortigern to his house to inspect this new building and the new soldiers who had landed. The king came immediately in private and praised the construction that had been completed so quickly and engaged the invited soldiers. When he had been refreshed by the royal banquet, the girl came out of the chamber carrying a golden goblet full of wine. She then approached the king, knelt down and said, 'Lord king, Wassail!' When he saw the girl's face he admired her great beauty and became excited. He then asked his interpreter what the girl had said and what he ought to reply to her. The interpreter told him, 'She called you "lord king" and honoured you with a word of greeting. You ought to reply to her with the word "Drink-hail".' And so in response Vortigern said 'Drink-hail', asking the girl to drink, and he took the goblet from her hands and kissed her and drank. From that day till this, this custom remains in Britain that at banquets the person who drinks says to the other,*

'Wassail! (Health to you!)' and when this one takes a drink after him, he replies, 'Drink-hail! (Drink good health!)'.

Arthur fights the Saxons, culminating in the battle of Badon Hill

[145] emensis postmodum paucis diebus urbem Kaerluideoit petunt a paganis **v.l. Kaerlwydcoed** quos supramemoravi obsessam. hec autem in Lindiseiensi provincia inter duo flumina super montem locata alio nomine Lindocolinum nuncupatur. ut igitur cum omni multitudine sua eo venerunt, preliati sunt cum Saxonibus inauditam cedem inferentes. ceciderunt nanque ex illis eadem die sex milia qui partim fluminibus submersi, partim telis percussi vitam amiserunt. unde ceteri stupefacti relicta obsidione fugam fecerunt. quos Arturus insequi non cessavit donec in nemore Colidonis venerunt. ibi ex fuga undique confluentes conati sunt Arturo resistere. conserto itaque prelio stragem Britonibus faciunt sese viriliter defendentes. usi etenim arborum auxilio tela Britonum vitabant. quod Arturus intuens iussit arbores circa illam partem nemoris incidi et truncos ita in circuitu locari ut egressus eis abnegaretur. volebat nanque ipsos inclusos tamdiu obsidere donec fame interirent. quo facto iussit turmas suas ambire nemus mansitque tribus diebus ibidem. cum igitur Saxones quo vescerentur indigerent, ne subita fame perirent pecierunt (pet-) eo pacto egressum ut relicto omni auro et argento cum solis navibus Germaniam redire sinerentur. promiserunt quoque se daturos tributum ex Germania obsidesque inde mansuros. tunc Arturus quesito consilio petitioni eorum adquievit. retinuit nanque ipsorum opes reddendique vectigalis obsides solumque abscessum largitus est.

[146] cumque illi in redeundo domum equora sulcarent, piguit peracte pactionis retortisque velis ambierunt Britanniam et Totonesium litus adiverunt. nacti deinde tellurem patriam usque ad Sabrinum mare depopulant, colonos letiferis vulneribus afficientes. inde arrepto itinere versus pagum Badonis urbem obsiderunt. idque cum regi nunciatum esset, admirans ultra modum ipsorum facinus iudicium fieri iussit de illorum obsidibus brevi hora suspendendis. pretermissa etiam inquietatione qua Scotos et Pictos opprimere inceperat obsidionem dispergere festinavit, maximis vero angustiis cruciatus quoniam Hoelum nepotem suum gravatum morbo in civitatem Aldclud deserebat. postremo Sumersetentem provinciam ingressus, visus cominus obsidione in hec verba locutus est: 'Quoniam impiisimi atque invisi nominis Saxones fidem mihi dedignati sunt tenere, ego fidem Deo meo conservans sanguinem concivium meorum hodie in ipsos vindicare conabor. armate vos, viri, armate et proditores istos viriliter invadite quos proculdubio auxiliante Deo triumphabimus.'

[147] hec eo dicente sanctus Dubricius[1] Urbis Legionum archiepiscopus ascenso cuiusdam montis cacumine in hunc modum celsa voce exclamavit: 'Viri christiana

---

1 Dubricius (Welsh, Dyfrig) was a sixth-century bishop, active in the area of the Welsh borders known as Archenfield (for which cf. Section II.4C) and said to be Bishop of Caerleon or Llandaff; cf. Benedict of Gloucester's *Vita Dubricii* (c.1150).

138 Twelfth Century

professione insigniti, maneat in vobis concivium vestrorum pietas et patrie qui
proditione paganorum exterminati vobis sempiternum erunt opprobrium nisi
ipsos defendere institeritis. pugnate pro patria vestra et mortem si supervenerit
ultro pro eadem patimini. ipsa enim victoria est et anime remedium. quicunque
enim pro confratribus suis mortem inierit vivam hostiam se prestet Deo Chris-
tumque insequi non ambigitur qui pro fratribus suis animam suam dignatus est
ponere. si aliquis igitur vestrum in hoc bello subierit mortem, sit ei mors illa omnium delictorum suorum penitentia et ablutio, dum hoc modo eam recipere non
diffugerit.' nec mora beati viri benedictione hylarati festinavit quisque armari se
et preceptis eius parere. ipse vero Arturus lorica tanto regi digna indutus auream
galeam simulachro draconis insculptam capiti adaptat: humeris quoque suis cli-
peum vocabulo Pridwen in quo imago sancte Marie Dei genetricis impicta ipsum
in memoriam ipsius sepissime revocabat. accinctus ergo Caliburno gladio optimo et in insula Avallonis fabricato lancea dextram suam decorat que nomine Ron
vocabatur. hec erat ardua lataque lancea, cladibus apta. deinde dispositis catervis
Saxones suo more in cuneos dispositos audacter invasit. ipsi tota die viriliter re-
sistebant Britones usque prosternentes. vergente tandem ad occasum sole proximum occupant montem pro castro eum habituri. multitudine etenim sociorum
confisis solus mons sufficere videbatur. at ut posterus sol diem reduxit, ascendit
Arturus cum exercitu suo cacumen sed in ascendendo multos suorum amisit.
Saxones nanque ex summitate occurrentes facilius ingerebant vulnera dum ipsos
citior cursus in descensu ageret quam eos in ascensu. Britones tamen cacumen
maxima vi adepti dextris hostium dextras suas confestim conferunt. quibus Saxones pectora pretendentes omni nisu resistere nituntur. cumque diei multum in
hunc modum preterisset, indignatus est Arturus ipsis ita successisse nec sibi victoriam advenire. abstracto ergo Caliburno gladio nomen Sancte Marie proclamat
et sese cito impetu infra densas hostium acies immisit. quemcumque attingebat
Deum invocando solo ictu perimebat. nec requievit impetum suum facere donec
quadringentos septuaginta viros solo Caliburno gladio peremit. quod videntes
Britones densatis turmis illum sequuntur stragem undique facientes. ceciderunt
ilico Colgrimus et Baldulfus eius frater et multa milia aliorum. At Cheldricus viso
sociorum periculo continuo in fugam cum ceteris versus est.

Translation: Geoffrey of Monmouth, *A History of the Kings of
Britain*

[145] *A few days later they made for the city of Kaerluideoit, which had been besieged
by the pagans, as I mentioned above. This is in Lindsey province, situated on a hill
between two rivers, and is also called Lincoln. When, therefore, they arrived there
with all their huge numbers, they fought the Saxons, inflicting unheard-of slaughter. For there fell on that day six thousand of them, some of whom were drowned
in the rivers, and some of whom lost their lives when wounded by weapons. The*

II.12 | Geoffrey of Monmouth, *The Kings of Britain* 139

rest were stunned by this, and abandoning the siege they fled. Arthur continued to pursue them until they reached the forest of Celidon. Gathering there from all directions they attempted to resist Arthur. Joining battle they defended themselves bravely and inflicted a massacre on the Britons. Using also the protection of the trees they avoided the Britons' weapons. When Arthur noticed this he gave orders for the trees in the surrounding forest to be chopped down and the tree trunks placed in a circle so that they could not get out. For he wanted to besiege them shut up in there for as long as it took for them to die of hunger. After doing this he ordered his troops to surround the forest and he remained there for three days. When, therefore, the Saxons needed something to eat, so as to avoid dying of hunger they asked for a way out on condition that they would leave behind all their gold and silver and would be allowed to return to Germany with just their ships. They also promised that they would give tribute from Germany and hostages from there who would remain. Then Arthur, after seeking advice, agreed to their request. For he kept their wealth and the hostages for the payment of tribute and only permitted their departure.

[146] While they were cutting a furrow through the seas on their return home, they regretted the treaty they had made and turning their sails round they headed for Britain and landed on the shore at Totnes. Then gaining control of the land they ravaged the country as far as the waters of the Severn, inflicting deadly wounds on the farming folk. Then marching towards the area around Badon they laid siege to the city. When the king received news of this, he was totally amazed at what they had done and he gave orders that their hostages should be sentenced to be hanged immediately. He abandoned the attacks with which he had begun to oppress the Scots and the Picts and hastened to break up the siege, tormented by terrible anguish because he was abandoning his nephew Hoel, who was seriously ill in the city of Aldclud. Then he entered the county of Somerset and after looking at the siege at close quarters, he spoke in the following words: 'Since the most wicked Saxons, of hateful reputation, have refused to keep faith with me, I will keep faith with my God and will try today to take revenge on them for the blood of my fellow citizens. Arm yourselves, my men, arm yourselves and attack these traitors bravely and we will, with God's help, undoubtedly triumph over them.'

[147] While he was saying this, the holy Dubricius, the Archbishop of the City of Legions, went up onto the top of a hill and shouted in a loud voice in the following manner: 'You men who have been marked with the sign of your Christian faith, may the love of your fellow citizens and your country remain in you: their deaths at the hands of the treacherous pagans will be an eternal source of shame to you if you do not undertake to defend them. Fight for your country, and if death should come then suffer it willingly for your country's sake. For death is itself a victory and a remedy for the soul. Anyone who dies for his compatriots offers himself as a living sacrifice to God, and he who thinks fit to lay down his life for his brothers does not hesitate to follow Christ. And so if any of you should be killed in this battle, may this death be for him a penance for all his sins, a means of washing them away, as long as he does not try to avoid receiving it in this way.' Immediately encouraged by

140 Twelfth Century

the holy man's blessing they hastened to arm themselves and obey his commands. Arthur himself was clad in chainmail worthy of such a great king: he fitted onto his head a golden helmet with an image of a dragon incised on it, and on his shoulders the shield named Pridwen on which the image of the holy Mary, mother of God, was painted, reminding him constantly of her. At his side he had his excellent sword, Caliburn, and a lance called Ron, made by craftsmen on the isle of Avalon, adorned his right hand. This was a long and broad lance, designed for serious fighting. Then, after arranging his troops he boldly attacked the Saxons who were arranged in their customary wedge formation. Right through the day they resisted bravely, laying low the Britons. When at last the sun was going down they took control of a nearby hill, intending to have it as a camp. The hill alone seemed to be enough for them, confident as they were in their many allies. But when the following sun brought back the daylight, Arthur climbed to the top of the hill with his army, but in climbing it he lost many of his men. For the Saxons, rushing down from the summit, inflicted wounds more easily since they could go down more quickly than the others could go up. However, the Britons took control of the summit with a huge show of force, engaging in hand-to-hand combat with the enemy. The Saxons, meeting them head on, strove with every effort to resist them. When most of the day had already been spent in this way, Arthur was furious that the Saxons had had such success and that he had not gained the victory. Pulling out his sword Caliburn he shouted the name of holy Mary and rushed forward into the dense enemy lines. Anyone he came across he would kill with a single blow, calling on God. And he did not rest from his attack until he had killed 470 men with his sword Caliburn alone. Seeing this the Britons formed their squadrons more densely and followed Arthur, slaughtering on every side. Colgrim and his brother Baldulf died on the spot, as well as many thousands of others. And Cheldric, seeing his companions' danger, straight away turned and fled with the rest.

Primary Sources and Related Texts

Wright, N. (ed.) (1985) *The Historia regum Britannie of Geoffrey of Monmouth*, vol. 1: *Bern Burgerbibliothek MS 568*, Cambridge.

Geoffrey of Monmouth, *The History of the Kings of Britain: an edition and translation of De gestis Britonum*, ed. M. Reeve and N. Wright, Woodbridge, 2007.

Historia Brittonum 56 (Section I.30).

William of Malmesbury, *Gesta regum* 1.7.

Further Reading

Crawford, T. (1982) 'On the linguistic competence of Geoffrey of Monmouth', *Medium Aevum* 51: 152–62.

Crick, J. (ed.) (1991) *The Historia regum Britannie of Geoffrey of Monmouth*, vol. 4: *Dissemination and reception in the later Middle Ages*, Cambridge.

Echard, S. (ed.) (2011) *The Arthur of medieval Latin literature*, Cardiff.

Henley, G. and Byron-Smith, J. (ed.) (2020) *A companion to Geoffrey of Monmouth*, Leiden.

Loomis, R. S. (ed). (1979) *Arthurian literature in the Middle Ages: a collaborative history*, Oxford.

Section II.13

Two Twelfth-Century Lives of St Frideswide
A: *Vita* A (*Vita S. Fritheswithe*) (excerpts: chapters 2–5, 12)
B: *Vita* B (excerpts: chapters 2, 3, 12, 15)

Date: *Vita* A: early twelfth century; *Vita* B: 1140–70.

Vita A is preserved only in BL MS Cotton Nero E.i (part 2), ff. 156–7 (1110–40), which may be based on the same source as the brief account by William of Malmesbury (*GP* 4.178). Parts 1 and 2 of this important MS contain a great number of documents relating to British saints. *Vita* B is found in three MSS, in Oxford, Cambridge and among the British saints' lives in Gotha, Forschungsbibliothek MS I.81.

Author: The author of *Vita* A is unknown, while *Vita* B is attributed to Robert of Cricklade (d. after 1188), the prior of St Frideswide's monastery in Oxford, who also wrote biblical commentaries and a lost Life of Thomas Becket which was translated into Old Norse and formed the basis of the Icelandic version, *Thomas Erkybiskups Saga*. The miracles of Thomas Becket recorded by Benedict of Peterborough (cf. Section II.50B(a)) include two miracles experienced by Robert of Cricklade (*RS* 67.2 (1876) 96–101).

Subject: Frideswide, or more accurately Frithuswith (650–727), a princess of west Oxfordshire on the borders of Mercia and Wessex, asked her father for permission to dedicate herself to the monastic life in a minster he then built for her, but she was pursued by King Algar of Leicester, who wanted to marry her,[1] forcing her to flee some miles to the west. She then lived as a solitary at Binsey outside Oxford, where her prayers brought forth a spring. The king was subsequently punished, and Frideswide was able to settle in Oxford, which became the focus of her cult. Christ Church Cathedral is probably built on the site of her minster. Frideswide's name occurs in many different spellings in the sources, partly due to confusion between the letter d and the OE letter ð (th). In the translations of the two Latin texts below, forms of the name reflecting the Latin are used.

---

1 The theme of the king who seeks to force nuns into sexual relationships occurs in documents relating to events in the eighth century, in Boniface's *Ep.* 75 and Alcuin's *Ep.* 16 (for which see Section I.21C and Section I.28A).

II.13 | Two Twelfth-Century Lives of St Frideswide 143

Work: The two Lives of Frideswide, written some half-century apart, both contain twenty-four chapters, but *Vita* B is longer, providing the story with slightly different details at each stage, and serving as the basis for later abridgements. Here parallel passages have been selected for comparison, focusing on Frideswide's education, dedication and (after Algar's attempts to force her into marriage) her time in hiding. In *Vita* A (12), Bampton is wrongly represented as close to Binsey, while in *Vita* B, her time in these places is recounted separately in chapters 12 and 15.

Two Middle English versions of Frideswide's Life appear in the South English Legendary of the fourteenth century, and she is called on as a saint in the Miller's Tale (3449) in Chaucer's *Canterbury Tales*. The health-giving spring mentioned in *Vita* B (15) is now known as St Margaret's Well, at Binsey outside Oxford; it was the inspiration for the 'treacle well' in *Alice's Adventures in Wonderland* by Lewis Carroll, where 'treacle' derives from the Greek *theriake*, meaning an antidote, though it is more commonly applied to a dark sugar syrup.

Linguistic points: *Vita* A is written in a less ornate style, with a number of biblical citations, and some snippets of direct speech. *Vita* B has many similarities of expression but shows a confident handling of longer sentences. *Vita* B follows A (23) in using the rare *scamnulus*, the diminutive of CL *scamnum*, i.e. a 'bench' or, as here in the context of a miracle, a 'support' allowing a cripple to walk. *Vita* B does not follow A in misapplying the reflexive pronoun in the phrase *rex dedit sibi ecclesiam* (4). Blair punctuates with a comma after *orationibus* (4); an alternative is to take *vigiliis et orationibus* as a dative phrase governed by *intendens*.

A: *Vita* A (*Vita S. Fritheswithe*) (excerpts: chapters 2–5, 12)

TEXT II.13A

Frideswide's early life and dedication to the monastic life
[2] igitur postquam populus Anglorum beati Augustini predicatione edoctus atque baptizatus est, constituti sunt presbiteri atque diaconi, ecclesieque constructe atque dedicate sunt per universam regionem illam. augebatur igitur credentium multitudo, et per universam terram Anglorum ecclesia nova prole **Acts 5:14** fecundabatur. post multum vero tempus fuit rex quidem Oxinefordie cui nomen erat Didanus. hic accepit uxorem nomine Sefridam, colentem Deum atque prudentem in omni opere bono, cunque simul gauderent flore iuventutis, donavit eis Dominus fecunditatem. concepit itaque venerabilis Sefrida, et post peractum tempus idoneum peperit filiam. cum hoc audisset supradictus rex, gavisus est valde, iussitque eam regenerari ex aqua et Spiritu Sancto. baptizatam itaque vocaverunt eam Fritheswitham.

144 Twelfth Century

[3] hec igitur regis filia diligenter enutrita est. transactis itaque quinque annis tradiderunt eam cuidam matrone, Aelfgive nomine, ad erudiendum litteras. virgo igitur, quam Deus iam providerat vas futurum Spiritus Sancti, ita animum stabilivit ad discendas litteras ut intra sex menses totum sciret psalterium. proficiebat igitur beata Fritheswitha virgo et crescebat, omnique animo nitebatur omnibus se amabilem facere, semperque prout valebat liminibus sancte ecclesie adherebat. sacrarum etiam scripturarum dicta in pectoris antro condebat, hanc sepe orationem repetens, ut inhabitare valeret in domo Domini omnibus diebus

Ps. 22:6 vite sue, videretque voluntatem eius atque impleret.

[4] prefata igitur mater eius, infirmitate corporis detenta febreque gravi correpta, mortua est. rex vero Didanus construxit ecclesiam, et dedicari fecit in honore Sancte Trinitatis et intemerate Virginis Marie Omniumque Sanctorum, in urbe Oxinefordia. venerabilis igitur Fritheswitha petiit patrem suum, videlicet Didanum regem, ut daret sibi ecclesiam. rex igitur dedit sibi ecclesiam. religiosa itaque virgo, post obitum matris sue, servire Deo studuit die noctuque vigiliis et orationibus semper intendens ita ut multotiens oblivisceretur cibum corporeum, totisque nisibus anhelaret cibum animarum. (…)

[5] beata igitur virgo rogavit patrem suum, dicens, 'O dulcissime pater, concede mihi ut sanctimonialem habitum adipisci merear et in templo Dei semper nomen eius laudare et benedicere.' rex autem Didanus, audiens propositum filie, gavisus est valde, et advocans quendam religiosum virum, Orgarum nomine, Lincoliensium pontificem,[2] fecit Deo filiam suam Fritheswitham consecrari. sacrate sunt itaque cum ea duodecim virgines, omnes nobili progenie. fecit itaque prefatus rex edificari domos que conveniunt sanctimonialibus, videlicet refectorium et dormitorium et claustra, virosque religiosos dedit ad serviendum eis. dedit etiam rex Didanus predia et villas Sancte Marie, tertiamque partem civitatis Oxinefordie, ad victum sanctimonialium. (…)

Translation: *Life of St Frideswide* (A)

[2] *So after the English people had been taught by St Augustine's preaching and been baptised, priests and deacons were appointed and churches built and consecrated all over that region. The number of believers was increasing and throughout the country of the English the Church was bringing forth new offspring. After a long period there was a king in Oxford whose name was Didanus. He took a wife called Sefrida who worshipped God and was clever at every type of good work, and since they both enjoyed the flower of youth the Lord granted them fertility. And so the venerable Sefrida conceived, and after the appropriate time had passed, she gave birth to a daughter. When he heard this, the king was very happy and ordered that*

---

2   This may be a reference to Eadgar, Bishop of Lindsey around 700.

she be reborn of water and the Holy Spirit. And when she was baptised they called her Fritheswith.

[3] *This daughter of the king was brought up with care. After five years she was entrusted to an older woman, called Ælfgiva, to be taught to read. The girl, whom God had already planned in advance as a future vessel of the Holy Spirit, concentrated so hard on learning her letters that within six months she knew all the psalms. And so the blessed Fritheswith, a virgin, made progress and grew, and with all her mind she strove to make herself loved by all and she always stayed within the church's boundary, as much as she could. She stored the sayings of holy Scripture in the chamber of her heart, often repeating this prayer, that she might be able to live in the house of the Lord all the days of her life, and might see and fulfil his will.*

[4] *Her mother, whom I mentioned, died after being confined with a physical infirmity and seized by a serious fever. King Didanus constructed a church and arranged for it to be dedicated in honour of the Holy Trinity and of the chaste Virgin Mary and all the saints, in the city of Oxford. Then the venerable Fritheswith asked her father, namely King Didanus, to give her the church. And so the king gave her the church. The devout girl, after her mother's death, devoted herself to serving God, spending all her time, day and night, in watching and praying, with the result that she often forgot bodily food, striving with all her might after spiritual food. (…)*

[5] *And so the blessed virgin asked her father, 'Dearest father, grant that I might be worthy to obtain a nun's habit and in God's temple always to praise and bless His name.' King Didanus, on hearing of his daughter's plan, was very pleased and, summoning a religious man named Orgar, the Bishop of Lincoln, he arranged for his daughter Fritheswith to be consecrated to God. With her were consecrated twelve virgins, all of noble birth. The king then arranged for buildings to be constructed which were suitable for nuns, namely a refectory and dormitory and cloisters, and he gave them religious men to serve them. King Didanus also gave estates and villages to Saint Mary, and a third part of the city of Oxford for the nuns' upkeep. (…)*

Frideswide seeks sanctuary at Bampton and Binsey after being harassed by the king

[12] surgens igitur beata virgo vocavit duas sanctimoniales secum virgines Deo dicatas, pervenientesque iuxta preceptum angelicum ad ripam Tamisie invenerunt naviculam, sedentemque iuvenem fulgentem angelico vultu, qui ita affatur virgines, 'Ingredimini in navim, virgines sacrate.' ingresse itaque in navim, in unius hore spatio venerunt ad villam que dicitur Bentonia, ducente Domino. egredientesque de navi, subito evanuit iuvenis ab oculis earum. beata igitur Fritheswitha cum suis virginibus, timens insidias nefandi regis, ingressa est in quodam nemore quod dicitur Benesia non longe a supradicta villa, inveneruntque ibi semitam que ducebat ad mansiunculam quam quondam fecerant subulci custodientes greges porcorum, coopertumque erat ex omni parte edera. In quam introivit sanctissima virgo cum suis virginibus, muniens se signaculo sancte crucis.

146 Twelfth Century

Translation: *Life of St Frideswide* (A)

[12] And so the blessed virgin got up and called two of the nuns who had been dedicated as virgins to God along with her, and when they reached the bank of the Thames as the angel commanded, they found a little boat and a young man seated in it, his face shining like an angel's. He addressed the virgins in this way: 'Climb into the boat, holy virgins.' And so they climbed into the boat, and in an hour they reached a village called Bampton, under the Lord's guidance. When they got out of the boat, the young man suddenly vanished from their sight. The blessed Fritheswith with her virgin companions, fearing an ambush from the wicked king, entered a wood called Binsey, not far from the village I mentioned, and there they found a path leading to a little cottage which some swineherds, looking after their herds of swine, had made at some point in the past, and it was covered all over with ivy. The most holy virgin went into it with her virgin companions, protecting themselves by making the sign of the holy cross.

B: *Vita B* (excerpts: chapters 2–3, 12, 15)

TEXT II.13B

Frideswide's early life and dedication to the monastic life

[2] anno itaque ab incarnatione Domini nostri Iesu Christi Regis omnium seculorum septingentesimo circiter vicesimo septimo, cum in effera gente Anglorum, que Brittanniam insulam invaserat, depopulaverat, dominatuique suo cruenta manu subiugaverat, verbum Dei effloruisset fructumque plurimum produxisset, subregulus quidam Didanus nomine, vir catholicus et omni morum honestate prestantissimus, civitatem que lingua Saxonica Oxenefordia denominatur, quod nos Latine Boum Vadum dicere possumus, incolatus sui frequentatione honestabat. hic nutu divino uxorem moribus suis congruam, Safridam nomine, accepit, de qua morum magis quam prediorum heredem suscepit, unicam videlicet filiam, quam fonte sacri baptismatis ablutam Fridesuuidam appellari precepit.

[3] transacto quippe quinquennio diligenti educatione, litterarum studiis erudienda traditur sub matrone cuiusdam admodum religiose disciplina, cui nomen Algiva. felicis quidem posteritatis quoddam quasi felicissimum presagium, in ipso eius discipline primordio adeo enituit, ut perspicuum foret omnibus quoniam mentem illius iamiam sibi habitaculum preelegerat Spiritus Sanctus. quis enim non obstupesceret quinquennem virgunculam in quinque fere mensibus psalmos Daviticos, qui centum quinquaginta sunt, didicisse, memorieque commendasse? (…)

Translation: *Life of St Frideswide* (B)

[2] *And so in about the 727th year since the Incarnation of our Lord Jesus Christ, the king of all ages, when among the wild English race which had invaded, devastated and subjugated the island of Britain to its domination, with bloody hands, the word of God had blossomed and produced a great deal of fruit, a certain minor king by the name of Didanus, a Catholic, outstanding for his honourable character, honoured with his regular residence the city named Oxeneford in the Saxon language but which we can call Boum Vadum (Oxen Ford) in Latin. By God's will he took a wife called Safrida, whose character made her suitable, by whom he had a child who inherited his character rather than his lands, namely an only daughter whom he ordered to be named Frideswide when she was washed in the spring of holy baptism.*
[3] *After she had been brought up carefully for five years, she was handed over to be taught the study of letters under the training of a very devout old woman called Algiva. In the very beginning of her training there shone forth some sort of very fortunate presage of a fortunate future, so that it was clear to all that the Holy Spirit had already chosen her mind as his dwelling. For who would not be amazed that a five-year old little girl had in about five months learned the psalms of David, all 150 of them, and knew them off by heart? (…)*

Frideswide seeks sanctuary at Bampton and Binsey after being harassed by the king
[12] Frideswida vero, gratias agens Deo, hylaris ab oratione surrexit duasque de sororibus suis secum assumens ad Thamesim usque pervenit et iuxta verbum angeli naviculam secus ripam repperit. quam ingresse, vident iuvenem in parte sedentem, habitu splendido vultuque venustissimo qui eas dulci demulcens affatu in naviculam collocavit. mira res, mirus impetus spiritus! sub unius hore spatio decem miliaria transferuntur et sub villa que Bentona dicitur exponuntur. exposite vero, nec navem nec itineris ducem uspiam conspiciunt. inventam ilico secus villam semitam pergunt et silvam non longe ab ea distantem ingrediuntur. sequentes autem semitam in profundum nemoris se protendentem, tandem mapale conspiciunt ad porcorum tutamen contra aeris intemperiem constructum sed multo iam tempore ab incolis derelictum, adeo ut hedera succrescente ex omni parte contectum occultato aditu ingredi volentibus negare videretur introitum. quod virgo cum suis ingressa sodalibus primum signo crucis munivit ac deinde qualiter ibidem Deo disponente manerent prout sibi oportunum videbatur statuit. (…)
[15] sed non virgo prudentissima sustinuit quoat adulationis procellosus favor vas olei e suis excuteret manibus, ut veniente Sponso non haberet unde lampadum suarum lumen informaret. unde et hominum pro facti magnitudine cum immani **Matt. 25** eam admiratione visere cupientium, laudes neuticam (-quam) sibi profuturas, fugere iudicavit utilius. convocatis igitur solitudinis sue consodalibus, 'Arbitror',

148 Twelfth Century

inquit, 'iam oportunum esse ut proprio appropinquemus cenobio. sorores namque nostre aut sollicite pro nobis, ut assolet, aut in absentia nostra in tristitie abyssum corruentes, a bono quod absit proposito fortasse destiterunt.' sic fatur, et naviculam preparatam cum sororibus conscendens, prepeti valde cursu ad predium civitati propinquum quod Buneseia dicitur, ope navigantium perducitur. e navi quippe progressa, locumque pervidendo permetiens, utile duxit tantillum a civitate defore, et dilecte quieti operam dare. quo et virginibus quas in cenobio dimiserat venire non esset onerosum, et civibus semper quod pro novitate stupeant querentibus minus aptum. erat in predicto predio locus multigenis arboribus consitus qui pro multitudine diversi generis spinarum lingua Saxonica Thornbiri nuncupabatur, solitarius siquidem et religioni aptissimus. in quo extemplo construxit oratorium, et quam plurima edificia sanctorum usibus competentissima. et quoniam fluminis alveus longius aberat, inoportunumque sibi videbatur quod sorores illuc usque ad hauriendum (aquam) procederent, fontem precibus impetravit qui nunc usque superest, plurimis prestans beneficia sanitatum potantibus. hic latere, hic dilecte quieti operam dare et hominum vitare frequentiam sperabat.

Translation: *Life of St Frideswide* (B)

[12] *Frideswide, giving thanks to God, got up cheerfully from her prayer and, taking two of her sisters with her, she went down to the Thames. Just as the angel told her, she found a little boat beside the riverbank. Getting into it, they saw a young man sitting in part of it wearing a shining robe and with the most attractive face. He soothed them with kind words and seated them in the boat. What a wonderful encounter! What a wonderful impulse of the spirit! Within an hour they had travelled ten miles and were put ashore near a village called Bampton. But when they got ashore they could see neither the boat nor their guide anywhere. They walked along a path they found near the village and entered a wood not far from it. Following the path, which led deep into the wood, they at last spotted a hut built to protect pigs against bad weather but abandoned by its inhabitants already long ago, so that it was covered all over with rampant ivy which concealed the entrance and seemed to deny entry to those who wished to go in. The virgin entered it with her companions and first made the sign of the cross for protection and then she decided that they would stay there, given that it seemed to be a suitable place, as God arranged. (…)* [15] *But the wise virgin did not allow the stormy approval of popular adulation to knock the oil jar out of her hands, which might mean that when the Bridegroom came she would have nothing to supply the light in her lamps. So when people, filled with huge admiration because of the greatness of her deed, desired to see her, she judged it more useful to flee their praise because it was of no benefit at all to her. So she summoned the women who shared her solitude and said, 'I think the time is right for us to move closer to our own monastery. For our sisters have perhaps given*

up – God forbid! – on their excellent plan, either because they are worried about us, as often happens, or they are falling into an abyss of sadness in our absence.' These were her words, and then she and her fellow sisters boarded the boat they had prepared, and very speedily, with the help of boatmen, reached the estate called Binsey, near the city. Leaving the boat they looked round and assessed the location and decided it would be useful to be a little way from the city, and to concentrate on the quiet life they loved. It would not be difficult for the virgins whom they had left in the monastery to come there, but less suitable for the townspeople, who were always looking for something new to marvel at. In this estate there was a place planted with many different kinds of trees which was called Thornbury in the Saxon tongue on account of the many thorn trees of various kinds, a remote place, certainly very well suited to the practice of religion. Here she immediately constructed an oratory and a number of buildings most suitable for the needs of the holy. And as the river channel was rather far away and she thought it was unsuitable for the sisters to have to go all the way there to draw water, she prayed and obtained a spring which still survives to the present day (i.e. St Margaret's Well), which provides health benefits to many who drink there. Here she hoped to remain concealed, to concentrate on the quiet life she loved and to avoid crowds of people.

Primary Sources and Related Texts

Blair, J. (ed.) (1987) 'Saint Frideswide Reconsidered', *Oxoniensia* 52: 71–127,
 including new editions of both versions: *Vita* A 93–101 (Latin 96–101); *Vita* B
 101–16 (Latin 103–16).
William of Malmesbury, *Gesta pontificum Anglorum* 4.178.
Miracles of St Frideswide, in *Acta sanctorum* for 19 October (*BHL* 3169).

Further Reading

Thompson, A. (1994) 'Shaping a saint's life: Frideswide of Oxford', *Medium
 Aevum* 63: 34–52.

Section II.14

Ælred of Rievaulx, *Letter Regarding the Nun of Watton Priory*

Date: c.1160.

This work survives in just three folios of a single Cambridge MS, namely CCC 139 (ff. 147r–149v), one of the most important post-Conquest manuscripts, containing among other things a unique version of Symeon of Durham's *History of the English and Danish Kings* (cf. Section II.11D). This account by Ælred seems to have been copied into the MS in the late 1160s, just a few years after the events recorded took place. It is sometimes referred to by the Latin title *De sanctimoniali de Wattun* or less specifically as *De quodam miraculo mirabili*.

Author: Ælred (1110–67) was the son of a priest but was given a classical education at Hexham and Durham before being attached to the court of King David I of Scotland, for whom he worked in an administrative and diplomatic capacity. In about 1134 he heard from Archbishop Thurstan of York (cf. Section II.11E) about the newly founded Cistercian monastery of Rievaulx, which he decided to join, taking with him his administrative and negotiating skills, which served him well when he became abbot, first of the daughter house, Revesby in Lincolnshire, and then of Rievaulx itself. Ælred also found time to write many works, mainly hagiographies, and spiritual writings, of which the most famous are the *De spiritali amicitia*, the *Speculum caritatis* and his many sermons.

Work: This brilliant but shocking short story, in the form of a letter to a friend but with something of the structure of Greek or Jacobean revenge tragedy and the flavour of a tale of the supernatural, is set in the double monastery of Watton near Beverley in Yorkshire, founded already in the seventh century but re-founded by Gilbert of Sempringham just a few years before these events. Focusing on the crime and punishment of a young girl, the work leaves the reader with much to ponder on, as to the course of events and the moral values of the human actions. On the face of it, it is an account of a miracle, but is there any saint involved? It can also be interpreted as a love story, or as the account of a rape followed by brutal revenge, as an admirable feminist act (but on whose part?) or as evidence of extreme devotion to Christ and to chastity. What is Ælred's own attitude to these events which he says he partly witnessed and partly heard about from reliable participants? Not only does he take account of the emotions of the characters, but he shows great psychological perceptiveness, imagination (in those scenes where no witnesses are present) and compassion, occasionally apostrophising the unnamed girl at the centre of the story. Certainly, the violent reaction to the love between a man and a woman is reminiscent of the exile of Eva from Wilton, as the result of her close friendship with Goscelin (Section II.3) and the castration of Abelard as the result of his relationship with Heloise. It is possible that Ælred's personal involvement in the incident recounted in this extract stimulated his writing of the *De institutione inclusarum*, about the female monastic life. Little has been omitted from the passage quoted below, because the account works so well as a complete text.

Linguistic points: The reader may gain the sense that each word within the balanced sentences is carefully chosen; there is much that is ambiguous, or viewed through the eyes of different protagonists at different moments, and the reader must therefore be careful when interpreting the narrative. The language (and citations) are largely biblical, and yet the atmosphere is often that of various genres of classical literature, with phrases such as *intempestae noctis silentio*, introducing the girl's vision, having an epic ring. Ælred uses wordplay and antithesis, as in *corripitur verbis, sed non corrigitur* and *dat signum praedae impiissimus praedo*. Indeed, antithesis is often essential to the story, bringing out the dangerously contrasting views of the protagonists, as in the way the young man and woman regard their relationship: *et ille stuprum meditabatur, illa vero postea dicebat, de solo cogitabat amore*. Note also the anguish of the threefold repetition of *egreditur*, in the highly rhetorical passage where the girl, starved of love, is torn between divine and human devotion. The use of *vir*, rather than a more precise object for the verb *abscidere* in describing the castration, is a euphemism.

TEXT II.14

Ælred addresses his friend on the importance of making God's miracles known
[1] miracula Domini et manifesta divinae pietatis indicia scire et tegere, portio sacrilegii est. quod enim esse potest praesentibus ad consolationem, ad aedificationem posteris, omnibus ad devotionem, indignum est cunctorum notitiae deperire. sed plerumque multorum nos terret ineptia, qui vel invidia tabescentes vel infidelitate languentes, de his quae bona sunt, vix de quoquam suis credunt oculis, ad credendum vero de quolibet ea quae mala sunt, levi tactu aurium inducuntur. hinc est quod rem mirabilem et nostris saeculis inauditam tibi potissimum, pater amantissime, credidi revelandam, cuius sancta simplicitas bene sentire de omnibus, de nullo absque certis indiciis sinistrum aliquid suspicari consuevit. nulla sit de verborum veritate cunctatio, cum ea quae dicenda sunt, ex parte propriis oculis viderim, omnia autem mihi tales personae retulerint, quas nec aetatis maturitas, nec spectata sanctitas, ulla sinerent ratione mentiri. (...)

Twelfth Century

Translation: Ælred, *The Nun of Watton Priory*

[1] *To know the miracles of the Lord and the clear indications of divine love and to conceal them has an element of sacrilege. For it is wrong for something that can be a consolation for those living now, a means of edifying those who live in the future, and an object of devotion to all, to escape everyone's notice. But often the stupidity of the majority deters us, for whether they are wasting away in envy or languishing in a lack of faith, they cannot believe their own eyes when it comes to things that are good, but are easily led to believe anything bad, even by the slightest gossip they may hear. That is why, dearest father, I thought I ought to reveal to you in particular a remarkable thing, unheard of in our time, since your holy simplicity tends to think well of all and not to have any suspicions of anything bad without definite proof. Let there be no doubt about the truth of my words, since what I have to tell I partly saw with my own eyes and everything was reported to me by people whose maturity and proven sanctity would never permit them to lie. (…)*

The child's arrival at Watton; she develops into a wilful young girl

[2] inter monasteria virginum quae vir venerabilis ac Deo dilectus, pater et presbyter Gillebertus per diversas Angliae provincias miro fervore construxit, unum in provincia Eboracensi situm est in loco qui aquis et paludibus septus ex re nomen accepit. dicitur enim Wattun, id est 'humida villa'.[1] qui quondam, ut refert **Bede, *HE* 5.3** in *Historia Anglorum* venerabilis presbyter Beda, magno sanctarum mulierum pollebat examine: ubi et beatus pontifex Joannes, puellam ob incautam sanguinis diminutionem fere desperatam, salubri tactu et oratione sanavit. (…) pontificante in ecclesia Eboracensi sanctae ac piae recordationis Henrico, puella quaedam quatuor ut putabatur annorum, ejusdem sancti patris precibus in eodem monasterio suscipitur nutrienda. quae mox ut infantilem excessit aetatem, cum puellaribus annis puellarem induit lasciviam. nullus ei circa religionem amor, nulla circa ordinem sollicitudo, circa Dei timorem nullus affectus. petulans illi oculus, sermo indecens, lascivus incessus. incedebat sacro tecta velamine, sed nihil tali dignum habitu praetendebat in opere. corripitur verbis, sed non corrigitur; urgetur verberibus, sed non emendatur. furabatur magistrarum oculis horas, ut vel indulgeret otio, vel signis inordinatis difflueret, aut vacaret fabulis, aut inutile aliquid aliis suaderet. disciplina ordinis premebatur, et ad exterioris hominis honestatem utcunque servandam cogebatur invita. omnia ei ex timore constabant, ex amore nihil. et jam nubilis facta, interioribus exteriora, otiosa quietis, seriis ludicra praeponebat.

---

1 An example of place-name etymology, referring to the English name of the site of the convent. Modern specialists have suggested other interpretations.

Translation: Ælred, *The Nun of Watton Priory*

[2] *Among the monasteries of virgins which the venerable father and priest Gilbert, dear to God, constructed with wonderful enthusiasm throughout various counties of England, there is one situated in Yorkshire in a place which takes its name from the fact that it is surrounded by waters and marshes, for it is called Watton, in other words, 'Wet Town'. It was once, according to the venerable priest Bede, in his History of the English, well known for the large number of holy women there, and it is where the blessed Bishop John (of Beverley) used a healing touch and prayers to cure a girl who was desperately ill as the result of an unexpected loss of blood. (…) While Henry (i.e. Henry Murdac, Archbishop of York 1147–53), of holy and pious memory, was bishop of the church of York, a girl thought to be four years old was received into this same monastery to be brought up there, at the request of this holy bishop. As soon as she had passed infancy, she began to behave in a naughty way, as girls often do. She had no love of the religious life, no concern for the monastic order, no feeling of fear of God. She had an insolent look, her speech was rude, and she walked in a provocative manner. She wore a holy veil but nothing she did was worthy of this garment. She was reproached by words but not reformed; she was punished by beatings but not corrected. She wasted hours in front of her teachers, either doing nothing or frittering away time making forbidden signs or spending time on stories or persuading others to do something useless. She was suppressed by the discipline of the rule and was forced against her will to observe outward decency to some extent, but she did everything out of fear, nothing out of love. And when she reached marriageable age she preferred outer things to inner, laziness to peace and silly things to serious.*

The girl falls in love with a young monk; their secret assignation
[3] accidit autem ut fratres monasterii quibus exteriorum commissa est cura, quidpiam operis facturi ingrederentur monasterium feminarum. quod illa perpendens accessit propius, et curiosius ipsorum opera contemplabatur et vultus. erat inter eos adolescens caeteris formosior facie et aetate nitidior. injecit in illum oculos misera, ipse vero intendebat in eam. aspiciunt se oculo blandiori; et mox serpens tortuosus, utriusque pectus ingrediens, laetiferum insibilat per cuncta vitalia virus. res primum nutibus agitur, sed nutus signa sequuntur. tandem rupto silentio conserunt de amoris suavitate sermonem. accendunt se mutuo, spargunt utrinque seminaria voluptatis, libidinis incentiva. et ille stuprum meditabatur, illa vero postea dicebat, de solo cogitabat amore. interim coalescunt affectus. sed ut sibi liberius colloquerentur vel se fruerentur uberius, de loco vel tempore in unam colere sententiam. abjicientibus itaque arma lucis, nox placebat obscurior. **Rom. 13:12** publicum fugitantibus locus secretior gratus habetur. dat signum praedae impiissimus praedo, ut ad sonitum lapidis quem vel in parietem vel tectum aedis in qua pausare consuevit, infelix se jactaturum promisit, de ejus adventu certissima egrederetur ad eum. (…) et tu, infelix, quid agis? quid cogitas? quid tam attente aures ad tegulas erigis? ubi timor, ubi amor, ubi illius sanctae congregationis

154   Twelfth Century

reverentia? ubi beati pontificis qui te huic monasterio tradidit suavis memoria? nihil horum a tanto te revocat scelere. deletis his omnibus, solus in corde turpis vivebat affectus. surgis misera, pergis ad ostium. conantem egredi vis divina repellit; tentans iterum, sed nihil profecisti. regressa modicum beatae virgini solitas vigilias cum duodecim lectionibus celebrasti. quid ultra tibi facere debuit Chris-

Isa. 5:4   tus et non fecit? o mira cordis excaecatio! quid denuo moliris egressum? (…) quid plura? heu! egreditur. claudite aures, virgines Christi, oculos operite. egreditur Christi virgo, adultera post modicum reditura. egreditur, et quasi columba

Hos. 7:11   seducta non habens cor mox accipitris excipitur unguibus. prosternitur, os ne clamaret obstruitur, et prius mente corrupta carne corrumpitur. experta voluptas nefas compulit iterare.

Translation: Ælred, *The Nun of Watton Priory*

[3] *It happened that the brothers of the monastery, whose duty it was to look after external matters, entered the women's monastery with the intention of carrying out some task. When the girl learned of this, she came closer and watched with curiosity their work – and their faces. Among them was an adolescent who was more good-looking than the others, with a youthful radiance. The poor girl turned her eyes on him, and he stared at her. They gave each other appreciative looks and immediately the insidious snake, penetrating the hearts of both, instilled with a hiss the deadly virus through their innermost parts. At first it was a matter of nods, but then signs followed the nods and finally the silence was broken and they talked of the sweetness of love. They inflamed each other, sprinkling the seeds of desire from both sides, the incitements to lust. And while the young man thought about sex, she – as she later said – was only thinking of love. Meanwhile their feelings merged and they agreed on a time and place so as to be able to speak together more freely or enjoy each other more fully. Abandoning the protection of light, they chose to meet at night because it was darker. A more secret place is preferable to those who shun a public one. The wicked predator gave a sign to his prey: at the sound of a stone that the unfortunate man promised he would throw on the wall or roof of the building where she slept, she should be sure he had arrived and come out to him. (…) And you, poor girl, what are you doing? What are you thinking? Why are you listening so carefully to the roof tiles? Where is your fear, your love, where your reverence for that holy congregation? Where is the sweet memory of the blessed bishop who entrusted you to this monastery? None of these things restrains you from such a crime. This was all forgotten, and all that was left in your heart was a shameful feeling. Miserable girl! You get up, you go to the door. The divine power pushes you back as you attempt to go out; you try again, but without success. You went back for a while and celebrated the customary vigils for the blessed Virgin with the twelve readings. What more should Christ have done for you that he did not do? What amazing blindness of heart! Why do you try to go out once again? (…) What next?*

Oh no! She goes out. Cover your ears, virgins of Christ, close your eyes! She goes out, a virgin of Christ; after a short while she will return an adulteress. She goes out and like a dove, deceived and without sense, she is caught by the hawk's talons. She is thrown down on the ground, her mouth covered so that she cannot cry out, and she who has already been corrupted in her mind, is corrupted in the flesh. The pleasure, once experienced, forced a repetition of the crime.

The aftermath: the nuns suspect, the young man flees, the girl reveals she is pregnant
[4] cum haec saepius agerentur, sorores sonitum quem crebro audiebant admirantes fraudem suspicabantur. illa maxime patuit suspicioni, cujus mores omnibus solebant esse suspecti. fuga etiam juvenis suspicionem adauxit. cum enim concepisse se adultero prodidisset, timens ne et ipse proderetur, relicto monasterio ad saeculum ire perrexit. tunc matronae sapientiores puellam conveniunt. illa ulterius celare non valens confitetur excessum. stupor autem apprehendit omnes quae audiebant verbum. exarsit mox zelus in ossibus earum, et aspicientes se mutuo, complosis manibus[2] irruunt super eam: extractoque ab ejus capite velo, aliae tradendam flammis, aliae vivam excoriandam, aliae impositam stipiti suppositis carbonibus assandam putarunt. fervorem adolescentium compescebant matronae. attamen spoliatur, extenditur, etiam absque ulla miseratione flagellis atteritur. praeparato ergastulo vincitur, intruditur; singulis pedibus duo annuli cum suis catenulis inducuntur; quibus duae non parvi ponderis catenae insertae, quarum una immani trunco clavis infigitur, altera per foramen extracta foris sera concluditur. sustentatur pane et aqua; quotidianis opprobriis saturatur. interea tumens uterus evolvit conceptum. o quantus tunc erat luctus omnium! quanta praecipue virginum lamenta sanctarum, quae suo timentes pudori unius crimen in omnibus metuunt impingendum, etiam quasi jam expositas se omnium oculis illudendas, quasi omnium traditas dentibus corrodendas sentirent! flebant omnes, flebant singulae; nimioque dolore succensae iterum irruunt in captivam. et nisi maturiores conceptui pepercissent, vix aliquando ab ejus poena quiescerent. illa universa haec mala patienter sustinet, majoribus se dignam clamat tormentis, credere se tamen caeteras pro ejus infidelitate nihil mali passuras.

Translation: Ælred, *The Nun of Watton Priory*

[4] *When this happened on several occasions, the sisters, wondering about the sound which they heard repeatedly, started to suspect deception. This girl was particularly under suspicion as it was her behaviour they all usually suspected. Their suspicion increased when the young man fled, for when the girl had revealed to the adulterer*

---

2   This action was a sign of extreme emotion, usually of sorrow or alarm; cf. Eadmer, *V.Osw.* 37: *complosis manibus lugubres eiulatus emittunt.*

that she was pregnant, he was afraid he would be betrayed and so he left the monastery and set off to return to secular life. Then the older and wiser women summoned the girl to a meeting. No longer able to conceal, the girl confesses her transgression. Shock seizes all the women who are listening to what she says. Immediately their zeal blazes up in their bones: looking at each other they smack their hands together in shock and rush upon her. Pulling the veil off her head, some say she should be thrown onto the flames, others that she should be flayed alive, others that she should be placed on a stake and roasted over the hot coals. The older women put a stop to the wild ideas of the younger ones. But she is nevertheless stripped, stretched out and mercilessly whipped. A prison is prepared and the girl is tied up and shoved into it; two rings with little chains are put one on each foot and two heavy chains are inserted into them, one of which is nailed to a huge log while the other is drawn through a hole and held by the bar on the door. She is kept alive on bread and water and each day she is served a surfeit of abuse. Meanwhile her swelling womb reveals her pregnancy. How great was the grief of all! How loud the laments especially of the holy virgins who, fearing for their modesty, were afraid that the one girl's sin would be imputed to them all; it was as if they already felt that they were being publicly ridiculed, as if they were being handed over to be gnawed at by everyone's teeth. They wept together, they wept singly and worked up by their excessive grief they fell once more upon the captive girl. And if the more mature women had not protected the foetus, they would have gone on punishing her almost forever. She endured all these terrible things with patience, crying out that she deserved worse torments, but she still believed that the other women would not suffer any bad effects as the result of her faithlessness.

The nuns plan harsh punishments for the girl and the young man

[5] deliberant[3] quid de his agendum. si expelleretur, in omnium hoc redundare infamiam, imminereque non parvum omnium animabus periculum, si destituta solatio mater cum sobole mortis discrimen incurreret; si servaretur, partum non posse celari clamabant. tunc una: 'Optimum', inquit, 'est, ut nequissimo juveni sua meretrix adulterino fetu gravida commendetur, ejusque dimittatur curae cujus consensit nequitiae.' ad haec infelix: 'Si hoc vobis poterit esse remedio, licet sciam hoc mihi futurum exitio, ecce adolescens nocte illa, hora illa, in loco nostrae iniquitatis conscio, mihi sicut promisit occurret; vestri tunc erit arbitrii me tradere illi. sicut fuerit voluntas in coelo, sic fiat.' continuo rapiunt verbum de ore ejus. jam jamque spirantes ultionem in juvenem, quaerunt ab ea de omnibus veritatem. confitetur illa, affirmans vera esse quae dixerat. tunc magister congregationis, ascitis quibusdam e fratribus, rem aperit. jubetque ut nocte illa unus tectus velamine caput, designato loco sederet, alios occulte praesentes adesse ut

1 Mcc. 3:60

---

3   Compare CL *deliberare*, as here, from *libra*, 'to deliberate', with LL *deliberare*, from *liber*, from which English derives 'to deliver' both in its sense of 'to free' and 'to deliver, hand over', for which see Section II.45D and Section II.49C.

venientem exciperent, attrectatumque fustibus vinctum tenerent. dixit et factum est ita. adolescens quid cum sua ageretur ignorans, non solum mente, sed etiam habitu saecularis, advenit. et ardens libidine, mox ut velamen aspexit, sicut equus et mulus quibus non est intellectus, irruit in virum quem feminam esse putabat.[4] **Ps. 31:9** at hi qui aderant, amarum ei cum baculis conficientes antidotum, conceptam febrem exstinguunt. res defertur ad virgines. mox quaedam zelum Dei habentes etsi non secundum scientiam, ulcisci cupientes virginitatis injuriam, petunt **Rom. 10:2** a fratribus juvenem sibi per modicum tempus dimitti, quasi secretum aliquid ab eo cogniturae. susceptus ab eis, prosternitur ac tenetur. adducitur quasi ad spectaculum, illa malorum omnium causa: datur ei in manibus instrumentum, ac propriis manibus virum abscidere invita compellitur. tunc una de astantibus, arreptis quibus ille fuerat relevatus, sicut erant foeda sanguine in ora peccatricis projecit. vides quo zelo urebantur aemulatrices pudicitiae, insectatrices immunditiae, Christi prae omnibus amatrices. (…) abscisus fratribus redditur, mulier in carcerem confusa retruditur.

Translation: Ælred, *The Nun of Watton Priory*

[5] *They debated what they should do. They cried out that if she was expelled, it would redound to the bad reputation of them all, and that there would be great risk to their souls if the mother was stripped of consolation and incurred death with her child; but if they kept them, the pregnancy could not be concealed. Then one of them said, 'The best is to hand over to that wicked young man this slut with his bastard offspring, so that the worry can be left to him, since it was he who consented to the wicked act.' The poor girl responded, 'If this might remedy things for you, although I know it will destroy me, look, the young man will be here tonight, this very hour in fact, to meet me as he promised in the place where our wicked act took place. Then you have the power to hand me over to him. May it happen as heaven wills it.' They immediately seized on her words and panting with desire to take revenge, now, this very moment, on the young man, they demand from her the truth on every point. She confesses, confirming that what she had said was true. Then the head of the community took some of the brothers into his confidence and revealed the situation to them. He gave orders that on that night one of them, his head covered with a veil, should sit in the appointed place and that the others should be there in secret to receive the man when he came; they should hold him fast, tie him up and beat him with cudgels. His orders were carried out precisely. The young man, unaware of what they were doing with his girlfriend, arrived, not only dressed but also thinking in a secular manner. On fire with lust, as soon as*

---

4 For confusion as to gender, cf. Section II.20 and the scene of the chancellor disguised as a woman on Dover Beach and wittily described as *cancellarius cancellaria*.

he caught sight of the veil, like a horse or mule devoid of reason, he fell upon the man he believed to be a woman. But the men who were there soon extinguished his fever, giving him a bitter medicine for it with their sticks. This was reported to the nuns. Immediately some of them, filled with zeal for God, even if it was not clever zeal, desiring to take revenge for the offence done to virginity, asked the brother to let them have the young man for a short while, pretending that they wanted to find out some secret from him. When they got hold of him they threw him to the ground and held him. Then the girl was also brought there, as if to watch some spectacle, she who was the cause of these terrible things. An instrument was put in her hands and she was forced against her will to castrate the man with her own hands. Then one of the women standing close by snatched what had been taken from him and hurled them, just as they were, foul with blood, in the girl's face. You see with what zeal they blazed, committed as they were to chastity, these lovers of Christ above all things. (…) The man, castrated, was handed back to the brothers; the woman, distraught, was pushed back into prison.

Two visions and a miraculous birth

[6] hactenus misera mulier, infelicitatis tuae historiam scripsimus, deinceps quemadmodum super te Christi stillaverit misericordissima pietas stylo prosequamur; **Rom. 5:20** ubi enim abundavit peccatum superabundavit et gratia. (…) jam infans in ventre vivebat, lac ex uberibus ubertim fluebat; adeo etiam uterus intumescere videbatur ut putaret geminos parituram. plumbeus color oculos circumfundit, faciem pallor invadit, et nunc vacuatis humore mamillis, post modicum solito liquore replebantur. jam eam vix capiebat ergastulum, jam partui necessaria praeparantur. cavent quantum possunt ne fletus infantis partum prodat. et ecce intempestae noctis silentio cum se misera sopori dedisset, videt in somniis assistere sibi pontificem, per quem, ut praediximus, in eodem monasterio divinis est officiis mancipata, amictum pallio, et monachico habitu subinduto. cumque severiori oculo aspiceret in eam: 'Quid est, inquit, quod me quotidie maledicis?' negavit illa nimio timore perterrita. tunc sanctus: 'Verum est,' ait, 'cur negas?' videns se deprehensam mulier, respondit: 'Vere domine, quia tu me huic monasterio tradidisti, in quo invenerunt me tanta mala.' ad haec antistes: 'Tibi hoc potius imputato quae peccata tua necdum ut oportet patri spirituali propalasti. sed vide ut quam citius poteris confitearis, et hoc a me suscipiens in mandatis, ut hos psalmos quotidie Christo decantes.' et mox ei numerum et nomen psalmorum describens disparuit. evigilans illa, et animaequior facta, visionem et psalmos commendat memoriae. sequenti vero nocte cum jam putaretur paritura, et amara videretur horae illius exspectatio, plus tamen timeretur ipsa partus editio, iterum venerabilis pontifex in somniis apparuit, desperanti duas secum adducens venusta facie mulieres. accessit ad miseram praesul, et super genua sua capite ejus supinato, pallio quo amiciebatur vultum operuit, increpans eam et dicens: 'Si fuisses vera confessione purgata, cerneres manifeste ea quae aguntur. nunc quidem senties beneficium, sed modum et

qualitatem facti scire non poteris.' erecta post modicum videt mulieres infantem, ut sibi videbatur, candido coopertum linteo in ulnis ferentes discedentem sequi pontificem, expergefacta nihil ponderis sensit in ventre. attrectat manu corpus, et totum vacuum reperitur.

Translation: Ælred, *The Nun of Watton Priory*

[6] *Thus far, poor girl, it is the story of your misfortune that we have been writing, but now we will continue by showing how Christ's merciful dew dropped down upon you. For grace is even more abundant where sin abounds. (…) Now the baby was alive in her womb, milk flowed in abundance from her breasts, and her womb also seemed to swell so much that you would have thought she was going to give birth to twins! A leaden colour suffused the area around her eyes, pallor spread over her face and now that her little breasts were emptied of moisture, they were filled after a while with the customary liquid. Now there was hardly room for her in the tiny prison, now the necessary preparations were made for the birth. They took all possible precautions so that the baby's cries should not reveal the birth. And now, in the silence of deepest night, when the wretched girl had succumbed to sleep, she saw in a dream, standing beside her, the bishop who, as we mentioned, had assigned her to the divine offices in that very monastery; he was clothed in a bishop's cloak but was wearing a monk's habit underneath. He looked at her severely and said, 'Why do you curse me every day?' The girl was terrified and denied it. Then the holy man said, 'It is true; why do you deny it?' Realising that she was trapped, the girl replied, 'Truly, my lord, it is because you handed me over to this monastery where I have suffered such terrible things.' The bishop's response to this was, 'You should rather blame yourself for this, since you have not yet confessed your sins as you should to your spiritual father. But make sure you confess as soon as possible and accept my orders, so that you chant these psalms for Christ every day.' And then he noted down the name and number of the psalms for her and vanished. When she awoke, she felt calmer and committed to memory the vision and the psalms. The following night, it was thought that she was going to give birth. The wait for that hour seemed bitter and yet the birth itself seemed even more frightening. It was then that the venerable bishop appeared once again in a dream bringing with him to the desperate girl two women of attractive appearance. The bishop went close to the poor girl and laid her head on his lap and covered her face with the cloak he was wearing; he reproached her, saying, 'If you had been purified by a true confession, you would see clearly what is happening. Now you will feel the benefit but you will not be able to understand what is done, or how it happens.' After a while she sat up and saw the women apparently carrying in their arms the baby, covered in a white linen cloth; they followed the bishop as he departed and when she woke up she could feel no weight in her stomach. She touched her body with her hand and found that it was completely empty.*

160 Twelfth Century

The miracle is investigated by the nuns and by Ælred, who reports to his friend

[7] mane autem facto, adsunt custodes, respicientes in illam, vident detumuisse uterum, vultum puellarem, ne dicam virginalem, induisse decorem, oculos perspicaces, plumbeum deposuisse colorem. et mox quasi propriis non credentes oculis: 'Quid est hoc?', inquiunt. 'An tot sceleribus tuis et hoc addidisti, ut tuum interficeres infantem?' statimque angustum ergastulum illud in quo catenata sedebat evertunt. nihil ibi latere pateretur angustia carceris, supellectilis vilitas, tenuitas stramentorum. 'Et quid,' inquiunt, 'misera, num peperisti?' ipsa se nescire respondit. 'Et ubi est', aiunt, 'infans tuus?' respondit 'Nescio.' referensque visionem, nihil amplius se scire professa est. non credunt rei novitate perterritae. palpant uterum, et ecce tumori successerat tanta gracilitas, ut dorso ventrem adhaerere putares. tentant ubera, sed nihil humoris eliciunt ex eis. nec tamen parcentes, fortius premunt, sed exprimunt nihil. per singulos artus currunt digiti, explorant omnia; sed nullum signum partus, nullum conceptus indicium repererunt. vocantur aliae, et post illas aliae, et unum inveniunt omnes. sana omnia, munda omnia, pulchra omnia; nihil tamen decernere, nihil sine patris auctoritate judicare praesumunt. adhuc tenetur in vinculis, adhuc circa pedes ferrum durat, strident catenae. duos divinae ministros clementiae sibi advenisse conspexit: et unus catenam qua arctius stringebatur arrepta socio comitante discessit.[5] sorores vero advertentes mane deesse catenam mirantur, causam inquirunt, audiunt, sed parum credentes scrutatae sunt omnem supellectilem ejus, sed nihil inveniunt. paulo post inveniunt de ejus pedibus unum de vinculis cecidisse. quod invenientes integrum, et in ea firmitate qua fuerat fabrilibus instrumentis, pedibus ejus innexum, admiratae sunt valde. sed quid multis morer? eodem ordine a caeteris absoluta, pes tantum unus uno compede tenebatur. interea sanctus pater adveniens, cum evidentibus signis ac veracissimis testibus omnia didicisset, sicut est mirae humilitatis homo, meam parvitatem de his omnibus credidit consulendam. veniens igitur ad nostrum monasterium servus Christi, cum mihi aperuisset secreto miraculum, rogat ut ancillis Christi meam non negarem praesentiam. libens annui. cum vero tam me quam itineris mei socios humanissime ac jucundissime suscepisset, imus ad cubiculum illud intra cubiculum ubi illa in suo antro sedebat inclusa. adsunt plures tam virgines quam viduae aevo jam graves, sapientia et discretione pollentes, spectabiles sanctitate et in regularibus disciplinis multum exercitatae. quae cum nobis omnia retulissent, coepi compedem propriis manibus attrectare, intellexique quod nec ab aliis nec ab ista sine Dei virtute posset absolvi. quaedam autem nec dum timore deposito quaesierunt a nobis, si alia ei vincula deberent imponi. prohibui, importunum hoc asserens, et quoddam infidelitatis indicium. exspectandum potius, et sperandum quod is qui eam liberavit ab aliis, ab hoc quoque quo adhuc tenetur eripiet. patre praeterea

---

5 *unus … discessit*: this is indeed the reading of the MS (f. 149v), but something seems awry with the construction.

praecipiente, relata sunt nobis multa aeterna memoria digna, quibus manifeste datur intelligi, quia beneplacitum est Domino super timentes eum, etiam in eis qui sperant super misericordia ejus. igitur commendantes nos sanctis orationibus **Ps. 146:11** earum, et eas prout potuimus verbo Domini consolantes, ad nostrum monasterium regressi sumus, laudantes et glorificantes Dominum in omnibus quae audi- **Luke 2:20** vimus et vidimus, et sanctae virgines narraverunt nobis. post paucos dies allatae sunt nobis viri illius venerabilis litterae, quibus significavit nobis, illum quo eam invenimus vinctam compedem cecidisse, et quid facto deinceps opus esset meam indignitatem consuluit. ego vero inter alia haec pauca verba rescripsi: Quod Deus **Acts 10:15** mundavit tu ne commune dixeris, et quam ipse absolvit, tu ne ligaveris. **Matt. 16:19**

[farewell] haec ideo tibi charissimo meo longe ab his partibus remoto maxime scribendum putavi, ut et invidis occasionem tollerem, et tamen Christi gloriam non tacerem. vale.

Translation: Ælred, *The Nun of Watton Priory*

[7] *When morning came, the guards appeared, and looking at her they saw that her stomach was no longer swollen, and that her face had taken on a girlish, not to say virginal beauty, her eyes were bright and she had lost the leaden colour. It was as if they could not believe their eyes and they immediately said, 'What is this? Have you added the murder of your own child to all your other crimes?' Straightaway they turned upside down the narrow little prison where the girl was sitting in chains. But the prison was too small, the contents too frugal, the straw bedding too thin to allow anything to be concealed. 'Well, you wretched girl, so then you haven't given birth?' She replied that she did not know. 'So where is your baby?' She replied, 'I do not know.' She told them of the vision and admitted that she knew nothing further. They did not believe her and were terrified by these strange events. They felt her stomach and noted that the swelling had been replaced by such slimness that you would have thought her stomach was stuck to her back. They touched her breasts but could squeeze no moisture out of them. Not sparing her, they squeezed harder but expressed nothing. Their fingers ran over each of her limbs, they explored everything, but could find no indication of a birth, no sign of a foetus. The other nuns are summoned, and after them, others, and they all find the same thing. Everything is restored, everything clean, everything lovely; but they dared not decide anything or make a judgement without the father's authority. The girl was still held in chains, the iron still remained round her feet, the chains still clanked. She saw two servants of God's mercy coming towards her and one of them removed the chain which bound her more tightly, and then left with his companion. The sisters were amazed when they noticed the next morning that the chain was missing and asked why. When they were told, they could not believe it and looked carefully around all the contents of the room but could find nothing. A little later they found one of the chains that had fallen from her feet. They found it unbroken and as strong as it had been when*

162 Twelfth Century

the blacksmith's tools made it, but not connected to her feet, and they were totally amazed. To cut a long story short, the girl had been freed from the rest in the same way, and only one foot was held by the fetter. Meanwhile the holy father arrived and when he had heard the whole story supported by clear proof and most reliable witnesses, as he is a man of marvellous humility, he thought that he had to ask advice about all this from me, insignificant though I am. So the servant of Christ came to our monastery and when he had confidentially revealed the miracle, he asked me to agree to come to the servant-women of Christ, and I willingly consented. When he had welcomed me and my travelling companions with the greatest kindness and joy, we went to that little room inside the room where the girl was sitting enclosed in her cell. There were many women present, both virgins and widows of advanced years, wise and full of discernment, of outstanding holiness and very experienced in the discipline of the Rule. When they had given us a full report, I began to handle the fetter with my own hands and I understood that it was impossible for it to have been undone by the other women or by the girl without God's power. Some of the women were still afraid and asked me if they should put other chains on the girl, but I forbade them, saying that it was inappropriate and rather a sign of lack of faith. I advised them to wait instead and to hope that he who had freed her from the other chain would release her also from the one which still held her. On the orders of the father, many things were told to us which deserve to be remembered eternally, by which we were clearly granted understanding that 'God is pleased with those who fear him and also with those who hope for his mercy.' And so, commending ourselves to their holy prayers and consoling them with the word of the Lord as far as we were able, we returned to our monastery, praising and glorifying the Lord in all that we had heard and seen and that the holy virgins had told us. A few days later a letter arrived for us from that venerable man in which he indicated to us that the fetter which we had found binding her had fallen off, and he asked my advice, unworthy though I am, as to what he should do next. Amongst other things I replied with this brief message: 'Do not call anything impure which God has made clean, and what he has released, do not bind.'

I thought I should write these things to you, my dearest friend, far removed as you are from these parts, particularly so as not give our enemies an opportunity to attack us, and yet not to remain silent about the glory of Christ. Farewell.

Primary Sources and Related Texts

De quodam miraculo mirabili in *Aelredi Rievallensis opera historica et hagiographica*, ed. D. Pezzini, *CCCM* 3, Turnhout, 2017. With introduction.

Ælred of Rievaulx, *De institutione inclusarum* (1162): two English versions, ed. J. Ayto and A. Barratt, EETS 287, Oxford, 1984.

Walter Daniel, *The Life of Ailred of Rievaulx*, ed. M. Powicke, OMT, Oxford, 1950, repr. 1978.

The Book of St Gilbert, ed. R. Foreville and G. Keir, OMT, Oxford, 1987.

Thomas Becket, *Letter* 44. In early 1165 Becket writes from exile, urging Gilbert to reform his order, after *maxima scandala*.

For examples of nuns unhappy in convents, or placed there for dubious reasons, see e.g. thirteenth-century Curia Regis Rolls, e.g. *CurR* 5.183–6; 9.66; 11 no. 1022.

For Joan of Leeds' dramatic escape from her convent in York to Beverley in 1318, see *The Register of William Melton, Archbishop of York*, 1317–40, vol. 6 (2011: 17–18); cf. The Northern Way: the Archbishops of York and the North of England (1305–1405), a research project of the University of York.

For checks by bishops on the physical state of nuns with the intention of finding evidence of moral corruption, see Matthew Paris, *Chronica majora* 5.226–7 on Bishop Grosseteste's visitations to convents in 1251: the use of words such as *quasi effractarius* and *tyrannis* imply that the bishop's behaviour was over-intrusive.

Further Reading

Boswell, J. (1988) *The kindness of strangers: the abandonment of children in western Europe from late antiquity to the Renaissance*, London.

Burton, J. (1999) *The monastic order in Yorkshire 1069–1215*, Cambridge.

Constable, G. (1978) 'Ælred of Rievaulx and the nun of Watton: an episode in the early history of the Gilbertine order' in *Medieval women*, ed. D. Baker, Oxford.

Elkins, S. K. (1988) *Holy women of twelfth-century England*, Chapel Hill, NC.

Love, R. (2013) '"Torture me, rend me, burn me, kill me!" Goscelin of Saint-Bertin and the depiction of female sanctity' in *Writing women saints in Anglo-Saxon England*, ed. P. Szarmach, Toronto.

Section II.15

William Fitzstephen, *A Description of London* (excerpts from his *Life of St Thomas*)

Date: c.1173.

Although it was originally composed as part of Fitzstephen's *Life of St Thomas*, the *Description* came to be copied separately, occurring in the following MSS: Bodleian MSS Douce 287 and Marshall 75; BL MS Lansdowne 398 and Corporation of London Record Office MS Cust. 6.

Author: Little is known about William Fitzstephen (died c.1190) except what he tells the reader in the prologue to his *Life of St Thomas*: he was a cleric who served Becket as an administrator for many years, both while Becket was chancellor and later archbishop. He accompanied him to the Council of Northampton in 1164 but did not go into exile with him; he was, however, with Becket in Canterbury Cathedral and witnessed his murder on 29 December 1170 (for which see Section II.16B(b)).

Work: Fitzstephen's *Life of St Thomas* is considered the best of the approximately ten contemporary biographies of Becket, all of which have historical and literary value. The work starts with a mention of Thomas' family, as the son of middle-class London citizens, neither practising usury nor trading professionally, but living respectably off their own income. There follows a series of vivid depictions of contemporary life, suggesting that William is writing as one who is intimately familiar with the city, and particularly of childhood pursuits there. The lively picture of children skating on the frozen marshland around Moorfields is renowned. For the topographical description of London and the Tower of London, cf. e.g. the description of Harfleur in 1415 (Section II.41B(a)).

Linguistic points: It is clear that William must have been trained in classical literature: his work contains allusions to such classical authors as Horace, Virgil and Persius, as well as to Christian writers; he is agile in adapting the quotes to fit grammatically into his text. He uses such rare words and technical terms as *ammentatus* and *paralogizare*. The description of London and the Thames (5–6) resembles the classical topos of *locus amoenus*, reinforced by the references to Virgil's *Georgics*. However, it also contains some words that are not classical, namely *foresta* (here probably referring to Waltham Forest) and *molinorum versatiles rotae*, i.e. 'water-mill wheels'. Although the common medieval term for

Shrove Tuesday was *Carniprivium* (as heralding the beginning of Lent, when meat-eating was not allowed), Fitzstephen provides the only attestation in BML of *Carnilevaria*, the ancestor of the modern word 'Carnival'.

TEXT II.15

Introductory description of London
[2] inter nobiles orbis urbes, quos fama celebrat, civitas Londoniae, regni Anglorum sedes, una est, quae famam sui latius diffundit, opes et merces longius transmittit, caput altius extollit. felix est aeris salubritate, Christiana religione, firmitate munitionum, natura situs, honore civium, pudicitia matronali; ludis etiam quam jocunda, et nobilium est foecunda virorum: quae singula semotim libet inspicere.
[3] ibi siquidem emollit animos hominum clementia caeli: non ut sint 'in Venerem putres', sed ne feri sint et bestiales, potius benigni et liberales. (...)   **cf. Pers. Sat. 5.58**

Translation: William Fitzstephen, *A Description of London*

[2] *Among the noble and famous cities of the world, London, the capital of the kingdom of the English, is the one that extends its reputation more widely, exports its wealth and merchandise further and raises its head higher than any other. It is fortunate in its healthy climate, Christian religion, strong fortifications, natural location, the high esteem of its citizens and the modest behaviour of its women. It is attractive for its sports and it produces many outstanding men. I would like to examine each of these things separately.*
[3] *There the mild weather certainly softens people's minds, not in a way that corrupts them with sex but which prevents them being wild and bestial, and instead makes them kind and generous. (...)*

St Paul's Cathedral and its rivalry with the archdiocese of Canterbury
[4] est ibi in ecclesia beati Pauli episcopalis sedes:[1] quondam fuit metropolitana, et adhuc futura creditur, si remeaverint cives in insulam; nisi forte beati Thomae martyris titulus archiepiscopalis et praesentia corporalis dignitatem illam Cantuarie, ubi nunc est, conservet perpetuam. sed cum utramque harum urbium sanctus Thomas illustraverit, Londoniam ortu, Cantuariam occasu; ipsius sancti intuitu, cum justitiae accessu, habet altera adversus alteram quod amplius alleget. sunt etiam quod ad Christianae fidei cultum pertinet, tum in Londonia tum in

---

1   St Paul's had been founded by King Æthelberht of Kent in 604 for the Bishop of the East Saxons (i.e. Essex); for William the Conqueror's grant to St Paul's, see Section II.2B.

166 Twelfth Century

suburbio tredecim majores ecclesiae conventuum, praeter minores parochianas centum viginti sex.

Translation: William Fitzstephen, *A Description of London*

[4] *The bishop there has his seat in St Paul's church: it was once the metropolitan church and it is still thought that it will be so again if citizens should return to the island; unless perhaps the title of the blessed martyr and archbishop Thomas and his bodily presence should preserve that high status for Canterbury, where it is at the moment. But since St Thomas has illuminated both these cities, London by his birth, Canterbury by his death, each city can make a claim against the other, with regard to the standing of the saint and the addition of justice. As regards the practice of the Christian faith, there are also thirteen larger conventual churches, both in London and in the suburbs, apart from the 126 smaller parish churches.*

The Tower of London, the river Thames and the suburbs
[5] habet ab oriente arcem palatinam maximam et fortissimam, cujus et area et muri a fundamento profundissimo exsurgunt, caemento cum sanguine animalium temperato: ab occidente duo castella munitissima; muro urbis alto et magno duplatis heptapylae portis intercontinuante, turrito ab aquilone per intercapedines. similiterque ab austro Londonia murata et turrita fuit; sed fluvius maximus piscosus, Thameses, mari influo refluoque, qui illac allabitur, moenia illa tractu temporis abluit, labefactavit, dejecit. item sursum ab occidente palatium regium eminet super fluvium eundem, aedificium incomparabile, cum antemurali et propugnaculis, duobus millibus ab urbe, suburbio frequenti continuante.
[6] undique extra domos suburbanorum horti civium, arboribus consiti, spatiosi et speciose, contigui habentur. item a borea sunt agri, pascuae, et pratorum grata planities, aquis fluvialibus interfluis; ad quas molinorum versatiles rotae citantur cum murmure jocoso. proxime patet ingens foresta, saltus nemorosi, ferarum latebrae, cervorum, damarum, aprorum, et taurorum sylvestrium. agri urbis **Virg. *Georgics*** sationales non sunt jejunae glareae, sed pingues Asiae campi 'qui faciant laetas **1.1; 2.517** segetes', et suorum cultorum repleant horrea 'Cerealis mergite culmi'. (...)

Translation: William Fitzstephen, *A Description of London*

[5] *On the east side it has a very large and strong royal castle, whose area and walls rise up from deep foundations which were made very strong with cement mixed with animal blood; on the west side are two well-fortified smaller castles, while a lofty and thick city wall runs between the seven double-layered gates, with towers at intervals on the north side. London was similarly walled and turreted on the south side, but a great tidal river full of fish, the Thames, glides by it on this side and*

washed away those walls in the course of time, undermining them and causing them to collapse. Again, upstream to the west, a royal palace looms over the same river, an incomparable building, with a barbican and bulwarks, two miles from the city, where the densely populated suburbs extend.

[6] On all sides outside the suburban homes are the citizens' gardens, close together and planted with trees, spacious and lovely. Again to the north there are fields and pastures and open areas of meadow, with streams flowing between them which set the water-mill wheels turning with a cheerful murmur. Close by, there extends a huge forest, with wooded groves, lairs of wild animals, forest stags and does, wild boar and bulls. The city's arable fields are not stony and barren but resemble the fertile fields of Asia which produce joyful crops and fill the farmers' barns with sheaves of Ceres' corn. (…)

The three principal schools at the churches of St Paul's, Bow and Martin-le-Grand: syllabus and competitions

[9] in Londonia tres principales ecclesiae scholas celebres habent de privilegio et antiqua dignitate. plerumque tamen favore personali alicujus notorum secundum philosophiam plures ibi scholae admittuntur. diebus festis ad ecclesias festivas magistri conventus celebrant. disputant scholares, quidam demonstrative, dialectice alii; hi rotant enthymemata, hi perfectis melius utuntur syllogismis. quidam ad ostentationem exercentur disputatione, quae est inter colluctantes; alii ad veritatem, ea quae est perfectionis gratia. sophistae simulatores agmine et inundatione verborum beati judicantur; alii paralogizant. oratores aliqui quandoque orationibus rhetoricis aliquid dicunt apposite ad persuadendum, curantes artis praecepta servare, et ex contingentibus nihil omittere. pueri diversarum scholarum versibus inter se conrixantur; aut de principiis artis grammaticae vel regulis praeteritorum vel supinorum, contendunt. sunt alii qui in epigrammatibus, rhythmis et metris utuntur vetere illa triviali dicacitate; licentia Fescennina socios suppressis nominibus liberius lacerant; loedorias jaculantur et scommata; salibus Socraticis sociorum, vel forte majorum, vitia tangunt; vel mordacius **Hor.** *Epist.* 1.18.82, dente rodunt Theonino audacibus dithyrambis.[2] auditores 'multum ridere parati, *Odes* 4.2.10 ingeminant tremulos naso crispante cachinnos'. **Pers.** *Sat.* 3.86-7

Translation: William Fitzstephen, *A Description of London*

[9] In London the three main churches have schools, famous for their ancient status and privilege. However, other schools are usually also permitted there through the personal favour of one of those notable for their philosophy. On feast days, at the patronal churches, the masters convene gatherings. The scholars dispute, some using

---

2 Cf. Lanfranc in *Letter* 19 (1073), who apparently uses the incorrect form *Theodino*.

168 Twelfth Century

demonstrative rhetoric, others dialectic; some argue using enthymemes, others perfect syllogisms with greater skill. Some are trained for display in competitive disputations, others for truth, that which is the grace of perfection. The sophistic tricksters are judged successful in the arrangement and flood of words, while others deceive with false arguments. Some orators occasionally say something in their rhetorical speeches that is persuasive, trying to observe the rules of the art and not to leave out any of the possibilities. Boys from different schools hold poetry competitions against each other and argue either about the rules of grammatical art or the rules of the past or supine. There are others who in rhythmical or metrical epigrams employ the traditional gibes of the trivium: with Fescennine licence they freely abuse their friends, without mentioning any names; they hurl abuse and insults; they allude to the vices of their friends or perhaps of their elders with Socratic wit or use audacious dithyrambs to criticise them rather caustically with Theon's tooth. The audience are ready to laugh a lot, and redouble their quivering guffaws while wrinkling their noses.

Fast food provision, excessive drinking and the risk of fires

[10] singulorum officiorum exercitores, singularum rerum venditores, singularum operarum suarum locatores, quotidiano mane per se sunt locis distincti omnes, ut officiis. praeterea est in Londonia supra ripam fluminis, inter vina in navibus et cellis vinariis venalia, publica coquina. ibi quotidie pro tempore est invenire cibaria, fercula, assa, pista, frixa, elixa, pisces, pisciculos, carnes grossiores pauperibus, deliciores divitibus, venationum, avium, avicularum. si subito veniant ad aliquem civium amici fatigati ex itinere, nec libeat jejunis exspectare ut novi cibi emantur et coquantur, 'dent famuli manibus lymphas, panesque canistris' interim ad ripam curritur, ibi praesto sunt omnia desiderabilia. quantalibet militum vel peregrinorum infinitas intrans urbem, qualibet diei vel noctis hora, vel ab urbe exitura, ne vel hi nimium jejunent, vel alii impransi exeant, illuc, si placet, divertunt, et se pro modo suo singuli reficiunt. que se curare volunt molliter, acciperensem vel Afram avem vel attagenem Ionicum non quaerant, appositis quae ibi inveniuntur deliciis. haec equidem publica coquina est, et civitati plurimum expediens, et ad civilitatem pertinens. hinc est quod legitur in Gorgia Platonis juxta medicinam esse cocorum officium, simulacrum et adulationem quartae particulae civilitatis. (...)

[12] non puto urbem esse in qua sint probabiliores consuetudines, in ecclesiis visitandis, ordinatis Dei honorandis, festis feriandis, eleemosynis dandis, in hospitibus suscipiendis, in desponsationibus firmandis, matrimoniis contrahendis, nuptiis celebrandis, conviviis ornandis, convivis hilarandis, etiam in exsequiis curandis et cadaveribus humandis. solae pestes Londoniae sunt immodica stultorum potatio et frequens incendium.[3] (...)

Virg. Aen. 1.702 (marginal reference to line "emantur et coquantur...")

Plato, Gorgias 464d (marginal reference to line "is juxta medicinam...")

---

3 Cf. the fire regulations of 1212 in Section II.47B.

Translation: William Fitzstephen, *A Description of London*

[10] *Each weekday morning the practitioners of all the different trades, the various salesmen, the various hired workmen are spread out all over the city according to their jobs. In addition there is in London, on the banks of the river, a public kitchen, amidst the wines for sale in the ships and the wine cellars. There, every day, according to the season, it is possible to find meals, dishes, roast, baked, fried and boiled food, fish, little fish, meat of inferior quality for the poor, of better quality for the rich, of venison, birds and little birds. If one of the citizens has an unexpected visit from some friends, tired out from their travels, and they do not want to wait, hungry, for fresh foods to be bought and cooked, 'let servants bring water for their hands and bread for the baskets'. Meanwhile someone runs down to the riverbank, where everything you could want is available. However many soldiers or travellers enter the city, or are just about to leave, at any hour of the day or night, they can go there, if they like, and each can get however much food they can manage, so that the former do not have to remain hungry for long and the others do not have to leave without dinner. Those who wish to eat fine food need not seek for a hawk or African bird or Ionian game birds, once the delicacies found here have been put before them. This, then, is the public kitchen which is so useful for the city and appropriate for a civilised life. That is why it is written in Plato's Gorgias, that a chef's profession is closest to that of the medic, an image and emulation of the fourth part of refinement.* (…)*
[12] I do not think there is a city in which there are more praiseworthy traditions when it comes to visiting churches, honouring God's ordained, celebrating feast days, giving alms, welcoming guests, confirming betrothals, contracting marriages, celebrating weddings, decorating banquets, making guests happy, as well as arranging funerals and burying corpses. The only things that plague London are stupid people's excessive drinking and frequent fires.* (…)

Sports and games, including skating on the ice
[13] Londonia pro spectaculis theatralibus, pro ludis scenicis, ludos habet sanctiores, repraesentationes miraculorum quae sancti confessores operati sunt, seu repraesentationes passionum quibus claruit constantia martyrum. praeterea quotannis, die quae dicitur Carnilevaria, ut a ludis puerorum Londoniae incipiamus (omnes enim pueri fuimus), scholarum singuli pueri suos apportant magistro suo gallos gallinaceos pugnaces, et totum illud antemeridianum datur ludo puerorum vacantium spectare in scholis suorum pugnas gallorum. post prandium vadit in suburbanam planitiem omnis juventus urbis ad lusum pilae celebrem.[4] singulorum studiorum scholares suam habent pilam; singulorum officiorum urbis exercitores suam fere singuli. majores natu, patres, et divites urbis,

---

4 Cf. *Historia Brittonum* 41: *pilae ludum faciebant pueri*, a ninth-century reference to children's ball games; for *HB* see Section I.30.

170 Twelfth Century

in equis spectatum veniunt certamina juniorum, et modo suo juvenantur cum juvenibus; et excitari videtur in eis motus caloris naturalis contemplatione tanti motus et participatione gaudiorum adolescentiae liberioris. (…)

[16] in festis tota aestate juvenes ludentes exercentur arcu, cursu, saltu, lucta, jactu lapidum, amentatis missilibus ultra metam expediendis, parmis duellionum. **Hor. *Odes*** puellarum Cytherea ducit choros usque imminente luna, et pede libero pulsatur **1.4.5, 1.37.2** tellus.

[17] in hieme (…) cum est congelata palus illa magna, quae moenia Urbis aquilonalia alluit, exeunt lusum super glaciem densae juvenum turmae. hi ex cursu moto captato citatiore, distantia pedum composita, magnum spatium latere altero praetenso perlabuntur; alii quasi magnos lapides molares de glacie sibi sedes faciunt; sessorem unum trahunt plurimi praecurrentes, manibus se tenentes. in tanta citatione lubrici motus aliquando pedibus lapsi cadunt omnes proni. sunt alii super glaciem ludere doctiores, singuli pedibus suis aptantes et sub talaribus suis alligantes ossa, tibias scilicet animalium, et palos ferro acuto supposito tenentes in manibus; quos cum aliquando glaciei illidunt, tanta rapacitate feruntur, quanta avis volans, vel pilum balistae. interdum autem magna procul distantia, ex condicto duo aliqui ita ab oppositis veniunt; concurritur, palos erigunt, se invicem percutiunt; vel alter vel ambo cadunt, non sine laesione corporali; cum post casum etiam vi motus feruntur ab invicem procul, et qua parte glacies caput excipit, totum radit, totum decorticat. plerumque tibia cadentis vel brachium, si super illud ceciderit, confringitur; sed aetas avida gloriae, juventus cupida victoriae, ut in veris praeliis fortius se habeat, ita in simulatis exercetur.

Translation: William Fitzstephen, *A Description of London*

[13] *Instead of theatrical spectacles and stage shows, London has sacred plays, reenactments of miracles that holy confessors have performed or representations of the sufferings and death that have made martyrs famous for their endurance. Moreover, every year, on the day known as Shrove Tuesday – to begin with children's games in London (for we have all been children) – each schoolboy brings to his master fighting cocks and the boys have the whole morning off to watch their cocks fighting in school. After lunch all the city's young men go to the open areas in the suburbs for the popular ball game. The scholars of each school have their own ball and the practitioners of almost all the different city trades each have their own ball. The older people, fathers and the wealthy citizens come on horseback to watch the young people's competitions and in their own way they join the young men in youthful behaviour; and it seems that their natural heat is stimulated into motion by watching so much movement and by participating in the enjoyment of youth's greater freedom. (…)*

[16] *On feast days throughout the summer the boys train in archery, running, jumping, wrestling, shot-put, wildly slinging missiles over the boundary, fighting with shields. Cytherea (Venus) leads the girls in dances until the moon appears, their feet freely tapping the beat on the ground.*

[17] *In winter (…) when the great marsh lapping at the walls on the north side of the city is frozen over, young people go out in close-packed gangs to play on the ice. Some take a run to get up speed and slide sideways, bracing themselves, across a large area, over a pre-arranged distance; others make themselves seats out of ice blocks like large millstones: several of them run ahead, holding on with their hands, pulling the one who is sitting on it. They all occasionally slip over and fall headlong when going so fast on the slippery surface. There are others who are more skilful at playing on the ice: they each fit bones, in other words animals' shin bones, to their feet, tying them under their soles, and hold poles with sharp metal tips in their hands, and when they strike these alternately on the ice they go as fast as a flying bird or crossbow bolt. Sometimes two of them come from a great distance, running at each other from opposite ends, lift up their poles and strike each other: either one or both fall over and are injured. Even after they fall they are carried by the force of their movement far from each other and wherever their head hits the ice, it is all scraped and grazed. It often happens that if someone falls he breaks his arm or leg, but youth is a time avid for glory and passionately keen to win, and just as it displays great courage in real battles, so also in pretend ones.*

Primary Sources and Related Texts

William Fitzstephen, *Life of St Thomas*, RS 67.3 (1877).

Stenton, F. (1934) *Norman London: an essay*, Historical Association Leaflets, repr. New York, 1990.

Historical descriptions of London, allegedly founded by Brutus after the fall of Troy and called Trinovantum, are given also by Geoffrey of Monmouth (*HRB* 22, 44) and by Gervase of Tilbury in his *Otia imperialia* (2.17). The foundation of London is also picked up in the *Letter* of 1301 from Edward I to the pope (Section II.31). A contemporary description of London to be compared with that of Fitzstephen is the satirical picture included by Richard of Devizes some twenty years later in his *Chronicle of the Reign of King Richard I* (Section II.18).

Further Reading

'Medieval sport' in *The Oxford handbook of sports history* (2017), ed. R. Edelman and W. Wilson, Oxford.

Haskins, C. H. (1927) 'The Latin literature of sport', *Speculum* 2.3: 235–52.

172 Twelfth Century

Keene, D. (2008) 'Text, visualisation and politics: London 1150–1250', *TRHS* 18: 69–99.

Murphy, J. (2005) 'The teaching of Latin as a second language in the twelfth century' in *Latin rhetoric and education in the Middle Ages and Renaissance*, Aldershot.

*Orme (1976).

Scattergood, J. (1996) 'Misrepresenting the city: genre, intertextuality and William FitzStephen's *Description of London* (c.1173)' in *Reading the past: essays on medieval and Renaissance literature*, Dublin.

Section II.16

Thomas Becket
A: Correspondence between Thomas Becket and the Empress
Matilda (excerpts: *Letters* 40 from Thomas and 49 from Matilda)
B: The Murder of Becket in Canterbury Cathedral: Two Eyewitness
Accounts (excerpts from the Lives of St Thomas (Becket) by
Edward Grim and William Fitzstephen)

A: Correspondence between Thomas Becket and the Empress Matilda (excerpts: *Letters* 40 from Thomas and 49 from Matilda)

Date: A(a): Letter 40 (December 1164); A(b): Letter 49 (July/August 1165)

See the introduction to the OMT edition for an account of the large number of
MSS.

Authors: Thomas Becket (c.1120–70) was born in London, the son of a merchant
(see Section II.15). He seems to have gained more education from the household
of the baron Richer, lord of L'Aigle (whose brother Geoffrey died in the wreck of
the White Ship, for which see Section II.11C) than from his schooling. His education led to work as a clerk, and he moved swiftly up from the household of Archbishop Theobald to become royal chancellor in 1154 for the newly crowned Henry
II, with whom he formed a close relationship. After Theobald's death in 1161, Henry decided to appoint Becket to succeed Theobald as Archbishop of Canterbury,
in the belief that Becket would support the king's political aims. Becket, however,
had his own agenda. Relations with the king became increasingly acrimonious,
as Becket failed to support the king's desire to reduce the Church's jurisdiction.
Becket went into exile in November 1164 after he clashed with Henry at the Council of Northampton, shortly before the letter excerpted here was written. Many
attempts to reconcile the king and the archbishop were made over the following
years. However, within a month of Becket's return to England in December 1170,
he was murdered in Canterbury Cathedral, a deed apparently prompted by the
king himself. A number of members of Becket's close entourage, including John
of Salisbury, William Fitzstephen and Herbert of Bosham, wrote biographies of
him after his death. The influence of Becket and his commitment to the freedom of the Church is seen even in the production of the Magna Carta, with its
opening clause on the king's obligation to preserve the liberties of the Church
(cf. Section II.25).

174 Twelfth Century

Matilda (1102–67) was the daughter of Henry I and Matilda, the sister of King David of Scotland. By the time her brother William was killed in the disaster of the White Ship (Section II.11) in 1120, she had been married to the future Holy Roman Emperor, Heinrich V. Trained for royal duties from a very early age, she acted as regent when necessary and became an expert in diplomacy between Church and state. When Heinrich died in 1125 she returned to England as her father's sole heir. It is at about this time that William of Malmesbury dedicated his *History of the English Kings* to the young *imperatrix* (*GR* 1, prefatory epistle). William describes her (*GR* 5.438) thus: *exhibebat patrem fortitudine, matrem religione; contendebat in ea pietas justitiae* ('she displayed her father's courage and her mother's devotion; in this woman piety vied with justice'). She was then married to Geoffrey of Anjou, and to them was born the future King Henry II in 1133. On the death of Henry I, however, it was her cousin Stephen who rushed to claim the English throne, and despite a good deal of support and military success, Matilda never managed to become queen of England, though she was accorded the title *Anglorum Domina* and coins were issued in her name. During the civil war between her and Stephen, in 1142, Matilda escaped from Oxford over the frozen Thames to Wallingford Castle. In 1148 she returned to Rouen in Normandy, but remained closely involved in British and European politics. She initially opposed the election of Becket as Archbishop of Canterbury, but when Becket went into exile in 1164 she attempted to mediate between him and her son, now Henry II of England, because she valued the freedom of the Church more highly than the king's wishes. However, despite her skills as a negotiator, she failed to bring Becket and Henry together. She died in 1167, having accomplished a vast amount as a politician, negotiator, benefactor and literary patron.

Work: Becket sent a letter to Matilda to ask for her assistance in persuading Henry II to bring about peace in the Church rather than oppressing the churches in England by attempting to reduce their powers. His letter and Matilda's response, given here, offer a rare example of correspondence between a powerful man and woman; with these may be compared the important letters between Matilda's mother of the same name and her spiritual mentor, Becket's predecessor Anselm, written some sixty years previously. The collection of Thomas Becket's correspondence is vast. Matilda's extant correspondence consists of seven other letters from her and five to her from papal, episcopal and royal correspondents.

Linguistic points: Becket's letter is grandiloquent, full of antitheses and biblical allusions. God is present throughout. There is no hint of a close relationship with the king – indeed the letter is extremely impersonal and stiff, as if the thought of Henry, and his recent treatment of Becket at Northampton, was still painful. Matilda's letter is in sharp contrast – more direct, conciliatory, practical and personal. She tells Becket that Pope Alexander III has asked her to mediate. She reminds Becket of the king's love for him and how he owes his high position to the king. She does not, however, tone down her son's accusations against Becket

II.16 | Thomas Becket   175

(*totum suum regnum ... adversus eum turbastis*), and her advice to Becket is blunt (*unum ... vobis veraciter dico ...*). While Thomas implies that the king needs the *humilitas* of the great men of old, Matilda repeats the word, telling him clearly that it is he who needs a large helping of the same. In Letter 41 of Becket's correspondence, the prior of Rouen recounts how, when the empress receives a letter, she asks the prior to read it to her in Latin and to expound it in French: this is likely to have been the normal procedure.

TEXT II.16A(a)

Letter 40: *Thomas to the Empress Matilda regarding her son, King Henry II's oppression of the Church*

[address] THOMAS Cantuariensis archiepiscopus, MATHILDI imperatrici.

gratias agimus Deo, qui nobilitatem vestram insignibus virtutis magis illustravit quam generis:[1] et quam sanguine clarissimam extulit in orbe Romano, bonis operibus clarificare non desinit in mundo. nam ab Oriente in Occidentem magnum est nomen vestrum in Domino, et eleemosynas vestras narrant ecclesiae sanctorum. quamvis enim Deo plurimum placeant subsidia temporalium, quae ei erogatis in membris suis, ei tamen minus placere non credimus sollicitudinem pacis et libertatis ecclesiasticae, quam tanto, ut fama est, zelatis affectu, ut cum Apostolo dicere valeatis: 'Quis infirmatur, et ego non infirmor? Quis scandalizatur, et ego non uror?' unde nos, qui ratione humanitatis et beneficii vestri merito **2 Cor. 11:29** nos vobis obnoxios esse recolimus, pro salute vestra, et filii vestri gloria, temporali pariter ac aeterna, de pace Ecclesiae fiducialius loquimur in auribus vestris, rogantes attentius, et obsecrantes in Domino, quatenus eum diligentius conveniatis, ut ea devotionis sedulitate pacem procuret Ecclesiae, qua sibi, haeredibus suis et terris suis per merita sanctorum pacem Dei desiderat procurari. nam unde plurimum contristamur, divulgatum est ab Oriente usque in Occidentem, quod ecclesias regni sui intolerabiliter affligit, et exigit ab eis inaudita quaedam et inconsueta. (...) non placent Deo sacrificia de rapina, nisi forte Patri placere possit, ut ei Filius immoletur. si resipuerit, Pater misericordiarum adhuc est promptus **2 Cor. 1:3** ad veniam: procul dubio judicium facturus sine misericordia in eos, qui non exercent misericordiam. potens est, et potentes potenter punit. terribilis, et aufert **Ps. 75:12–13** spiritum principum, ut fortioribus instet fortior cruciatus. tetendit arcum suum, **Sap. 6:9** et paravit illum, et in eo posuit vasa mortis, jaculaturus in brevi, nisi sponsam **Ps. 7:13–14**

---

1   Cf. the lines from one of the epitaphs for Matilda written by Arnulf of Lisieux (*PL* 201.199D) in which he addresses her as *regis mater ... et regibus orta Mathildis | ... egregia virtutum laude coruscans | fortunam generis vicerat et tori* ('Matilda, mother of a king and sprung from a line of kings, ... in the illustrious reputation of her outstanding virtues exceeded the fortune her family and marriage gave her').

176 Twelfth Century

suam, pro cujus amore mori dignatus est, liberam esse permiserint, et privilegiis ac dignitatibus, quas sanguine suo ei comparavit in cruce, sustinuerint honorari. debetis autem, si placet, in eo revocando, et matris diligentiam adhibere, et dominae auctoritatem: ut quae ei regnum et ducatum multis laboribus acquisistis, et ad eum haereditaria successione jura transmisistis, quorum occasione nunc premitur et conculcatur Ecclesia, proscribuntur innocentes, et pauperes intolerabiliter affliguntur. nos quod possumus pro salute vestra et illius, animo libenti facimus, Dei misericordiam precibus, quibus possumus, jugiter implorantes: fiducialius oraturi, si pace ecclesiis reddita ad auctorem et benefactorem suum Deum prompta devotione redierit. nec pudeat eum coram Deo humiliari per poenitentiam, cum antiquis regibus, quorum memoria in benedictione est, nihil magis ad gloriam ascribatur, quam poenitentiae titulus, legis divinae zelus, veneratio sacerdotii, et fidelissima virtutum custos, humilitas. talibus enim hostiis **Hebr. 13:16** David, Ezechias, Josias, et Constantinus Domino placuerunt, et gloriam assecuti **Exod. 17:16** sunt apud homines a generatione in generationem.

Translation: Thomas Becket, *Letter to Empress Matilda*

THOMAS Archbishop of Canterbury, to Empress MATILDA.

We give thanks to God, who has honoured your nobility with the insignia of virtue rather than of birth; and she whom He has exalted to the heights of nobility of birth in the Roman world He does not cease to honour with good works in the world. For from east to west your name is great in the Lord and the churches of the saints tell of your charitable giving. For although the support of temporal things pleases God greatly, which you grant to Him in His members, yet we do not believe that He is any less pleased by your commitment to the peace and freedom of the Church, which, so it is said, you are passionate about, so that you can say with the Apostle, 'Who is weak and I am not weak? Who stumbles and I do not burn with indignation?' And so we who are aware that we are rightly indebted to you as the result of your kindness and generosity, for the sake of your salvation and the glory of your son, both his temporal and eternal glory equally, are speaking loyally to your ears about the peace of the Church, begging and beseeching you in the Lord to urge him earnestly to procure peace for the Church by means of that assiduous devotion by which he desires to procure God's peace for himself, his heirs and his lands by the merits of the saints. What particularly saddens us is that the rumour goes from east to west that he is putting intolerable pressure on the churches of his kingdom, demanding from them unheard-of amounts, to which they are not accustomed. (...) God is not pleased with sacrifices from plunder, unless perhaps God could be pleased that His Son was sacrificed. If he (the king) should come to his senses, the Father of mercies is still ready to forgive, but He will undoubtedly pronounce judgement without mercy on those who do not practise forgiveness. He is powerful and punishes the powerful with power. He is terrifying and takes away the spirit of the princes so that a stronger torment may oppress the strong. He stretched his bow and prepared it and put instruments of death in it, ready to shoot His arrow in a short while, unless they allowed His bride, for whose love He thought fit to die, to go free, and unless they permitted her to be honoured with the privileges and honours which He gained for her by His blood on the cross. But you ought, if it pleases, to restrain him with the care of a mother and the authority of a powerful woman, since it was you who acquired for him a kingdom and a dukedom by many efforts, and transferred to him hereditary rights of succession, as the result of which the Church is now oppressed and trampled upon, innocent people are outlawed and the poor are intolerably afflicted. We are gladly doing what we can for your well-being and his, continually imploring the mercy of God by all possible prayers; we will pray with greater confidence, if once peace is returned to the churches, he returns to God, his author and benefactor, with ready devotion. Nor should he be ashamed to be humbled before God by penitence, since the ancient kings, whose memory is blessed, have nothing greater accorded them than the title of penitence, a passion for the divine law, veneration of the priesthood, and the most faithful humility, guardian of the virtues. For by means of such sacrifices, David, Hezekiah, Josiah and (Emperor) Constantine pleased the Lord and gained glory among men from generation to generation.

TEXT II.16A(b)

Letter 49: *The Empress Matilda to Thomas, warning him to act with restraint if he wishes for reconciliation*

[address] THOMAE Cantuariensi archiepiscopo MATILDIS imperatrix.

mandavit mihi dominus papa, et in remissionem peccatorum meorum injunxit, quatenus de pace et concordia inter filium meum regem et vos reformanda intromitterem, et vos ipsum eidem reconciliari satagerem. inde etiam, sicut scitis, me requisistis. unde majore affectione tam pro honore Dei, quam pro honore sanctae Ecclesiae rem istam incipere et tractare curavi. sed multum grave videtur regi, et baronibus suis, atque consilio, sicut vos dilexit, et honoravit, atque dominum totius regni sui, et omnium terrarum suarum constituit, et in majorem tandem honorem, quem habebat in tota terra sua, vos sublimavit, ut de caetero vobis securius debeat credere, praecipue cum asserant quod totum suum regnum, quantum potuistis, adversus eum turbastis, nec remansit in vobis, quin ad eum exhaeredandum pro viribus intenderitis. eapropter mitto vobis fidelem et familiarem nostrum Laurentium archidiaconum, ut per eum sciam voluntatem vestram super his omnibus, et cujusmodi animum vos habetis erga filium meum, et qualiter vos continere volueritis, si contigerit, quod petitionem meam et precem

178 Twelfth Century

de vobis ad plenum exaudire voluerit. unum quoque vobis veraciter dico, quia nisi per humilitatem magnam, et moderationem evidentissimam, gratiam regis recuperare non poteritis. verumtamen quid super hoc facere volueritis, nuntio proprio, et litteris vestris mihi significate.

Translation: Empress Matilda, *Letter to Thomas Becket*

To Thomas, Archbishop of Canterbury, the Empress Matilda (sends greetings).

The lord pope has charged me and ordered me, for the remission of my sins, to intervene to restore peace and concord between my son the king and you and to attempt to reconcile you to him. As you know, you also asked me about that matter. And so I have taken care to set this matter in motion and to deal with it with great affection both for God's honour and for the honour of the holy Church. But the king and his barons and his council consider it a very grave matter, since he loved you and honoured you and appointed you as the lord of his whole kingdom and of all his lands and finally promoted you to the highest position he had in all his lands, so that he should henceforward believe you more confidently, especially since they allege that you have stirred up his whole kingdom against him, to the best of your abilities, and that you are pretty much doing your best to disinherit him. For this reason I am sending to you our loyal and close friend, the archdeacon Laurence, so that I may know from him your wishes on all these matters and what your attitude is to my son, and how you wish to act, if it should happen that he is willing to listen in full to my petition and the request from you. One thing I must tell you honestly: you will not be able to regain the king's grace except by great humility and very obvious restraint. Anyway, please let me know by means of my personal envoy and your letters what you wish to do in this matter.

Primary Sources and Related Texts

The correspondence of Thomas Becket, Archbishop of Canterbury, 2 vols, ed. A. Duggan, OMT, Oxford, 2000.
William of Malmesbury, *Historia novella*.
Gesta Stephani.

Further Reading

Chibnall, M. (1991) *Empress Matilda: queen consort, queen mother and lady of the English*, Oxford.
*Tyler (2017).

B: The Murder of Becket in Canterbury Cathedral: Two Eyewitness Accounts (excerpts from the Lives of St Thomas (Becket) by Edward Grim and William Fitzstephen)

Date: B(a): 1171–2; B(b): 1173–4.

Grim's version survives in numerous MSS, but as a complete work only in three British Library MSS: MS Arundel 27, MS Cotton Vespasian E.x and MS Cotton Vitellius C.xii. In the case of Fitzstephen's *Life of St Thomas*, there are in fact two versions of the Life, version B including many extra passages, many of them critical of King Henry II. Version A, which may be the earlier version, exists only in Bodleian MS Douce 287, of the twelfth century, and in the fifteenth-century BL MS Lansdowne 398, part 1.

The murder of Archbishop Thomas Becket in Canterbury Cathedral on 29 December 1170 greatly affected contemporaries. This shocking episode engendered about ten Lives of Becket, most of which were written soon after Becket's death: from John of Salisbury's short account in a letter written as soon as early 1171, to that of Herbert of Bosham, dating from the 1180s. These Lives were written for the most part by people who had worked with Becket in different capacities and who were able to give an eyewitness account of various episodes in his life, including his murder, at which Edward Grim, Benedict of Peterborough and William Fitzstephen were present, while William of Canterbury and John of Salisbury fled the scene in terror. Herbert of Bosham was a devoted companion of Becket for many years, being one of the few who accompanied him into exile in the 1160s. Although Herbert was not present at the murder, he gives an account of it in Book 6 of his Life. These literary accounts occasionally draw on each other, but each is distinctive in style and detail. Herbert of Bosham's version, and his related work, the neglected *Liber melorum*, an allegory of Becket's life in musical terms, are particularly original, with their lengthy digressions and theological interpretations of Thomas' life, but their complexity and prolixity make them less suitable for inclusion in an anthology. These writers supplemented their eyewitness accounts with oral tradition as well as references to Becket's correspondence. The Life by Edward Grim, who only joined Becket's entourage near the end of the archbishop's life, is the earliest of the biographies. The Life by William Fitzstephen is regarded as containing the most interesting details about Thomas, drawing on William's long service with Becket, but was in fact less influential than that of Grim. In 1198–9 an influential composite text of these various Lives was produced, known as the *Quadrilogus*, which was translated into English in the thirteenth century. Thomas' cult status was assured not only by these works but also by the miracles associated with him from the time of his death, some of which were recorded by Benedict of Peterborough and William of Canterbury. As a result of the miracles and the cult that quickly developed at Canterbury, Becket was canonised unusually soon after his death, on 21 February 1173.

180 Twelfth Century

Work: Here two excerpts, full of drama and urgency, from the longer murder accounts within the Lives of Becket by the secular clerks Edward Grim and William Fitzstephen have been selected for literary comparison. Despite the differences between these two versions, which are arguably the best accounts of the murder, they both focus in detail on the events in Canterbury Cathedral immediately before the murder, portraying them in terms of the similarities with Christ's arrest and trial on the day of His crucifixion, as in the Gospel of John, chapters 18–19. As the murderous knights approach with noise and violence, Becket stands firm, rejecting his friends' attempts to persuade him to hide somewhere in the vast cathedral and remaining calm but also provocative (especially in Grim's version) when faced with his enemies.

Linguistic points: These authors both create well-crafted accounts of Becket's life, and in these excerpts, showing the knights closing in on Becket, they both use antitheses to contrast Becket and his attackers as powerfully as possible, together with quotations (Grim more from the Bible, Fitzstephen also from classical poetry). Grim uses more religious imagery (e.g. sheep and wolves, the red and white flowers associated with martyrdom and innocence) while both use assonance and wordplay, as in Grim's *liberius ac licentius* and Fitzstephen's *renitere/ retinere*, or *adoraturus et oraturus*. In this passage Fitzstephen cites a saying that he claims is by Basil of Caesarea (in Cappadocia) but is in fact from another Christian Greek writer, Eusebius of Caesarea (in Palestine).

B(a): Edward Grim, *Life of St Thomas* (*Vita S. Thomae*) (excerpts: 80–2)

TEXT II.16B(a)

The knights pursue the monks into the cathedral in search of Becket
[80] postquam autem intra fores ecclesiae monachi se receperant, jam dicti milites quatuor cursu rapidissimo post terga secuti sunt. affuit inter illos subdiaconus quidam, eadem qua milites armatus malitia, Hugo Malus-clericus merito suae nequitiae cognominatus, qui nec Deo nec sanctis reverentiam exhiberet. quo sequens factum probavit. intranti vero monasterium sancto archiepiscopo, omissis vesperis quas Deo libare inceperant, occurrunt monachi glorificantes Deum quod patrem suum quem exstinctum audierant, vivum cernerent et incolumem. valvas etiam ecclesiae repagulando hostes a nece pastoris arcere festinant. ad quos conversus athleta mirabilis imperat ecclesiae januas aperiri, 'Non decet', inquiens, 'orationis domum, ecclesiam Christi, turrem facere, quae etsi non claudatur, suis sufficit ad munimen; et nos patiendo potius quam pugnando triumphabimus hostem, qui et pati venimus, non repugnare.' nec mora, sacrilegi gladiis evaginatis ingrediuntur domum pacis ac reconciliationis, solo quidem aspectu

et armorum strepitu non modicum horroris cernentibus ingerentes. turbatisque qui aderant ac tumultuantibus (jam enim qui vespertinis intenderant laudibus ad lethale spectaculum accurrerant) in spiritu furoris milites exclamaverunt, 'Ubi est Thomas Beketh, proditor regis et regni?' quo non respondente, instantius vociferati sunt, dicentes, 'Ubi est archiepiscopus?' ad hanc vocem intrepidus quidem et, ut scriptum est, 'justus quasi leo confidens absque terrore erit', occurrit e gradu **Prov. 28:1** quo delatus fuerat a monachis metu militum, et satis audibili sermone respondit, 'Ecce adsum, non regis proditor sed sacerdos; qui me quaeritis?' et qui se eos non timere jam antea dixit, adjunxit, 'Ecce praesto sum in nomine Ejus pati qui me sanguine suo redemit; absit ut propter gladios vestros fugiam, aut a justitia recedam.' quo dicto divertit in dextram sub columna, hinc habens altare beatae Dei genetricis et perpetuae virginis Mariae, illinc vero sancti confessoris Benedicti; quorum exemplo et suffragiis crucifixus mundo et concupiscentiis ejus, tanta animi constantia ac si in carne non esset, quicquid carnifex inferebat, sustinuit ac superavit. quem insecuti carnifices, 'Absolve', inquiunt, 'et communioni restitue quos excommunicasti et ceteris officium redde qui suspensi sunt.' quibus ille, 'Nulla', ait, 'satisfactio praecessit nec eos absolvam.' 'Et tu', inquiunt, 'modo morieris, suscipiens quod meruisti.' 'Et ego', ait, 'pro Domino meo paratus sum mori, ut in meo sanguine ecclesia libertatem consequatur et pacem; sed meis sive clerico sive laico, in nomine Dei omnipotentis interdico ne in aliquo noceatis.' quam pie suis, quam prudenter sibi, providit martyr egregius, ne videlicet laederetur proximus, innocens opprimeretur, ne gloriam properantis ad Christum proximi casus tristior obfuscaret! decuit plane ducis sui militem martyrem salvatoris inhaerere vestigiis, qui cum quaereretur ab impiis, 'Si me', inquit, 'quaeritis, sinite hos abire.' **John 18:8**

Thomas prepares to die in the face of the knights' violence
[81] igitur facto impetu manus sacrilegas injecerunt in eum, durius illum contrectantes et trahentes, ut extra fores ecclesiae aut jugularent aut vinctum inde asportarent, sicut postmodum confessi sunt. sed cum facile non posset a columna moveri, unum ex ipsis acrius insistentem et accedentem propius a se repulit, lenonem appellans, dicensque, 'Non me contingas, Reinalde, qui fidem ex jure debes et subjectionem; insipienter agis cum tuis complicibus.' miles vero pro repulsione furore terribili totus incanduit, ensemque vibrans contra sacrum verticem, 'Non fidem', ait, 'non tibi subjectionem debeo contra fidelitatem domini mei regis.' cernens igitur martyr invictus horam imminere quae miserae mortalitati finem imponeret, paratam sibi et promissam a Domino coronam immortalitatis jam proximam fieri, inclinata in modum orantis cervice, junctis pariter et elevatis sursum manibus, Deo et sanctae Mariae et beato martyri Dionysio[2] suam et ecclesiae causam commendavit.

---

2 St Denis of Paris was a third-century martyr who, like Becket, suffered decapitation. To St Denis is dedicated the church in Paris where many of the kings of France are buried.

182 Twelfth Century

The knights attack, and the writer of this account is wounded in protecting Becket
[82] vix verbum implevit et metuens nefandus miles ne raperetur a populo et vivus evaderet, insiliit in eum subito, et summitate coronae, quam sancti chrismatis unctio dicaverat Deo, abrasa, agnum Deo immolandum vulneravit in capite, eodem ictu praeciso brachio haec referentis. is etenim, fugientibus tam monachis quam clericis universis, sancto archiepiscopo constanter adhaesit, et inter ulnas complexum tenuit, donec ipsa quam opposuit praecisa est. ecce simplicitatem

Matt. 10:16 columbae, ecce serpentis prudentiam, in hoc martyre, qui corpus percutientibus opposuit, ut caput suum, animam scilicet vel ecclesiam, conservaret illaesam, nec contra carnis occisores, quo magis hac necessitate careret, cautelam vel insidias machinatus est! o pastorem dignum qui ne oves laniarentur, seipsum luporum morsibus tam confidenter opposuit! et quia mundum abjecerat, mundus eum volens opprimere nescius sublimavit. deinde alio ictu in capite recepto adhuc quoque permansit immobilis. tertio vero percussus martyr genua flexit et cubitos, seipsum hostiam viventem offerendo, dicens submissa voce, 'Pro nomine Jesu et ecclesiae tuitione mortem amplecti paratus sum.' at tertius miles ita procumbenti grave vulnus inflixit, quo ictu et gladium collisit lapidi, et coronam, quae ampla fuit, ita a capite separavit, ut sanguis albens ex cerebro, cerebrum nihilominus rubens ex sanguine, lilii et rosae coloribus virginis et matris ecclesiae faciem confessoris et martyris vita et morte purpuraret. quartus miles supervenientes abegit ut ceteri liberius ac licentius homicidium perpetrarent. quintus vero, non miles, sed clericus ille qui cum militibus intraverat, ne martyri quinta plaga deesset, qui

John 19:34 in aliis Christum fuerat imitatus, posito pede super collum sancti sacerdotis et martyris pretiosi (horrendum dictu) cerebrum cum sanguine per pavimentum spargens, ceteris exclamavit, 'Abeamus hinc, milites, iste ulterius non resurget!'

Translation: Edward Grim, *Life of St Thomas*

[80] *After the monks had withdrawn inside the doors of the church, these four knights now followed behind them at great speed. Among them there was a certain sub-deacon, armed with the same malice as these knights, who was fittingly named Hugh Mauclerc because of his wickedness; he showed no respect either for God or for the saints, as was proved by what ensued. The monks had abandoned the office of Vespers which they had begun to offer to God and they then came to meet the holy archbishop as he entered the monastery; they glorified God when they saw their father alive and safe after hearing that he was dead. They hastened to bolt the doors of the church to bar their enemy from killing their shepherd, but the wonderful athlete turned to them and gave orders that the doors of the church be opened: 'It is not right', he said, 'to make the house of prayer, Christ's church, into a fortified building, for even if it is not locked, it provides sufficient protection for its people. We will triumph over our enemy by suffering rather than fighting, for we have come to suffer, not to offer resistance.' Without delay those sacrilegious men drew their*

swords and entered the house of peace and reconciliation: just the sight and sound of their weapons caused the onlookers a great deal of terror. Those who were there (for those who were already taking part in Vespers had run up to watch the deadly spectacle) were thrown into confusion and a disturbance broke out among them, and in their fury the knights shouted at them, 'Where is Thomas Becket, traitor to king and kingdom?' When they refused to answer, these men shouted more insistently saying, 'Where is the archbishop?' Fearless (for as it says in Scripture, 'the righteous will be fearless as a bold lion'), he responded to this question by coming down from the steps where he had been taken by the monks, in their fear of the knights, and in a clear voice he replied, 'Here I am, not a traitor to a king, but a priest; who is looking for me?' And he who already earlier had said that he was not afraid of them, added, 'Here I am, ready to suffer, in the name of Him who redeemed me by His blood; far be it from me to run away from your swords or to withdraw from justice.' With these words he turned aside to the right, at the foot of a pillar with the altar of the blessed mother of God and perpetual virgin Mary on one side, and that of the holy confessor Benedict on the other. By their example and with their support he had died to the world and its desires, and with great firmness of mind as if he was not in the flesh, he endured whatever the torturer inflicted – endured, and overcame. The torturers pursued him, saying, 'Absolve and restore to communion those whom you have excommunicated and restore to their positions those you have suspended.' He replied to them, 'They need to give satisfaction first, and so I will not absolve them.' 'Then,' they said, 'you will die now, and get what you deserve.' 'And I', he said, 'am ready to die for my Lord so that in my blood the Church may gain freedom and peace; but I forbid you, in the name of almighty God, to harm in any way those with me, whether clergy or laity.' How gently the outstanding martyr took care of his friends, how wisely he took care of himself, to prevent his neighbour being hurt, or an innocent person being crushed, to prevent a tragic outcome from darkening his glory as he hastened to Christ. It was right for the soldier martyr to follow closely in the footsteps of the Saviour, who was leading him, who when he was sought by the wicked, said, 'If it is me you are looking for, let these people go.'

[81] The knights then rushed at him, grabbing him with their sacrilegious hands, handling him roughly and dragging him, intending either to murder him outside the doors of the church or tie him up and take him away from there, as they later admitted. But since he could not easily be moved from the pillar, one of them was pushing him more violently and getting closer, but Becket pushed him away, calling him a pimp, and said, 'Don't touch me, Reginald, you who owe me faith and obedience by law; you and your accomplices are behaving like fools.' The knight became totally incensed with a terrible rage at being pushed back. Brandishing his sword at the sacred head, he said, 'I don't owe you faith or obedience when it clashes with my loyalty to my lord king.' When the unconquered martyr saw that the hour was at hand which would put an end to his wretched mortality and realised that the crown of immortality prepared for him and promised by the Lord was now very close, he bent his head as if in prayer, put his hands together and raised them on high,

184 Twelfth Century

entrusting his cause and that of the Church to God and holy Mary and the blessed martyr Denis.

[82] He had hardly finished speaking when this terrible knight, fearing that Thomas might be snatched by the people and get away alive, leapt at him suddenly and, slicing off the top of his skull, which had been dedicated to God with the anointing of the holy chrism, he inflicted a wound in the head of the lamb which was to be sacrificed to God. With the same blow he first slashed the arm of the person who is writing this account. For this person, when the monks as well as all the clerics were running away, stuck closely to the holy archbishop and held him in his arms until the arm with which he tried to protect him was slashed. Behold the simplicity of the dove, behold the wisdom of the serpent in this martyr who put his body in the way of the killers so that he might preserve his head, in other words his soul and his Church, unharmed, and did not devise a trap or a trick for the killers of the flesh so as to avoid this horror. O worthy shepherd who put himself so boldly in the way of the wolves' jaws, so that the sheep would not be torn to pieces! And because he had renounced the world, the world, wishing to crush him, unknowingly exalted him. Then Becket received a second blow on his head but he still would not be moved. But when the martyr was struck a third time he bent his knees and arms, and offering himself as a living sacrifice, he said in a low voice, 'For the sake of Jesus and the protection of the Church, I am ready to embrace death.' Then the third knight inflicted a serious wound on him as he lay there; with this blow he shattered the sword on the stone paving and separated the broad crown from the head in such a way that the blood turned white from the brain and the brain turned red from the blood and with the colours of the lily and the rose, the colours of the virgin and the mother, the face of the Church was brightened through the life and death of the confessor and martyr. The fourth knight drove away those who were arriving on the scene, so that the others could carry out the murder more freely and without hindrance. The fifth, not a knight but a cleric who had entered together with the knights, so that the martyr would receive a fifth blow because in other ways, too, he had imitated Christ, put his foot on the neck of the holy priest and precious martyr (dreadful to relate), spreading brains and blood over the paving, and shouted to the others, 'Let's get away from here, fellow knights! This one won't be getting up again!'

B(b): William Fitzstephen, *Life of St Thomas (Vita S. Thomae)* (excerpt: sections 138–41)

TEXT II.16B(b)

Despite the monks' anxiety for him, Becket refuses to flee as the armed knights arrive
[138] intratum est in ecclesiam ipsam. monachi ecclesiae, pro tali et tanto tumultu tam pavidi quam attoniti, relictis et non percantatis vesperis, domino

archiepiscopo in ecclesiam intrante, a choro exeunt ei obviam, gaudentes et Deo gratiam habentes quod eum vivum cernunt et recipiunt, quam jam detruncatum audierant. et cum alii prae gaudio vel timore flerent, alii hoc, alii illud suaderunt, ut Petrus Domino dicens, 'Propitius esto tibi,' ille, pro ecclesiae Dei libertate et causa non timidus mori, jussit eos abire et a se recedere: utique ne impedirent passionem ejus, quam futuram praedixerat et imminere videbat. iturus ad aram superius, ubi missas familiares et horas solebat audire, jam quatuor gradus ascenderat, cum ecce ad ostium claustri, quo veneramus, primus adest Raginaldus Ursonis loricatus, ense evaginato et vociferans, 'Nunc huc ad me, homines regis!' nec multo post adduntur ei tres praedicti socii ejus, similiter loricis contecti corpora et capita, praeterquam oculos solos, et ensibus nudatis. plurimi etiam alii sine loricis, armati, de sequela et sociis suis; et aliqui de urbe Cantuariae quos coactos secum illi venire compulerant. die illo et quatriduo post ad vicina castra Dovrae, Hastingae et ceterorum, ut praedictum est, erant milites habentes custodias: et ad portus transmarinos regis erant domestici; comes Willelmus ad Witsant, Saierus de Quinci, Ricardus de Humet, alibi: forte si mare attentasset archiepiscopus, appulsus hic vel ibi caperetur. visis, inquam, illis armatis, voluerunt monachi ostium ecclesiae obfirmare: sed bonus homo, fiduciam habens in Domino, et non expavescens repentino terrore irruentes potentias impiorum, e gradibus descendit regressus, prohibens ne ostium ecclesiae clauderetur, et dicens, 'Absit ut de ecclesia Dei castellum faciamus; permittite intrare omnes ecclesiam Dei intrare volentes: fiat voluntas Dei.' eo tunc a gradibus descendente versus ostium, ne clauderetur, Johannes Saresberiensis et alii ejus clerici omnes, praeter Robertum canonicum et Willelmum filium Stephani et Edwardum Grim, qui novus ad eum venerat, praesidia captantes, et se in tuto collocare curantes, relicto ipso, petiverunt alii altaria, alii latibula.

cf. Luke 18:13

Becket refuses to hide in the cathedral and confronts the knights calmly
[139] et quidem si vellet archiepiscopus declinare, et se fugae praesidio liberare, optime uti posset, non quaesita sed oblata occasione temporis et loci. vespera erat, nox longissima instabat; crypta erat prope, in qua multa et pleraque tenebrosa diverticula. item erat ibi aliud ostium prope, quo per cochleam ascenderet ad cameras et testudines ecclesiae superioris; forte non inveniretur, vel interim aliud fieret. sed nihil horum voluit. non declinavit, non percussoribus supplicavit, non murmur edidit, non querimoniam in tota sua agonia: sed extremam horam quae imminebat, pro Christo et causa ecclesiae patienter exspectans, fortitudine et constantia mentis, corporis et sermonis, qualem de aliquo martyrum maiorem nunquam audivimus, usus est, donec totum consummaretur. ecce jam illi spiculatores, furia invecti, praeter spem apertum cernentes cursim ostium intrant ecclesiae. 'Quo, quo, scelesti, ruitis?' 'Quis furor, o miseri! quae tanta licentia ferri!' quidam autem illorum monachis dixit, qui cum eo astabant, 'Ne vos moveatis.' et quidem quasi confusi et attoniti, a reverentia vultus ejus illi grassatores primo retulerunt pedem, viso archiepiscopo. postea clamavit aliquis, 'Ubi est ille

Hor. *Epode* 7.1/
Lucan, *Pharsalia* 1.8

186 Twelfth Century

proditor?' archepiscopus, suam in patientia animam possidens, ad verbum illud non respondit. aliquis item: 'Ubi est archiepiscopus?' ille: 'Ecce ego, non proditor sed presbyter Dei; et miror quo in tali habitu ecclesiam Dei ingressi estis. quid placet vobis?' unus grassator: 'Ut moriaris; impossibile est ut vivas ulterius.' at ille, 'Et ego in nomine Domini mortem suscipio, et animam meam et ecclesiae causam Deo et beatae Mariae et sanctis hujus ecclesiae patronis commendo. absit ut propter gladios vestros fugiam; sed auctoritate Dei interdico, ne quempiam meorum tangatis.' aliquis eorum bisacutam et gladium simul habuit, ut in securi et bisacuta, si eis obfirmaretur, ostium dejicerent ecclesiae; sed retento gladio, bisacutam, quae adhuc ibi est, deposuit.

The knights resort to violence
[140] quidam eum cum plano ense caedebat inter scapulas, dicens, 'Fuge; mortuus es.' ille immotus perstitit et cervicem praebens, se Domino commendabat; et sanctos archiepiscopos martyres in ore habebat, beatum Dionysium et sanctum Ælfegum Cantuariensem. aliqui dicentes, 'Captus es, venies nobiscum', injectis manibus, eum ab ecclesia extrahere volebant; nisi timerent quod populus eum esset erepturus de manibus eorum. ille respondens, 'Nusquam ibo; hic facietis quod facere vultis et quod vobis praeceptum est', quod poterat, renitebatur; et monachi eum retinebant: cum quibus et magister Edwardus Grim qui et primum a Willelmo de Traci in caput ejus vibratum gladii ictum brachio objecto excepit; eodemque ictu et archiepiscopus in capite inclinato, et ipse in brachio, graviter est vulneratus. 'O', ut ait sanctus Basilius, 'bestiarum feritas in Dei virtute mansuescit; humana rabies nec ferarum mitescit exemplis.'[3]
[141] archiepiscopus a capite defluum cum brachio detergens et videns cruorem, gratias Deo agebat, dicens, 'In manus tuas, Domine, commendo spiritum meum.' datur in caput ejus ictus secundus quo et ille in faciem concidit, positis primo genibus, conjunctis et extensis ad Deum manibus, secus aram, quae ibi erat, sancti Benedicti; et curam habuit vel gratiam ut honeste caderet, pallio suo coopertus usque ad talos, quasi adoraturus et oraturus. super dextram cecidit, ad dextram Dei iturus. eum procumbentem Ricardus Brito percussit tanta vi ut et gladius ad caput ejus et ad ecclesiae pavimentum frangeretur.

Translation: William Fitzstephen, *Life of St Thomas*

[138] *The knights entered into the church itself. The monks of the church were both terrified and shocked by this great disturbance. They abandoned Vespers before they had finished chanting it, and when the lord archbishop entered into the church,*

---

3 This saying comes from Rufinus' Latin translation (c.402) from the Greek of Eusebius' *Church History* (8.74; ed. T. Mommsen in *GCS* 2.2: 755).

they left the choir to meet him, rejoicing and giving thanks to God because they saw and welcomed him alive, although they had heard that he had already been cut to pieces. And while some were weeping for joy or fear, and some were advising one thing, others something else (as when Peter said to the Lord, 'May he be merciful to you!'), Thomas, who was not afraid to die for freedom's sake and for the cause of the Church of God, ordered them to go away and leave him, no doubt so that they would not prevent his suffering, which he had predicted would happen and saw was imminent. He was about to go up to the altar where he was in the habit of hearing the customary Masses and hours. He had already ascended four steps when behold, at the door of the cloister, to which we had come, there appeared first Reginald Fitzurse, clad in armour, with his sword drawn from its scabbard and shouting, 'Now follow me, you who are the king's men!' Immediately after came his three companions, their heads and bodies similarly covered in armour except for their eyes alone, and with bare swords. Along came also many others from their retinue and their allies, without armour but with weapons. Some of them, whom they had rounded up and forced to join them, had come from the city of Canterbury. On that day and for the next four days there were knights keeping guard at the neighbouring castles of Dover, Hastings and other places, as stated earlier. And at the overseas ports were waiting members of the king's household: Earl William at Wissant (Pas-de-Calais, France), Saher de Quincy and Richard de Humet at other places; perhaps if the archbishop had ventured upon the sea, he would have been driven to one of these places and been captured. When, as I said, these armed men appeared, the monks wanted to lock the doors of the church; but this good man who had faith in the Lord and was not terrified by the force of these wicked men as they rushed in, came back down the steps, forbidding them to close the church door and saying, 'God forbid that we should turn the church of God into a fortification; allow all those to enter who wish to enter the church of God. God's will be done!' As he was going down the steps towards the door to prevent it being closed, John of Salisbury and all the other clerics except Canon Robert, William Fitzstephen and Edward Grim (who had recently joined him) deserted Thomas, for they were desperate for protection and anxious to find somewhere safe. Some sought protection at the altars, others looked for somewhere to hide.

[139] Indeed, if the archbishop had been willing to turn aside and gain freedom for himself by fleeing, he could have made good use of the opportunity which he had not sought but which time and place presented to him. It was now evening and a very long night was approaching. The crypt was close by and in it were numerous dark recesses. There was also another door close at hand which led to a spiral staircase going up to the rooms and vaults of the upper church: perhaps he would not be found or something might happen in the meantime! But he did not want any of these possibilities. He did not turn aside, he did not beg for mercy from his attackers, he uttered not a murmur, not a complaint during his whole agony. Instead he patiently awaited his final hour which was drawing near, for the sake of Christ and the cause of the Church. Right to the end, he displayed a greater fortitude and

188 Twelfth Century

constancy of mind, of body and of speech, than we have heard of in any other martyr. Look! those executioners, carried away by their fury, now noticed that the door of the church was unexpectedly open and entered at a rush. 'Where, where are you rushing to, you wicked men?' 'What is this madness, you wretches? What this great frenzy of slaughter?' One of the knights shouted to the monks who were standing with the archbishop, 'Don't move!' The predators actually seemed rather confused and shocked, and at first they recoiled when they came face to face with Becket, out of reverence. Then one of them shouted, 'Where is that traitor?' The archbishop, controlling his soul in patience, did not reply. Then another called out similarly, 'Where is the archbishop?' and Becket answered, 'Here I am, no traitor but a priest of God; and I am amazed that you have entered the church of God clad in that manner. What do you want?' One of the villains said, 'We want you to die. It is impossible that you should live any longer.' But the archbishop replied, 'And I accept death in the name of the Lord and I commend my spirit and the cause of the Church to God and the blessed Mary and the patron saints of this church. I will certainly not flee on account of your swords; but I forbid you, in the name of God's authority, to touch any of my men.' One of them had both a two-edged axe and a sword, intending to use them to break down the door of the church, had they found it locked; but keeping hold of his sword, he laid down his axe, which is still lying there.

[140] One knight struck him between the shoulders with the flat blade, saying, 'Run now! you are dead.' He stayed where he was, motionless and presenting his neck; he then commended himself to the Lord, and on his lips were the names of the archbishops who had been martyred, St Denis and holy Ælfege of Canterbury. Some of the knights said, 'You have been captured; you will come with us,' and taking hold of him they would have dragged him out of the church, if they had not been afraid that the people were going to pull him from their grasp. He answered, 'I am going nowhere; do here what you want and have been ordered to do.' He resisted as much as he could and the monks restrained him. Among them was master Edward Grim, who first received on his arm a sword blow, which William de Tracy had brandished at his head; with the same blow the archbishop and Edward Grim were seriously wounded, the archbishop on his head as he bent it forward and Grim on his arm. As St Basil says, 'God's power makes fierce animals become gentle but human fury is not softened by the example of wild animals.'

[141] The archbishop wiped away the drips from his head with his arm and when he saw that it was blood, he gave thanks to God, saying, 'Into your hands, Lord, I commend my spirit.' A second blow fell on his head and he fell on his face, first dropping to his knees with his hands together and extended towards God, beside the altar of St Benedict which stood there. And he took care or had the grace to fall decently, covered with his robe down to his ankles, as if he was about to worship and pray, and he fell on his right side as he was on the point of going to the right hand of God. Richard Brito struck him as he lay face down with such force that the sword smashed against his head and the church paving.

Primary Sources and Related Texts

Edward Grim, *Life of St Thomas*, RS 67.2 (1876).
William Fitzstephen, *Life of St Thomas*, RS 67.3 (1877).
Staunton, M. (2001) *The Lives of Thomas Becket*, Manchester.

Further Reading

Duggan, A. (2004) *Thomas Becket*, London.
López Sabatel, J. A. (2021), 'The analysis of the work of William fitz Stephen as a historical source in relation to the life of Thomas Becket', *Academia Letters*, Article 736. DOI: 10.20935/AL736.
O'Reilly, J. (2019) '*Candidus et rubicundus*: an image of martyrdom in the Lives of Thomas Becket' in *History, hagiography and biblical exegesis*, ed. M. MacCurran and D. Scully, London.
Staunton, M. (2006) *Thomas Becket and his biographers*, Woodbridge.

Section II.17

Glanvill, *The Laws and Customs of the Kingdom of England* (*Tractatus de legibus et consuetudinibus regni Anglie*) (excerpts: prologue and 1.1–7)

Date: c.1188.

Two different textual traditions are found, each surviving in several MSS. Since the edition of Woodbine, these have been referred to as the *alpha* and *beta* traditions, though scholars have disagreed as to which version is more likely to be closer to the original.

Author: Although the work is referred to as Glanvill, it is unlikely that the author was Ranulph Glanvill, justiciar from 1180. One alternative is Hubert Walter, whose name is also cited in the text and margins as an authority. Justiciar from 1190 and chancellor, as well as crusader to the Holy Land with Richard I, and Archbishop of Canterbury (1193–1205), he was a key figure, along with Glanvill, in the development of the royal administration at the end of the twelfth century. However, Hubert Walter was criticised by his contemporaries, including Gerald of Wales, for his lower standard of Latin. Another alternative as author is Godfrey de Luci, later Bishop of Winchester (1189–1204), one of those also involved in the downfall of William de Longchamp, chancellor of the Exchequer (for which, see Section II.20), who had the requisite legal expertise.

Work: This work stands at the opposite end of the twelfth century from the *Laws of Henry I* (cf. Section II.10B): both works intend to provide an account of English law at the time. Glanvill's work deals with civil cases in the king's court, rather than criminal law, and it provides explanations and examples of many elements of legislation and custom. It shows that English law had changed over the course of the twelfth century, for by the time of Henry II there was a permanent court of justice at the Exchequer in London and regular local court sessions around the country, using a system of initiating writs followed by inquests with juries of twelve men. In addition, the increasing influence of Roman and canon law was being felt (though this never replaced the common law, worked out in Anglo-Saxon times): the preface of Glanvill, for example, contains passages of Justinian's *Institutes*. This summary of the common law of England acts as a counterpart to the account of the workings of the Exchequer found in the contemporary *Dialogue of the Exchequer* (Section II.4B). In the late thirteenth century Henry

II.17 | Glanvill, *Laws and Customs of England* 191

Bracton drew on Glanvill extensively in his multi-volume work on the laws and customs of England which would replace Glanvill as the primary authority. It was in the second half of the thirteenth century, too, that French began to be used as the language of certain legal documents and teaching manuals; this change is alluded to in the Latin text known as the *Modus componendi brevia* (c.1285), which provides advice on the formulation of pleas and writs, as had Glanvill in the excerpt quoted here.

The *alpha* and *beta* texts differ in that *beta* is usefully divided into books and chapters. There are also some stylistic differences. Woodbine believed that *beta* had been given a stylistic makeover by someone outside the English court, but more recently it has been argued that *alpha*, the longer and more elegant text, is earlier than the more workmanlike *beta* text, and indeed it is more common for a longer text to be abbreviated.[1] However, a close stylistic comparison of the two remains to be done, as also between this work and the *Dialogue of the Exchequer*.

Linguistic points: The work is written in elegant and well-crafted Latin, clear, concise and pertinent. In the prologue the author claims to have chosen to use *stilo vulgari et verbis curialibus* because it is good for those unused to such language to become familiar with it: by this he probably means the routine language and legal terminology of the judicial courts. The author's claim can be compared with the interlocutor's insistence in the prologue to the approximately contemporaneous *Dialogue of the Exchequer* that *communia verba* should be used for the customs and laws of the Exchequer. If the authors of these works had problems defining and defending the language they used, the modern reader can find it problematic, too, when determining the precise definitions of the words they used. Certainly, both works show evidence of the influence of Anglo-Norman French on the new technical terminology which was to become the everyday language of the royal administration, pervading all walks of medieval life.

Examples of legal technical terms deriving from French (and often ultimately from a Germanic word) are *deforciare* (i.e. *diffortiare*; cf. OF 'desforcier'), *replegiare*, *saisina*, *essonium* (excuse for non-appearance in court), where the OF 'essoine' derives from a Germanic word, 'sunni'), *roberia* (cf. the form *robaria* in the *Laws of Henry I*, for which see Section II.10B), *mellitis*, i.e. *medlea* or *medleta*, which gives English both 'medley' and 'mêlée', and *purprestura*. *relevium* has various senses in BML (relating to CL *(re)levare*) but is most commonly used, as here, for the payment made by an heir on taking possession of his inheritance.[2] The spelling of *octavus* as *octab-* is common when used in phrases designating time,

---

1   Cf. R. Southern (1950) 'A note on the text of Glanville, *De legibus et consuetudinibus regni Anglie*', *EHR* 65: 81–9.

2   For another sense of *relevium*, cf. Section II.49B.

192 Twelfth Century

particularly as a substantive meaning the eighth day or the eight days (inclusive) after a religious feast day. *breve de recto* refers to a specific legal writ (involving a claim to property) issued by the king. Other names for specific writs are often based on the imperative form of the verb, as in the case of *breve de liberate*, or simply *praecipe*.

TEXT II.17

The importance of laws for justice and peace

Prologus: regiam potestatem non solum armis contra rebelles et gentes sibi regnoque insurgentes oportet esse decoratam, sed et legibus ad subditos et populos pacificos regendos decet esse ornatam, ut utraque tempora, pacis scilicet et belli, gloriosus rex noster ita feliciter transigat, ut effrenatorum et indomitorum dextra fortitudinis elidendo superbiam et humilium et mansuetorum equitatis virga moderando iusticiam, tam in hostibus debellandis semper victoriosus existat quam in subditis tractandis equalis iugiter appareat. (…) leges autem Anglicanas licet non scriptas leges appellari non videatur absurdum, cum hoc ipsum lex sit, 'quod principi placet, legis habet vigorem',[3] eas scilicet quas super dubiis in concilio diffiniendis, procerum quidem consilio et principis accedente auctoritate, constat esse promulgatas. si enim ob solum scripture defectum leges minime censerentur, maioris proculdubio auctoritatis robur ipsis legibus videretur accommodare scriptura quam vel decernentis equitas aut ratio statuentis.

leges autem et iura regni scripto universaliter concludi nostris temporibus omnino quidem impossibile est, tum propter scribentium ignoranciam tum propter eorundem multitudinem confusam. verum sunt quedam in curia generalia et frequenter usitata, que scripto commendare non mihi videtur presumptuosum, sed plerisque perutile et ad iuvandum memoriam admodum necessarium. horum utique particulam quandam in scripta redigere decrevi, stilo vulgari et verbis curialibus utens ex industria ad eorum noticiam comparandam eis qui in huiusmodi vulgaritate minus sunt exercitati. ad quorum evidentiam causarum secularium genera in hunc modum duxi distinguendum.

Translation: *The Laws and Customs of the Kingdom of England*

Prologue: Royal power should not only be decked with arms against rebels and peoples attacking it or the kingdom, but it is right that it should also be adorned with laws to govern subject and peaceful people, so that our glorious king might

---

3 Cf. Ulpian, *Dig.* 1.4.1; J. Sal. *Polycraticus* 689A.

negotiate periods both of peace and war so successfully that by crushing the pride of the unbridled and untamed with the right hand of strength and tempering justice for the humble and meek with the rod of fairness, he may always both be victorious in subduing the enemy and appear fair in dealing with his subjects. (...) Although the laws of England are not written down, it does not seem absurd to call them laws, namely those known to have been promulgated regarding problems decided in council with the magnates' advice and the prince's supporting authority. For the statement 'what pleases the prince has the force of law' is in itself a law. If they were not regarded as laws just because of the lack of writing, then writing would seem to accord the laws a force of greater authority than either the justice of the one who decrees them or the reason of the person establishing them. It is, however, utterly impossible for the laws and legal code of the kingdom to be entirely confined to writing in our time, both because of the scribes' ignorance and because of the confusingly large number of laws. It is true that there are some general rules frequently used in the court which I think it is not presumptuous to commit to writing; indeed it is very useful to many people and necessary as an aide-memoire. I have decided to edit at least a small part of these in writing, intentionally using an everyday style and forensic terms so as to provide knowledge of them to those who are not trained in this kind of everyday language. In order to clarify these matters, I thought that the kinds of secular cases should be distinguished in the following way.

The division of secular cases into civil and criminal etc.

[1.1] distinctio causarum secularium: placitorum aliud criminale aliud civile. item placitorum criminalium aliud pertinet ad coronam domini regis, aliud ad vicecomites provinciarum. ad coronam domini regis pertinent ista:

[1.2] crimen quod in legibus dicitur crimen lese maiestatis, ut de nece vel seditione persone domini regis vel regni vel exercitus; occultatio inventi thesauri fraudulosa; placitum de pace domini regis infracta; homicidium; incendium; roberia; raptus; crimen falsi, et si qua sunt similia: que scilicet ultimo puniuntur supplicio aut membrorum truncatione. excipitur crimen furti quod ad vicecomites pertinet et in comitatibus placitatur et terminatur. ad vicecomites etiam pertinet per defectum dominorum cognoscere de mellitis, de verberibus, de plagis etiam nisi accusator adiciat de pace domini regis infracta.

[1.3] distinctio causarum civilium: placitum civile aliud in curia domini regis tantum placitatur et terminatur, aliud ad vicecomites provinciarum pertinet. in curia domini regis habent ista tractari: placitum de baroniis; placitum de advocationibus ecclesiarum; questio status; placitum de dotibus[4] unde mulieres ipse nihil penitus perceperunt; querela de fine facto in curia domini regis non observato;

---

4   The *dos* usually refers to a portion of the husband's land, granted at marriage, to which a woman is entitled after her husband's death; cf. Glanvill 6.1 and 7.1.

194 Twelfth Century

de homagiis faciendis et releviis recipiendis; de propesturis; placitum de debitis laicorum. et ista quidem placita solummodo super proprietate rei prodita sunt. de illis autem que super possessione loquuntur et per recognitiones terminantur inferius suo loco dicetur.

[1.4] ad vicecomites pertinent ista: placitum de recto de liberis tenementis per breve domini regis ubi curie dominorum probantur de recto defecisse, quod qualiter fieri debeat inferius dicetur; placitum de nativis, sed per breve domini regis.

The discussion of pleas

[1.5] cum quis clamat se domino regi aut eius iusticiis de feudo vel libero tenemento suo, si fuerit loquela talis quod debeat vel dominus rex velit eam in curia deduci, tunc is qui queritur tale breve de submonitione habebit:

[1.6] Breve de prima summonitione facienda: 'rex vicecomiti salutem. Precipe N. quod iuste et sine dilatione reddat R. unam hidam terre in illa villa unde idem R. queritur quod predictus N. sibi deforciat. et nisi fecerit, summone eum per bonos summonitores quod sit ibi in crastinum post octabas clausi Pasche coram me vel iusticiis meis ostensurus quare non fecerit. et habeas ibi summonitores et hoc breve. teste Rannulfo de Glanvill' apud Clarendunam.'

[1.7] summonitus autem ad diem prefixum aut venit aut non venit. item si non venit, aut nuncium aut essonium mittit aut neutrum. si neque venit neque mittit, adversarius eius qui petit adversus eum die statuta coram iusticiis appareat et se adversus eum liti offerat, et ita in curia per tres dies expectabit. (…) et ita tribus summonitionibus sub hac forma emissis, si nec ad terciam summonitionem venerit neque miserit, capietur terra in manum domini regis et ita per quindecim dies remanebit. et si infra illos quindecim dies non venerit, adversario eius adiudicabitur saisina ita quod de cetero non audietur nisi super proprietate per breve de recto. si vero infra illos quindecim dies venerit volens replegiare tenementum, precipietur ei quod ad quartum diem veniat et habebit quod de iure habere debebit, et ita poterit saisinam recuperare si venerit.

Translation: *The Laws and Customs of the Kingdom of England*

[1.1] *The division of secular cases: some pleas are criminal, others civil. Some criminal pleas belong to the crown of the lord king, others to the sheriffs of the counties. The following belong to the crown of the lord king:*

[1.2] *the crime which in the laws is called the crime of lèse-majesté, namely the killing of the person of the lord king or the betrayal of the kingdom or the army; fraudulent concealment of treasure trove; the plea of breach of the lord king's peace; homicide, arson, robbery, rape, the crime of falsifying and any similar crimes, for which the punishment is capital punishment or the cutting off of limbs. The crime of* theft is excluded because it belongs to the sheriffs and is pleaded and decided in the counties. If there are not sufficient lords, it is also up to the sheriffs to exercise jurisdiction over brawls, beatings, and even wounds unless the accuser adds a breach of the peace of the lord king.

[1.3] The division of civil cases: some civil pleas are pleaded and decided only in the court of the lord king, while others belong to the sheriffs of the counties. The following must be dealt with in the court of the lord king: pleas regarding baronies, pleas regarding advowsons of churches, inquiries into legal status, pleas of dower where the women have received nothing at all from it; complaints regarding failure to keep an agreement made in the court of the lord king; regarding homage and receiving relief payments; pleas regarding purprestures and laymen's debts. And these pleas only concern the right of ownership indicated in the matter at issue. Those pleas which deal with possession and are decided by formal investigations will be discussed in their proper place further on.

[1.4] The following belong to the sheriffs: pleas concerning the right of free tenement through a writ of the lord king where the lords' courts are proved to have defaulted from what is right, which will be discussed further on as to how they should be dealt with; pleas concerning villeins, but (instigated) through a writ of the lord king.

[1.5] When someone complains to the lord king or to his justices regarding his fee or free tenement, if the case is such as it should be or if the king agrees for it to be tried in his court, then the complainant will have the following writ of summons:

[1.6] The writ for making the first summons: 'The king to the sheriff (sends) greetings. Order N. to render to R. justly and without delay one hide of land in the village which this same R. complains that N. is withholding from him. If he does not do so, summon him by means of trustworthy summoners to appear before me or my justices on the day after the octave of the end of Easter to show why he has not done so. And have the summoners and this writ there. Witness, Ralph de Glanvill at Clarendon.

[1.7] The person who has been summoned either comes or does not come on the appointed day. If he does not come, then he sends either a representative or an essoiner or neither. If he neither comes nor sends anyone, his opponent who is claiming against him should appear before the justices on the appointed day and present himself for a lawsuit against this man, and he will wait for three days in court. (...) And so when three summonses have been sent out in this way, if he neither comes at the third summons, nor sends anyone, his land will be taken into the lord king's hand and will remain there for a fortnight; and if he does not come within that fortnight, possession will be adjudged to his opponent, and he will not be heard again, except regarding ownership by means of a writ of right. But if the tenant comes within the fortnight and wishes to recover possession of the property, he will be ordered to come on the fourth day, when he will be given justice, and so he can regain possession then, if he comes.

196 Twelfth Century

Primary Sources and Related Texts

The Treatise on the Laws and Customs of the Realm of England, commonly called Glanvill, ed. G. Hall, OMT, Oxford, 1965/1993. This gives the *alpha* text, as opposed to the *beta* text given in the 1932 edition of G. Woodbine, and includes a section by M. Clanchy: Guide to further reading.

Richard Fitzneale, *Dialogus de Scaccario*, ed. E. Amt and S. Church, OMT, Oxford, 2007.

Henry Bracton, *De legibus et consuetudinibus Angliae.*

EHD 2.495–513.

Further Reading

Brand, P. (1993) *The making of the common law*, London.

McSweeney, T. J. (2022) 'Those things which are written in Romance: language and law teaching in thirteenth-century England', *American Journal of Legal History* 62.4: 1–20.

*The Oxford history of the laws of England, vol. 2 (2004).

Pleas before the king or his justices 1198–1202, vol. 1, Selden Society 67 (1953).

Royal writs from Conquest to Glanvill, Selden Society 77 (1959).

Section II.18

Richard of Devizes, *Chronicle of the Reign of King Richard I* (*Chronicon de tempore regis Ricardi I*) (excerpt: 64–7)

Date: before 1198.

The chronicle is found only in Cambridge MS CCC 339, ff. 25r–43v (which is in the author's own hand) and BL MS Cotton Domitian A.xiii, ff. 70r–87r, a fair copy of the Cambridge MS.

Author: Richard of Devizes (c.1150–c.1200) was a Benedictine monk at Winchester, as we learn from his own work. He was loyal to King Richard and contemptuous of secular clergy such as Hugh Nonant, Bishop of Coventry, though he shares Hugh's antipathy towards Richard's chancellor, William de Longchamp (Section II.20). He claims that the aim of his work is to portray the fickleness (*mobilitas*) of the world and particularly the royal court, with which he seems familiar, so as to reinforce his friend's commitment to the monastic life.

Work: This work covers only the period from the coronation of Richard I in 1189 down to 1192, where it stops abruptly. It is unusual in having a secular slant despite being written by a monk, and in not being derived from obvious sources. Comparison with contemporary works and documents confirms the information it gives, such as the killing of the Jews that started on the day of Richard's coronation. The work is a mixture of satire and seriousness, and like his contemporary Walter Map (Section II.19) the author blends fact and fiction. The excerpt selected here is the satirical passage on London and other cities around England (Winchester alone is praised, because it did not take part in the violence against the Jews), with amusing stereotypes of their inhabitants; this passage was recently cited in English in M. Beaumont (2015) *Nightwalking: a nocturnal history of London*, London. It forms part of a speech by a French Jew, giving advice to the Christian boy who becomes the protagonist of the story told after this excerpt. In the story the boy is apparently murdered by the Jews of Winchester, with which one may compare the strange legal case, recorded in Curia Regis Rolls 15 no. 1320, when some Jews in Norwich in 1240 were accused of abducting a little boy and forcibly circumcising him. Devizes appears sceptical about the truth of such stories, and here the long story ends abruptly with the Jew being acquitted of the charge of murder, partly because the witnesses, a boy and a woman, were not believed.

198 Twelfth Century

Linguistic points: Richard's language shows him to be an outspoken writer with startling, original ways of expressing himself and some unusual vocabulary, apparently inventing compounds and diminutives, for example. Indeed, he shares the linguistic ebullience of his contemporaries Walter Map and Gerald of Wales, though each displays this ebullience in different ways. Richard alludes extensively to classical literature, particularly Horace and Juvenal, and uses occasional Greek words, alongside some biblical allusions. The passage quoted here has much in common with Horace's *Satire* 1.2 and even more so with Juvenal's third *Satire* with its theme of Rome's undesirability as a place to live. The reader will notice Richard's tendency toward short sentences and the staccato effect this produces.

TEXT II.18

A Christian boy is sent from France to the Jews of Winchester
[64] quia Wintonia non debuit debita sibi mercede privari pro servata, ut (in capite libri) prepositum est, pace Iudeis, Wintonienses Iudei civitatis sue Iudaico more studentes honori, etsi factum forte defuerit, plurimis facti indiciis celebrem sibi famam de martirizato a se in Wintonia puero confecerunt. casus erat huiusmodi. puerum quendam Christianum artis sutorie sciolum Iudeus quidam in familiare familie sue consciverat ministerium. non ibi continuum residebat ad opus, nec magnum aliquid semel sinebatur explere, ne provisam sibi cedem probaret cohabitatio, et ut pro modico labore melius ibi quam pro multo alibi remuneratus, domum demonis donis eius et dolis illectus libentius frequentaret. fuerat autem Francus genere, pupillus et orphanus, abiecte condicionis et paupertatis extreme. has huius miserias (in Francia) male miseratus, quidam Iudeus Francigena crebris ei monitis persuasit ut Angliam peteret, terram lacte et melle manantem; Anglos liberales predicavit et dapsiles; ibi nullum qui niteretur ad probitatem pauperem moriturum. puer promtulus, ut naturaliter Francorum est, ad velle quicquid volueris, assumpto secum comite quodam coetaneo suo et compatriota, ad peregre proficiscendum precinctus est, nichil in manibus habens preter baculum, nichil in sytarchia preter subulam. valedixit Judeo suo.

The French Jew gives the boy advice on different towns in England, a land flowing with milk and honey
cui Iudeus, [65] 'Vade', ait, 'viriliter. Deus patrum meorum deducat te sicut desidero.' et impositis manibus super capud eius, ac si esset hircus emissarius,[1]

---

1   Cf. Lev. 16 for the 'scapegoat' ritual on a real goat.

II.18 | Richard of Devizes, *The Reign of Richard I* 199

post stridores quosdam gutturis et tacitas imprecationes, iam de preda securus, adiecit, 'Forti animo esto; obliviscere populum tuum et terram tuam, quia omnis terra "forti patria est, ut piscibus equor, ut volucri vacuo quicquid in orbe patet". **Ovid,** *Fasti* **1.493–4** Angliam ingressus, si Londoniam veneris celeriter pertransibis. Multum enim michi displicet illa polis. omne hominum genus in illam confluit ex omni natione que sub celo est. omnis gens sua vitia et suos mores urbi intulit. nemo in ea sine crimine vivit. non omnis in ea vicus non habundat tristibus obscenis. eo ibi quisquis melior est quo fuerit maior in scelere. non ignoro quem instruo. habes supra tuam etatem fervorem ingenii, frigiditatem memorie, ex utrinque contrariis temperantiam rationis. nichil de te michi metuo, nisi cum male viventibus commoreris. ex convictu enim mores formantur. esto, esto. Londoniam venies. ecce predico tibi. quicquid in singulis, quicquid in universis partibus mundi mali vel malitie est, in una illa civitate repperies. lenonum choros non adeas. ganearum gregibus non immiscearis. vita thalum et tesseram, theatrum et tabernam. plures ibi quam in tota Gallia trasones offendes. gnatorum autem infinitus est numerus. histriones, scurre, glabriones, garamantes, palpones, pusiones, molles, mascularii, ambubaie, farmacapole, crissarie, phitonisse, vultuarie, noctivage, magi, mimi, mendici, balatrones: hoc genus omne totas repplevere domos. ergo, **Hor.** *Sat.* **1.2.1–2** si nolueris habitare cum turpibus, [66] non habitabis Londonie. non loquor in litteratos vel religiosos, sive Iudeos, quamvis et ex ipsa cohabitatione malorum, minus eos ibi quam alibi crediderim esse perfectos. nec eo pergit oratio ut in nullam te recipias civitatem, cum meo consilio nusquam tibi sit nisi in urbe manendum; refert tamen in qua. si igitur circa Cantuariam appuleris, iter habebis perdere, si vel per eam transieris. tota est in illa perditorum collectio, ad suum nescio quem, nuper deificatum, qui fuerat Cantuariorum archipresbiter, quod passim pre inopia panis et otio per plateas moriuntur ad solem. Rofecestria et Cicestria viculi sunt, et cur civitates dici debeat preter sedes flaminum nichil obtendunt. Oxonia vix suos homines non dico satiat sed sustentat. Exonia eodem farre reficit homines et iumenta. Batonia in imis vallium, in crasso nimis aere et vapore sulphureo posita, immo deposita, est ad portas inferi. sed nec in arctois sedem tibi legeris urbibus, Wigornia, Cestria, Herefordia, propter Walenses vite prodigos. Eboracus Scottis habundat, fedis et infidis homuncionibus. Heliensis pagus perpetuo putidus est pro circumfusis paludibus.[2] in Dunelmo (Norhwico) sive Lincolnia, perpaucos de potentibus de tua conditione, nullum penitus audies Romane loquentem. apud Bristollum nemo est qui non sit vel fuerit saponarius, et [67] omnis Francus saponarios amat ut stercorarios. post urbes, omne forum, villa vel opidum incolas habet rudes et rusticos. omni insuper tempore pro talibus Cornubienses habeto, quales in Francia nosti nostros Flandrenses haberi. ceterum regio ipsa generaliter in rore celi et in pinguedine terre tota beatissima

---

2   Cf. Felix, *Life of Guthlac* (Section I.20) for mention of the fens around Ely.

200 Twelfth Century

est. in singulis etiam locis aliqui boni sunt, sed multo minus in omnibus quam in una, Wintonia. Hec est in partibus illis Iudeorum Ierosolima; in hac sola perpetua pace fruuntur.'

Translation: Richard of Devizes, *Chronicle*

[64] *Because Winchester ought not to be deprived of its due reward for keeping peace with the Jews, as told at the beginning of this book, the Jews of Winchester, keen to work for the honour of their city, as is the Jewish custom (even if what was done perhaps undermined it), made themselves famous for having martyred a boy in Winchester, with plenty of proofs of this deed. The case was as follows: a certain Jew had decided to bring a Christian boy, skilled in the cobbler's craft, into his household to work as a domestic servant. The boy did not live there continuously for his work, nor was he allowed to complete any major project at one go, in case his living there with them might prove that his murder was premeditated; but he was happy to frequent the devil's house, seduced by his gifts and trickery, for he got paid more there for just a little work than he would have got elsewhere for a lot of work. This boy was French by birth, a minor and an orphan from an extremely humble and impoverished background. A certain French Jew had (with evil intentions) taken pity on the boy's unhappy situation in France and had persuaded him, by means of repeated advice, to go to England, a land flowing with milk and honey. He claimed that the English were generous and lavish: no one who strove to make an honest living there would die poor. The boy was ready to agree to anything (a natural characteristic of the French), and so taking with him a friend of his own age, a fellow Frenchman, he prepared to set off abroad, taking nothing apart from a staff and with nothing in his satchel except an awl. He said goodbye to his Jewish friend, who said to him, [65] 'Be strong on your journey. May the God of my fathers lead you as I wish.' Laying his hands on the boy's head, as if he were a scapegoat, after some grating noises in his throat and silent prayers, already certain of his victim, he added, 'Be brave; forget your people and your country, because every country "is a homeland to the strong person, as the sea is to the fishes and the vast empty skies are to the bird". When you reach England, if you come to London, pass through it quickly, for I really dislike that city. People of all types flood into it from every nation under heaven. Every nationality brings its own vices and habits to the city. No one lives in it innocently. Every street abounds in grim obscenities. The more of a criminal someone is, the more highly he is regarded there. I am aware who I am instructing: you have a hotter intelligence and a cooler memory than is usual at your age, and these contrasting characteristics give you well-balanced rational qualities. I fear nothing for you unless you get into bad company, for behaviour is formed by those you live with. Well, be that as it may, you will get to London, and I warn you that you will find in that one city all the evil and wickedness to be found*

in any part of the world. Do not go near the gangs of pimps, and do not get caught up with the crowds of harlots; avoid dice and gambling, the theatres and the taverns. You will come across more braggarts than in the whole of France, and there are innumerable parasites. Actors, jesters, gay young men, black people, flatterers, young boys, effeminates, butch men, courtesans, sellers of drugs, various kinds of sorceress, people wandering around at night, magicians, mime artists, beggars and buffoons: the houses are filled with all these types. And so, if you don't want to live with wicked people, [66] do not live in London. I am not speaking against educated or religious people, or against Jews, although I think that these are less perfect than elsewhere, just because they live in close contact with bad people. I do not go so far as to say that you should avoid going to any city, since my advice is that you must not stay anywhere except in a town, but it just depends which one. If you land near Canterbury, or if you pass through it, you will waste time. There is a large number of those abandoned by their recently deified leader (the former Archbishop of Canterbury): they are now dying in the open everywhere throughout the city through lack of food and employment. Rochester and Chichester are just villages, and there is no reason for them to be called cities except that they are bishops' seats. Oxford can hardly sustain its own population, let alone satisfy them. Exeter feeds its men and beasts alike on grain, while Bath is set or rather deposited at the bottom of a valley in an atmosphere of dense air and sulphurous vapour, as if it stood at the gates of hell. And do not choose to settle in any town to the north, in Worcester, Chester or Hereford, because of the Welsh, who are prodigal of others' lives. York is full of Scots, foul and faithless and scarcely human. The area around Ely stinks perpetually on account of the surrounding fens. In Durham, Norwich or Lincoln there are very few people of your sort among those with power, and you will not hear French spoken at all. In Bristol there is no one who is not or has not been a soap-seller, and [67] every Frenchman loves soap-sellers as he does dung-collectors. Outside the towns, every marketplace, estate or village is inhabited by uncouth and rustic people. In addition, at all times judge people from Cornwall like our Flemish friends in France. In other respects, the country is in general totally blessed with dew from heaven and for the richness of its soil. In each place there are some good people but far fewer in all of these put together than in the single city of Winchester. That city is the Jerusalem of the Jews in those parts; in that city alone do they enjoy perpetual peace.'

Primary Sources and Related Texts

Cronicon Richardi Divisensis de tempore regis Richardi Primi, ed. J. Appleby, London, 1963.
Walter Map, *Courtiers' Trifles* (Section II.19).
EHD 3.59–63.

Further Reading

Partner, N. (2011) 'Richard of Devizes, the monk who forgot to be medieval' in *The Middle Ages in texts and texture*, ed. J. Glenn, Toronto.
Rees-Jones, S. and Watson, S. (ed.) (2013) *Christians and Jews in Angevin England: the York massacre of 1190, narratives and contexts*, Woodbridge.
Rexroth, F. (2007) *Deviance and power in late medieval London*, Cambridge.
*Staunton (2017).

Section II.19

Walter Map, *Courtiers' Trifles (De nugis curialium)* (excerpt: 1.25)

Date: 1181–2.

Courtiers' Trifles survives only in the important Bodleian MS 851, where part 1 (fourteenth century) also contains other works of medieval Latin satire such as Nigel of Canterbury's *Speculum stultorum*, while part 2 (fifteenth century) comprises the 'Z' text of Langland's *Piers Plowman*.

Author: Possibly from a Welsh family living around Hereford, Walter Map (c.1140–1210) was educated first in Gloucester. He then studied for several years in Paris before entering royal service as a secular clerk back in England in the early 1170s. He also worked for Gilbert Foliot, Bishop of London (1163–87) and opponent of Thomas Becket. In 1179 he was one of the royal representatives at the Third Vatican Council. After the death of Henry II in 1189 he moved to Lincoln and served in various cathedral roles under Bishop Hugh. In his last years he became Archdeacon of Oxford.

Work: Walter Map's combination of satire, anecdote and recent history in his *Courtiers' Trifles* provokes questions of the relations between fact and fiction, between what teaches and what amuses. Part of the *Courtiers' Trifles*, the so-called *Dissuasio Valerii* (4.3) in which the author warns his friend against marriage by giving examples of 'wicked wives' from the Bible and classical literature, drawing on Ovid and on Jerome's tract *Against Jovinianus*, took on a life of its own: this short work circulated separately in more than fifty MSS, but not under Walter's name; it was printed in Rome before 1468 as a work of Jerome but was in fact the first work by a British author to be printed. John of Salisbury, writing a few years before Walter, had given his *Policraticus* the subtitle *De nugis curialium et vestigiis philosophorum*. Both the *Policraticus* and the roughly contemporaneous first book of *De principis instructione* by Walter's friend Gerald of Wales share elements of hilarious satire and criticism of the court with Walter's *Courtiers' Trifles*; indeed, in his *Speculum Ecclesiae* (3.14) Gerald actually refers to Walter's witty criticism of religious orders.

Although the *Courtiers' Trifles* does not seem to have been widely known, as indicated by the paucity of MSS, Map's name was somehow connected with satire, and much satirical verse was attributed to him. The name Walter Map occurs in a number of MSS associated with satirical poems attributed to him in Gerald of

204 Twelfth Century

Wales' *Speculum Ecclesiae*. In the remarkable Bekynton Anthology (named from its fifteenth-century owner and editor, the English humanist Thomas Bekynton) in Bodleian MS Add. A.44, which still awaits an editor, such popular poems as *A tauro torrida* and *Sit Deo gloria*, the latter an anti-marriage tract, are attributed to 'Magister Walter Mape'.[1] Although it is unlikely that Map really wrote these poems, there is one poem in Goliardic verse that is apparently by an Englishman called Richard. He writes to the Goliardic fraternity in France to find out the rules by which he would have to live if he joined them:[2] it begins *omnibus in Gallia Anglus Goliardus* and uses the rare word *harlotus*; cf. the use of this word by Gerald of Wales (*Spec. Eccl.* 3.20, p. 251) with the equally rare and interesting *ribaldus*, both of which have the sense 'vagabond'. In the passage below, part of a scathing digression on the monastic life, Map directs his criticism against the Cistercians, who had suffered a decline in their reputation since their foundation in 1098 as a reformed Benedictine order: here he reveals the limitations of their generosity and austerity.

Linguistic points: Map cites both the Bible and works of classical literature, particular those of Horace, Ovid, Virgil and Juvenal. His Latin is largely classical. He does, however, include some rare words, like *anclare* (*NC* 7.9) and *runcator* (1.25), perhaps derived from glossaries. He also inserts neologisms such as *inolibilis*, *intumbare*, *transcorporare*, formed from CL. Map uses some Latin words formed from borrowings, such as *baro* ('baron') and *baco* ('bacon') derived from Frankish (in BML from the eleventh century), or *cnipulus* ('knife') from OE 'cnif' (in BML from the mid-twelfth century), or *brathanum* ('cloth') associated with Welsh 'brethyn'. The Latin form of this Welsh word occurs only in Walter Map and Gerald of Wales, an example of a regional Latin word. Note the characteristic wordplay with *deliciari* and *delectare*.

TEXT II.19

Walter mocks the Cistercians' claims of generosity and austerity

[1.25] primum pauperibus habent (i.e. Cistercienses) manus apertas, at parce: dis-

Ps. 111:9 pergunt quidem et dant, sed non reficiunt, quia singuli modicum quid accipiunt et cum neque secundum suam ditent habundanciam neque secundum pauperum indigenciam, sinistra dare videntur, non dextra. sed tamen ut omnia vere, nichil sophistice faciant, nullatenus equabunt Domino quod abstulerunt, quod vel nullus est vel pauci sunt eorum conventus, qui non plures fecerint egenos

---

1 Cf. A.G. Rigg (1977) 'Golias and other pseudonyms', *Studi Medievali* 18: 65–109.

2 T. Wright (1841) *The Latin poems commonly attributed to Walter Mapes*, Camden Society 16: 69.

quam exhibeant. hospitales invicem, id est inter se, sine murmure possunt esse, sed non nobis, Domine Deus noster, non nobis. his quos timore potestatis vel emun-gendos or e-mungendos suscipiunt, toto splendore popine propiciantur, tota vultus et verborum adest leticia; ipsis eorum tam benigne, tam misericorditer apertus est sinus, tam simpliciter, tam ydiotice cuncta profusa, credas angelos esse non homines, et in abcessu tuo miraberis laudes eorum. nos autem Egipcii et vagi, qui pro Deo solo suscipimur, nichil nisi caritatem allegantes, illuc ultra non revertimur, dum alias alique patuerint porte vel burse, que respondere possint. post ymnos vespertinos neminem nostrum aut vocant aut trahunt aut hospicium paciuntur ingredi, cum post longas dietas magis eo tempore quies optetur et refeccio, sitque repulsa molestior. **Ps. 113:9**

A comparison between the Cistercians and the Welsh
de vestibus eorum et cibo et labore diuturno dicunt (quibus ipsi boni sunt, quia nichil eis mali facere possunt), quod vestes non sufficunt ad frigus nec cibus ad esuriem, labor autem immensus; et inde michi faciunt argumentum quod cupidi non sunt quia sibi ad nullas delicias acquisita perveniunt. O quam facilis ad hoc responsio! feneratores et quicunque avaricie deserviunt, nonne parcissime se vestiunt et viliter exibent? et thesauris incumbunt morientes avari; non congregant ut delicientur sed delectentur, non ut utantur sed conservent. si de labore, de frigore, de cibo contendas, Walenses in omnibus hiis gravius affliguntur;[3] isti multas habent tunicas, illi nullam; isti pellicias non habent, nec illi; isti non utuntur lino, nec illi lana, preterquam in curtis palliolis et simplicibus; isti calceos habent et caligas, illi nudis pedibus et tibiis incedunt; isti non vescuntur carne, nec illi pane; isti dant elemosinam, illi non habent cui dent; cum sint apud eos cibi communes, nemo inter eos cibum petit: nemo in hac gente mendicus. omnium enim hospitia omnibus sunt communia, sed sine prohibicione sumit; illi tamen inverecundius et manifestiore vi captivant et interficiunt homines quam isti; illi semper in tabernaculis sunt aut sub divo, isti domibus eburneis delectantur.

Cistercian policy on undergarments leads to a humorous incident
et in hac districcione vestium de femoralibus admirandum duco, quod eis uti oportet in altaris obsequio et cum inde recesserint deponuntur. sacrarum vestium hec est dignitas; hec autem sacra non est nec inter sacerdotalia vel levitica computatur aut benedicitur; typica vero est et pudenda contegit, venerisque secreta signare videtur et castigare ne prodeant. cur ab illis abstinendum sit quidam michi racionem dedit, ut scilicet circa loca illa frigeant, ne prosiliat ardor vel fiat impetus in incestum. absit hoc! et decurtentur interiores a zona tunice, manente suprema, et non decalventur a veste venerabili et ab omni alias

---

3 These claims about Welsh austerity and generosity are supported by Map at 2.20–1 of this same work and by Gerald of Wales in his *Descriptio Kambriae* (*Description of Wales*) 1.9–10.

206 Twelfth Century

approbata religione loca celanda. dominus rex Henricus secundus nuper, ut ei mos est, totam illam infinitatem militum et clericorum suorum precedens, cum domino Rerico monacho magno et honesto viro verbum faciebat, eratque eis ventus nimis et ecce monachus albus in vico pedes negociabatur, respiciensque divertere properabat; offendit ad lapidem nec portabatur ab angelis tunc et coram pedibus equi regii corruit; ventus autem vestes eius in collum propulit, ut domini regis et Rerici oculis invitis manifesta fieret misera veritas pudendorum. rex, ut omnis facecie thesaurus, dissimulans vultum avertit et tacuit. Rericus autem intulit secreto 'Maledicta religio que develat anum!'[4] ego verbum audivi et dolui quod derisa est sanctitas, licet ventus non iniuste in loca sibi concessa impegerit. verumtamen si cibi parcitas et vestis aspera gravisque labor, qualia describunt hec singula, modum carni sue ponere non possunt, desideraturque ventus pro freno Veneri, bonum est ut braccis careant et insufflentur. scio quod caro nostra, mundana scilicet non celestis, tantis non eget ad hec bella clipeis, quia sine Cerere et Baco nostra friget Venus; sed forsitan forcior in eos insurgit hostis, quos firmius novit clausos. monachus tamen qui cecidit honestius surrexisset, si corporaliter clausus est.

Terence, *Eun.* 732

Translation: Walter Map, *Courtiers' Trifles*

[1.25] *Firstly, the Cistercians are open-handed to the poor, but only slightly; to be sure, they hand out and they give, but they do not revive, because each person only receives a little, and since they provide funds neither in proportion to their own wealth nor to the needs of the poor, they seem to give with their left hand, not their right. But still, even if they did all this sincerely and without pretence, they will in no way equal for the Lord what they have stolen, because there is no monastery of theirs, or only a few, which has not made more people destitute than they sustain. They can be hospitable, that is, to each other, without grumbling, but not to us, O Lord our God, not to us. Those whom they welcome out of fear of their power or because they intend to fleece them, they propitiate with all the glamour of the canteen, while their words and faces give an impression of pure joy; they dip their hands deep in their pockets for these people, showing kindness and compassion, pouring forth everything so disingenuously and simply that you could believe they were angels, not men, and when you leave you are amazed at their effusive words. But we, Egyptians and wanderers as we are, who are received for God's sake alone and have no claim apart from that of charity, will not go back there again, as long as other doors are open to us elsewhere and there are other purses from which to pay us. After the evening hymns they do not invite or draw any of us in or even allow us to*

---

4 Cf. *Speculum stultorum* (lines 2141–8) on the Cistercians' lack of undergarments and Gerald of Wales, *Spec. Eccl.* 3.20 on *femoralia*.

enter their guesthouse, although after a long day's journey it is at that moment that we long for rest and refreshment and so their rejection is all the more painful. As for their clothes and food and long working days, those to whom they are kind (because they do not harm them) say that their clothing is insufficient to combat cold, their food insufficient to combat hunger and their hard work unceasing. Such people try to prove to me that the Cistercians are not greedy on the grounds that their acquisitions are not used for luxuries. How easy it is to respond to this! Do not usurers and those who are enslaved to avarice wear cheap clothes and give an impression of poverty? On their deathbeds misers pore over their treasures; they do not collect them so as to lead a life of luxury but to take delight in them, not to use them but to save them. If you argue about the hard work, the cold and the food, the Welsh suffer in every respect much more than these people. The Cistercians wear many coats, the Welsh none; they do not have furs, but neither do the Welsh; they do not use linen, well, the Welsh do not use wool, except for short, unlined cloaks. The Cistercians have sandals and boots, while the Welsh go around with bare feet and legs; they do not eat meat, while the Welsh have no bread; they give money to the poor, but the Welsh have none to give to, for as they share all their food, not one of them has to beg for food but can just help himself. The Cistercians capture and kill men more shamefully and with more open violence than the Welsh; while the monks delight in buildings of ivory, the Welsh always live in tents or out in the open.

With regard to their clothing regulations, I think it is surprising that they have to wear undergarments when serving at the altar and then take them off afterwards. That is the privilege of sacred vestments, but this garment is not sacred, nor is it reckoned among the garments of the priests or Levites, nor is it blessed; it is symbolic, concealing the private parts and, as it were, putting a seal on Love's secrets, restraining them so that they do not reveal themselves. Someone explained to me why undergarments are not used by the Cistercians: it is so that the monks should be cool in that part of the body, to prevent heat erupting and possibly sparking a sexual impulse. No, that cannot be the case. The inner tunics could be shortened from the belt downwards, retaining the upper part; the parts that need to be concealed should not be stripped of a venerable garment, otherwise approved by every religion. The lord king, Henry II, was recently riding ahead of the whole infinite array of his knights and clerics as was his custom, while talking to Lord Reric, a distinguished monk and an honourable man. A strong wind was blowing while a monk in white robes (i.e. a Cistercian) was making his way on foot down the street. Looking round he hastened to get out of the way, but oh no! he tripped on a stone and at that moment was not being supported by angels, and so he fell flat on his face in front of the hooves of the king's horse. The wind propelled his habit up over his neck so that the wretched truth of his private parts was exposed to the unwilling gaze of the lord king and Reric. The king, being a veritable treasury of politeness, turned his face away and said nothing; but Reric whispered, 'Cursed be this religion that bares his bottom!' I heard what he said and I was embarrassed that something holy could be mocked, although the wind had a perfect right to intrude there. However, if meagre *food and rough clothing and heavy labour, as they list them, cannot put a brake on their fleshly desires, and if wind is needed to restrain Venus, then it is a good thing that they go without breeches and feel a draught. I know that our flesh, our earthly flesh, that is, not the heavenly one, has no need of such things to protect it in these battles, because without Ceres and Bacchus, Venus is cold; but perhaps the enemy attacks these monks more fiercely just because it knows they are more firmly enclosed. Anyway, the monk who fell over would have got up with less embarrassment if his body had been enclosed by more clothes.*

Primary Sources and Related Texts

Walter Map, *De nugis curialium*, ed. M. R. James (rev. C. Brooke and
    R. Mynors), OMT, Oxford, 1983.
Jankyn's Book of Wikked Wyves, vol. 2: seven commentaries on Walter Map's
    Dissuasio Valerii, ed. T. Lawler and R. Hanna III, Athens, GA, 2014.
Gerald of Wales, *Speculum Ecclesiae*, for disparagement of the Cistercian order.
Peter of Blois, *Letter* 14, for criticism of life at court.

Further Reading

Bayless, M. (1996) *Parody in the Middle Ages: the Latin tradition*, Ann Arbor.
Coxon, S. (2012) 'Wit, laughter and authority in Walter Map's *De nugis
    curialium*' in *Author, reader, book: medieval authorship in theory and practice*,
    ed. S. Partridge and E. Kwakkel, Toronto.
*Rigg (1992).
*Staunton (2017).

Section II.20

Hugh Nonant, Bishop of Coventry, *Letter* Recounting the Spectacular Downfall of Chancellor William de Longchamp (excerpts from pp. 125–9)

William de Longchamp (d. 1197), from a humble French family, became Chancellor of England and Bishop of Ely (1190–7) under Richard I. Among his misdemeanours was the persecution of Richard's half-brother Geoffrey, who became Bishop of York in 1190: the hostility between them (part of the wider political picture) and Longchamp's downfall in October 1191 were treated by many contemporary historians. In his *Gesta Ricardi* 2.214 Roger of Howden, for example, wittily summarised Longchamp's undoing in the phrase *cancellarius cancellatus* ('the cancelled chancellor'). Roger also records the letter of Hugh Nonant, who gives a detailed account of events leading up to the chancellor's ignominious fall from power. Other contemporaries were more supportive of Longchamp: Peter of Blois expresses his shock at Nonant's depiction of Longchamp in a letter (*Ep.* 87) laden with biblical references, also recorded by Roger (*Chr.* 3.148), while Nigel of Canterbury dedicated his satirical epic poem *Speculum stultorum* to Longchamp. Surprisingly, Longchamp returned to England from exile to serve the king on Richard's return from the Crusades.

Date: late 1191.

Nonant's letter is contained in the British Library and Bodleian Library MSS of Roger of Howden's *Gesta Regis Ricardi* and his *Chronica*; for the complex MS situation see *Episcopal Acta* 17, p. 125. The letter exists also in Bodleian MS Add. A.44, ff. 219r–222r (s.xiii, i.e. contemporary with the events concerned), art. 101. This MS also contains the Bekynton Anthology (cf. Section II.19), with its many satirical poems, including a rhythmic and rhyming poem of 172 lines on the same subject, containing classical and biblical references, published by C. Kingsford (1890) 'Some political poems of the twelfth century', *EHR* 5: 317–19.

Author: Hugh Nonant (d. 1198 at Bec Abbey), a nephew of Arnulf of Lisieux (cf. Section II.16, n. 1), came from Normandy to serve Thomas Becket (even going into exile with him) and later worked as a diplomat for Henry II. After he was made Bishop of Coventry (1188–98) his behaviour became less diplomatic, arousing the hostility of many when he replaced the monks with secular canons. Gervase of Canterbury sums Hugh up (*Chr.* 1.349) as *acer ingenio, captiosus in verbo, promptus ad maledicendum ut timidos faceret, mollibus utens ut firmos subverteret*

210 Twelfth Century

('intellectually sharp, verbally subtle, quick to insult so as to intimidate, using weak people to destroy the strong'). Gerald of Wales discusses him in his *Speculum Ecclesiae* (2.23–4): William de Longchamp had been his friend until 1191, but as Devizes (p. 48) puts it, *pessima pestis est familiaris inimicus* ('the worst plague is a close friend turned enemy'). In the letter excerpted below, Hugh excoriates William for his pride and for abuse of power.

Work: The long letter in which Hugh traces Longchamp's rise and fall as a cautionary tale, a kind of anti-saint's Life, is quoted in full by Roger of Howden in both his *Gesta* and *Chronica*. It is a brilliant work of vitriolic rhetoric, culminating in the ludicrous description of Longchamp's capture on Dover beach as he tried to escape to France dressed as a woman. It formed the basis for many other contemporary accounts of this episode: for a slightly different, if similarly rhetorical treatment of this episode, one may compare Gerald of Wales in his *Life of Geoffrey of York* (*V.Galfridi* 2.12) and Richard of Devizes (pp. 48–54); for less lurid versions, see William of Newburgh (*Historia rerum Anglicarum* 4.17), Ralph of Diceto (*Ymagines historiarum* 2.97–101) and Gervase of Canterbury (*Chr.* 1.504–8), each in his own style. Matthew Paris includes the episode in his *Chronica majora* 2.380–2, choosing to change *femoralia* to the Gaulish-derived CL synonym *bracae* (for which, cf. Section II.19)

Linguistic points: The author uses such rhetorical devices as antithesis, assonance and wordplay (e.g. *accusatorem, immo destructorem* or *usibus sed abusibus et lusibus*), as well as the tricolon and concatenations such as *abstractum fortiter vinxit, vinctum turpiter traxit, tractum incarceravit*. One of the few borrowings from the vernacular is *garcio* (originally meaning a 'ruffian', but developing the sense of 'servant lad') from French (as in modern French 'garçon'), going back to the Frankish form 'wrakkjo'; *garcio* is first attested in BML in Orderic Vitalis (*HE* 6.458), who was of course writing in Normandy at the beginning of the twelfth century. Hugh quotes plentifully from the Bible, but also refers to the Roman emperor Tiberius. According to Nonant's comment, Longchamp was entirely ignorant of the English language: if this is so, it is an interesting indication of the linguistic situation in government at the end of the twelfth century, if the Chancellor of England could perform his role without knowing English.

TEXT II.20

William de Longchamp's rise to power
[p. 125 Franklin] casum itaque Eliensis episcopi ad notitiam omnium litteris instantibus volumus in posterum consignari, ut in hoc exemplari semper inveniat et humilitas quod prosperet, et superbia quod formidet. erat enim ille vir magnus inter omnes occidentales, utpote qui regni potestatem et sedis apostolicae auctor-

itatem quasi ambidexter habebat, et regis sigillum super omnem terram gestabat, ut pro sua voluntate posset impetrare, et de potestate valeret omnia affectu mancipare, ut pariter rex et sacerdos haberetur et esset; (…) quia nec venatio in terris, nec piscatio in aqua, nec volatus in aere qui suae non cogerentur mensae servire: ut partitus videretur fuisse elementa cum Deo, coelum tantum celi Domino relinquens, cetera tria suis usibus sed abusibus et lusibus profutura reservans. huic omnes filii nobilium serviebant vultu demisso, nec in celum aspicere audebant, nisi forte ab eo vocati et si aliter attentassent aculeo pungebantur quem dominus prae manibus habebat, memor piae recordationis avi sui, qui servilis conditionis in pago Belvacensi, et aratrum ducere et boves castigare consueverat. qui tandem ad remedium libertatis ad fines Normannorum transvolavit. hujus nepotes et consanguineas sive quascunque propinquas de paupere tugurio procreatas, comites et barones regnique magnates sibi summa aviditate in matrimonium copulare ardebant, gloriosum reputantes quocunque titulo familiaritatis ejus gratiam adquisissent; nec erat rusticus qui agrum, nec civis qui fundum, nec miles qui praedium, nec clericus qui ecclesiam, nec monachus qui abbatiam affectaret, quem in jus et potestatem ejus transire non oporteret. licet enim flexo genu tota Anglia ei deserviret, ad Francorum tamen libertatem semper aspirans, apud Oximum milites deservientes omnemque suam familiam abstrahebat, et spreta in omnibus gente Anglorum, stipatus agmine Francorum et Flandrensium pompatice incedebat, subsannationem in naribus, cachinnum in ore, derisum in oculis, supercilium in fronte gestans pro lamina sacerdotis. hic ad augmentum et famam sui nominis emendicata carmina et rhythmos adulatorios comparabat, et de regno Francorum cantores et joculatores muneribus allexerat, et de illo canerent in plateis; et jam dicebatur ubique quod non erat talis in orbe. et revera si tempus Caesaris fuisset, se Deum vivum cum Tiberio appellari fecisset. (…)

Translation: Hugh Nonant on Longchamp's Downfall

And so we wish, by means of the present letter, to pass on to all future generations an awareness of the Bishop of Ely's downfall, so that in this example humility may always find support and pride may find a warning. For William de Longchamp was a powerful man among all the people of the west, in that he held power ambidextrously over the secular realm and the authority of the papal see, and wielded the king's seal over all the land, so that he could govern as he wished. His power allowed him to grant all things according to his desire, so that he was considered to be, and indeed he was, both a king and a priest; (…) Because there was no game on land nor fish in the sea, nor birds in the air that were not compelled to serve his table, he seemed to have divided up the elements with God, leaving only the heavens for the Lord of heaven, keeping the remaining three as profitable for his own uses, or rather his abuses or sport. All the sons of the nobility served him with downcast eyes, not daring to look up towards the heavens unless by chance they were summoned by

212 Twelfth Century

him; and if they tried to do something else they were whipped with the goad which their lord had in his hand, remembering his grandfather of blessed memory, of servile status in the region of Beauvais, who used to drive his plough and whip his oxen and who finally fled into Normandy to regain his freedom. Earls and barons and the magnates of the kingdom greedily desired to be joined in matrimony to this man's grandchildren and relations or any close female relatives who sprang from that poor cottage, for they considered it was a way of gaining high status to win the favour of a close connection with him by whatever title. For there was no farm-worker who desired land, no town-dweller who desired some property, no knight an estate, no cleric a church, no monk who desired an abbey, who was not obliged to become subservient to his authority and power. Although the whole of England submitted to him on bended knee, he always longed for the freedom of the French and dragged the knights in his service and his whole household to 'Oximum'; showing contempt for the English people in all things, he used to process ostentatiously, closely surrounded by a throng of French and Flemish supporters, his nostrils curled with contempt, a scornful smirk on his lips, a look of derision in his eyes, an attitude of superciliousness in place of priestly adornments. This man paid beggars to compose songs and adulatory verses to make him more of a celebrity and increase his reputation and he used bribes to lure singers and entertainers from France to sing about him in the town squares. Already people everywhere were saying that there was no one like him in the world. To be sure, if it had been the time of the Caesars, he would have arranged for himself to be called the living God, like Tiberius. (…)

England can bear his arrogant power no longer; the struggle over Archbishop Geoffrey of York brings about Longchamp's downfall

[p. 126] cum igitur Anglia sub tam gravi onere et jugo importabili diutius laboras-

Jonah 3:8   set, ingemiscens tandem propter opera, clamavit in fortitudine et ascendit clamor ejus ad Dominum (…) cum igitur homo tantus ab homine non posset superari,

2 Cor. 1:3   Pater misericordiarum et Deus totius consolationis venit in adjutorium populo suo supplicanti, et in affectum ejus manum misericordiae supponens, dejecit illum a potestate, et accusatorem, immo destructorem, in eum spiritum vertiginis

Exod. 9:12   induxit, a quo reverti non posset vel resurgere; sed ita induravit cor, excaecavit

2 Cor. 4:4/   mentem, infatuavit consilium illius, quod archiepiscopum Eboracensem in ec-

2 Sam. 15:31   clesia prius obsedit, postmodum cepit, captum violenter extraxit, abstractum fortiter vinxit, vinctum turpiter traxit, tractum incarceravit. (…) [p. 127] ergo per totam insulam a laicis publice proclamatur, 'Pereat qui cuncta perdere festinat,

Luke 23:31   opprimatur ne omnes opprimat; quia si in viridi haec fecit, in arido quid faceret?'

Ps. 106:3   et ecce, Spiritu Sancto ducente, ab aquilone et mari et ex omni parte insulae totius, concurrunt et confluunt universi, ut archiepiscopus ille posset liberari. verum funiculis peccatorum suorum ipsum constringentibus cancellarium, et conscientia sua eum vehementius accusante, fugit loricatus a facie hominum, et se abscondit et inclusit cum hominibus suis in turre Lundoniarum. nobis autem introeuntibus civitatem in sero, plures de familia ejus armati cum gladiis exsertis nos invaserunt, et nobilem de nostris militem interfecerunt et plures vulneraverunt. mane ergo habito consilio cum omnibus fere magnatibus regni, praesente domino Johanne fratre regis et Rothomagensi et Eboracensi archiepiscopis, episcopis etiam praesentibus Dunelmensi, Lundoniensi, Wintoniensi, Bathoniensi, Rofensi, Norwicensi, Lincolniensi, Herefordensi, Menevensi, Coventrensi, factoque consilio coram omni populo totius civitatis, praesentibus quoque justiciariis domini regis et approbantibus, de consilio universorum statuimus, ne talis de caetero in regno Angliae dominetur, per quem ecclesia Dei ad ignominiam et populus ad inopiam esset redactus. ut enim caetera omittam, ipse et garciones sui totum regnum exhauserant, nec viro balteum nec feminae monile remanserat, nec annulus nobili nec quodlibet pretiosum alicui etiam Judaeo. (...) super quo et fratres suos et camerarium suum obsides dedit, et Cantuariam properavit, ut ibi sicut decebat crucem acciperet peregrinationis, et deponeret crucem legationis, quam per annum et dimidium anni, post mortem papae Clementis in praejudicium Romanae ecclesiae et detrimentum Anglicanae portaverat. (...)

Translation: Hugh Nonant on Longchamp's Downfall

And so when England had suffered for too long beneath such a heavy burden and an unbearable yoke, at last groaning at his deeds, she cried out with all her strength and her cry went up to the Lord. (...) Since such a powerful man could not be overcome by man, the Father of mercies and the God of all consolation came to the assistance of his people as they cried for help; placing the hand of mercy on their emotion, he hurled Longchamp down from power and introduced a spirit of vertigo into that accuser, or rather destroyer, so that he could neither return nor rise again. But his heart was hardened, his mind blinded and his wisdom turned to folly to such an extent that he first laid siege to the Archbishop of York in a church, then captured him, and after capturing him he dragged him out violently, and after dragging him out he bound him strongly, and when he was bound he dragged him shamefully, and after dragging him he locked him in prison. (...) And so it was publicly proclaimed by the lay people all over the island, 'Death to the one who hastens to destroy everything! Let him be crushed to stop him crushing everyone! For if this is what he has done when things are fresh, what would he do when they are dry?' See how under the guidance of the Holy Spirit everyone comes running, converging from the north and the sea and from every part of the whole island to allow that archbishop to be freed. But when the ropes of his crimes began to tighten round the chancellor and his conscience started to accuse him forcefully, he fled in chainmail from the sight of men and went into hiding, shutting himself up with his men in the Tower of London. When we entered the city late that evening, a large number of his household, armed and with swords drawn, attacked us and killed one of our noble knights and wounded several. In the morning, a meeting was held with almost all the magnates of the kingdom, in the presence of the lord John, the king's brother, and

214 Twelfth Century

the archbishops of Rouen and York, and also with the bishops of Durham, London, Winchester, Bath, Rochester, Norwich, Lincoln, Hereford, St David's and Coventry; then a meeting was held in front of all the people of the whole city, in the presence also of the lord king's justiciars, who gave their approval. We decided unanimously that from now on such a man should not be in control in the kingdom of England, for he had caused the Church of God to be reduced to shame and the people to poverty. In short, he and his henchmen had drained the whole kingdom and there remained no belt for a man, no necklace for a woman and no ring for a nobleman nor anything valuable for anyone, even a Jew. (...) In addition he gave his brothers and his chamberlain as hostages and hurried to Canterbury so that he might take up the cross of pilgrimage, as was fitting, and lay down the cross of his legate's office, which he had carried for a year and a half after the death of Pope Clement, to the disadvantage of the Roman Church and the detriment of the English Church. (...)

William de Longchamp attempts to flee but is exposed on Dover Beach
cum autem in castello Doroberniae aliquot diebus commoratus fuisset, immemor suae professionis et fidei obligationis quam [p. 128] fecerat, oblitus etiam fratrum suorum quos obsides datos morti turpiter exponebat, navigare proposuit. et cum hoc aperte non auderet, novum genus fraudis invenit, et sese foeminam simulavit, cujus sexum semper odit, vestemque sacerdotis in habitum convertit meretricis. proh dolor! vir factus est foemina, cancellarius cancellaria, sacerdos meretrix, episcopus scurra. ergo de castello superiori licet claudus esset, pedibus praelegit properare ad littus, tunica foeminea viridi et enormiter longa, pro tunica sacerdotis hyacinthina indutus; cappam habens ejusdem coloris deformiter manicatam pro planeta, peplum in capite pro mitra; pannum lineum in manu sinistra quasi ad vendendum, pro maniplo; virgam venditoris in dextera, pro baculo pastorali. talibus ornatus antistes descendit ad mare et qui loricam militis saepius gestare solebat, mira res quod tam effoeminati animi factus, animum foemineum praelegit. cum enim sederet in littore supra petram, piscator quidam, qui statim deputans scortum propius accessit; et qui quasi nudus de mari descenderat calefieri cupiens, cucurrit ad monstrum, et manu sinistra collum complectens, dextra partes inferiores rimatur. cumque tunicam subito sublevasset, et nimis inverecunde ad partes verecundas manum extendisset audacter, femoralia sensit et virum in foemina certis argumentis agnovit; et vehementer admirans, retro prosiliens totus attonitus, voce magna proclamat, 'Venite omnes et videte mirabilia, quia in foemina inveni virum!' protinus servientes ejus et noti qui stabant a longe accesserunt et modesta quadam violentia eum repulerunt et increpaverunt ut taceret; tacuit ergo piscator et clamor ille quievit, et sedebat hermaphroditus exspectans. interim mulier quaedam exiens de villa, videns pannum lineum quem ille vel illa gestabat, expositum venditioni, et procedens coepit inquirere quanti esset pretii et pro quanto ulnam daret? ille non respondebat quia linguam Anglicanam prorsus ignorabat. at illa magis instabat; et continuo supervenit alia mulier, illud idem instanter inquirens et plurimum instans ut ei pretium venditionis aperiret. cum-

que ille nihil responderet sed magis subrideret, coeperunt interesse et fabulari et quaerere quidnam esset. et dolum arbitrantes projecerunt manus ad peplum quo facies tegebatur, et submittentes a naso usque deorsum viderunt faciem hominis nigram et noviter rasam. stupescere coeperunt ultra modum et corruentes eum ad terram, voces ad sidera tollunt, dicentes, 'Venite, lapidemus hoc monstrum qui deformavit utrumque sexum!' et facta est statim multitudo virorum ac mulierum extrahentium de capite peplum et trahentium eum prostratum in terram per manicas et caputium, per arenam ignominiose, et per saxa non sine laesione. servientes autem sui bis aut ter impetum fecerunt in turbam ut eum liberarent; sed non potuerunt, quia totus populus eum insatiabili corde persequens, et verbis et alapis et sputis, pluribusque modis turpiter tractavit per totam villam; et sic tractatum, immo distractum, in [p. 129] quodam cellario tenebroso eum quasi sub carcerali custodia inclusit. tractus est igitur qui traxerat; captus est qui vi ceperat; ligatus est qui ligaverat; incarceratus qui incarceraverit; ut secundum quantitatem culpae commensurabilis videretur quantitas poenae. (…)

Translation: Hugh Nonant on Longchamp's Downfall

When he had stayed for a few days in Dover Castle, ignoring his profession of obedience and the bond of faith he had made, and forgetting also his brothers whom he had given as hostages and shamefully exposed to death, he decided to set sail. Since he did not dare to do this openly, he found a new type of deception and pretended he was a woman, whose sex he had always hated, and changed his priestly robes for a prostitute's clothing. Alas! The man became a woman, the male chancellor a female one, the priest a prostitute, the bishop a scoundrel. Although he was limping, he chose to rush down from the upper castle to the shore on foot, dressed in a woman's green tunic which was enormously long, instead of a priest's blue tunic; he had a hooded cloak of the same colour shamefully provided with sleeves instead of a chasuble, a veil on his head instead of a mitre; linen cloth in his left hand as if he were selling it, instead of a maniple; the rod of a seller in his right hand instead of a pastoral staff. Dressed like this the bishop went down to the sea, and the strange thing was that he who often used to wear a soldier's chainmail had become so effeminate that he preferred a feminine attitude. For while he was sitting on a rock on the shore, a fisherman who immediately thought he was a prostitute came up closer to him, and as he had come out of the sea more or less naked and wanted to be warmed, ran to the monster and putting his left arm round his neck, he began to grope down below with his right hand. When he suddenly lifted the tunic and boldly put out his hand to touch the shameful parts very shamelessly, he felt the breeches and recognised from clear proof that the woman was a man; and he was very surprised and leapt back, totally shocked, and shouted loudly, 'Come here everyone and see something amazing! I have found a man in a woman!' The bishop's servants and friends, who were standing at some distance, immediately came over and drove the man away with a

216 Twelfth Century

degree of violence and rebuked him to make him keep quiet. So the fisherman shut up and stopped shouting, and the hermaphrodite sat waiting. Meanwhile a woman coming out from the town, seeing the linen cloth he, or she, was carrying, laid out as if for sale, went up and began to ask the price and how much it cost per yard. He did not answer, because he knew no English at all. But the woman persisted and then another woman came up, too, asking insistently the same thing and insisting that he reveal to her the price it cost. When he made no reply but smiled instead, they began to get involved and to converse and to try to find out what was going on. Thinking it might be a trick they stretched out their hands to the veil covering his face and pulling it down from his nose they saw the face of a man, swarthy and newly shaved. They were extremely shocked and pulling him to the ground they raised their voices to heaven, saying, 'Come on! Let's stone this monster who has disfigured both sexes!' And immediately a crowd of men and women gathered, pulling the veil from his head and ignominiously dragging him headlong onto the ground by his sleeves and hood, over the sand and the rocks, injuring him. His servants attacked the crowd two or three times to try and release him, but they were unable to do so, because all the people were pursuing him and would not give up, insulting and beating him, spitting at him, treating him shamefully in many different ways, right through the town; finally after dragging, or rather tearing him apart in this way, they shut him up in a dark cellar, as if he were in custody in prison. And so the man who had dragged was himself dragged, the one who had captured by force was himself captured, he who had bound was bound and he who had imprisoned was imprisoned, so that the amount of punishment seemed proportionate to the amount of blame. (…)

Primary Sources and Related Texts

English Episcopal Acta 17: Lichfield and Coventry 1183–1208, ed. M. Franklin, Oxford, 1998: 124–31.
Roger of Howden, *Gesta Ricardi Primi*, RS 49.2 (1867) 215–20.
Roger of Howden, *Chronica*, RS 51.3 (1870) 141–7.

Further Reading

Desborough, D. (1991) 'Politics and prelacy in the late twelfth century: the career of Hugh de Nonant, Bishop of Coventry 1188–98', *Historical Research* 64: 1–14.

THIRTEENTH CENTURY

Section II.21

Gerald of Wales (Giraldus Cambrensis)
A: *An Account of Gerald's Achievements* (*De gestis Giraldi*) (excerpt: 3.1–2)
B: *The Jewel of the Church* (*Gemma ecclesiastica*) (excerpt: 2.35–6)

These excerpts provide various examples of the difficulties experienced by clergy and laity alike in mastering the Latin language.

Author: Much of what we know about Gerald derives from his autobiographical work, the *Account of Gerald's Achievements*. Gerald de Barri (1146–1223) was born in Wales and educated at Gloucester Abbey under Abbot Hamelin (the dedicatee of Osbern of Gloucester's lexicographical work, the *Derivationes*) and at the University of Paris. His career was spent in the service of the king and bishops, but his hopes of ecclesiastical preferment (above all, of gaining the archbishopric of St David's, a controversial position at the time) were repeatedly dashed, largely because of his disputatiousness, though he suggests that it was also because of his Welsh heritage and his opponents' jealousy of his cleverness. An illustration of this may be seen in the angry exchange of letters between Gerald and Hubert Walter, Archbishop of Canterbury at the time, and Hubert's brilliantly rhetorical letter to the pope decrying Gerald's election to the bishopric of St David's; Gerald was never consecrated to the post. His background and education meant that Gerald was multilingual, in French, Welsh, English and Latin. He had a strong interest in comparative linguistics, as well as in other aspects of culture, in the state of the Church and in contemporary politics. He travelled to Rome several times, and his knowledge of Wales, and his travels round Ireland, allowed him to write colourful ethnographic works, with fascinating details, about these countries. Gerald combined strongly held views with a vitriolic sense of humour, as demonstrated in particular in his works *Speculum Ecclesiae*, *Speculum duorum* and *Topographia Hibernica*. His works are full of allusions to classical literature, both prose and verse, and to patristic writings, especially those of Jerome, whose literary qualities as well as his bitterness no doubt attracted Gerald. Like his friend Walter Map, Gerald was skilled at inserting anecdotes that reflected his critical acumen, while teasing the reader on the fine line between fact and fiction.

220 Thirteenth Century

A: *An Account of Gerald's Achievements* (*De gestis Giraldi*)
(excerpt: 3.1–2)

Date: 1208–16.

The early thirteenth-century BL MS Cotton Tiberius B.xiii is one of only two that preserve this work.

Work: As an author Gerald is often strongly present in his work, particularly so in the autobiographical writing, the *Account of Gerald's Achievements* (*De gestis Giraldi*, also known as *De rebus a se gestis*), which is built around the theme of life at court and his own experiences, and yet he chooses to write about himself (i.e. the archdeacon (of Brecon) in the passage below) in the third person, even at one point drawing a distinction between the archdeacon and himself. In this passage Gerald wants to take time out from court life to devote himself to his studies. He visits his friend, the anchorite Wecheleu from Llowes near Hay-on-Wye, to ask for help in understanding the Scriptures, but his friend points out that knowledge alone is dangerous. Gerald enquires about Wecheleu's strange way of speaking Latin. The anchorite explains that on his return from pilgrimage God granted him the ability to speak a simplified form of Latin to enable basic communication. It is possible that there is a connection here with a basic Romance lingua franca apparently used by international pilgrims and crusaders at this period.[1] It is to be noted that Wecheleu 'learns' Latin not as the result of academic study (which is being denigrated in this passage) or through written texts but by a miraculous gift from God. With this may be compared the experience of Godric, who, through the agency of the Holy Spirit, was able to understand the monks' discussion in Latin despite his lack of learning.[2]

Linguistic Points: The opening section of this passage is clearly rhetorical, but even the account of Wecheleu continues the rhetorical antitheses, and the theme of what is *vanus*, moving from the quotations from classical literature to those from the Bible and Christian writings. The uneducated Wecheleu temporarily challenges Gerard's admiration for learning by his ability to communicate by means of uninflected verbs – using just the infinitive (except in idiomatic phrases like *hora comedendi* and *sicut mihi videbatur*). The only vernacular Wecheleu uses is 'och', the Welsh for 'alas!' Gerald himself rarely uses non-classical vocabulary, though occasionally one comes across post-Conquest words that had become

---

1 See K. Mallette (2004) 'Lingua franca' in *A companion to Mediterranean history*, ed. P. Horden and S. Kinoshita, Chichester, 330–44.

2 Reginald of Durham, *Life and Miracles of Godric, Hermit of Finchale*, ed. M. Coombe, OMT, Oxford, 2022: 79.170.

part of BML lexis at an early stage, such as *foresta* (for which see Section II.44), and (borrowed from the vernaculars) *cnipulus* (based on OE 'cnif'), also used by Walter Map (Section II.19), and *warnisona* (from AN 'garnisun', deriving from a Germanic word).

TEXT II.21A

Gerald decides to withdraw from court life to devote himself to study
[3.1] considerans autem Giraldus vanam ex toto curiae sequelam, vanas omnino promissiones, vanas et indignas nec juxta merita promotiones; quod olim mente conceperat ac paulatim jam inceperat, a curiae strepitu tanquam tempestuoso pelago penitus se retraxit; et ad scolas ac studium tanquam portum quietum et tranquillum salubriori consilio se transferre curavit, illud Plinii Secundi saepius ad animum revocando: 'Strepitus inanesque discursus et ineptos labores, ut primum occasio fuerit, relinque; teque studiis trade; quia dulce honestumque otium ac pene omni negotio pulcrius est studere'. et illud ejusdem: 'Humiles et sordidas curas aliis manda; ipse te in arduo et sublimique secessu studiis asseris.'[3]

Gerald learns from the anchorite that knowledge and grammar are not essential
[3.2] in hoc itaque proposito firmiter constitutus, ad amicum suum anachoritam suo non procul a Vagae fluvio, cui nomen Wecheleu, virum bonum et sanctum, licentiam ac benedictionem suam accepturus, accessit. quem cum inter caetera rogaret attentius, ut oraret pro ipso, quatinus Sacram Scripturam, cui indulgere volebat, scire salubriter et intelligere posset; respondit vir sanctus, manum archidiaconi sua tenens et stringens: 'Och, och, noli dicere scire sed custodire: vana vana est scire nisi custodire.' talis enim erat ei loquendi modus semper per infinitivum nec casus servabat; et tamen satis intelligendi poterat. quare magis admirandum, unde viro simplici et idiotae scientia talis, quod vana sit scientia non custodienti, quinetiam et periculosa; quia qui sciens et prudens peccat, graviter peccat. cui nimirum plus committitur, merito et ab ipso plus exigitur. quo **Luke 12:48** enim quisque melius sapit, eo deterius delinquit; et ubi majus donum scientiae, ibi transgressor majori subjacet culpae.[4] Unde Ysaias, 'Qui vides multa, non custodies?' non igitur ab homine est sententia talis sive scientia sed a Deo, cujus **Isa. 42:20** revera spiritu plenus erat. archidiaconus autem hoc audito correctus plurimum et

---

3 Both quotes derive from Pliny the younger, *Letters* 1.9 and 1.3.

4 This sentence combines two statements from medieval Latin that became almost proverbial: the first part is taken from Gregory the Great, *Regula pastoralis* 3.22, while the second appears in the *Glossa ordinaria* and is then cited as an authoritative text by a number of authors from the twelfth century, who attribute the saying to various Church Fathers. A different version is found in Bede's commentaries on Luke (*PL* 92.394D) and Mark (155B): *ubi scientiae donum maius, ibi gravius est inexcusabilis noxae periculum.*

222 Thirteenth Century

ad lacrimas commotus, supplicavit ei tunc attentius, ut oraret, quatinus Sacram Scripturam divinam non solum scire sed etiam summopere custodire valeret. requirenti vero archidiacono unde ei verba Latina, cum non didicerit, respondit in hunc modum (sua enim ipsius verba ponam, sicut ea libenter archidiaconus et frequenter retractare et recitare consuerat): 'Ego', inquit, 'ire Hierosolimam et visitare sepulchrum Domini mei; et quando redire ego ponere me in hoc carcere pro amore Domini mei qui mori pro me. et multum ego dolere, quod non posse intelligere Latinum neque missam nec evangelium; et multotiens flere et rogare Dominum dare mihi Latinum intelligere. eandem vero cum uno die hora comedendi vocare ad fenestram servientem meum semel et iterum et pluries, et non venire; propter taedium simul et famem ego dormire et quando vigilare, ego videre super altare meum panem jacere. et accedens benedicere panem et comedere; et statim ad vesperas ego intelligere versus et verba Latina quae dicere sacerdos, et mane similiter ad missam sicut mihi videbatur. et post missam ego vocare presbyterum ad fenestram cum missali, et rogare ipsum legere evangelium illius diei. et ipse legere et ego exponere; et dicere sacerdos quod recte; et postea loqui cum presbytero Latinum et ipse mecum. et ab illo die ego sic loqui; et Dominus meus qui dedit mihi Latinam linguam, non dedit eam mihi per grammaticam aut per casus, set tantum ut intelligi possem et alios intelligere.'

Translation: Gerald of Wales, *An Account of Gerald's Achievements*

[3.1] *When Gerald thought about the vanity of the court's retinue as a whole, the totally empty promises, the worthless and unworthy promotions unrelated to merit, he withdrew utterly from the noisy court as from the stormy sea, this being an idea he had conceived some time ago and had already made a gradual start on; and in accordance with this plan, more conducive to his well-being, he arranged to transfer to the schools as if to a calm harbour, to study there, often recalling to mind what Pliny the Younger had written: 'Leave behind the noise and the futile rushing around and useless tasks as soon as you have a chance. Devote yourself to your studies because study is a delightful and honourable way to spend your time and more attractive than any occupation.' And in another letter, 'Hand over the unimportant and squalid tasks to others and devote yourself to your studies in that lofty and sublime retreat of yours.'*
[3.2] *Resolute in this decision he went to visit his friend the anchorite not far from his river, the Wye. This man's name was Wecheleu, a good and holy man, and Gerald wanted to receive his permission and a blessing from him. When Gerald asked him, among other things, earnestly to pray for him that he might know and understand the Holy Scriptures in a manner useful to his soul, which he wished to benefit, the holy man took Gerald's hand in his and squeezed it, saying in reply, 'Oh dear, oh dear! Do not say "to know" but "to observe", for knowledge is useless unless (you) observe the Scriptures.' For his way of talking involved always using the infinitive,*

*not the cases; and yet one could understand him well enough. So it is rather sur-
prising how this simple and unlearned man had got the knowledge that knowledge
is worthless, indeed dangerous, unless you observe it; because he who sins when he
knows and is wise, commits serious sin. To the person to whom more is entrusted,
from him more is justifiably demanded. For the more someone knows, the worse he
sins; and where there is a greater gift of knowledge, there the transgressor is liable
for greater blame. That is why Isaiah says, 'You who see much, do you not observe?'
And so this saying or knowledge was not from a man but from God, with whose
Spirit Wecheleu was indeed filled. When the archdeacon heard this he felt sharply
corrected and was moved to tears. He begged the anchorite then earnestly to pray
that he might not only know God's Holy Scripture but also observe it properly. When
the archdeacon asked where he got the Latin words, since he had not learned Latin,
Wecheleu answered in the following way (for I will give his own words, just as the
archdeacon was in the habit of reviewing and reciting them willingly and frequently): '(I) go to Jerusalem and visit my Lord's tomb; and when (I) return (I) put myself
in this prison for the sake of the Gospel; and very often (I) weep and ask the Lord to
grant an understanding of Latin. At last, when one day it was time to eat (I) call my
servant at the window once and again and several times but (he does) not come; out
of tiredness together with hunger (I) sleep and when (I) wake (I) see my bread lie
on the altar. And approaching the bread (I) bless and eat it and immediately in the
evening (I) understand the verses and Latin words which the priest says, and in the
morning the same happened at Mass, as it seemed to me. And after Mass (I) call the
priest at the window with the missal and ask him to read the Gospel of that day. And
(he) reads and (I) explain and the priest says (I) read it correctly; and afterwards
(I) speak Latin with the priest and he with me. And from that day (I) speak in this
way; and my Lord who granted me the Latin language did not give it to me with
grammar and cases but only to be able to be understood and understand others.'*

B: The Jewel of the Church (*Gemma ecclesiastica*)
(excerpt: 2.35–6)

Date: 1197.

The sole surviving MS is Lambeth Palace Library 236, a MS of the late twelfth century, written under Gerald's supervision. It has been suggested that the presence
of salt water (perhaps indicative of a sea-crossing to the Continent) on the middle
leaves may mean that this is the copy presented to Innocent III in 1199, a journey
alluded to in Gerald's *De gestis Giraldi* 1.119. According to Gerald, Pope Innocent
III liked this book so much he would not let it out of his sight.

Work: This work is a collection of more or less satirical anecdotes and diatribes
against the Church. It was probably written during his withdrawal from court

224 Thirteenth Century

life, as mentioned in Section II.21A. These excerpts are selected to show examples of what were regarded as errors in the Latin of churchmen. Admittedly Gerald is as much amused as shocked by these errors. Gerald blamed the low standard of Latin on the popularity of logic, or of vocational subjects such as law and medicine in the schools, which attracted students away from the study of grammar and rhetoric.

Linguistic points: The errors arise from confusion of near homonyms, from ignorance of Latin grammar or vocabulary, or from confusion between like-sounding words in French and Latin with different senses ('repentir'/*repente*). Such errors often lead to misinterpretation of biblical texts or to the preface of the Mass, regarded as a serious failing in a priest. All the errors are due to *illiteratura*, a 'lack of education'; formed from CL *illiteratus*, *illiteratura* is a word that Gerald uses several times, but it is not found in any other writer. Gerald does in fact occasionally introduce words like *antecubitus*, formed from classical components, but apparently not occurring elsewhere in BML. *obtinere* is here used absolutely, i.e. without an object, as it can be in CL, to mean 'to win his case, prevail'. *sterlingus* is thought to be a creation of late Old English, to mean a pound of English coins, later becoming the term for the English currency. However, it first occurs in a charter from the years after 1066, quoted by Orderic Vitalis (*HE* 3.234) with the spelling *sterilensium* for *sterlingorum*; it is not attested in English until the end of the thirteenth century. It is noteworthy that the clerics seem to gloss the Latin passages from the Bible using French (*Gallice*).

TEXT II.21B

[2.35] qualiter autem evangelia sacramque scripturam hodie presbyteri parochianis suis exponant per exempla quaedam ostendemus. exemplum de presbytero qui, sermonem faciens ad populum de sancto Barnaba, inter caetera dixit, 'bonus vir erat et sanctus sed tamen latro fuerat', auctoritatem sumens de evangelio hoc, John 18:40   scilicet, 'erat autem Barabbas latro', inter Barnabam et Barabban male distinguens. item exemplum de sacerdote qui sermonem faciens de muliere Cananea, dixit eam partim canem esse, partim mulierem, inter Cananeam et caninam non bene distinguens. (…)

    item exemplum de presbytero, qui, sermonem faciens de illo evangelio, 'duo debitores erant',[5] in quo legitur 'alii donavit quingenta, alii quinquaginta', etc., exposuit de eodem numero, scilicet quinquagenario; cui praepositus villae ait,

---

5 See Luke 7:41–3, in which the creditor cancels the debts of two men, for fifty and five hundred denarii respectively, and the question is, who is more grateful to him? Here the incompetent Latinist translates both numbers as fifty, thereby cancelling the point of the parable; when he realises this, he tries to claim that as the fifty coins were in

II.21 | Gerald of Wales 225

'Neutri ergo plusquam alteri donavit cum utrique l. nec plura.' presbyter autem, se deprehensum sentiens, subintulit: 'Sed alii denarii Andegavenses erant, alii vero sterlingi.' (…) item exemplum de presbytero denuntiante bestiam[6] sancti Johannis ante portam Latinam, et dicente 'Quoniam Johannes ille primo Latinam linguam in Angliam portavit'; sic enim exposuit 'ante' id est 'primo', 'portam' 'portavit', 'Latinam' supple 'linguam'. (…)

[2.36] non solum autem in minoribus sacerdotibus sed etiam in majoribus, abbatibus scilicet, prioribus, magnis ecclesiarum decanis, episcopis et archiepiscopis tales interdum defectus invenies. (…) [RS p. 346] item exemplum de abbate Malmesburiensi Roberto qui nostris diebus accusatus a monachis suis super illiteratura et a judicibus a papa Alexandro III delegatis, Bartholomeo scilicet Exoniensi et Rogero Wigorniensi, ex hoc probatus: 'factus est repente de coelo sonus' etc. cum cetera Gallice interpretatus esset, veniens ad 'repente', stetit et **Acts 2:2** haesitavit, tandem vero dixit, 'repente, *il se repenti*'. quidam autem assessorum, scilicet Johannes Cumin[7] qui postmodum archiepiscopus Dublinensis in Hibernia factus est, abbatem quia non plane legibus potuit, saltem exemplo iuvare volens, retulit de quodam abbate quem vidit in curia Romana coram Alexandro III et cardinalibus super illiteratura similiter a monachis suis accusatum et de canone missae probatum, hoc loco 'vere dignum et justum est, aequum et salutare', qui cum exposuisset, 'vere dignum et justum est', *'veraiment dignum et juste'*, veniens ad 'aequum' dixit, 'equum', *ceo est cheval* et 'salutare' *'saillavit'*. et cum putarent multi eum deponendum, quia tamen bonus dispensator erat, et domui suae bene praepositus, judicio summi pontificis obtinuit et abbas remansit. similiter et iste quoniam bonus erat in rebus gerendis et gubernatione domus et exteriorum administratione, contra monachos obtinuit, priori autem et subpriori defectus eius in spiritualibus injunctum est ut supplerent.

Translation: Gerald of Wales, *The Jewel of the Church*

[2.35] *We will show by means of certain examples how priests nowadays explain the Gospels and Holy Scriptures to their parishioners. There is the example of a priest who, when he was giving a sermon on St Barnabas to the people, said amongst other things, 'He was a good and holy man but he had been a thief', deriving his authority from this passage in the Gospel, namely 'For Barabbas was a thief', because he could not distinguish between Barnabas and Barabbas. There is also the example of the*

---

different currencies, the value was different – but of course he makes another mistake by assuming that contemporary currencies were used in the time of Christ.

6 sic *RS*; ?l. festum. Cf. *RS* 21.7 (1877) 21: *festa Johannis*. I am grateful to Thomas Charles-Edwards, Paul Russell and Jacob Currie for their advice on this reading.

7 John Cumin (Comyn) (d. 1212) was also Archdeacon of Bath and a supporter of Henry II in the dispute with Thomas Becket during the 1160s.

226 Thirteenth Century

priest giving a sermon about the woman at Canaan who said that she was part dog, part woman, not being able to distinguish between Cananeam and caninam. (...)

There is also the example of the priest who was preaching on the Gospel passage about the two debtors, in which it says that one owed five hundred and the other fifty, but he gave the same number, namely fifty, in both cases. Then the village reeve said to him, 'So neither gave more than the other since both gave fifty and no more?' The priest, realising that he had been caught out, added that one was in the currency of Anjou and the other in sterling. (...) There is also the example of the priest preaching on the feast of St John before the Latin gate, who claimed that John was the first to bring the Latin language to England. For he interpreted 'ante' as 'first', 'portam' as 'carried' and added the word 'language' to 'Latin'. (...)

[2.36] You will sometimes find these sorts of mistakes not only in the minor orders but also in the higher ones, namely in abbots, priors, great deans of churches, bishops and archbishops. (...) There is also the example of Robert, Abbot of Malmesbury, who in our time was accused by his own monks for his lack of literacy. He was examined by the judges appointed by Pope Alexander III, namely Bartholomew of Exeter and Roger of Worcester, and was given the following text as a test: 'And suddenly there came a sound from heaven' etc. When he had translated the rest into French he came to the word 'repente', and stopped and hesitated; at last he said, 'repente, repented'. One of his examiners, namely John Cumin, afterwards Archbishop of Dublin in Ireland, wanting to help the abbot at least with an example, and because he could not do so openly according to the laws, told the story of a certain abbot whom he saw in the Curia at Rome, in the presence of Alexander III and his cardinals, and who was similarly accused of a lack of literacy by his monks. He was tested on the canon of the Mass, and he came to the passage 'It is truly meet and just, right and salutary'. When he had glossed 'vere dignum et justum est' as 'it is truly meet and just', he took the word 'aequum' as 'equum', that is 'horse', and for 'salutare' he said 'he jumped'. Cumin said that many considered that this abbot ought to be deposed from office, but because he was a good administrator and managed his abbey well, he won his case before the pope and remained an abbot. And in fact Robert of Malmesbury, because he was good at managing things and at governing his abbey and administering external affairs, also won his case against the monks, and the prior and sub-prior were told to make up for his deficiencies in the spiritual interpretation of the Bible.

Primary Sources and Related Texts

Giraldi Cambrensis Opera, 8 vols, RS 21 (1861–91).
De gestis Giraldi, ed. T. Charles-Edwards, P. Russell and J. Currie, OMT, Oxford, 2023.
Giraldus Cambrensis, *De rebus a se gestis*, RS 21.1 (1861).
Giraldus Cambrensis, *Gemma ecclesiastica*, RS 21.2 (1862).

Gerald of Wales, *The Jewel of the Church*, transl. J. Hagen, Leiden, 1979: 259–65.
Gesta Sancti Albani 2.113–14 on Hugh de Eversden, Abbot of St Alban (1308).
Gerald of Wales, *Instruction for a ruler*, ed. R. Bartlett, OMT, Oxford, 2018.

Further Reading

Bartlett, R. (2006) *Gerald of Wales: a voice of the Middle Ages*, Stroud.
Clanchy, M. (1981) 'Literate and illiterate; hearing and seeing: England 1066–1307' in *Literacy and social development in the West*, ed. H. Graff, Cambridge.
Henley, G., and McMullen, A. (2018) *Gerald of Wales: new perspectives on a medieval writer and critic*, Cardiff.
La Vere, S. (2018) '"A priest is not a free person": condemning clerical sins and upholding higher moral standards in the *Gemma ecclesiastica*' in *Gerald of Wales: new perspectives on a medieval writer and critic*, ed. G. Henley and A. J. McMullen, Cardiff.
*Staunton (2017).
Zimmer, S. (2003) 'A medieval linguist: Gerald de Barri', *Études celtiques* 35: 313–50.

Section II.22

Jocelin of Brakelond, *The Chronicle of the Deeds of Abbot Samson* (*Cronicon de rebus gestis Samsonis abbatis*)
(excerpts: pp. 11–13 and 39–41)

Date: c.1203.

This work is extant in full only in the so-called *Liber Albus* of Bury St Edmunds (BL MS Harley 1005, ff. 121–63). It is likely to be a copy made from Jocelin's autograph. A slightly earlier copy (BL MS Cotton Vitellius D.xv) was pretty much destroyed in the Cotton Library fire of 1731.

Author: Jocelin of Brakelond (died c.1215) was a monk at Bury St Edmunds from about 1173, but we know little of his background or earlier education. He clearly knew the Bible well and was familiar with some classical literature. He held various offices within the monastery, including that of chaplain to Abbot Samson, 'noting many things and storing them in his memory' and using them later in his depiction of the abbot.

Work: In the *Chronicle*, his only surviving work, Jocelin combines history and biography in presenting a vivid picture of life in his monastery and also of the town of Bury St Edmunds between 1173 and 1202. The author includes many different topics, from interactions between the king and the abbot, as well as information about Abbot Samson's many disputes over his rights, regarding which the abbot kept a detailed inventory of the revenues due to him, in his Kalendar, a document mentioned by Jocelin and which was discovered by chance in the nineteenth century, to the transportation of eels and the sale of herring by the townspeople. He sometimes refers to himself in the first person, as having been present in certain episodes. Jocelin claims to include negative things *ad cautelam* ('as a warning') and positive things *ad usum* ('for the benefit they may bring'), for he shares his contemporaries' belief in the moral purpose of historiography. Despite being entitled *Chronicle*, his work is not intended as a record of national history. The passages here contain the discussions about the desired qualities of the new abbot, and a description of Samson, the abbot subsequently elected. This description may be compared with, for example, the famous literary portraits of Henry II by Walter Map, Peter of Blois and Gerald of Wales.

Linguistic points: As a writer Jocelin has been compared with his contemporaries Gerald of Wales and Adam of Eynsham (who wrote a biography of St Hugh of Lincoln), but his language is more direct, more engaged with the details of life around him, so despite the fact that he occasionally quotes both from Scripture (especially in the monastic discussions he reports) and from classical writers such as Horace, Ovid and Virgil, and sometimes uses rare words found in classical Latin, his Latin is anything but formal or highly literary. At this period around 1200 BML was being infused with vernacular words to a greater degree than at any other time. Jocelin's writing is one of the outstanding examples of a Latin that is both lucid and filled with words derived from early Germanic roots, from English (e.g. *hustingum*, *husebondus*) and primarily from French (e.g. *appruntare*/*appromptare*, related to French 'emprunter', 'to borrow'). Certain words (e.g. *berefredum*, related to 'belfry', and *froccus*, 'robe') are attested also in Continental medieval Latin. Some are attested here for the first or only time, as for example *reclutare*, 'to patch together', from CL prefix *re-* and infinitive suffix *-are* added to the English word 'clout', i.e. 'piece of cloth' (in its early ME form 'clut', which would have been the usual form in Jocelin's time; cf. Section II.45E). With reference to *discus* for 'dish', the CL word has an interesting morphological and semantic development. It is one of the Latin words taken into Old English at an early stage, with 'disc' for 'dish', but later appears in various senses in modern English as 'dish', 'disk', 'desk' and 'dais'. Two words designating troublemakers are introduced to BML by Jocelin: *baratator* and *paltenarius* (cf. p. 42 Butler, *paltenarium et baratorem de Norfolchia*), both of which have an interesting Continental history and also appear for a time in English (cf. *OED s.v.* barrator, pautener). Such a high degree of vernacular-derived words is otherwise only found at this period in the administrative and legal Latin generated at the English royal court, and is striking in an author who is likely to have spent all his life in Bury St Edmunds, albeit in a powerful and well-documented monastery. Jocelin also provides information about the linguistic skills and attitudes of some of his contemporaries, both religious and secular, with regard to the three main languages, English, French and Latin, and to local dialects. Abbot Samson, for example, was born in Norfolk and continued to speak in that dialect when he moved to Suffolk.

TEXT II.22

The monks argue as to what kind of person would make a good abbot
[p. 11 Butler] vacante abbatia, sepe, sicut decuit, rogavimus Dominum et sanctum martirem Aedmundum,[1] ut nobis et ecclesie nostre congruum darent pastorem,

---

1 The reference is to Edmund, king of the East Saxons, who was killed by the Danes in 870 according to the *Anglo-Saxon Chronicle*. He was buried in what is now the town of Bury St Edmunds in Suffolk. In the eleventh century an abbey dedicated to Edmund was established here: this is the focus of Jocelin's *Chronicle*. On the life and death of

230 Thirteenth Century

singulis ebdomadibus ter cantantes vii psalmos penitenciales[2] prostrati in choro, post exitum in capitulo: et erant aliqui, quibus si constaret quis futurus esset abbas, non ita devote orassent. de eligendo abbate, si rex nobis liberam concederet electionem, diversi diversis modis loquebantur, quidam publice, quidam occulte; **Terence,** et 'quot homines tot sententie'. dixit quidam de quodam: 'Ille, ille frater, bonus *Phormio* **454** monachus est, probabilis persona; multum scit de ordine et consuetudinibus ecclesie: licet non sit tam perfectus philosophus sicut quidam alii, bene potest esse abbas. abbas Ordingus homo illiteratus fuit, et tamen fuit bonus abbas et sapienter domum istam rexit: legitur etiam in fabulis, [p. 12] melius fuit ranis eligere truncum in regem, super quem confidere possent, quam serpentem, qui venenose sibilaret, et post sibillum subiectas devoraret.'[3] respondit alter: 'Quomodo potest hoc fieri? quomodo potest facere sermonem in capitulo, vel ad populum **Matt. 16:19** diebus festivis, homo qui literas non novit? quomodo habebit scientiam ligandi et solvendi, qui scripturas non intelligit? cum sit ars artium, scientia scientiarum, regimen animarum, absit ut statua muta erigatur in ecclesia sancti Aedmundi, ubi multi literati viri et industrii esse dinoscuntur.'

item dixit alius de alio: 'Ille frater vir literatus est, eloquens et providus, rigidus in ordine; multum dilexit conventum, et multa mala pertulit pro bonis ecclesie: dignus est ut fiat abbas.' respondit alter: 'A bonis clericis libera nos, Domine: ut a baratoribus de Norfolchia nos conservare digneris, te rogamus, audi nos.' item dixit de quodam: 'Ille frater bonus husebondus est: quod probatur ex warda sua et ex obedienciis quas bene servavit, et edificiis et emendacionibus quas fecit. multum potest laborare et domum defendere, et est aliquantulum clericus, quamvis **Acts 26:24** nimie litere non faciant eum insanire: ille dignus est abbatia.' respondit alter: 'Nolit Deus ut homo, qui non potest legere nec cantare nec divina officia celebrare, homo inprobus et injustus et excoriator pauperum hominum, fiat abbas.' item dixit aliquis de aliquo: 'Ille frater homo benignus est, affabilis et amabilis, pacificus [p. 13] et conpositus, largus et liberalis, vir literatus et eloquens, et satis idonea persona in vultu et in gestu, et a multis dilectus intus et extra; et talis homo ad magnum honorem ecclesie posset fieri abbas, si Deus vellet.' respondit alter: 'Non **Ovid,** *Heroides* honor esset sed onus de homine qui nimis delicatus est in cibo et potu; qui vir- **9.31** tutem reputat multum dormire, qui multum scit expendere et parum adquirere; qui stertit quando ceteri vigilant; qui semper vult esse in habundantia, nec curat de debitis quae crescunt de die in diem, nec de expensis unde adquietari possint; solicitudinem et laborem odio habens, nichil curans, dummodo unus dies vadat

---

Edmund, see the *Passio sancti Eadmundi* written by Abbo of Fleury during his stay at Ramsey Abbey (985–7).

2 I.e. Psalms 6, 31, 37, 50, 101, 129, 142 in the Vulgate numbering.

3 Aesop's fable *The Frogs Who Desired a King* is first found in the Latin writer Phaedrus (1.2) of the first century AD.

et alter veniat: homo adulatores et mendaces diligens et fovens; homo alius in verbo et alius in opere. a tali prelato defendat nos Dominus!' etc. (…)

Translation: Jocelin of Brakelond, *Chronicle*

During the abbot's vacancy we often, as was appropriate, asked the Lord and the holy martyr Edmund to give us a shepherd who was suitable for us and our church: every week we chanted the seven penitential psalms three times, prostrate in the choir, after the departure, in the chapter. And there were some who, if it had been clear who would be the abbot, would not have prayed so devoutly. Regarding the choice of an abbot, if the king had granted us a free election, different people would have said different things, some in public, some in private; and there would have been as many different views as there were people. Someone said about one of them, 'That one, that brother, is a good monk and a commendable priest; he knows a lot about the order and the customs of the church; he may not be as perfect a philosopher as some others but he could perfectly well be an abbot. Abbot Ording was illiterate and yet he was a good abbot and governed this house wisely: one can even read in the fables that it was better for the frogs to elect as their king a log which they could trust, than a snake that hissed poisonously and after hissing devoured its subjects.' Another person replied, 'How can this be done? How can a person who does not know his letters give a sermon in chapter or to the people on feast days? How will he know how to bind and loose, if he does not understand the Scriptures? Since the government of souls is the art of arts, the science of sciences, God forbid that a dumb statue should be set up in the church of St Edmund, where there are known to be many literate and industrious men.' Again another person said about someone else, 'That brother is a literate man, eloquent and far-sighted, and strict in the Rule; he loves the religious community very much and has endured many difficulties for the good of the church: he deserves to be made abbot.' Someone else replied, 'Free us, Lord, from good clerics! Please preserve us from Norfolk troublemakers, we ask you, hear our prayer!' Then he said about another, 'That brother is a good steward, as is proved by his wardenship and the monastic dependencies he has kept well and the buildings he has made and repairs he has carried out. He can work hard and protect the house and he is not a bad cleric, although too much learning has not driven him insane: he would make a good abbot.' The other man replied, 'God does not want a man who cannot read or sing or celebrate the divine office, an unprincipled and unjust person who fleeces the poor, to be made abbot.' Again someone said of someone, 'That brother is a kind person, affable and likeable, peaceable and composed, generous and munificent, educated and eloquent, and he looks and behaves as a priest should and he is loved by many both within and outside the community; such a person, if elected abbot, could be a great honour to the Church, if God so wishes.' The other replied, 'Such a man would not be a benefit but a burden, for he is too fussy about what he eats and drinks; he considers it a virtue to sleep a lot, and knows how

232 Thirteenth Century

to spend a lot but brings in little; he snores when others are awake and always wants to be surrounded by abundance and does not care about the debts which mount up day by day or how the expenses can be paid; he hates anxiety and hard work, cares about nothing, as long as one day goes and the next comes; he is a person who loves and indulges admirers and liars, a man who says one thing and does another. May the Lord protect us from such a prelate!' (…)

The result of the election: a description of Abbot Samson
[p. 39] Abbas Samson mediocris erat stature, fere omnino calvus, vultum habens nec rotundum nec oblongum, naso eminente, labiis grossis, oculis cristallinis et penetrantis intuitus, auribus clarissimi auditus, superciliis in altum crescentibus et sepe tonsis; ex parvo frigore cito raucus; die eleccionis sue quadraginta et septem annos etatis habens et in monachatu decem et septem annos; paucos canos habens in rufa barba, et paucissimos inter capillos nigros, et aliquantulum crispos; set infra xiiii annos post eleccionem suam totus albus efficitur sicut nix; homo supersobrius, nunquam desidiosus, multum valens et volens equitare vel pedes ire, donec senectus prevaluit que talem voluntatem temperavit; qui, audito rumore de capta cruce et perdicione [p. 40] Jerusalem, femoralibus[4] cilicinis cepit uti et cilicio loco staminis, et carnibus et carneis abstinere; carnes tamen voluit sibi anteferri sedens ad mensam, ad augmentum scilicet elemosine. lac dulce et mel et consimilia dulcia libencius quam ceteros cibos comedebat. mendaces et ebriosos et verbosos odio habuit; quia 'virtus sese diligit, et aspernatur contrari-

Boethius, *De topicis differentiis* 1184a15 um'. murmuratores cibi et potus et precipue monachos murmuratores condempnans, tenorem antiquum conservans quem olim habuit dum claustralis fuit: hoc autem virtutis in se habuit quod nunquam ferculum coram eo positum voluit mutare. quod cum ego novicius vellem probare si hoc esset verum, forte servivi in refectorio, et cogitavi penes me ut ponerem coram eo ferculum quod omnibus aliis displiceret in disco nigerimo et fracto. quod cum ipse vidisset, tanquam non videns erat; facta autem mora, penituit me hoc fecisse, et statim, arepto disco, ferculum et discum mutavi in melius et asportavi: ille vero emendacionem talem moleste tulit iratus et turbatus. homo erat eloquens, Gallice et Latine, magis rationi dicendorum quam ornatui verborum innitens. scripturam Anglice scriptam legere novit elegantissime, et Anglice sermocinare solebat populo (set secundum linguam Norfolchie, ubi natus et nutritus erat), unde et pulpitum iussit fieri in ecclesia et ad utilitatem audiencium et ad decorem ecclesie. videbatur quoque abbas activam vitam magis diligere quam contemplativam, quia bonos obedienciales magis commendavit quam bonos claustrales; et raro aliquem propter solam scientiam literarum approbavit, nisi haberet scientiam rerum secularium; et cum audiret forte aliquem prelatum [p. 41] cedere oneri pastorali et fieri anachoritam, in hoc eum non laudavit. homines nimis benignos laudare noluit, dicens: 'Qui

---

4 Cf. Section II.19 on the Cistercian use of this garment.

omnibus placere nititur, nulli placere debet.' primo ergo anno suscepte abbatie omnes adulatores quasi odio habuit, et maxime monachos; set in processu temporis videbatur eos quasi libentius audire et magis familiares habere. unde contigit quod, cum quidam frater noster, hac arte peritus, curvasset genua ante eum, et sub optentu consilii dandi auribus eius adulacionis oleum infudisset, subrisi ego stans a longe: eo vero recedente, vocatus et interrogatus quare riserim, respondi mundum plenum esse adulatoribus. et abbas: 'Fili mi, diu est quod adulatores novi, et ideo non possum adulatores non audire. multa sunt simulanda et dissimulanda, ad pacem conventus conservandam. audiam eos loqui, set non decipient me, si possum, sicut predecessorem meum, qui consilio eorum ita inconsulte credidit, quod diu ante obitum suum nichil habuit quod manducaret vel ipse vel familia sua, nisi a creditoribus mutuo acceptum.'

Translation: Jocelin of Brakelond, *Chronicle*

Abbot Samson was of medium height, almost completely bald, with a face that was neither round nor oblong, a prominent nose, thick lips, eyes as clear as crystal with a penetrating look, ears that could hear very clearly, arching eyebrows that were always trimmed; when it was a bit cold he quickly got a bad throat; on the day of his election he was forty-seven years old and had been a monk for seventeen years; he had a few grey hairs in his reddish beard and a very few in his hair, which was mostly black and a bit curly, though within fourteen years after his election it turned completely white as snow. He was an extremely temperate man, never lazy, very able, enjoying riding and walking until old age forced him to moderate this kind of enjoyment. When he heard that the cross had been captured and Jerusalem had been lost, he began to wear underclothes made of hairshirt material and a hairshirt instead of an undergarment of cloth, and to abstain from meat and meaty things; and yet he wanted meat to be placed before him when he sat at table, to increase the amount that was given in alms. His favourite food was sweet milk and honey and other sweet things rather than other kinds of food. He hated people who lied or got drunk or were verbose, because virtue loves itself and despises its opposite. He condemned people who grumbled about the food and drink and especially monks who complained, and he preserved the old regime which he had maintained in the past when he was prior: he had this virtue, that he never wanted to change a dish that was put before him. When I was a novice I wanted to test to see if this was true and by chance I was serving in the refectory and I had the idea of putting before him some food which everyone else disliked on a dish that was very black and broken: when he saw it, it was as if he did not see it. After a while I regretted what I had done and quickly whisked away the dish and changed the food and the dish for a better one and brought it to him: he was irritated by this improvement and got angry and upset. He was an eloquent man, both in French and Latin, putting more effort into the argument of what he wanted to say than the ornamentation of the

234 Thirteenth Century

words. He could elegantly read the Scriptures written in English and used to preach to the people in English (but in the Norfolk dialect, because that is where he had been born and brought up). And so he ordered a pulpit to be made in the church both for the benefit of the audience and for the adornment of the church. The abbot also seemed to prefer the active to the contemplative life, because he praised the good obedientiaries more than the good monks; and he rarely praised anyone just for their literary knowledge unless he had a knowledge of secular matters; and when he happened to hear that some prelate was renouncing his pastoral commitment to become an anchorite, he did not praise him for this. He refused to praise people who were too kind, saying, 'He who strives to please everybody is bound to please no one.' And so in the first year that he undertook the position of abbot, he seemed to hate all who flattered him, and especially the monks; but in the course of time he seemed to listen to them more willingly and to be more friendly to them. And so it happened that when a certain brother of ours, skilled in this, bent his knee before him and under the pretext of giving him advice poured into his ears the oil of flattery, I smiled from where I was standing at a distance. When this man had withdrawn, the abbot called me over and asked why I was smiling, and I replied that the world was full of flatterers. Then the abbot said, 'My son, I have known flatterers for a long time and therefore I cannot avoid listening to flatterers. One has to pretend and disguise many things in order to preserve peace in the community. I will listen to them speak, but if possible I will not let them deceive me as they deceived my predecessor. He trusted their advice so rashly that long before his death neither he nor his household had anything to eat, except as a loan from his creditors.'

Primary Sources and Related Texts

Jocelin of Brakelond, *Cronica de rebus gestis Samsonis abbatis monasterii S. Edmundi*, ed. H. Butler, Oxford, 1949.

Jocelin of Brakelond, *The Chronicle of the Abbey of Bury St Edmunds*, transl. D. Greenway and J. Sayer, Oxford, 1989.

The Kalendar of Abbot Samson of Bury St Edmunds, Camden Society 3rd ser. 84, 1954.

Further Reading

Carlyle, Thomas, *Past and present*, Book 2: *The ancient monk*, Berkeley, 2005.

Gransden, A. (1974) 'Historical writing at Bury St Edmunds in the thirteenth century' in *Gransden (1974).

Scarfe, N. (1997) *Jocelin of Brakelond*, Leominster.

Section II.23

Scientific Teaching of the Twelfth Century
A: Adelard of Bath, *Questions on Natural Science* (*Quaestiones naturales*) (excerpt: 41)
B: *The Salernitan Questions* (*Quaestiones Salernitanae*) (excerpts: B14 and B104)

These texts provide examples of some of the many scientific questions that were being asked in the twelfth century, at a time when scientific texts were being translated from Arabic and Greek into Latin, many more works of Aristotle were being rediscovered, and further progress was being made in practical medicine. Following Adelard, other British scholars such as Alfred of Shareshill and Robert of Ketton were prominent in the field of translation from Arabic, not only of scientific texts, but also, in the case of Robert of Ketton, of the Qur'an: his Latin version was printed at Basle in 1550.

A: Adelard of Bath, *Questions on Natural Science* (*Quaestiones naturales*) (excerpt: 41)

Date: c.1140.

This work survives in nearly thirty MSS, of which seven are now in British libraries; it was printed in Louvain c.1475.

Author: Adelard of Bath (1080–1152) has been called the first English scientist. With his interest in mathematics, astronomy, philosophy and medicine, he was a forerunner of the very prolific thirteenth-century writers Robert Grosseteste and Roger Bacon. Adelard was one of the first to make translations, most notably of Euclid's *Elements*, translating from the Arabic version, itself a translation from the Greek. Adelard had a classical education in England before travelling around the Mediterranean and the Middle East to learn from the cultures he encountered. One of the places he visited was Salerno in Italy, where he probably came across the question cited here regarding the transmission of leprosy, for it occurs, too, in the *Quaestiones Salernitanae*.

Work: Adelard's most famous original works are the *De eodem et diverso* (modelled on Boethius' *De consolatione philosophiae*) and the *Questions on Natural*

Science, in dialogue form, which discusses the causes of things, and can be compared with Seneca the younger's work of the same name. Adelard's *Questions* are full of allusions to classical Latin literary texts, and also to philosophical works such as Cicero's *De natura deorum*, the works of Macrobius and Boethius and Calcidius' translation of Plato's *Timaeus*, with which he was familiar. He also speaks of his *magistri Arabici* (6). Adelard introduces a number of scientific technical terms into BML, such as *complexionalis* ('relating to temperament'), or (from Greek) *eclipticus* ('ecliptic') and *aplanes* ('firmament' of fixed stars). The short section below has been selected because of its parallel with one of the *Salernitan Questions*. Adelard's answer leads his nephew to ask about the question of women's reputation for lustfulness: how can this be so, if women are by nature colder than men? Adelard replies that it is the *humiditas* rather than the *frigiditas* which is responsible.

Linguistic points: Adelard refers here to the technical terms describing the qualities of the four temperaments: *calidus, frigidus, siccus, humidus,* according to the system developed by Hippocrates in the fifth century BC. He gives synonymous phrases for sexual intercourse: *ad mulierem accedere* and *mulierem cognoscere,* both of which occur equally in classical Latin and that of the biblical translations. Adelard uses the term *elephantiosus,* found in LL, for a leper, i.e. one suffering from a form of elephantiasis, while *leprosus* is the equivalent in the *Salernitan Questions.* This is the only instance in BML of CL *affectio* in the sense of disease.

TEXT II.23A

If a woman sleeps with a leper, why does she not get leprosy, but when she then sleeps with another man, he gets leprosy?

[41] Nepos: quia de humana natura sermo nobis susceptus est, accidit in ea quiddam quod cum taciturnitate pretereundum non est: cur scilicet ad mulierem sanam si vir elephantiosus accedat, non ipsa mulier, set qui eam deinde primus cognoverit, morbum sustinebit?

Adelardus: plangenda quidem non ammiranda est hec translatio. cuius causam si cognoscere cupis, utriusque sexus proprietatem prius cognoscas. est igitur virilis quidem natura secundum esse calidior, muliebris vero frigidior, et virilis quidem ad siccitatem pertinet, muliebris vero ad humiditatem. unde si quando elephantiosi semen suscipiat, frigida et humida proprietas a tali eam affectione defendat. in qua tamen cum pars seminis inefficax remaneat, cum ad eandem vir accedit, cum siccitate tum calore ingruente ex similitudine qualitatum affectionem sibi accidit ut inducat. sicut enim frigiditas et humiditas expellunt, ita caliditas et siccitas suapte natura attrahunt.

Translation: Adelard, *Questions on Natural Science*

[41] *Nephew: Since we have started to discuss the inherent qualities of human beings, there is something that happens which we should not pass over in silence: namely, why is it that if a man with leprosy has sex with a healthy woman, it is not the woman, but the man who next has sex with her, who will be smitten with the disease?*

Adelard: One should be saddened rather than surprised at this transference. If you wish to know the reason for it, you must first recognise the property of each sex. Man's nature, according to his essence, is hotter, while that of women is colder, and man's nature is associated with dryness, that of women with moisture. So if at some point a woman receives the semen of a man with leprosy, her cold and moist property protects her from this disease. But since a bit of the semen remains inactive in her, when a man has sex with this woman, as the dryness and heat increase it happens that he attracts the disease to himself because of the similarity of the qualities. For just as coldness and moisture expel, so heat and dryness by their very nature attract.

Primary Sources and Related Texts

Adelard of Bath, *Conversations with his nephew*, ed. and transl. C. Burnett, Cambridge, 1998.

Further Reading

Adams, J. N. (1982) *The Latin sexual vocabulary*, London.
Burnett, C. (1987) *Adelard of Bath: an English scientist and Arabist of the early twelfth century*, London.
—— (1997) *The introduction of Arabic learning into England*, London.
Langslow, D. (2000) *Medical Latin in the Roman empire*, Oxford.

B: *The Salernitan Questions (Quaestiones Salernitanae)*
(excerpts: B14 and B104)

Date: ?late twelfth century.

The collection appears in various forms in a number of MSS. The questions given here come from Bodleian MS Auct. F.3.10, written in the hand of an English scholar in about 1200.

238 Thirteenth Century

Work: This particular collection of fascinating questions and answers regarding a wide range of scientific and medical subjects derived from various earlier writers, both classical and medieval. The collection, though likely to have been formulated by an English writer, is so called because many of the questions come from the great medical teaching centre of Salerno. For the second question one may compare Pliny (*Natural History* 7.17), who claims in contrast that men's corpses float face up, women's face down, with the explanation that nature is thus protecting women's modesty.

Linguistic points: This text uses such medical technical terms as *complexio*, a synonym of *temperamentum*, i.e. a proportionate combination of the different qualities. The use of the suffix -*ositas* to form neologisms is particularly prevalent in scientific and medical texts from this period onwards, using abstract nouns to describe the qualities of physical nature. *Incurtare*, formed from CL *curtare*, can mean 'to shorten' in a medical context, or 'to lag behind' in an astronomical context. Like Adelard, the anonymous writer uses synonymous phrases for sexual intercourse.

TEXT II.23B(a)

If a woman sleeps with a leper, why does she not get leprosy, but when she then sleeps with another man, he gets leprosy?
[B14] queritur si leprosus accedit ad mulierem mulier non leditur, qui vero post illum prius ad eam accedit quare leprosus efficitur?
Responsio: constat et evidenti patet ratione quod quelibet mulieris complexio frigida est <et> humida, dicit autem Ypocras calidissima mulier frigidior <est> viro frigidissimo. talis complexio dura est et corruptioni maxime virili inobediens et omnino fere repugnans. putrida tamen materia ex coitu leprosi remanet in matrice. cum autem vir ad eam intrat, virilis virga que ex nervis consistit matricem intrat, corruptionemque vi attractiva attrahit atque ad membra quibus adheret transmittit. et ita materia corrupta repit ad alia et ea inficit, et ita de membro in membrum transiendo totum corpus inficit, inficiendo leprosum reddit.

Translation: *The Salernitan Questions*

[B14] *Question: If a man with leprosy has sex with a woman and the woman is not affected, why does the man who has sex with her after him become a leper?*
Answer: It is accepted and evident from clear reason that a woman's constitution is cold and moist; indeed, Hippocrates says that the hottest woman is colder than the coldest man. Such a constitution is tough and especially resistant to male corruption and is able to defend itself almost completely against it. However, putrid matter

remains in the womb after sex with a leper. When a man has sex with her, the male member, which consists of sinews, enters the womb and attracts the corruption by means of its attractive force and transmits it to the parts of the (man's) body with which it is in close contact. And so the corrupt matter creeps to other parts and infects them, and in this way, passing from one bodily part to another, it infects the whole body, and by infecting it, it makes the man leprous.

TEXT II.23B(b)

When a woman drowns, why is she found face up, while a man is found face down?
[B104] queritur quare mulier submersa inveniatur supina, vir autem pronus? Responsio: in maribus thoracis latitudo et pectoris eminentia multam in se ossuositatis copiam obtinet. que ossa cum sint magna et de complexione frigida et sicca et quantitate et qualitate, plurimam in se continent ponderositatem. sui sarcinositate motum de centro consequitur, unde partem anteriorem versus inferiora dum contrahunt, virum in aqua mortuum pronum reddunt. est et alia ratio, nervus quidam in masculis a prora capitis, scilicet ab anteriori parte, usque ad extrema digitorum pedum protenditur, qui dum frigiditate et siccitate contrahitur, corpus in aqua secundum se incurtatum pronum in aqua reddit. mulier vero supina invenitur duplici de causa, et propter matricis concavitatem et mamillarum spongiositatem, quarum utraque in anteriori parte continetur. matrix namque cum multam in se habeat vacuitatem, quamplurimum in ipsius concavitate concipit aeris, ex cuius aeris presentia alleviatur; et quia est in anteriori parte, quod satis apparet in pregnantibus, in anteriori parte elevatur. mamille etiam cum sint spongiose et multum in se habeant aereitatis, satis ad hoc operantur ut anteriora magis eleventur. et quod superius dictum est in viro de nervo contrahente et corrugante, e contrario assignari potest de muliere.

Translation: *The Salernitan Questions*

[B104] *The question is why, when a woman drowns, is she found face up, while a man is found face down?*
Answer: In men the broad thorax and prominent chest contain a good deal of boniness. As these bones are large and are of a cold and dry complexion both as regards quantity and quality, they have a lot of heaviness in them. This heavy burden causes a movement from the centre, and the front is pulled down towards the lower parts, causing the dead man to lie face down in the water. There is also another reason: in men a nerve extends from the front of the head, in other words from the anterior part, right down to the tips of the toes, and when this contracts as the result of cold or dryness, it causes the body which has contracted to lie face down in the water. But a woman is found face up for two reasons, both because of the womb's cavity and

240 Thirteenth Century

the spongy nature of the breasts, both of which are situated at the front. For since the womb has a large empty space inside it, it fills up with a great deal of air in this cavity, and the presence of this air makes the womb lighter; and because it is at the front, as is obvious in pregnant women, it rises up at the front. Since the breasts, too, are spongy and contain a great deal of air, they have the effect of making the front rise up higher. And what was said above about the nerve contracting and folding up in a man, works the other way round in a woman.

Primary Sources and Related Texts

The Prose Salernitan Questions, ed. B. Lawn, Auctores Britannici medii aevi 5, Oxford, 1979.

Further Reading

Garcia-Ballester, L. (ed.) (1994) *Practical medicine from Salerno to the Black Death*, Cambridge.
Wallis, F. (ed.) (2010) *Medieval medicine: a reader*, Toronto.

Section II.24

Matthew Paris, *The Major Chronicles* (*Chronica majora*): King John Offers His Kingdom to the Caliph of Morocco (excerpt: 2.559–61)

Date: 1240–59.

The *Major Chronicles* exists as an illustrated autograph MS in three volumes: Cambridge MS CCC 26 covers the period from Creation to 1188, MS CCC 16 covers 1189–1253, and coverage of the years 1254–9 is in BL MS Royal 14.C.vii, ff. 157–218.

Author: Matthew Paris (c.1200–59) spent his life as a monk at the great monastery of St Albans from about 1217, though he was sent by the pope to visit King Haakon in Norway in the late 1240s. Matthew wrote a number of historical works, the greatest being the *Major Chronicles*, which follows the work of another St Alban's monk, Roger of Wendover (d. 1236), who had written an original history (*Flores historiarum*) covering the years down to 1235. From 1236–59 Matthew gives a detailed and independent account of contemporary events, based on oral and documentary evidence drawn from his many connections. Matthew wrote several shorter historical works and a few saints' Lives, some in AN verse for a lay audience. He is also famous as an illustrator and cartographer, whose work can be seen in the MSS mentioned above.

Work: This episode is not found in any of Matthew's sources, but it was included also in the *Gesta abbatum monasterii Sancti Albani* (1.236–42, from the BL MS Cotton Claudius E.iv), presumably also by Matthew as the chronicler of that abbey. It is part of Matthew's account of King John's secret mission to the fourth Almohad caliph, Emir Muhammad al-Nasir (d. 1213), who was the Commander of all Muslim believers at the time. In 1211–12 John was looking for foreign support against the French threat to England. In his anger with the pope and the barons, King John has apparently offered to hand over his kingdom to the Emir and to convert to Islam. On enquiry the first envoy, the knight Thomas Hardington, describes England and the English in very positive terms, but the Emir is suspicious: why would a great king in a successful country offer to betray his country and religion? Dismissing two of the envoys, the Emir then has a frank conversation in private with Robert of London, who reveals a more damning portrait of John. The desire to rebel against fellow Christians and an appreciation of Muslim tolerance of other religions, as apparently felt by King John, had already surfaced among frustrated Christians: Abelard in his letter known as the *Historia calamitatum* says that he often thought of moving to a non-Christian country *atque ibi quiete sub quacunque tributi pactione inter inimicos Christi christiane vivere* ('and to lead a quiet Christian life there among the enemies of Christ, paying any tribute necessary'),[1] while in 1168 Henry II's envoys threatened Pope Alexander III with the claim that the king would rather follow the religion of Nur ad-Din, the Sultan of Aleppo and uncle of Salah ad-Din (Saladin), than allow Thomas Becket to continue as Archbishop of Canterbury (John of Salisbury, *Ep.* 272, p. 561). Comparison may also be made with the attempt of the Protestant Queen Elizabeth I in 1599 to make an alliance with the Muslim Mehmet III, the Ottoman Caliph in Istanbul, in the face of the Catholic Habsburgs' power. Some modern historians have doubted the veracity of Matthew's account, but there is independent evidence for the existence of the people mentioned, for example in Pipe Rolls and Curia Regis Rolls, and Matthew claims to have heard the account from the cleric Robert, whom John rewarded by foolishly granting control of St Alban's Abbey. As a further chapter in the history of international diplomacy it has been suggested that Robert, emboldened by the favour shown to him by the caliph, turns up again, in 1243, as the envoy of the Tartar Khan when the Tartars attack central Europe; in a letter quoted by Matthew (4.274) he is referred to as *Anglicum natione, sed propter quaedam maleficia de regno Angliae perpetua banniatione proscriptum* ('of English nationality but permanently banished from England on account of certain crimes').

This episode also has a connection with the maps produced by Matthew Paris in his manuscripts: the label in Anglo-Norman, *e tute la terre l'Amiral Murmelin k'em apele Miramumelin e la terre de Marroch ke sue est* occurs on f. 4a of BL MS Royal 14.C.vii in the description of the territories mentioned with reference to the *Itinerary from London to Jerusalem*. The passage has been selected as revealing a somewhat surprising episode of British history, involving the mutual attitudes of Muslims and Christians. The depiction of diplomatic communication in early thirteenth-century Morocco provides plausible information about foreign attitudes to England, and about the multilingual situation at the time. For the description of England, compare the description of the island of Britain by Gildas in the sixth century (Section I.2), followed by Bede (*HE* 1.1).

Linguistic points: King John's envoy states proudly that England in his day is a trilingual country where the inhabitants know Latin, French and English.

The term *admirallus* appears in BML from the twelfth century in various forms, and with the sense both of an Arab ruler and of a naval commander, i.e. English 'admiral'. Compare, for example, Matthew Paris, *Maj.* 1.272 *s.a.* 622: *Ma-*

---

1 *The letter collection of Peter Abelard and Heloise*, ed. D. Luscombe and transl. B. Radice, OMT, Oxford, 2013: 92 (ch. 59).

II.24 | Matthew Paris, *The Major Chronicles* 243

chometus ... in regno Saracenorum pretores statuit, quos admiralios vocavit ('Muhammad called the rulers he appointed in the Saracen realm "admirals"'). The Latin noun seems to be influenced in sense and spelling by Latin *admirari*, by French 'a(d)miral' (in various spellings) and Arabic 'emir': for the complex etymology, cf. *OED s.v.* admiral.

TEXT II.24

King John's ambassadors arrive at the Emir's palace in Morocco
[*RS* 2.559] misit igitur nuncios secretissimos cum festinatione summa, videlicet Thomam de Herdintona et Radulfum filium Nicholai milites et Robertum de Londoniis clericum ad admiralium Murmelium, regem magnum Affricae, Marrochiae, et Hyspaniae, quem vulgus Miramumelinum vocat;[2] significans eidem, quod se et regnum suum libenter redderet eidem et dederet et deditum teneret ab ipso, si placeret ei, sub tributo. nec non et legem Christianam, quam vanam censuit, relinquens, legi Machometi fideliter adhaereret. quod cum dicti nuncii secretius relaturi ad curiam dicti principis [p. 560] pervenissent, invenerunt ad primam portam aliquot milites armatos, introitum arctius custodientes, gladiis evaginatis. ad secundum vero ostium, scilicet palatii, plures invenerunt milites ad unguem armatos et prioribus elegantius, ensibus strictis ingressum diligenter custodientes, et, ut censeri potuit, aliis fortiores ac nobiliores. in ostio vero thalami inferioris, multo secundum apparentiam robustiores et ferociores et plures prioribus.

Translation: Matthew Paris, *The Major Chronicles*

And so with all haste King John sent in great secrecy envoys, namely Thomas of Erdington and Ralph, son of Nicholas, both knights, and Robert, a London cleric, to the Emir Murmelinus, the great king of Africa, Morocco and Spain who is generally called Miramumelinus, to indicate to him that he would willingly give himself and his kingdom to him and would submit to him and would be held subject by him, should he wish, under tribute. Indeed, he would also abandon the Christian religion, which he considered worthless, and faithfully conform to the Islamic religion. When these envoys who were to report in great secrecy arrived at the court of this ruler, they found a number of armed soldiers at the first gate, guarding the entry closely, their swords drawn. At the second gate, in other words the palace gate, they

---

2 The title Murmelinus (for which the text of Matthew Paris gives corrupt versions) is the Latin equivalent of the Arabic 'amir al-mu'minin' ('commander of the faithful'), referring to Muhammad al-Nasir, caliph from 1199–1213. Cf. Hugeburc, *Life of Willibald* (Section I.24) chapter 4, where the 'king of the Saracens' is referred to as Myrmumni.

244 Thirteenth Century

found many soldiers armed to the teeth and more elegantly dressed than the previous ones, carefully guarding the entrance with drawn swords, and as far as one could assess, more powerful and more noble than the others. At the gate of the lower chamber they were in appearance much more robust and fierce than the previous ones, and there were also more of them.

The Emir responds politely to the English envoys
cum autem pacifice introducti, ex licentia ipsius admiralii quem Regem Magnum vocant, ipsi nuncii et vice domini sui, regis scilicet Angliae, reverenter salutassent, exposuerunt causam adventus sui plenius, cartam regiam ei porrigentes; quam quidem interpres qui praesens vocatus aderat, evidenter patefecit. quo intellecto, rex librum quem inspexerat clausit; sedit enim ad pulpitum suum studens, vir aetate et statura mediocris, et gestu maturus et verbis facundus et circumspectus. et cum paulisper quasi secum deliberans respondisset, modeste dixit: 'Modo inspexi librum in Graeco scriptum cujusdam Graeci sapientis et Christiani, nomine Pauli,[3] cuius actus et verba mihi optime complacent, et accepto; unum tamen de ipso mihi displicet, quod in lege sub qua natus erat non stetit, sed ad aliam tanquam transfuga et inconstans avolavit. et id dico de domino vestro Anglorum rege, qui relicta piissima et mundissima lege Christianorum sub qua nascebatur, cereus, et instabilis gliscit transmeare.' et addidit, 'Novit qui nihil ignorat Deus omnipotens omnium Creator, si exlex essem, illam prae omnibus eligerem, et acceptans amplexarer.'

Translation: Matthew Paris, *The Major Chronicles*

When, after being led inside in a peaceable manner, the envoys, with the permission of the Emir whom they called the Great King, greeted him with respect on behalf of their lord, the king of England, they explained in greater detail the reason why they had come, and handed to him the king's document which the interpreter, who had been summoned to attend, explained clearly. When he understood it, the king closed the book he had been looking at, for he was sitting at his desk studying, a man of middle age and medium height, of mature bearing, eloquent and discreet in his words. He seemed to ponder a while before replying, saying modestly, 'I have just

---

3   The Emir is able to read St Paul's letters in the original Greek; if the English wished to read the Islamic text, the Qur'an, there was by this time a translation from Arabic to Latin undertaken by an Englishman, Robert of Ketton, in the 1140s at the instigation of Peter the Venerable of Cluny: see T. Burman (2007) *Reading the Qur'an in Latin Christendom 1140–1560*, Philadelphia. There is as yet no modern edition of the translation, but Robert's prefatory letter to Peter is included in D. Howlett (2003) *Insular inscriptions*, Dublin, 168–75. In the Cambridge MS CCC 184, the Latin translation is presented in a periodic rather than paratactic structure.

II.24 | Matthew Paris, *The Major Chronicles*   245

been looking at a book written in Greek by some Greek wise man, a Christian by the name of Paul, by whose deeds and words I am most impressed, and I approve them. But one thing about him that I do not approve is the fact that he did not stand firm in the religion into which he was born: he did not remain constant but fled to another like a fugitive. And I say the same about your lord, the king of England, who resembles wax in lacking firmness, given his eagerness to cross over to another religion, abandoning the most pious and pure Christian religion into which he was born.' He added, 'God, the omnipotent creator of all, who is ignorant of nothing, knows that if I were without a religion, I would choose this one before all others and would embrace it with approval.'

An envoy gives a description of England; the Emir is sceptical
postea vero sciscitabatur, cujus conditionis esset rex Angliae et regnum ejus; respondit Thomas, utpote nunciorum facundissimus, 'Egregie et ingenue atavis **Hor. *Odes* 1.1.1** regibus magnis procreatus, terra ejus opulenta et suis contenta bonis, culturis, pascuis, pratis et silvis abundat. ex ea etiam omne genus metallorum studio conflatili eliquatur. gens nostra [p. 561] speciosa et ingeniosa tribus pollet idiomatibus erudita, scilicet Latino, Gallico et Anglico, et omni arte liberali et mechanica plenius erudita. veruntamen vinearum aut olivarum copiam ex se terra nostra non producit vel abietum, sed ea ex vicinis regionibus commercio sibi adquirit abundanter; aer salubris et temperatus; inter occidentem sita et septentrionem, ab occidente calorem, a septentrione sumens frigiditatem, temperiem sortitur gratissimam. undique mari vallatur, unde insularum regina meruit appellari. regnum etiam ab inuncto et coronato gubernatum, ab antiquo liberum esse dinoscitur et ingenuum, ad nullius praeterquam Dei spectans dominationem. ecclesia etiam et nostrae cultus religionis plus quam in aliqua mundi parte ibidem prosperatur, et papalibus ac regiis legibus pacifice gubernatur.' tracto igitur ab alto praecordiali suspirio, respondit rex, 'Nunquam legi vel audivi quod aliquis rex, tam prosperum regnum possidens subjectum et obediens, suum sic vellet sponte pessundare principatum, ut de libero faceret tributarium, de suo alienum, de felici miserum; et se alterius tamquam sine vulnere victum dedere voluntati (…)'

Translation: Matthew Paris, *The Major Chronicles*

Then the Emir asked the envoy to describe the king of England and his kingdom. Thomas, being the most eloquent of the envoys, replied: 'He is born from a noble and outstanding ancestral line of mighty kings; his country is wealthy and self-sufficient; it abounds in arable land, pasture, meadows and woodland. Every kind of metal is crushed from it by means of the smelting process. Our people are attractive and clever and excel in being trained to speak three languages, namely Latin, French and English; they are also highly educated in every liberal art and mechanical skill. But our country is not able to produce an abundance of vines or olives or pine timber, but imports these things in large amounts from neighbouring countries by means of trade. The climate is healthy and temperate; situated between west and north, taking heat from the west and cold from the north it acquires a very pleasant temperature. On all sides it is enclosed by sea, which means it deserves the title "Queen of Islands". The kingdom is ruled by an anointed and crowned king and from ancient times it is famous for being free and of noble stock, respecting no one as its lord except God. The Church, too, and the practise of our religion prosper there more than in any part of the world, peacefully governed by the laws of the pope and the king.' Drawing a sigh from the depths of his heart, the Emir responded, 'I have never read or heard that any king who possesses as his obedient subject such a prosperous kingdom would of his own will agree to destroy his dominion so as to make it a tributary state instead of a free one, to give it to someone else instead of having it as his own, to make it unfortunate instead of fortunate; and to surrender himself to someone else's will as if he had been beaten without putting up a fight (...)'

Primary Sources and Related Texts

Matthew Paris, *Chronica majora*, 7 vols, RS 57 (1872–83).
Gesta abbatum monasterii Sancti Albani, RS 28 (1867) 1.236–42.

Further Reading

Church, S. (ed.) (1999) *King John: new interpretations*, Woodbridge.
Daniel, N. (1975) *The Arabs and medieval Europe*, London.
Mitchell, J. (1933) 'The Matthew Paris maps', *Geographic Journal* 81: 27–34.
Ronay, G. (1978) *The Tartar Khan's Englishman*, London.
Shoval, I. (2016) *King John's delegation to the Almohad court (1212): medieval interreligious interactives and modern historiography*, Turnhout.
Vaughan, R. (1958) *Matthew Paris*, Cambridge.
Vincent, N. (2021) *John, an evil king?* Harmondsworth.

Section II.25

Magna Carta, the Great Charter (excerpts from the 1225 version: chapters 7, 9, 23, 25, 29, 30)

Date: versions exist from 1215, 1216, 1217 and 1225.

Four original copies of the 1225 version of the Charter survive, two in the British Library, one in Lincoln and one in Salisbury.

Magna Carta is perhaps the most famous historical document in Britain. The necessity for such a document, a kind of Bill of Rights, grew out of the tensions between King John and his barons, which had been increasing throughout his reign as the king became more demanding and suspicious while the barons became less willing to cooperate and more determined to cling to what they had. Gradually the barons unified in their hostility, giving them the power to demand reforms regarding fair treatment, not only for the barons themselves, but for other lay people lower down on the social scale. In many instances the Fine Rolls of the period can provide evidence of the extent to which the most important clauses of Magna Carta were obeyed.

Work: The first version of Magna Carta, a document of some 3,550 words, was a series of statements drawn up under pressure from the barons and agreed by both parties on 15 June 1215 at Runnymede on the banks of the Thames. It was based on Henry I's influential coronation charter of 1100, itself a continuation of Anglo-Saxon laws. Despite its long-term celebrity status as a guarantor of the people's rights, in the short term it failed to bring about peace between the king and the rebels. At first it was referred to as *carta de libertatibus communibus*, then came to be known as *magna carta*, originally to distinguish it from the shorter charter about forest law (Charter of the Forest). The title was applied to the 1225 version that became definitive. The charter is extant in several thirteenth-century copies, each on a single sheet. The sections below are excerpted from the 1225 version, which was addressed to 'all' and not just 'all free (men)', as in the 1215 version: so the unfree and the peasants and women were granted certain benefits, as well as the Church, the nobility, the free men. This charter was authenticated by the Great Seal of Henry III. It was signed by, amongst others, Archbishop Stephen Langton, who had helped to persuade the king to reissue the Magna Carta. Mindful of the stance of Thomas Becket (cf. Section II.16) regarding the rights of the Church, his successor as Archbishop of Canterbury was keen to see the king agree to maintain the liberties of the Church, as stated in the opening section of the Charter: it is no coincidence that these were the years when Langton

248 Thirteenth Century

was arranging the splendid ceremony in Canterbury Cathedral for the translation (moving) of Becket's body from the crypt to a new chapel, which took place in 1220, fifty years after Becket's murder.

In the chapters excerpted below we find a number of issues addressed that are still relevant and sometimes controversial, with regard to women's incomes, the right to basic maintenance, standardisation of weights and measures, the problems caused by obstructions in rivers, each person's right to a swift and fair trial, and freedom of movement for foreign traders.

Linguistic points: King John and the barons would have probably spoken French in discussing the terms of the Magna Carta, but the final document was recorded in Latin. This Latin version, in all its succinctness, was soon translated into French, as *La graunt chartre des fraunchises*. There is no extant English translation from before the sixteenth century. This document, as is the case with the Domesday Book some 130 years earlier, contains many words that had appeared for the first time in BML during the previous decades, as the result of legal and administrative developments. Some of these new words, such as the legal sense of CL *distringere*, had already appeared in Glanvill (see Section II.17). Most of these derive from French/Anglo-Norman, with the French forms usually deriving either from an earlier Latin or Germanic word. Examples are *mesagium*<AN 'messuage'<*mansio* + *-agium*: 'tenement'; *estoverium*<AN 'estovoir' ('to be necessary')<*est opera*: 'maintenance'; *kidellus*<AN/ME 'kidel': 'weir' for catching fish; *costera*<AN 'costere'<CL *costa*: 'coast'; *toltis* (*malis*)<AN 'tolte' (cf. CL *tollere*): 'unjust tax', 'maltolt'; *gwerra*<AN/ME 'werre', OF *guerre*: 'war'; *gwerrinus*<*gwerra* + CL *-inus*: 'of war'; *attachiare*<OF 'atachier' (which occurs in the *Chanson de Roland*, line 3737), cf. ME (1325) 'to attach': 'to bind by pledge to appear in court' (cf. *OED s.v.* attach). As for *halbergettus* (*haub-*), the term is only attested in the period 1196–1228; it appears to refer to a twill weave resembling chainmail (cf. 'hauberk').

There are also new words derived from English, as for example *lista*<OE/ME 'liste': 'border', 'selvedge': even though the English word occurs already around 700 in the so-called Épinal-Erfurt Latin–Old English glossary, possibly compiled for Aldhelm at Malmesbury, it does not make the transition into BML until the early thirteenth century.

The *maritagium* is the property assigned to a woman by her family at her marriage. The word can also signify 'marriage', 'wedding' and 'the right to give in marriage'.

TEXT II.25

[address] Henricus Dei gratia rex Anglie. dedimus et concessimus archiepiscopis, episcopis, abbatibus, prioribus, comitibus, baronibus et omnibus de regno nostro has libertates subscriptas tenendas in regno nostro Anglie in perpetuum.

Henry, by the grace of God, king of England. To the archbishops, bishops, abbots, priors, earls, barons and all those from our kingdom we have given and granted these liberties, as mentioned below, to be held in perpetuity in our kingdom of England.

[7] vidua post mortem mariti sui statim et sine difficultate habeat et hereditatem suam, nec aliquid det pro dote sua, vel pro maritagio suo vel hereditate sua, quam hereditatem maritus suus et ipsa tenuerunt die obitus ipsius mariti, et maneat in capitali mesagio ipsius mariti sui per quadraginta dies post obitum ipsius mariti sui, infra quos assignetur ei dos sua, nisi prius ei fuerit assignata, vel nisi domus illa sit castrum; et si de castro recesserit, statim provideatur ei domus competens in qua possit honeste morari, quousque dos sua ei assignetur secundum quod predictum est; et habeat rationabile estoverium suum interim de communi. assignetur autem ei pro dote sua tercia pars tocius terre mariti sui que sua fuit in vita sua, nisi de minori dotata fuerit ad hostium ecclesie. nulla vidua distringatur ad se maritandum, dum vivere voluerit sine marito, ita tamen quod securitatem faciet quod se non maritabit sine assensu nostro, si de nobis tenuerit, vel sine assensu domini sui, si de alio tenuerit. [Magna Carta 1215: 7–8]

[7] *After her husband's death, a widow is to have her marriage portion and her inheritance at once and without any hindrance; nor should she pay anything for her dower, her marriage portion or her inheritance which she and her husband held on the day of her husband's death; and she may stay in her husband's house for forty days after his death, within which period her dower is to be assigned to her, unless it was assigned to her previously or unless her home is a castle; and if she withdraws from the castle, a suitable house should immediately be provided for her, in which she can live respectably until her dower is assigned to her according to what was said previously; and she should have her reasonable maintenance from the common land. There should be assigned to her for her dower a third part of all her husband's land which was hers during her lifetime, unless she was given a smaller dower at the door of the church. No widow is to be compelled to marry so long as she wishes to live without a husband, provided that she gives security that she will not marry without our consent if she holds (land) of us, or without the consent of her lord, if she holds (land) of another.*

[9] civitas London' habeat omnes antiquas libertates et liberas consuetudines suas. preterea volumus et concedimus quod omnes alie civitates et burgi et ville et barones de Quinque Portubus et omnes portus habeant omnes libertates et liberas consuetudines suas. [1215: 13]

[9] *The city of London must have all its ancient liberties and free customs. Furthermore, we wish and grant that all other cities, boroughs, towns, barons of the Cinque Ports and all ports are to have all their liberties and free customs.*

[23] omnes kidelli decetero deponantur penitus per Tamisiam et Medewayeiam et per totam Angliam, nisi per costeram maris.[1] [1215: 33]

[23] *All kiddles (fish weirs) are henceforth to be completely removed from the Thames and the Medway and throughout England, except on the sea coast.*

[25] una mensura vini sit per totum regnum nostrum, et una mensura cervisie, et una mensura bladi, scilicet quarterium London', et una latitudo pannorum tinctorum et russetorum et halbergettorum, scilicet due ulne infra listas; de ponderibus vero sit ut de mensuris. [1215: 35]

[25] *There should be a single measure of wine throughout the kingdom and one measure of ale and one measure of corn, namely the London quarter, and one width of cloth whether dyed, russet or halberjet, namely two ells within the selvedges. Let it be the same for weights as with measures.*

[29] nullus liber homo decetero capiatur vel imprisonetur aut disseisiatur de aliquo libero tenemento suo vel libertatibus vel liberis consuetudinibus suis, aut utlagetur aut exulet aut aliquo alio modo destruatur, nec super eum ibimus nec super eum mittemus nisi per legale judicium parium suorum vel per legem terre. nulli vendemus, nulli negabimus aut differemus rectum vel justiciam [1215: 39–40]

[29] *No free man is to be arrested or imprisoned or dispossessed of any free tenement of his or of his liberties or free customs, or outlawed or exiled or in any way ruined, nor will we go to fetch him or send for him except by the lawful judgement of his peers or by the law of the land. To no one will we sell, to no one will we deny or delay right or justice.*

[30] omnes mercatores, nisi publice antea prohibiti fuerint, habeant salvum et securum exire de Anglia et venire in Angliam et morari et ire per Angliam, tam per terram quam per aquam, ad emendum et vendendum sine omnibus toltis malis, per antiquas et rectas consuetudines, preterquam in tempore gwerre, et si sint de terra contra nos gwerrina, et si tales inveniantur in terra nostra in principio gwerre, attachientur sine dampno corporum vel rerum, donec sciatur a nobis vel a capitali justiciario nostro quomodo mercatores terre nostre tractentur, qui tunc invenientur in terra contra nos gwerrina; et si nostri salvi sint ibi, alii salvi sint in terra nostra. [1215: 41]

---

1   Cf. *CurR* 17 no. 117 (1242–3), *diligenter inquireret qui fecerunt kidellos in Sabrina post perhibicionem* (?*pro-*) *domini regis* ('he should carefully enquire who has made the fish weirs in the Severn after the lord king's prohibition').

[30] *All merchants, unless they have previously been publicly forbidden, are to be safe and secure in leaving England and entering England and in staying and travelling in England, both by land and by water, to buy and sell free from all unjust taxes, according to the ancient and rightful customs, except, in time of war, if they come from a country that is at war with us. And if such are found in our country at the outbreak of war, they should be detained without damage to their bodies or goods until we or our chief justiciar know how the merchants of our country who are at that time to be found in the country that is at war with us are being treated; and if ours are safe there, the others should be safe in our country.*

Primary Sources and Related Texts

Latin text from 1225 version (based on 1215 version), printed in *Statutes of the Realm* 1.22–5, London, 1810.

Holt, J. C. (ed.) (2015) *Magna Carta*, 3rd ed., Cambridge: 420–8.

Further Reading

Annesley, S. (2007), 'The impact of Magna Carta on widows: evidence from the Fine Rolls, 1216–1225', Henry III Fine Rolls Project, Fine of the month for Nov. 2007, https://finerollshenry3.org.uk

Bogdanor, V. (2015) 'Magna Carta, the rule of law and the reform of the constitution' in *Magna Carta and its modern legacy*, ed. R. Hazell and J. Melton, Cambridge.

Magna Carta, ed. D. Carpenter, Harmondsworth, 2015. With chapters on the society and the royal administration of the time, and a glossary of terms and a section on 'The nature of the 1225 charter' (424–9).

Linebaugh, P. (2008) *The Magna Carta manifesto: liberties and commons for all*, Berkeley.

Loengard, J. S. (1993) '*Rationabilis dos*: Magna Carta and the widow's "fair share" in the earlier thirteenth century' in *Walker (1993).

Vincent, N. (2015) *Magna Carta: origins and legacy*, Oxford.

Section II.26

Roger de Montbegon: a Life in Administrative Documents
A: 1199 *Rotuli de oblatis et finibus* 41–2 (TNA: C60/1A): Marrying an Heiress
B: 1207–10 Curia Regis Rolls (Plea Rolls), Pipe Rolls and Pedes finium (Feet of Fines): Disputes about the Right to Nominate Priests to Vacant Churches
C: 1215–20 Magna Carta, Close Rolls, Fine Rolls, Pedes finium: Magna Carta and Its Aftermath
D: 1225–36 Fine Rolls and Pedes finium: Roger's Death and Beyond

This sample of administrative documents in which one person, the landowner Roger de Montbegon, makes an appearance over the course of some twenty-five years is intended to give an idea of the range of different kinds of documents that make use, in everyday contexts, of the language and technical terms we have seen in the Domesday Book, Glanvill and the Magna Carta, relating to the complex administrative processes governing matters of law, taxation, feudal rights etc. These procedures, often provoked by some minor dispute or subsequent to everyday events such as marriage or death, and involving many royal officers in London and throughout the country, might drag on for many years, as can be seen below.

Roger de Monte Begonis (c.1165–1226), from a Norman family granted land in England after 1066 across the north of England (as recorded in DB), was a troublesome character whose name appears in many different documents in various contexts: the excerpted examples below are not exhaustive. Initially a supporter of John against King Richard, he became disillusioned and joined other baronial opponents of John leading up to the issuing of the Magna Carta, for which he was appointed as one of the twenty-five enforcers. Although his primary estate was Hornby Castle in Lancashire, on the edge of the Lake District, like most landowners of Norman stock he held properties in many different counties, some of which are mentioned below. The indexes to the printed volumes of these sources make it possible to track individuals and places.

A: 1199 *Rotuli de oblatis et finibus* 41–2 (TNA: C60/1A): Marrying an Heiress

Here Roger appears in 1199 paying a 'fine' of 500 marks to King John for marriage to an heiress and widow, Olive (née Fitzjordan). He will also receive her lands and inheritance. The payment seems also to secure for Olive the dower owing to her from her previous husband. The document in which this is recorded is in the series known as *Rotuli de oblatis et finibus* (later regarded as Fine Rolls), recording offers of money to the king for concessions or favours. The *fines* in the title refer to the agreement made to pay, or as a semantic extension, the payment itself, from which comes the modern English sense of a fine. For a contemporary description of these rolls, which started to be produced by the Exchequer perhaps in the 1170s, see the *Dialogue of the Exchequer* (cf. Section II.4B) 2.24. The word *scaccarium* used in the first excerpt as a term for the Exchequer originally referred to a checked cloth, like a chessboard, used for computing before the adoption of Arabic numbers.

TEXT II.26A

Rogerus de Munbegun dat domino Regi d. marcas argenti pro habenda Oliva que fuit uxor Roberti de Sancto Johanne cum tota terra sua et hereditate et mandatum est G. filio Petri quod accepta securitate ab eo de c marcis reddendis ad scaccarium ad mediam Quadragesimam proximo futuram et de c marcis solvendis ad clausum Pasche proximo sequens et de residuis ccc marcis reddendis per c. marcas de scaccario in scaccarium, tunc ei de prefata Oliva cum tota terra et hereditate sua plenariam saisinam sine dilatione habere faciat et faciat habere eidem Olive rationabilem dotem suam de terra que fuit Roberti de Sancto Johannis quondam viri sui secundum rationabilem cartam suam quam inde habet.

Translation: *Rotuli de oblatis et finibus*

Roger de Montbegon gives the lord king 500 marks of silver to have Olive, who was the wife of Robert of St John, with all her land and inheritance, and once Geoffrey fitzPeter receives surety from Roger that he will pay 100 marks at the Exchequer at next mid-Lent and 100 marks one week after next Easter and the remaining 300 marks at the rate of 100 marks at each Exchequer session, then Geoffrey is ordered to arrange for Roger to have full seisin without delay of the aforesaid Olive with all her land and inheritance and for Olive to have her reasonable dower from the lands which belonged to her late husband Robert of St John, according to the reasonable charter which he has concerning this matter.

B: 1207–10 Curia Regis Rolls (Plea Rolls), Pipe Rolls and Pedes finium (Feet of Fines): Disputes about the Right to Nominate Priests to Vacant Churches

A few years later Roger turns up in a dispute with the abbot of Barlings Abbey in Lincolnshire as to who is going to nominate the priest to the vacant church of Broughton in the same county; the fact that the church is vacant is known from the form of action taken. Here are documents spanning the period 1207–10, from the

254 Thirteenth Century

Curia Regis Rolls, the Pipe Rolls and the so-called Feet of Fines. Three years after the initial court case both men are paying the king half a mark to be allowed to come to an agreement which will stop the plea between them which had started in 1207. Neither of the men pays immediately, for the sum is recorded later that year (1210) in a Pipe Roll as being due for collection by the local sheriff. This is a roll resembling a pipe, made up of lengths of parchment sewn together at their heads and then rolled up: on each were recorded the king's income and expenses for one financial year, from Michaelmas (29 September) to Michaelmas. Unpaid debts can often be followed through several consecutive Pipe Rolls, with the earliest surviving Pipe Roll dating from 1130. Then in a document from the series known as Pedes finium or Feet of Fines, a conclusion ('final concord') to their dispute is recorded whereby the abbot on one side, and Roger and Olive on the other, agree in effect to exchange the advowsons of Broughton and Tuxford. Such a final concord often marked the end of the kind of dispute recorded in the Curia Regis Rolls. From 1195 the Feet of Fines were produced in three copies, one for each of the parties (both written on the upper part of the piece of parchment, with one on the left and one on the right, then divided by a wavy cut so that they could be proved to belong together, and the third copy written on the lower bit which was separately deposited in the court of Common Pleas (now referenced as CP 25 or 27 in the National Archives). Note CL *advocatio*, whose semantic development in BML was to produce the AN form 'avouson' and the English 'advowson'; also the phrase *quietum clamare*, meaning 'to renounce one's claim'. *persona* is seen here on its semantic journey from CL to modern English 'person' and 'parson'. *Deforciare* (*diffort-*) as a legal term occurs in the handbook known as Glanvill (cf. Section II.17). Not only individual words but also phrases recur in many types of legal document.

Texts II.26B

1207 Curia Regis Rolls 5.56
abbas de Berlinges optulit se iiij die versus Rogerum de Munbegun de ecclesia de Brocton', scilicet quare ipse non permittit abbatem ipsum presentare idoneam personam ad ecclesiam illam; et ipse non venit vel se essoniavit et summonicio etc. et ideo attachietur quod sit in octabis sancti Martini etc. Et abbas ponit loco suo Walterum Mauclerc.

Translation: Curia Regis Rolls

The abbot of Barlings Abbey appears in court on the fourth day against Roger de Montbegon regarding Broughton church, namely as to why he does not permit the abbot to present a suitable parson to that church; and he does not turn up or essoin himself, and a summons (was issued) etc. And therefore he should be attached so as to be in court in the Octave of St Martin, etc. And the abbot puts in his place Walter Mauclerc.

1210 Curia Regis Rolls 6.41
Abbas de Berlinges dat dimidiam marcam pro licencia concordandi. Rogerus de Munbegun dat dimidiam marcam pro licencia concordandi cum abbate de Berlinges de ecclesia de Briucton'.[1]

Translation: Curia Regis Rolls

The abbot of Barlings Abbey gives half a mark for permission to reach an agreement. Roger de Montbegon gives half a mark for permission to reach an agreement with the abbot of Barlings Abbey regarding Broughton Church

1210 Pedes finium no. 309 (TNA: CP 25/1/127/10 m. 4)[2]
Hec est finalis concordia facta in curia domini regis apud Westmonasterium a die Pasche in tres septimanas anno regni [regis] Johannis xj^{mo} coram ipso domino rege, Simone de Pateshull', Jacobo de Poterna, Henrico de Ponte Aldemer' iustic' et aliis fidelibus domini regis tunc ibi presentibus, inter Robertum abbatem de Berlinges petentem et Rogerum de Monte Begonis et Olivam uxorem suam deforciantes per Willelmum filium Radulfi et Adam de Tid' positos loco eorum ad lucrandum vel perdendum de advocacione ecclesie de Broctan', unde placitum fuit inter eos in eadem curia, scilicet quod predictus abbas remisit et quietum clamavit de se et successoribus suis predictis Rogero et Olive et heredibus ipsius Olive totum ius et clamium quod habuit in advocacione predicte ecclesie inperpetuum. et predicti Rogerus et Oliva remiserunt et quietum clamaverunt de se et heredibus ipsius Olive predicto abbati et successoribus suis et ecclesie beate Marie de Berlinges totum ius et clamium quod habuerunt vel habere potuerunt in advocacione ecclesie de Tufford inperpetuum.

Translation: Pedes finium

This is the final agreement made in the court of the lord king at Westminster three weeks after Easter Day in the eleventh year of the reign of King John, in the presence of the lord king, the justices Simon of Pattishall, James of Potterne, Henry de Pont-Audemer, and other subjects of the lord king who were present there at the time, between Robert, abbot of Barlings, the demandant, and Roger de Montbegon

---

1   Cf. Pipe Roll 12 John (n.s. 26) 39 (Michaelmas 1210): *Rogerus de Monte Begonis debet dim. m. pro licencia concordandi cum abbate de Berling'*.

2   Cf. the picture in the frontispiece to this volume, showing a similar Pedes finium (Feet of Fines) document from 1296 (TNA: CP 25/1/245/35 (20)). This document includes the first evidence, in a Latin matrix, of the English word 'pasteymaker', with the profession used as a surname, and (as often at this period) preceded by the French article *Le* (for which see the lemma in *DMLBS*).

256   Thirteenth Century

and Olive his wife, the party allegedly withholding the advowson, through William son of Ralph and Adam de Tid' appointed as their attorneys, to win or lose the plea regarding the advowson of Broughton Church. And so legal action took place between them in this same court, to the effect that the aforesaid abbot remitted and quitclaimed all right and claim which he had in the advowson of this church in perpetuity, with respect to himself and his successors, to Roger and Olive and to Olive's heirs. And Roger and Olive remitted and quitclaimed all right and claim which they had or could have in the advowson of the church of Tuxford in perpetuity, with respect to themselves and Olive's heirs, to this abbot and his successors and to the church of St Mary at Barlings.

C: 1215–20 Magna Carta, Close Rolls, Fine Rolls, Pedes finium: Magna Carta and Its Aftermath

Then in 1215 Roger appears as one of twenty-five barons appointed to ensure that King John observed the terms of the Magna Carta: indeed, he was one of four barons witnessing a royal charter at Runnymede five days after the king put his seal on the Magna Carta, at a point when both king and rebels still hoped each side would get what it wanted. The following year, during John's campaign in the north of England, an entry in the Close Rolls for 1216 records John's instructions to various sheriffs, including that of Nottinghamshire, regarding some of Roger's many land-holdings, especially in the north of England; to these he adds specific orders regarding the lands at Oswaldbeck and Wheatley in Nottinghamshire. Here these names are given as 'Oswardebec' and 'Watelegh': note the various spellings of these place names in the documents. Similar letters, from a king to his sheriffs regarding the restoration of confiscated lands, are frequently to be found in the royal records of the thirteenth century after periods of strife between king and barons. Note the word *bailla* or *balliva* used here in a Close Roll and in a Fine Roll, meaning a particular area of jurisdiction, and related to the English 'bailiff': it is derived from the CL *bajulus*, via the OF/AN form 'baillie'; the word is also related to the English legal term 'bail'.

TEXTS II.26C

1216 Close Rolls (RC) 1.244
Rex vicecomiti Kancie etc. scias quod Rogerus de Monte Begonis venit ad fidem et servicium nostrum et nos ipsum in graciam nostram suscepimus. et ideo tibi precipimus quod eidem Rogero de omnibus terris suis in bailla tua sine dilacione plenam saisinam habere facias. et si quid de terris suis ammotum fuerit post suscepcionem litterarum istarum eidem Rogero reddi facias. apud Pontem Fractum ij die Januarii.

Translation: Close Roll

The king to the Sheriff of Kent, etc. You should be aware that Roger de Montbegon came to our allegiance and service and we welcomed him into our favour. And so we order you to arrange for this same Roger to have full seisin, without delay, of all his lands in your bailiwick. And if any of his lands has been removed after the receipt of this letter, arrange for it to be returned to Roger. Pontefract, 2 January.

In the following year, 1217, the new king, Henry III (also in a royal writ to the Sheriff of Nottingham, recorded at Close Rolls (RC) 1.339a), repeats his father's instructions regarding 'Oswaldebec' and 'Wethele', referring to his father's writ granting possession to Roger. But by April 1220 it would seem that although Roger had got these places back, he had then been dispossessed again by the Constable of Nottinghamshire, Peter Marc, on the orders of the infamous Sheriff of Nottinghamshire, Philip Marc, for these places are included among the possessions Roger sues for in that year. This appears in a letter preserved among the Ancient Correspondence (i.e. *Royal Letters*), from the Constable of Nottingham to the Sheriff of Nottinghamshire reporting on Roger's recent appearance in the county court. *averia* from French 'aveir' (deriving from CL *habere*) is used for property or livestock: it occurs in an early twelfth-century Norman charter, but only enters common usage in the early thirteenth century. In the commonly used phrase *per vadium et plegium*, the two nouns are synonymous. *Vadium* derives from an early Germanic word, *wadi*. In the eighth-century Reichenau Glossary, *wadius* had been glossed by CL *pignus*. *Wadi* is the source of such modern English words as 'gage', 'wage' (via OF/AN forms) and 'wedding'.

1217 *Royal Letter* no. 86 (TNA: SC 1/11/68)
noveritis, domine carissime, quod dominus Rogerus de Monte Begoniae venit ad comitatum die lunae in crastino clausi Paschatis et petiit averia sua aut quieta (quia dicebat ea vi et injuste esse capta) aut per vadium et plegium. (…)

Translation: *Royal Letter*

You know, my dearest lord, that Lord Roger de Montbegon came to the county court on the Monday, the day after the end of Easter, and he demanded his livestock should either be released free (because he said that they had been taken by force and unjustly) or by surety and pledge. (…)

Roger claimed that his livestock had illegally been taken from various places including 'Oswandebec' and 'Wheatele', but the court countered that these had been justly taken because of the serious transgressions he had committed. Roger refused to admit any fault, and stormed off without regard to the king's orders or

258 Thirteenth Century

the law. The court agreed that *nisi fuisset tam magnus homo et baro domini regis, per corpus eius pro tantis transgressionibus juste deberet retineri* ('if he were not such an important person and a baron of the lord king, he ought to be justly held in person for such great transgressions'). Only a few days later King Henry seems to have heard of the debacle in Nottingham county court, for the livestock crop up in his instruction to the Sheriff of Nottingham once again to grant Roger the land. The king writes rather tetchily:

1220 Close Rolls 1.415a

Rex vicecomiti Noting' salutem. scias quod inspeximus cartam domini Johannis regis patris nostri quam fecit Rogero de Monte Begonis de terra de Oswaldebec cum pertinentiis suis quam ei concessit tenendam in feodo et hereditate per servicium unius militis sicut illam prius concesserat dum fuit Comes Moreton' per cartam suam quam similiter inspeximus; et per eandem cartam quam inspeximus concessit idem dominus Johannes Rex pater noster eidem Rogerio manerium de Watelegh quod fuit Johannis Malherbe fratris sui tenendum sibi omnibus diebus suis quoad vixerit, ita tunc quod post decessum ipsius Rogeri manerium illud de Watelegh ad nos revertatur vel heredes nostros. et ideo tibi precipimus quod predictam terram de Oswaldebec et predictum manerium de Watelegh cum pertinenciis suis eidem Rogero in pace habere permittas retenta in manu nostra terra de Claworth cum pertinenciis suis. homines et averia predicti Rogeri de Monte Begonis que cepisti occasione contentionis mote inter te et servientes tuos et predictum Rogerum et servientes suos pro saisina ei facienda de terris predictis de Oswaldebec et de Watelegh, eidem Rogero sine dilacione et difficultate aliqua deliberes, ita quod amplius inde clamorem non audiamus. teste Henrico etc. ut supra.

Translation: Close Roll

The king sends greetings to the Sheriff of Nottingham. You should be aware that we have inspected the charter of the lord king John, our father, which he made for Roger de Montbegon regarding the land of Oswaldbeck with its appurtenances which he granted to him to be held in fee and inheritance for the service of one knight just as he had previously granted it when he was Count of Mortain by means of his charter, which we have likewise inspected; and by means of that same document which we have inspected, this same lord king, John, our father, granted to this same Roger the manor of Wheatley which belonged to John Malherbe, his brother, to be held for all the days of his life, in such a way that then, after the death of Roger, this manor of Wheatley should revert to us or our heirs. And so we order you to allow Roger to hold this land of Oswaldbeck and the manor of Wheatley with its appurtenances in peace, while we retain in our control the land of Claworth with its appurtenances.

You must without delay or hindrance release to Roger the men and livestock belonging to this same Roger de Montbegon which you took on the occasion of the dispute arising between you and your servants, and Roger and his servants, regarding giving seisin to him of the lands of Oswaldbeck and Wheatley. Please do this in such a way that we do not hear any further claims regarding this matter. Witness, Henry etc. as above.

D: 1225–36 Fine Rolls and Pedes finium: Roger's Death and Beyond

In March 1225 an instruction is copied onto a Fine Roll shortly after Roger's death, indicating that his lands, held in various counties, should immediately be taken into the hands of the king (as was the royal prerogative until the king ordered their release) apart from the inheritance belonging to Roger's wife, perhaps from her first marriage, to which the king is not entitled. The Fine Rolls come in the form of a roll of documents attached head to foot in a continuous roll, in this case about 15 inches wide with tiny brown script.

TEXTS II.26D

1225 Fine Roll 10 Hen III (1225/6) no. 128 (TNA: C60/24 m. 7 for 30 March)
Mandatum est vicecomiti Lancast' quod statim visis literis istis capiat in manum domini regis totam terram quam Rogerus de Monte Begonis qui mortuus est tenuit in balliva sua excepta hereditate uxoris sue et eam salvo custodiat donec dominus rex aliud inde preceperit.

Translation: Fine Roll

Order to the Sheriff of Lancaster that immediately after having viewed these letters, he is to take into the king's hand all the land that Roger de Montbegon, who is dead, held in his (i.e. the sheriff's) bailiwick, except the inheritance of his wife, and to keep it safely until the king orders otherwise.

As for Olive de Montbegon, a further Fine Roll (TNA: C60/32), on 4 November 1232, records that the Sheriff of Nottinghamshire should stop the annual payment of £20 from Oswaldbeck because the king has arranged for her to have one third of Hornby Castle in the name of her dower. In 1236 she agrees a final concord with Henry of Monewden (Roger's distant relative and heir), relinquishing her right of dower at Hornby Castle in exchange for an annual payment.[3] Soon Henry of Monewden sold the castle to Hubert de Burgh, who had been Chief Justiciar of England and had earlier built Hadleigh Castle, for which see Section II.36, where it becomes the home of Duke Humfrey in 1405.

Primary Sources

Rotuli de oblatis et finibus, ed. T. Duffus Hardy, RC, London, 1835.
*Curia Regis Rolls.
*Pipe Rolls.
Magna Carta, see Section II.25.
*Close Rolls.
Royal and other historical letters illustrative of the reign of Henry III, 1216–1235, RS 27.1 (1862).
*Fine Rolls.
Feet of Fines for Lincolnshire 1199–1216, London, 1954.

Further Reading

The Victoria history of the county of Lancaster, London, 1906–14, repr. 1990–3.
    Vol. 1: 319–26 on the Montbegon family.
Calendar of the Fine Rolls of the reign of Henry III, vol. 1, ed. D. Carpenter,
    P. Dryburgh, B. Hartland, Woodbridge, 2007.
https://finerollshenry3.org.uk.
The Oxford companion to local and family history (2008).
The new Oxford history of England (2000) 1:696–9 on types of royal documents.
Carpenter, D. (2007) 'The Henry III Fine Rolls', *History Today* 57.5.
Crook, D., and Wilkinson, L. (ed.) (2015) *The growth of royal government under Henry III*, Woodbridge.
Dryburgh, P., 'The language of making fine', Fine of the Month for June 2007, *Fine Rolls Project*, https://finerollshenry3.org.uk.
Loengard, J. S. (1993) '*Rationabilis dos*: Magna Carta and the widow's "fair share" in the earlier thirteenth century' in *Walker (1993). Cf. Section II.25.

---

3 W. Farrer (ed.) (1899) *Final Concords of the county of Lancaster*, Part 1 (1189–1307), Record Society of Lancs and Chesh 39, Edinburgh: 147. The TNA references for the many final concords (or 'Feet of Fines') in the period 1195–1377 start with CP 25 and are grouped by county.

Section II.27

Edmund of Abingdon
A(a): *Speculum religiosorum* (Latin original of section 77: early thirteenth century)
A(b): *Mirour de seinte Eglyse* (French translation: thirteenth century)
A(c): *Speculum Ecclesiae* (translation from French into Latin: fourteenth century)
A(d): *The Myrrour of Seynt Edmonde* (translation from French into English: fourteenth century)
B(a): *Speculum religiosorum* (Latin original of section 93: early thirteenth century)
B(b): *Speculum Ecclesie* (translation into Latin from French version: fourteenth century)

Date: c.1220.

The original Latin work, entitled the *Speculum religiosorum*, survives in six MSS: the text below is from Bodleian MS Hatton 26, part 3. The fourteenth-century Latin version, the *Speculum Ecclesie*, occurs in more MSS, listed in Forshaw's edition.

Author: Edmund of Abingdon (c.1174–1240), also known as Edmund Rich and Edmund of Canterbury, is famous for his asceticism, for being one of the most important early teachers at Oxford University (and a proponent of the teaching of Greek, like his contemporaries Grosseteste and Bacon) and for being Archbishop of Canterbury (1234–40) at a time of political and ecclesiastical upheaval. Matthew Paris wrote a Life of Edmund, in Latin prose and in AN verse.

Work: The *Speculum religiosorum* is a collection of spiritual exercises, including meditation and contemplation of nature, Scripture and God. It draws on patristic writers and on Hugh of St Victor. Aimed at those in the religious life, it was written in the early thirteenth century at about the same time as another spiritual guide which underwent multiple translations within Britain, namely the Middle English guide for anchoresses, the *Ancrene Wisse*, which was translated from the original ME into Latin and French and from French back into English. Some half-century after Edmund completed the *Speculum* while at the monastery of Pontigny where his predecessor Thomas Becket had spent his exile, the work was translated into Anglo-Norman but then, in the fourteenth century, translated back into Latin in a slightly different version (sometimes referred to as the 'vulgate' text), with the

262 Thirteenth Century

alternative title *Speculum Ecclesie* deriving from the AN title. In the fifteenth century it seems that both the AN and the Latin texts were translated several times into English: a ME translation of the first Latin excerpt is included here.

The first excerpt comes from the discussion of the importance of the Lord's Prayer; the second, from the section that guides the reader to contemplate God's humanity, focusing on the conditions at the Nativity, which seems to be imagined in terms of an English location, in freezing weather. On the Nativity, compare Section I.4A, where Theodore of Canterbury gives an interpretation of these events in the *List of Malalas*.

Linguistic points: The first excerpt (77) is given in the original early thirteenth-century Latin (with modern translation), followed by the Anglo-Norman translation of the Latin, the fourteenth-century Latin translation based on the French, and finally the Middle English translation, so as to allow comparison of language and methods of translation. Note that the French translates *carminibus theatralibus* with the rare 'guliardie', which the *Speculum Ecclesie* then adopts in the Latin form *goliardia*, which is only attested here in BML, and once in the *Novum Glossarium* from the statutes of the Synod of Cahors, where it is glossed with *histrionatus*. The second excerpt (93) is given in its two Latin versions to show how they differ slightly in their choice of expressions, e.g. in the use of the imperative, or the jussive subjunctive. The later version adds a phrase glossing the derivation of *diversorium* (the word often translated as 'inn' in English versions of the Nativity narrative at Luke 2:7), with which the translator glosses Edmund's original *casa sine pariete* ('house without walls'), explaining that it is a covered passage where people shelter from bad weather; for this gloss, cf. Petrus Comestor, *Historia scholastica* (*PL* 198.1540A), who explains that Mary and Joseph, *in communi transitu, qui erat inter duas domus, operimentum habens, quod diversorium dicitur, se receperunt, sub quo cives ad colloquendum vel ad convisendum in diebus otii, vel pro aeris intemperie divertebant* ('found shelter in a common passage between two houses, with a roof which is called a *diversorium*; people stand under it when they chat or meet up in their spare time or when it is raining').

TEXTS II.27A

A: *Speculum religiosorum* (section 77)

A(a): *Speculum religiosorum* (Latin original of section 77: early thirteenth century)

In praise of the Lord's Prayer
hec oracio cunctas alias excellit oraciones, tam dignitate quam auctoritate. dignitate quidem precellit alias oraciones et utilitate racione auctoris qui eam instituit, et ipsam dicendum docuit, Iesus Christus. ideoque tali magistro magnum

dedecus et irreverenciam ingerit, qui mentem ponit in verbis rithmicis aut cu-
rioso dictamine compositis, contempta verborum serie postposita vel mutata,
quam posuit ipse Deus et docuit, qui totam Patris novit voluntatem totamque
nostram necessitatem, et pretactam oracionem pre ceteris magis acceptat, quam
nobis miseris plus expedit frequentare. unde multi decipiuntur propter oracionum multiplicacionem qui quando putant puram habere devocionem, frequenter
impuram et carnalem habent affectionem. omnis enim carnalis animus in carnali
lingua magis delectatur. et ideo te scire volo quod quedam sordida luxuria est in
carminibus theatralibus delectari. (…)

Translation: *Speculum religiosorum* 77

*This prayer (i.e. the Lord's Prayer) surpasses all other prayers, both in importance
and in authority, because of the author who composed it and taught that one must
say it, namely Jesus Christ. And so anyone who concerns himself with rhythmic
words or ones composed with elaborate construction demonstrates great dishonour
and disrespect to such a teacher, showing disdain for the word order by neglecting
or changing it although God himself put it there and taught it, he who knows everything the Father wishes and everything we need. He approves this prayer above all
others and it is right for us, wretched as we are, to repeat it. Many people are deceived on account of the large number of prayers. When they think their devotion is
pure, their emotions are actually impure and carnal. For all carnal impulse delights
more in a carnal tongue, and that is why I want you to know that to take delight in
songs for entertainment shows a disgusting lack of self-restraint. (…)*

A(b): *Mi` de seinte Eglyse* (French translation: thirteenth century)

[17, ANTS p. 47] *Ceste oreysun surmunte chescun autre oreysun en digneté e en
utilité, en digneté pur ço ke Deu meymes la fist. Et pur ço fet celuy grant hunte et
grant irreverence a Jhesu le Fiz Deu ki se prent as paroles rimees e curioses, et let
la priere ke celi nus aprist ke set tote la volunté Deu le Pere, et quele ureysun plus
li vient a pleysir, e quele chose nus cheytifs avuns mester a prier. Kar ausi cum
jo vus ay dist, il sul set tote sa volunté e tote nostre necessité. E pur ço sunt cent
mil hommes deceuz par multiplicacion de oreysuns. Kar quant il quident k'il eient
devociun, si unt une orde e charnele affection, pur ço ke chescun charnel curage de
delite natureument en teu turnis language. E pur ce seez garnie, kar seurement le
vus di, ce est une orde lecherie pur deliter en teu manere de guliardie.*

A(c): *Speculum Ecclesie* (translation from French into Latin: fourteenth century)

[17] ista oracio superat et excellit omnem aliam oracionem in dignitate et
utilitate. in dignitate quia ipsemet Deus illam fecit; et ideo facit ille magnum

264 Thirteenth Century

dedecus et magnam irreverenciam Iesu Dei Filio qui sibi accipit verba ritmica et curiosa, dimittitque et relinquit oracionem quam ipsemet composuit, qui scit totam voluntatem Dei Patris, et que oracio maxime sibi placet, et pro quibus nos miseri maxime indigemus deprecari. nam sicut prius dixi, ille solus scit totam Dei Patris voluntatem, et totam nostram necessitatem. igitur centum milia hominum decipiuntur per multiplicacionem oracionum. cum enim putant se habere devocionem, habent unam vilem carnalem affectionem, quia omnis carnalis animus naturaliter delectatur in tali loquela curiosa. ideo sis providus et discretus, nam certissime tibi dico quod est una turpis luxuria ita delectari in tali modo guliardie.

Translation: *Speculum Ecclesiae 77*

This prayer exceeds and surpasses every other prayer both in importance and in usefulness. In importance because God himself made it; and so the person who takes for himself rhythmic and strange words and rejects and leaves the prayer which He composed who knows the whole will of God the Father and what prayer pleases Him most, and for what things we wretched creatures especially need to pray, does a great dishonour and shows great lack of respect to Jesus, Son of God. For as I said before, He alone knows all that God the Father wishes and all that we need. And so a hundred thousand people are deceived by the large number of prayers. For when they think they have devotion, they have a vile carnal affection, because all carnal impulse naturally delights in such strange speech. So be provident and discreet, for I say to you most definitely that to find enjoyment in such a manner is an example of shameful self-indulgence.

A(d): *The Myrrour of Seynt Edmonde* (translation from French into Middle English: fourteenth century)

Now, my dere frende, thou sall wyt that this oryson passes all other prayers, pryncypally in twa thynges, that es to say, in worthynes and in profyte. In worthynes, for that God Hym-selfe mad it; and for-thi do thay gret schame and gret unreverence till Ihesu, Goddes son, that takes tham till wordis rynnand and curius, and leves the prayere that He us kennede, that wate all the will of Godd the ffadir, and the whilke orysone commes mare till His plesynge, and whate thynges the wrechede caytyfe has myster at prayer fore. Alswa, als I hafe sayde, He wate anely all the Fadir wyll, and he wate all our nede; and thare-for a hundrethe thousande er dyssayved with multyplicatione of wordes and of orysouns; for when thay wene that thay hafe grete devocyon, than hafe thai a fulle fleschely lykynge, forthy that ilk a fleschely lykynge delytes tham kyndely in swylke turnede langage; and thare-fore I walde that thou war warre, for I say the sykerly, that it es a foule lychery for to delyte in rymmes and slyke gulyardy.

B: *Speculum religiosorum* (section 93)

B(a): *Speculum religiosorum* (Latin original of section 93: early thirteenth century)

A guide to meditation on Christ's Nativity

ante matutinas sive nocte media cogitare debes de tempore, loco et hora in quibus Christus natus est. tempus erat hiemale, quando maxima frigiditas solet dominari; hora noctis media, periculosior, durior seu gravior aliis horis, ideo dicitur intempestatum; locus erat in via, in casa sine pariete. pannis involutus, instita ligatus, in presepe positus ante bovem et asinum erat Iesus, quia non erat ei locus in diversorio. ibi cogita de matris sollicitudine circa filium; de coniuge Ioseph; quantum erat eis gaudium; de devocione et devota relacione pastorum; de dulci cantico angelorum; et attolle cor tuum ad laudes eorum et cum illis cantica, 'Gloria in excelsis Deo!'

Translation: *Speculum religiosorum* 93

Before matins or in the middle of the night you ought to think about the season, place and hour in which Christ was born. For it was the winter season when the most intense cold usually prevails; the time was the middle of the night, a more dangerous, harsh and serious time than others, which is why it is called untimely; the place was on a street, in a small building without walls. Jesus was wrapped in cloths, bound with strips, laid in a manger in front of an ox and an ass, because there was no room at the inn. There think about his mother's worry about her son, about her husband Joseph, how great their joy was, about their devotion and the shepherds' devout account; of the sweet singing of the angels; and raise your heart to praise them and sing with them, 'Glory to God in the highest!'

B(b): *Speculum Ecclesie* (translation into Latin from French version: fourteenth century)

ante matutinas de nativitate Domini primo debes cogitare, et postea de eius passione. de nativitate debes cogitare diligenter tempus, locum et horam in quibus natus fuit Dominus noster Iesu Christus dulcis. tempus fuit in medio hyemis, quando maximum frigus fuit; hora erat in media nocte que est hora durissima; locus erat in media via, in una domo sine pariete, que dicitur diversorium a divertendo: nam illic homines divertebantur pro pluvia et aliis tempestatibus. in qua fuit pauperrimis panniculis involutus, cum una fascia ligatus, et in presepe positus, coram bove et asino, quia non habuit alium locum in diversorio. hic debes cogitare de diligenti cura beate Marie circa puerum suum Iesum; et de Ioseph, marito suo, quomodo habuit magnum gaudium. cogita eciam de devocione pastorum et de dulci turba angelorum; erigeque cor tuum ad Deum et cantica cum illis, 'Gloria in excelsis Deo', etc.

266 Thirteenth Century

Translation: *Speculum Ecclesiae* 93

Before matins you ought first of all to think about the Lord's birth and then about his passion. Regarding his birth, you ought to ponder carefully the season, place and time in which our Lord, sweet Jesus Christ, was born. The season was midwinter, when the cold is most intense; the time was the middle of the night, which is the hardest time; the place was right on the road, in a building without walls which is called a 'diversorium' from 'divertendo' because people turn in there on account of the rain and other storms. Here he was wrapped in tattered cloths, bound with bands of cloth and placed in a manger, in front of the ox and the ass because there was no other room in the inn. At this point you should think about blessed Mary's careful concern for her son Jesus, and about Joseph, her husband, how he had a great joy. Think also about the devotion of the shepherds and the lovely host of angels; raise your heart to God and sing with them, 'Glory to God in the highest', etc.

Primary Sources and Related Texts

Edmund of Abingdon, *Speculum religiosorum and Speculum Ecclesie*, ed. H. Forshaw, Auctores Britannici Medii Aevi 3, Oxford, 1973.

Mirour de seinte Eglyse (c.1250?), ANTS, London, 1982.

The Myrrour of Seynt Edmonde (1350?) in *Religious pieces in prose and verse from Robert Thornton's MS*, EETS 26, 1867, 15–47.

Matthew Paris, *Life of St Edmund of Abingdon* in *Edmund of Abingdon*, ed. C. H. Lawrence, Oxford, 1960.

Anselm of Canterbury, *Proslogion* (Section II.7B) for meditation on mankind and contemplation of God.

Ælred of Rievaulx, *De institutione inclusarum* (1162): two English versions of the fourteenth century, ed. J. Ayto and A. Barratt, EETS 287, Oxford, 1984.

Further Reading

The Cambridge companion to medieval English mysticism, ed. S. Fanous and V. Gillespie, Cambridge, 2011.

Barratt, A. (2008) 'Spiritual writings and religious instructions' in *The Cambridge history of the book in Britain*, vol. 2: *1100–1400*, ed. N. Morgan and R. Thomson, Cambridge.

Lawrence, C. H. (1960) *Edmund of Abingdon: a study in hagiography and history*, Oxford.

Section II.28

The Study of Latin and Other Languages
A: John of Garland, *Dictionary* (*Dictionarius*) (excerpts)
B: Alexander Neckam, *The Priest at the Altar* (*Sacerdos ad altare*) (excerpt: chapter 8)
C: Roger Bacon, *The Usefulness of Studying Languages* (*De utilitate grammaticae*) from the *Opus majus*, part 3 (excerpts from vol. 1, pp. 66–70; variant readings from vol. 3, pp. 80–4)

In the thirteenth century, Latin vocabulary was usually taught with the help of wordlists and imaginary lexicographical narratives providing a setting for interesting words, both rare and mundane, often grouped around specific themes. These followed on such works of the Anglo-Saxon period as the Corpus and Leiden glossaries and the *Glossary*, *Grammar* and *Colloquy* of Ælfric (for which see Section I.39). Examples of this narrative type are the works of Adam of Balsham in the twelfth century, and John of Garland and Alexander Neckam in the thirteenth century, all of whom had studied in Paris. Their works are important as providing much everyday Latin vocabulary, showing the semantic and not merely morphological/etymological relations between Latin and French; the glosses (by the author himself in the case of Neckam) provide a variety of synonyms, and this can assist in the modern study of the development of both Latin and Anglo-Norman.

A: John of Garland, *Dictionary* (*Dictionarius*) (excerpts)

Date: c.1220.

The most important of the many MSS of this work are Cambridge MS Gonville and Caius College 385/605 (also containing some glosses, and other grammatical and lexicographical works) and Bruges MS 546.

Author: John of Garland (c.1195–c.1272), probably born near Wantage in Berkshire, studied at Oxford and then moved to Paris, where he stayed for the rest of his life, teaching and writing, apart from a few years as master of grammar in the new university at Toulouse. He wrote many works on Latin vocabulary and grammar, basing his teaching on the writings of a wide range of classical authors, with a particular emphasis on poetry. In the *Integumenta Ovidii* he gives allegorical interpretations of stories from the *Metamorphoses*. He also wrote two long

268 Thirteenth Century

poems, the *Epithalamium Virginis Mariae* and the *De triumphis ecclesie*. Modern scholars have largely neglected Garland's pedagogical works (indeed, some are as yet unprinted), despite the fascinating material many of them offer to students of the history of Latin language and literature.

Work: The *Dictionary* (c.1230), which provides the earliest evidence for the use of the word 'dictionary', was written to teach students Latin vocabulary by grouping the words according to different subjects – a popular pedagogical method of the time. In this excerpt the vocabulary is based on a description of everyday life in the streets of Paris. However, there is little in the way of explanation, and the student is presumably supposed to understand the words from their context. The fact that later MSS of this work are heavily glossed (mainly in AN) shows that a need was felt for translation and interpretation: the glosses would have been useful both for those who knew more French than Latin and as a means of teaching a bit of French, as another second language, to those educated in Latin. Further work is required on both Garland's text and the glossed MSS. The *Dictionary* demonstrates how dominant the French language was as a medium for the learning of Latin, and offers a rich and early source of French words, as well as of Latin neologisms. In common with many educational works, the *Dictionary* contains humorous elements to amuse the students, as in section 65, where women's favourite tools are listed.

Linguistic points: There is much of linguistic interest in this text: *liripipium*, for which the derivation is unknown, is here part of a shoe, though it is also interpreted as the pointed tippet of a hood or part of a head garment, as in Knighton's *Chronicle* (Section II.34A: *liripiis ad modum cordarum circa capud advolutis*). *fultrum* ('felt', or an article made of felt) occurs in BML in various spellings (filt-, felt-, fult-, feut-) from the thirteenth century, deriving from a Germanic word that gives OE 'felt' and French 'feutre'. The use of *de* with ablative of material from which something is made (e.g. *pilleola de lana*) occurs at least as early as Virgil's *Georgics* (3.13, *templum de marmore*). *pollitrudiare* is a common word for 'to sieve', combining CL *pollen* and *trudere*. *machaera* and *mensacula* are CL words deriving from Greek words for a 'dagger' and 'javelin' respectively, here used as words for a 'knife'. A few of the later glosses have been inserted in the text below to give an indication of how they were applied. The list of fish names in section 72 is commonly found in such works, as in Ælfric's *Glossary* (Section I.39A(b)): that large quantities of fish were caught around Britain is clear also from the text *De halimoto et statutis piscenariorum* in *Munimenta Gildhallae Londoniensis* 1.374–9 of the late thirteenth century, with amounts of tax to be paid by fishmongers on different kinds of fish, given randomly with Latin or English names, or English names in Latin form. *lucibruciunculum* ('sleekstone') also occurs in various glossaries, in one of which is also found the verb *lucibrucinare*, glossed with ME 'sleght' ('slighten') i.e. 'to smooth'. The CL word for 'herring', (*h*)*allec*, was used

II.28 | The Study of Latin and Other Languages 269

right through the period of BML, while *harengus*, based on the French 'harenc', first occurs in a Latin form in the late twelfth century, in texts relating to France. The OE 'hæreng', which like the French form derived from a Germanic word, seems not to have crept into BML.

TEXT II.28A

Everyday life in early thirteenth-century Paris
[9] [p. 122 Wright] unus vicinorum nostrorum tulit hodie ad vendendum in pertica una sotulares ad laqueos cum liripipiis, et ad plusculas, tibialia, cruralia, et crepitas femineas et monachales. (…)

[9] *Today one of our neighbours carried shoes to sell on a pole: laced shoes with elongated points and shoes with buckles, boots and leggings and the boots worn by women and monks. (…)*

[17] [p. 124] eruginatores (ae-) gladiorum cumulant denarios, vendendo gladios bene exeruginatos, qui habent tholos et capulos rutilantes et novas vaginas.

[17] *Furbishers of swords heap up pence by selling well-polished swords that have gleaming pommels and hilts and new sheaths.*

[18] mercatores habitantes super Magnum Pontem vendunt capistra, lumbaria, ligulas, marsupia de corio cervino, ovino, porcino.

[18] *Merchants living on the Grand Pont (i.e. Pont Notre-Dame) sell halters, belts, straps and purses made of deerskin, sheepskin and pigskin.*

[19] cirothecarii decipiunt scolares Parisius vendendo eis cirothecas simplices et furratas pellibus agninis, cuniculinis, vulpinis et mitas de corio factas.

[19] *Glovers defraud the Parisian students by selling them unlined gloves, gloves lined with lambskin, rabbit fur and fox fur and mittens made of leather.*

[20] capellarii faciunt capella de fultro, sive centone[1] et de pennis pavonis et pillea de bombace et quedam pilleola de lana et pilis.

[20] *Hatters make hats of felt and peacock feathers and caps of cotton and little caps of wool and fur.*

---

1 *cento* is glossed as OF 'feutre', i.e. 'felt', in Neckam's *De nominibus utensilium*; it is likely to be given here as a synonym for *fultrum* (i.e. *filtrum*, derived from a Germanic word).

270 Thirteenth Century

[21] ad portam Sancti Lazari manent architenentes qui faciunt balistas et arcus de acere, viburno et taxo, tela et sagittas de fraxino. (…)

[21] *At the Porte Saint-Lazare live the bowyers, who make crossbows and bows of maple, viburnum and yew, and bolts and arrows of ash. (…)*

[24] [p. 125] pictaciarii viles sunt qui consuunt sotulares veteres renovando pictacia et intercutia, soleas et inpedias.

[24] *There are wretched cobblers who stitch together old shoes, renewing the patches, the welts, the soles and the uppers.*

[29] [p. 126] precones vini clamant gula hyante vinum attaminatum in tabernis ad quatuor denarios et ad sex et ad octo et ad duodecim, portando vinum temptandum fusum in craterem a lagena.

[29] *Wine-criers, with mouths agape, proclaim their wine that was broached in the taverns, at fourpence, sixpence, eightpence and twelvepence, carrying wine poured from a gallon jug into a cup for tasting.*

[30] precones nebularum et gafrarum pronunciant de nocte nebulas et gafras et artocreas vendendas in calathis, velatis albo manutergio, et calathi vero frequenter suspenduntur ad fenestras clericorum, perditi senione.

[30] *Street sellers of light pastries and wafers proclaim their light pastries and wafers and rissoles at night, selling them from baskets covered with a white towel, and the baskets are often hung at the windows of clerks, forfeited by the throw of a die.*

[31] auctionarii mittunt servos et servas per vicos ad discipiendum clericos quibus vendunt nimis care cerasa, pruna alba et nigra et poma immatura et pira et lactuca et nasturcia et cerfolia. (…)

[31] *Retailers send out their male and female servants into the streets to cheat the clerks to whom they sell, at too high a price, cherries, white and black plums, unripe apples and pears and lettuce, cress and chervil. (…)*

[33] [p. 27] pistores[2] Parisius pinsunt pastam et formant panes quos cocunt in furno mundato cum tersorio. vendunt autem panes de frumento, de siligine, de ordeo, de avena, de acere et frequenter de furfure. pistores habent servos et servas qui pollitrudiant farinam grossam cum pollitrudio delicato et inmittunt paste

---

2 For some less honest practices of bakers, cf. the Assize of Bread, Section II.49D.

II.28 | The Study of Latin and Other Languages 271

fermentum ut elevet panem in alveo. archas etiam radunt aliquando cum costa pastali.

[33] *The bakers of Paris knead dough and form loaves which they bake in an oven that has been wiped clean with a cloth. They sell bread made of wheat, rye, barley, oats, chaff and frequently of bran. The bakers have male and female servants who sift the coarse flour with a fine sieve and mix the yeast into the dough to make the bread rise in the trough. Sometimes they also scrape out the bins with a dough-scraper.*

[34] pastillarii quam plurimum lucrantur, vendendo clericis pastillos de carnibus porcinis et pullinis et de anguillis cum pipere, cum exponendo tartas (gl. ME *ab-pel chake*) et flacones[3] fartos caseis mollibus et ovis sanis et frequenter immundis.

[34] *Pie-makers make a huge profit by selling to clerks pork pies, chicken pies and eel pies seasoned with pepper, and displaying for sale tarts and flans stuffed with soft cheeses and eggs, healthy but often dirty.*

[35] coquinarii vertunt et cocunt verubus colurnis anseres et columbas, altilia sed frequenter vendunt carnes crudas simplicibus mancipiis scolarium cum salsa-mentis et alliatis male distemperatis. quibus invident carnifices in macellis suis, vendentes carnes grossas bovinas et ovinas et porcinas, aliquando lepra percus-sas, macheras et mensaculas scolaribus incutientes. sed mactatores a scolaribus animosis mactantur propter hillas inmundas et salsucias et tuceta (gl. ME *pud-dings*) et scruta, que popello conveniunt tunicato. (…)   Hor. *Epist.* 1.7.65

[35] *Cooks turn and roast geese, pigeons, and capons on hazelwood spits, but often they sell raw meat, badly seasoned with sauces and garlic, to the foolish servants of the students. The butchers in their meat market hate them, selling them coarse flesh of beef, mutton and pork, sometimes measled, brandishing their cleavers and great knives at the students. But these slaughterers are slain by the angry students because of the filthy meat-stuffed intestines, sausages, black puddings and tripe that are suit-able for the impoverished rabble. (…)*

[65] hec sunt instrumenta mulieris convenientia: forcipes et acus, theca et fusus, vertebrum et colus, mataxa, trahale, girgillus et excudia, rupa, feritorium (gl. *bateldore*), linipulus et cupatorium, cum lexiva et lexivatorio, calotricatorium et licinitorium (gl. anglice *slicston*) quod monachi dicunt lucibruciunculum. set plus diligunt instrumenta viri pendentia grossa et rigida. (…)

---

3   The correct reading may be *flatones* (with c for t), i.e. *flado*, a LL word from Frankish.

[65] *These are the instruments suitable for a woman: scissors and needle, container and spindle, spindle whorl and distaff, silk thread, skein-winding reel, yarn-winder, hemp-beater, flax-breaker, battledore, hank of flax and weaver's trough, with lye and a washing tub, a smoothing-iron and a sleekstone, which the monks call a 'lucibruciunculum'. But even more they love a man's instrument, hanging down, big and stiff. (…)*

[72] piscatores vendunt salmones, truttas, murenas, morium, pectines, anguillas quibus associantur lucii, rocie, stincti, ragadie, allecia, mulli. ipsi vero piscatores capiunt cum hamis et rethibus perchas gobiones et gamaros, quia canes marini ab equore devehuntur.

[72] *Fishermen sell salmon, trout, lampreys, cod, plaice, eels together with pike, roach, tench, ray, herring and mullet. The same fishermen catch perch, gudgeon and sprats with hooks and nets, and porpoises are taken from the sea.*

Primary Sources and Related Texts

Hunt, T. (1991) *Teaching and learning Latin in thirteenth-century England*, 3 vols, Cambridge; text in vol. 1: 196–203, glosses in vol. 2: 125–56. Page numbers are given according to the edition of T. Wright (1857) *A volume of vocabularies*, Liverpool, vol. 1: 120–38.

John of Garland, *Opus synonymorum*, giving Latin synonyms in hexameter verse.

Adam of Balsham, *De utensilibus*, giving both everyday and esoteric words.

Alexander Neckam, *De nominibus utensilium* (a dictionary of vocabulary of everyday life, arranged by topic).

Isidore of Seville, *Etymologiae*, book 10 (on the etymology of words).

Further Reading

*The Oxford history of classical reception in English literature, vol. 1: *800–1558* (2016).

Les manuscrits des lexiques et glossaires de l'antiquité tardive à la fin du Moyen Âge, ed. J. Hamesse, Louvain-la-Neuve, 1996.

Carlin, M. (2007) 'Shops and shopping in the early 13th century: three texts' in *Money, markets and trade in late medieval Europe*, ed. M. Elbl, Leiden.

Orme, N. (2006) *Medieval schools: from Roman Britain to Renaissance England*, London.

Weijers, O. (1989) 'Lexicography in the Middle Ages', *Viator* 20: 139–54.

B: Alexander Neckam, *The Priest at the Altar* (*Sacerdos ad altare*) (excerpt: chapter 8)

Date: early thirteenth century.

This work is known only from the Cambridge MS Gonville and Caius College 385/605, attributed there to John of Garland; C. H. Haskins has, however, shown that Neckam is the likely author.

Author: Alexander (1157–1217) studied in his home town of St Alban's and later went to Paris to study theology, law and medicine, also gaining some competence in Hebrew. After teaching theology for a time at Oxford he became Abbot of the Augustinian Canons at Cirencester, where he wrote numerous works (some lost and some hitherto unprinted) on a variety of subjects, including teaching works on grammar and vocabulary (e.g. *De nominibus utensilium*), on the natural world (e.g. the *Laus sapientiae divinae* in verse) and theology, as well as many biblical commentaries (including a three-book commentary on Ecclesiastes), alongside two books on natural science in the *De naturis rerum*. His tomb is in Worcester Cathedral.

Work: This work of twenty chapters, known by the first words of its text, *sacerdos ad altare* (*accessurus*), in the manner of papal bulls, is described in the MS as a *Dictionarius*, like that of Garland above, though in the case of Garland the lexical glosses in French and English were added by later scribes, whereas Neckam provides his own Latin commentary, occasionally referring to vernacular words. Neckam discusses subjects relating to the Church and monasteries (including the facilities these should offer), and to the court and education. By providing brief information on these subjects and Latin terms relevant to life in these contexts, this textbook aims to raise the standard of Latin education of the clergy. The text consists of short essays on particular topics, followed by a section of glosses of various lengths by Alexander, on individual words in the essay. This section, a sort of etymological commentary, draws on works by the seventh-century scholar Isidore of Seville (e.g. Book 10 of the *Etymologiae* (or *Origines*) and the influential *Liber derivationum* (or *Panormia*) of Osbern of Gloucester, compiled in the twelfth century, but also adds points on Latin grammar and quotations from a wide range of classical and medieval literature. This passage has been selected to give an example of a recommended reading list for a student of classical literature in the early thirteenth century. Note that no distinction is made between Seneca the elder, who wrote the speeches, and Seneca the younger, who wrote the other works mentioned.

Linguistic points: The lexicographical and etymological aspects of the work include references to Greek and French words (for which see the *Index verborum Franco-Gallicorum* in the *CCCM* edition). The rare word *volaria*, a compound

274 Thirteenth Century

based on CL *vola*, is glossed by *ferula*. Below is given the gloss on CL *fragum* (to warn of a possible confusion with CL *fragus*), including the French word for 'strawberry'. Note the spelling *eroum* as the gen. pl. of *heros*, and Liphius for Livius. For an example of a more complex gloss, involving also the pronunciation of words related to *pila* and *pilus*, see Neckam on *pila*, when discussing ball games at court (pp. 133–4 Wright), and compare with the *DMLBS* entries for these words.

TEXT II.28B

What students need for their education

[8] [pp. 174–5] scolaris liberalibus educandus artibus dipticas gerat quibus scitu digna scribantur. ferat palmatoriam sive volariam vel ferulam qua manus puerilis leniter feriatur ob minores excessus, virgis vero cedatur cum res id fieri desideraverit. absint flagella et scorpiones, ne modum excedat castigando. postquam alphabetum didicerit et ceteris puerilibus rudimentis imbutus fuerit, Donatum et illud utile moralitatis compendium quod Catonis esse vulgus opinatur et ab Egloga Theodoli transeat ad egglogas Bucolicorum, prelectis tamen quibusdam libellis informationi rudium necessariis. deinde satiricos et ystoriographos legat, ut vitia etiam in minori etate addiscat esse fugienda et nobilia gesta eroum desideret imitari. a Thebaide iocunda transeat ad divinam Eneida, nec necgligat vatem quem Corduba genuit, qui non solum civilia bella describit, set et intestina. Iuvenalis moralia dicta in archano pectoris reservet et flagitium nature summopere vitare studeat. sermones Oratii et epistolas legat et Poetriam et Odas cum libro Epodon. Elegias Nasonis et Ovidium Metamorfoseos audiat, sed et precipue libellum De remedio amoris familiarem habeat. placuit tamen viris autenticis carmina amatoria cum satiris subducenda esse a manibus adolescentium ac si eis dicatur 'Qui legitis flores et humi nascentia fraga,* | frigidus, o pueri, fugite hinc, latet anguis in **Virg. *Eclogues*** herba.' librum Fastorum non esse legendum nonnullis placet. Statius Achilleidos **3.92–3** etiam a viris multe gravitatis probatur. Bucolica Maronis et Georgica multe sunt utilitatis. Salustius et Tullius De oratore et Thuscanarum et De amicitia et De senectute et De fato multa commendatione digni sunt et Paradoxe. liber inscriptus De multitudine deorum a quibusdam reprobatur. Tullius De officiis utilissimus est. Martialis Cocus et Petronius multa continent in se utilia sed multa auditu indigna. Simachi breve genus dicendi admirationem parit. Solinum De mirabilibus mundi et Sydonium et Suetonium et Quintum Curtium et Trogium Pompeium et Cris(i)p(p)um et Titum Liphium commendo, sed Senecam ad Lucilium et De questionibus phisicis et De beneficiis relegere tibi utile censeas. Tragedium ipsius et Declamationes legere non erit inutile. (…)

Ovid, Met. 1.104 [p. 185] *hoc fragum -gi, i. *frese*, unde Ovidius Methamorphoseon, 'montanaque fraga legebat'. Hic fragus -gi est recurvatio poplitis vel ipse poples, unde et suffragines poplites specialiter dicuntur.

Translation

[8] *A student who is to be educated in the liberal arts should carry a wax tablet on which anything noteworthy can be written. The teacher should carry a stick, cane or ferule with which to smack the children's hands lightly for minor transgressions, but this should be replaced by a rod when the situation demands. There should be no whips or lashes, to avoid excessive punishment. After the student has learned the alphabet and has been steeped in other basic matters suitable for children, he should learn Donatus and that useful compendium of moral teaching which is generally attributed to Cato; he should move from the Eclogues of Theodulus to those of the Bucolics, although he should first read certain short books necessary for the instruction of beginners. Then he should read the satirists and historians so as to learn at a young age that vices are to be avoided and so as to desire to imitate the noble deeds of heroes. From the amusing Thebaid he should move on to the divine Aeneid, without omitting the poet born in Cordova who describes not only the civil wars but also the internal ones. He should keep Juvenal's moral sayings in the secret recess of his heart and make a great effort to avoid the sin against nature. He should read the Satires of Horace together with his Epistles and Ars poetica and Odes together with the book of Epodes. He should listen to the elegies of Naso and Ovid's Metamorphoses, but should be particularly familiar with his Remedies for Love. Yet the authorities thought that love poems and satires should be kept out of the hands of young people, as if they were being told, 'You who pick flowers and strawberries* growing close to the ground, get away from here, boys, for a cold snake is hiding in the grass.' Some think that the book of Fasti should not be read. Men of great seriousness also approve of the Achilleid of Statius. Virgil's Eclogues and Georgics are very useful. Sallust, and Cicero's The Orator, Tusculan Disputations, On Friendship, On Old Age and the work On Fate are very worthy of approval, as also his Paradoxes. Many criticise the book entitled The Many Gods (i.e. De natura deorum). The most useful work is the De officiis. Martial the cook and Petronius contain many useful things but also many that are shocking to hear. Symmachus' succinct style is admired. I recommend Solinus' On the Miracles of the World, and Sidonius and Suetonius and Quintus Curtius and Pompeius Trogus and Chrysippus and Titus Livy, but you may consider it worthwhile to reread Seneca's letters to Lucilius and the work On Natural Phenomena (i.e. Quaestiones naturales; cf. Section II.23A) or the dialogue On Benefits. It will be useful to read Seneca's tragedies and his speeches. (…)*
*fragum, -i, a neuter noun, in other words, strawberry, which is why Ovid in his Metamorphoses writes, 'he used to pick the mountain strawberries'. fragus, -i as a masculine noun is the hollow behind the knee or the knee itself, which is why knee joints are also referred to as knees.

Primary Sources and Related Texts

Alexandri Neckam Sacerdos ad altare, ed. C. McDonough, *CCCM* 227, Turnhout, 2010.

John of Garland, *Commentarius*, with words related to the nobility and the Church, and some French glosses.

Osbern of Gloucester, *Derivationes: Derivazioni*, ed. P. Busdraghi et al., 2 vols, Spoleto, 1996.

Bede, *De orthographia* (Section I.10A).

Further Reading

Copeland, R. (2010) 'Naming, knowing and the object of language in Alexander Neckam's grammar curriculum', *JML* 20: 38–57.

—— (2012) 'Alexander Neckam, a list of textbooks (from *Sacerdos ad altare*) c.1210' in *Medieval grammar and rhetoric: language, arts and literary theory, AD 300–1475*, ed. R. Copeland and I. Sluiter, Oxford.

Haskins, C. H. (1924) 'A list of text-books from the close of the twelfth century' in *Studies in the history of mediaeval science*, Cambridge, MA.

Hunt, R. W. (1994) *The schools and the cloister: the life and writings of Alexander Nequam*, Oxford.

C: Roger Bacon, *The Usefulness of Studying Languages* (*De utilitate grammaticae*) from the *Opus majus*, part 3 (excerpts from vol. 1, pp. 66–70; variant readings from vol. 3, pp. 80–4)

Date: c.1267.

The primary MSS are Vatican MS 4086, BL MS Cotton Julius D.v and Bodleian MS Digby 235.

Author: Roger Bacon (c.1215–92) studied and taught philosophy and science at Oxford and in Paris, and did private research before becoming a Franciscan in about 1256, following in the footsteps of Robert Grosseteste and Adam Marsh. The work of this hugely prolific writer dealt with many of the contemporary intellectual controversies. He also prepared the way for the fourteenth-century English philosophers Duns Scotus and William of Ockham and influenced many others in areas of experimental science such as optics, medicine and astrology. The saying 'Knowledge of languages is the door to wisdom', often quoted in contemporary media, is attributed to Bacon. It comes from his *Opus* *tertium* (*Tert.* 28, p. 102), in which he also devotes chapters to the importance of learning languages: he writes, *notitia linguarum est prima porta sapientiae et maxime apud Latinos qui non habent textum theologiae nec philosophiae nisi a linguis alienis* ('A knowledge of languages is the first door to wisdom and especially among Latin speakers who derive their theological and philosophical texts only from foreign languages'). This belief is also the theme of the passage below.

Work: As a whole the *Opus majus* ranges over many subjects, such as physics, mathematics, logic, grammar and philosophy, boldly setting out what Bacon regards as the flaws in contemporary learning and educational methodology. The section *The Usefulness of Studying Languages* is one of the seven parts of this work. Bacon believed in the practical importance of high linguistic standards for the Church, and considered Latin to be a universal technical language, but he also thought that a wider knowledge of such languages as Greek, Hebrew, Aramaic and Arabic was essential, particularly since Latin was formed on the model of the grammars of Greek and Hebrew. He gives eight reasons (of which four are mentioned below) why a knowledge of languages other than Latin is necessary for the study of wisdom. In the final chapters of this section he shows how such knowledge is useful for understanding the liturgy, for running the state and for converting non-Christians. He also discusses the difficulty of producing accurate translations to aid study, but without which the originals cannot be understood. Although the period between 1150 and 1250 had seen the production of more translations into Latin of Aristotle, in addition to those produced by Marius Victorinus and Boethius in late antiquity, these often lacked clarity and accuracy. Bacon sums up the problem (*Tert.* 10, p. 33) of obtaining good technical translations: *quia interpres debet scire scientiam, quam vult transferre, et linguam a qua tranfert, et aliam in quam transfert* ('because the translator needs to know the science which he is translating, the language from which he is translating and the other one into which he is translating').

Linguistic points: Bacon here records how he told his students that the Latin word *belenum* for 'henbane', found in the Latin translation (made by the Englishman Alfred of Shareshill) of the Arabic version of the pseudo-Aristotelian work *De vegetabilibus et plantis*, was an Arabic technical term, but his students disabused him: it was in fact from the Spanish 'beleño' (also modern Spanish). Bacon observes that each language has its own idiom, and indeed even different dialects can be mutually incomprehensible, as he shows by reference to various French regional dialects. Bacon uses *scientialis*, a new formation of thirteenth-century scientists and philosophers, here meaning 'scientific' or 'technical'. *hujusmodi* occurs as an indeclinable noun, as becomes common in the thirteenth century.

278 Thirteenth Century

TEXT II.28C

The usefulness of the study of language and grammar for the acquisition of knowledge

[p. 66 Bridges] declarato igitur quod una est sapientia perfecta quae sacris literis continetur, per jus canonicum et philosophiam, qua mundus habet regi, nec alia requiritur scientia pro utilitate generis humani, nunc volo descendere ad ea huius sapientiae magnifica quae maxime valent exponi. et sunt quinque sine quibus nec divina nec humana sciri possunt, quorum certa cognitio reddit nos faciles ad omnia cognoscenda.

et primum est grammatica in linguis alienis exposita, ex quibus emanavit sapientia Latinorum. impossibile enim est quod Latini perveniant ad ea quae eis necessaria sunt in divinis et humanis nisi per notitiam aliarum linguarum, nec perficietur eis sapientia absolute, nec relate ad Ecclesiam Dei et reliqua tria praenominata. quod volo nunc declarare et primo respectu scientiae absolutae. nam totus textus sacer a Graeco et Hebraeo transfusus est, et philosophia ab his et Arabico deducta est.

Translation: Bacon, *De utilitate grammaticae*

After stating that there is a single perfect wisdom contained in the Scriptures by which the world must be directed by means of canon law and philosophy, and that no other science is needed for the benefit of the human race, I now wish to turn to those valuable parts of philosophy which it is most useful to explain. There are five of these, without which neither divine nor human matters can be known. An assured knowledge of these prepares us to know all things.

First there is grammar, set out in the foreign languages from which the wisdom of the Latins is derived; for it is impossible for the Latins to achieve what is necessary for them in divine and human matters without knowing other languages, nor will they gain perfect wisdom either absolutely or in relation to the Church of God and to the three other things mentioned above. I now wish to set this out, first with respect to absolute knowledge. For the whole sacred text is drawn from Greek and Hebrew, and philosophy is derived from these sources and from Arabic.

The difficulties of translation

sed impossibile est quod proprietas unius linguae servetur in alia. nam et idiomata ejusdem linguae variantur apud diversos sicut patet de lingua Gallicana quae apud Gallicos et Picardos et Normannos et Burgundos multiplici variatur idiomate. et quod proprie dicitur in idiomate Picardorum horrescit apud Burgundos, immo apud Gallicos viciniores: quanto igitur magis accidet hoc apud linguas diversas? quapropter, quod bene factum est in una lingua, [p. 67] non est possibile ut transferatur in aliam secundum ejus proprietatem quam habuit in priori.

II.28 | The Study of Latin and Other Languages 279

unde Hieronymus in epistola de optimo genere interpretandi[4] sic dicit: 'si ad verbum interpretor, absurdum resonat. (...) quod si cuiquam non videtur linguae gratiam interpretatione mutari, Homerum ad verbum exprimat in Latinum. plus aliquid dicam; eundem in sua lingua prosae verbis interpretetur, videbit ordinem ridiculum et poetam eloquentissimum vix loquentem.' quicunque enim aliquam scientiam ut logicam vel aliam quamcumque bene sciat, eam, etsi nitatur in linguam convertere maternam, videbit non solum in sententiis sed in verbis deficere. et ideo nullus Latinus sapientiam sacrae scripturae et philosophiae poterit ut oportet intelligere, nisi intelligat linguas a quibus sunt translatae.

Translation: Bacon, *De utilitate grammaticae*

But it is impossible for the particular quality of one language to be preserved in another, for even dialects of the same language vary among different people, as is clear from the French language, which is divided into many dialects among the Gauls, Picards, Normans, Burgundians and others. An expression that is appropriate and comprehensible in the Picard dialect is considered rebarbative to the Burgundians, or even to their closer Gaulish neighbours. Is this then not even more true between different languages? For this reason something that is well expressed in one language cannot be transferred into another in accordance with the particular quality it possessed in the original language.

This is why Jerome, in his letter on the best method of translating, writes, 'If I translate literally, the result sounds absurd. (...) But if anyone thinks the beauty of a language is not altered by translation, let him translate Homer literally into Latin. I will go further and say, if someone translates this author into his own language, he will see that the order is ridiculous and that the most eloquent poet can hardly speak.' Let anyone with an excellent knowledge of some science like logic or any subject whatsoever make an effort to translate it into his mother tongue, and he will realise that it lacks not only the statements but even the words. As a result no Latin speaker will be able to understand as he ought the wisdom of the sacred scripture and of philosophy unless he understands the languages from which they were translated.

The lack of Latin technical terms necessitates the use of the vernacular
et secundo considerandum est quod interpretes non habuerunt vocabula in Latino pro scientiis transferendis quia non fuerunt primo compositae in lingua Latina. et propter hoc posuerunt infinita de linguis alienis quae sicut nec intelliguntur ab eis qui linguas ignorant, sic nec recte proferuntur nec scribuntur ut decet; atque, quod vile est, propter ignorantiam linguae Latinae posuerunt His-

---

4 Jerome, *Ep.* 57.5: Jerome is quoting from his preface to his translation of Eusebius' *Chronicon*; Bridges' edition fails to indicate the full quote.

280 Thirteenth Century

panicum et alias linguas maternas, quasi infinities pro Latino. nam pro mille millibus exemplis unum ponatur de libro vegetabilium Aristotelis ubi dicit, 'Belenum
in Perside pernitiosissimum, sed transplantatum Jerusalem fit comestibile.' hoc
vocabulum non est scientiale laico Hispanicorum. nam jusquiamus vel semen
cassilaginis est nomen eius in Latino. quod sicut multa alia prius ab Hispanis
scholaribus meis derisus cum non intellegebam quae legebam, ipsis vocabula linguae maternae scientibus, tandem didici ab eisdem.

Translation: Bacon, *De utilitate grammaticae*

Secondly one must consider the fact that translators did not have the Latin terms
for translating scientific works because they were not originally composed in Latin,
and so for this reason they used many words from other languages. Just as these
words are not understood by people ignorant of these languages, neither are they
pronounced correctly or written as they should be. And what is despicable, owing
to their ignorance of Latin they have almost exclusively used Spanish and other na-
tive languages in place of Latin. Let one example out of all these thousands suffice,
from Aristotle's book on plants where he says 'Belenum, which is very harmful in
Persia, becomes edible when transplanted to Jerusalem.' This word (belenum) is not
the scientific term but colloquial Spanish. For its name in Latin is jusquiamus [i.e.
henbane] or the seed of the cassilago. When I did not understand what I was read-
ing, my Spanish students, who were familiar with the words of their own language,
laughed at me, and so I finally learned from them the meaning of this word and of
many more besides.

Translators need to understand the subject as well as the languages
tertio, oportet quod interpres optime sciat scientiam quam vult transferre et
duas linguas a quibus et in quas transferat. solus Boethius primus interpres novit plenarie potestatem linguarum. et solus dominus Robertus, dictus Grossum
Caput,[5] novit scientias. alii quidem mendici translatores (ut Gerardus Cremon-
ensis, Michael Scotus, Aluredus Anglicus, Hermannus Alemannus quem vidimus Parisius) [p. 68] defecerunt multum tam in scientiis quam in linguis; quod
ostendit ipsorum translatio. nam tanta est perversitas et horribilis difficultas,
maxime in libris Aristotelis translatis, [p. 69] quod nullus potest eos intelligere.
sed quilibet alii contradicit et multiplex reperitur falsitas, ut patet ex collatione
diversorum interpretum et textuum diversarum linguarum. et similiter in textu
sacro inveniuntur falsa et male translata quamplurima. nam Hieronymus probat translationem LXX interpretum (i.e. the Septuagint Greek version of the Old

---

5 Robert Grosseteste (1170–1253) was Bishop of Lincoln from 1235 and the author of
   many works on theology and science. He also produced translations of many classical
   and Byzantine works, and commentaries.

II.28 | The Study of Latin and Other Languages   281

Testament) et Theodotionis et Aquilae multas habuisse falsitates quae fuerunt
vulgatae per totam Ecclesiam. et omnes stabant maxime pro translatione LXX
sicut pro vita, et reputabatur Hieronymus falsarius et corruptor scripturarum,
donec paulatim claruit veritas Hebraica per solum Hieronymum in Latinum con-
versa. ne tamen nimia novitate deterreret Latinos, ideo ut ipse scribit, aliquando
coaptavit se LXX interpretibus et aliquando Theodotioni, aliquando Aquilae, et
ideo multa dimisit ut fuerunt per alios translata et propter hoc remanserunt plura
falsa. nam ut Augustinus probat de doctrina Christi libro secundo male transla- ***DDC* 2.12.18**
tum est quod habetur in libro Sapientiae, 'Spuria vitulamina non dabunt radices **Sap. 4:3**
altas.' nam debent esse spuriae plantationes, ut Augustinus probat per Graecum.[6]
et tamen Hieronymus dimisit hoc sicut alia propter pacem Ecclesiae et doctorum.
atque scitur manifeste quod Hieronymus, humanum aliquid passus, aliquando in
translatione sua oberravit, sicut ipsemet pluries confitetur. (…)

Translation: Bacon, *De utilitate grammaticae*

*Thirdly, although the translator ought to be well acquainted with the subject he
wishes to translate as well as the two languages between which he is translating,
Boethius alone, the first translator, was fully aware of the power of languages, and
Master Robert, known as Grosseteste, the recent Bishop of Lincoln, alone knew the
sciences. Certain other misleading translators (such as Gerard of Cremona, Michael
Scot, Alfred the Englishman, Herman the German, whom we saw in Paris) have
fallen short both in the languages and the sciences, as their translation shows. There
is so much that is incorrect and terribly difficult, particularly in the translated works
of Aristotle, that no one can understand them. Each one contradicts the other and
numerous false statements are found, as is clear from a comparison of the different
translators and of the texts in the different languages. Similarly in the sacred text
many statements are found that are false or badly translated. For Jerome proves
that the translation of the Seventy interpreters and those of Theodotion and Aquila
contained many errors, and since these errors were spread throughout the whole
Church and everyone defended the translation of the Septuagint as they would their
own life, Jerome was considered a falsifier and a corrupter of the Scriptures until
gradually the truth of the Hebrew became clear when Jerome alone translated it
into Latin. However, not wishing to create problems for the Latins by altering too
much, he himself tells us that he sometimes accepts the readings of the translators
of the Septuagint, sometimes of Theodotion and sometimes of Aquila, and so he has*

---

6   Certain Latin translators of the Greek Septuagint seem to have been confused by the
    similarity between *moscheumata*, meaning 'seedling', and *moschus*, meaning 'calf': they
    invented the word *vitulamen* as a calque on *moscheumata* to replicate the apparent
    link between *vitulamen* and the Latin for 'calf', *vitulus*; others give the slightly clearer
    adulterinae plantationes.

282 Thirteenth Century

left much as it was translated by others with the result that many false statements remain. For as Augustine demonstrates in Book 2 of 'On Christian Doctrine' the translation given in the Book of Wisdom is wrong: 'illegitimate seedlings will not produce deep roots', for it should read, 'spurious plantings' as Augustine proves by reference to the Greek. And yet Jerome let this pass like many other passages for the sake of peace in the Church and among the Doctors. And it is well known that Jerome, subject to human frailty, sometimes made mistakes in his own translation, as he himself often admits. (...)

The lack of philosophical and theological works in Latin

[p. 70] quarta causa est et ratio hujus rei quod quamplurima adhuc desunt Latinis tam philosophica quam theologica. nam vidi duos libros Machabaeorum in Graeco, viz. tertium et quartum, et Scriptura facit mentionem de libris Samuel et Nathan et Gad videntis, et aliorum quos non habemus. atque cum tota certificatio historiae sacrae sit a Josepho in Antiquitatum libris, et omnes sancti expositionum suarum radices accipiant a libris illis, necesse est Latinis ut habeant illum librum incorruptum; sed probatum est quod codices Latini omnino sunt corrupti in omnibus locis in quibus vis historiae consistit, ita ut textus ille sibi contradicat ubique, quod non est vitium tanti auctoris; igitur ex translatione mala hoc accidit et ex corruptione ejus per Latinos. nec est remedium nisi de novo transferantur vel ad singulas radices sufficienter corrigantur. similiter libri doctorum magnorum, ut beatorum Dionysii, Basilii, Johannis Chrysostomi, Johannis Damasceni et aliorum multorum deficiunt; quorum tamen aliquos dominus Robertus praefatus episcopus vertit in Latinum et alii quosdam alios ante eum; cujus opus est valde gratum theologis. et si libri istorum translati essent, non solum augmentaretur sapientia Latinorum sed haberet Ecclesia fortiora adjutoria contra Graecorum haereses et schismata, quoniam per sanctorum eorum sententias, quibus non possunt contradicere, convincerentur. similiter fere omnia secreta philosophiae adhuc jacent in linguis alienis. nam solum quaedam communia et vilia ut in pluribus translata sunt; et de hujusmodi etiam multa desunt.

Translation: Bacon, *De utilitate grammaticae*

The fourth reason for this situation is the fact that the Latins down to the present time lack many philosophical and theological works. For I have seen two books of the Maccabees in Greek, namely the third and fourth, and Scripture mentions the books of Samuel and Nathan and Gad the seer and others that we do not have. And since the whole authorisation of sacred history comes from Josephus in his books on Antiquities, and all the sacred writers take those books as the basis for their expositions, the Latins need that work in an uncorrupted form. But it has been shown that the Latin manuscripts are completely corrupt in all the passages which are the basis for history, so the text is everywhere self-contradictory. This is not the fault of this great author, but results from a bad translation and corruption by the Latins and the only remedy would be a new translation or adequate and fundamental correction. Similarly the books of the great teachers like the blessed Dionysius (i.e. Ps.-Dionysius the Areopagite), Basil, John Chrysostom, John of Damascus and many others are missing; some of them, however, have been translated into Latin by Master Robert, and other people before him translated other works: his work is very welcome to theologians. If these authors' books had been translated, not only would the learning of the Latins be increased but the Church would have stronger support against the heresies and schisms of the Greeks, since they would be convinced by the sayings of their sacred writers whom they cannot contradict. Similarly, almost all the secrets of philosophy up to the present lie hidden in foreign languages. In many instances only what is ordinary and unimportant has been translated and much even of this kind of material is missing.

Primary Sources and Related Texts

R. Bacon, *Opus majus*, ed. J. Bridges, 3 vols, Oxford, 1897–1900, vol. 1 (revised version in vol. 3).

Cf. Bacon's summarised version in chapter 25 of the *Opus tertium*, RS 15 (1859).

On the importance of learning Greek for the study of the Bible and for critique of earlier Latin translations, cf. Augustine, *De doctrina Christiana* 2.11.16 and Robert Grosseteste's proemium to his *Hexaemeron*.

Further Reading

A companion to philosophy in the Middle Ages, ed. J. Gracia and T. Noone, Oxford, 2003.

Latham, J. D. (1972) 'Arabic into medieval Latin', *Journal of Semitic Studies* 17: 30–67; (1976) *Journal of Semitic Studies* 21: 120–37; (1989) *Journal of Semitic Studies* 34: 459–69. Latham's articles cover the letters A–F for words contained in the *DMLBS*.

Mallette, K. (2021) *Lives of the great languages: Arabic and Latin in the medieval Mediterranean*, Chicago.

White, C. (2013) 'Technical terms in British medieval Latin and some European links', *ALMA* 71: 27–35.

Section II.29

A Miracle Associated with St John of Beverley: a Boy Falls from the Minster Roof

(excerpt: *RS* 71.1, pp. 328–30)

Date: c.1275.

This short set of miracles survives only in the *Acta sanctorum* for 7 May (*BHL* 4344), which was printed on the basis of an unknown English MS.

Author: These accounts of miracles attributed to St John of Beverley (d. 721) were written by an anonymous writer.[1]

Work: This miracle is taken from a collection (referred to as *Alia miracula* III) recording events between 1211 and 1219. This section tells of the drama of a boy falling from the highest point inside the Minster at Beverley. Such accidents were not uncommon in an age when so many churches and cathedrals were being built,[2] but this accident is different, occurring during the performance of a religious drama to which people have excitedly flocked. The specifics of the setting and the perceptive details about human emotions suggest that the author was an eyewitness. The dramatic structure of the episode is brilliant, with the focus gradually moving from the huge crowds to the single individual, the young man who is about to fall, and the fall described, as it were, in slow motion. In a coda the drama is said to be an analogy of the drama of Christ's Passion and Resurrection, with reference also to the biblical typology which was such a popular interpretative device in the Middle Ages: an episode in the Old Testament (here, Abraham's attempt to sacrifice his son Isaac) is taken as foreshadowing the experience of Christ. This account of the miracle provides evidence of the performance in the thirteenth century of religious drama, with which one might compare the later evidence of such productions in the York Mystery Plays or the fourteenth-century

---

1 Cf. Bede, *HE* 5.2–6; also Section II.14 where Ælred refers to a miracle of John of Beverley that had occurred at Watton, and Section II.31 for a reference to this saint's involvement in Æthelstan's victory at the battle of Brunanburh in 937.

2 For accounts of similar accidents, cf. e.g. Wulfstan's *Life of Æthelwold* (34; for this work see Section I.40A) with reference to the reconstruction of the Old Minster at Winchester before 980, and Gervase of Canterbury (Section II.47A) with reference to the rebuilding of Canterbury Cathedral after the fire of 1174.

II.29 | Miracle Associated with St John of Beverley 285

Ordinalia (in Middle Cornish, preserved in Bodleian MS 791), which contains a Passion and a Resurrection drama.

Linguistic points: The author states in his preface that he needs to bring these miracles into the open so as to strengthen and spread the Christian faith, but he eschews *pomposas verborum phaleras* ('the pompous trappings of words') which just obfuscate the truth. He does, however, intersperse biblical allusions. In the case of the following miracle he combines the description of the action with a broader theological vision of the episode, using biblical allusion and typology (indicated by the word *typus*). Allegory is also conveyed by the parallel between the stone that falls without being touched by human hand and the virgin birth. *persona* is here used in its basic CL sense, as a character in a drama, but cf. its use as 'parson' in Section II.26B. This is the only known example of *dialogus* used in the context of a drama. The author uses several unusual words, e.g. *polyandrium*, which is a LL word for a cemetery, derived from Greek, and *matricularius*, a LL word that here refers to a churchwarden: by the third century *matrix* ('womb') comes to signify a list or register, with *matricula* as its diminutive, and *matricularius* is developing as someone in charge of a (church) register (as here), or a poor person inscribed on the church list as eligible for charity. Another rare LL word is *expalmare* from CL *palmare*.

TEXT II.29

Crowds flock to watch the Church drama performed in the cemetery
[*RS* p. 328] contigit ut tempore quodam aestivo intra septa polyandri ecclesiae Beati Johannis, ex parte aquilonari, larvatorum (ut assolet) et verbis et actu fieret representatio Dominicae resurrectionis. confluebat eo copiosa utriusque sexus multitudo, variis inducta votis, delectationis videlicet, seu admirationis causa, vel sancto proposito excitandae devotionis. cum vero, prae densa vulgi astante corona, pluribus, et praecipue statura pusillis, desideratus minime pateret accessus, introierunt plurimi in ecclesiam; ut vel orarent, vel picturas inspicerent, vel per aliquod genus recreationis et solatii pro hoc die taedium evitarent.

Translation: A Miracle Associated with St John of Beverley

It happened that one summer, within the confines of the cemetery of St John's Church, on the northern side, a dramatisation of the Lord's Resurrection took place, with masked actors speaking and acting, as was the custom. A large crowd of men and women came flooding there, drawn by different motives, for pleasure no doubt, or out of wonder and with the holy intention of stimulating their devotion. On account of the dense crowd of people standing round, many, and especially those of

286 Thirteenth Century

smaller stature, were unable to get a good view as they had hoped; so a large number of them went into the church, either to pray or to look at the wall paintings or so as to avoid boredom on that day by means of some kind of recreation and consolation.

The boys climb up inside the church to get a better view
ingressi igitur ecclesie limina adolescentuli quidam, casu fortuito ostium quoddam reperiunt semiapertum, quo per gradus ascenditur ad superiora murorum. eo accurrentes levitate puerili, gradatim insuper murales ascendebant basilicae testudines,[3] ea ut reor intentione, ut per altas turriculorum fenestras, seu si qua vitrearum fenestrarum essent foramina, liberius personarum et habitus et gestus respicerent et earundem dialogos auditu faciliori adverterent; Zaccheum in hoc imitantes qui cum esset statura [p. 329] pusillus, ut videret Jesum, arborem as-

Luke 19:3–4 cendit sycomorum.

Translation: A Miracle Associated with St John of Beverley

Some young teenagers entered the church and happened to find a half-open door through which stairs led up to the higher parts of the walls. They rushed up there in a spirit of boyish fun, and gradually climbed up above the vaulting of the basilica, with the intention, I believe, of getting a better view of the actors' costumes and gestures and of hearing their dialogue more easily through the high turret windows or any gaps in the glass windows; in this they were imitating Zacchaeus who, because he was of small stature, climbed the sycamore tree to see Jesus.

The churchwardens chase them, and one boy falls to the paving beneath
sed, ecce! intimatum est matriculariis quod agebatur ab adolescentulis, qui nimirum verentes ne puerorum indiscretio, desiderio videndi personas, quarum officio praetaxata transigebatur repraesentatio, fenestras vitreas perforaret, vel aliquo modo detereret, illos insequebantur cursu pernici; ipsosque temeritatis argutos, alapis gravioribus expalmatos coegerunt reverti.

quidam vero puerorum poena sociorum conspecta, in insequentium manus formidans incidere, superiores secessit in partes, quoadusque deveniret cursu praerapido ultra crucem magnam, tunc temporis collocatam in altaris B. Martini confinio. ibi vero stans et deorsum aspiciens, quadrato cuidam lapidi pedem imposuit incautius; qui a muro solutus et decisus, non sine fragore magno super lapideum decidit pavimentum; et, non obstante duritia, in infinitas partes est comminutus. adolescentulus vero suo destitutus fulcimine, horrendo stupore

---

3 Cf. Section II.16B(b) for this word, with reference to Canterbury Cathedral.

II.29 | Miracle Associated with St John of Beverley 287

percussus, solotenus corruit, et ibi per aliquantum temporis articulum exanimis jacuit, et mortuo simillimus.

Translation: A Miracle Associated with St John of Beverley

But look! someone pointed out to the churchwardens what the boys were doing: they were afraid that the boys' foolish behaviour, driven by a desire to see the actors who were performing the aforementioned play, might cause the glass windows to be broken or damaged in some way, and so they ran in hot pursuit of them and accusing them of recklessness they gave them a hard smack and forced them to come back down.

But one of the boys, seeing his friends' punishment and terrified of falling into the hands of his pursuers, withdrew to the higher parts until he very quickly reached a position above the large cross at that time situated near the altar of St Martin. Standing there and looking down, he recklessly put his foot on a square stone, which came away from the wall and fell down on the stone pavement below with a great crash. Despite the stone's hardness, it shattered into an infinite number of pieces. The teenager, suddenly losing his footing, was paralysed with terror and hurtled to the ground, where he lay for a time without moving, looking very much as if he were dead.

Reaction and resurrection
circumstabant plurimi graviter suspirantes, de casu tali miserabiliter ingemiscentes, dolores suos lacrymarum exuberantia protestantes. parentes ejus ejulabant, laniabant capillos, clamorem et ululatum crebris interrumpebant singultibus; ignorantes, quia in brevi divina dispensatione tristitia in gaudium, ploratus in risum esset convertendus. non passus namque Deus ecclesiam, in sui et confessoris honore dedicatam, quasi caede humana pollui; sed volens eam majoris in posterum auctoritatis haberi, volens etiam testimonium perhibere veritatis, illi quae interim fiebat suae resurrectionis repraesentationi, in omnium qui aderant conspectu adolescentulum, qui mortuus credebatur, erexit incolumem adeo ut nec aliquam in toto corpore suo esset perpendere laesionem. factum est ergo ut qui prae [p. 330] populi multitudine extra ecclesiam repraesentationi non poterant interesse, mirabilius viderent resurrectionis indicium intra corpus ecclesiae; et non tantum resurrectionis, sed passionis Dominicae. per decisionem namque lapidis, sine manu decidentis a muro, plane indicabatur sine admixtione virili, ex virgine Dominica incarnatio; per utriusque casum, scilicet et lapidis et pueri, significabatur passio eiusdem, hominis et Dei. veruntamen lapis cadendo confractus typum gessit arietis occisi; adolescens vero typum Isaac permanentis illaesi. unde **Gen. 22** cuius passionis secundum humanitatem signum fuit ruina, ejus etiam resurrectionis secundum divinitatem signum exstitit erectio miraculosa.

Translation: A Miracle Associated with St John of Beverley

A crowd gather around him, sighing deeply and lamenting wretchedly at this accident, their floods of tears testifying to their grief. His parents were wailing, tearing their hair and interspersing their shouts and wails with sobs; they were unaware that by divine dispensation their sadness would shortly be turned into joy, their lament into laughter. For God did not allow the church which was dedicated in his honour and that of his confessor to be polluted by a human killing, as it were; but wishing to increase this church's authority for the future, wishing also to provide a witness to the truth, which was just then being shown in the drama of the Resurrection, in the sight of everyone there he raised the young man, who was thought to be dead, so completely unharmed that there was no sign of injury anywhere on his body. And so it happened that those who were unable to see the play outside the church, because of the crowds, saw a more amazing indication of the Resurrection within the body of the church; and not only of resurrection, but of the Lord's passion. For the loosening of the stone which fell from the wall without human intervention was a clear indication of the Lord's incarnation from the Virgin without sexual intercourse with a man; the fall of both things, namely of the stone and the boy, signified the passion of the Lord, both man and God. And indeed the stone which smashed when it fell bore the image of the slaughtered ram; the teenager, the image of Isaac who remained unharmed. And so just as the fall was a sign of the Lord's passion according to his humanity, so the miraculous raising was a sign of his Resurrection according to his divinity.

Primary Sources and Related Texts

Historians of the church of York, RS 71.1 (1879) 327–47 (i.e. Mir. J. Bev.C).

Further Reading

Wilson, S. (2006) *The life and after-life of St John of Beverley: the evolution of the cult of an Anglo-Saxon saint*, Aldershot.
——. *Resurrection: representation v. reality in a miracle of St John of Beverley*, Medieval Forum, www.sfsu.edu/~medieval/Volume%201/Wilson.html.

Section II.30

The 1297 Visitation of Chiswick Church by the Authorities of St Paul's Cathedral (excerpts)

Date: 1297.

The record of this visitation is in the St Paul's Cathedral MS, now in the London Metropolitan Archives, with the reference CLC/313/L/F/002/MS25516.

Work: The visitation was carried out by the Dean of St Paul's, travelling around the counties encircling London to update detailed inventories of the possessions of churches granted to St Paul's Cathedral in previous centuries and to record the state of the buildings and contents. The record of the 1297 visitation is an early example of this genre of documents. Chiswick in Middlesex is the last church on the Dean's circuit.

With these lists one may compare, for example, the later examples such as the Visitations of Southwell Minster (1469–1542), where the accounts focus on human behaviour (mainly sexual relations – including a woman's testimony, card-playing, chatting or sleeping during the service and the occasional instance of sorcery) in church and community rather than on church furniture or the lack of it; or the Visitation of Godstow Nunnery (1432), a report on lax discipline among the nuns for whom the *Register of Godstow* was translated from Latin to English in about 1450.

Linguistic points: This text is of interest as providing Latin terms for ecclesiastical furniture and vestments. CL *cancellus* ('rail' or 'lattice') extends its meaning to the railed-off part (chancel) of a church. *barrare* here has its basic sense of 'to fit with bars', a verb formed from the noun *barra*, which surfaces in BML at the end of the twelfth century, deriving from OF 'barre'. *descha* ('desk') is one of the forms developing from CL *discus* (cf. Sections II.22 and II.36); it is sometimes synonymous with *lectrina*. *sconsa* is a screened ('hidden') light: like the ME 'scons', it is an aphaeretic form related to OF 'esconse', from *absconsa*. *hercia* is a type of frame for candles (around a bier), in a form that develops from CL *irpex* ('agricultural harrow'), via *herpex/herpica*, and OF 'herce'; in modern times the word ('hearse') is transferred to a means of transporting the coffin. *rochetum* develops from French 'rochet', associated with Germanic/OE 'rocc'. *siclatun* is a variant spelling of *cyclaton*, from Arabic 'siqlatun', meaning a silken cloth woven with gold (cf.

OED s.v. ciclatoun); here the word is used without Latin inflection as the name of a type of cloth. Cloth *de opere saraceno* was another rich silk material, with its name giving English 'sarsenet'; the cloth is also found in a Latin document of 1397 in the form *sarsinettum. samitum* too is a rich silk, with a name that developed from Greek *hexamitos* into Latin *hexamitum* and AN/ME 'samit': it has given the modern names for velvet in, for example, German ('Samt'), Swedish ('sammet') and Polish ('aksamit'). *Placebo* and *Dirige* are terms for the evening and morning offices for the dead, so called from the initial words of their respective antiphons, based on Psalm texts (Ps. 114:9 and Ps. 5:9), and a common component of the primers that people would carry around.[1]

TEXT II.30

The contents of Chiswick church in 1297
Ecclesia de Chesewich visitata die Jovis proxima post festum Sancti Luce Ewangeliste anno domini millesimo cc^mo nonagesimo septimo.

cimiterium sufficienter clausum. navis ecclesie male cooperta. item campanarium cum duabus campanis non bene cordatis. (...) item cancellum bene opertum cum fenestris bene vitreatis et barratis, j descha, ij lectrina. j ordinale de usu Sarum cum kalendario et historiis beati Thome martiri. item j psalterium bonum cum kalendario et ympnario, Placebo et Dirige (...) item legenda temporalis et sanctorum plenarium. item deficit martilogium. item ij gradualia cum processionali. item j troparium. item deficit secundum troparium. item missale moniale non notatum. item aliud missale antiquum debile. item j manuale bonum de usu Sancti Pauli. item deficiunt statuta sinodalia et statuta J. de Pecham, articuli conciliorum et Capitula Octoboni.

item deficit pannus lectrinus. item j velum quadragesimale competens. item j superpellicia bonum et ij debilia. item j rochetum. item ij manutergia ablata per fenestram navis ecclesie. item ij abstersoria. item unum frontale de siclatun. (...) item unum vestimentum festivale cum paruris, albe de viridi pallo, cum stola, manipula de opere saraceno, et casula de rubeo samitto, parura amicti broidata. (...) item vestimentum feriale debile, cum casula rubea debili de *fusteyn.* (...) item ij sconse. (...) item j lucerna, j hercia.

---

1 Cf. Langland, *Piers Plowman*, C-text, passus 5, line 46; E. Duffy (1992) *The stripping of the altars: traditional religion in England 1400–1580*, New Haven, CT: 220. *dirige*, an imperative form of the Latin verb, is the derivation of the English noun 'dirge'. The adverb *item* is often used, as here, in a list, as in an inventory or will; in modern English it is used primarily as a noun.

Translation: Visitation of Chiswick Church

The church of Chiswick inspected on the Thursday immediately after the feast of St Luke the Evangelist in the year of the Lord 1297.

The cemetery was adequately enclosed. The nave of the church badly roofed. Also the belfry with two bells not properly fitted with ropes. (…) Also the chancel with a good roof (and) with windows fitted with glass and bars in good condition, 1 desk, 2 lecterns. 1 ordinal of the Use of Sarum with a calendar and accounts of the blessed martyr Thomas. Also 1 good psalter with a calendar and a hymnal, the Placebo and Dirige. (…) Also a legendary pertaining to the days of the year that are not saints' days and a comprehensive volume of the saints. The book of martyrs is missing. Also 2 graduals with a processional. Also 1 book of tropes. Also the second book of tropes is missing. Also a nun's missal not noted. Also another old missal which is falling to pieces. Also 1 manual in good condition, of the Use of St Paul's. Also missing are the statutes of the synods, the statutes of John Peckham, the articles of the councils and the chapters of Ottoboni. Also a cloth for the lectern is missing. Also 1 Lent-cloth, satisfactory. Also 1 good surplice and 2 in poor condition. Also one rochet. Also 2 hand-towels removed through the window of the nave of the church. Also 2 napkins. Also one frontal of silk woven with gold. (…) Also one vestment for feast days with embroidery, albs of green cloth, with a stole, a maniple of sarsenet and a chasuble of red samite, with the ornament of the amice embroidered. (…) Also a vestment for use on ordinary days in poor condition, with a red chasuble of fustian in poor condition. (…) Also 2 sconces. (…) Also 1 lamp, 1 candelabrum.

Primary Sources and Related Texts

Visitations of Churches Belonging to St Paul's Cathedral in 1297 and 1458, Camden Society n.s. 53, 1895, 57–8.

Further Reading

Encyclopaedia of dress and textiles of the British Isles c.450–1450 (2012).
Medieval dress and textiles in Britain: a multilingual sourcebook (2014).
Brown, C., Davies, G. and Michael, M. (ed.) (2016) *English medieval embroidery: Opus Anglicanum*, New Haven, CT.
Forrest, I. (2013) 'The transformation of visitation in thirteenth-century England', *Past and Present* 221: 3–38.

FOURTEENTH CENTURY

Section II.31

King Edward I, *Letter* to Pope Boniface VIII on Relations between England and Scotland (excerpt: pp. 97–9)

Date: 1301.

The letter is preserved among the Close Rolls (TNA: C54/118 m. 10d and 9d)

Author and addressee: Edward, king of England (1272–1307), writes to Pope Boniface VIII (pope from 1294–1303). Boniface (aka Benedetto Caetani) had in fact spent some years in England in the 1260s, helping Cardinal Ottobono to oppose the barons after Simon de Montfort's death at the battle of Evesham (see Section II.48); he was even rector of St Lawrence's Church in Towcester, Northamptonshire for a time. At the end of his life he was placed by the poet Dante among the fraudsters in the *Inferno*.

Work: This long letter, dated 7 May 1301, gives an account of the relations between Scotland and the kings of England, culminating in a description of John de Balliol's savage attacks on northern England, including the burning of 200 children in their primary school at Hexham. As well as the copy of this letter among the Close Rolls, there is a draft in French among the Scottish documents in the National Archives at Kew: E39/99/48–51 and E39/1/18. The letter was written in response to a papal bull (TNA: SC7/6/10) of 27 June 1299 in which the pope ordered Edward to release certain Scottish churchmen and to abandon the war in Scotland on the grounds that he had no rights over that country: the pope claimed sovereignty over Scotland, thereby pushing out English claims. There is also the Baron's Letter of 1301 (TNA: E26) repudiating papal involvement in the affairs of Scotland and asserting English sovereignty. It is not clear that this letter was ever sent to the pope. The miracle performed apparently through the intercession of John of Beverley when King Æthelstan asked God for a sign in support of his victory against the Scots is recorded in a thirteenth-century anonymous collection of miracles attributed to this saint (*Historians of the church of York*, RS 71.1 (1879) 296–7).

Linguistic points: The account of the relations between England and Scotland in the distant past reads like an official summary of parts of Geoffrey of Monmouth's *HRB*. It contains both anaphora and widespread use of the ablative absolute but is more syntactically varied and complex than Geoffrey's text. Note the way in which the long final sentence is constructed, from *Adelstanus ...*, and the phrase

296 Fourteenth Century

in the middle of it, *extracto gladio de vagina, percussit in silicem qui lapis ad ictum gladii, Dei virtute agente, ita cavatur ut ...*, where *qui lapis*, referring to *silex*, neatly turns the object into the subject.

TEXT II.31

How the kings of England gained control over Scotland from the earliest times
[p. 97] sub temporibus itaque Ely et Samuelis prophete vir quidam strenuus et insignis, Brutus nomine, de genere Trojanorum post excidium urbis Troje cum multis nobilibus Trojanorum applicuit in quandam insulam tunc Albion vocatam, a gigantibus inhabitatam, quibus sua et suorum devictis potencia et occisis eam nomine suo Britanniam sociosque suos Britones appellavit et edificavit civitatem quam Trinovantum nuncupavit que modo Londonia nominatur. et postea regnum suum tribus filiis suis divisit, scilicet Locrino primogenito illam partem Britannie que nunc Anglia dicitur, et Albanacto secundo natu illam partem que tunc Albania a nomine Albanacti nunc vero Scotia nuncupatur, et Cambro filio minori partem illam nomine suo tunc Cambria vocatam que nunc Wallia vocatur, reservata Locrino seniori regia dignitate. itaque biennio post mortem Bruti applicuit in Albania quidam [p. 98] rex Hunorum nomine Humber et Albanactum fratrem Locrini occidit, quo audito Locrinus rex Britonum prosecutus est eum qui fugiens submersus est in flumine quod de nomine suo Humber vocatur et sic Albania revertitur ad dictum Locrinum. item Dunwallo rex Britonum Staterium regem Scocie sibi rebellem occidit et terram in dedicionem recepit. item duo filii Dunwallonis scilicet Belinus et Brennius inter se regnum patris sui diviserunt ita quod Belinus senior diadema insule cum Britannia, Wallia et Cornubia possideret; Brennius vero sub eo regnaturus Scociam acciperet. petebat enim Trojana consuetudo ut dignitas hereditatis primogenito perveniret.

From King Arthur to Æthelstan: victories over Scotland
item Arturus rex Britonum princeps famosissimus Scociam sibi rebellem subjecit, et pene totam gentem delevit et postea quemdam nomine Anguselum in regem Scocie prefecit et cum postea idem rex Arturus apud civitatem Legionum festum faceret celeberimum interfuerunt ibidem omnes reges sibi subjecti inter quos Anguselus rex Scocie servicium pro regno Scocie exhibens debitum gladium regis Arturi detulit ante ipsum et successive omnes reges Scocie omnibus regibus Britonum fuere subjecti. succedentibus autem regibus Anglis in predicta insula et ipsius monarchiam et dominium optinentibus subsequenter Edwardus dictus senior filius Elvredi (Alf-) regis Anglie Scotorum, Cumbrorum et Stregwallorum reges sibi tanquam superiori domino subjectos habuit et submissos. Adelstanus rex Anglie Constantinum regem Scotorum sub se regnaturum [p. 99] constituit dicens, 'Gloriosius est regem facere quam regem esse' et est dignum memoria quod idem Adelstanus, intercedente sancto Johanne de Beverlaco quondam

archiepiscopo Ebor', Scotos rebellantes ei dimicavit qui gracias Deo devote agens Deum exoravit, petens quatinus interveniente beato Johanne sibi aliquod signum evidens ostenderet quatinus tam succedentes quam presentes cognoscere possent Scotos Anglorum regno jure subjugari, et videns quosdam scopulos juxta quemdam locum prope Dumbar in Scocia prominere, extracto gladio de vagina, percussit in silicem qui lapis ad ictum gladii, Dei virtute agente, ita cavatur ut mensura ulne longitudini possit coaptari, et hujus rei hactenus evidens signum apparet et in Beverlac' ecclesia in legenda sancti Johannis quasi singulis ebdomadis per annum ad laudem et honorem sancti Johannis pro miraculo recitatur, et de hoc exstat celebris memoria tam in Anglia quam in Scocia usque ad presentem diem. (…)

Translation: Letter from King Edward I to the Pope

And so in the time of Eli and of Samuel the prophet, after the fall of the city of Troy, a vigorous and outstanding man called Brutus, a Trojan by birth, landed with many noble Trojans at an island called Albion at that time, inhabited by giants. When he had defeated and slain them by his own strength and that of his men, he called it Britain after his own name and called his companions Britons, and he built a city which he called Trinovantum, now called London. Afterwards he divided his kingdom between his three sons: he gave that part of Britain which is now called Anglia to his firstborn, Locrinus, and to Albanact, his second son, he gave that part then known as Albany after the name Albanact but which is now called Scotland, and to Cambrus, his youngest son, he gave the part then called Cambria after him but now called Wales; for the rank of king was reserved for Locrinus, the eldest. But two years after Brutus' death, a king of the Huns called Humber landed in Albany and slew Albanact, Locrinus' brother. On hearing this Locrinus, king of the Britons, pursued him; he fled but was drowned in the river called the Humber after his name, and so Albany reverted to Locrinus. Likewise Dunwallo, king of the Britons, slew Stater, king of Scotland, who had rebelled against him, and took his land in surrender. Next the two sons of Dunwallo, namely Belinus and Brennius, divided their father's kingdom between them so that Belinus, the elder one, possessed the crown of the island, with Britain, Wales and Cornwall, while Brennius received Scotland to rule it under his brother, for Trojan custom demanded that the dignity of the inheritance should go to the firstborn. Next Arthur, king of the Britons, the most famous leader, subjected Scotland when it rebelled against him, and destroyed almost the whole nation and then put someone called Anguselus in charge of the kingdom of Scotland, and when King Arthur afterwards held a celebrated feast at Caerleon, all the kings who were subject to him were present there, among whom were Anguselus, king of Scotland, who carried King Arthur's sword before him, as an indication of the service due for the kingdom of Scotland; and in succession all the kings of Scotland were subject to all the kings of the Britons. The succeeding English kings in

298 Fourteenth Century

this island obtained both its monarchy and dominion, and subsequently Edward, known as 'the Elder', son of King Alfred, king of England, kept the kings of the Scots, the Cumbrians and the people of Strathclyde subject and submissive to himself as the superior lord. Æthelstan, king of England, appointed Constantine as king of the Scots to rule under him, saying, 'It is a greater cause for pride to make a king than to be one.' It is worth remembering that this same Æthelstan, on the intercession of St John of Beverley, formerly Archbishop of York, defeated the Scots when they rebelled against him, and then thanking God devoutly he prayed to God, asking that through the intervention of John he would give him a clear sign so that people in future as well as at the present time would be able to know that the Scots were justly subject to the kingdom of the English. Seeing some overhanging rocks at a place near Dunbar in Scotland, Æthelstan drew his sword from its sheath and struck the rock. At the sword's blow, through God's providence, such a big hole was made in the stone that the measure of an ell's length could be fitted into it. Clear evidence of this incident is still visible, and at the church of Beverley the deed is recounted as a miracle every week throughout the year in John's saint's Life, in praise and honour of St John, and the memory of this has spread far and wide both in England and Scotland down to the present day. (…)

Primary Sources and Related Texts

Anglo-Scottish relations, 1174–1328, ed. E. Stones, OMT, Oxford, 1965: no. 30.
The History of the Britons (cf. Section I.30).
Geoffrey of Monmouth, *A History of the Kings of Britain* (cf. Section II.12).
Henry of Huntingdon, *A History of the English* (cf. Section II.4A).

Further Reading

Goldstein, R. J. (1991) 'The Scottish mission to Boniface VIII in 1301', *Scottish Historical Review* 70: 1–15.

Section II.32

The Trial of Alice Kyteler on a Charge of Witchcraft (excerpt: pp. 1–3)

Date: 1324.

The proceedings are preserved in part 2 of BL MS Harley 641, from the early fifteenth century.

Author: Richard Ledrede (c.1275–1360) is thought to be the author of the account of the trial of Dame Alice Kyteler and her son, William Outlaw, on charges of heresy and witchcraft in Kilkenny in south-east Ireland. Ledrede was an Englishman, a Franciscan, Bishop of Ossory from 1317 until his death, and also the author of Latin hymns (see the *Red Book of Ossory*). He had spent time in Avignon, where he witnessed the trial of Templars, at which demonic association was one of the charges. When he later investigated Alice Kyteler on charges of sorcery, he was keen to charge her also with demonic association (see the second, third, fifth and seventh charges), which was the first time a woman had been accused of this. Although Ledrede saw himself as a defender of the faith, his heavy-handed treatment of his opponents led to him going into exile.

Defendant: Alice Kyteler was a shrewd businesswoman in Kilkenny, who managed to make a lot of money and a number of enemies, including among the members of her family. It was her stepchildren from her four marriages who reported her. It seems that Alice escaped to England, but her accomplice Petronilla was, according to this text, the first witch to be burned in Ireland.

Work: The excerpt here forms the opening of Ledrede's careful account of his investigation of Alice and the other eleven people charged, including her son William Outlaw. Here the seven charges relating to sorcery are listed, with mention made of many of the attributes commonly associated with medieval witchcraft. A century later (1412–20) Lydgate gives a description, in Middle English, of a sorcerer in his *Troy Book*.

Linguistic points: The description of the defendants' alleged behaviour is more shocking than the language used, which is an example of clear official writing, enumerating the charges point by point. Robin Filius Artis, as a name of the Devil, is one of several uses of the name Robin in the context of sorcery. *incubus* here

300 Fourteenth Century

signifies a demon, and it is clear from the context that it was thought to have sexual relations with women.[1]

TEXT II.32

The background to the trial
[p. 1] tempore huius papae contigerunt in Hybernia quae sequuntur. visitante venerabili patre fratre Ricardo (Ledrede) episcopo Ossoriensi suam diocesim, invenit per inquisitionem solennem, in qua erant quinque milites et alii nobiles in magna multitudine, quod in civitate Kilkenniae erant a magnis temporibus et adhuc sunt haeretici sortilegae quamplures, diversis utentes sortilegiis, quae sapiebant diversas haereses, ad quorum investigationem procedens episcopus prout ex officii [debi]to tenebatur, invenit quandam dominam divitem, quae vocatur domina Alicia Kyteler, matrem Willelmi Outlawe, cum suis multis sodalibus, haeresibus variis irretitam.

Translation: The Trial of Alice Kyteler

In the time of this pope (John XXII), the following events took place in Ireland. When the venerable father, Brother Richard, Bishop of Ossory, was visiting his diocese, he found, by means of an official investigation in which there were five knights and other nobles in great numbers, that in the city of Kilkenny there had been for a long time, and still are, a number of heretical sorcerers, using various kinds of spell which smack of various heresies. The bishop, proceeding to investigate them as he was bound to do by his office, found a certain wealthy lady called Lady Alice Kyteler, the mother of William Outlaw, ensnared in various different heresies together with her many companions.

The seven charges against Alice Kyteler
primo scilicet, quod ad obtinendum intenta per sua nefaria sortilegia, fidem Christi et ecclesiae abnegabant ex toto per mensem vel per annum, secundum quod obtinendum per sortilegium erat majus vel minus, ita quod durante illo tempore in nullo crederent quod ecclesia credit nec corpus Christi adorarent ullo modo nec ecclesiam intrarent nec missam audirent nec panem sumerent benedictum nec aquam benedictam.

---

1 Cf. Augustine (*De civitate Dei* 15.23), who refers to raunchy fauns *quos vulgo incubos vocant*. In the twelfth century Gervase of Tilbury (*Otia imperialia* 1.17) cites Geoffrey of Monmouth's *History of the Kings of Britain* (107), who had referred to Apuleius' *De deo Socratis* on the subject, in suggesting that an incubus was involved in Merlin's conception.

II.32 | The Trial of Alice Kyteler 301

secundo, quod sacrificia dabant demonibus in animalibus vivis, quae divide-
bant membratim et offerebant distribuendo in quadruviis cuidam daemoni [p. 2]
qui se facit appellari Artis Filium ex pauperioribus inferni.

?l. profundioribus

tertio, quod consilia et responsa per sua sortilegia petebant a daemonibus.

quarto, quod jurisdictionem et claves ecclesiae usurpabant in suis conven-
ticulis de nocte, cum candelis de cera accensis, sententiam excommunicationis
fulminando, etiam in viros proprios, a planta pedis usque ad verticem capitis
per omnia membra expressa nominatim et singillatim, et in fine cum extinctione
candelarum dicendo 'fi, fi, fi: amen'.

quinto, quod de intestinis et interioribus gallorum daemonibus, ut praemitti-
tur, immolatorum, cum quibusdam vermibus horribilibus, herbis variis, ac etiam
unguibus mortuorum, crinibus posteriorum crebro et pannis puerorum dece-
dentium sine baptismo, ac etiam aliis detestabilibus quamplurimis in testa capitis latronis cuiusdam decollati super ignem de lignis quercuum bullitis, varios
foverunt pulveres, unguenta et pixides, ac etiam candelas de pinguedine in dicta
testa bullita cum suis variis incantationibus, ad concitandum amores et odia, ad
interficiendum ac etiam ad affligendum corpora fidelium christianorum, et alia
innumera optinenda.

sexto, quod filii et filiae quatuor maritorum dictae dominae publicis instabant
clamoribus apud episcopum, remedium et auxilium postulantes contra eam, publice coram populo allegantes quod ipsa per huiusmodi sortilegia patres eorum
quosdam interfecerat, quosdam infatuaverat et ad tantam sensus stoliditatem
duxerat quod omnia bona sua sibi et filio suo dederant, ad perpetuam filiorum
suorum et haeredum depauperationem, unde et vir ejus qui nunc est, miles dominus Johannes le Power, per huiusmodi pulveres et pixides ac etiam sortilegia in
tali statu positus est, quod totus est extenuatus, ungulis privatus, et toto corpore
depilatus, sed per ancillam quandam eiusdem dominae praemunitus, ablatis violenter clavibus cistarum dictae dominae de manibus ejusdem et cistis apertis,
invenit dictus miles unum saccum plenum de huiusmodi horribilibus et detestabilibus in eisdem, quem cum inventis per manus duorum religiosorum sacerdotum episcopo transmisit supradicto.

septimo, quod dicta domina daemonem quendam [p. 3] habuit incubum,
a quo cognosci carnaliter se permittit, qui Filius Artis se facit appellari, et aliquando Robinum filium Artis; qui etiam quandoque sibi apparet in specie cati,
quandoque in specie canis nigri et pilosi, quandoque in specie cuiusdam aethi-
opis cum duobus sociis ipso majoribus et longioribus, quorum quilibet virgam
ferream portant in manibus; cui etiam se et omnia sua committit; a quo etiam
omnes suas divitias et ea quae possidet recepisse se recognoscit.

Translation: The Trial of Alice Kyteler

*Firstly, namely, that in order to obtain their goals by means of their wicked spells
they completely renounced their faith in Christ and the Church for a month or for*

a year, depending on whether what they wanted to obtain by their spell was larger or smaller, in such a way that during this period they believed in nothing that the Church believes in nor did they worship the body of Christ in any way nor did they enter the church or hear Mass or take the bread or water that had been blessed. Secondly, that they made sacrifices to demons of living animals, dividing them up limb by limb, and offered them by distributing them at the crossroads to some demon who had himself called the Artisson by the poor inhabitants of hell. Thirdly, that they sought advice and answers from demons by means of their spells. Fourthly, that they appropriated the jurisdiction and keys of the church in their illegal gatherings at night, with lighted wax candles, fulminating the sentence of excommunication, even against their own husbands, naming each and every part of the body from the soles of the feet to the top of the head and at the end, saying 'Fi, fi, fi, amen' as they blew out the candles. Fifthly, that with the intestines and innards of cockerels sacrificed to demons, as mentioned, together with some horrible worms, various herbs and even dead men's nails, frequently with the hair of the posterior and the cloths of babies dying without baptism, and also many other disgusting things boiled together over a fire made with oak logs, in the skull of some thief who has been beheaded, they produced various different powders, ointments and (boxes for) charms and also candles made of tallow boiled in this same skull, together with their different incantations, in order to arouse love and hatred, to kill and also to cause suffering to the bodies of faithful Christians, and to obtain innumerable other things. Sixthly, that the sons and daughters of the four husbands of this lady were making importunate requests, shouting publicly in front of the bishop, demanding legal redress and assistance against her, publicly alleging before the people that she, by means of spells of this kind, had killed some of their fathers and sent others mad and had brought them to such a state of stupidity, that they had given all their possessions to her and her son, causing the permanent impoverishment of their children and heirs. For this reason her present husband, the knight, Lord John le Power, by means of powders and charms of this kind and also spells, was placed in such a position that he was completely worn out, his nails fell out, and his body lost all its hair. But when he was warned by one of this lady's maidservants, he violently snatched the keys of this lady's chests from her hands, and when the chests were opened this knight found in them a sack full of horrible and disgusting things of this kind which, with their contents, he arranged for two religious priests to deliver to the aforementioned bishop. Seventhly, that this lady had a demon (which had itself called Son of Art or sometimes Robin Artisson) as an incubus, which she allowed to have sex with her: sometimes it also appeared to her in the form of a cat, sometimes in the form of a furry black dog, sometimes in the form of a black man with two companions larger and taller than him, some of whom carried an iron wand in their hands; she also entrusted herself and all her things to him and acknowledged that she had received from him also all her wealth and everything she possessed.

Primary Sources and Related Texts

A contemporary narrative of the proceedings against Dame Alice Kyteler, prosecuted for sorcery in 1324 by R. de Ledrede, Bishop of Ossory, Camden Society 24, 1843.

The sorcery trial of Alice Kyteler: a contemporary account (1324) together with related documents in English translation, with introduction and notes, ed. L. Davidson and J. Ward, Binghamton, NY, 1993.

Curia Regis Rolls 16 no. 1403 (1237–42) for suspicion of death by witchcraft.

Theodore's *Penitential* 1.xv.4 for seventh-century punishments for sorcery.

William of Malmesbury, *GR* 2.204 on the sorceress of Berkeley.

Further Reading

Kors, A. and Peters, E. (ed.) (2001) *Witchcraft in Europe, 400–1700: a documentary history*, Philadelphia, PA.

Neary, A. (1983) 'The origins and character of the Kilkenny witchcraft case of 1324', *Proceedings of the Royal Irish Academy* 83C: 333–50.

Section II.33

John of Gaddesden, an Operation to Remove a Cataract, from
Rosa Anglica (*The English Rose*) (excerpt: f. 110v.1 in 1502
edition; f. 141v in 1492 Pavia edition)
A: Dedicatory Letter by Phillip Schopff in the 1595 Edition of *Rosa Anglica* (excerpts: ff. 3r–4r)
B: John of Gaddesden, *On the Cataract* (*De cataracta*)

Date: c.1313.

The numerous MSS of this work are listed in *Sharpe (1997); most of them are in Britain, but some are now in Continental libraries.

Author: John of Gaddesden (c.1280–1349) studied at Oxford in the new faculty of medicine between 1307 and 1316, during which time he wrote the *English Rose* (*Rosa Anglica*, also known as *Rosa medicinae*). He was then in royal service as a physician but also held various ecclesiastical posts, some by royal and papal appointment. Gaddesden was the first English, Oxford-trained physician to have an international reputation, though the French physician Guy de Chauliac later scorned his lack of originality. He is mentioned, along with the earlier English physician Gilbertus Anglicus, by Chaucer in line 434 of the prologue to the *Canterbury Tales*, and it is possible that he was the model for Chaucer's 'doctour of phisike'. His death in 1349 was possibly the result of the plague.

Work: The *English Rose* is a compendium of information on the treatment of many ailments, starting with those of the head and moving down the body. It draws on many earlier authorities, from Galen (in new Latin translations from the Arabic versions of this Greek text), Constantinus Africanus and the Arabic Avicenna to more contemporary medics of Paris and Montpellier. However, there is evidence of its English origin, as for example on f. 50 when he mentions certain pustules *et vocantur anglice 'mesles'* (f. 40v.2), and more personally, it contains many comments offering Gaddesden's own experience and views, as when he writes of cataract operations, *ista passio est communis ... et cum possit hoc curare hic habebit pecuniam quasi infinitam* (f. 110v.1, 'this is a common ailment ... and anyone who can cure this will earn a more or less unlimited amount of money'). It was first printed in Pavia in 1492. A fifteenth-century Irish translation of part of the text survives. Here the section with directions for a cataract operation is given in the early fourteenth-century text of Gaddesden as printed in a 1502 edition, together with notes from the 1595 edition of the text (pp. 185–6) by the physician Philipp Schopff which alters the text in line with the principles of humanist Latin: this enables the reader to see some of the minor ways in which medieval Latin was regarded as in need of refinement by post-Renaissance scholars.

Linguistic points: Gaddesden uses the word *cataracta* for 'cataract of the eye' but also the word *aqua*, which was more common at this time when new technical terms were just coming into Latin from Greek and Arabic. *plumaceolum*, as a pad used by doctors, occurs only in medical texts: Gaddesden also uses another diminutive, *pulvillus*, as a synonym (f. 122v.2). As noted in the linguistic discussions of Roger Bacon (Section II.28), technical terms were sometimes taken over in their original language and sometimes replaced by neologisms or calques in Latin. The passage from Schopff's later edition of the *English Rose* provides evidence of an awareness, as also seen in Bacon's work, of the problems involved in writing scientific Latin.

A: Dedicatory Letter by Phillip Schopff in the 1595 Edition of *Rosa Anglica* (excerpts: ff. 3r–4r)

TEXT II.33A

Scientific Latin deemed uncouth by the highly educated needs to be revised, but one should be wary of the pitfalls which can distort the message of the text
at multi sunt qui barbarorum doctorum scripta, quales superiora tempora tulere, legere non possunt: eo quod a Latinae linguae puritate atque elegantia abhorrent, et quod nauseam fastidiumque pariunt illius linguae studiosis (...). quaedam sermone latino puriori reddita sunt ne politioris literaturae viri ab illius lectione avocerentur; nonnulla etiam artis vocabula aut loquendi formas (etsi horridiores essent) intactas reliquimus ne si ornatum verborum studeremus, rerum veritatem amitteremus aut mentem auctoris minus dextre interpretaremur.

Translation

There are many who are unable to read the works of barbarous doctors such as earlier times produced because these works are at variance with the purity and elegance of the Latin language and because they engender disgust and distaste in those who are learned in that language (...). Some things are rendered in a purer Latin style so that men of a more refined education might not be put off reading this work;

306   Fourteenth Century

we have also left some technical terms or expressions untouched, even if they are somewhat unrefined, lest we should concentrate on the embellishment of the words to the detriment of the truth of the matter or should fail to interpret the author's intention correctly.

B: John of Gaddesden, *On the Cataract* (*De cataracta*)
f. 110v.1 (Schopff's 'improved' Latin readings or an indication that something has been omitted are given in brackets; Gaddesden's original versions of Schopff's readings are italicised)

TEXT II.33B

Instructions on how to remove a cataract from the patient's eye
tamen (Schopff 1595: attamen) ante operationem cum ferro nihil comedat illo die *stante* (constante) virtute. sedeat *ergo* (autem) patiens inter manus doctoris et plumaceolum planum in loco lucido *cum radio solis* (radiante sole) absque nebula. colligantur et genua eius usque ad pectus et ligentur; sedeat super scamnum *quasi* (quodammodo) supinus et convertat patiens intuitum suum ad nasum, aperiendo oculum lesum; et *serviens* (servus) teneat caput eius *posterius* (ad posteriora inflexum) et elevet palpebram. deinde *accipe* (sume) instrumentum vel acum ferream cum capite rotundo *et* (,) acuto et incipe perforare ex parte silvestri lachrymali, in ipsa coniunctiva, cum violentia impellendo versus pupillam, incipiendo a cauda oculi *et perforet* (eo usque perforet) *usque quo veniat* (donec venerit) supra uveam et *supra* (om.) pupillam *perforando intra tunicam et tunicam* (inter duas tunicas) *quousque veniat ad vacuum oculi* (ad vacuum usque oculi penetrando) quod est ante pupillam. *et teneat medicus* (teneatque chirurgus) oculum *quousque perforatio facta sit* (donec absoluta fuerit perforatio) *et comprimat* (prematque) aquam deorsum cum instrumento et occultet eam sub cornea. et quod instrumentum sit in foramine, scietur ex *tactu* (tractu) *policis* (pollicis) super locum *et* (sed) non extrahatur statim instrumentum illud *sed* (verum) maneat aliquantulum ut aqua superius non revertatur et itera *deponens illius aquam* (aque illius depositionem) frequenter, *si vis* (pro necessitate et arbitrio tuo); elevetur igitur acus et postea comprimatur et involvatur ibi; deinde extrahatur. ex parte inferiori oculi non fiat perforatio ne humor albugineus exeat sed in

?l. elogio   angulo eque alto cum pupilla. interea confortetur patiens cum *bono elogo* (bonis verbis) et mitigetur timor eius et *quaeras si videat aquam depositam* (quaere num aquam depositam sentiat). si sic, bene *est* (se res habet). si *non* (minus), non est tunc (om.) complete *deposita* (aqua educta) vel est error in perforando (sed vel error est commissus in perforando) vel (quia) materia ista dimissa est *et tunc* (om.) *redeundum est* (redeundum ad illius pleniorem dispositionem) *et deponatur melius* (om.). deinde *emplastrum fiat super oculum* (supra oculum ponatur emplastrum) *de* (ex) vitello ovi, oleo rosato et violarum *superponatum* (et su-perimponatur) *cum pulvillo* (pulvillus) de *stupa* (stuppa). *stet* (versetur) in loco obscuro per 7 dies (septem diebus), vitet motum *et* (,) sternutationem et tussim.

Translation: John Gaddesden, *The English Rose*

However, before an operation with a metal instrument (the patient) should not eat anything on that day, if he is strong enough. The patient should sit between the doc-tor's hands and a flat feather pad in a brightly lit place facing the sunlight without any cloud, and his knees should be bent up to the chest and tied. The patient should sit on a stool, leaning right back, and he should focus on his nose, with the damaged eye open while the assistant holds his head back and lifts the eyelid. Then take the instrument or metal needle with a sharp, rounded point and begin to make a hole on the outer side by the lachrymal gland in the conjunctive membrane by pushing it with some force towards the pupil, starting from the outer corner of the eye; the needle should drill through until it reaches the area above the uvea and above the pupil, making a hole between the two tunics until it comes to the empty area in front of the pupil. And the doctor should hold the eye until the drilling is completed and he should press the cataract downwards with the instrument and conceal the cataract beneath the cornea. He will know when the instrument is in the aperture by placing his thumb on the spot; he must not pull the instrument out immediately but let it remain there for a while so that the cataract does not come up again: he should repeat this several times, pushing the cataract down, as he considers neces-sary; and so the needle should be raised and then pressed down and twirled there and then pulled out. The hole should not be made on the lower part of the eye to prevent the aqueous humour seeping out, but rather in the corner on a level with the pupil. Meanwhile the patient should be comforted with kind words and his fears calmed; ask whether he can see that the cataract has been removed: if he can, that is good, but if not, then the cataract has not been completely removed or there has been an error made in the drilling or there has been a discharge of that fluid and the doctor must start again and remove the cataract more successfully. Then put a dressing on the eye, made of egg yolk, oil of roses and violets, with a compress of hemp. The patient should remain in a dark room for seven days, avoid movement and sneezing and coughing.

Primary Sources and Related Texts

John of Gaddesden, *Rosa Anglica*, Venice, 1502.
John of Gaddesden, *Rosa Anglica practica medicine a capite ad pedes, noviter impressa et perque diligentissime emendata*, ed. P. Schopff, Augsburg, 1595.
Roger Bacon, *Opus majus*, part 5 on optics.

Further Reading

Demaitre, L. (2013) *Medieval medicine: the art of healing, from head to toe*, Santa Barbara, CA.

Eldredge, L. (1997) 'The anatomy of the eye in the thirteenth century', *Micrologus* 5: 145–60.

Gaye, F. (1998) *Medicine in the English Middle Ages*, Princeton, NJ.

Grant, E. (ed.) (1974) *A sourcebook in medieval science*, Cambridge, MA.

Langslow, D. (2000) *Medical Latin in the Roman Empire*, Oxford.

Leffler, C. T. et al. (2021) 'The first cataract surgeons in the British Isles', *American Journal of Ophthalmology* 230: 75–122.

McVaugh, M. (2001) 'Cataracts and hernias: aspects of surgical practice in the fourteenth century', *Medical History* 45: 319–40.

Section II.34

Historians of the Fourteenth Century
A: Henry Knighton, *Chronicle* (*Chronicon*) (excerpt: pp. 92–4)
B: Thomas Walsingham, *The Major Chronicles* (*Chronica majora*)
(excerpts: vol. 1, pp. 496–500, 544–6)

This section presents excerpts from the historical works of some of the many
Latin writers of the fourteenth century who were contemporaries of such English writers as Geoffrey Chaucer and John Gower. The passage from Knighton's
Chronicle describes an event in 1348, just before the coming of the Black Death,
and the passages from Thomas Walsingham's *Major Chronicles* deal with some
events during the Peasants' Revolt of 1381.

A: Henry Knighton, *Chronicle* (*Chronicon*) (excerpt: pp. 92–4)

Date: c.1390.

BL MS Cotton Tiberius C.vii is one of two MSS containing the *Chronicle*: it was
revised under Knighton's supervision and contains some lines possibly in his own
hand, on f. 62. The slightly later BL MS Cotton Claudius E.iii is regarded as de-
rivative.

Author: Knighton (died c.1396) was one of a number of chroniclers of the reign
of Richard II. He was associated with Leicester, where he was a canon at the Augustinian abbey of St Mary of the Meadows.

Work: Knighton's *Chronicle* covers English history from a brief introduction on
the century before the Conquest down to the end of the fourteenth century, partly using Ralph Higden and Walter of Guisborough as sources. His account of the
last half-century, dealing with events in Knighton's own lifetime, including the
rise of Lollardy and the Peasants' Revolt of 1381, is particularly vivid. He was also
interested in social history, as his treatment of the Black Death shows (Section
II.43A). Here a passage from 1348 has been selected, recording a tabloid-hitting
feature involving women dressed as men presenting themselves on horseback at
tournaments, an episode regarded as typical of this turbulent period.

Linguistic points: Knighton's Latin contains much of linguistic interest as far as
vocabulary goes, for the very readable Latin actually contains many borrowings

Fourteenth Century

and neologisms, as well as rare classical words like *clepere*, derived from Greek. In the first passage is found *liripipa*, associated with extravagantly pointed headgear, rather than with shoes as in John of Garland (cf. Section II.28A). *hastiludium*, compounded of *hasta* and *ludus*, is the usual Latin word for a tournament in BML. Its synonym *torneamentum* occurs already in William of Malmesbury (*GR* 3.257: *in quodam quod vocant torniamento ad mortem laesus*) though throughout the twelfth century the word is referred to as slightly unfamiliar, from the French vernacular 'tournai', which would give the standard English word, 'tournament', rather than the rare 'hastilude'. *secta* here occurs with the sense of a set of artefacts or pieces of cloth, in an idiomatic phrase meaning 'matching'. *secta* in BML in fact has a range of meanings which give English the useful words 'suit', 'suite', 'sect' and 'set', for which compare *discus* and the English words deriving from it (cf. Section II.22). *daggerius* is apparently derived from English, in which language its first appearance is in the Latin context of a Coroner's Roll in 1349: *Willelmum felonice interfecit cum quodam cultello qui vocatur 'daggere'* ('he killed William feloniously with a knife that is called a "dagger"'). Shortly afterwards it appears in Knighton in the Latin form *daggerius*, though the context, *cultellos quos daggerios vulgariter vocant*, shows that it is felt as a vernacular word. In Walsingham's *Major Chronicles* 1.838 it occurs in the form *extracto cultello daggardo*, though the form 'daggard' in English is rare and later. *powchia* is one of the variants of *poca*, related to French 'poche' (possibly deriving from a north Germanic word) but with a pronunciation that relates it to modern English 'pouch', whereas the form *poca* survives in the noun 'poke', as in the expression 'a pig in a poke'.

TEXT II.34A

An unusual tournament

[*s.a.* 1348, p. 92] illis diebus ortus est rumor et ingens clamor in populo eo quod ubi hastiludia prosequebantur, quasi in quolibet loco dominarum cohors affuit, quasi comes interludii in diverso et mirabili apparatu virili, ad numerum quandoque quasi xl, quandoque l dominarum, de speciosioribus et pulcrioribus, non melioribus tocius regni, in tunicis partitis scilicet una parte de una secta, et altera de alia secta, cum capuciis brevibus et liripiis ad modum cordarum circa capud advolutis, et zonis argento vel auro [p. 94] bene circumstipatis in extransverso ventris sub umbilico habentes cultellos quos daggerios wlgariter dicunt, in powchiis desuper impositis. et sic procedebant in electis dextrariis vel aliis equis bene comptis de loco ad locum hastiludiorum. et tali modo expendebant et devastabant bona sua et corpora sua ludibriis et scurilosis lasciviis vexitabant, ut rumor populi personabat. et sic nec Deum verebantur nec verecundam populi vocem erubescebant, laxato matrimonialis pudicicie freno. (…) sed Deus in hiis sicud in

l. liripipiis

cunctis aliis affuit mirabili remedio, eorum dissipando dissolucionem. nam loca et tempora ad hec vana assignata imbrium resolucione tonitrui et fulguris coruscacione et variarum tempestatum mirabili ventilacione preocupavit.

Translation: Knighton, *Chronicle*

In those days a rumour arose and great to-do among the people because when tournaments were held, a troop of ladies turned up in nearly every place, as if they were part of the entertainment for the interlude, dressed in various kinds of men's clothes, which was rather shocking, up to forty or fifty of them, very handsome and beautiful, but not of the kingdom's better ranks, in matching particoloured tunics, with short hoods and liripipes wound round their heads like ropes, with belts beautifully studded with gold and silver across their stomachs, with knives (commonly known as daggers) to hand below their waists in pouches strung onto the belts. Dressed like this they rode on choice chargers or other beautifully groomed horses from one tournament to the next. And in this way they spent and used up their money and tormented their bodies with wanton and scurrilous acts of unrestrained behaviour, as announced by popular rumour. And so, once they had slipped the bridle of matrimonial modesty, they neither feared God, nor did the people's outcry at their lack of propriety cause them to feel shame. (…) But God, in this as in all other things, came with a wonderful remedy to dispel their followers' dissolute behaviour. He forestalled the times and places organised for these frivolous events with a downpour and thunder and lightning as an extraordinary number of different storms blew over them.

Primary Sources and Related Texts

Knighton's Chronicle (1337–1396), ed. G. Martin, OMT, Oxford, 1995.
For the appearance of the women at the tournaments, cf. the account in the *Chronicle of Meaux*, RS 43.3 (1868) 69.
For the inundation of 1348, cf. Walsingham, *Chronicon Angliae* 26; for a downpour in seventh-century Jerusalem, cf. Adomnán, *The Holy Places* (Section I.5A).

Further Reading

Gransden, A. (1982) 'Chroniclers of the reign of Richard II' in *Gransden (1982).
Netherton, R. (2005) 'The tippet: accessory after the fact?' in *Medieval clothing and textiles* (2005–), vol. 1.

312 Fourteenth Century

B: Thomas Walsingham, *The Major Chronicles* (*Chronica majora*) (excerpts: vol. 1, pp. 496–500, 544–6)

Date: c.1400.

This work is contained in BL MS Royal 13.E.ix, which goes up to 1392, while Bodleian MS 462 continues until 1420.

Walsingham's *Major Chronicles* are a continuation of the thirteenth-century work of the same name by Matthew Paris. As the complete form of the text does not exist in any single MS, and occurs in a long and a short form, it is found confusingly dispersed and variously titled, also in printed form, made up of *Chronicon Angliae* (1328–88), *Historia Anglicana* (1272–1422), *Annales Ricardi II et Henry IV* and the *St Alban's Chronicle 1406–20*. The first three titles in this list were published in the Rolls Series. The *Major Chronicles* have now been edited in the OMT series under the title *The St Alban's Chronicle: the Chronica maiora of Thomas Walsingham*.

Author: Thomas Walsingham (c.1340–c.1422) was a monk of St Albans who is known as a great chronicler of his monastery and of British history of the long fourteenth century, but he also wrote works on music theory and was interested in classical literature and mythology, as demonstrated by the work *Archana deorum*, a commentary on Ovid's *Metamorphoses*. Walsingham's historical writings were used as sources by such chroniclers as Froissart in the fourteenth century and Holinshed in the sixteenth.

Work: Walsingham's account of the Peasants' Revolt, which grew out of dissatisfaction with the social conditions and new laws and taxes after the Black Death, is one of the most important in Latin, alongside the accounts of Knighton and the Westminster Chronicle, together with the French *Anonimalle Chronicle* and the *Chronicle* of Froissart.

The passages here selected tell of the rebels' murderous fervour against learning, and give the confession, in the first person, of the rebel leader Jack Straw regarding the insurgents' plans, including killing the king and burning down London. This is followed by a summary of the sermon of the wandering priest John Ball at Blackheath, in London, on the words from the popular English rhyme, 'When Adam delved and Eve span'. Ball's sermon culminates with the slogan of liberty and equality of rank, dignity and power that summed up the social demands of the rebels, *equa libertas, eadem nobilitas, par dignitas, similisque postestas*. In July 1381 Ball was captured in Coventry and executed at St Albans.

Linguistic points: The confession of Jack Straw includes an unusual series of contracted forms of the pluperfect subjunctive (*conflassemus* etc.), which are suitable for expressing the unfulfilled past plans of the peasantry. *tricen(n)alis*, from the CL distributive *triceni*, i.e. 'thirty each', became a technical term as adjective or noun to refer to a series of thirty masses for a recently deceased person, payment for which went to the Church; the word also exists in the form *trentale*, closer to the AN/ME form 'trental'. The passage about John Ball's final weeks contains the description of his execution, involving 'dragging' (*tractio*), hanging, decapitation, disembowelling (*exenteratio*) and quartering (*quarterizatio*): these Latin nouns appear to occur first in Walsingham.

TEXT II.34B

The insurgents' plans to eradicate learning in the Peasants' Revolt: anyone with an inkpot was a target

[vol. 1, p. 496] ex operibus quippe iudicandi sunt quia patrem tocius cleri et **Rev. 20:13** caput ecclesie Anglicane, archiepiscopum Cantuariensem, occiderunt.[1] in fidei quoque detrimentum quid fecerunt? magistros scolarum grammaticalium iurare compulerunt se nunquam parvulos instructuros in arte prefata. amplius quid fecerunt? munimenta vetera studuerunt dare flammis et ne de novo quis reperiri valeret qui vetera sive nova de cetero posset vel nosset commendare memorie, huiusmodi trucidabant. periculosum erat agnosci pro clerico, set multo periculosius si ad latus alicuius atramentarium inventum fuisset; nam tales vix aut nunquam ab eorum manibus evaserunt.

Translation: Thomas Walsingham, *The Major Chronicles*

By their works they must be judged, for they murdered the father of all the clergy, the head of the church, the Archbishop of Canterbury. What else did they do to destroy the faith? They forced the masters of the grammar schools to swear that they would never teach young boys the art of grammar. What more did they do? Their aim was to burn ancient documents, and so that no one could be found again who had the ability or knowledge in future to commit to memory old things or new, they murdered men of this sort. It was dangerous to be recognised as a clerk, but far more dangerous if an inkpot were found at someone's side; for such men hardly ever, or never, escaped from their clutches.

---

1 For the ecclesiastical penalties of murdering Archbishop Simon Sudbury (1375–8) meted out to those responsible, see *Sermon* 99 of Thomas Brinton, Bishop of Rochester (1373–89).

Jack Straw's Confession

[p. 496 cont.] quid in regni destruccionem cogitaverant, probat confessio Johannis Straw, qui fuit, post Walterum Tylere, maximus inter illos. hic cum captus esset et Londoniis maiore dictante sentenciam, capite privandus esset, maior Londoniarum, postquam dampnatus fuisset, puplice eum taliter est allocutus, 'Johannes,' inquit, 'ecce mors tua instat absque dubio, et nullam sperare potes viam evadendi. quapropter in adiutorium tui exitus, et pro salute anime tue, absque mendacio narra nobis propositum quod inter vos concepistis, ad quem finem turbam comunium commovistis.' cumque aliquandiu hesitaret et differret loqui, maior subiunxit, 'Scias firmissime, o Johannes, que precipio, si hiis parueris, in anime tue comodum conversura; set et ego in adiutorium anime tue plures tricennales missas faciam celebrari.' multique qui aderant ex civibus idem promiserunt, unusquisque pro persona. ipse vero, iam animatus tam pulchris pollicitacionibus, ita cepit:

Jack Straw: [p. 498] 'Iam', ait, 'mentiri non expedit, nec fas est falsa proferre; presertim cum ea noverim spiritum meum tormentis artioribus deputandum et quia duplex spero comodum ex veritate dicenda; primo, quia reipublicae profectura sunt que dicam et postea iuxta promissa vestra, post mortem vestris suffragiis adiuvari, sine fuco eloquar falsitatis. eo tempore quo ad le Blakehethe convenimus, quando pro accersiendo rege destinavimus, propositi nostri fuerat, cunctos milites, armigeros et ceteros generosos qui cum eo venissent, morti subito tradidisse; ipsum quoque regem, inter nos regaliter exhibitum in universis, nobiscum de loco ad locum traduxisse ut, eo viso, omnes et precipue commune vulgus ad nos et nostram turbam transmigrare debuissent audacius, qui viderent ipsum regem esse velut auctorem nostrae commotionis. cumque innumerabilem turbam conflassemus per omnes patrias comunis plebis, repente dominos mortificassemus, in quibus consilium contra nos vel resistencia esse potuisset; et primo et principaliter, destruccioni Hospitulariorum vacassemus. postremo regem occidissemus, et cunctos possessionatos, episcopos, monachos, canonicos, rectores insuper ecclesiarum, de terra delevissemus. soli mendicantes vixissent super terram qui suffecissent pro sacris celebrandis aut conferendis universe terre. cum vero nullus maior, nullus fortior, nullus sciencior, nobis superfuisset, leges condidissemus ad placitum, quibus subiecti regulati fuissent. nam et reges creassemus, Walterum Tylere in Cantia, et in ceteris comitatibus singulos, prefecissemus. set quia istud nostrum propositum impeditum fuit per archiepiscopum, maiori odio exarsimus contra eum, et cicius studuimus tradere eum morti. rursum, eo die advesperascente quo occisus est Walterus Tylere, proposuimus quia comune vulgus Londoniensium nobis favebat, et precipue pauperiores, iniectis ignibus in quatuor partibus civitatis, urbem repente cremasse, et omnia preciosa reperta inter nos pro libito divisisse.' (...) post hanc confessionem factam, decapitatus est et capud eius [p. 500] positum super pontem Londoniis, iuxta capud college sui, Walteri Tylere.

Translation: Thomas Walsingham, *The Major Chronicles*

What their plan was for the destruction of the kingdom is proved by the confession of Jack Straw, who was, after Wat Tyler, the greatest of the rebels. After Straw had been arrested and was going to be beheaded in accordance with the sentence given by the mayor of London, the mayor addressed him publicly as follows:

'John, you see that your death is assuredly at hand and you cannot hope for any means of escape. And so, to assist your departure and for the salvation of your soul, tell us without any lies the plan you had concocted together and what your goal was in stirring up the common people.' When Jack hesitated for a time and delayed speaking, the mayor added, 'You know very well, John, that if you obey my instructions it will benefit your soul; but I too will help your soul by arranging to have a large number of trental masses celebrated.' Many of the citizens present made similar promises, each individually. Then Jack, encouraged by such attractive promises, began to speak thus: 'It no longer serves me to lie, nor is it proper to speak falsehoods, especially as I know my soul would be subjected to harsher torments if I did so. Moreover, I hope for two benefits if I speak the truth: firstly because what I say may be of use to the country and also because, according to your promises, I will have the support of your prayers after my death. When we assembled at Blackheath in order to arrange to meet with the king, our plan was to kill all the knights, squires and other gentlemen who came with him. Then we would have taken the king around with us from place to place in the sight of all so that when everybody, and especially the common people, saw him, they would willingly have joined us and our band, for it would have seemed to them that the king supported the rebellion. And when we had assembled an enormous crowd of common people throughout the country, we would immediately have murdered all those lords who could have opposed or resisted us. First and above all we would have proceeded to the destruction of the Hospitallers. Then we would have killed the king and driven out of the land all possessioners, bishops, monks, canons and rectors of churches. Only the mendicants would have been allowed to survive, for they would have been useful for celebrating services and conferring the sacraments throughout the country. Since there would have been no one left who was more powerful, stronger or more knowledgeable than us, we would have made laws to suit ourselves, by which all subjects would be ruled. Moreover, we would have appointed Wat Tyler as a king in Kent and a separate king in each of the other counties. Because this plan of ours was stopped by the archbishop, he was the object of our greatest hatred and we wanted to kill him as soon as possible. Again, on the evening of the day that Wat Tyler was killed, since the common people of London, especially the poor, were on our side, we planned to set fire to the city in four areas and to burn it down and to divide amongst ourselves everything valuable we found in it as we wished.' (…) After he had made his confession Jack Straw was beheaded and his head was placed on London Bridge next to that of his colleague, Wat Tyler.

316 Fourteenth Century

John Ball's sermon at Blackheath to 200,000 commoners
[p. 546] ut sua doctrina plures inficeret, ad le Blakheth, ubi ducenta millia hominum communium fuere simul congregata, hujuscemodi sermonem est exorsus: *Whan Adam dalf and Eve span | wo was þanne a gentilman?* continuansque sermonem inceptum, nitebatur per verba proverbii quo pro themate sumpserat, introducere et probare ab inicio omnes pares creatos a natura, servitutem per iniustam oppressionem nequam hominum introductam contra Dei voluntatem; qui, si Deo placuisset servos creasse, utique in principio mundi constituisset quis servus, quisve dominus, futurus fuisset. considerarent igitur iam tempus a Deo datum eis in quo, deposito servitutis iugo diutinae, possent, si vellent, libertate diu concupita gaudere. quapropter monuit ut essent viri cordati, et amore boni patrisfamilias excolentis agrum suum, et extirpantis ac resecantis noxia gramina que fruges solent opprimere, et ipsi in presenti facere festinarent. primo, maiores regni dominos occidendo, deinde iuridicos, iusticiarios et iuratores patrie, perimendo, postremo quoscunque scirent in posterum comunitati nocivos, tollerent de terra sua; sic demum et pacem sibimet parerent et securitatem in futurum, si, sublatis maioribus, esset inter eos equa libertas, eadem nobilitas, par dignitas, similisque potestas. cum haec et plura alia deliramenta praedicasset, commune vulgus eum tanto favore prosequitur, ut acclamarent eum archiepiscopum futurum et regni cancellarium.

John Ball is executed and disembowelled
[p. 544] hoc die (…) Johannem Balle presbiterum captum a viris Coventrensibus et pridie ductum ad Sanctum Albanum et regis presenciam, cuius maiestatem convictus est lesisse enormiter, auditum et confessum turpissima scelera, traxioni, suspendio, decollacioni, exentracioni et quarterizacioni, ut usu vulgari loquar, idem Robertus adiudicavit.

Translation: Thomas Walsingham, *The Major Chronicles*

So as to infect more people with his teaching, he preached a sermon at Blackheath, where 200,000 commoners had gathered at the same time, and he began his sermon with these words: 'When Adam delved and Eve span, who was then the gentleman?' Continuing the sermon he had begun, he attempted to use the words of the proverb he had taken as his theme, to propose and prove that all from the beginning were created equal by nature and that servitude was introduced, against the will of God, as the result of the unjust oppression of wicked men. If God had wished to create serfs he would definitely have appointed, already at the beginning of the world, who was to be a servant, who a master. They should therefore consider that God had now granted them time in which, having thrown off the yoke of their long-standing servitude, they could, if they wanted, enjoy the freedom they had long desired. He therefore advised them to be sensible and to hasten to act like a good head of the

*family who out of love tills the land and pulls up and cuts down the harmful weeds
which tend to choke the crops. Firstly killing the important people of the realm, then
killing the lawyers, judges and juries of the land, they should finally remove from
their country those who they know would be harmful in future to the common-
wealth. In this way they would at last acquire peace for themselves and security for
the future, if, once the nobles had been removed, they could all have equal freedom,
similar nobility, matching dignity and the same power. When he had preached these
and many other mad ideas, he became so popular among the common people that
they acclaimed him as a future archbishop and chancellor of the realm.*

*On that day (…) the priest John Ball, who had been captured by the men of
Coventry and taken on the previous day to St Alban's, into the king's presence, was
convicted of heinously committing treason against his majesty. He was heard and
confessed the most wicked crimes, and then Robert Tresilian sentenced him to be
drawn, hanged, beheaded, disembowelled and quartered, if I may use the everyday
terms.*

Primary Sources and Related Texts

The St Albans Chronicle: the Chronica Majora of Thomas Walsingham, vol. 1
(1376–94), vol. 2 (1394–1422), ed. J. Taylor, W. Childs and L. Watkiss, OMT,
Oxford, 2003, 2011.
The Chronica majora of Thomas Walsingham 1376–1422, transl. D. Preest,
Woodbridge, 2005.
John Gower, *Vox clamantis*, Book 1 (*Visio Anglie*), *The complete works of John
Gower*, ed. G. C. Macaulay, Oxford, 1899-1902.
The Anonimalle Chronicle (French).
Jean Froissart, *Chroniques* (French).

Further Reading

Clark, J. (2004) *A monastic renaissance at St Albans: Thomas Walsingham and
his circle (c.1350–1440)*, Oxford.
*Gransden (1982).
Justice, S. (1994) *Writing and rebellion: England in 1381*, Berkeley.
O'Brien, M. (2016) *When Adam delved and Eve span: a history of the Peasants'
Revolt of 1381*, London.

Section II.35

Wills of Lay Men and Women
A: Three Yorkshire Wills of the Late Fourteenth Century
B: A London Will of the Fifteenth Century (excerpt: pp. 549, 551)

A person's last will and testament can shed light not only on the life of the testator but also on the society of the time: on funeral arrangements, church services for the dead, the various people and institutions that have been important to the testator, as well as details about crafts, houses, furniture, clothes, textiles etc. Whereas in the Anglo-Saxon period it was the tradition to write wills in OE, after 1066 wills appear in both Latin and English or a combination of these languages.

Work: The majority of surviving wills are those left by men of the church and the aristocracy. Here are selected four examples of wills left by lay men and women. It is likely they were written by a clerk on the instructions of the testator.

Linguistic points: Latin wills, despite tending towards a formulaic nature (with terms like *mortuarium, aisiamentum* and *acquietatio* here), do present a certain variety, depending on the personal status of the testator, which may affect not only the personal possessions which are being bequeathed, but also the language and spelling in which this is recorded. In the following four wills are found such words of linguistic interest as the late form *blodius* ('blue'), which only appears in BML in the fourteenth century, though the alternative LL form *blavus* is attested in the seventh century. The ultimate origin of this colour word is unclear. *tristellum* ('trestle'; cf. Section II.36) is the medieval Latin form of 'trestle', the form common to AN and ME, which may itself derive from a diminutive form of Latin *transtrum* ('beam'). *braciatrix* is a feminine noun usually meaning a 'female brewer' or 'ale wife', but here it is used in apposition with *domus* (f.) to signify a 'brewhouse'. *grocerus* reflects the modern spelling 'grocer', but both the Latin and English forms are derived from Latin *grossarius*, one of whose senses is a wholesale dealer in everyday foodstuffs. *grossarius* itself was formed by adding the suffix *-arius* (denoting an agent) to *grossus*, a LL adjective with a plethora of senses that would produce such English words as 'gross' in the sense of 'large' or 'coarse', and in the sense of 'wholesale', and as a noun for the number 144, as well as 'groat' (via the Dutch 'groot') for a specific coin.

Wills can sometimes read like a lexicon of rare words. *pandoxatio* is one of a large number of words related to brewing, common in later BML, deriving from LL *pandochium* (from the Greek for an inn) but it may here be regarded as rare, for it seems that *seu bracione* is a kind of gloss to explain it: such a use of *seu* is common in BML when dealing with slightly unfamiliar words. It is common for vernacular words to appear in wills, sometimes as a gloss to the Latin, occasionally flagged as non-Latin by the use of *Anglice* ('in English'), and at other times just set within the Latin matrix but without any Latin termination. Examples of these are *skreu, breuled in fournes* (i.e. 'brew-lead in the furnace') and ME *maskfat* (i.e. 'mash vat'), this latter being a word used in Scotland and northern England, as here, in a document from York. CL *epitogium* ('overcoat'), which is indeed glossed by the educational writers Garland and Neckam (cf. Section II.28) with the French 'surcot', is here glossed with the English word 'courtepy', which appears in Chaucer's Friar's Tale, both roughly contemporary with this will. For *sterlingus*, cf. Section II.21B. As in many types of non-literary texts, the spelling can vary, even within a single text: here *cervisia* ('ale') occurs alongside *servisia*. *braseum* and *brasiare* are given as not uncommon alternatives for *bracium* and *braciare*, formed from OF. *shopa* occurs here in the 1437 will, in a recognisable form of what was originally an OE word, 'scoppa'. The Latin word occurs in many different spellings, only in post-Conquest texts; cf. Section II.47E for an example from 1405: in general at this period it signifies a workshop.

A: Three Yorkshire Wills of the Late Fourteenth Century (from *Testamenta Eboracensia*, vol. 1, Surtees Society 4 (1836))

TEXT II.35A(a)

17 August 1369: *The will of Emma, widow of John of Stonegate* (no. 66)
[p. 87] ego Emma Relicta Johannis de Stayngate quondam civis Ebor. xvii Aug. 1369. volo quod ipsa Agnes (filia Thomae Papenham) serviens mea juxta disposicionem executorum meorum totum braseum meum brasiet, et servisiam bonam faciet, et pecuniam inde levatam, deductis expensis racionalibus, liberet executoribus meis. item do et lego eidem Agneti melius plumbum meum, Anglice *breuled in fournes* cum cacabo quod fuerat suum, et unum *maskfat*. et volo quod ipsa Agnes habeat omnia utensilia ad domum braciatricem pertinencia usque ad finem anni primi post diem obitus mei et tenementum quod inhabito integrum. ita quod dicti executores pro dicto tenemento ad opus dictae Agnetis de bonis meis propriis pro firma illius tenementi satisfaciant vicariis dicti chori B. Petri Ebor. item volo quod ipsa Agnes juret, tactis sacrosanctis Evangeliis, quod durante anno predicto, de qualibet pandoxacione sive bracione, quam continget ipsam braciare pro anima mea animabusque omnium fidelium defunctorum, quatuor lagenas de meliori servisia pauperibus ad hostium ubi solebam trahere moram fideliter donet. et quod executores mei dictae Agneti de bonis meis satisfaciant pro cervisia predicta. lego Sibillae de Kent unum epitogium, Anglice *courteby*.

Translation

I, Emma, the widow of John de Stayngate formerly a citizen of York, 17 August 1369. I wish that Agnes (the daughter of Thomas Papenham), my servant, according to the arrangement of my executors should brew all my malt and make a good ale and she should pay to my executors the money raised from this, after reasonable expenses have been deducted. Also I give and bequeath to this same Agnes my better lead vessel, in English 'brew-lead in the furnace', together with the cauldron which had been hers and one mash vat. And I wish that this Agnes should have all my utensils belonging to the brewhouse until the end of the first year after the day of my death and the whole tenement which I live in, in such a way that the said executors for this tenement, for the use of the said Agnes, should make a payment, for the rent of this tenement, out of my own goods, to the vicars of the said choir of St Peter of York. Also I wish that this Agnes should swear, with her hand on the holy Gospels, that during the aforementioned year, from whatever act of brewing or brew which it happens that she brews for my soul and the souls of all the faithful departed, she will faithfully donate four gallons of superior-quality ale to the poor people at the door where I used to spend time. And that my executors should pay the said Agnes from my possessions for this ale. I bequeath to Sibyl de Kent one gown, in English a courtepy.

TEXT II.35A(b)

1393: *The will of John de Ryell, tailor (no. 154)*
[p. 194] Die Mårcur' proxime ante F.(estum) S.(ancti) Thomae A(nno) 1393 ego Johannes de Ryell cissor sepeliendum in cimiterio S. Augustini de Eden. Johanni filio meo unum *skreu* ferreum,[1] post decessum Margaretae uxoris meae, forpices meas, una cum tabula lata super quam sedebam ad suendum, unam sellam novam, unum arcum, meum gladium cum *bokeler*, et unam tabulam mensalem cum tristellis.

Translation

On the Wednesday just before the feast of St Thomas in the year 1393. I, John de Ryell, tailor, to be buried in the cemetery of St Augustine at Hedon. To my son John (I bequeath) one iron 'skreu', after the death of my wife Margaret, my shears, together with a broad table on which I used to sit to sew, one new saddle, a bow, my sword with a buckler and one board used as a table, with trestles.

---

1 For the English word 'skreu', set within the Latin matrix, see W. Skeat, *An etymological dictionary of the English language*, 1882–4 *s.v.* screw.

TEXT II.35A(c)

3 June 1397: *The will of Alice Mustardmaker of Ripon* (no. 172)
[p. 221] ego Alicia Mustardmaker de Ripon, sanae mentis, necis morsum michi attendens inevitabiliter imminere, condo et ordino testamentum (...) sepeliendum in cimiterio ecclesiae B(eati) P(etri) Apostoli Ripon. item lego unum equum pro mortuario meo. item lego quinque libras cerae ardendae circa funus meum, die sepulturae meae. item lego pro exequiis meis vij d. item lego Aliciae de Ripon tunicam de blodio. item volo ut una acra terrae, quae jacet in campo de Sharowe, venundatur et cum precio inde levato unus presbiter celebret per certum tempus pro anima mea. et residuum Thomae et Agneti uxori Johannis de Stayvlay filiis meis junioribus.

Translation

I, Alice Mustardmaker of Ripon, being in full possession of my faculties and of sound mind, considering that death's bite is inevitably closing in on me, draw up and prepare my will (...) that I should be buried in the cemetery of the church of St Peter the Apostle in Ripon. Also I bequeath one horse for my mortuary fee. Also I bequeath five pounds of wax to be lighted around my corpse, on the day of my burial. Also I bequeath for my funeral, 6d. Also I bequeath to Alice of Ripon a blue tunic. Also I wish that one acre of land, which lies in the field of Sharowe, should be sold and with the price raised from this, one priest should celebrate (Mass) for a definite period for my soul. And the remainder should go to Thomas and to Agnes, the wife of John de Stayvlay, my younger children.

B: A London Will of the Fifteenth Century (excerpt: pp. 549, 551)

TEXT II.35B

2 March 1437: *The will of Robert Otley*
[p. 549] in Dei nomine Amen. ego Robertus Oteleye civis et grocerus London' compos mentis et in bona mea memoria existens duodecimo die mensis Septembris anno Domino millesimo cccc^{mo} xxxvj^{to} anno regni regis Henrici sexti post conquestum[2] quinto decimo, condo et ordino presens testamentum meum

---

2 The numbering of kings from the Norman Conquest has encouraged a view of British history that excludes the period between the Roman settlement and the Conquest: it is interesting to note that this phrase becomes common in the fifteenth century.

322 Fourteenth Century

in hunc modum. (...) [p. 551] item voluntas mei predicti Roberti Oteleye talis est, scilicet quod predicti executores mei tam cicius (cit-) quo melius fieri poterit post meum obitum vendant omnia terras et tenementa mea vocata le Barge in Bokeleresbury.[3] in parochia Sancti Stephani de Walbrok London' ut in domibus, mansionibus, shopis, celariis, solariis, gardinis, viis, introitibus et aisamentis et aliis suis pertinenciis universis et quod ipsi qui mecum ex confidencia et ad usum meum feoffati existunt de et in omnibus eisdem terris et tenementis cum suis pertinenciis faciant inde statum illi vel illis cui vel quibus dicta vendicio fiat cum inde debite requisiti fuerint per dictos executores meos. et de pecunia de huius modi vendicione proveniente lego magistro et confratribus ecclesie Sancti Thome martiris de Acon[4] iuxta conductum[5] London' centum marcas sterlingorum ad exorandum devote perpetualiter pro anima mea et anima Johanne nuper uxoris mee animabusque parentum et benefactorum nostrorum et omnium fidelium defunctorum. et totum residuum eiusdem pecunie lego tam ad perimplendum istud testamentum quam ad faciendum et disponendum per dictos executores meos pro anima mea et aliis animabus predictis ut in distribucione pauperum domorum tenencium qui bona sua per adversitatem mundi amiserunt ac in acquietacione incarceratorum in prisonis pro debito detentorum, emendacione viarum concavatarum et magis profundarum circa London' et alibi in patria ac in maritagiis pauperum puellarum bone fame et in aliis operibus caritativis prout iidem executores mei melius viderint et sperent Deo placere et saluti anime mee et aliarum animarum predictarum proficere.

Translation

In God's name, Amen. I, Robert Otley, citizen and grocer of London, being of sound mind and having a good memory, on 12 September in the year of the Lord 1436 in the fifteenth year of the reign of King Henry, the sixth since the Conquest, compose and prepare this present will of mine in this way: (...) This is the wish of the aforesaid Robert Otley, namely that the aforementioned executors of mine, the sooner the better after my death, should sell all my lands and tenements called le Barge in Bucklersbury in the parish of St Stephen Walbrook in London, as for example in houses, dwellings, shops, cellars, upper storeys, gardens, roads, entrances and subsidiary buildings and all other things belonging to them. It is also my wish that those

---

3 Cf. Section II.47E for mention of Bucklersbury in the city of London in 1405.

4 This was the church dedicated to St Thomas Becket in London; it was independent of the monks of Canterbury who controlled Becket's shrine at the cathedral. On the site of the church in Cheapside now stands the Mercers' Hall.

5 This refers to the so-called Great Conduit, a man-made channel bringing water from Tyburn springs to Cheapside in the City of London.

who are enfeoffed with me, of and in each and all these same lands and tenements
with their appurtenances, on trust and for my benefit, should make an estate to the
person or persons to whom the said sale is to be made, when duly required to do so
by these executors of mine. And from the money deriving from a sale of this kind I
bequeath to the master and brothers of the church of St Thomas the martyr of Acon,
near the conduit in London, one hundred marks sterling so that they might pray devotedly and in perpetuity for my soul and the soul of Johanna, my former wife, and
for the souls of our parents and benefactors and of all the faithful departed. And all
the rest of this money I bequeath both to carry out this will and to do and dispose
by means of my said executors on behalf of my soul and the other souls mentioned,
as for example for the distribution to poor tenants of houses who have lost their
possessions through the world's adversity and for the release of those incarcerated in
prisons, detained for debt; for mending roads that have become hollowed out and
too deep around London and elsewhere in this country, and for the marriage portion of poor girls of good reputation and for other charitable works, as these same
executors of mine may see fit and may hope to please God and benefit the salvation
of my soul and the other aforementioned souls.

Primary Sources and Related Texts

A: *Testamenta Eboracensia* (1350–1500), 6 vols, Surtees Society (1836–1902).
B: Canterbury and York Society 42: Register of Henry Chichele, Archbishop of
    Canterbury (1414–43), vol. 2, 549–53.
Calendar of wills proved and enrolled in the Court of Husting (1258–1688), ed. R.
    Sharpe, 2 vols, London, 1889–90.
Bishops' registers are also a source of testamentary texts, as wills were often
    proved before the bishop.
Magna Carta (1215) 7–8 (cf. Section II.25).
Glanvill 7.5–6 on women and wills.

Further Reading

*Medieval dress and textiles in Britain: a multilingual sourcebook (2014).
Barron, C. (2017) 'The will as autobiography: the case of Thomas Salter, priest,
    died November 1558' in *Medieval London: collected papers of Caroline M.
    Barron*, ed. J. Rosenthal and M. Carlin, Kalamazoo, MI.
Helmholz, R. H. (1993) 'Married women's wills in later medieval England' in
    *Walker (1993).
Jefferson, L. (2022) *The Register of the Goldsmiths' Company: deeds and
    documents, c.1190–1666*, Woodbridge.

324 Fourteenth Century

Wray, S. K. and Cossar, R. (2012) 'Wills as primary sources' in *Rosenthal (2012).

Wright, L. (2011) 'On variation and change in London medieval mixed-language business documents' in *Code-switching in early English*, ed. H. Schendl and L. Wright, Berlin and Boston, 191–218, esp. 192–200 on a mixed-language will of 1425 from *London Metropolitan Archives* 7086/1.

FIFTEENTH CENTURY

Section II.36

Duke Humfrey Sets Up Home: the King's Grant of Furniture to His Son

Date: 4 March 1405.

TNA: C66/372 m. 5.

Work: This Patent Roll records the armour, weapons, furniture and kitchen-ware bought for Humfrey, Duke of Gloucester (1390–1447), by his father, King Henry IV, in preparation for Humfrey's move into a household of his own at Hadleigh Castle in Essex, above the Thames estuary. That he considered this his home for some time is shown by the fact that he was married in the village church here in 1422. Humfrey was to spend his life supporting his brother Henry V and acting as protector for the young Henry VI, his nephew, while involved in military, administrative, political and cultural affairs. The abbreviated phrase *ad quos etc.* is very common at the start of documents, standing for *ad quos hae literae pervenerint* ('to those who receive this letter') or similar. There is ellipsis of the expected verb of sending after *salutem*. The abbreviated phrase *in cuius etc.* is common at the end of documents: it stands for *in cujus rei testimonium, has litteras nostras fieri fecimus patentes* ('as witness to this we have arranged for this letter patent to be made') or some similar second clause. Indeed, a version of this phrase occurs in the first Letter Patent (in the TNA series C66) from 1201.

Linguistic points: This royal text perhaps surprisingly contains a combination of kinds of words that occur also in many other texts: Latin words formed from the vernaculars (often with Germanic origins), e.g. *bundellus* and *gunna* from English, *stuffura* and *harnesium* via French (both meaning 'equipment' and both of unknown origin); Latin words formed from a vernacular but ultimately derived from Latin, e.g. *parcella* from AN 'parcel', derived from the LL diminutive *particella*, and *standardum* (AN 'standard'), i.e. aphetic forms of OF 'estandard', ultimately from CL *extendere*. *sausaria*, here probably a pewter vessel rather than a salt cellar, has associations with CL *salsarius* but is affected by the French and English forms saus- or sauc-, from which modern English derives 'saucer', now specifically a small dish under a cup. Then there is the LL word derived from Greek, as many Late Latin words were: e.g. *creagra*, which is attested in BML from the eighth to the fifteenth centuries, predominantly in glossaries. Note the

328 Fifteenth Century

parallel of *grossa plumba in fornacibus posita* here with Section II.35A, *plumbum meum*, Anglice 'breuled in fournes', referring to a vessel essential for brewing ale. The twenty-three *paria cirotecarum de plate* are paralleled in a Latin will of the same period (*Test. Ebor.* no. 144) by *j payr glovys de playt quas lego Ricardo de Thryston*: note the use of French *de* in both, which means that both phrases are a mixture of Latin, English ('plate', i.e a thin piece of iron or steel) and French. These are but two of the many non-integrated vernacular words, both French and English, in this inventory.

TEXT II.36

A list of the Duke's household furniture

De Stuffura pro Castro de Hadlegh

[address] Rex omnibus ad quos etc. salutem.

sciatis quod de gratia nostra speciali concessimus carissimo filio nostro Humfredo Parcellas et Hernesia subscripta pro Stuffura castri nostri de Hadlegh ordinata, videlicet, Viginti et quinque *Doublettes*, Viginti et quatuor *Jakkes*, Sex *Basynettes*, Septem *Vysers*, Undecim *Palettes*, Viginti et Tria Paria Cirotecarum de *Plate*, Tresdecim Loricas, Quinque *Aventailles*, Quadraginta Arcus, Centum et Quatuor Bundellos de *Bykeryngtakell*, Decem Balistas, Quatuor Cophinos cum Quarellis, Tria *Banderikes* (?*baud-*), Viginti et novem *Pavisses*, cum Armis Sancti Georgii depictos, et quindecim *pavisses*, cum Armis Oxon. et Deverosse depictos, Tria Standarda, Unum Vexillum cum Armis Regis, Unum Cadum pro Armatura, Unam Tabulam pro Altari, cum diversis Ymaginibus depictam, Unum longum Ferrum pro Gunnis opturandis, Unum parvum Plumbum, ad similitudinem unius Tubbae factum, Diversas Parvas Pecias Telarum Plumbi, Unum Par Bilancium de Ferro, Quatuor veteres Tabulas pro Camera et Aula cum Septem longis Formellis et quatuor curtis Formellis, Unum vetus *Cupburd*. Duo Grossa Plumba in Fornacibus posita, cum Uno Parvo Plumbo, Unam Crucem Processionariam de Auricalco, Duo *Chargeours*, Quinque Duodenas Discorum, Tres Duodenas et Octo Sausarias de *Peutre*, Duas Magnas Ollas, cum quatuor Parvis Ollis de Aere, cum Uno Magno *Chaufour*, Quinque Patellas, Tres Cacabos Aereos, Quatuor Pelves, Duo Lavatoria de Auricalco, Unam Creacram, Quatuor Verna ferrea, Unum Par de *Rakkes*, Unam Craticulam, Unum *Fyrepanne*, Duo Paria de *Andeins*, Unum *Fryngpanne* ferreum, Unam Scalam, Unum Lectrum, Duos *Desques*, Et Tria Paria Tristellorum, Habendorum de Dono nostro. In cuius etc. Teste Rege apud Westmonasterium, quarto die Martii. Per ipsum regem.

Translation: Patent Roll for 1405, Duke Humfrey's Furniture

Regarding the provisions for Hadleigh Castle

The king (sends) greetings to all to whom (these letters arrive).

You should know that from our own special grace we grant to our dearest son, Humfrey, the items and equipment listed below for the provisions arranged for our castle of Hadleigh, namely: Twenty-five doublets, twenty-four jakkes, six basinets, seven vysers, eleven headpieces, twenty-three pairs of gloves of plate, thirteen suits of chainmail, five mouthpieces for helmets, forty bows, one hundred and four bundles of bickering-tackle (i.e. skirmishing weapons), ten crossbows, four leather boxes with crossbow bolts, three baldrics, twenty-nine pavises (large shields) painted with the arms of St George and fifteen pavises painted with the arms of Oxfordshire and Devereux, three standards, one standard with the king's arms, one container for armaments, one table for the altar painted with various images, one long piece of iron for stopping up the guns, one small lead vessel, made like a tub, various small pieces of lead weapons, one pair of iron scales, four old tables for the chamber and hall with seven long benches and four short benches, one old cupboard, two large lead vessels placed in furnaces, with one small lead vessel, one processional cross of brass, two chargers, fifteen dozen plates, three dozen and eight pewter sauce boats, two large pots with four small pots of bronze with one large vessel for heating water, five pans, three bronze cauldrons, four basins, two brass washbasins, one flesh-hook, four iron spits, one pair of racks, one gridiron, one firepan, two pairs of andirons, one iron frying pan, one balance, one lectern, two desks, and three pairs of trestles, to be received as a gift from us. In (witness) whereof etc. Witnessed by the king at Westminster, on 4 March. By the king himself.

Primary Sources and Related Texts

Foedera 8.314 (*Foedera, Conventiones et cujuscunque generis acta publica*, ed. T. Rymer, 20 vols, 1704–35). This is a massive source for a wide range of public documents, down to 1654; it can be consulted in this original edition, or in the 10 vols of the 3rd ed., published in the Hague (1739–45) or in the RC edition of 1816–69 (4 vols in 7).

Further Reading

Saygin, S. (2002) *Humphrey, Duke of Gloucester (1390–1447) and the Italian humanists*, Leiden.

Section II.37

The *Pennal Letter* from Owain Glyndŵr, Prince of Wales, to the King of France (excerpt: from part 2)

Date: 31 March 1406.

The *Pennal Letter* is preserved in Paris, Archives nationales MS J516.B.40 (part 1) and J516.A.29 (part 2), as its addressee was the king of France, Charles VI.

Author: Owain Glyndŵr (c.1359–c.1416), prince of Wales, the Welsh leader who fought for Welsh independence against the English.

Work: The *Pennal Letter* (named after the place in Wales where it was composed) is in two parts: the first (J516.B.40) is addressed to Charles VI, king of France, in which Owain pledges to give his allegiance to the pope at Avignon, who was regarded by many as the antipope, i.e. an illegitimate rival to the true pope. The second part (excerpted here) is a much longer letter in which he sets out the terms of that allegiance, regarding the state of the Welsh church and universities. Owain Glyndŵr offers to support the schismatic pope, Benedict XIII, based at Avignon, in opposition to the English Crown's support for the pope in Rome, Innocent VII. He will back Benedict as *verum Christi vicarium* ('Christ's true deputy') and trusts that Charles will speak on his (Glyndŵr's) behalf regarding the following twelve articles concerning the state and reform of Wales. Glyndŵr needs to regain control, as his ascendancy after his rebellion has begun to wane. He wishes to strengthen Welsh independence against England, primarily by furthering the use of the Welsh language and founding two universities, in the north and south. Henry of Lancaster, the 'usurper' mentioned in the document, is Henry Bolingbroke, who was currently King Henry IV of England. Note that there is still dispute over the relation between the church of St David's in Wales, and Canterbury, as at the time of Gerald of Wales (Section II.21), and anger against the barbarian English. This document, with its anti-English tone, has been referred to as 'the Welsh "Elgin Marbles"', in that it is a cultural artefact of importance which is preserved in a foreign collection and which should, it is felt, be returned to its country of origin.

Linguistic points: *data* with reference to *littera* means 'issued', being the past participle of *dare*; sometimes it occurs in the neuter rather than feminine, depending on what kind of document it refers to. This Latin past participle of this verb was most productive, providing other languages with several nouns: OE 'datarum', and ME and modern English 'date', as well as 'datum' in a number of European languages; in its neuter plural form it has of course provided modern English with 'data'. The *Pennal Letter* contains lengthy sentences, particularly characteristic of documents associated with the papacy, as is evident in the collection of *Vetera monumenta Hibernorum et Scottorum historiam illustrantia (1216–1547)*, ed. A. Theiner, Rome, 1864. *ambaxiatores* (*ambasc-*) only appears in BML at the end of the thirteenth century, but in Continental sources from the twelfth; it is not attested in English before Chaucer. Note the orthographic variations of s for c (*sensura*), and i for e (*evinire/heridibus/quartirizare*): such spellings are in fact more characteristic of the BML of the eighth century than the fifteenth, but may reflect regional spellings. For *quarterizare*, cf. the noun used in Section II.34.

TEXT II.37

Owain Glyndŵr makes demands of the French king regarding the ecclesiastical and cultural independence of Wales with regard to English overlordship

et primo si sensure ecclesiastice contra nos et subditos nostros seu terram nostram per prefatum dominum Benedictum aut Clementem predecessorem suum late existant, quod ipse Benedictus eas relaxet. item quod quecumque et qualiacumque juramenta per nos seu quoscumque alios principatus nostri illis qui se nominaverunt Urbanum et Bonifacium nuper deffunctos seu eisdem adherentibus qualitercumque prestita relaxet. item quod confirmet et ratificet ordines collatos, titulos prelatorum, dispensacionesque et officia tabellionum ac alia quecumque in quibus periculum animarum aut prejudicium nobis et subditis nostris in ea parte evinire seu generari possent a tempore Gregorii xi. item quod ecclesia Menevensis que a tempore sancti David archiepiscopi et confessoris fuit metropolitana et post obitum ejusdem successerunt eidem archiepiscopi ibidem xxiiij, prout in cronicis et antiquis libris ecclesie Menevensis nomina eorumdem continentur et hic pro majori evidencia eadem exprimi fecimus, videlicet Eliud, Keneu, Morwal, Menevie, Haerunen, Elwayd, Gvrnuen, Llevdiwyt, Gvrwyst, Cledavc, Ainan, Elave, Maesyswyd, Sadernuen, Catullus, Alathvy, Nouis, Sadernuen, Diochwael, Asser, Arthuel, David secundus, et Sampson, pristina statui restituatur; quequidem ecclesia metropolitana infrascriptas habuit et habere debet ecclesias suffraganeas, videlicet, Exoniensem, Battoniensem, Herefordensem, Wygorniensem, Legicestrensem, cujus sedes jam translata est ad ecclesias Coventrensem et Lichfeldensem, Assavensem, Bangorensem et Landavensem; nam ingruente rabie barbarorum Saxonum qui terram Wallie eisdem usurparunt, ecclesiam Menevensem predictam suppeditarunt et eam ancillam ecclesie Cantuariensis de facto ordinarunt.

332 Fifteenth Century

item quod idem dominus Benedictus provideat de metropolitano Menevensi ecclesie et aliis ecclesiis cathedralibus principatus nostri, prelaturis, dignitatibus et beneficiis ecclesiasticis, curatis scientibus linguam nostram dumtaxat. item quod dominus Benedictus in corporaciones, uniones, annexiones, et appropriaciones ecclesiarum parrochialium principatus nostri, monasteriis et collegiis Anglicorum quorumcumque auctoritate hactenus factas revocet et annullet et quod veri patroni earumdem ecclesiarum locorum ordinariis ydoneas personas presentare valeant ad easdem seu alias conferre. item quod dominus Benedictus concedat nobis et heredibus nostris principibus Wallie quod capella nostra de cetero sit libera et gaudeat privilegiis, exempcionibus et immunitatibus quibus gaudebat temporibus progenitorum nostrorum principum Wallie. item quod habeamus duas universitates sive studia generalia, videlicet unum in Northwallie et aliud in Swthwallie, in civitatibus, villis seu locis per ambaxiatores et nuncios nostros in hac parte specifiendis et declarandis. item quod dominus Benedictus contra Henricum Lencastrie intrusorem regni Anglie et usurpatorem corone ejusdem regni et sibi adherentes, eo quod ecclesias tam cathedrales quam conventuales et parochiales voluntarie combusit et comburi procuravit, archiepiscopos, episcopos, prelatos, presbyteros, religiosos tam possessionatos quam mendicantes inhumaniter suspendi, decapitari et quartirizari fecit et fieri mandavit et quod scismaticus existit, cruciatam concedere dignetur in forma consueta. item quod idem dominus Benedictus concedat nobis et heridibus nostris, subditis et adherentibus nobis cujuscumque nacionis fuerint dumtamen fidem teneant ortodoxam, qui guerram contra prefatum intrusorem sustinemus plenam remissionem omnium peccatorum et quod remissio hujusmodi duret guerra inter nos, heredes et subditos nostros et prefatum Henricum, heredes et subditos suos durante.

in cujus rei testimonium, has litteras nostras fieri fecimus patentes. data apud Pennal ultimo die Macii anno a Nativitate Domini millesimo quadringentesimo sexto et principatus nostri sexto.

Translation: The *Pennal Letter*

Firstly, if ecclesiastical censures broadly exist against us and our subjects or our country by the aforesaid lord Benedict or his predecessor Clement, we ask that Benedict should cancel them. Also that he cancel all the oaths of whatever kind made in whatever manner by us or any others of our principality to those who called themselves Urban and Boniface, recently deceased, or to the adherents of these men. Also that he should confirm and ratify the orders that have been conferred, the titles of the prelates, the dispensations and offices of the notaries and other such things from the time of Gregory XI from which there could arise or be produced spiritual danger and prejudice to us and our subjects in this matter. Also that the church of

St David's should be restored to its original status which has been the metropolitan church since the time of St David, the archbishop and confessor, and after his death twenty-four archbishops succeeded him there, just as their names are contained in the chronicles and ancient books of the church of St David's, and here we have had these same names written down as stronger evidence, namely Eliud, Ceneu, Morfaell, Mynyw, Haerwnen, Elwaed, Gwrnwen, Llewdwyd, Gwrwyst, Glydâwg, Aman, Elias, Maeslyswyd, Sadwrnwen, Cadell, Alaethwy, Novis, Sadwrnwen, Drochwel, Asser, Arthwael, David the second, and Samson. This same metropolitan church had and ought to have the following suffragan churches, namely Exeter, Bath, Hereford, Worcester and Leicester (the see of which has already been translated to the churches of Coventry and Lichfield), St Asaph, Bangor and Llandaff; for as the fury of the barbarian Saxons increases, they have appropriated the land of Wales for themselves, trampled underfoot the church of St David's and made it in reality subordinate to the church at Canterbury. Also that the same lord Benedict should provide the metropolitan church of St David's and other cathedral churches of our principality, with prelates, dignitaries and ecclesiastical benefices, and curates who at least know our language (i.e. Welsh). Also that lord Benedict should revoke and annul the incorporations, unions, annexations and appropriations of the parochial churches of our principality, made hitherto with the English monasteries and colleges by any authority whatsoever, and that the true patrons of these same churches should be able to present to the ordinaries of those places suitable beneficed persons to these same churches or appoint others. Also that lord Benedict should concede to us and to our heirs, the princes of Wales, that our chapels should henceforth be free and enjoy privileges, exemptions and immunities which they enjoyed in the times of our ancestors, the princes of Wales. Also that we should have two universities or 'studia generalia', namely one in North Wales and another in South Wales, in cities, towns or places to be specified and announced by our ambassadors and envoys in this matter. Also that lord Benedict should be good enough to grant a crusade in the usual form against Henry of Lancaster, the usurper of the kingdom of England and the usurper of the crown of this kingdom and his adherents, because he has of his own will burned churches – cathedral and conventual and parochial churches – and arranged for them to be burned, has inhumanely hanged, decapitated and quartered archbishops, bishops, prelates, priests, religious, both priests with a benefice and mendicants, and has ordered it to be done, and because he is a heretic. Also that the same lord Benedict should grant to us and our heirs, subjects and our adherents of whichever nation they may be, as long as they hold the orthodox faith, who wage war against the aforesaid usurper, full remission of all sins and that this remission should last as long as the war between us, our heirs and subjects, and the aforesaid Henry, his heirs and subjects, lasts.

In testimony to this, we have arranged for this letter patent to be made. Dated at Pennal on the last day of March in the 1406th year since the birth of the Lord, and the sixth year of our rule as prince.

334 Fifteenth Century

Primary Sources and Related Texts

Rees, D. and Jones, J. G. (ed.) (2010) *Thomas Matthews's Welsh Records in Paris: a study in selected Welsh medieval records*, Cardiff. Latin text, pp. 42–54; English translation, pp. 85–99.

Livingstone, M. and Bollard, J. (ed.) (2013) *Owain Glyndŵr: a casebook*, Liverpool.

Further Reading

Pryce, H. (ed.) (2005) *The acts of Welsh rulers 1120–1283*, Cardiff. Includes earlier grants, letters and agreements, mostly in Latin.

Section II.38

Sermon Writing
A: Thomas of Chobham, *Sermon* 23 for Palm Sunday (excerpt)
B: A Macaronic Sermon in Latin and English
C: A Ghost Story in a Preacher's Commonplace Book

The sermon has been a form of oral or written discourse used throughout the history of Christianity as a means of teaching, whether by explaining the biblical text or discussing theological and moral themes. Its prototype is Christ's Sermon on the Mount (Matt. 5–7), but as the Church developed, the sermon primarily found a place within the liturgy in church. Examples survive from late antiquity onwards, and indeed the sermons of, for example, Augustine were hugely influential. Sermons usually focused on the explanation of a particular biblical text, but in explaining one text, the author would range all over Scripture, introducing allusions and citations to make his point. Nevertheless, the sermon might vary considerably as to its language and register, depending on the intended audience/readership: for example, while Augustine's *Enarrations on the Psalms* and his *Tractates on St John* are literary texts of profound theology, his sermons, delivered before his congregation at Hippo in North Africa, contain more everyday language, with lively imagery and wordplay to make his message clear and memorable.

In Britain, Bede was particularly influenced by Gregory the Great in writing his *Homilies*, which take the form of biblical commentaries. In the twelfth and thirteenth centuries there was a flowering of this genre, as a vehicle of spiritual writing, with collections made, for example, of the sermons of the Cistercians Ælred of Rievaulx and John of Ford, the Carthusian Adam of Dryburgh, and Thomas of Chobham.

Further Reading

Charland, T. (ed.) (1936) *Artes praedicandi* in *Publications de l'Institut d'études médiévales d'Ottawa 7*, Paris. With works by Robert of Basevorn and Thomas Waleys.

Thayer, A. (2012) 'The medieval sermon: text, performance and insight' in *Understanding medieval primary sources: using historical sources to discover medieval Europe*, ed. J. Rosenthal, London.

336 Fifteenth Century

A: Thomas of Chobham, *Sermon* 23 for Palm Sunday (excerpt)

Date: c.1220.

This sermon from Thomas' collection was written into the thirteenth-century Cambridge MS CCC 455, ff. 89v–94v, immediately after his *Summa de arte prae-dicandi*. The passage below starts on f. 91r.

Author: Thomas (c.1168–c.1235) was a subdean of Salisbury who wrote a *Summa de arte praedicandi* advising preachers on both form and content, as well as a volume on penance (*Summa confessorum*) and one on virtue and vice (*Summa de commendatione virtutum et extirpatione vitiorum*). His sermons contain many biblical references as well as quotes from the Church fathers and from classical writers, e.g. Seneca the younger, Juvenal, Horace; Thomas also includes many interesting facts about the natural world.

Work: This is the sermon written for Palm Sunday, expounding the text of the Song of Songs 2.11–12. Thomas considers the passing of winter and the coming of spring, but warns that the flowers that appear are not all good. In this passage he interprets the first three of the seven bad kinds of flowers according to the moral ('tropological') sense as relating to worldly prosperity. He proceeds to discuss the three good kinds of flowers, interpreting them as those of innocence, penitence and patience. In this sermon Thomas shows how each biblical phrase, indeed, even a single word, can spark references to phrases from all over the Bible, which the author considers helpful in explaining the text. The sermon contains, besides the biblical allusions, references to Augustine, to Jerome's book on the interpretation of Hebrew names and to Gregory the Great's homily (1.6) on Ezechiel, as also to the *Distichs of Cato* (a popular teaching text in the medieval period), Juvenal's *Satires*, Horace's *Epistles*, Lucan's *De bello civili* (i.e. *Pharsalia*), Seneca's *Epistulae ad Lucilium* and Apuleius' *De deo Socratis*. For the range of his reading at this period, cf. Neckam's educational work *The Priest at the Altar* (Section II.28B).

Linguistic points: The reader enters a world of metaphor and allegory, led by the author from one biblical reference to another. The language and cadences are biblical, and yet the author does also refer to the literary classics of antiquity. The problem for the reader lies in following the train of thought from one image to another, rather than in deciphering rare words or deconstructing complex syntax. Thomas appears to use the otherwise unattested *enigrare* ('to blacken') but it is possible that since the text reads *ad enigranda*, the scribe was misled into thinking he had written the more common *denigrare* in its literal sense. Note the spelling *innoscencia*.

TEXT II.38A

Sermon for Palm Sunday
Sermo in ramis palmarum: iam hyems transit et ymber abiit et flores apparuerunt in terra nostra.

What do the flowers in the biblical text represent?
[Morenzoni p. 238] *flores apparuerunt in terra nostra.* sed sciendum est quod **Cant. 2:12** sunt boni flores et mali. de malis [p. 239] dicitur in Ysaia XL° *exsiccatum est* **Isa. 40:7** *fenum et cecidit flos.* et in Mattheo VII *a fructibus eorum cognoscetis eos.* non dicit **Matt. 7:20** 'a floribus' quia sepe pulcriores flores habet arbor que generat fetidos fructus quam illa que parturit bonos fructus. sicut flos sambusce pulcrior est quam flos vinee, sed tamen botri sambusce fetidi sunt et ad nichil valent nisi ad enigranda calciamenta, botri vinee dulces sunt et exhyllarant.

The seven flowers of worldly prosperity
septem sunt flores prosperitatis mundane quos multi preponunt floribus divinis. primus flos est sanitas corporis et decor eius; secundus nobilitas generis; tercius habundantia temporalium; quartus dignitas sive potentia secularis; quintus scientia; sextus facundia; septimus securitas status sui. ista septem videntur esse florida hic omnibus. de hiis in Ysaia XI: *percuciet Dominus flumen terrenorum, percuciet Dominus in predictis septem rivis.* est autem flumen Egypti Gyon quod **Isa. 11:15** sonat turpitudinis et significat prosperitatem mundanam quia sicut fluvius quanto magis crescit tanto magis turbidus est, ita prosperitas mundi quanto magis crescit tanto magis conturbationem habet. de primo flore, id est de sanitate vel decore corporis, XIII Job: qui *quasi flos egreditur et conteritur* etc. iste flos ad modicum **recte, Job 14:2** frigus periit et ad minimum estum marcescit et ad impetum venti cadit. unde Job: *egreditur* (quia perit per frigus etatis) *et conteritur*, quia sepe marcescit per estum egritudinis, cadit per ventum extremi flatus. de secundo flore, id est de nobilitate generis, legitur in Johanne I quod Dominus tales elegit *qui non ex sanguinibus* **John 1:13** *neque etc.* sed illos qui sunt *sine patre et matre*, ut Melchisedec, ad Hebreos VII. **Hebr. 7:3** de hoc legitur in Genesi XXXV quod ait Jacob ingredienti in Efratham, *mortua* **Gen. 35:19** *est uxor mea Rachel.* sic potest exponi: cum aliquis ingreditur Efratham, id est ascribit nomen suum inter potentes ratione sanguinis sui, moritur ei *Rachel,* que interpretatur *ovis,*[1] id est perit in eo simplicitas et innoscencia. hunc florem reprehenderunt antiqui philosophi. unde poeta, 'stemmata quid faciunt, quid prodest, Pontide, longo sanguine censeri generis', scilicet [p. 240] 'pictosque ostendere **Juv. Sat. 8.1–3** vultus maiorum', et post concludit, 'nobilitas animi sola est atque unica virtus'. **Juv. Sat. 8.20** et vulgariter dicitur, reprehensibilis est illa nobilitas que nascitur ex renibus.

---

1 Cf. Jerome, *Liber de nominibus Hebraicis* (PL 23.783).

338 Fifteenth Century

Ps. 149:8
(Septuagint)
Matt. 19:6
1 Cor. 7:27

Dominus piscatores elegit ut preessent imperatoribus non imperatorem piscatoribus, sicut ait Augustinus.[2] *piscatores regibus honera imponunt, quia alligant reges in compedibus et nobiles in manicis ferreis.* quis enim regum hoc iugum solvere audet? *quod Deus coniunxit, homo non separet,* ut in Matheo XIX. *alligatus es uxori? noli querere absolutionem,* ut prima ad Corinthios VII. si exempla antiquorum recte inquisiveris, melius per innobiles quam per nobiles, sicut ait, gubernata est ecclesia.

Eccl. 5:12
Juv. *Sat.* 10.22
Hor. *Epist.* 1.18.29

tercius flos sunt divicie seculares, sicut ait Salomon in Ecclesiaste V: *infirmitas pessima est quam vidi sub sole divicias congregatas in malum domini sui.* divitibus enim semper instant insidie, sed cantabit vacuus coram latrone viator; stulticiam paciuntur opes, sicut ait philosophus. sepe deficeret iniquitas si deesset facultas etc.

Translation: Thomas of Chobham, Sermon

Sermon for Palm Sunday: Now the winter is gone and the rain is past and flowers have appeared in our land.

(…) But one must be aware that there are good flowers and bad ones. Of the bad ones, it is said in Isaiah 40 (verse 8): 'the grass dries out and the blossom falls'. And in Matthew 7 (20): 'from their fruits you will know them'. He does not say 'from their flowers', because a tree that produces disgusting fruits often has lovelier flowers than one which brings forth good fruits, just as the flower of the sambuca is lovelier than the flower of the vine and yet the sambuca's berries are disgusting and only useful as black shoe polish, while the grapes on the vine are sweet and bring joy.

There are seven flowers of worldly prosperity which many people value more than divine flowers. The first flower is physical health and attractiveness; the second is nobility of birth; the third is an abundance of temporal belongings; the fourth is high rank or secular power; the fifth is knowledge; the sixth is eloquence; the seventh is security of one's position. Everyone considers these seven to be the most important. It is about these that it is written in Isaiah 11 (15): 'the Lord will strike the river of earthly things; the Lord will strike in these seven streams'. There is a river in Egypt called Gyon, which means 'wickedness', and it signifies worldly prosperity because just as the more the river swells, the more turbulent it is, so the more worldly prosperity increases, the more turbulence there is. Regarding the first flower, i.e. physical health and attractiveness, it is written in the thirteenth chapter of Job: 'he who goes out like a flower and is crushed etc.' This flower dies at the slightest cold and fades in the slightest heat and collapses when pushed by the wind. And so Job says: 'it goes out', because it dies in the chill of age and 'is crushed' because it often fades in the heat of illness, and it falls in the wind of extreme blasts. Regarding the second flower, i.e. nobility of birth, one reads in John 1 (13) that the Lord chose people who are

---

2 Augustine's actual words, in his *Enarratio* on Ps.149, are *elegit (Christus) prodesse imperatori de piscatore, non piscatori de imperatore* (CCSL 40.2188).

'not from blood relations nor etc.' but those who are without father and mother, like Melchizedek, in Hebrews 7 (3). In this connection one reads in Genesis 35 (16–19) that when Jacob was on his way into Efratha, he said, 'My wife Rachel has died.' This can be explained as follows: when someone enters Efratha, in other words, he enters his name among the powerful by reason of his blood, Rachel dies to him; since Rachel means 'sheep', this means that simplicity and innocence die in him. The ancient philosophers are critical of this flower, which is why Juvenal says: 'What do family trees matter, what good does it do, Pontidus, to be regarded as being from a long and noble line, namely to show the portraits of your ancestors?' And afterwards he concludes that nobility of soul is the one and only virtue. It is commonly said, that the nobility that is due to one's birth is reprehensible. The Lord chose fishermen so that they might rule over emperors, not an emperor to rule over fishermen, as Augustine puts it. The fishermen impose burdens on kings because they bind kings in fetters and noblemen in iron handcuffs. For who among kings dares to undo this yoke? 'What God has joined, let man not separate', as it says in Matthew 19 (6). 'Are you bound to a wife? Do not seek a divorce', as it says in 1 Corinthians 7 (27). If you rightly ask for some examples from the people of the past, the Church has been governed better by those who are not noble than by the noble, as he says.

The third flower consists of worldly wealth, as Solomon says in Ecclesiastes 5 (12): the worst sickness I have seen beneath the sun is wealth heaped up for the owner to his detriment. For rich people always live with the threat of sudden attack, while a person who travels empty-handed will sing when faced with a robber; wealth permits folly, as the philosopher said. If the opportunity did not arise, wickedness would rarely succeed.

Primary Source

T. Chobham, *Sermones*, ed. F. Morenzoni, *CCCM* 82A, Turnhout, 1993: 238–40.

Further Reading

Evans, G. (1985) 'Thomas of Chobham on preaching and exegesis', *Recherches de théologie ancienne et médiévale* 52: 159–70.

Morenzoni, F. (1995) *Des écoles aux paroisses: Thomas de Chobham et la promotion de la prédication au début du XIIIe siècle*, Paris.

B: A Macaronic Sermon in Latin and English

The medieval period in Britain is studded with texts using more than one language in various ways and for various reasons. Examples of English texts

340 Fifteenth Century

containing Latin tags and quotations are the *Ancrene Wisse* (indeed, this work can be regarded as bilingual) and *Piers Plowman* as well as many ME sermons. Here is an example of a kind of text in which occasional words and phrases from a second language (here, English) are integrated into a primarily Latin text. This kind of code-switching is often referred to as 'macaronic', but here it lacks the riotous humour often associated with the term. This text is one of a number of sermons dating from the period 1350–1450 and is an example of a more extreme form of the mixture of languages: the Latin is dominant, but the English is syntactically integrated and is not restricted to glosses or to marking divisions in the carefully structured text. The question of what these texts say about the linguistic abilities of those who wrote them down and whether they were composed and/ or delivered in Latin, English or in both languages is still open for discussion. However, the recent work both of sociolinguists studying code-switching in vernacular languages and of, e.g., Laura Wright on mixed-language texts, has shown how those who are thoroughly bi- or trilingual move easily between languages, using a word or phrase from another language not because of any lack of linguistic skills: this was clearly the case in certain fields particularly in the late medieval period, where specialists moved fluidly between one language and another, aided by the frequent similarities between Latin, French and English. The audience for these sermons is likely to have been ecclesiastical or academic, though some such sermons are specified as being directed also to a lay audience.

Sermon O-07 from the collection in Bodleian MS 649 (excerpt: lines 155–66, 180–214)

Date: early fifteenth century.

Bodleian MS 649 (early fifteenth century) ff. 40v–48.

Work: This MS contains a large number of fully macaronic sermons. This anonymous sermon has an unusually high ratio of English words which are not technical terms or glosses, though the matrix is always Latin. The preacher gives an allegorical interpretation of the spiritual vine which must grow with the strong branches of justice and mercy in the vineyard representing the fertile realm of England. The sermon is based on the text 'De caelo querebant' ('they asked him (for a sign) from heaven') (Luke 11:16). The section excerpted here, in which the learned writers Robert Grosseteste, Johannes de Sacrobosco (both English of the early thirteenth century) and Isidore of Seville are referred to, opens a lengthy comparison between the sky and the Church, with the striking image of Christ as a stonemason with his compass, or himself a compass made of two parts, his humanity and divinity, moving across the heavens through the signs of the zodiac in his different attributes.

The MS makes no visual difference between the Latin and the English, but here the English is highlighted in italics to help the reader.

Linguistic points: In texts such as these there is a greater than average ratio of English words within the Latin. Each language keeps to its own morphology and syntax during the integration of the inflected and non-inflected languages. There appears to be no grammatical awkwardness in the way the two languages are intertwined.

TEXT II.38B

The Church is compared to the starry firmament, and the life of faith to the zodiac traced on the heavens by Christ himself
ut magnus clericus Lincolniensis dicit in suis Dictis, dicto 168,[3] per illud *briȝt schyninge* celum quod clerici vocant celum stellatum possumus bene intelligere Ecclesiam, que recte ut celum semper movetur super duos polos, fidem et spem, *arayid* septem stellis septem sacramentorum, and *piȝt ful* fixis stellis omnium aliarum virtutum. iam diffundit suum lumen in terram humane anime per *prechinge and techinge.* ibidem iam per influenciam exempli facit illam germinare virtutibus et fructus producere bone vite. in isto lucido celo Ecclesie *is* corpus perfectum *þe nurchinge sunne* curatorum *with his bemis al brennyng.* in isto est eciam mater *and succur* noctis, *þe variand mone* divitum *in briȝtnes al schynynge.* et in isto celo et planeta *ful briȝt* Mercurius, *of smale vitrileris ful besy in mevynge.* (...) iste sol curatorum fulgebat olim *ful briȝt* in celo Ecclesie, quia sicut materialis sol *goth* suum cursum per omnia duodecim signa in zodiaco, qui est circulus in firmamento, dare lumen toti mundo, sic spiritualis sol curatorum et doctorum olim movebatur continue in circulo zodiaci. ut auctor *De spera* dicit,[4] capit suum nomen ab isto termino greco *zoe* quod interpretatur vita. quid melius potest comparari huic circulo vite quam fides que vivificat animam humanam et est vera vita cuiuslibet Christiani, secundum quod Apostolus dicit ad Hebreos X, 'iustus autem ex fide vivit'? istum circulum vite Christus protraxit ipsemet in firmamento **Hebr. 10:38** Ecclesie. et sicut latomus faciendo circulum capit *a cumpas, set* unam partem firmiter in uno puncto, and *drawþe toþer partie al abowte,* sic quando Christus noster geometer fuit in hoc mundo, habuit *a crafti cumpas made of twey partes,*

---

3 Of the 147 extant *Dicta* attributed to Robert Grosseteste, Bishop of Lincoln (1235–53), the most relevant seems to be no. 137, in which clerics are likened to the starry firmament.

4 Johannes de Sacrobosco, *Sphaera mundi* 2; Grosseteste also wrote a work on this topic around the same time, but in it he derives 'zodiac' from the Greek word for 'animal' (*De sphaera* 14).

de benedicta deitate et humanitate *knyt togedur in o persone.* unam partem huius *cumpas,* scilicet benedictam deitatem, *he set perfecte* in uno puncto beatitudinis. *þis was piȝt so sadlich in þis* puncto quod nulla miseria huius mundi, *no sikenes ne mischef myȝt hit touche ne meve.* altera parte istius *cumpas,* sua humanitate, *he drow þis* circulum vite. *þis parti he drow about* in hoc mundo *in muche woo, payn and travail. herwith he gravyd* in hoc seculo omnia duodecim signa zodiaci, omnes duodecim articulos fidei, quia quando suscepit carnem et sanguinem ex Beata Virgine, domina sancta Maria, *he gravid* in isto circulo signo virginis, *þe signe of þe maide, þe article* sue pure incarnacionis. quando ponebatur in cruce et optulit *up* sanguinem cordis sui patri suo pro redempcione generis humani, sculpsit in illo signum tauri, *þe signe of þe bole,* articulum sue acerbe passionis, *and scylfullich* offerendo seipsum sculpsit signum tauri quia communiter in veteri lege tauri offerebantur in sacrificiis. tertia die resurgens a mortuis, *he gravid* in illo signum leonis, *þe signe of þe lionn,* articulum sue gloriose resurreccionis. et racionabiliter isto tempore sculpsit signum leonis quia sicut Izodorus dicit 12 *Ethimologiarum,* sicut catulus leonis noviter *welpit* iacet tribus diebus sine vita et erigitur ad vitam per *rorynge noyse* antiqui leonis, sic Christus, leo de tribu Iuda, iacuit mortuus, secundum comunem modum loquendi doctorum, tribus diebus in suo sepulcro et tertia die virtute deitatis (…) suum corpus et anima revivebantur *and rose fro deth to lyve.* (…)

Isid. Etym. 12.2.5

Translation: Macaronic Sermon

As the great cleric of Lincoln says in his Sayings, no. 168, by that bright shining heaven which scholars call the starred sky we can clearly understand the Church, which just like the heavens always moves on two poles, faith and hope, arrayed with the seven stars of the seven sacraments and set fully with the fixed stars of all the other virtues. Already it sheds its light onto the earth of the human soul by means of preaching and teaching. There, through the influence of its example, it makes the earth germinate with virtues and produce the fruits of the good life. In this bright heaven of the Church is the perfect body, the nourishing sun of the priests, with its beams all on fire. In it is also the mother and succour of the night, the changing moon of the wealthy people, all shining in brightness. And in that heaven is the planet Mercury, outstandingly bright, of common victuallers very busy in action. (…) This sun of the priests used to shine so brightly in the heaven of the Church, for just as the material sun moves on its course through all the twelve signs on the zodiac, which is a circle in the firmament, to give light to the whole world, so the spiritual sun of the priests and learned men used to move continually on the circular track of the zodiac. As the author of The Sphere says, the zodiac takes its name from the Greek word 'zoe', which means 'life'. What can better be compared with this circle of life than faith, which gives life to the human soul and is the true life of every Christian according to what the Apostle says to the Hebrews, 10: 'the just man lives by faith'? Christ traced this circle of life Himself on the firmament of the Church. And as a stonemason tracing a circle takes a compass, places one part firmly on one point and draws the other part all around, so when our Christ was a surveyor in this world, He had a well-made compass of two parts, of blessed divinity and humanity joined together in one person. He placed one part of this compass, namely His blessed divinity, perfectly on one point of blessedness. This was set so firmly on this point that no unhappiness of this world, no sickness or mischief could touch or move it. With the other part of this compass, His humanity, He traced this circle of life. This section He drew around in this world in much woe, pain and travail. With it He engraved in this world all twelve signs of the zodiac, all the twelve articles of the faith, because when He took on flesh and blood from the blessed Virgin, the holy lady Mary, He engraved in that circle the sign of Virgo, the sign of the maiden, the article of His pure incarnation. When He was placed on the cross and offered up His blood to His father for the redemption of mankind, He engraved in it the sign of the bull, the article of His bitter suffering. And with good reason did He engrave the sign of the bull by offering Himself, for bulls are commonly offered in sacrifice in the Old Testament. On the third day rising from the dead He engraved the sign of Leo, the article of His glorious resurrection. And He appropriately engraved the sign of Leo at that time, because as Isidore says in Book 12 of his Etymologies, just as the newly whelped lion cub lies for three days without life and is stimulated to life by the roaring noise of the old lion, in the same way Christ, the lion of the tribe of Judah, lay for three days dead in His tomb, according to the common way of speaking of the Doctors (of the Church), and on the third day, by virtue of His divine nature, (...) His body and soul were revived and rose from death to life. (...)

Primary Sources and Related Texts

Horner, P. (ed. and transl.) (2006) *A macaronic sermon collection from late medieval England: Oxford, MS Bodley 649*, Toronto: Sermon 7.

Wenzel, S. (1994) *Macaronic sermons: bilingualism and preaching in late medieval England*, Ann Arbor: Sermon O-07, pp. 268–307.

Further Reading

Halmari, H. and Regetz, T. (2011) 'Syntactic aspects of code-switching in Oxford, MS Bodley 649' in *Code-switching in early English*, ed. H. Schendl and L. Wright, Berlin.

Pahta, P., Skaffari, J. and Wright, L. (2018) *Multilingual practices in language history: English and beyond*, Berlin and Boston.

Schendl, H. (2013) 'Code-switching in late medieval macaronic sermons' in *Jefferson and Putter (2013).

344 Fifteenth Century

Wenzel, S. (2005) 'The arts of preaching' in *The Cambridge history of literary criticism* (2005).

C: A Ghost Story in a Preacher's Commonplace Book

Date: 1373.

This story is only found in Oxford MS Trinity College 7, ff. 49r–50r.

Work: Preachers often drew on popular tales in order to teach some point about morality or the spiritual life. It is thought, for example, that the *Gesta Romanorum*, a Europe-wide collection of tales, was used for this purpose, for each tale is followed by a brief moral explanation. Here is included an otherwise unknown ghost story, involving an event that took place in Haydock, Lancashire in 1373, written into a Trinity College, Oxford MS in the fifteenth century as a moralising tale to show the efficacy of the Mass for remission from purgatory. The MS is thought to be a preacher's commonplace book, as it comprises hymns, prayers, saints' legends, a few sermons, proverbial verses etc., in English, French and Latin.

Linguistic points: Note the spelling *terribulis* for *terribilis*. Also noteworthy are the words and phrases *prope et longe* (possibly a calque on the English phrase 'near and far', evident from the thirteenth century), and *cavillus* (cf. AN 'cheville', possibly from CL *clavicula*, but cf. also *OED s.v.* kevel, a Scottish and Northern dialect word meaning a peg of some sort, there said to be of ON provenance). The use of *pro* with the gerund or gerundive as a purpose clause occurs in both pre- and post-Conquest BML.

TEXT II.38C

The ghostly woman and her strange request

per magistrum Ricardum de Puttes &c.

narracio de celebracione misse. anno domini mccclxxiij, quidam homo de Haydok in comitatu Lancastrie tenuit vnam concubinam de qua generauit pueros. obiit illa mulier & vir duxit aliam mulierem in vxorem. contigit postea quod is vir iuit quadam die ad quendam fabrum pro ferris aratri, scilicet cultro & vomere, corrigendis siue acuendis. qui quidem faber manebat in alia villa vocata Hulme que distat a Haydok predicta per duo miliaria. qui cum reuerteretur in nocte veniebat per quandam crucem stantem in via que dicitur Newton cros, & ibi inuasit eum horror terribulis. et sic perterritus respiciens circa se vidit quasi vmbram obscuram quam coniurauit ne sibi noceret sed ut diceret quid esset; et respondit vox ex illa vmbra et dixit illi, 'Ne timeas. ego sum illa mulier que quondam fui amasia tua, et permissa sum venire ad te pro auxilio a te habendo.' quesiuit ab illa vir quomodo esset secum. que respondit, 'Male. sed si vis, potes me juvare.' respondit vir, 'Libenter faciam quidquid potero, si dicas mihi quomodo.' at illa, 'Per missas celebrandas a bonis presbiteris potero liberari a magna pena quam patior.' cui ille, 'Et ego faciam missas pro te celebrari, eciam si contigerit me expendere omnia bona mea vsque ad vltimum denarium' et tunc illa dixit, 'Ne timeas, sed pone manum tuam ad capud meum & accipe quod ibi inueneris.' et ille posuit manum suam ad capud illius, et accepit ibidem quasi fere dimidium manipulum pilorum valde nigrorum. mulier tamen in vita sua habuit crines in capite croceos et satis pulcros. tunc dixit mulier, 'Si feceris tot missas pro me celebrari quot ibi sunt capilli, tunc liberabor a pena.' quod concessit; et tunc dixit illa, 'Venias ad istum locum tali hora et scies tunc de statu meo'; et sic euanuit. et ipse dictos pilos firmauit cum cauillo in foramine cuiusdam postis, et statim aliquam partem bonorum suorum vendidit, & monetam leuauit, & profectus est prope & longe pro presbiteris querendis, & plures missas fecit celebrari. quo facto respexit capillos supradictos, & inuenit plures eorum mutatos in colorem croceum secundum numerum missarum celebratarum; & sic iterum fecit plures missas celebrari, & iterum et sic quousque omnes capilli supradicti essent mutati in croceum colorem. postea ad tempus assignatum venit ad crucem supradictam, & expectauit per tempus modicum, et vidit eminus quoddam lumen versus ipsum mouens festinanter. et cum venerit ad ipsum, vox de ipsa loquebatur, regracians illi, & dixit, 'Benedictus sis inter omnes homines quod me liberasti de maxima pena, & nunc tendo ad gaudium'; & brevi colloquio inter eos habito, recessit ab eo motu velocissimo. supple de virtute misse &c.

Translation: A Ghost Story

From Master Richard de Puttes etc., a narrative concerning the celebration of the Mass.

In the year of the Lord 1373, a man from Haydock in Lancashire kept a mistress who had borne him children. That woman died and the man married another woman. It happened later that this man went one day to a blacksmith to have the metal parts for his plough, namely the coulter and ploughshare, mended or sharpened. This blacksmith lived in another village, called Hulme, which was about two miles from Haydock. When the man was returning during the night he came past a cross standing on the road which was known as Newton Cross and there a terrifying horror seized him; utterly terrified, he looked round and saw a sort of dark shadow which he conjured not to harm him but to tell him what it was; and a voice from this shadow replied and said to him, 'Do not be afraid. I am that woman who was once your lover, and I have been allowed to come to you get help from you.' The man asked her how she was and she answered, 'I am in a bad way, but if you want, you

346 Fifteenth Century

*can help me.' The man replied, 'I will gladly do whatever I can, if you tell me how.'
She said, 'By means of Masses celebrated by good priests, I can be released from the
great punishment I am suffering.' To which he replied, 'I will arrange for Masses to
be celebrated for you, even if I have to spend everything I have, down to the last
penny.' Then she said, 'Do not be afraid, but place your hand on my head and take
what you find there.' He placed his hand on her head and took from there about half
a handful of the blackest hair; and yet the woman had had beautiful yellow hair in
her lifetime. Then she said, 'If you arrange for as many Masses to be celebrated as
there are hairs there, then I will be released from my punishment.' The man agreed
and then she said, 'Come to this place at such and such a time, and you will learn
about my condition,' and then she vanished. And the man fastened these hairs with
a peg into a crack on a post and immediately sold part of his property and raised
some money and journeyed near and far to look for priests and arranged for several
Masses to be celebrated. When he had done this, he looked again at the strands of
hair and found that the number of them that had turned yellow corresponded to the
number of Masses said; and so he again arranged for many Masses to be said and
again and again until all those hairs had turned yellow. Later on, at the designated
time, he came to the cross and waited there for a while and saw from afar a light
moving quickly towards him. And when it reached him, a voice spoke to him out of
it, thanking him and saying, 'Blessed be you among all men for releasing me from
the most severe punishment, and now I am making progress towards happiness.' After they had had a short conversation, the light receded at great speed. Understand
this as referring to the effectiveness of the Mass etc.*

Primary Sources and Related Texts

Blakiston, H. (1923) 'Two more medieval ghost-stories', *EHR* 38: 85–7 for the
  story printed here.
James, M. R. (1922) 'Twelve medieval ghost-stories', *EHR* 37: 413–22.
For more medieval tales of the supernatural, such as the story of the green
  children at Woolpit in Suffolk, see e.g. William of Malmesbury, *GR*; William
  of Newburgh, *HA*; Gervase of Tilbury, *Otia imperialia*; Ralph de Coggeshall,
  Chronicon Anglicanum; Walter Map, *Courtiers' Trifles*; and Gerald of Wales,
  Itinerarium Kambriae.
The Anglo-Latin Gesta Romanorum, ed. P. Bright, OMT, Oxford, 2019.

Further Reading

Watkins, C. (2007) *History and the supernatural in the Middle Ages*, Cambridge.

Section II.39

An Heir Proves He Can Inherit: Oral Testimony of Witnesses in Proof of Age Texts. The Case of Thomas Baldyngton: May 1425

The proof of age texts preserved in the series of documents known as the Inquisitions post mortem throw up interesting information about the lives of the witnesses who are called to swear before a jury that the heir has reached the legal age (21 in the case of a man, or 16 in the case of a single woman, 14 for a married woman) when they are entitled to enter into their inheritance, which has been in the hands of the king since the death of the previous owner, if he was a tenant in chief of the king. The events that are cited as proof of age are those that took place when the heir in question was born or baptised, this system being necessary as births were rarely officially registered at the time. It is a system that relates to questions of memory and literacy as well as circumstances of everyday life which are often referred to as part of the oral testimony, associated with the community and therefore held in the common memory, even many years after the event. It is true that the oral testimony would have been given in English, and then translated into Latin. When written down it may have been adapted slightly, resulting in a rather formulaic format; occasionally the texts are so similar in their details that one suspects that, for whatever reason, they have been copied by the clerk with only the name of the witness changed. In many cases it is possible to trace a series of different documents relating to the proof of age text for a particular heir: such documents might be various kinds of writ instructing the local sheriff to make inquiry, immediately after the death of a tenant in chief, into the property held when he died, so as to establish exactly what he owned, what he owed to the king, who his heir was, and to make arrangements (if the heir was under age) for the property to be administered by a guardian until the heir came of age.

Selected here as an example of this type of text are three of the twelve witness accounts at the *Probatio aetatis* inquest of Thomas Baldyngton, son and heir of William Baldyngton, who had died on 25 October 1419. The text, as preserved among the Inquisitions post mortem, is given together with references, in chronological order, to a series of different documents relating to this case.

Linguistic points: *torcha* derives from French 'torche', and *grangia*, via French 'grange', from ML *granica*, formed from CL *granum* or the later feminine form *grana*. Note also *data*, as feminine form of the past participle of *dare*, as 'date', for which the neuter is often used.

348 Fifteenth Century

Dates and Documents Relating to Thomas Baldyngton

1400 7 September *The marriage of Thomas Baldyngton's parents.* Dower is assigned to Joan, widow of Thomas Quatermaynes, for her marriage to William Baldyngton, as witnessed by R. Quatermaynes, one of the witnesses at the proof of age inquest twenty-five years later. List of buildings, lands and rents (TNA: C137/29/71 in *CIPM* 18 no. 534).

1419 ?25 October *The death of William Baldyngton, Thomas' father.*

1420 27 April *Inquest to determine the lands held by William Baldyngton at his death* (Inquisition post mortem, TNA: C138/45/21 in *CIPM* 21 no. 412).

1420 23 November *The lands of William Baldyngton are committed to guardians until Thomas comes of age.* The king arranges for the property to be granted to J. Wilcote, J. Cottesmore and N. Dixon for a fee of £40 to be paid to the king, together with suitable maintenance to the heir, and a pledge to maintain the buildings (Patent Roll, TNA: C66/403 m. 10 in *CalPat* (1416–22) 307).

1424 24 November *Replacement writ for that issued in 1419* (Inquisition post mortem, TNA: C139/15/22 mm. 1–2 in *CIPM* 22 no. 415). Delayed inquest held on 25 April 1425 to determine the lands held from the king by William Baldyngton.

1425 *Proof of age inquest for Thomas Baldyngton.* Writ issued on 5 May instructing inquest to be held on the 12 May. N. Dixon and J. Cottesmore are to be informed, but they do not appear. Witness accounts of twelve witnesses (Inquisition post mortem, TNA: C139/20/48 mm. 1–2 in *CIPM* 22 no. 528).

1425 14 June *Thomas Baldyngton inherits.* Writ to the escheator in Oxfordshire, ordering him to give Thomas possession of his father's lands, apart from the dower due to his mother, as he has proved his age, and the king has taken his homage and fealty.

1425 16 June Writs to the escheators of Oxfordshire and Buckinghamshire to grant Joan, Thomas' mother, her dower, once she has taken her oath (Close Roll, TNA: C54/275 m. 5 in *CalCl* (1422–9) 172).

1425 22 October *Thomas' mother granted a licence to remarry.* Licence for 100s. paid in the Hanaper Office for Joan, wife of William Baldyngton, to marry John Cotes esquire (Patent Roll, TNA: C66/418 m. 10 in *CalPat* (1422–9) 321).

TEXT II.39

Proof of age text: the testimony of three of the twelve witnesses (C139/20/48 mm. 1–2)

[1425] Probacio etatis Thomae Baldyngton filii et heredis Willelmi Baldyngton (…) per sacramentum xii proborum et legalium hominum subsequentium:

Richard Quatermaynes: Ricardi Quatermaynes etatis lii annorum et amplius, juratus et per se separatim examinatus de et super etate predicti Thomae Baldyngton qui de etate eiusdem Thome Baldyngton ac de die anno et loco nativitatis eiusdem concordat cum prefato Thomae Wykham et requisitus qualiter hoc scit dicit quod in festo nativitatis sancti Johannis Baptistae ipsemet Ricardus duxit in uxorem quandam Sibyllam nuper uxorem suam apud Wynelcote predict' ad tunc sociam Joannae matris predicti Thomae Baldyngton et in festo sancti Petri quod dicitur Advincula extunc proximo sequente idem Thomas Baldyngton fuit natus et in festo nativitatis Joannis Baptistae ultimo predicto ante datam capcionis ipsius probatoris xxi anni elapsi fuerunt ex quo idem Ricardus duxit ipsam Sibyllam in uxorem et pro eo bene constat ei de etate predicti Thomae Baldyngton.

Robert Quynaton: Roberti Quynaton etatis lx annorum et amplius, juratus et per se separatim examinatus de et super etate predicti Thomae Baldyngton qui de etate eiusdem Thomae Baldyngton et de die anno et loco nativitatis eiusdem concordat cum predicto Thomae Wykham et requisitus qualiter hoc scit dicit quod ipse Robertus Quynaton apud Balscote in comitatu Oxon, in festo nativitatis sancti Johannis Baptistae anno quarto supradicti regis Henrici quarti fugavit quandam carectam suam carcatam cum feno a prato dominicali manerii de Balscote predicte ville in grangiam manerii et ipse Robertus Quynaton super carectam predictam sic cum predicto feno cariato in grangea predict' stabat et de carecta illa subito cecidit usque ad terram et per casum illius brachium suum sinistrum ibidem fregit et in festo sancti Petri quod dicitur Advincula extunc proximo sequente natus fuit predictus Thomas Baldyngton et in festo nativitatis Johannis Baptistae ultimo predicto ante datam capcionis istius probatoris xxi anni elapsi fuerunt ex quo brachium suum sic fregit per quod bene recolit de etate predicti Thomae Baldyngton.

Thomas Coventry: Thomae Coventre etatis lx annorum et amplius, juratus et per se separatim examinatus de et super etate predicti Thomae Baldyngton qui de etate eiusdem Thomae Baldyngton et de die anno et loco nativitatis eiusdem concordat cum predicto Thomae Wykham et requisitus qualiter hoc scit dicit quod in festo sancti Petri quod dicitur Advincula anno quarto supradicti regis Henrici quarti immediate post baptismum predicti Thomae Baldyngton apud villam de

350 Fifteenth Century

Wynelcote ipse Thomas Coventry ludebat cum aliquibus sociis suis ad pilam ped-
alem et idem Thomas Coventry ibidem sic ludens tibiam sinistram suam fregit[1]
et fuerunt xxi anni elapsi in festo sancti Petri (…) quod dicitur Advincula (…) ex
quo hoc decidebat per quod bene recolit de etate predicti Thomae Baldyngton.
(…)

Translation: Proof of Age Text

*Proof of age of Thomas Baldyngton, the son and heir of William Baldyngton, (…)
by means of the oath of the following upright and law-worthy men.*

*Richard Quatermaine, aged 52 years and more, having taken an oath, and exam-
ined on his own and separately about and regarding the age of the aforesaid Thomas
Baldyngton (TB), agrees with the said Thomas Wykham about TB's age and the
day, year and place of his birth. And asked how he knows this, he says that on the
feast of the nativity of John the Baptist, he, Richard, married a certain Sibyl, his late
wife, at Wilcote. At that time she was a companion of Joan, TB's mother, and on the
following feast of St Peter which is called Ad Vincula, this same TB was born, and
on the last feast of the nativity of St John, before this inquest as to proof of age, 21
years had passed since this same Richard married Sibyl, and for that reason he is
very clear as to TB's age.*

*Robert Quynaton, aged 60 years and more, having taken an oath, and examined
on his own and separately about and regarding the age of the aforesaid TB, agrees
with the aforesaid Thomas Wykham about TB's age and about the day, year and
place of his birth. Asked how he knows this, he says that he, Robert Quynaton, at
Balscote in the county of Oxfordshire, on the feast of the birth of St John the Baptist
in the fourth year of the abovementioned King Henry IV, was driving a cart loaded
with hay from the demesne manor at Balscote to the manor grange, and he Robert
Quynaton, was standing on this cart with the hay that was being transported to the
grange and he fell suddenly from the cart to the ground, and in the fall he broke his
left arm there, and on the next feast of St Peter which is called Ad Vincula, TB was
born, and on the last feast of the nativity of John the Baptist before the date of the
inquest as to proof of age, 21 years had passed since he broke his arm in this way, so
he can clearly remember TB's age.*

*Thomas Coventry, aged 60 years and more, having taken an oath, and examined on
his own and separately about and regarding the age of TB, agrees with the aforesaid
Thomas Wykham about TB's age and about the day, year and place of his birth.*

---

1 For another injury sustained during a football match, see the miracle apparently
performed by King Henry VI, recorded in Section II.42.

Asked how he knows this, he says that on the feast of St Peter which is called Ad Vincula, in the fourth year of the aforesaid King Henry IV, immediately after the baptism of this TB, in the village of Wilcote, he, Thomas Coventry, was playing football with some friends of his and while he was playing there he broke his left leg and on the feast of St Peter (…) known as Ad Vincula, twenty-one years had passed (…) since this happened, which is how he remembers well the age of TB. (…)

Primary Sources and Related Texts

TNA: C139/20/48 mm. 1–2, calendared in *CIPM* 22 no. 528.
www.inquisitionspostmortem.ac.uk.
www.british-history.ac.uk/inquis-post-mortem.
EHD 3.826–7 for a proof of age text from 1304.

Further Reading

Bedell, J. (1999) 'Memory and proofs of ages in England', *Past and Present* 162: 3–8.

Carpenter, C. (2003) 'General introduction' in *Calendar of Inquisitions post mortem*, vol. 22, Woodbridge.

Deller, W. S. (2016) 'Proofs of age 1246–1430: their nature, veracity and use as sources' in *The later medieval Inquisitions post mortem: mapping the medieval countryside and rural society*, ed. M. Hicks, Woodbridge.

McGlynn, M. (2009) 'Memory, orality and life records: proofs of age in Tudor England', *The Sixteenth Century Journal* 40.3: 679–97.

Rosenthal, J. (2017) *Social memory in late medieval England: village life and proofs of age*, Basingstoke.

Walker, S. S. (1973) 'Proof of age of feudal heirs in medieval England', *Mediaeval Studies* 35: 306–23.

Section II.40

A Woman Is Tried for Heresy at Norwich: a Court Record
(excerpts: pp. 43–5, 46, 49)

Date: 1428.

The text is preserved in the Westminster Diocesan Archives, MS B.2.

Work: This is regarded as the most important record of heresy investigations in Britain prior to the Reformation, preserved in a paper courtbook probably written by a cleric working for the bishops of Norwich as a notary public. It shows how the Church authorities dealt with what they regarded as heretical beliefs and practices, here in the case of fifty-one men and nine women accused of being Lollards (i.e. followers of the teachings of John Wyclif, who had died in 1384) in the villages between Norwich and the coast. The excerpted passage focuses on Margery Baxter who, in conversation with her friends while doing 'women's work' around the fire, comes across as a passionate teacher of anti-clerical views with a sharp tongue that lays into many of the tenets of Christian theology: according to her, it is the Catholic Church that is heretical. The scene is set in the bishop's court in Norwich, where Margery's friend accuses her of spreading shocking beliefs regarding the sacraments and the veneration of the Church, e.g. that the Eucharist is nothing but bread that passes through the body and there is no more value in venerating the crucifix than the gallows on which ordinary people die, or that baptism and marriage are unnecessary.[1] The excerpt finishes with Margery's brazen claim that she will not be burned at the stake. It seems that despite being deeply involved in the Lollard movement she escaped execution.

Linguistic points: The passage comes from the report made to the bishop. It is likely to have been noted first in English and then translated into Latin, but some of Margery's forceful language has been retained in English. She uses bold images to convey her beliefs. The unusual Latin word *mametria* (i.e. *mahometria*, from 'Mahomet') is formed from the AN form 'maumetrie', from which ME derived 'mammetry' (maum-) to mean 'idolatry'. 'Lollard' (from the Dutch word for 'mumbler') was adopted into English around 1400 as a term of contempt for followers of John Wyclif, deemed by the Church to be heretical: Latin forms

---

1 On baptism by lay people in emergencies, see Section II.50A.

II.40 | A Woman Is Tried for Heresy at Norwich 353

appeared immediately.[2] By the mid-fifteenth century the word was used of heresy more generally, though presumably Margery did not consider her own views heretical. The phrase *carta salvationis* refers to a sort of 'Get out of jail free' card, the implication being that a woman could not be executed while she was pregnant.

TEXT II.40

Depositions against Margery Baxter: 1 April 1429

The court convenes in the chapel of the Bishop's palace
[p. 43] die prima mensis Aprilis anno Domini millesimo cccc^mo xxix° Johanna Clyfland, uxor Willelmi Clifland, commorans in parochia Sancte Marie Parve in Norwico, citata comparuit personaliter coram reverendo in Christo patre et domino, domino Willelmo Dei gracia Norwicensi episcopo, in capella palacii sui iudicialiter sedente. et de mandato dicti patris iuravit ad sancta Dei evangelia per ipsam corporaliter tacta de veritate dicenda in et super omnibus et singulis interrogandis ab eadem que concernunt materiam fidei.

Johanna Clifland speaks as a witness, citing Margery Baxter's claims about the Church and sacraments
quo quidem iuramento sic prestito, ipsa Johanna Clifland dixit quod die Veneris proximo ante festum Purificacionis Beate Marie [p. 44] ultimum, Margeria Baxter, uxor Willelmi Baxter, *wright*, nuper commorantis in Martham Norwicensis diocesis, sedens et suens cum ista iurata in camera eiusdem iuxta camenum in presencia istius iurate ac Johanne Grymell et Agnetis Bethom, serviencium istius iurate, dixit, et informavit istam iuratam et servientes suas predictas quod nullo modo iurarent, dicens in lingua materna: 'Dame, bewar of the bee, for every bee will styngge, and therefore loke that ye swer nother be Godd ne be Our Ladi ne be non other seynt, and if ye do the contrarie the be will styngge your tunge and veneme your sowle.' deinde dicit ista iurata quod prefata Margeria quesivit ab ea quid ipsa fecit sic omni die in ecclesia. et ista respondebat sibi dicens quod primo post introitum suum in ecclesiam ipsa solebat, genuflectendo ante crucem, dicere in honore crucifixi quinquies Pater Noster et totidem Ave Maria in honore Beate Marie, matris Christi. et tunc dicta Margeria, increpando, dixit isti iurate, 'Vos male facitis sic genuflectendo et orando coram ymaginibus in talibus ecclesiis quia Deus nunquam erat in tali ecclesia nec unquam exivit nec exibit de celo, nec vult magis meritum tibi prebere vel concedere pro talibus genufleccionibus, adoracionibus vel oracionibus factis in talibus ecclesiis quam lumen accensum

---

2 Cf. Thomas Elmham, *Historia monasterii S. Augustini Cantuariensis* 209 for more fanciful etymologies of the word, associating it with *lolium* and *loligo*.

354 Fifteenth Century

et sub lata coopertura fontis baptismalis undique absconditum potest tempore nocturno prebere lumen existentibus in ecclesia quia non est maior honor exhibendus ymaginibus in ecclesiis nec ymaginibus crucifixi quam est exhibendus furcis super quas frater vester esset suspensus', dicens in lingua materna, '*Lewed wrightes of stokkes hewe and fourme suche crosses and ymages, and after that lewed peyntors glorye thaym with colours*, et si vos affectatis videre veram crucem Christi ego volo monstrare eam tibi hic in domo tua propria.' et ista iurata asseruit se libenter videre velle veram crucem Christi. et prefata Margeria dixit, 'Vide', et tunc extendebat brachia sua in longum, dicens isti iurate, 'hec est vera crux Christi, et istam crucem tu debes et potes videre et adorare omni die hic in domo tua propria, et adeo tu in vanum laboras quando vadis ad ecclesias ad adorandas sive orandas aliquas ymagines vel cruces mortuas.'

Margery's claims about the sacraments: Eucharist, baptism and marriage
et deinde dixit ista iurata quod prefata Margeria quesivit ab ea quomodo ipsa credidit de sacramento altaris. et ista iurata, ut asseruit, sibi respondebat dicens quod ipsa credidit quod illud sacramentum altaris post consecracionem est verum corpus Christi in specie panis. et tunc dicta Margeria dixit isti iurate, 'Tu male credis quia si quodlibet tale sacramentum esset [p. 45] Deus et verum corpus Christi, infiniti sunt dii, quia mille sacerdotes et plures omni die conficiunt mille tales deos et postea tales deos comedunt et commestos emittunt per posteriora in sepibus turpiter fetentibus, ubi potestis tales deos sufficientes invenire si volueritis perscrutari; ideoque sciatis pro firmo quod illud quod vos dicitis sacramentum altaris nunquam erit Deus meus per graciam Dei, quia tale sacramentum fuit falso et deceptorie ordinatum per presbiteros in Ecclesia ad inducendum populum simplicem ad ydolatriam, quia illud sacramentum est tantum panis materialis.'[3] (…) [p. 46] item dixit ista iurata quod prefata Margeria dixit sibi quod nullus puer sive infans natus habens parentes Christianos debet baptizari in aqua secundum usum commune quia talis infans sufficienter baptizatur in utero matris, et ideo illa mamentria et idolatria quas isti falsi et maledicti sacerdotes faciunt cum intingunt infantes in fontes in ecclesiis, hoc tantum faciunt ad extorquendas pecunias a populo ad manutenendos ipsos sacerdotes et concubinas eorundem. item quod eadem Margeria dixit isti iurate tunc ibidem quod solus consensus mutui amoris inter virum et mulierem sufficit pro sacramento matrimonii, absque expressione aliorum verborum et absque solennizacione in ecclesiis. (…) [p. 49] dixit eciam eadem Margeria isti iurate quod ipsa Margeria non deberet comburi, licet ipsa fuerit convicta de lollardiis, quia ipsa Margeria, ut asseruit isti iurate, habuit et habet unam cartam salvacionis in utero suo.

---

3   Cf. Section I.8: Anon. of Whitby, *Life of Gregory the Great* (20) on the woman persuaded by a miracle to believe that the bread was the Body of Christ.

Translation: A Heresy Trial at Norwich

On 1 April in the year of our Lord 1429, Johanna Clyfland, the wife of William Clifland, resident in the parish of St Mary the Less in Norwich, was summoned and appeared in person before William, the reverend lord in Christ, father and lord, by God's grace Bishop of Norwich, seated according to correct judicial procedure in the chapel of his palace, and on the order of the said father she swore on the holy Gospels of God, while in physical contact with them, to speak the truth in and about each and every thing to be asked of her, concerning the matter of the faith.

When the oath had been given in this way, this Johanna Clifland said that on the last Friday before the most recent feast of the Purification of the Blessed Mary, Margery Baxter, wife of William Baxter, wright, formerly resident in Martham in the diocese of Norwich, sitting and sewing with Johanna (who had taken the oath) in this same woman's chamber beside the fire in the presence of Johanna and Johanna Grymell and Agnes Bethom, servants of this Johanna, spoke and informed this Johanna and her servants that they should in no way take an oath, saying in her mother tongue, 'Lady, beware of the bee, for every bee wants to sting, so be careful that you do not swear either by God or by our Lady or by any other saint, and if you do the contrary, the bee will sting your tongue and poison your soul.' Then this Johanna says that this Margery asked her what she did all day in church and she replied and said to her that first after she entered the church she would bend the knee in front of the cross and say the Our Father five times in honour of the one who was crucified, and the Ave Maria the same number of times in honour of blessed Mary, the mother of Christ, and then the said Margery, rebuking her, said to Johanna, 'You do wrong to bend the knee and pray in this way before the images in such churches, because God was never in such a church and he never left or will leave heaven. He does not want to give or grant to you more merit for such genuflections, adoration or prayers made in such churches than a light lit and hidden on all sides under the broad covering of the baptismal font is able to provide light at night to those in the church, because greater honour is not to be shown to images in churches nor to images of the crucified one than is to be shown to the gibbet on which your brother was hanged.' In her mother tongue she said, 'Carpenters from the laity cut and shape crosses and images like this out of logs and after that, painters from the laity decorate them with colours, and if you are keen to see a true cross of Christ I am willing to show it to you here in your own home.' And Johanna stated that she would be very happy to see a true cross of Christ. Then Margery said, 'Look', and she stretched out her arms wide, saying to Johanna, 'This is the true cross of Christ! You ought to and can see this cross and adore it all day here in your own home. You are wasting your time when you go to churches to worship or pray to some lifeless images and crosses.' Then Johanna said that Margery asked her what she believed about the sacrament of the altar and Johanna, according to her statement, answered her by saying that she believed that the sacrament of the altar, after the consecration, is the true body of Christ in the appearance of the bread, and then Margery said to Johanna, 'You are wrong to believe this, because if some such sacrament is God and the true body of Christ, then there are infinite gods, because a thousand priests and more, every day, consecrate a thousand such gods and afterwards they eat these gods and after they have eaten them they pass them through their backsides in the hedges, which stink in a disgusting way. You can find such gods in plenty if you are willing to look for them; and so you can be sure that what you call the sacrament of the altar will never be my God by the grace of God, because such a sacrament was falsely and deceitfully decided on by the priests in the Church to lead the simple people into idolatry, because that sacrament is only bread made of matter.' (…) Again the sworn witness said that this Margery said to her that no child or infant having Christian parents when it was born ought to be baptised in water according to common practice, because such a baby was adequately baptised in its mother's womb and so it is maumetry and idolatry that these false and accursed priests practise when they dip the babies in the church fonts, for they only do it to extort money from the people to maintain these priests and their mistresses. Then this Margery said to Johanna at that time in that same place that the agreement of mutual love between a man and a woman alone was sufficient for the sacrament of marriage, without the saying of any words and without a church ceremony. (…) This same Margery also said to Johanna that she, Margery, ought not to be burned, even if she were convicted of Lollardy, because she, Margery, as she stated to Johanna, had and has a ticket of salvation in her womb.

Primary Sources and Related Texts

Heresy trials in the diocese of Norwich 1428–1431, Camden Society 4th ser. 20, 1977.
Ralph de Coggeshall, *Chronicon Anglicanum*, RS 66 (1875) 121–5. On the heretics of Rheims (1176–80).

Further Reading

Butler, S. M. (2018) 'Pleading the belly: a sparing plea? Pregnant convicts and the courts in medieval England' in *Crossing borders: boundaries and margins in medieval and early modern Britain*, ed. S. M. Butler and K. J. Kesselring, Leiden.
Cross, C. (1978) 'Great reasoners in Scripture: the activities of women Lollards 1380–1530' in *Medieval women*, ed. D. Baker, Oxford: 359–80.
Hornbeck II, J. P. (2013) 'Love and marriage in Norwich heresy trials 1428–1431', *Viator* 44.3: 237–55.
McSheffrey, S. (1995) *Gender and heresy: women and men in Lollard communities 1420–1530*, Philadelphia, PA.
Thomson, J. (1965) *The later Lollards 1414–1520*, Oxford.

Section II.41

Military Historiography
A: The Battle of Bannockburn (1314) in the *Chronicle of Lanercost*
(*Chronicon de Lanercost*) (excerpt: 225–6)
B: The Siege of Harfleur and the Battle of Agincourt (1415) in *The Deeds of Henry V* (*Gesta Henrici quinti*) (excerpt: ch. 4, pp. 26–30); Thomas Elmham's *Metrical Book on Henry V* (*Elmhami Liber metricus de Henrico quinto*) (excerpt: lines 509–20); Titus Livius, *The Life of Henry V* (*Vita Henrici quinti*) (excerpt: pp. 19–21); Ps.-Elmham, *Life and Deeds of Henry V* (*Vita et gesta Henrici V*) (excerpts: pp. 65, 67)
C: The Battle of Bosworth Field (1485) in Polydore Vergil's *English History* (*Anglica historia*) (excerpt: 25.25)

A: The Battle of Bannockburn (1314)

The English and Scots had been fighting over Scotland since 1297, with control of the country alternating between them. Bannockburn was the site (its exact location disputed) of a victory of the Scots, after a two-day battle under their leader Robert the Bruce, over the English under King Edward II. In 1328 the Treaty of Edinburgh–Northampton was signed, which gave Scotland its independence.

The Chronicle of Lanercost (*Chronicon de Lanercost*) **(excerpt: pp. 225–6)**

Date: mid-fourteenth century.

The *Chronicle of Lanercost* is preserved only in BL MS Cotton Claudius D.vii, of the late fourteenth or early fifteenth century.

Work: This chronicle, covering the period 1201–1346, may be the work of a monk at the monastery of Lanercost in Cumbria, who based it on that of a Franciscan chronicler with a particular interest in military history. The account of the battle of Bannockburn (pp. 225–8) is derived at least partly from eyewitnesses whom the author considered reliable. Alternative accounts can be found in *Gesta Edwardi de Carnarvan* (i.e. Edward II) by a canon of Bridlington (46); Walter Bower, *Scotichronicon* 12.20, with sections in rhyming verse; Adam of Murimuth, *Chr.* 20–1 and in a more rhetorical version by John de Trokelowe in the *Annals of St Albans* (pp. 84–6). An Anglo-Norman version is provided by the *Scalachronica* of

358 Fifteenth Century

Thomas Grey, written in the mid-fourteenth century. Geoffrey le Baker (*Chronicon 7*) adds the detail that before the battle *vidisses illa nocte gentem Anglorum non angelorum more vivencium set vino madencium, crapulam eructantium, Wassayl et Drinkhail plus solito intonancium*, contrasting the drunken behaviour of the English with the Scots, who were praying and fasting in silence, and using the recurring wordplay of the antithesis between *angeli* and *Angli* ('angels' and 'the English') which goes back at least as far as Gregory the Great's words as recorded by the author referred to as Anonymous of Whitby (9) around 700 (cf. Section I.8).

Linguistic points: The account has a tendency towards parataxis, moving towards a doom-laden statement, from the English point of view, at the end of each section. The style is not unlike that of Geoffrey of Monmouth in the *History of the Kings of Britain*. In general the author uses few non-classical words apart from the occasional word derived from French, e.g. *cussinus* ('cushion'), while from English comes *baldus* ('bold'), in a spelling perhaps reflecting a northern ME form of the fifteenth century.

TEXT II.41A

The battle of Bannockburn

[p. 225] ante festum autem nativitatis sancti Johannis Baptistae, collecto in unum toto exercitu suo, appropinquavit rex cum pompa praedicta versus castrum de Strivelyn ad amovendam obsidionem et pugnandum cum Scottis qui ibi erant in tota sua fortitudine congregati; et in vigilia Nativitatis predictae, post prandium venit exercitus regis juxta silvam de Torres; et audito quod Scotti essent in silva, prima acies regis, quam duxit dominus de Clifforde, voluit circuire silvam ne forte Scotti evaderent fugiendo. Scotti autem hoc permiserunt, donec essent multum a sociis elongati, et tunc ostenderunt se et dividentes illam primam aciem regis a media acie et extrema, irruerunt in eam et quosdam occiderunt et in fugam alios converterunt, et ab illa hora factus est timor inter Anglicos et major audacia inter Scottos. in die autem crastina quae fuit Anglicis dies mala, infelix nimis et infausta, cum se praepararent ex utraque parte ad proelium, exierunt sagittarii Angliae ante aciem, quibus occurrerunt sagittarii Scottorum et ex utraque parte fuerunt aliqui vulnerati et aliqui interfecti; sed sagittarii regis Angliae cito alios fugaverunt. cum autem duo exercitus multum appropinquassent, posuerunt se omnes Scotti in genibus suis dicendo 'Pater noster' et recommendaverunt se Deo et de coelo auxilium petiverunt; quo facto, audacter contra Anglicos processerunt. ordinaverunt autem sic exercitum suum, quod duae acies ejus praeirent tertiam, una ex qua latere alterius, ita quod neutra aliam praecederet; et tertia sequeretur in qua erat Robertus. quando vero ambo exercitus se mutuo conjunxerunt et

II.41 | Military Historiography 359

magni equi Anglorum irruerunt in lanceas Scottorum, sicut in unam densam silvam, factus est sonus maximus et horribilis ex lanceis fractis et ex dextrariis vulneratis ad mortem, et sic steterunt in pace ad tempus. Anglici autem sequentes non potuerunt attingere ad Scottos propter primam aciem interpositam nec in aliquo se juvare et ideo nihil restabat [p. 226] nisi ordinare de fuga. istum processum audivi a quodam fidedigno, qui fuit praesens et vidit. (…) aliud etiam infortunium accidit Anglicis quia cum paulo ante transissent unam foveam magnam in quam intrat fluxus maris nomine Bannokeburne, et jam confusi vellent redire, multi nobiles et alii prae pressura cum equis in illam ceciderunt et aliqui cum difficultate magna evaserunt et multi nunquam se explicare de fovea potuerunt; et ideo Bannokeburne in ore Anglicorum erat per multos annos sequentes.

Translation: *Chronicle of Lanercost*: the Battle of Bannockburn

Before the feast of the Nativity of St John the Baptist, the king, having gathered his whole army, advanced with great pomp towards Stirling Castle, to raise the siege and to engage with the Scots who were assembled there with all their forces. On the evening before 24 June, the king's army arrived after dinner near the forest of Torwood, and on hearing that there were Scots in the wood, the king's advance guard, led by Lord de Clifford, began to make a circuit of the wood to prevent the Scots escaping by flight. The Scots allowed this until they (the English) were far ahead of the main body, and then they revealed themselves. Cutting off the king's advance guard from the central and rear columns, they charged at them and killed some of them and put the others to flight. From that moment panic broke out among the English, while the Scots grew bolder. The next day – an evil, wretched and calamitous day for the English – when both sides were preparing for battle, the English archers emerged in front of the line and the Scottish archers engaged them, and some were wounded and others killed on either side; but the king of England's archers quickly put the others to flight. Now when the two armies had come very close to each other, all the Scots knelt down to say the Our Father, commending themselves to God and seeking help from heaven; after which they advanced boldly against the English. They had so arranged their army that two columns went side by side, in advance of the third, in such a way that neither should be in front of the other; and the third followed, in which was Robert the Bruce. When the two armies engaged and the great horses of the English charged the pikes of the Scots, as if into a dense forest, there arose a great and terrible crash of broken spears and of destriers fatally wounded; and so they stood still and quiet for a while. Now the English in the rear could not reach the Scots because the first column was in the way, nor could they do anything to help themselves, and so nothing remained but to make arrangements for flight. I heard this account from a reliable person who was there as an eyewitness. (…) Another misfortune that befell the English was that, whereas they had shortly before crossed

360 Fifteenth Century

a great ditch called Bannockburn, into which the tide flows up from the sea, they now in their turmoil were desperate to cross back. Many nobles and others fell into it with their horses in the crush. Some escaped only with great difficulty, while many never managed to extricate themselves from the ditch. As a result, for many years after, Bannockburn was a subject on the lips of the English.

Primary Sources

Chronicon de Lanercost, ed. J. Stevenson, Edinburgh, 1839.
The Chronicle of Lanercost 1272–1346, transl. H. Maxwell, repr. Glasgow, 2010.
Geoffrey le Baker of Swinbrook, *Chronicon*, transl. D. Preece, Woodbridge, 2008.

B: The Siege of Harfleur and the Battle of Agincourt (1415)

These events of the autumn of 1415 occurred in the context of the Hundred Years' War (1337–1453) between England and France. The young King Henry V (1386–1422), wanting the crown of France as well as peace with that country, invaded at Harfleur on the coast of Normandy, and after besieging that town, he forced the citizens to capitulate before moving north to the village of Agincourt (the English version of the French place name, Azincourt, currently the home of the Centre historique médiéval d'Azincourt), where he engaged, and overcame, the far more numerous French army. The battle of Agincourt is probably the most famous battle in English history after the battle of Hastings. As a victory over the French it is now regarded as more important for English self-mythology than for any political effect.

The texts excerpted below are the *Deeds of Henry V*, Thomas Elmham's *Metrical Book on Henry V*, Titus Livius' *Life of Henry V*, and the Ps.-Elmham, *Life and Deeds of Henry V*, all written during the first half of the fifteenth century by writers who were closely involved with Henry V, his brother Duke Humfrey of Gloucester, and Humfrey's nephew, Henry VI. With regard to the battle of Agincourt, comparison should also be made with the contemporary account of Thomas Walsingham, in his *Major Chronicles*, where he liberally weaves into his text quotations from classical Latin satirical and epic poets such as Virgil, Statius, Lucan, Persius and the author of the *Ilias Latina*. As well as providing detailed accounts of sieges and battles of the period, these writers share a desire to produce positive propaganda of their subjects, both for an English and a Continental audience, in the context not only of English claims to the French crown, but also of heresy and papal schism affecting a number of European countries at the time.

Further Reading

Curry, A. (2009) *The battle of Agincourt: sources and interpretations*,
 Woodbridge. For translations of historians and administrative sources.
—— (2010) 'Languages in the military profession in later medieval England' in
 The Anglo-Norman language and its contexts, ed. R. Ingham, York.
Gransden, A. (1982) 'The biographies of Henry V' in *Gransden (1982).

B(a): *The Deeds of Henry V* (*Gesta Henrici quinti*) (excerpt: ch. 4, pp. 26–30)

Date: 1416–17.

This work survives in two fifteenth-century MSS in the British Library: BL MS
Cotton Julius E.iv (also contains Ps.-Elmham, *Life and Deeds of Henry V* and
Thomas Elmham's *Metrical Book on Henry V*) and MS Sloane 1776.

Author: Although this work is anonymous, it seems that it was written by a chaplain at Henry's court who accompanied Henry to France and was indeed present
at the siege of Harfleur and the battle of Agincourt, for he often speaks in the
first-person plural. For a time it was thought that Thomas Elmham might be the
author, after Thomas Hearne's attribution of the later work *Life and Deeds of Henry V* to Elmham (published in 1727) was rejected by nineteenth-century scholars:
the *Life and Deeds* is now regarded as anonymous and referred to as Ps.-Elmham,
for which, see below, Section II.41B(d).

Work: This work covers the years 1413–15. It opens with a description of Henry's
coronation. The topographical description of Harfleur on the estuary of the tidal
river Seine, and the course of the siege in 1415, leading to surrender by the French,
is given in chapters 4–8, while the battle of Agincourt is described through a
first-person narrative in chapters 12–14 (cf. *Liber metricus* 485–560). In general
the author stresses God's constant support of the English.

Linguistic points: The unknown author of the *Deeds of Henry V* provides a clear
topographical description, with a number of sometimes rather periphrastic
technical terms associated with civic and military architecture. Mentioning the
water mills, he uses the medieval word *multura* (a spelling of *molitura*), derived
from CL *molere*, for the process of grinding. The medieval term *fortalitium*,
used also on the Continent, is applied to the massive fortification which, he
says, 'we call a Barbican, but which is generally called a Bulwark' – this being the
earliest attestation of the word 'bulwark' in English. With regard to the weap-
onry, *canellus*, derived from CL *canalis* via OF/AN 'cha-/canel', for a 'channel',
here occurs in a secondary sense, as a 'tube', i.e. a small cannon; the author then
adds the gloss, *quas in nostro vulgari 'Gunnys' vocamus*, introducing the English

362 Fifteenth Century

word 'gun', of obscure derivation, which is first attested in the mid-fourteenth century, also within a Latin text. In describing the bridges linking the tower with the outside, he mentions a smaller wooden bridge *qui ad voluntatem hostium poni et retrahi potuit*, preferring this circumlocution to the more technical terms current at the time, whereby various adjectives based on *tract-*, *torn-*, *(e)leva-*, *versa-*, or the term *coleicius* (associated with '(port)cullis') were used with *pons* to denote a drawbridge. In general the few non-classical words used by the author are already current in BML, such as *harnesium*, i.e. 'harness' (used in this text in its sense of 'armour'), a word that comes into Latin in the twelfth century from French: it occurs in many European languages, but its ultimate origin is obscure.

TEXT II.41B(a)

A description of Harfleur, besieged by Henry V in 1415

[4] situatur enim villa [de Harfleu] in extremitate vallis, super crepidinem Secani fluminis, per quod mare fluit ultra medium ville, et refluit ad unum miliare et ultra. descendit eciam fluvius dulcis per mediam vallem, replens fossas in bona profunditate et latitudine extra de sub muris ex parte vallis et ex parte illa ubi se rex monstravit usque ad latus contiguum aque Secane qui et intrat divisim sub muris per medium ville in una ianua fluviali et duobus collateralibus alveolis testudinatis, claudendis vel aperiendis pro toto vel parte ad libitum incolarum. et intra sub muris due molendine volvuntur impetu introeuntis aque, servientes pro multura in alimentum urbanorum et plebium. et transcursis molendinis fluvius ab alveolis se remergit (re-emerg-) in ampnem et pleno alveo per medium ville percurrit ad portum. pars vero altera ville opposita regi sicca est set munita fossa duplici, quarum interior inestimate profunditatis est et latitudinis competentis. villa quidem non est nisi modica set pulcra valde, armata et circumcincta muris externis angularibus et idcirco, secundum magistrum Aegidium,[1] difficilioribus ad impugnandum ac facilioribus et caucioribus (caut-) ad resistendum, cum turribus altis et decentis structure, aliisque inferioribus intermediis fortaliciis, habens tres portas pro introitu et exitu, unam ex parte illa ubi rex se monstravit et duas ex parte opposita, quarum utramque coni circumducentis aque in dictis fossis a nostris accessibus protegebant. et ante introitum cuiuslibet ipsarum portarum prius fabricaverat hostilis caliditas unum forte fortalicium quod nos *Barbican* set communes *Bulwerkis* appellamus, et illud ex parte regis fuit fortissimum et maximum eorum, armatum exterius rotundis et grossis arboribus fere ad altitudinem murorum ville affixis in circuitu, constrictisque fortiter et ligatis; interius vero meremio, terra et tignis excisis in antris et diverticulis

---

1 I.e. Aegidius Romanus (d. 1316), *De regimine principum* 3.3.20.

II.41 | Military Historiography 363

pro recepcione hostium et hostilium, ac rimis, angulis et porosis mansiunculis per que in canellis suis, quas in nostro vulgari *Gunnys* vocamus, ac telis balistis et offensivis aliis nos afficere potuerunt. et erat structura eius orbicularis, plus continens in diametro quam iactus lapidis quo vulgus nostrum in Anglia se solet ad limites recreare. et circuiebat illud aqua magne profunditatis et latitudinis duarum, ubi strictius, lancearum, habens pontem pro introitu et exitu versus villam et ponticulum ligneum versus extra, qui ad voluntatem hostium poni et retrahi potuit, quociens eis videretur expediens irrumpere in nostrates. interius vero villa ornatur perpulcris edificiis prope sitis et solum unica parochiali ecclesia decoratur.

Translation: *The Deeds of Henry V*, the Siege of Harfleur

The town of Harfleur is situated on the edge of a valley on the banks of the river Seine, through which the sea flows up beyond the town centre and flows back more than a mile. A freshwater river also flows down through the middle of the valley, filling the ditches to a good depth and breadth outside below the walls on the valley side and on the side where the king mustered his army, as far as the wide expanse close to the River Seine, which divides and enters beneath the walls through the town centre in one water gate and two adjoining vaulted channels: these are closed or opened fully or in part as the inhabitants decide. Within the town beneath the walls two mills are turned by the force of the incoming water, helping to grind food for both the upper and lower classes of townspeople. And when the river has flowed past the mills it re-emerges from the channels into a stream and runs through the town centre with a full channel to the port. The other part of the town opposite where the king was mustered is dry but protected by a double ditch, of which the inner one is of an unknown depth and a substantial width. The town is only relatively small but it is very attractive, well protected and surrounded with outer polygonal walls which are therefore, according to Master Giles, more difficult to storm and easier and better prepared to offer resistance, with their high towers of an appropriate structure, and other, lower fortifications in between. It has three gates by which to enter and leave, one on the side where the king mustered and two on the opposite side, both of which are protected from our approaches by the bastions of the surrounding water in the aforementioned ditches. In front of each of these gates the enemy's cunning had previously constructed a strong fortress which we call a barbican but people in general call a bulwark. The one on the king's side was the strongest and largest of them, protected on the outside by massive circular tree trunks, almost to the level of the town walls, and set in a closely packed circle, tightly bound together; but inside it was protected with wood, earth and beams cut out in caves and recesses to hold the enemy and allow its hostile attacks. It had slits, corners and little shelters with many openings through which they were able to assail us with their tubes (which we call 'guns' in our vernacular), and with their arrows and crossbows and other

364 Fifteenth Century

offensive weapons. There was also a circular structure with a diameter wider than the distance our common people in England often toss the stone put when training on the sports field. This was surrounded by very deep water, as wide, at its most narrow, as two lances, with one bridge facing the town by which to enter and leave and a small wooden bridge facing the outside: this one could be lowered or raised as our enemy decided, whenever they thought it was expedient to rush out against us. On the inside the town is adorned with very beautiful buildings situated close together and honoured with just a single parish church.

Primary Sources and Related Text

Gesta Henrici quinti, ed. F. Taylor and J. Roskell, OMT: Oxford, 1975.

Thomas Walsingham, *The St Albans Chronicle: the Chronica majora of Thomas Walsingham*, vol. 2: *1394–1422*, eds. J. Taylor, W. Childs and L. Watkiss, Oxford, 2011: 666–72.

Thomas Walsingham, *Ypodigma Neustriae* 459–62.

For the king's speech before the battle of Harfleur, cf. Shakespeare, *Henry V* Act III, scene 1: 'Once more unto the breach, dear friends, etc.', and scene 3; *Historia Henrici quinti* by Richard Redman (d. 1540) in *Memorials of Henry the Fifth*, RS 11 (1858) 43–4 for a Latin version of this speech.

B(b): Thomas Elmham's *Metrical Book on Henry V* (*Elmhami Liber metricus de Henrico quinto*) (excerpt: lines 509–20)

Date: c.1418.

Despite or perhaps because of the cryptic nature of the poem, it seems to have found an appreciative audience: nine fifteenth-century MSS survive, of which BL MS Cotton Julius E.iv contains the fullest version.

Author: Thomas Elmham was born in 1364 and died in about 1427. He was a monk at St Augustine's, Canterbury, but also, according to a letter of Henry V, seemed to have acted as royal chaplain for a while. At the end of his life he was in charge of Cluniac monasteries in England and Scotland. He is thought to be the author of an impressive history of St Augustine's Abbey, sometimes known as the *Speculum Augustinianum*, a chronicle of the kings of England (hitherto unprinted), based on Geoffrey of Monmouth, and Lives of Henry V, both in prose and verse, though only the verse version excerpted here survives.

Work: This poem in elegiac couplets, written in about 1418, is said to be an abbreviation of a prose work, probably Elmham's own (lost) version based on the

Deeds of Henry V. It gives an account of events down to 1418. Elmham states in the preface that he is writing in verse because it is more obscure, and he probably felt this was appropriate for one of the major themes of the poem, an attack on the Lollards. The short excerpt here gives King Henry V's speech rousing the English troops as they go into battle at Agincourt, with emphasis placed on the righteousness of the English cause.

Linguistic points: Elmham adds to the cryptic nature of the poem by using cryptograms and wordplay, as when he refers to Wyclif in the Latin form of his name, *Mala Vita*. An example of an obscure couplet is: *mox rex pro villis Nel misit redimendis; | non respondetur pir datur inde per ir*, where *pir* and *ir* are transliterations of the Greek words for 'fire' and 'hand' respectively. This use of learned and cryptic language is common in the political poems of the fourteenth and fifteenth centuries, which often contain an apocalyptic or prophetic element. Elmham also uses biblical allusions plentifully, as is appropriate for his primarily clerical audience.

Further Reading

*Gransden (1982: 206–10).

TEXT II.41B(b)

The king rallies his troops
[**509**] rex dixit reliquis, 'Consortes, arma parate! (…)
[**515**] Anglia non planget me captum sive redemptum;
praesto, paratus ero juris agone mori.
Sancte Georgi! Sancte Georgi, miles, adesto!
Anglis in jure, Sancte Maria, fave! (…)
[**519**] hac hora plures pro nobis corde precantur
Anglorum justi: fraus tua, France, ruet!' (…)

Translation: *Metrical Book on Henry V*

[**509**] *The king said to the rest: 'Fellow-fighters, prepare your weapons!' (…)*
[**515**] *England will not bewail my capture or my ransom;*
I will be at hand, ready to die in the struggle for what is just.
St George! St George! be with us, knight!
Holy Mary, take the side of the English who are in the right! (…)

366 Fifteenth Century

[519] *At this moment large numbers of righteous English
are praying intensely for us. Frenchman, your treachery will fail! (…)*

Primary Source and Related Texts

Thomas Elmham, *Liber metricus de Henrico quinto*, in *Memorials of Henry the
Fifth*, RS 11 (1858): 120–2 for the battle of Agincourt.
Political poems and songs relating to English history (1327–1483), 2 vols, RS 14
(1859–61); cf. Shakespeare, *Henry V* Act III, scene 1: 'Follow your spirit, and
upon this charge | Cry "God for Harry! England and Saint George!"'

B(c): Titus Livius, *The Life of Henry V* (*Vita Henrici quinti*) (excerpt: pp. 19–21)

Date: c.1437.

The work is found in four MSS, namely BL MS Cotton Claudius E.iii and MS
Arundel 12 in the College of Arms in London (a copy written for Duke Humfrey),
and two in Corpus Christi College, Cambridge.

Author: Titus Livius was born near Ferrara in Italy soon after 1400; he travelled
widely round the Mediterranean, teaching and writing, before coming to England, where from 1436 he was attached to the household of Duke Humfrey, acting
as writer-in-residence for a few years, before returning to Italy, where he died in
about 1456. Some of his Latin comedies and praise poems also survive.

Work: Titus Livius wrote this work at the behest of, and with information provided by, Duke Humfrey, the younger brother of Henry V, whose life Henry saved
at Agincourt. It has been described as a typical work of Renaissance humanism,
partly because of the panegyric form, which was popular among Renaissance
writers. Livius' work was a primary source for the first English Life of Henry V,
dating to about 1514. There has been much discussion as to which work came first:
this one by Titus Livius or Ps.-Elmham's *Life and Deeds*, below. A comparison of
the two is instructive.

Linguistic points: Although Titus Livius is usually regarded as a humanist writer,
the syntax is often strained and less than clear. The author uses classical technical
terms such as *fetialis* here, and elsewhere *senatores* for the councillors of London,
though he glosses this with *quos aldermannos vocant* (p. 22), where *aldermannus*
is derived from English. *fetialis* was a CL term for a member of a college of priests
in Rome, but it came to mean a herald or ambassador. It was not unknown in
earlier BML, for it crops up in glossaries, but Titus Livius is the earliest writer to
use it within a narrative text.

TEXT II.41B(c)

The heat of the battle at Agincourt

[Hearne p. 19] et cum ad viginti passus ad oppidum Agincourt ad Gallos hostes devenissent, cum tubicinum clangor maximus ad proelium omnium animos excitat, occurrunt hostes, initur proelium. erat Anglicis acies quantum campus ille patiebatur lata, Gallis vero duobus factis acutis cuneis tanquam duobus cornibus, se versus [se] semper in latius extendentibus in hostes in medium accipiendos irruunt. turbatus fuisset et a Gallis equitibus Anglicorum ordo, nisi sagittis et arcubus pars maxima tum mortui tum vulnerati, reliqui perterriti in suos redire compulsi. fixerat Anglicus unusquisque terrae pro se palum acutum [utriusque] pro scuto, ut insultans hostilis equus vel metu retrocederet vel ipso infixus vulneratus caderet, vel ab Anglico cum equite conficeretur. simul accenditur proelium, instat et viro vir, nec pes pedi cedit, sed ad tres horas quo concurritur loco quisquis aut caedit aut caeditur. nemo praedam sed victoriam spectat. capitur nullus. caeduntur multi. Anglicus vero postquam jam in medium acceptus est, ad caedem acrius accenditur, ut cui nulla praeterquam [p. 20] in victoria salutis spes reliqua videbatur. caedunt immaniter propinquos, quos et alii subsequuntur. brevique nullus e Gallis ad pugnam sed ad caedem satis et sua superbia singuli ducuntur et innumeri. vero cum Galli iam leto dediti forent, et ipsa victoria certa videretur Anglicis, ecce caedi parcitur, Galli capiuntur, principes domini nobiles quamplurimi. nec inclitus unquam rex proelio laboribusve pepercit, nec pericula vitaeque discrimina devitans suis defuit, sed ut invictus leo tunc animo pugnans ardentissimo in hostes, in ipsa galea et armorum reliquo plures ictus accepit. ecce dum impetu valido regis frater serenissimus Humfredus Gloucestriae dux incautius forte pugnaret, in iliis mucrone transfixus, semianimis ad terram prosternitur: ipse vero rex frater Humfredi cruribus intra suos pedes repositis. ceciderat namque dux inclitus ad suos obverso capite, sed pedibus ad hostes, ubi rex diu fortissime pugnans frater fratrem ab hostibus tutatus inter suos reportari fecit.

King Henry gains victory

obtenta tandem victoria, fuso, caeso, prostratoque Gallorum exercitu, statim et illic hostium non minor exercitus se parat ad pugnam, putantes jam fessos Anglicos tam dira et longa poena, quem ut viderunt Anglici, qui plures multo captivos habebant quam ipsimet numero forent, timentes hac in nova pugna, ne sibi simul cum captivis et hostibus decertandum esset, plurimos quanquam dites et nobiles morti dedere. rex praeterea prudentissimus feciales ad Gallos, novum exercitum, mittit, ut statim aut ad pugnam veniant aut retrocedant, scientes quod si differant vel ad proelium veniant, mox omnes de suis capti simul et quotcumque capientur ex ipsis nulla misericordia gladiis omnes caedentur. quae quidem sententia regia ut statim innotuit illis, cum vires Anglicas tum sibi et suis timentes, moesti pudore maximo redierunt. rex tunc tanta victoria potitus maximas Deo gratias agit. et cum eo die beatorum Crispini et [p. 21] Crispiani commemoratio fiebat

368 Fifteenth Century

ab ecclesia, quorum suffragiis a Deo victoriam tantam de hostibus obtinuisse sibi videbatur, statuit ut quoad viveret singulis diebus in missa quam audiret eorundem beatorum commemoratio fieret.

Translation: Titus Livius, *The Life of Henry V*

When within twenty paces of the town of Agincourt they came upon the French enemy and the strident noise of trumpets roused everyone's spirits to battle, the enemies rushed at each other and battle commenced. The English battle line was as wide as the field allowed, while the French had made two sharp wedges like two horns, extending all the wider as they rushed forward towards the enemy to catch them in the middle. The English lines would have been thrown into disarray by the French knights if the majority of them had not been killed and wounded by bows and arrows, and the rest terrified and forced to turn back towards their own lines. Each Englishman had fixed stakes in the ground in front of him as a shield so that when the enemy cavalry leaped forward they would either recoil in terror or fall, pierced and wounded by the stakes, or would be killed by the English, together with their riders. At that moment the battle flared up, with one man pushing forward onto another and no one giving an inch, but for three hours each man either killed or was killed as they clashed there. No one looked for spoils, only victory. No one was captured, but many were slaughtered. But after the English were drawn into the centre, the slaughter became more intense, as if no one thought there was any hope left of safety except in victory. They brutally slaughtered those closest to them and then those who came up behind these. In short, the French came in vast numbers, drawn by their arrogance, not to battle but to slaughter. As the French surrendered to death, and victory seemed certain for the English, behold! the English cease the slaughter, the French are captured, a vast number of leaders, lords and nobles. The celebrated king never spared himself from the toil of battle, never avoided danger or risk to his life, nor did he fail his men, but like an unvanquished lion, fighting the enemy with indomitable spirit at that moment, he received many blows on his helmet and the rest of his armour. And look! while the king's most serene brother, Humfrey, Duke of Gloucester, was fighting bravely and perhaps rather incautiously, as he rushed forward he was pierced in the intestines by a sword and fell to the ground, half dead. His brother, the king, straddled Humfrey's legs, for the noble Duke had fallen with his head towards his own men and his feet towards the enemy. Then the king, fighting bravely for a long time, managed to protect his brother from the enemy and get him carried back to his own side.

When the victory was won at last, and the French army had been routed, slaughtered and brought down, immediately another enemy army, no smaller, prepared to fight, thinking that the English were now exhausted by such a dreadful and lengthy torment. When they saw this, the English, who were holding more men captive than the number of men in their own army, fearing that in this new battle they would have to fight with the captives and the enemy at the same time, put to death a large number even of wealthy and noble men. Meanwhile the king, acting very wisely, sent heralds to this new French army, to tell them either to come to battle or withdraw immediately, and that they should bear in mind that if they dispersed or entered the battle, all of their men who had been captured and all those who would be captured would immediately be put to death by the sword without mercy. As soon as the king's decision was reported to them, fearing the English forces for themselves and their own men, they departed in sorrow and great shame. The king, having gained such a great victory, gave great thanks to God, and since that day was observed by the church as a feast day for the blessed Crispin and Crispian, whose intercession with God, it seemed to him, had helped him to gain such a great victory over the enemy, he arranged that for as long as he lived, these blessed saints would be commemorated every day when he heard Mass.

Primary Sources and Related Texts

Titi Livii Foro-Juliensis Vita Henrici quinti, regis Angliae, ed. T. Hearne, Oxford, 1716.

Thomas Walsingham, *Ypodigma Neustriae* 463–8.

Thomas Walsingham, *The St Albans Chronicle: the Chronica majora of Thomas Walsingham*, vol. 2: *1394–1422*, eds. J. Taylor, W. Childs and L. Watkiss, Oxford, 2011: 672–82.

Polydore Vergil, *Anglica historia* 22.7–9, for an account of the battle of Agincourt.

The first English Life of King Henry the Fifth, ed. C. Kingsford, Oxford, 1911.

Henry of Avranches, *Passio sanctorum Crispini et Crispiniani*, ed. M. Allen, *Analecta Bollandiana* 108 (1990) 357–86.

EHD 5.130–7.

Further Reading

Gransden, A. (1982) 'The biographies of Henry V' in *Gransden (1982).

Rundle, D. (2008) 'The unoriginality of Tito Livio Frulovisi's *Vita Henrici quinti*', *EHR* 123: 1109–31.

Weiss, R. (1957) 'Humphrey, Duke of Gloucester and Tito Livio Frulovisi' in *Fritz Saxl (1890–1948): a volume of memorial essays from his friends*, ed. D. Gordon, London.

Cf. Shakespeare, *Henry V* Act IV, scene 3, 'This day is call'd the feast of Crispian, etc.'

370   Fifteenth Century

B(d): Ps.-Elmham, *The Life and Deeds of Henry V* (*Vita et gesta Henrici V*) (excerpts: pp. 65, 67)

Date: c.1446.

Work: Thomas Hearne judged this work to be by Thomas Elmham, who also wrote the *Metrical Book on Henry V*, but it is now accepted that the author is unknown and is referred to as Ps.-Elmham. It covers the years 1387–1422, in other words the whole of Henry V's life. The relation between this work and the biography of Henry V by Titus Livius (for which, see above, Section II.41B(c)) is controversial. The earlier part of the work is closer to that of Livius in its factual content, but later the author draws on other sources, such as Lord Hungerford, to whom the first recension of the work is addressed.

Linguistic points: The author has been accused of long-windedness, but he controls the long sentences in an impressive manner and communicates the dramatic scene with multi-sensory clarity. He combines such rhetorical devices as the personification of abstracts (a form of prosopopoeia), like Disease, with realistic details drawn from eyewitness accounts, as in the description, later in the work, of Henry V's death in 1422 outside Paris. The excerpt here is particularly rhetorical, with wordplay (*in Martis, immo mortis obsequium*) and apostrophe, culminating in the long list of emotions, noises and actions (starting from *o letale bellum*), to convey the murderous turmoil of the battle.[2] *Invasivus*, in the sense 'offensive', of weapons, occurs in BML from the mid-fourteenth century, as also in English in the sixteenth century, though it is later replaced in English by 'offensive'. The form *herodum* ('herald') reflects the pronunciation of the AN and ME form 'heraud', possibly derived from a Germanic word; it was not until the sixteenth century that English adopted the form 'herald'.

TEXT II.41B(d)

The horrors of battle at Agincourt
[Hearne p. 65] cumque usque ad distanciam viginti passuum non procul de Agincourt versus acies hosticas appropinquassent, et lituorum sonitus, aeris viscera maximo reboatu dilacerans, animos bellatorum in proelium invitasset, ipsa pars adversa, jam primo se movens, Anglis se dirigit in occursum. nec mora, furor bellicus gravissimus invalescit, cum istac, in primaevo concursu tantorum forcium armatorum, lancearum diris impulsibus, mucronum impetuosis aggressibus et aliis variis Marcialibus insaniis, tam validorum armorum compaginibus

---

2   Cf. Section I.20 for a similar description of the noise of the unclean spirits in hell, in the eighth-century *Life of Guthlac*.

violenter diruptis, viri praenobiles letalia vulnera alterutrum infligerent et causarent. illac vero architenencium cunei bellicosi, forti et multiplici tractu suo aera nebulis vestientes, ut nubes imbrifera stillas pluviales, pungencium sagittarum intolerabilem multitudinem emittentes, in Martis, immo mortis obsequium totis nisibus hanelabant. qui, in primo acierum concursu, equites Gallicanos, ad ipsos transcurrendum et a tergis Anglicos impugnandum dispositos, impetu multiplici sagittarum equis vulnera imprimentes, aut in terram dejecerunt aut retrocedere coegerunt, et sic ipsorum tam grave et timendum propositum in pugnae facie est cassatum. o letale bellum, dira strages, clades mortalis, fames mortis, sitis cruoris insaciabilis, furibundus impetus, furor impetuosus, insania vehemens, crudelis conflictus, inmisericors ulcio, lancearum fragor inmensus, sagittarum garritus, securium concussus, ensium vibracio, armorum dirupcio, vulnerum impressio, effusio sanguinis, induccio mortis, corporum dissolucio, nobilium occisio, aer fragoribus horrendis tonitruat, nubes missilia impluunt, tellus cruorem absorbet, spiritus a corporibus evolant, semiviva corpora proprio sanguine volutant, cadaveribus occisorum terrae superficies operitur. iste invadit, ille cadit, iste aggreditur, ille moritur, iste animum revocat, ille animam cum cruore simul eructat, occisor irascitur, occisus moerore conteritur, victus reddi desiderat, victorum impetus reddicionis tempora non exspectat, saevicia regnat, pietas exulat, fortes et strenui opprimuntur et montes cadaverum cumulantur, multitudo maxima traditur morti, principes et magnates ducuntur captivi. (…)

The king takes control and gains victory
[p. 67] nobilis etiam dux Gloucestriae, frater regis, Gallicorum feriencium ictibus, se forsan animosius equo promovens in conflictum, vulneratus graviter erat ad tellurem prostratus, in cujus proteccionem regia victoriosa nobilitas commota, super uterino fratre visceribus pietatis modo militari contra hostes insilit, obumbracione proprii corporis ipsum defendit, et ab hostium saevienti malicia, in ictuum multitudine gravissima, Marcia, vix tolerabilia, perpessus pericula, eruit et custodit. contigit eciam ut victoriosissimus princeps cum ipsa acie, cui ipsemet praeerat, aciem sibi oppositam primo devicit. quibus dispersis, cum ipse rex cum suis se in praeviae suae aciei, non dum a pugna cessantis, auxilium divertisset, vidit coram se alium numerosum cuneum Gallicorum, se in campo adversus se et suos in proelia praeparantem, ad quos ipsum regem, cum sibi assistentibus, necessario intendere oportebat. post pauca tamen omnes acies regis, tam praeviae quam subsequentes, et ala utraque, prostratis hostibus, victrices in proelio sunt effecta, putantesque Anglici, jam lassati, et armis invasivis plurimum destituti, per ipsos Gallicos, se in proelia disponentes, novum inire conflictum, timentes ne captivi quos duxerant in ipsos irruerent cum pugnarent, multos eorum, licet nobiles, in ore gladii trucidabant. sed regalis summa nobilitas ipsis Gallis qui adhuc rura ut praediximus occupabant, herodum secundum legacionem mandavit ut aut in bellum venirent aut a conspectu suo se retraherent festinanter, scientes quo, si in novum proelium se disponerent pugnaturos, tam ipsi quam captivi ad

372 Fifteenth Century

huc superstites, absque misericordia, dirissima vindicta quam Angli possent infligere, interirent. nec mora, tam gravis decreti sentenciam formidantes, omnes adversarii timore, pudore et dolore confusi, a campis unanimiter recesserunt. et divina miseracione glorioso potitus triumpho, rex magnificus, hostibus superatis, in campo quo proelium committebatur exspectans, non ingratus dememinit tantae victoriae gracias devotissime reddere largitori. et qui in festo sanctorum Crispini et Crispiniani tanta victoria sibi datur, omni die, durante vita sua, memoriam de eisdem in una missarum suarum audivit.

Translation: Ps.-Elmham, *Life and Deeds of Henry V*

When they had approached and were only twenty paces from the enemy lines, not far from Agincourt, and as the sound of trumpets, rending the sky itself, so loud was their sound, had roused the fighters' spirits to battle, the enemy side now first moved forward to meet the English. Immediately the madness of war greatly increased in strength when on that side in the first clash between so many strong-armed men, with terrible hurling of spears, with impetuous sword strikes and various other insanities of war, and when the close fastenings of robust armour had been violently torn apart, these noble men caused deadly wounds, inflicting them on each other. But on the English side the warlike and close formations of bowmen, covering the sky with clouds of arrows as they powerfully drew their bows in vast numbers, put all their efforts into sending forth an unbearable number of pointed arrows like a rain-bearing cloud sending rain drops, in obedience to Mars, or rather to death. The French horsemen were drawn up to go past the English and to attack them from behind, inflicting many wounds on their horses by means of a shower of arrows. But the English managed either to throw them to the ground or to force them to retreat, and so the dreadful and terrifying plan of the French came to nothing. O deadly war, terrible slaughter, mortal disaster, hunger for death, insatiable thirst for blood, raging attack, violent madness, powerful insanity, cruel conflict, merciless revenge, great crashing of lances, arrows whistling, axes clashing, swords reverberating, armour smashing, inflicting wounds, blood pouring, the causing of death, bodies hacked to pieces, noblemen killed, the sky thundering with horrendous crashes, clouds raining missiles, the earth absorbing bloody gore, souls flying out of their bodies, half-dead bodies rolling in their own blood, the surface of the ground covered with the corpses of the dead. One attacks, another falls, one assails, another dies, one regains his strength, another belches forth his last breath together with bloody gore, the killer is enraged, the killed is crushed by grief, the victim longs for surrender, but the onslaught of the victors does not allow any time for the return of the dead, cruelty reigns, love goes into exile, brave and vigorous men are crushed and mountains of corpses pile up, a great multitude is handed over to death, and princes and leaders are taken captive. (…)

The noble Duke of Gloucester, the king's brother, also moved forward on his horse too vigorously into the conflict and was seriously wounded and thrown to the ground by the blows of the attacking French. The noble and victorious king, motivated by a desire to protect him, attacked the enemy like a good soldier and out of compassion stood above his brother's body to protect him, defending him by putting his own body in the way and pulling him away from the raging cruelty of the enemy: in the midst of a very dangerous onslaught of blows, enduring the dangers of war which are scarcely bearable, Henry saved Humfrey. It happened also that the most victorious prince, together with the battle line of which he was in charge, was the first to overcome the battle line ranged before him. When they had been scattered and the king had turned aside with his own men to assist the battle line in front, which had not yet ceased fighting, he saw before him another troop of numerous French soldiers, preparing on the field to fight against him and his men; the king and the men assisting him had necessarily to deal with these. But before long the enemy was laid low and all the king's battle lines, both in front and behind, and both wings, were victorious. But the English were exhausted and, deprived of offensive weapons, they were afraid to see the French arranging themselves to go into battle once more, for they feared that the French captives they had taken would rush upon them while they were fighting. And so they massacred many of them at swordpoint, despite the fact that the captives were noblemen. But the cream of the royal nobility sent a message to the French who were still occupying the field, as we mentioned, telling them either to come into battle or swiftly to withdraw from their sight, bearing in mind that if they were disposed to fight a new battle, both they and the captives who were still alive would die without mercy, with the most brutal vengeance the English could inflict. Immediately all the enemy, fearing this severe announcement, thrown into disarray by fear, shame and grief, agreed unanimously to withdraw from the battlefield. After gaining a glorious triumph by divine mercy, the magnificent king, his enemy vanquished, remained on the battlefield, remembering gratefully to give most devout thanks for such a great victory to the one who had granted it, and because such a great victory occurred on the feast of St Crispin and St Crispinianus, every day for the rest of his life he listened to an account of them in one of his Masses.

Primary Sources and Related Texts

Thomae de Elmham Vita et gesta Henrici quinti, ed. T. Hearne, Oxford, 1727.

Titus Livius, *Vita Henrici quinti*.

Thomas Walsingham, *The St Albans Chronicle: the Chronica majora of Thomas Walsingham*, vol. 2: *1394–1422*, eds. J. Taylor, W. Childs and L. Watkiss, Oxford, 2011: 672–82.

374 Fifteenth Century

Further Reading

Rundle, D. (2008) 'The unoriginality of Tito Livio Frulovisi's *Vita Henrici quinti*', *EHR* 123: 1109–31.

C: The Battle of Bosworth Field (1485)

This was the final battle (1485) in the Wars of the Roses, at which the House of Lancaster won a victory over the House of York and King Richard III was killed, allowing Henry VII to become the first Tudor king.

Polydore Vergil, *English History* (*Anglica historia*) (excerpt: 25.25)

Date: c.1531.

An autograph MS of the first version of this work (dated 1531) survives in two volumes in the Urbino collection in the Vatican Library.

Author: Polydore Vergil (c.1470–1555), born in Urbino, wrote a work *De inventione rerum* and a collection of Latin proverbs, the *Adagia*, before coming to England in 1502 in the service of an Italian cardinal. In England he had some success as a diplomat and administrator and as Archdeacon of Wells, and became a member of the humanist circle around Thomas More and John Colet. Later he fell foul of Cardinal Wolsey and was imprisoned in the Tower of London for a while. The first edition of the *English History* was finished in 1512–13, but there were also later printed editions. In 1525 Polydore Vergil brought out the first critical edition of a British historical text, namely of Gildas' *The Destruction of Britain*. He left England for Italy in 1553.

Work: Polydore Vergil wrote his *English History*, in twenty-seven books, the most famous of his works in England, for Henry VII. He took his information from eyewitnesses as well as from British (Gildas), English, Scottish and French written sources and arranged the work biographically, king by king, in the manner of Suetonius. This became an important source particularly for the period of English history 1460–1537, including the Wars of the Roses, from which the passage below is taken. Book 25 contains the life of Richard III (1452–85): elements of Polydore Vergil's description of Richard III will be familiar, for Polydore's work was used by the English historians on whom Shakespeare drew for his history plays. The passage excerpted here is the last chapter in the book about Richard: it describes him at the end of the battle, with a hint of admiration for his spirit amid the grim portrayal of his character and looks (including the curvature of the spine causing one shoulder to be higher than the other). The author sees his description of Richard's character and his ignominious end as an example to deter people from such behaviour, as it were, the opposite of a saint's Life. This chapter also shows Henry rejoicing in his victory and making arrangements for both the dead and the survivors.

Linguistic points: Polydore Vergil's style is very smooth, with the order of words and phrases often apparently inverted, with for example the object at the beginning of the sentence or an ablative absolute or two at the end of a sentence. The use of *fugere*, in the sense 'to escape the notice of', synonymous with *latere*, is only found in BML in the fifteenth century.

TEXT II.41C

The battle of Bosworth field: the defeat of Richard III by the future Henry VII
[25.25] Ricardus potuit, ut fama est, salutem fuga quaerere. nam qui circa eum erant, ubi videretur militem iam inde ab initio certaminis languide ac segniter arma movere, atque alios clam praelio excedere, fraudem suspicati, hortati sunt eum ad fugam, et cum iam manifeste res inclinata esset, equum velocem adduxerunt. ille vero, quem non fugiebat populum sibi infestum esse, spe deposita omnis posthac futuri eventus, fertur respondisse se eo die aut bellorum aut vitae finem facturum, adeo magna ferocia magnaque vis animi in eo fuit. qui propterea sciens certo illum diem vel regnum sibi deinceps pacatum redditurum vel perpetuo adempturum, corona regia redimitus in certamen descendit, ut aut initium finemve regnandi ex illo faceret. ita miser subito similem exitum habuit atque iis accidere solet qui ius, qui fas, qui honestum pro eo habent ac voluntatem, impietatem, improbitatem. sane ista sunt exempla longe hominum vocibus vehementiora ad deterrendum eos qui nullam horam vacuam a scelere, crudelitate, flagitio praeterire patiuntur. Henricus adeptam statim victoriam Deo optimo maximo multis precibus acceptam retulit, dein incredibili laetitia perfusus in proximum collem se recepit, ubi postquam collaudavit milites iussitque curari vulneratos atque occisos sepeliri, immortales omnibus principibus gratias egit, pollicitus se memorem beneficiorum fore, milite interea eum magno clamore regem salutante, plaususque libentissimo animo dante. quo viso, Thomas Stanleius coronam Ricardi inter spolia repertam capiti protinus imposuit, perinde ac si iam populi iussu rex fuisset more maiorum renuntiatus, atque id primum fuit felicitatis omen. post haec Henricus, collectis omnibus sarcinis, cum victore exercitu Lecestriam ad vesperam perrexit, ubi reficiendi a labore militis itinerisque Londinum versus parandi causa duos moratur dies. interim Ricardi corpus, cuncto nudatum vestitu ac dorso equi impositum, capite et brachiis ac cruribus utrinque pendentibus, Lecestriam ad coenobium Franciscanorum monachorum deportatur, spectaculum mehercule miserabile sed hominis vita dignum, ibique sine ullo funere honore biduo post terra humatur. regnavit annos duos et totidem menses,

376 Fifteenth Century

plusque die uno. statura fuit pusilla, corpore deformi, altero humero eminentio-
re, facie brevi ac truculenta, quae olere malitiam et dolum ac fraudem clamitare
videretur. dum in cogitatione aliqua versabatur, inferius labrum assidue morde-
bat quasi ita fera in eo corpusculo natura in seipsam furente. simul pugionem
quem semper gestabat dextra manu ex vagina dimidio tenus pariter recondendo
atque condendo. ingenium vero habuit acutum, sagax, versutum, ad simulandum
atque dissimulandum aptum. animum autem elatum ac ferocem, qui eum etiam
non defecit in morte, quam destitutus a suis maluit per ferrum capere quam per
turpem fugam, incertae ac fortasse post paulo morbo vel supplicio interiturae
vitae parcere.

Translation: Polydore Vergil, *English History*

*[25.25] It is said that Richard could have saved himself by fleeing. For when it
seemed that the soldiers were already from the beginning of the battle fighting feebly
and without energy and that others were leaving the battle furtively, his entourage
suspected treachery and urged him to flee. And when things were now clearly going
downhill, they brought him a swift horse. He had not failed to notice that the people
were hostile to him, and having lost all hope of future success, he is said to have
replied that he would that very day either bring the fighting or his life to an end,
so fierce and spirited was he. Consequently he was aware that that day would definitely either give him the kingdom with future peace or it would snatch it from him
forever, and so he went into battle wearing the royal crown, so as to make either a
beginning or an end to his reign. The wretched man soon suffered the same outcome
as usually affects those who believe justice, right and honesty to be synonymous with
desire, wickedness and dishonesty. Examples like this are undoubtedly much more
powerful than human voices in deterring those who permit no hour to pass free of
crime, cruelty and shameful acts. Henry announced that the victory he had gained
so quickly had been won by means of their many prayers to God Almighty. Then,
filled with incredible happiness, he withdrew to a nearby hill, where, after praising
his troops and giving orders for the wounded to be cared for and the dead to be
buried, he gave everlasting thanks to all his nobles, promising to remember their
support. Meanwhile Henry's soldiers greeted him as their king with a great shout,
applauding him enthusiastically. Seeing this, Thomas Stanley promptly placed Richard's crown, discovered among the spoils, on Henry's head, just as if he had been
acclaimed king by the will of the people, in the traditional manner. This was the first
sign of his good fortune. Henry then collected together all his baggage and reached
Leicester that evening with his victorious army, staying there for two days so that his
soldiers could recover from their hard work and prepare for the journey to London.
Meanwhile Richard's body, stripped of all its clothing and slung over a horse, his
head and arms and legs dangling down on both sides, was transported to Leicester
to the monastery of the Franciscan friars – a wretched sight, but appropriate in view*

*of the man's life. There he was buried two days later without a funeral ceremony.
He had reigned for two days and as many months, and one additional day. He was
small of stature, with a deformed body, one shoulder higher than the other, a squat
and cruel face which seemed to stink of malice and to proclaim trickery and deceit.
While he pondered something, he would constantly bite his lower lip as if the wild
nature in that little body was raging at itself. At the same time, the dagger he always
carried he would pull halfway in and out of the sheath with his right hand. He had
a very sharp mind, was shrewd, cunning and good at pretence and concealment. His
spirit, haughty and fierce, did not fail him even in death, for when he was deserted
by his own men he preferred to incur death by the sword than to choose shameful
flight to save his life, which was anyway uncertain as it could soon be extinguished
by illness or punishment.*

Primary Sources and Related Texts

Polydore Vergil, *Anglica historia, libri XXVII*, ed. D. Sutton, www.philological
.bham.ac.uk/polverg/.
The Anglica historia of Polydore Vergil A.D. *1486–1537*, ed. D. Hay, London, 1950.
Thomas More, *History of King Richard III*, ed. R. Sylvester, New Haven, CT, 1963.

Further Reading

Gransden, A. (1982) 'The humanist historians' in *Gransden (1982).
O'Connor, S. (ed.) (2021) *Polydore Vergil's Life of Richard III: an edition of the
original manuscript*, Richard III Society.

Section II.42

A Miracle Associated with King Henry VI: a Painful Football Injury Is Healed (excerpt: 3.91)

Date: c.1500.

The edition is based on BL MS Royal 13.C.viii, written in the hand of the translator; the MS later belonged to Thomas Cranmer.

Author: There is no agreement as to who might have composed this Latin, though various known names, e.g. John Blakman, the author of *De virtutibus et miraculis Henrici VI* (c.1483), are proposed in the introduction to the edition.

Work: This series of 174 miracles attributed to King Henry VI after his death is a Latin translation of a lost English original, compiled as part of the beatification process, which was set in motion in 1494 by the pope. However, the process petered out as the Reformation took hold in England under Henry VIII. Henry is appealed to as a saint in the hymn *Rex Henricus, sis amicus*, included by S. Gaselee in his *Anthology of medieval Latin* (London, 1925).

This miracle consists of an account of a nasty accident on the football field and the subsequent healing attributed to King Henry. It is one of the earliest descriptions of a football match and is described as if the reader may not know about this shocking (*execrabilis*) game which involves rolling the ball rather than throwing it in the air; the writer says that 'some people call it *pedipiludium*', a compound of the Latin words for 'foot' (*pes*), 'ball' (*pila*) and 'game' (*ludus*). Rowdy games in public places, including churchyards, were repeatedly banned.

Linguistic points: The commentary on this informal village football match is hardly colloquial, but the rather high-flown language befits the account of a healing miracle attributed to a holy king to which this incident leads. The excerpt contains the only attestation of the noun *pedipiludium*, though *pila pediva* is attested in a document from 1363. In late medieval glossaries are found *pedilusor* ('footballer') and *pedipilare* ('to play football'): no doubt the game was played more often than it was written about. *gravedo* occurs here in the otherwise unattested sense 'discomfort' or 'injury', for which the CL *gravamen* is more commonly used. There is probably wordplay detectable in the phrase *cum virga ipsa pene (ut aiunt) semicisa, penas illi gravissimas ...*, possibly highlighted by *ut aiunt*, i.e. 'so to speak'.

TEXT II.42

A misjudged kick causes injury on the football pitch

qualiter Willelmus Bartram, pede cuiusdam secum ludentis percussus verenda, intolerabiles inde et diuturnos dolores sustinuit, sed viso in sompnis glorioso rege Henrico, subito sanitatis beneficium est adeptus. (…) cum enim esset hic villicule cuiusdam habitator, cui vocabulum Cawnton, exeunte dudum in campos, xiiii° videlicet kalendas Marcii, turba non modica vicinorum, sub obtentu pariter captandi solacii, contigit et illum, societatis gratia, commigrasse. porro ludus ad quem mutue recreationis gracia excercendum convenerant, a quibusdam pedipiludium dicitur. est enim quo solent adolescentes rustici et lascivi ingentem pilam non iactando in aera, sed solotenus volutando, nec manibus quidem sed pedibus pulsitando atque versando, propellere; ludus, inquam, execrabilis satis et, meo sane iudicio, omni genere ludorum rusticior, inhonestior quoque et vilior, qui et raro absque ipsorum ludencium dampno, calamitate aut dispendio aliquo terminatur. sed quid? iam assignatis limitibus et ludo inito, cum contra se invicem calcitrantes fortiter concertarent, et is, de quo nobis sermo est, concertantibus se medium miscuisset, ecce unus, nescio quis, colludencium ex adverso veniens, frustrata percussione in pilam, fortuitu in hominem pedem dedit, ictuque adeo vehementi et infausto verenda eius conquassavit ut ille perinde mortis periculo premeretur. nam quid testiculi, facile iudicatur, cum virga ipsa pene (ut aiunt) semicisa, penas illi gravissimas atque acerbissimas generaverunt, tantundemque molestie intulisse homini perhibentur, ut duodecim saltem dierum et totidem noctium spacio pre magnitudine doloris continui sompnum vel modicum capere eius oculi non valerent. unde re vera preter tenerrimi membri intolerabiles torturas, quas nemo sedare tanto tempore potuit, ob defectum quietis naturalis et debite digestionis, homo iam pene in non hominem versus defecerat.

Translation: A Miracle of Henry VI

How William Bartram, kicked in the private parts by one of his fellow players, sustained unbearable and long-lasting pains therefrom, but after seeing the glorious King Henry in his dreams, he was suddenly healed. (…) For while he was living in a small village called Cawnton [Caunton, Notts.], a substantial number of his neighbours went out into the fields, on 14 March, with the intention of relaxing together, and it happened that he went along with them because they were his mates. The game which they had gathered to play for some shared recreation is called by some 'football'. For it is a game in which rowdy young men, in the countryside, propel a large ball, not by throwing it in the air, but rolling it on the ground, striking and turning it not with their hands but their feet. It is a dreadful game, in my opinion, rougher, rowdier and more uncivilised than any other game, and it usually

380 Fifteenth Century

ends with injury, damage and disaster for the players. But what happened? The boundaries had already been determined and the game had started: as they kicked there was strong competition between them, and the man who is the subject of my account had thrown himself into the midst of the players when one of his fellow players, I do not know which one, came to tackle him but failed to strike the ball and instead happened to kick the man and smashed his private parts with such a powerful and unfortunate blow that this man was thereby in mortal danger. For it is easy to judge what very serious and excruciating pains his testicles generated when his penis (so they say) was almost ripped off, and it is said that the man suffered such a terrible injury that for at least twelve days and nights he was unable to get a wink of sleep because of the continuous and terrible pain. And so in truth, on top of the unbearable torments of his badly bruised penis, which no one could alleviate for all that time, this man had now almost become non-human and wasted away on account of the lack of natural sleep and proper digestive process.

A miracle follows

quod et ipse demum perpendens animo, sui scilicet imminere dispendium, mente admodum suppplici et devota, predilecti famuli Christi regis Henrici imploravit auxilium, firmataque in ipso, imo in Christi misericordia, ancora sue spei, eius oportuno tempore sanctum sacrarium discalciatus et nudipes visitando honorare devovit. sed nec satis id fore ad promerendam tanti beneficii graciam arbitratus, statuit sibi, quoad viveret, eius ob honorem qualibet tercia feria fore ieiunandum et ab omni specie carnium penitus abstinendum. quantum ergo vel devota sanctorum locorum frequentacio vel corporis per ieiunium extenuacio, divine sit placita pietati, dubitare quis poterit? presertim si qualem perinde graciam homo iste fuerit assecutus, dignetur advertere. mox enim ut hec humillima vota perfecte rationis confirmasset, vidit in spiritu adesse sibi gloriosum regem Henricum, ipsiusque sancti viri presencia vel virtute omnem prorsus a se pristini doloris molestiam aufugisse. quod utrum fantasma an veritas fuerit, nec ipse quidem, quamdiu sompno oppressus iacuerat, scire potuit. ilico autem expergefactus vero visionis agnovit effectu quid in se divine clemencie fuerat operata dignacio, cum nichil prorsus prioris gravedinis in suo corpore repperiisset, sed nec lesionis vestigium. erat enim ex hac sola visione beati viri, sanitati plenissime restitutus. quod ipse quidem, oblacione facta, quibusdam reverendis viris iuxta ipsum sacrati regis reclinatorium, ore suo sub assercione fidei patefecit ad laudem et gloriam summi regis omnium seculorum, qui in sanctis suis semper est mirabilis.

Translation: A Miracle of Henry VI

When he at last realised that he was close to death, he begged very humbly and devotedly for help from King Henry, Christ's beloved servant, and with the anchor of his hope firmly attached in him, or rather in Christ's mercy, he made a vow that he would honour Henry by visiting his sacred shrine without shoes and barefoot, at a suitable time. But believing that this would not be enough to obtain the grace of such a benefit he decided that for as long as he lived he would fast and completely abstain from all types of meat every Tuesday. Who could doubt that God's love was greatly pleased that he visited the holy places devoutly and that his body grew thinner as he fasted? Especially if one takes the trouble to consider what kind of grace this man thereby obtained. For as soon as he had confirmed these most humble prayers of perfect reason, he realised that the glorious King Henry was present in the spirit, and that as the result of the holy man's presence or virtue, absolutely all the trouble caused by his earlier pain had vanished from him. Whether this was an illusion or the truth, not even he could know, while he lay in a deep sleep. But as soon as he woke up he realised, because of the effect of the vision, what the graciousness of God's mercy had worked in him, since he could find in his body absolutely nothing of his former discomfort and not even a trace of the injury. For he was completely restored to health simply by this vision of the holy man. When he had made an offering, he revealed to some worthy men next to the tomb of the blessed king what had happened, in his own words, asserting that they were true, to the praise and glory of the highest king of all ages who is ever wondrous in his saints.

Primary Sources and Related Texts

Henrici VI Angliae regis miracula postuma, ed. P. Grosjean, Brussels, 1935.
Knox, R. and Leslie, S. (ed.) (1923) *The miracles of King Henry VI, being an account and translation of 23 miracles taken from the MS in the British Museum (Royal 13 C viii)*, Cambridge.
Munimenta Gildhallae Londoniensis 3.439–41. Anglo-Norman proclamation of 1314 against rowdy football games in London.

Further Reading

Craig, L. A. (2003) 'Royalty, virtue, and adversity: the cult of King Henry VI', *Albion: A Quarterly Journal Concerned with British Studies* 35: 187–209.
Duffy, E. (2005) *The stripping of the altars: traditional religion in England 1400–1580*, 2nd ed., New Haven, CT.
Magoun, F. (1929) 'Football in medieval England and in medieval English literature', *American Historical Review* 35.1: 33–45.
Mommsen, T. (1941) 'Football in Renaissance Florence', *Yale University Library Gazette* 16: 14–19.
Theilmann, J. (1980) 'The miracles of King Henry VI of England', *The Historian* 42.3: 456–71.

Section II.43

The Black Death and Its Effects
A: Henry Knighton, *Chronicle* (*Chronicon*) (excerpt: pp. 94–6, 98–104)
B: *The Ordinance of Labourers* of 1349 (excerpts)

Further Reading

Bailey, M. (2021) *After the Black Death: economy, society and the law in fourteenth-century England*, Oxford.
Horrox, R. (ed.) (1994) *The Black Death*, Manchester.

A: Henry Knighton, *Chronicle* (*Chronicon*) (excerpt: pp. 94–6, 98–104)

Author: See Section II.34.

Work: Knighton's interest in social history is revealed here in his account of the economic effects of the plague, as well as the record of statistics of deaths by region. He also records the different reactions of various countries, who often view it as divine punishment on themselves or their enemies. One of the unforeseen cultural consequences of the plague was that the Church, having lost many clergy to the disease, as a result of which chaplains became an expensive commodity, then experienced a flood of applications for ordination from men, rendered widowers by the plague, who were, if not illiterate, without a sufficient understanding of Latin. Some of the colleges at Oxford and Cambridge, e.g. Trinity Hall, Cambridge, were founded in the aftermath of the Black Death specifically to replenish the clergy.

Linguistic points: *artificiarius*, as an alternative for *artifex* as 'craftsman', does not occur before the mid-fourteenth century. *hameletta* is the Latin form of 'hamelet', which occurs in both AN (which also has the slightly earlier form 'hamel') and ME, a double diminutive evolving (via 'hamel' and 'hamelet') from the Frankish 'haim' meaning a small village; an alternative form is *hamellus*. Note the occasional spelling with a single consonant, e.g. *ocupare*, and the spelling *wlg-* for *vulg-*. Knighton gives an English translation of the oath, *per fedam mortem Anglorum*, i.e. 'by the foul death of England', presumably because this was originally a spoken English phrase used by the Scots.

TEXT II.43A

The plague spreads from the east

[*s.a.* 1348, p. 94] isto anno et anno sequenti erat generalis mortalitas hominum in universo mundo. et primo incepit in India, deinde in Tharsis, deinde ad Saracenos postremo ad Cristianos et Iudeos. ita quod in spacio unius anni, videlicet a Pascha usque ad Pascham ut rumor in curia Romana procrepuerat, mortui sunt **?l. per-** in illis remotis regionibus viij millia legiones preter Cristianos quasi subita morte. rex Tharsus videns tam subitam et inauditam stragem suorum, iter arripuit cum multitudine copiosa nobilium versus Avinoniam ad papam disponens se Cristianum fieri et baptizari a papa, credens vindictam Dei [p. 96] populum suum enervasse propter eorum malam incredulitatem. igitur cum fecisset viginti dietas itinerando, audivit quod lues mortaliter invaluit inter Cristianos sicud inter alias naciones, verso calle ultra non progreditur in illo itinere, set repatriare festinavit. Cristiani vero a tergo eos insequentes, occiderunt de illis quasi ij millia. (…)

Translation: Knighton, *Chronicle*

In this year and the following one there was a general plague among humankind throughout the world. It first started in India, then it spread to Tartary, then to the Saracens and finally to the Christians and Jews, with the result that in the course of a single year, namely from one Easter to the next, 8,000 legions of people had died suddenly in those remote regions, besides Christians, according to the report that had spread through the Roman curia. The king of Tartary, seeing such a sudden and unparalleled massacre of his people, travelled with a large number of his nobles to Avignon, intending to become a Christian and to be baptised by the pope, for he believed that God's revenge had weakened his people because of their wicked lack of faith. When he had travelled for twenty days, he heard that the plague was as deadly among Christians as among other nations; he decided to go no further in that direction and turned round, and hastened to return home. The Christians pursued them and slew about 2,000 of them. (…)

The plague reaches southern England and spreads through the country

[p. 98] tunc pestis dolorosa penetravit maritima per Southamtonam et venit Bristollam et moriebantur quasi tota valitudo ville quasi subita morte preocupati. nam pauci erant qui lectum ocupabant ultra iij dies, vel duos dies, aut dimidium diem. deinde mors ipsa seva prorupit circumquaque secundum cursum solis. et moriebantur apud Leycestriam in parva parochia Sancti Leonardi plus quam xix xx. in parochia Sancte Crucis plusquam cccc. in parochia Sancte Margarete Leycestrie plusquam vij c. et sic in singulis parochiis in magna multitudine. (…) [p. 100] eodem anno fuit magna lues ovium ubique in regno, adeo quod in uno

384 Fifteenth Century

loco moriebantur in pastura una plusquam v millia ovium. et in tantum putrescebant quod nec bestia nec avis tangere volebat.

Translation: Knighton, *Chronicle*

Then the lamentable plague penetrated the coastal areas by way of Southampton and reached Bristol, where almost the whole population of the city died, suddenly snatched away. For there were few who took to their beds for more than three or two days, or even half a day. Then that cruel death burst forth everywhere, following the course of the sun. And at Leicester in the tiny parish of St Leonard more than 380 died, and in the parish of St Cross more than 400, in the parish of St Margaret, Leicester, more than 700, and similarly in every parish, in great numbers. (…) In the same year there was a great plague among sheep throughout the kingdom, so much so that in one place, more than 5,000 sheep died in a single pasture. And the animals were so putrid that neither wild animals nor birds would touch them.

Economic effects of the plague
[p. 100 cont.] et erat leve precium de cunctis rebus, pre mortis timore. nam valde pauci erant qui de diviciis vel quibuslibet rebus curam agerent. nam homo posset habere unum equum qui ante valuerat xl solidos pro dimidia marca, j bovem crassum et pinguem pro iiij s., j vaccam pro xij denariis, j iuvencam pro vj d., j agnum pro ij d., j magnum porcum pro v d., j petram lane pro ix d. et oves et boves per campos et inter segetes vagabant errantes et non erat qui eas agendo fugaret aut coligeret. sed in sulcis deviis et sepibus morte perierunt, numero incomputabili per universas regiones pre defectu custodis. quia tantus defectus extitit servorum et famulorum quod non erat quis qui sciret quid facere deberet. nam non occurrit memoria tam rigide mortalitatis et tam seve, a tempore Vortigerni regis Brito**Bede, *HE* 1.14** num, in cuius tempore, ut testatur Beda de gestis Anglorum, vivi non sufficiebant sepelire mortuos. in autumpno sequenti non potuit quis habere unum messorem minor precio quam viij d. cum cibo, unum falcatorem, quam xij d. cum cibo. quam ob causam multe segetes perierunt in campis pre defectu colectoris. sed in anno pestilencie ut supradictum est de aliis rebus, tanta habundancia erat omnis **?l. nullus** generis bladorum quod ullus de eis quasi curavit.

Translation: Knighton, *Chronicle*

The fear of death caused the price of everything to fall, for there were very few who cared for wealth or possessions. A man could get a horse which had been worth 40s. for half a mark, a heavy and fat ox for 4s., a cow for 12d., a heifer for 6d., a stone of wool for 9d. And sheep and cattle wandered aimlessly through the fields

II.43 | The Black Death and Its Effects 385

and crops because there was no one to drive them or round them up, and they died in out-of-the-way furrows and hedges, in numbers beyond reckoning throughout the country as the result of a lack of people to watch over them. There was such a shortage of servants and farmhands that there was no one who knew what needed to be done. For there was no memory of such a severe and cruel plague since the time of Vortigern, king of the Britons, in whose time, as Bede records in the Deeds of the English, there were not enough living people to bury the dead. In the following autumn no one could hire a mower for less than 8d. with his food, or a reaper for less than 12d. with his food. So, many crops rotted in the fields as the result of the shortage of harvesters. But in the year of the plague, as mentioned already in another connection, there was too much grain of every variety for anyone to take care of it.

The plague reaches Scotland
[p. 100 cont.] Scoti audientes de crudeli peste Anglorum, suspicati sunt de manu Dei vindici hoc eis evenisse. et sumpserunt in iuramentum prout wlgaris rumor aures Anglorum personuit, sub hac forma, quando iurare volebant, 'per fedam mortem Anglorum', Anglice '*be þe foul deth of Engelond*' et sic Scotti credentes vindictam Dei horribilem Anglos obumbrasse, convenerunt in foresta de Selfchirche in proposito invasisse totum [p. 102] regnum Anglie. supervenit seva mortalitas et ventilavit Scotos subita et immanis mortis crudelitas. et moriebantur in parvo tempore circiter v millia. reliqui vero quidem debiles, quidam fortes repatriare se disponebant set Angligene eos preocupaverunt insequentes et occiderunt ex eis multos nimis. (…)

Translation: Knighton, *Chronicle*

The Scots, hearing of the savage plague among the English, attributed it to the avenging hand of God and adopted it as an oath, according to a widespread rumour that reached the ears of the English, and when they wished to swear they would do so in these words: 'By the foul death of England'. And so the Scots, believing that God's dreadful judgement had cast a shadow over the English, gathered in the forest of Selkirk, planning to invade the whole kingdom of England. A savage pestilence arrived and a sudden and massive death cruelly scattered the Scots. In a short space of time about 5,000 died and the rest, some feeble and some strong, decided to return home, but the English pursued them and attacked them, killing a large number of them. (…)

One effect is a dearth of priests, leading to higher wages and a rush of poorly educated candidates
[p. 102] eodem tempore tanta penuria erat sacerdotum ubique quod multe ecclesie viduate erant carentes divinis officiis, missis, matutinis, vesperis, sacramentis

386 Fifteenth Century

et sacramentalibus. vix posset homo habere unum capellanum infra x libras vel x marcas ministrare alicui ecclesie. et ubi homo posset habere unum capellanum pro v aut iiij marcis, vel pro ij marcis cum mensa, quando copia extitit sacerdotum ante pestilentiam, vix erat in isto tempore qui acceptare vellet unam vicariam ad xx libras aut xx marcas. sed infra breve confluebant ad ordines maxima multitudo quorum uxores obierant in pestilencia, de quibus multi illiterati et quasi meri laici, nisi quatenus aliqualiter legere sciebant licet non intelligere.

Translation: Knighton, *Chronicle*

At that time there was such a shortage of priests everywhere that many churches had been left bereft and lacked divine offices, Masses, matins, vespers, the sacraments and sacramental rites. A man could scarcely retain a single chaplain to serve a church for less than £10 or 10 marks. And where a man could have a chaplain for five or four marks, or for two marks with his board, when there were plenty of priests before the plague, there was in these times hardly anyone willing to accept a vicar's position for £20 or 20 marks. But in a short space of time there was a flood of ordinands whose wives had died in the plague; many of them were illiterate and, as it were, pure laymen, who could perhaps read a little but without understanding.

The Ordinance of Labourers: attempts to keep wages down
[p. 102 cont.] coria boum sub vili precio scilicet ad xij denarios, et j par sotularios ad x d., xii d. vel xiiij d. j par ocriarum ad iij s. et iiij s. interim rex misit in singulos comitatus regni quod messores et alii operarii non plus caperent quam capere solebant, sub pena in statuto limitata, et ex hoc innovavit statutum. operarii tamen adeo elati et contrariosi, non advertebant regis mandatum. sed si quis eos habere vellet, oportuit eum eis dare secundum suum velle et aut fructus suos et segetes perdere aut operariorum elatam et cupidam voluntatem ad vota implere. [p. 104] (...) deinde rex fecit attachiare laborarios quamplures et misit eos in carcerem et multi tales retraxerunt se et abierunt ad silvas et boscos pro tempore. et qui capti erant, graviter sunt amerciati. et maiores sunt iurati quod ultra antiquam consuetudinem stipendia diurna non caperent et sic sunt liberati de carcere. simili modo fiebat de aliis artificiariis in burgis et villis. (...)

Translation: Knighton, *Chronicle*

Ox hides were dirt cheap, namely about 12d., and a pair of shoes cost 10d., 12d. or 14d. One pair of leather leggings cost 3s. or 4s. Meanwhile the king sent a message to every county in the kingdom to the effect that reapers and other workers should

*not be paid more than they used to be paid, under the penalties set out in that stat-
ute, and he brought out a new statute on this matter. However, the workers were so
full of self-importance and antagonistic that they took no notice of the king's order.
If anyone wanted to hire them, he had to give them what they asked for and either
lose his fruit and crops or give in to the demands of the self-important and greedy
workers. (...) Then the king had many labourers arrested and sent them to prison.
Many ran away and went off into the woods and forests for a time. Those who were
caught were given a heavy fine. Most were made to swear that they would not take
more than the old established rate, and so they were released from prison. The same
thing happened with the other workmen in the boroughs and towns. (...)*

Deserted villages throughout the country and high inflation
[p. 104 cont.] post predictam pestilenciam multa edificia tam maiora quam mi-
nora in omnibus civitatibus, burgis et villis collapsa sunt et ad terram penitus
diruta pre defectu habitatoris. similiter multe villule et hamilette desolate sunt,
nulla in eis relicta domo, sed mortuis omnibus qui in eis habitarent et verisimile
erat quod multe tales villule non essent habitande pro perpetuo. in yeme sequenti
tanta erat penuria servorum in omnibus agendis quod vix ut homo credebat retroactis temporibus tanta carencia fuerat. (...) et sic cuncta necessaria adeo cara
devenerunt quod id quod retroactis temporibus valuit unum denarium, iam isto
tempore valuit iiij d. aut v.

Translation: Knighton, *Chronicle*

*After this plague many buildings, both large and small, in all the cities, boroughs
and towns collapsed and were utterly razed to the ground, because of a lack of
inhabitants. Similarly many villages and hamlets were deserted, without a single
house remaining, for all the inhabitants were now dead; it was likely that many of
these villages would never be inhabited again. In the following winter, there was
such a shortage of servants for every kind of work that it was almost universally believed that there had never existed such a shortage in the past. For cattle and all the
livestock which someone might possess were wandering around without anyone to
tend them, and there was no one to look after anything that anyone owned. (...) As
a result all the necessities of life became so expensive that what in the past had been
worth 1d. now cost 4d. or 5d.*

Primary Source and Related Texts

Knighton's Chronicle (1337–1396), ed. G. Martin, OMT, Oxford, 1995.
TNA: Nonae Rolls of 1340–1.

388 Fifteenth Century

B: *The Ordinance of Labourers* of 1349 (excerpts: pp. 307–8)

Date: 18 June 1349.

Close Roll, TNA: C54/185 m. 8d.

Work: This document takes the form of a writ from King Edward III, sent to the Sheriff of Kent (and similarly to all sheriffs throughout England). This ordinance, reinforced by the *Statute of Labourers* in 1351, set out new regulations which introduced a maximum wage to counter the increased power of the workers now that there were fewer of them; it tried to restrict the inflation of food prices and laid down that male and female workers had to continue working till the age of 60. It also became illegal to give support to able-bodied beggars, who must be encouraged to join the labour market, given that 'the devil finds work for idle hands to do'. The situation was clearly being regarded from the viewpoint of the upper classes, adversely affected by the lack of servants but unwilling to pay what they regarded as 'excessive' wages. The ineffectiveness of this statute and its unpopularity with the labourers who wanted higher wages was shown by the fact that many abandoned the countryside and headed for the cities to seek better-paid work. There are also numerous documents recording court cases involving noncompliance. John Gower, in Book 5 of his work *Vox clamantis*, in Latin elegiac couplets, attacks agricultural and urban labourers for their laziness and insubordination: in lines 577–8 he says of the common people (*plebs*), *sunt enim tardi, sunt rari, sunt et avari;* | *ex minimo quod agunt premia plura petunt* ('they are lazy, scarce and grasping; they demand very high pay for the very little they do').

Linguistic points: This document contains a large number of words for different professions, most of which are the CL terms or derived from CL nouns (e.g. *carectarius* and *pulletarius*, from CL *carrus* and *pullus*, via diminutive forms), while some are ML words derived from the vernacular, e.g. *batellarius* (see Section II.48D) and *braciator* (see Section II.47B), with the appropriate CL suffixes. With regard to the words used for payments to workers, some like *salarium* and *merces* are CL senses, while *liberatio* shows semantic extension, and *vadium* is a post-classical word (cf. Section II.26C). This text also contains two medieval words for 'prison' that would pass into modern English: *gaola* is said to derive, via French, from LL *caveola*, while *imprisonamentum* is based on *priso/prisona*, deriving, again via French, from CL *prensio*.

TEXT II.43B

Rural workers: statute to put pressure on rural workers to seek employment
[p. 307] quia magna pars populi et maxime operariorum et servientium jam in ista pestilencia est defuncta, nonnulli videntes necessitatem dominorum

II.43 | The Black Death and Its Effects 389

et paucitatem servientium servire nolunt nisi salaria recipiant excessiva et alii mendicare malentes in ocio quam per laborem querere victum suum, nos pensantes gravia que ex carencia presertim cultorum et operariorum hujusmodi pervenire possent incommoda, super hoc cum praelatis et nobilibus et peritis aliis nobis assistentibus deliberacionem habuimus et tractatum, de quorum unanimi consilio duximus ordinandum:

quod quilibet homo et femina regni nostri Anglie, cujuscumque condicionis fuerit liber vel servilis, potens in corpore et infra etatem sexaginta annorum, non vivens de mercatura nec certum exercens artificium, nec habens de suo proprio unde vivere vel terram propriam circa culturam cujus se poterit occupare, et alteri non serviens, si de serviendo in servicio congruo considerato statu suo fuerit requisitus, servire teneatur illi qui ipsum sic duxerit requirendum; et percipiat dumtaxat vadia, liberaciones, mercedes seu salaria que in locis ubi servire debeat consueta sunt prestari anno regni nostri Anglie vicesimo vel annis communibus quinque vel sex proxime praecedentibus. (…) et si messor, falcator aut alius operarius vel serviens, cujuscumque status fuerit seu condicionis, in servicio alicujus retentus, ante finem termini concordati, a dominico servicio sine causa rationabili vel licencia recesserit, penam imprisonamenti subeat (…)

Translation: *The Ordinance of Labourers*

A large part of the population and particularly workers and servants have already died in this plague, and some people, noticing the difficulties of the masters and the reduced numbers of servants, refuse to serve unless they receive excessive wages, while others prefer to remain unemployed and to beg rather than earning their living through employment. As a result, we have considered the serious problems which could result in particular from the lack of agricultural labourers and workers, and we have had discussions with the prelates and nobles and other experts assisting us. As the result of these negotiations, on their unanimous advice we have decided that it must be decreed that:

Each man and woman of our kingdom of England, whether of free or servile status, physically strong and under the age of 60, not living from trade or practising a specific skill, and not having their own means to live off or their own land to cultivate, and not in service to another, if such a person is required to serve in appropriate service taking their status into account, he or she should be bound to serve the one who considers him or her to be needed in this way, and he or she should at least receive the wages, payments, rewards or fees which were customarily provided in the places where they might serve, in the twentieth year of our reign in England or in the five or six most recent normal years preceding (…) and if a harvester, scyther or other worker or servant, of whatever status or condition he may be, retained in someone's service, should withdraw from his lord's service before the end of the agreed term, without good reason or permission, he must be imprisoned as a penalty. (…)

390 Fifteenth Century

Urban workers: statute to keep wages and prices down, while taking the notion of 'food miles' into consideration
[p. 308] item sellarii, pelletarii, allutarii, sutores, cissores, fabri, carpentarii, cementarii, tegularii, batellarii, carectarii et quicumque alii artifices et operarii non capiant pro labore et artificio suo ultra id quod dicto anno vicesimo et aliis communibus annis precedentibus, ut premittitur, in locis quibus eos operari contingit, talibus solvi consuevit et si quis plus receperit, gaole proxime modo quo premittitur committatur. item quod carnifices, piscenarii, hostellarii, braciatores, pistores, pullettarii et omnes alii venditores victualium quorumcumque teneantur hujusmodi victualia vendere pro precio rationabili, habita consideracione ad precium quo hujusmodi victualia in locis propinquis venduntur, ita quod habeant hujusmodi venditores moderatum lucrum, non excessivum, prout distancia locorum a quibus victualibus hujusmodi cariantur duxerit rationabiliter requirendum; (…)

Translation: *The Ordinance of Labourers*

Also saddlers, tanners, cordwainers, tailors, smiths, carpenters, masons, tilers, shipwrights, carters and any other craftsmen and workmen should not receive for their work and their craft in excess of what was usually paid to such as these in the said twentieth year and the other normal years preceding, as stated above, in the places where they happen to work, and if anyone receives more he should be committed to the nearest gaol in the manner stated above. Also that butchers, fishmongers, innkeepers, brewers, bakers, poultrymongers and all other sellers of whatever kind of food are bound to sell foodstuffs of this kind for a reasonable price, taking into consideration the price at which foodstuffs of this kind are sold in neighbouring places, so that sellers of this kind should receive a moderate, not excessive profit, to the degree they consider reasonably required by the distance between the places from which foodstuffs of this kind are transported. (…)

It is illegal to give money to a beggar who is healthy enough to work
[p. 308 cont.] (…) et quia multi validi mendicantes, quamdiu possent ex mendicatis elemosinis vivere, laborare renuunt, vacando ociis et peccatis et quandoque latrociniis et aliis flagiciis, nullus sub pena imprisonamenti predicta, talibus qui commode laborare poterunt, sub colore pietatis vel elimosine quicquam dare seu eos in sua desidia confovere presumat, ut sic compellantur pro vite necessario laborare.

Translation: *The Ordinance of Labourers*

(…) and because many strong people are begging and refuse to work as long as they are able to live from the handouts they receive from begging, spending their time

doing nothing or doing sinful things and sometimes even stealing and committing other crimes, no one, on pain of imprisonment, should dare, under the pretext of piety or alms-giving, to give anything to such people who can find suitable work, or to indulge them in their idleness. The intention is that they should thus be forced to work for the necessities of life.

Primary Sources and Related Texts

Statutes of the Realm 1. 307–8, London, 1810.

Further Reading

Bailey, M. (2021) *After the Black Death: economy, society and the law in fourteenth-century England*, Oxford.

Britnell, R. (1994) 'The Black Death in urban towns', *Urban History* 21.2: 195–210.

Putnam, B. (1908) *The enforcement of the statutes of labourers during the first decade after the Black Death 1349–59*, New York.

Section II.44

Forest Documents
A: Richard FitzNigel, *The Dialogue of the Exchequer* (*Dialogus de Scaccario*) (excerpt: 1.12–13, OMT p. 93)
B: A Letter of Mandate from Waleran de Beaumont, Count of Meulan
C: *The Charter of the Forest* (*Carta de foresta*) (excerpts: clauses 1, 4, 7, 9, 12–15)
D: A Plea of the Forest Regarding the Taking of a Deer (excerpt: pp. 106–7)
E: The King Grants Firewood to His Daughter

Soon after the Norman Conquest, William the Conqueror arranged for vast tracts of land (not only woodland) to be converted into royal forests to be used as hunting grounds for him and his barons, subject to special laws. The most famous of these is the New Forest in Hampshire, one of the forests mentioned in Domesday and in Henry of Huntingdon, *HA* 6.39. There is controversy over how these lands were managed from an ecological point of view, but it is clear that the king withdrew them from the use of those who had traditionally exploited their resources. This caused resentment, which the *Charter of the Forest*, an offshoot of the Magna Carta, was intended to mitigate with its regulations as to rights and duties. The letter of Waleran de Meulan shows this baron granting forest land that he had from the king, in the period before the *Charter of the Forest* of 1217. The next excerpt, a court case from 1253, shows how the regulations as to forest use were infringed, and the infringements punished. Finally, the royal grant from the Patent Rolls of 1292 shows King Edward I using his forest rights to supply wood for fuel for the household of his young daughter.

Further Reading

Aberth, J. (2013) *An environmental history of the Middle Ages: the crucible of nature. Part II: Forest*, London.

Grant, R. (1991) *The Royal Forests of England*, Stroud.

Rackham, O. (1983) 'Wooded forests: the king's wood-pasture' in *Trees and woodland in the British landscape*, London.

Wilson, D. (2004) 'Multi-use management of the medieval Anglo-Norman forest', *Journal of the Oxford University History Society* 2, https://sites.google.com/site/jouhsinfo/wilson01.pdf.

A: Richard FitzNigel, *The Dialogue of the Exchequer* (*Dialogus de Scaccario*) (excerpt: 1.12–13, OMT p. 93)

Work: For information about this work, see Section II.4B. This excerpt shows the master defining to his pupil the nature of royal forest and related concepts.

Linguistic points: The author of the *Dialogue* suggests that 'forest' is associated with *ferus* ('wild animal') and *statio*, whereas modern etymologists dispute whether the word has a Latin or Frankish origin: some suggest a connection with *foris* ('outside', i.e. *forestam silvam*, 'woodland outside the ordinary laws'). *essarta* is thought to derive from a hypothetical LL form *exsartum* (modern English 'assart'), a past participle of CL (*ex*)*sarire* ('to clear for plantation'); the author regards it as synonymous with CL *occatio*, though this is not exactly what Isidore says at *Etym.* 17.2.4. The master defines the term *vastum* (regarding this as a shortened form of *vastatum*) as woodland that has been more radically cleared of trees. The use of CL *pecunialiter* here is the earliest in BML.

TEXT II.44A

The definition of royal forest

[1.12, OMT p. 93] Magister: foresta regis est tuta ferarum mansio, non quarumlibet set silvestrium, non quibuslibet in locis set certis et ad hoc idoneis. unde foresta dicitur, e mutata in o, quasi feresta, hoc est ferarum statio.

Discipulus: numquid in singulis comitatibus foresta regis est?

Magister: non, set in nemorosis ubi et ferarum latibula sunt et uberrima pascua. nec interest cuius sint nemora, sive enim regis sint sive regni procerum, liberos tamen et indempnes habent fere circumquaque discursus. (…) [1.13] essarta vero vulgo dicuntur que apud Ysidorum occationes nominantur, quando scilicet foresta nemora vel dumeta quelibet pascuis et latibulis oportuna succiduntur; quibus succisis et radicitus avulsis terra subvertitur et excolitur. quod si nemora sic excisa sint ut subsistens quis in vix extanti succise quercus vel alterius arboris stipite circumspiciens, v. succisas viderit, vastum reputant, hoc est vastatum, per sincopam sic dictum. excessus autem talis, etiam in propriis cuiuslibet nemoribus factus, adeo gravis dicitur ut nunquam inde per sessionem scaccarii liberari debeat, set magis juxta sui status possibilitatem pecuniariter puniri.

Translation: *The Dialogue of the Exchequer*

[1.12] *Teacher: The king's forest is the preserve of wild animals, not just any kind, but woodland creatures, and not everywhere, but in certain places that are suitable for*

394　Fifteenth Century

them. That is why it is called 'forest', the e of 'feresta', i.e. a place for wild animals,
having been changed into an o by syncope.
Student: Does every county have some royal forest?
Teacher: No, only wooded ones, where wild animals have their lairs and plenty of
food. It makes no difference who owns the woods, the king or his nobles; the wild
animals still have free run of them and safe refuge there. (…) [1.13] Assart is the
common name for what Isidore calls 'occationes', namely when forests, woods or
any thickets offering lairs or food for animals are cut down; after the trees have been
felled and uprooted, the land is ploughed and cultivated. But if the woods are cut
down in such a way that someone standing by the trunk of a felled oak or any other
kind of tree and looking round can see five other felled trees, it is called 'waste', which
is short for 'devastated'. Moreover, such an offence, even if it is committed in one's
own woods, is regarded as so serious that it cannot be excused by the privilege of the
exchequer, but instead is punished by monetary means according to the perpetra-
tor's rank and ability to pay.

Primary Source

Richard Fitzneale, *Dialogus de Scaccario*, ed. E. Amt and S. Church, OMT, Oxford, 2007.

B: A Letter of Mandate from Waleran de Beaumont, Count of Meulan

Date: 1146–7.

This letter survives only in a (slightly faulty) copy made from the original (now lost) by Elias Ashmole: MS Ashmole 833 (p. 14) in the Bodleian Library.

Author: Waleran de Beaumont, Count of Meulan (1104–66), was the son of Robert de Beaumont, who fought with William the Conqueror at Hastings and whose tragic experiences were used as an example by Henry of Huntingdon in his *Contempt for the World* (cf. Section II.11F). Waleran, who became first Earl of Worcester, was first married to Matilda, the infant daughter of King Stephen, but she died as a child and Waleran married Agnes, a member of the de Montfort family. He led a politically risky but generally successful life in Normandy and England, in both of which he held extensive lands. He was also remarkable for being a highly educated layman: Orderic Vitalis says that he was trained in philosophy and the classics, Stephen of Rouen states that he wrote Latin verse, and in 1136 Geoffrey of Monmouth dedicated the first version of his *History of the Kings of Britain* (cf. Section II.12) jointly to Waleran and to Robert of Gloucester. At about the same time, Waleran was granted lands in England, including Worcestershire, by King Stephen. During the civil war he supported the empress Matilda (Section II.16A). In 1147 Waleran joined the Second Crusade with Louis VII of France (as alluded to in this letter).

Work: This is one of a few letters (printed in Crouch's appendix (2009)) among the many acts that survive from Count Waleran's household. It was written, possibly while Waleran was in France, in response to a request for help from the monks of Worcester Cathedral priory, and is addressed to William Beauchamp, himself a baron and Sheriff of Worcestershire, who was managing Waleran's lands in his absence. The copy made in the seventeenth century of the lost original has been checked, particularly in connection with the ambiguous syntax in the final sentence; the MS version abbreviates a number of words, particularly relative pronouns, which can cause confusion.

Linguistic points: The letter is largely formulaic, but provides an example of the use of such legal and feudal terms as *clamare quietos, foresta, geldum*. Whereas *clamare* on its own here means 'to claim', with the adjective *quietos* it means 'to exempt'. *forestagium* is one of the many compounds using the suffix *-agium* (from Latin *-aticum*) in BML to indicate a specific tax or toll: this suffix is seen in such English words as 'passage', originally a toll on a ferry crossing. Since earls were exempt from paying the *geldum*, a tax due to the king, Waleran can grant it to his friends, the prior and monks, instead. Both *iter* and *peregrinatio* are used for his travels, with the latter being more specifically applied to a Crusade. With regard to syntax, in the final sentence it would seem that the first *ut* means 'as', rather than being dependent on the verb *rogo*; instead this verb goes with *quod*, which then requires a subjunctive, supplied by reading *curetis* instead of Crouch's *cuius*; *curetis* takes the object *eos* rather than *eos et omnia sua* (i.e. *et* here introduces a new clause); of the following subjunctive verbs *manuteneatis* and *custodiatis* (still dependent on *rogo quod*), *manuteneatis* takes the object *omnia sua*, while *custodiatis* introduces a new *ut* clause with the subjunctive *valeat*.

TEXT II.44B

[address] G. comes Mell(enti) Willelmo de Bellocampo filio suo salutem.

mando vobis et precipio quatenus clametis priorem et monacos ecclesie sancte Marie Wigornensis quietos de forestagio de Tabrituna et de omnibus placitis illius foreste ita ut nullum ius de forestis quod ad illam villam pertinet amodo clamabatis quia sciatis quod pro remedio anime mee et Agnetis comitisse uxoris mee et Rodberti filii mei et pro animabus patris et matris mee concedo et perdono priori et monachis geldum regis quod ad me pertinet et omnes

Fifteenth Century

consuetudines et servitia et iura forestaria que prius regis erant et postea mea in illa villa. de terra autem pro qua miserunt ad me, scilicet pro una carrucata terre que est de feudo episcopi, non possum intermitere pro itinere meo sed quicquid frater meus comes de Leircestra et vos faciatis ex mea parte do et concedo priori et monachis quia sciatis quod non sunt monachi in tota terra mea quos tantum diligo nec in quibus orationibus plus confido et si dederit mihi Deus ut possim de hac peregrinatione sanus et incolumis redere bene illis monstrabo. quapropter

sic MS, l. curetis rogo vos ut filium karissimum quod cuius eos et omnia sua pro amore meo in loco meo manuteneatis et custodiatis ut amor meus illis valeat. testibus Willelmo capellano, Radulfo de Auromonte, Hugone filio Galer'i et Gervasio preposito de Inkit(berga).

Translation: Waleran de Meulan, Letter

Count Waleran de Meulan sends greetings to his son(-in-law) William de Beauchamp.

I direct and instruct you to exempt the prior and monks of the Church of St Mary of Worcester from the forest dues and all pleas in the forest of Tibberton, so that from now on you claim no forest rights pertaining to that estate; for you should be aware that for the sake of my soul and that of my wife, Countess Agnes, and of Robert my son and those of my father and mother I grant and donate to the prior and monks the king's geld which belongs to me together with all customs and services and forest rights which were formerly the king's and then mine on the said estate. As to the land regarding which they sent to me, namely the one carucate of the bishop's fee, I am unable to get involved because of my journey. But whatever my brother (Robert) the Earl of Leicester and you do on my part, I give and grant to the prior and monks. For you should know that there are no monks in all my domains whom I love so much, nor in whose prayers I trust so much; and if God grant that I return from this pilgrimage safe and sound, I will make this very clear to them. So I ask you, as my dear son, that you will look after them and manage in my place all their business for the love of me and that you will make sure that my love benefits them. Witnesses, William the chaplain, Ralph de Auromonte, Hugh son of Waleran and Gervase, the prior of Inkberrow.

Primary Sources and Related Texts

Crouch, D. (2009) 'Between three realms: the Acts of Waleran II' in *Records, administration and aristocratic society in the Anglo-Norman realm*, ed. N. Vincent, Woodbridge.

English lawsuits from William I to Richard I, Selden Society 106–7 (1990–1).

Further Reading

Crouch, D. (1986) *The Beaumont twins: the roots and branches of power in the twelfth century*, Cambridge.

King, E. (1985) 'Waleran de Meulan' in *Tradition and change: essays in honour of Marjorie Chibnall*, ed. D. Greenway, C. Holdsworth and J. Sayers, Cambridge.

C: *The Charter of the Forest* (*Carta de foresta*) (excerpts: clauses 1, 4, 7, 9, 12–15)

Date: 1217.

Three copies of the 1217 document survive, preserved in Durham, Lincoln and Sandwich. A copy of the 1225 version is MS Add. Ch. 24712 in the British Library.

Work: 'Forest' was originally a term applied to areas of land consisting of woodland, heath, arable and even villages, which the king cleared of villagers to reserve them as hunting grounds for himself. However, by the end of the twelfth century about one quarter of the land in England was under forest law, with many restrictions on the use of the natural resources by those who lived in these areas who had traditionally had the right to use a reasonable amount of wood for burning, beechmast for feeding pigs etc. This provoked the grievances which were addressed first in the Magna Carta of 1215 and then in the separate, expanded document of 1217 named the *Charter of the Forest*, addressed by Henry III to all the secular, ecclesiastical and judicial leaders. It can be regarded as one of the first statutes to deal with environmental law and heritage, re-establishing rights of access for free men to land that had been set aside exclusively for royal use. In section 12, the reference to a marl pit (not a marsh pit, as often erroneously in modern translations) is to a source of chalky stone applied as a kind of fertiliser, not, as has recently been suggested (cf. article cited at Section II.45B), a clay to be used for building: this is corroborated by contemporary documents in which the agricultural context is clear.

Linguistic points: This text is full of legal terms relating to forests: *afforestare*: 'to put under forest laws', i.e. to expand the Royal Forest; *disafforestare<dis-* + *afforestare* (cf. AN 'desafforester'): 'to remove (land) from forest status', i.e. to restore the rights of the commoners; *purprestura<*AN 'purpresture', perhaps associated with CL *praestare*: 'encroachment' or 'illegal enclosure'. For the terms *vastum* and *assartus*, see Section II.44A. *bedellus* ('bedel', 'manorial official') comes from OE 'bydel'/AN 'bedel', both of which derive from a Germanic word; the term is still used in certain contexts in modern English in the form 'beadle'. A *scot-ale* was a particular kind of community drinking party that was part of medieval society,

398 Fifteenth Century

involving compulsory contributions of money (cf. Section II.47B for an urban context). Formed from ME 'scotale', the BML word appears in a wide variety of declensions and genders, and here it could be either third declension neuter (as elsewhere), or the vernacular. The word is often given with Latin synonyms such as *potatio, cervisiae* or *fustales* (i.e. 'filstales', a term that could be ME or third-declension Latin). Note that *reguardorum* is from third declension *reguardor* ('official in charge of inspecting a forest'), not from second declension *reguardum* ('inspection'): both can be spelled *reward-* and are associated with AN 'regarder/rewarder' ('to inspect', or 'to reward'). *agistare* as a verb ('to use (land) as pasture' or 'to put (animals) to pasture') is related to AN 'giste' (i.e. 'gîte') meaning 'lodging', going back to CL *jacere*: modern English 'to agist' is still current in Australia. *pannagium* ('pannage', i.e. the right to collect food for pigs in the forest) derives via AN 'pannage/pasnage' from a hypothetical form *pastionaticum. occasionare* is a ML verb <CL *occasio* + *-are* (cf. AN 'occasioner'), occasionally used as 'to cause', but more frequently taking on a legal sense: 'to institute legal proceedings against'. *marlera* (AN 'marler') comes from the CL form *marga*, which may originally be Gaulish; cf. Section II.45B(b) for the use of marl in agriculture. *cooperatus* (CL *cooperire*) is used as an adjective with *boscus* or as a neuter or feminine noun to mean a place 'covered' with woodland, a 'covert'; it also occurs in BML as *covertum*, based on the French form 'covert'. *espervarius* ('sparrowhawk') derives its form from AN 'esperver/sperver' but may also be associated with OE 'spearwa' (going back to Old High German) + CL *-arius*; indeed, *spervarius* occurs already in the *Lex Salica*. The English word 'heron' does not occur until the mid-fourteenth century (as ME 'heyrone'), but in this early thirteenth-century text is the first example of the Latin word *heyronus*, associated with AN 'heiron', but attested slightly later than the Latin. *chiminagium* (also *chem-*), related to AN 'cheminage' from 'chemin' + *-agium*, means a payment for permission to use a path through the forest; it goes back to *caminus*, meaning 'road', used in BML documents relating to Gascony, and possibly derived from Gaulish; it has no connection to the other, more common BML *caminus* ('chimney'), derived from CL and Greek. *busca* ('firewood') is related to and exists alongside CL *boscus*, but enters BML via the AN form 'busche'. *forisfacere*, a common word in BML, is a compound of CL *foris* + CL *facere*, meaning 'to commit an offence' (here with dative of person affected); as one might expect from BML, there is also the form *forfaitare* from the AN 'forfaiter', giving English 'forfeit', but this seems to be much rarer. For this word and words morphologically related to it, see Section II.4C, II.46A and II.46D.

TEXT II.44C

1. in primis omnes foreste quas Henricus rex avus noster afforestavit, videantur per bonos et legales homines; et si boscum aliquem alium quam suum

dominicum afforestaverit ad dampnum illius cuius boscus fuerit, deafforestentur. et si boscum suum proprium afforestaverit, remaneat foresta, salva communa de herbagio et aliis in eadem foresta illis qui eam prius habere consueverunt. (…)

4. archiepiscopi, episcopi, abbates, priores, comites et barones et milites et libere tenentes qui boscos suos habent in forestis, habeant boscos suos sicut eos habuerunt tempore prime coronacionis predicti regis Henrici avi nostri ita quod quieti sint in perpetuum de omnibus purpresturis, vastis et assartis factis in illis boscis, post illud tempus usque ad principium secundi anni coronacionis nostre. et qui de cetero vastum, purpresturam vel assartum sine licencia nostra in illis fecerint, de vastis et assartis respondeant. (…)

7. nullus forestarius vel bedellus de cetero faciat scotale, vel colligat garbas vel avenam vel bladum aliud vel agnos vel porcellos nec aliquam collectam faciant; et per visum et sacramentum duodecim reguardorum quando facient reguardum, tot forestarii ponantur ad forestas custodiendas quot ad illas custodiendas racionabiliter viderint sufficere. (…)

9. unusquisque liber homo agistet boscum suum in foresta pro voluntate sua et habeat pannagium suum. concedimus eciam quod unusquisque liber homo possit ducere porcos suos per dominicum boscum nostrum, libere et sine impedimento ad agistandum eos in boscis suis propriis vel alibi ubi voluerit. et si porci alicuius liberi hominis una nocte pernoctaverint in foresta nostra, non inde occasionetur ita quod aliquid de suo perdat. (…)

12. unusquisque liber homo decetero sine occasione faciat in bosco suo vel in terra sua quam habet in foresta, molendinum, vivarium, stagnum, marleram, fossatum vel terram arabilem extra coopertum in terra arabili, ita quod non sit ad nocumentum alicuius vicini.

13. unusquisque liber homo habeat in boscis suis aerias ancipitrum espervariorum, falconum, aquilarum, et de heyrinis, et habeat similiter mel quod inventum fuerit in boscis suis.

14. nullus forestarius de cetero qui non sit forestarius de feudo, firmam nobis reddens pro balliva sua, capiat chiminagium aliquod in balliva sua; forestarius autem de feudo, firmam nobis reddens pro balliva sua, capiat chiminagium, videlicet, pro careta per dimidium annum duos denarios. (…) illi autem qui portant super dorsum suum buscam, corticem vel carbonem ad vendendum, quamvis inde vivant, nullum decetero dent cheminagium.

15. omnes utlagati pro foresta tantum a tempore regis Henrici avi nostri usque ad primam coronacionem nostram, veniant ad pacem nostram sine inpedimento, et salvos plegios inveniant quod decetero non forisfacient nobis de foresta nostra.

Translation: *The Charter of the Forest*

1. Firstly the forests which King Henry (II) our ancestor put under forest laws should be inspected by good men possessing legal rights; and if he has put some other woodland than his own demesne under forest laws, occasioning loss to the person whose wood it was, it should be removed from forest status. And if he has put his own wood under forest laws it should remain subject to forest law, saving the common right of pasturage etc. in this same forest for those who used to have it previously. (...)

4. The archbishop, bishops, abbots, priors, earls and barons and knights and free tenants who hold their woodlands in the forests should have their woodlands in the same way as they had them at the time of the first coronation of the aforesaid King Henry our ancestor, in such a way that they are permanently exempt from all purprestures, wastes and assarts made in their woods, after that time until the beginning of the second year of our coronation. And those who henceforward cause there to be uncultivated land, encroachment or assart in them without our permission must answer regarding the uncultivated land and assarts. (...)

7. No forester or agent should hold a scot-ale in future, or raise a levy on sheaves of corn or on oats or other crops or lambs or piglets nor make any levy; and by the survey and oath of twelve inspectors when they make an inspection, the same number of foresters should be set to protect the forests as they consider reasonably sufficient to protect them. (...)

9. Each free man must assess his own woodland for pasture in the forest as he wishes and must have the right to feed his pigs on mast. We also grant that each free man should be able to take his pigs through our demesne woods, freely and without impediment to pasture them in his own woods or anywhere else he wants. And if the pigs of some free man should spend one night in our forest, legal proceedings should not be instituted against him as a result so that he should lose anything of what is his. (...)

12. Each free man may in future make, without a pretext, in his wood or on the land which he has in the forest, any of the following: a mill, fishpond, pool, marl pit, ditch or arable land outside the covert on the arable land, as long as it does not harm any neighbour.

13. Every free man shall have the eyries of hawks, sparrowhawks, falcons, eagles and herons in his woods, and likewise honey found in his woods.

14. No forester who is not a tenured forester, paying us a rent for his area of jurisdiction, should in future receive any payment for right of way in his area of jurisdiction; but the tenured forester from a fee, paying us a rent for his area of jurisdiction, should receive payment for right of way, namely 2d. for each cart, every half-year. (...) But those who carry on their backs firewood, bark or coal for sale, even though they gain their living from this, should not in future pay for a right of way.

15. All who have been outlawed for a breach against forest law only from the time of King Henry our grandfather up to our first coronation should peacefully acknowledge our authority without hindrance and must find reliable guarantors that they will not commit an offence against us in the future in respect of our forest.

II.44 | Forest Documents   401

Primary Sources and Related Texts

Carta de foresta in *Statutes of the Realm* 1.20–1, London, 1810.
Holt, J.C. (ed.) (2015) *Magna Carta*, 3rd ed., Cambridge, 429–33.
Select Pleas of the Forest, Selden Society 13 (1901) cxxxvii.
Fleta, prologue and Books 1 and 2, Selden Society 72 (1953) 2.40–1.
Leges Henrici Primi 17, on problems dealt with by forest courts.

Further Reading

Hazell, R. and Melton, J. (ed.) (2015) *The Magna Carta and its modern legacy*,
    Cambridge.
Robinson, N. (2014) '*The Charter of the Forest*: evolving human rights in nature'
    in *Magna Carta and the rule of law*, ed. D. Magraw et al., Chicago.
    https://earlyenglishlaws.ac.uk/reference/essays/forest-law/.

D: A Plea of the Forest Regarding the Taking of a Deer (excerpt: pp. 106–7)

Date: 1253.

TNA: E32/65 (Forest proceedings of the Treasury of the Receipt).

Work: This book deals with the state of the English forests in the period after
the issuing of the *Charter of the Forest* in 1217. It contains examples of court cases
regarding breaches of forest law, e.g. the harming of animals. This excerpt mentions two of the officers involved in managing the king's forest of Rockingham in
Northamptonshire, namely the verderer and the forester, who were involved in
the inquest by the four neighbouring townships into the case of the dead deer.
The case involves suspicious behaviour at night and witness statements by various
villagers in and around Brigstock, which was at the time an administrative hub
for the forest surrounding it.

Linguistic points: The word *spaula* ('shoulder') is connected to AN 'espaule',
deriving from CL *spatula*, but may also be associated with CL *scapula*. *corbel-
lis* ('basket') derives from AN 'corbeil', itself from CL *corbicula*: in BML it is a
good example of a multi-gender, multi-declension noun, appearing between the
twelfth and fourteenth centuries in all three genders and as a first-, second-, and
(as here) third-declension declension noun. In addition, it here bears the suffix
-es, which is usefully multilingual, used as a plural in AN, ME and Latin. There

402 Fifteenth Century

are numerous words for 'basket' in BML, as is clear from a search of the English word in the online *DMLBS*. For *prisona*, cf. Section II.43B. For *cervisia* as an 'ale feast', cf. Section II.49B, and cf. *scotale*. *tina* occurs in BML in the sense of a 'tub', or a liquid measure, much more frequently than either in AN ('tine') or in CL.

TEXT II.44D

The suspicious death of a doe, found in the possession of Geoffrey Catel
[p. 106] accidit die Martis proxima ante Dominicam palmarum anno eodem infra noctem quod Willelmus de Rode forestarius pedites de parco venit in villa de Brixstok ita quod obviavit Galfrido Catel de eadem et Petro Welp intrantibus villam. et Galfridus tulit unam damam integram wlneratam per medium capud cum quadam sagitta. et dictus Willelmus cepit dictum Galfridum et interrogavit eum, ubi habuit dictam damam; et ipse dixit quod venit in parco apud Hassok' eodem die et invenit dictam damam mortuam in cava quercu, et traxit illam in quendam dumetum, et accessit ad villam de Brixstok' et obviavit Johanni Prentut, forestario equiti, et Colino de Geytington', forestario pediti, et Thome Stule, garcioni Johannis Prentut, et Petro Welp, qui perceperunt super eum pilum bestialem. et interogaverunt eum unde ille pilus fuit. et ipse dixit quod invenit unam damam mortuam in parco et eam abscondit. et ipsi promiserunt ei quod nunquam haberet inde malum, condicione, quod reduceret eos ad damam predictam. et ipse retornavit ducens eos ad damam. et ipsi preceperunt ei ferre predictam damam ad domum Petri Welp in Brixstok' et promiserunt ei spaulas et collum. postea die Jovis proxima sequenti, convocatis forestariis viridariis et quatuor villatis, scilicet Brixstok', Stanerne, Grafton, et Suburg' apud Brixstok', ad inquisicionem super hoc faciendam. Brixstok', iurata, dicit per sacramentum suum quod bene sciunt quod dictus Galfridus invenit predictam damam mortuam set nesciunt quis eam occidit, et quod dictus Galfridus voluit tulisse eam ad domum suam propriam et non ad domum Petri Welp. et dicunt per sacramentum suum quod bene sciunt quod totum falsum esset quicquid [p. 107] inponebat forestariis et Petro Welp. et bene sciunt quod Petrus Welp venit de cervisia eadem hora ante Willelmus cepit eundem Galfridum. et nullam suspeccionem habent versus aliquem vel aliquos de malefacto predicto nisi versus eundem Galfridum qui captus est. Stanerne, iurata, dicit idem. Grafton', iurata, dicit idem. Suburg', iurata, dicit idem. Dominus Mauricius Daundely, viridarius, dixit quod predicti forestarii comederunt eodem die Martis cum Radulfo de Craneford' apud Craneford et fuerunt ad domum suam usque ad occasum solis. dictus Galfridus dedixit etc. coram quatuor viridariis et quatuor villatis quicquid prius dixerat coram senescallo et forestariis et quatuor viridariis; et dixit quod Willelmus de Rode, qui eum cepit, fecit eum per vim dicere hoc quod dixit super forestarios et Petrum Welp. dictus Galfridus commissus fuit ad prisonam Norhampt'; tunc vicecomes dominus Willelmus

de Insula. catalla eius capta fuerunt in manu domini regis, videlicet due parve bovette femelle et quatuor oves matrices tondentes et quatuor iuvenes agni, toti de precio iiij s. et una vetus tina, et due veteres corbelles de precio iij d. et commissa fuerunt toti villate ut respondeant de precio coram iusticiariis. coreus dami commissus fuit Geroudo filio Roberti de Suburg' in Brixstok' ad tenendum coram iusticiariis. caro data fuit leprosis pro anima domini regis.

Translation: Pleas of the Forest

It happened on the last Tuesday before Palm Sunday in the same year, during the night, that William de Rode, the forester, came on foot from the park in the village of Brigstock and happened to meet Geoffrey Catel from the same village and Peter Welp, who were coming into the village. And Geoffrey was carrying a whole doe, wounded in the middle of its head with an arrow. Then the said William took hold of Geoffrey and interrogated him, as to where he had got this doe; and he said that he came from the park at Hassok that same day and found this doe dead in a hollow oak tree, and he dragged it into a thicket and went on to the village of Brigstock and met John Prentut, the forester, on horseback, and Colin of Geddington, the forester, on foot, and Thomas Stule, John Prentut's servant-boy, and Peter Welp, who found animal hairs on him. And they asked him where that animal hair came from. And he said that he found a dead doe in the park and hid it. And they promised him that he would not get into any trouble as a result, on condition that he led them back to this doe. And he turned back and took them to the deer. And they told him to take this deer to Peter Welp's house in Brigstock and they promised him the shoulders and neck. Then on the next Thursday following, the foresters, verderers and representatives of four villages, namely Brigstock, Stanion, Grafton and Sudborough, were gathered at Brigstock to carry out an investigation of this matter. The Brigstock jury say on oath that they know well that this Geoffrey found this deer dead but they do not know who killed it, and that this Geoffrey wanted to take it to his own home and not to Peter Welp's home. They say on oath that they know well that whatever he accused the foresters and Peter Welp of was totally false. They know very well that Peter Welp was coming back from the ale that same hour before William took hold of this same Geoffrey. And they do not suspect anyone of the aforesaid crime apart from Geoffrey who was caught. The juries of Stanion, Grafton and Sudborough said the same. Lord Maurice Daundely, the verderer, said that these foresters were eating on that Tuesday with Ralph de Craneford at Craneford and they were at his house until sunset. The said Geoffrey denies etc. in front of the four verderers and the representatives of the four villages what he had previously said in front of the seneschal and foresters and four verderers; he said that William de Rode, who took hold of him, forced him to say what he said about the foresters and Peter Welp. The said Geoffrey was committed to prison in Northampton; at the time Lord William

404 Fifteenth Century

de Insula was the sheriff. Geoffrey's belongings were taken into the hands of the lord king, namely two small female heifers and four grazing ewes and four young lambs, valued together at 4s., and one old tub and two old baskets, valued at 3d. They were handed over to the whole village to answer to their value before the justices. The deer's hide was entrusted to Gerald, son of Robert of Sudborough in Brigstock, to be held before the justices. The meat was given to the lepers for the soul of the lord king.

Primary Source

Select Pleas of the Forest, Selden Society 13 (1899).

Further Reading

Young, C. R. (1974) 'The forest eyre in England during the thirteenth century', *American Journal of Legal History* 18.4: 321–31.

E: The King Grants Firewood to His Daughter

Date: 2 January 1292.

Patent Roll, TNA C66/111.

Work: This document includes mandates (on a schedule (i.e. a slip of parchment) attached to membrane 27) to the keepers of the forests, to the sheriffs of Southampton and Wiltshire, to arrange transport from the forests of Chute and Buckholt to the convent of Amesbury. The king, Edward I, is, as it were, setting up a standing order, granting a regular supply of fuel and wine for the use of his daughter Mary (1279–1332), soon after she took the veil at the age of twelve. Amesbury Priory was a convent with strong royal connections and a daughter house of the order of Fontevraud, based in the Loire valley in France. Mary stayed at Amesbury for the rest of her life, dying there forty years later. The king sensibly allocates wood from two forests in Wiltshire, not too far from Amesbury. Mary was also granted a good supply of wine. With regard to the forest of Buckholt, two years earlier the king had granted the prioress of Amesbury the right to disafforest the northern section, thereby releasing it from the royal forest laws.

Linguistic points: The letter patent opens with the standard, impersonal address from the king in making a grant. CL *dolium* ('cask') is here used, as commonly, for an ample measure of wine. The bailiff (cf. Section II.26C) was an agent of the king, here perhaps organising the sending of the wine casks from the port at Southampton.

TEXT II.44E

The king instructs his officials to deliver firewood and wine to his daughter

[address] rex omnibus ad quos, etc. salutem.

sciatis nos dedisse et concessisse pro nobis et haeredibus nostris, carissimae filiae nostrae Mariae, sanctimoniali Fontis Ebroldi apud Ambresbur' commoranti, quadraginta robora, singulis annis percipienda, in forestis nostris de Chut et Bokholte, per manus custodum earumdem forestarum qui pro tempore fuerint, ad focum suum, in camera sua, quamdiu moram fecerit apud Ambresburiam, percipienda. in cujus etc.[1] teste rege, apud Westm' decimo die Augusti. dedimus etiam et concessimus pro nobis et haeredibus nostris praedictis eidem filiae nostrae viginti dolia vini, singulis annis percipienda, per manus ballivorum nostrorum Southamptoniae, qui pro tempore fuerint (unam videlicet medietatem in quindena Paschae et aliam medietatem ad festum sancti Martini in hyeme) ad sustentationem camerae suae, quamdiu moram fecerit infra regnum nostrum Angliae. in cujus, etc. teste rege apud Westmonast', ii die Januarii, anno etc. vicesimo.

Translation: Patent Roll

The king sends greetings to all those to whom etc.
Please be aware that we have given and granted, for our sake and that of our heirs, to our dearest daughter Mary, a nun of Fontevraud residing at Amesbury, forty three trunks to be taken each year, in our forests of Chute and Buckholt, by the hand of those who are guardians of those forests at the time, for the hearth in her chamber, to be taken for as long as she resides at Amesbury. As a witness to this, the king, at Westminster, on the 10th day of August. We have also given and granted on behalf of us and our heirs, as mentioned, to this same daughter of ours twenty tuns of wine, to be received each year, by the hand of those who are our bailiffs at Southampton at the time (namely one half on the fifteenth day of Easter and the other half at the feast of St Martin in the winter) for the sustenance of her chamber, as long as she resides within our kingdom of England. In witness to this etc., the king at Westminster, on 2 January in the twentieth year etc.

---

1   For this abbreviated phrase cf. Section II.36.

406 Fifteenth Century

Primary Sources and Related Texts

Calendar of Patent Rolls (1281–92) 464–5.
Foedera 1.758 (RC edition, 1816–69).

Further Reading

Victoria history of the county of Wiltshire, vol. 3, 1956. On Amesbury priory, see
    pp. 242–59.

Section II.45

Manorial and Agricultural Documents
A: The Cartulary of St Peter's, Gloucester (excerpt: 3.213)
B: Estate Management in the Letters of Ralph Neville and Simon of Senliz
C: The Custumals of Battle Abbey (1283–1312) (excerpt: pp. 88–90)
D: *Fleta* on the Role of the Reeve of the Manor (excerpt: 2.82)
E: Records of Elton Manor: the Reeve's Accounts (excerpts: pp. 212, 214–15)
F: Assessment of the Royal Estates in the Channel Islands (excerpt: *Extente de l'île de Jersey*, pp. 8–9)

Alongside the records dealing with the legal and financial aspects of the king's court, there exist numerous records, often preserved in local archives all over Britain, for the administration of the manors which managed the land, those who lived on it, and its products. The feudal system had developed a hierarchy of officers and workers under the lord of the manor, each of whom had both rights and responsibilities which were set out in so-called customaries. Below are excerpts from various texts, of different genres (e.g. rules, accounts, letters), demonstrating different aspects of the workings of the manor. Perhaps surprisingly, Latin is the primary language of manorial documents. As these texts deal with a world of numerous technical terms, often vernacular words used by rural workers, they provide a rich source of Latin forms of mostly English words, or of calques, or of what are supposedly synonyms, or of code-switching.

Further Reading

Bailey, M. (ed.) (2002) *The English manor c.1200–c.1500*, Manchester.
Ingham, R. (2009) 'Mixing languages on the manor', *Medium Aevum* 78: 80–97.
Slavin, P. (2012) 'The sources for manorial and rural history' in *Rosenthal (2012).

A: The Cartulary of St Peter's, Gloucester (excerpt: *RS* 3.213)

Date: thirteenth century.

TNA: C 150.

408 Fifteenth Century

The cartulary of St Peter's Abbey, Gloucester is an illuminated MS of 337 vellum leaves, containing transcripts of such documents as charters, customaries and 'extents' (i.e. valuations for tax purposes) from the period 1100–1400. It was intended as a presentation volume. The passage here excerpted contains advice on estate management which seems to have been written before such didactic treatises as Walter of Henley's *Husbandry* were available, for these are not referred to. In this short excerpt the reeve of the manor is instructed to record things properly on a roll, in other words to provide a weekly ledger for auditing purposes, and by reading them out clearly and frequently to remind his co-workers of their responsibilities and the heavy penalty of failing to comply. This instruction is followed by pages of rules regarding everything on the manorial estate (pp. 213–21).

Linguistic points: *aperte faciat recitari* expresses the correlative of the much-used phrase *audire compotum* (i.e. 'to hear an account read out', for which see e.g. *Fleta* 2.89ff., and Simon of Senliz in *Royal Letters* (*RS* 27.1) nos 241 and 410) applied to the checking of accounts, from which English derives the verb 'to audit'.

TEXT II.45A

The reeve's duty to read out the regulations and to observe them
praepositus quolibet mense semel ad minus articulos istius scripti distincte coram eo et socio suo messore aperte faciat recitari, et formam praeceptorum in eo contentam cum summa diligentia et sollicitudine sub poena restitutionis omnium obmittendorum pro posse suo ad plenum observabit, nisi manifesta commoditas vel urgens necessitas sive aliqua alia causa rationabilis ipsum excuset, ostendenda coram suo superiori cum super hoc fuerit requisitus.

Translation: Cartulary of St Peter's, Gloucester

At least once a month the reeve should arrange for the articles of this document to be recited clearly and distinctly in his presence and that of his colleague the reaper, and he will fully observe, to the best of his ability, the form of regulations contained in it with all diligence and care, on pain of restitution of all the things omitted, unless it is clearly appropriate and urgently necessary to excuse him or there is any other reasonable cause, which must be demonstrated to his superior in person when he is required to do so.

Primary Source and Related Texts

Historia et cartularium monasterii S. Petri Gloucestriae (12–14c.), 3 vols, *RS* 33 (1863–7).

II.45 | Manorial and Agricultural Documents   409

Further Reading

Oschinsky, D. (1947) 'Medieval treatises on estate accounting', *Economic History Review* 17.1: 52–61.

Sabapathy, J. (2014) *Officers and accountability in medieval England, 1170–1300*, Oxford.

B: Estate Management in the Letters of Ralph Neville and Simon of Senliz

Date: early thirteenth century.

The original letters are preserved in the National Archives (TNA: SC1/6/3 and SC 1/6/132).

Authors: Ralph Neville, of an unknown background, worked his way up to a position of great wealth and power in royal service from the early years of the thirteenth century. He was Bishop of Chichester from 1222 and Chancellor of England from the mid-1220s until 1244, but the first letter here was written before he was accorded these titles.

Simon of Senliz came from the English branch of a noble French family in which most males were called Simon. This Simon came from an illegitimate line, but he became steward to Ralph Neville and later to the Archbishop of Canterbury.

Work: These letters between Ralph Neville and his land agents provide evidence of how well-educated people wrote to each other on everyday business, giving orders in an unofficial manner and reporting on business relating to Neville's lands. Although the focus here is mainly on Sussex, it is clear that business was done over a wide area of the country, involving a good deal of travel. Note the hurried postscript to the first letter, occasioning a repeated *valete*. The second letter offers an example of the lands of a recently deceased lord (here, Amaury de Craon, who died in 1226) being entrusted to a guardian (i.e. Neville) until he reaches the age of 21, for which cf. Section II.39. The letter proves that marl was used to spread on arable land to improve its yield, as is supported also by *Fleta* 2.76, where the benefits of marl are mentioned.

Linguistic points: While CL *paenula* occurs in BML glossaries both pre- and post-Conquest in its original sense as a cloak, it is more often used in everyday life as the lining or trim of a cloak. *bissus* (from French 'bis') refers to the fur of a hind or squirrel, but has also been taken to refer to the colour of the fur, as *OED s.v.* byse. *ascer-* is one of the spelling variants for *acerum*, related to *aciarium* ('steel'). *bruillus* (in various spellings) is related to AN 'bruil', apparently

410 Fifteenth Century

from a hypothetical form 'brogilos', possibly originally a Gaulish word, meaning a wooded thicket or deer park. The Latin word occurs on the Continent (also as *brolium*) at an early date, but in Britain not until after the Conquest, in DB, and then becomes popular in the thirteenth century: the name Broyle survives in place names in Sussex. *meheremium* is one of the many possible spellings of *maeremium* (cf. Section II.47E); it refers to the timber used for building etc. rather than *boscus*, which is used for the smaller branches for light construction and firewood. The word only appears in the late twelfth century, taking over from such words as *lignum* and *robur*.

B(a): *Royal Letter* **no. 165**

Date: 1214–22.

TNA: SC1/6/3.

TEXT II.45B(a)

Ralph Neville writes to his land agent about wheat prices and the delivery of 5,000 herrings

[address] R. de Nevill, decanus Lichefeldenis fideli suo G. Salvage, salutem.

quod bladum meum de Thorp vendidistis pro xxii marcis sicut mihi mandastis ex quo pro majori precio vendi non potuit, placet mihi quod ita vendatur. de perquisitis eciam vestris de quibus me certificari voluistis prudentiam vestram commendo, rogans quatinus agendis meis intendatis, quod grates vobis sciam. sciatis quod locutus sum cum domino Ricardo Duket, quod faciet mihi habere quinque milia allecis, et cc cere et unam penulam de bisis et de ferro et ascero ad carrucas meas et ideo vobis mando quod quam cito poteritis ad eum accedatis, **?l. Norwicensis** et de his omnibus eum conveniatis. mementote de allece quem Prior Nuwicensis mihi dedit, scilicet quinque milia, ad quem recipiendum oportet quod sitis apud Norwic vel tertia die ante festum Sancti Martini vel tercia die post festum Sancti Martini; de alio allece quod scitis totum relinquo discretioni vestre. valete. literas Abrahe de Cruezford deperdidi, quarum tenorem penitus ignoro. valete.

Translation: Letter of Ralph Neville

R. de Nevill, Dean of Lichfield, (sends) greetings to his faithful G. Salvage.
As for the fact that you have sold my wheat from Thorp (?Morningthorpe in Norfolk) for 22 marks as you told me, because it could not be sold for a higher price, I am

II.45 | Manorial and Agricultural Documents 411

content that it should be sold like that. Regarding your purchases also, concerning which you wished to inform me, I commend your prudence, asking you to manage my affairs in such a way that I may be grateful to you. Please be aware that I have spoken with Sir Richard Duket, that he may let me have 5,000 herrings and 200 wax candles and a grey cloak and some iron and steel for my ploughs; and therefore I order you to go to him as soon as you can and ask him about all these things. Remember the herring which the prior of Newark (?Norwich) gave me, namely 5,000: in order to receive them you must be at Norwich either on the third day before or the third day after the feast of St Martin. Regarding the other herring which you know about, I leave it all to your discretion. Farewell. I have lost the letters of Abraham de Cruezford, and have no idea of their content. Farewell.

B(b): *Royal Letter* no. 239

Date: ?1226–7.

TNA: SC 1/6/132. Some of the letters by Simon are autographs.

TEXT II.45B(b)

Simon of Senliz reports to Ralph Neville about timber, wheat, marl and a windmill

[address] reverendo domino suo R. gratia Dei Cycestrensi episcopo domini regis cancellario, devotus suus S[imon] de Senliz salutem et tam devotum quam debitum in omnibus famulatum.

sciatis, domine, quod emi ad opus vestrum xii acras de maremio in brullio Cycestriae de domino Willelmo de S. Johanne, de meliore maremio in electione mea, quamlibet acram pro xl s. et hoc de consilio liberorum et legalium hominum vestrorum, qui firmiter asserunt quod quelibet acra valet iv marcas, et bene credo quod W[illelmus] de S. Johanne dabit nobis aliquantum de meheremio suo in dicto Bruillo. nolo etiam vos latere, quod bladum in singulis maneriis vestris in episcopatu vestro bene et fructuose ad commodum vestrum colligitur, et absque pluvie inundacione in horrea vestra salvo deponitur. nihil ex eo erit ad colligendum in crastino decollationis Beati Johannis Baptiste. gratia Dei enim singula negocia vestra prospere procedunt in Sussex, et laborabo pro viribus ne aliter procedant. marlare facio apud Seleseiam cum duabus carretis, quoniam ut dicitur marla ibi inventa optima est, unde si videritis expedire ut marlare faciam cum pluribus caretis, consulo ut perquiratis de domino Godescallo vel alibi xii equas ad trahendum in caretis; quoniam expedit vobis, ut in partibus illis illas perquiratis, quoniam ut aurum emantur in Sussex. loquimini, si placet, domine, cum domino ut committat vobis custodiam terre domini Amauri de Croun, usque

412 Fifteenth Century

ad plenam etatem heredis, quoniam tunc commode possem ad utilitatem vestram maneriis providere de instauro et de aliis negociis. similiter marlare facio apud Watresfeld cum v caretis, et bene spero quod cedet ad utilitatem vestram. molendinum etiam ad ventum ibidem promptum est et bene paratum et molit. dominus W[illelmus] de S. Johanne benigne michi respondet quod animo libenti voluntatem vestram et beneplacitum de negocio de quo ut colloquium haberem cum eo michi precipistis, et sicut alias vobis significavi, adimplebit. super predictis et aliis voluntatem vestram michi significare dignemini. desidero de statu vestro et incolumitate certitudinem audire. Dominus conservet vos per tempora longa.

Translation: Letter of Simon of Senliz

To his reverend lord Ralph, by the grace of God Bishop of Chichester and chancellor of the lord king, his loyal servant Simon of Senliz sends greetings and service as devoted as is due in all things.
Please be aware, my lord, that I have bought for your use from Lord William de St John 12 acres of woodland in the Chichester Broyle of the best timber I have to choose from, at 40s. for each acre, on the advice of your freemen and liegemen, who resolutely claim that each acre is worth 4 marks, and I well believe that W. de St John will give us some of his own timber in the said Broyle. I wish you to know that the wheat in each of your manors in your diocese is being gathered in efficiently and in abundance for your benefit, and is being safely deposited in your granaries so as not to be damaged by heavy rain. There will be nothing left to gather the day after the beheading of St John the Baptist. By the grace of God all your affairs are proceeding prosperously in Sussex and I will make every effort to see that they continue to do so. I am using marl at Selsey with two carts, as it is said that the marl found there is the best; and so if you think it useful for me to use marl with more carts, I advise you to procure, from Lord Godescall or elsewhere, twelve mares to be placed in the carts to pull them, seeing that it is worth your procuring them in those parts, because they are as expensive as gold in Sussex. Please, my lord, speak with the lord king, asking him to entrust to you the wardship of Lord Amaury de Craon's land, until his heir reaches adulthood, since I could then conveniently look after the stock and other business for your manors to your advantage. In like manner I am using marl at Watresfield with five carts, and I hope greatly that this will have an advantageous result for you; furthermore, the windmill there is ready and suitably fitted and it is now grinding. Sir W. de St John answers me kindly that he is happy to carry out your request and your wishes regarding the business which you told me to discuss with him, and as I have informed you elsewhere. Concerning the matters mentioned, as well as others, please let me know what you want. I desire also to receive assurance concerning your situation and well-being. May the Lord preserve you for many years to come.

II.45 | Manorial and Agricultural Documents 413

Primary Sources and Related Texts

Royal Letters (1216–35), RS 27.1 (1862) nos 165 and 239.
Calendar of Patent Rolls (1225–32) 52: (1226) the king grants broyle at Chichester
to William of St John; *Calendar of Close Rolls (1227–1231)* 272: (1229) the king
transfers broyle from William of St John to Ralph Neville.

Further Reading

Carlin, M. and Crouch, D. (2013) *Lost letters of medieval life: English society,
1200–1250*, Philadelphia.
Riggulsford, M. (2017) 'Common as marl', *The Geoscientist*, 16–19.
Stone, J. and Stone, L. (1984) 'Bishop Ralph Neville, chancellor to King Henry
III, and his correspondence: a reappraisal', *Archives* 16.71: 227–57.
Vincent, N. (1996) *Peter des Roches: an alien in politics, 1205–38*, repr.
Cambridge, 2002.
https://sites.uwm.edu/carlin/selected-correspondence-of-ralph-de-
neville-d-1244/, where this letter is given as no. 3.

C: The Custumals of Battle Abbey (1283–1312) (excerpt: pp. 88–90)

Work: A custumal is a document which in a manorial context records the tenants
of the manor and the conditions of their tenure. The introduction to the cited
edition opens with the claim that 'a very complete and interesting picture of agricultural life in England during the latter part of the thirteenth century … may be
obtained by a careful study of the records … bearing on the subject of customary
tenures'. Such documents include the *Inquisitiones Hundredorum* in the Hundred
Rolls of 7 and 8 Edward I (extant for five counties), but also the monastic records
as to the amount and value of work exacted by the lord of the manor and what
recompense the different classes of tenants were entitled to; as often, these documents record the names of many individuals of all ranks. The records excerpted
here, dating to the end of the reign of Edward I and concerning the lands held by
Battle Abbey (built near the site of the battle of Hastings) in Sussex, are taken from
the *Liber regius de Bello* (i.e. vol. 57 of the Augmentation Books listed as E315 in
the National Archives), ff. 56–7. This excerpt relates to the manor of Crowmarsh
in Oxfordshire, and can therefore be compared with the material for Oxfordshire
in the Hundred Rolls (2.763b–764a). Note that many of the tenants are women.

Linguistic points: Note the varied and confusing spelling of the place name, a
characteristic feature of medieval documents: in the Custumal Crowmarsh is
written Craumareys and in the Hundred Rolls it occurs as Prustecromse (for

414 Fifteenth Century

Preston Crowmarsh). This excerpt shows some of the many manorial and agricultural terms not found in these forms or senses in CL, e.g. *messuagium* ('dwelling'), a common spelling ultimately deriving from *mansio*; *pannagiare* ('to pay for pannage' (i.e. the right to collect food for swine, probably deriving from an early form, *pastionaticum*)). *falda* is the BML word for '(sheep)fold', derived from OE 'fald', whereas the modern English derives from the ME 'fold'; despite the connection with the OE word it does not occur in BML until after the Conquest. Note also the variant spellings of *arrare* (*ar-*), *curtilagium* (*curt-* being the AN form of the OF *cort-*) and *sommonere* (for *submon-*): the latter two display the common interchange between o and u. The term for 'church tax' occurs here in the ME form 'cherset', which was one of the corrupt forms from OE 'ciricsceat'; it also appears with Latin terminations in many different spellings, for which see *DMLBS s.v. cyricsceattum*. *communere* ('to exercise the right of common pasturage') appears as a verb in the late thirteenth century. Note the French definite article, often used, as here, in place names. 'Forsettere' (a strip of ploughed land at the edge of a field) is here ME, though it does occur in an integrated Latin form as *foresheta*, in another Oxfordshire text (*Ambrosden*, ed. W. Kennett, 1818). Here it occurs alongside *foretata*, which may be a past participle like *fimata* and *faldata*, from an otherwise unattested *forerare*, or more plausibly a form of *forera*, also meaning the edge of a field, which may be etymologically related to 'forest'.[1]

TEXT II.45C

The tenants of Crowmarsh, Oxfordshire: their rights and responsibilities
[p. 88] Alicia et qui secuntur debent omnia servitia sicut Thomas le Neweman, excepto quod non debent triturare. Matilda, relicta Johannis, tenet ij acras et dimidiam, reddens per annum xiij d. et iij d. de *cherset*. ista debet metere in autumpno per vj dies et ligare; et ad iij[es] precarias inveniet quolibet die j hominem et ad iiij[tam] precariam unum hominem usque nonam. et fenum vertere debet et levare, cum communi villatae. Radulphus de Northene tenet per Agnetem uxorem suam ij acras et dimidiam et unum curtilagium. et debent xiiij d. et iij d. de *cherset* et omnia servitia ut praedicta Matilda; idem tenet unam acram de terra le Deen, de dimissione H. Abbatis, et debet per annum iiij d. Mabilia, relicta Johannis, tenet ad terminum vitae viij acras terrae de tenemento quod fuit Thomae North, quod est in manu nostra de dimissione Agnetis filiae suae cum toto. quas quidem viij acras dominus Abbas ei concessit ad terminum vitae, reddens per annum xx d. [p. 89] Johannes le Wyte tenet de terra Thomae North ij acras et j messuagium

---

1 Cf. the version in the Hundred Rolls, 1.764[a] (1279): *item omnes habebunt unam acram bladi quam eligere voluerint post primam precariam autumpni ita quod non sit fortsetere fimata nec forera super dominicum domini.*

II.45 | Manorial and Agricultural Documents 415

de venditione praedicti Thomae et reddit per annum xij d. memorandum quod omnes tenentes debent pannagiare porcos suos, pro porcos plenariae aetatis j d. et pro minore aetatis secundum portionem; debent denarios dare Sancti Petri. item non debent maritare filias suas extra libertatem sine licentia, nec etiam bovem suum vel equum sine licentia vendere.

Food allowances for the tenants, and rights on common land
debent etiam omnes custumarii habere in autumpno cibum suum ad precarias, bis per diem; scilicet ad nonam, panem de frumento, cervisiam et caseum et ad vesperas, panem, cervisiam, potagium, carnem vel alleces secundum quod dies fuerit, et caseum, et dicunt quod debent habere potationem post nonam. debent etiam habere unam acram de frumento post primam precariam, quam eligere voluerint, ita tamen quod non sit fimata nec faldata nec forsettere nec foretata super dominicum mensurata sicut jacet in campo; debent etiam communere super stipulam quam cito blada domini colliguntur et in una pastura quae vocatur Heycrofte; et post festum Sancti Martini arrabunt domino j acram que vocatur Grasherxe qui habent carrucas; qui vero non habent carrucas, tunc primo communent in omnibus locis infra et extra; et debent colligere stipulam super dominicum post festum Sancti Martini ad opus eorum et propter hoc dabunt *cherset*; dicunt etiam quod quaelibet virgata potest habere sexdecim bidentes ad faldam suam per tempus; dicunt etiam omnes custumarii debent sommoneri per ij dies antequam debent sarclare, falcare et metere, ut sint parati cum instrumentis opera domini perficere et qui non habet falcem debet falcatoribus j d.

Translation: The Custumals of Battle Abbey

Alice and those who follow owe all services just as Thomas le Newman, except that they do not have to thresh. Matilda, the widow of John, holds 2½ acres, returning 13d. a year, and 3d. in church tax. She is obliged to reap in the autumn for six days, and to bind; and on the four days of customary work she must find one man each day and on the fourth day of customary work one man until noon. And she must turn the hay and lift it, with the commons of the village. Ralph of Northene holds, through his wife Agnes, 2½ acres and 1 curtilage. And they owe 14d., and 3d. of church tax and all the services, like the aforesaid Matilda. The same man holds 1 acre of the le Deen land, by the grant of Abbot H., and he owes 4d. a year. Mabilia, the widow of John, holds until the end of her life 8 acres of land from the tenement which belonged to Thomas North, which is in our hand by the grant of Agnes her daughter, with the entirety. The lord Abbot granted these 8 acres to her till the end of her life, returning 20d. a year. John le Wyte holds 2 acres from the land of Thomas North and a tenement from the sale of the aforesaid Thomas, and he returns 12d. a year. It is to be remembered that all the tenants must pay pannage for their pigs, 1d. for full-grown pigs and pro rata for

416 Fifteenth Century

a younger one. They must give St Peter's pence; in addition, they must not give their daughters in marriage outside the domain without permission, nor sell their cow or horse without permission. All customary tenants must also receive their food on the days of customary work in autumn, twice a day; namely at noon, bread made of wheat, ale and cheese, and in the evening, bread, ale, soup, meat or herring depending on what day it is, and cheese, and they say that they should have the drink after noon. They should also have 1 acre of wheat (as it lies in the field), which they can choose, after the first day of customary work, as long as it is not manured or enclosed as a sheepfold, and it is not a headland nor a strip round a field measured out on the demesne land; they should also have right of common on the stubble as soon as the lord's cereal crop is gathered in and in one pasture called Heycroft; and after the feast of St Martin those who have ploughs will plough for the lord 1 acre called Grasherxe; those who do not have ploughs will first have right of common in all the places within and outside; and they must collect stubble on the demesne land after the feast of St Martin for their work, and on account of this they will pay church tax; they say also that each virgate can have sixteen sheep in a sheepfold for a time; they say also that all customary tenants must be summoned two days before they have to hoe, mow and reap so that they may be ready with the tools to carry out the lord's works, and anyone who does not have a scythe owes 1d. to the mowers.

Primary Sources and Related Texts

Custumals of Battle Abbey (1283–1312), Camden Society n.s. 41 (1887).
The Chronicle of Battle Abbey, ed. E. Searle, Oxford, 1980.

Further Reading

Birrell, J. (2014) 'Manorial custumals reconsidered', *Past and Present* 224.1: 3–37.
Searle, E. (1974) *Lordship and community: Battle Abbey and its banlieu*, Toronto.

D: *Fleta* on the Role of the Reeve of the Manor (excerpt: 2.82)

Date: c.1290.

The text survives only in BL MSS Cotton Julius B.viii and Cotton Nero D.vi.

Author: *Fleta* was compiled by an anonymous lawyer, written around 1290 in the Fleet Prison, from which it is thought to derive its Latin title.

Work: *Fleta* is a conflation of earlier reference books for estate managers, primarily *Seneschaucy* and Walter of Henley's *Husbandry* (both in AN, written in the late thirteenth century), which along with the *Anonymous Husbandry* and the *Rules* of Robert Grosseteste (*Regulae ad custodiendum terras*) are the prime examples of such works, written not by academics but by lawyers and estate managers based on their experience on lay or ecclesiastical estates. The author draws also on the huge legal work of Bracton. The work is aimed at lawyers who work as estate managers. This excerpt is a postscript to 2.76, where the author describes the reeve's work: here he returns to the reeve's duties at the manor. He is expected to safeguard his lord's produce and maximise his income: this even includes preventing anyone begging a bit of cheese or butter from the dairymaid, just as the bailiff must stop threshers from stealing corn in their shoes, gloves or satchels. Despite being a legal text, it is full of perceptive details of the realities of everyday life, including advice on the ideal personalities for the jobs of shepherds and dairymaids. *melius est in tempore occurrere quam post causam vulneratam cause remedium adhibere* is the reeve's version of the proverb 'a stitch in time saves nine'.

Linguistic points: With regard to syntax, this text is rich in jussive subjunctives, as appropriate when giving the reeve's duties; *debet* or *officium prepositi* with the infinitive are alternatives. Note also the list of past participles used to describe all the things that might need mending. With regard to vocabulary, the text is particularly rich in words derived from French (often going back to a CL or a Germanic word). *appruator* ('improver, enricher, manager') is formed from *approvare*, a popular word in the context of land-cultivation: it is related to AN 'approver', retaining an echo in *OED s.v.* approve v. 2, meaning to make a profit by increasing the value of land. *warantum* (related to modern English 'warrant', 'warranty', 'guarantee') comes into BML after the mid-twelfth century, but goes back to a Germanic word that had passed into French, 'garant/warant'. *warantum* also forms the basis of the verb *warantare* and its common variant *warantizare*. *dissaisina* means 'dispossession', but the context here implies that it is a disreputable event that the estate officers should not attend. *drasca* (AN 'drasche') signifies the malt 'dregs'. *misa* (here in the sense 'expense') derives from AN 'mise', from 'mettre', ultimately deriving from CL *mittere*. *daieria* ('dairy') occurs in ME ('deierie') as well as AN ('daierie'), going back to OE 'dæge' ('servant-girl'; *OED s.v.* dey) with the Romance suffix '-erie' from Latin *-arius* (see also Section II.45E). CL *detegere* is here applied in its original literal sense of 'to take the roof off'. *deliberare* is here the LL rather than the CL word, signifying 'to free' or 'to deliver' rather than 'to deliberate'. It is possible that the non-classical word goes back to Tertullian's paraphrase of Ps. 32:19 in *Against Marcion* 2.19, *ad deliberandas animas de morte*, with *deliberare* as the equivalent of *eruere*.

TEXT II.45D

The many and various duties and responsibilities of the reeve on his lord's estate
[2.82] nullus prepositus ultra unum annum remaneat irremotus, nisi pro fideli ac optimo appruatore, set, cum in prepositura remanserit, diligenter defectus videat in curia subortos, utpote de domibus detectis, muris fractis, fossatis obstructis, sepibus dirutis, carucis ruptis, carectis disiunctis et fractis, ovilibus derelictis et huiusmodi, quibus cum celeritate manus adiutrices apponat ne negligencia eius domino sit dampnosa. quod enim hodie posset de uno denario corigi, in fine forte anni de xij denariis non poterit emendari, ideoque melius est in tempore occurrere quam post causam vulneratam cause remedium adhibere. prospiciat sibi tamen de waranto inde habendo, alioquin voluntaria erit allocacio predictorum, eo quod huiusmodi misas esse falsas supponunt auditores compotorum. nec fiant sepes de pomariis, piris, cerisariis vel prunariis, set de salicibus et alba spina construantur. et caveat sibi prepositus ne alicui extraneo vel domini familiari supervenienti quicquam inveniat sine waranto vel mandato. nec eciam permittat quod aliquis vel aliqua ad caseatricem accedat ne quicquam casei, lactis, butiri vel huiusmodi deportet quod cedere posset parve familie in comodum seu casei butiri vel daerie in decrementum. nec eciam sustineat quod aliquis alicui officio deputatus, de nocte vel de die, ferias, mercatos, disseysinas, vigilias, luctas adeat vel tabernas, set quod omnes constanter suis intendant officiis, nec licencia hac vel illac cuiquam vacandi concedatur priusquam substitutum pro quo voluerit respondere, suo duxerit officio collocare. si custos namque ovium vel porcorum vel huiusmodi vacaret nullo sibi substituto, possibile esset huiusmodi pecora per loca diversa deviare et dispergere et dampnum facere domino vel vicinis pluraque alia inde possent dampna evenire.

et qualibet septimana debet prepositus cum ballivo conputare consuetudines ebdomadis operacionesque talliare ut de arreragiis operacionum perinde cerciorientur que si in denarios convertentur poterit sic redditus augmentari. item nec permittatur quod ignis deferatur in stabulum vel boveriam seu lumen candele, nisi ob necessitudinem, nec tunc per minus quam per duos homines portari sustineatur. item prepositi scire est quociens carecte per diem cariagia sua comode facere valeant ad fenum, turbam, maheremium, boscum, fimum, marlam et huiusmodi, ut si cariatores de ceteris diebus secundum illius diei laborem non responderint, penam compoti se voluerint incursuros. item officium prepositi de toto exitu grangiarum se onerare, necnon et de omnibus receptis et de omnibus empcionibus et vendicionibus intrinsecis et forinsecis, tam bladi quam instauri, item bladum ad furnandum et braseum et braciandum per tallias pistori deliberare et exitum eorundem, videlicet furfur, a pistore recipere, ac draschiam, per visum ballivi, custodi carucarum per talliam et mensuram liberare ac furfur eciam pistori ac marescallo, ad panem garcionum et familie et ad pastum canum, similiter per talliam et mensuram debet liberare.

Translation: *Fleta*

[2.82] *Let no reeve remain for more than a year without being removed from office, except in the case of one who is trustworthy and highly skilled at improving the estate; but while he remains in the position of reeve, he should diligently watch out for defects arising in the manor house, such as buildings without a roof, cracked walls, blocked ditches, torn-down hedges, broken ploughs, carts that have fallen apart and are broken, derelict sheepfolds and suchlike, to which he should speedily give a helping hand so that his lord does not lose money as the result of his negligence. For something that one might mend today for 1 penny will not be able to be put right for 12 pence at the end of the year, and so it is better to come forward with help in good time than to apply a remedy once the damage has been done. Let the reeve take the precaution to have authorisation for this; otherwise any allowance for these things will be voluntary, with the result that the auditors of the accounts allege that these expense claims are false. Hedges should not be made of apple, pear, cherry or plum, but should be constructed of willow or hawthorn. The reeve must be careful that he has authorisation and instructions in providing anything for any stranger or for anyone of the lord's household who happens to arrive. Nor should he allow anyone, whether man or woman, to visit the dairymaid, in case this person takes some cheese, milk, butter or suchlike to help a small household, but which reduces the yield of cheese, butter or dairy products. Nor should he put up with anyone, appointed to any position, going off by night or by day to visit a fair or market or confiscation of property, or revels, fights or pubs; instead everyone should constantly concentrate on their duties. The reeve must not allow anyone to take time off until he has arranged for a substitute, for whom he is willing to answer, to take over his duties. If the shepherd or swineherd or suchlike should take time off without a substitute, it is possible that the cattle will stray, wandering off in different directions and causing their lord and his neighbours to lose money and many other losses to occur.*

And each week the reeve ought to account to the bailiff for the weekly services and make a tally of the customary works so that the arrears of works due may be ascertained in this way; if these are converted into money, then the revenue can be increased. Again, he should not allow fire or lighted candles to be taken into the stable or cowshed, except when indispensable, and then it should not be permitted to be carried by fewer than two men. Next it is the duty of the reeve to know how many times a day the carts can conveniently carry loads of hay, turf, timber, wood, dung, marl and suchlike, so that if the carters are not answerable on other days at the rate of that day's labour, then they should be ready to incur a penalty at the time of the account. Then it is the duty of the reeve to take responsibility for all the produce of the barns, and for all the receipts and purchases and sales, both at the manor and away from it, both of corn and stock; and also to supply, by means of tallies, the baker with corn for baking and malt for brewing, and to receive their by-products

420 Fifteenth Century

(namely bran) from the baker, to be inspected by the bailiff, and to supply malt dregs to the man in charge of the ploughs, by tally and measure, and bran also to the baker and horse-servant, for bread for the grooms and the household and to feed the dogs, similarly by tally and measure.

Primary Sources and Related Texts

Fleta, prologue and Books 1 and 2, Selden Society 72 (1953).
Rules of Robert Grosseteste and *Seneschaucy* (chapter 100) in Oschinsky, D. (1971) *Walter of Henley and other treatises on estate management and accounting*, Oxford.
Rectitudines singularum (a late eleventh-century estate text, giving duties of the thegn/*villanus*, etc.) in **Die Gesetze der Angelsachsen* 1.444–5.

Further Reading

Oschinsky, D. (1956) 'Medieval treatises on estate management', *Economic History Review* n.s. 8: 296–309.

E: Records of Elton Manor: the Reeve's Accounts (excerpts: pp. 212, 214–15)

Date: 1313–14.

TNA: SC 6/884/4 m. 5d and m. 6, a series of narrow membranes joined at the top and rolled up.

This set of reeve's accounts from the manor of Elton belongs to the series of ministers' accounts in the National Archives: this series is a rich source of words for agricultural implements. The manor of Elton, now in Cambridgeshire, belonged to Ramsey Abbey from before 1066, and is mentioned in the Domesday Book; these excerpts show that material for the manor was sourced from Peterborough (Burgum) and nearby Fotheringhay Castle. Later in the same document under the years 1349–50 there are brief allusions to the effects of the plague in the repeated phrase *causa mortalitatis accidentis anno precedente* ('by reason of the plague that hit in the preceding year'). Note the mention of parchment, presumably bought to record the accounts.

Linguistic points: Note that the Roman numeral for hundred, namely 'c', here indicates the medieval 'long hundred', i.e. 120. These excerpts provide an excellent

II.45 | Manorial and Agricultural Documents 421

example of the lexical mixture so characteristic of BML texts, and in particular agricultural accounts. One finds a combination of CL terms (e.g. *collare* and *capistrum*), also with semantic extension (e.g. fourth declension *tractus*, extended to mean the straps on a horse's collar, i.e. modern English 'traces'), integrated vernacular words, i.e. with Latin word-final suffixes (e.g. *stottus* from OE 'stot', *cluta* from ME 'clut (clout)' or *fagotus* from AN 'fagot'), or abbreviations/suspensions which left the ending – and indeed the language of the word – ambiguous. For example, *brodd'* could be English ('brad-nail') or its borrowing into Latin, *broddum*, in whatever case was needed: in other account rolls this word does appear with a Latin suffix. In addition there are non-integrated vernacular terms like 'stroknayl' or 'chyrne'. *dynelegg* seems to be a version of *douellegia* (ME 'doulegge'), i.e. 'duledge' or 'dowel-edge' for the metal edge of a cartwheel. The form *saii* occurs twice but remains a mystery.[2] One might expect a word in the ablative here, like *sarculo*; there may be a connection with CL *sarire*. *canopus* and *canobus* are versions of CL *cannabis*, which can signify 'hemp', 'tow' or 'canvas'. The spelling with initial double f, as in *ffodr*, indicates an initial capital F.

TEXT II.45E

The accounts for agricultural tools and equipment

[p. 212] idem computat in virgis emptis pro carectis fimorum emendandis et reparandis post festum sancti Michaelis iiij d. In palis emptis pro predictis carectis fimorum ij d. In xxiiij clutis ad carectas emptis post festum sancti Michaelis xi-iij d. In cc brodd' ad idem emptis iij d. (…) In xxx wynding' emptis ibidem xij d. In uno novo ferramento ad carectam empto circa Purificationem cum toto necessario ad idem viij s. iij d. In uno carpentario conducto per duos dies ad mensam domini pro viij axibus de novo faciendis de meremio (maer-) domini ij d. In ij veteribus rotis emendandis et ligandis de ferro domini vij d. In palis pro vj carectis emptis vj d. In coriis unius pulli masculi et duorum stottorum de morina dealbandis ad harnesium xvj d. In uno pare rotarum de novo ferrando post Pascham vij d. In ij peciis ferri emptis pro vinculis faciendis ad veteres rotas vj d. ob. In dictis veteribus rotis ligandis et emendandis de predicto ferro vj d. In c de spyk' empta ad carectas fimorum post Pascham ij d. ob. In lx de *stroknayl* emptis apud Undele circa hok' xij d. In ij paribus rotarum ferratarum et ij paribus rotarum nudarum emptis apud Sanctum Neotum die Ascensionis domini xij s. In iiij cordis ad carectas et iiij paribus tractuum emptis ibidem iij s. iij d. In iij sellis nudis ad carectas emptis ibidem vij d. ob. In una corda ad carectam et vij capistris de canopo domini faciendis iij d. In ij ulnis canobi emptis ad harnesium contra

---

2   Gratitude is due to Richard Sharpe and James Willoughby for confirming that the reading is a mystery.

422 Fifteenth Century

autumpnum v d. In iij colariis ad equos carectarios emptis contra autumpnum ij s. ix d. In uno pare de basses empto eodem tempore vj d. In lx de *stroknayl* emptis eodem tempore xij d. In ij kyppelyn' emptis eodem tempore j d. ob. (…) In una pecia ferri empta pro dynelegg' faciendis iiij d. ob. In uno pare rotarum de novo ferrando post Gulam augusti ad mensam domini ix d. (…)

Translation: Records of Elton

The same accounts for rods bought for mending and repairing the dung-carts after the feast of St Michael, 4d. For stakes bought for the aforesaid dung-carts, 2d. For 24 (metal) patches for carts bought after the feast of St Michael, 14d. For 240 brad-nails bought for the same, 3d. (…) For 30 cartwheels bought at the same place, 12d. For one new set of ironwork for a cart bought around the Purification with all that is necessary for the same, 8s. 3d. For one carpenter hired for two days (with food) at the lord's table to make 8 new axles from the lord's timber, 2d. For mending and binding with the lord's iron 2 old wheels, 7d. For stakes bought for 6 carts, 6d. For white-tawing the hides of one male colt and of two stots (dead) of disease, for a harness, 16d. For making new iron tyres on one pair of wheels after Easter, 7d. For 2 pieces of iron bought for making bands for old wheels, 6½ d. For binding and mending the said old wheels with the aforesaid iron, 6d. For 120 spike-nails bought for the dung-carts after Easter, 2½ d. For 60 strake-nails bought at Oundle around Hock-day, 12d. For 2 pairs of wheels fitted with tyres and 2 pairs of wheels without tyres bought at St Neots on the day of the Ascension of the Lord, 12s. For 3 cords for carts and 3 pairs of traces bought at the same place, 3s. 3d. For 3 bare seats bought there for the carts, 7½ d. For one rope for a cart and for making 7 halters from the lord's tow, 3d. For 2 ells of tow bought for a harness against the autumn, 5d. For 3 collars for carthorses bought against the autumn, 2s. 9d. For one pair of cart-horse collars bought at the same time, 6d. For 60 strake-nails bought at the same time, 6d. For 2 harness-cords bought at the same time 1½d. (…) For one piece of iron bought for making the duledge, 4½ d. For fitting with new tyres one pair of wheels after the Gule of August (with food) at the lord's table, 9d. (…)

[p. 214] idem computat in virgis emptis pro animalibus ligandis in bostaribus suis iij d. In una sporta empta iij d. In ferramento unius vange et duorum trobulorum (trib-) faciendo de ferro domini iij d. In iij^m vj^c turbarum emptis ad ffocale ij s. xj d. In veteri Busca ad ffocale empta xviij d. In duobus saticulis emptis iiij d. ob. In vij presuris emptis et factis ad dayeriam domini xiij d. ob. et ij caseos de rewayn. In iiij ulnis panni ad dayeriam emptis vij d. [p. 215] In ij patellis et iij ollis luteis emptis ad dayeriam pro lacte iiij d. In iiij^{xx} x ffagettis emptis in parco de ffodr' (i.e. Park of Fotheringhay) v s. In uno chyrne ad dayeriam empto ad Gulam Augusti ix d. In una pecia ferri empta pro uno 'saii' faciendo ad querendum petram in campis iiij d. ob. In dicto 'saii' faciendo ad taschiam iij d. de predicto ferro. In iij furcis ferreis emptis pro garbis levandis in autumpno iij d. ob. q. In diversis animalibus cindendis (scind-) et castrandis per annum ex convencione xij d. ad Pascham. In pergameno empto iiij d. In herbagio super stagnum molendinorum empto ad vaccas domini x s. In busca empta ad ffocale post autumpnum viij s. Summa xxxiij s. vij d. q.

Translation: Records of Elton Manor

The same accounts for rods bought for fastening the animals in their byres, 3d. For one basket bought, 3d. For making the ironwork for one spade and two shovels out of the lord's iron, 3d. For 3,600 turves bought for fuel, 2s. 11d. For old brushwood bought for fuel, 18d. For two seed-baskets bought, 4½ d. For 7 cheese presses bought and made for the lord's dairy, 13½ d. and 2 'rowen' cheeses. For 4 ells of cloth bought for the dairy, 7d. For 2 pans and 3 earthenware jars for milk bought for the dairy, 4d. For 90 faggots bought in the park of Fotheringhay, 5s. For one churn bought for the dairy at the Gule of August, 9d. For one piece of iron bought for making one 'saii' (a tool) for collecting stone in the fields, 4½ d. For making the said 'saii' by piecework from this iron, 3d. For 3 iron forks bought for lifting the sheaves in the autumn, 3d. For cutting and gelding diverse animals during the year by agreement, 12d. at Easter. For parchment bought, 4d. For herbage above the millpond bought for the lord's cows, 10s. For brushwood bought for fuel after the autumn, 8s.
Total: 33s. 7¼ d.

Primary Sources and Related Texts

Elton Manorial Records 1279–1351, Roxburghe Club, Cambridge, 1946, with
    introduction.
Domesday Book f.204c: Huntingdonshire (Adelintune = Elton).
Cartulary of Ramsey Abbey, *RS* 79.3 (1893) 257–60 (Æthelingtuna).

Further Reading

Karakacili, E. (2004) 'English agrarian labor productivity rates before the Black
    Death: a case study', *Journal of Economic History* 64.1: 24–60.
Oschinsky, D. (1947) 'Medieval treatises on estate accounting', *Economic History
    Review* 17.1: 52–61.
Wright, L. (2017) 'Non-integrated vocabulary in the mixed-language accounts of
    St Paul's Cathedral, 1315–1405', in *Ashdowne and White (2017).

424   Fifteenth Century

F: Assessment of the Royal Estates in the Channel Islands
(excerpt: *Extente de l'île de Jersey*, pp. 8–9)

Date: 1331.

TNA: E101/89/15.

This is an account of the king's rights and duties with regard to land and to his tenants. Its content is similar to that of the Custumals of Battle Abbey (Section II.45C).

Linguistic points: This Latin text was clearly written in a French-speaking area, namely the Channel Islands, off the coast of France. *bussellus* (AN 'boissel') is both a bowl and a measure of dry goods, giving modern English 'bushel'. *cabotellus* (AN 'cabotel'), also a dry measure, only appears in texts from the Channel Islands. *caput stanni* ('mill-head') is glossed with the French word 'escluse', from which modern English derives 'sluice'. *exclotura*, a watergate (associated with French 'esclotoire'), is another word only attested in texts from the Channel Islands. The king is responsible for supplying the trundle-head (*torta*) and the cogs (*alleucho*) for the mill: *torta* occurs in this sense only here, apparently as a transferred sense of the LL word for a round loaf of bread, while *alleucho* (various spellings) is a rare word from OF 'aleuchon', which is always associated with mills. *roetum*, attested here only, is the Latin form of AN 'roet', from *rotulatum*. For *guerra*, cf. Section II.11.

TEXT II.45F

Feudal obligations in the parish of St Martin, with reference to the upkeep of the mill tenentes de dictis bovetis qui habent messuagia in eisdem debet sectam ad magnum molendinum *des grans vaus* in parochia S. Salvatoris pro molendo ibi omnia blada sua et illi qui non habent ibi messuagia debent ibi venire ad molendum ter in anno videlicet ad festum Omnium Sanctorum cum duobus boissellis bladi, ad festum Nativitatis Domini cum duobus boissellis et ad festum Pasche cum duobus boissellis, quae si defecerint debent solvere pro quolibet termino quartam partem cabotelli bladi communis et illi qui habent messuagia in eisdem bovetis de consuetudine patrie secundum considerationem juratorum curie domini regis, si deficerent de secta praedicta facienda debent puniri. item tam residentes in eisdem bovetis quam tenentes et alibi residentes debent invenire totum meremium ad dictum molendinum et adducere ad locum sumptibus suis propriis, quilibet ipsorum secundum portionem tenementi quod tenet de dictis bovetis. item ipsi debent invenire cooperturam ad dictum molendinum et petram pro faciendo parietes quocienscumque necesse fuerit et cariare ad locum dicti molendini sumptibus suis propriis et debent etiam facere caput stanni quod vulgariter *escluse* nuncupatur, pro conservando aquam pro dicto molendino excepto quod dominus rex debet facere circa excloturam in viciniori parte dicte excloture unam brachi(ari)am. cetera omnia ad dictum molendinum spectantia in materia et factura dominus rex tenetur invenire. et de meremio dicti molendini quod superius exprimi debuisset dominus rex debet invenire tortas et allechones pro roeto, et dicti tenentes debent cariare molas et alia necessaria ad dictum molendinum faciendum; quod si praedictum molendinum per tempestatem aut guerram comburetur aut aliter destruetur, dominus rex illud tenetur facere de novo sumptibus suis excepto cariagio de quo supra fit mentio. et de valore istius molendini habetur plenius in extenta facta de molendinis istius insule.

Translation: Assessment of the Island of Jersey

The tenants of these bovates who have tenements in them owe suit to the big mill des grands vaus in the parish of the Holy Saviour to grind all their corn there, while those who do not have tenements there must come to the mill three times a year, namely at the feast of All Saints with two bushels of corn, at the feast of the Lord's Nativity with two bushels and at Easter with two bushels, and if they fail to do this they must pay at each term day a quarter of a caboteau of common corn, and those who have tenements in these bovates must be punished according to the local custom and at the discretion of the jurors of the lord king's court, if they fail to perform this suit. Also both those residing in these bovates and the tenants and those residing elsewhere must find all the timber for this mill and bring it to the place at their own expense, each of them according to the portion of the tenement which he holds from these bovates. Also they must find roofing for this mill and the stone to make the walls whenever necessary and must transport it to the mill's location at their own expense and they must also make the dam which is commonly called 'escluse' to contain the water for this mill, except that the lord king must make a subsidiary outlet around the floodgate in the neighbouring part of this floodgate. The lord king is responsible for finding everything else pertaining to this mill, both material and labour. Regarding the timber of this mill, which should have been mentioned earlier, the lord king must find the trundle-heads and cogs for the cogged millwheel and these tenants must transport the millstones and other things necessary to make this mill; but if this mill is burned down or otherwise destroyed by storm or war, the lord king is responsible for rebuilding it at his own expense apart from the transport costs mentioned above. Regarding the value of this mill further details can be found in the assessment produced of this island's mills.

426 Fifteenth Century

Primary Sources and Related Texts

Extente de l'île de Jersey, 1331. Société jersiaise 1 (1876) 8–9.
Sausmarez, H. (ed.) (1934) *The extentes of Guernsey of 1248 and 1331*, Societé guernesiaise, Guernsey.

Further Reading

Everard, J. and Holt, J. C. (2004) *Jersey 1204: the forging of an island community*, London.
Lennard, R. (1929) 'What is a manorial extent?', *EHR* 44.174: 256–63.

Section II.46

Town Life and Trade: Administrative Documents
A: Newcastle upon Tyne: an Early Municipal Charter
B: Sourcing Food for the King (excerpt: *Calendar of Patent Rolls*, p. 175)
C: Records of Leicester: a Guild Meeting (excerpt: p. 105)
D: The King Settles the Price of Wine in London (excerpt: *Foedera* 2.268)
E: Imports and Exports: Customs Accounts

The documents that deal with aspects of urban life and trade complement those associated with manorial life (Section II.45). Again there are rules and regulations, taxes and tolls to be paid or received and a balance between the duties and privileges or rights of people in different layers of society, as well as attempts to balance the requirements of different groups of people and to maintain standards.

A: Newcastle upon Tyne: an Early Municipal Charter

Date: reign of Henry I.

TNA: Miscellanea of the Chancery, C47/34/1/15.

Work: This text, which appears in slightly different forms in different documents, appears to show the situation regarding property, trade and the legal rights of its citizens under King Henry I (mentioned in the first line), but recorded in a charter of Henry II from about 1175: it lists those areas of civic regulation which could be dealt with by local government. Newcastle was part of Northumberland, which was granted by King Stephen as an earldom to Henry, son of King David I of Scotland, in 1139 in the Treaty of Durham: between 1139 and 1153 Newcastle was treated as part of Scotland. David based the laws for Edinburgh, Roxburgh, Berwick and Stirling on the customs of Newcastle. Although Henry II then took the city back into English possession, he did allow the laws and customs of Stephen's reign to continue to pertain, as is clear from this charter. Note the appearance of herrings again, as in Brakelond's *Chronicle of the Deeds of Abbot Samson* (Section II.22) and in the correspondence of Ralph Neville (Section II.45B): in all three texts, the context for the herring is the east coast of England, along which the bulk of this commodity was sourced.

428 Fifteenth Century

Linguistic points: *surgere* is here used as a synonym of the more common *oriri* in the sense of 'to arise'. *refluxio* is a characteristic medieval formation from the supine of the CL verb *refluere* with the noun suffix *-io*.[1] *burgum, burgensis*, and *burgagium* are associated with a Germanic word (OE 'burh/burg') from which modern 'borough' is derived. *namium* and the related verb *namiare* derive from an old Germanic word signifying 'taking' (of property as compensation). This text uses *villanus* for an 'unfree tenant', for which *nativus* and *rusticus* are synonyms. The term *forisfactum*, a substantive formed from *forisfacere*, is here used in connection with women involved in the production and sale of bread and ale: it means both an offence, and then the punishment for that offence. As often in legal texts (cf. Section II.2 and II.10), the vernacular is here used for technical feudal terms, e.g. 'merchet' and 'heriet (heriot)'; the latter had appeared in the eleventh-century *Laws of Cnut* in the OE form 'heregeata'. As for syntax, the subject matter calls for a large number of conditional sentences, using various tenses of both indicative and subjunctive.

TEXT II.46A

Municipal charter for Newcastle upon Tyne

hae sunt leges et consuetudines quas burgenses Novi Castelli super Tinam habuerunt tempore Henrici Regis Angliae et habere debent. burgenses possunt namiare foris habitantes infra suum forum et extra et infra suam domum et extra et infra suum burgum et extra sine licentia praepositi, nisi comitia teneantur in burgo, et nisi in exercitu sint vel custodia castelli. super burgensem non potest burgensis namium capere sine licentia prepositi. si burgensis foris habitantibus de suo accommodaverit in burgo, ipse debitor si concedat reddat, si negaverit in burgo faciat rectum. placita que in burgo surgunt ibidem teneantur et finiantur, preter illa que sunt corone regis. si aliquis burgensis de aliqua loquela appelletur, non placitabit extra burgum nisi ex defectu curie. nec debet respondere sine die et termino, nisi prius in stultam responsionem inciderit, nisi de rebus que ad coronam pertinent. si navis apud Tinemue aplicuerit que velit discedere, licet burgensibus emere quod voluerint. inter burgensem et mercatorem si placitum oriatur, finiatur ante tertiam refluxionem maris. quidquid mercature navis per mare advexerit ad terram debet ferri preter sal; et allec debet vendi in navim. si quis terram in burgagio uno anno et una die juste et sine calumnia tenuerit, non respondeat calumnianti, nisi calumnians extra regnum Anglie fuerit, vel nisi sit puer non habens etatem loquendi. si burgensis filium habuerit in domo sua ad mensam suam, filius ejus eandem habeat libertatem quam et pater suus. si rusticus in burgo veniat manere, et ibi per annum unum et diem sicut burgensis

---

1 On tides and their terminology, see Section I.10B.

maneat in burgo, ex toto remaneat, nisi prius ab ipso vel domino suo praelocutum sit ad terminum remanere.[2] si quis burgensem de re aliqua appellaverit, non potest super burgensem pugnare, sed per legem se defendat burgensis, nisi sit de proditione, unde debeat se defendere bello. nec burgensis contra villanum poterit pugnare nisi prius de burgagio exierit.

mercator aliquis, nisi burgensis, non potest extra villam emere nec lanam nec coria nec mercatoria alia nec infra burgum nisi burgensibus. si forisfactum contigerit burgensi, dabit vj oras preposito. in burgo non est *merchet*, nec *heriet*, nec *blodwit*, nec *stengesdint*. unusquisque burgensis potest habere suum furnum et molam manualem si velit, salvo jure furni regis. si femina sit in suo forisfacto de pane vel de cervisia, nullus debet intromittere nisi prepositus. si bis forisfecerit, castigetur per forisfactum. si tertio forisfecerit, justitia de ea fiat. nullus nisi burgensis poterit emere telas ad tingendas nec facere nec secare. burgensis potest dare terram suam et vendere et ire quo voluerit libere et quiete, nisi sit in calumnia.

Translation: Charter for Newcastle upon Tyne

These are the laws and customs which the burgesses of Newcastle upon Tyne had in the time of Henry, king of England, and ought to have. The burgesses may distrain (i.e. punish by seizing property) those living outside within their market and without, and within their houses and without, and within their borough and without, and they may do this without the reeve's permission, unless the courts are being held within the borough, or unless they are on army service or on castle-guard. But a burgess may not distrain on another burgess without the reeve's permission. If a burgess lends anything in the borough to someone living outside it, the debtor should repay the debt if he admits it, or if he denies it he should make amends in the borough court. Pleas which arise in the borough shall be held and concluded there, apart from those that belong to the king's crown. If any burgess is sued in respect of any plaint, he shall not plead outside the borough except for default of court; nor does he need to answer except at a stated time and place, unless he has already made an invalid response or unless the case concerns matters pertaining to the crown.

If a ship comes to Tynemouth and wishes to depart, the burgesses will be permitted to purchase what they want. And if a dispute arises between a burgess and a merchant, it shall be settled before the third low tide. Whatever merchandise a ship

---

2 This has been seen as a reference to the medieval principle that 'town air makes you free after a year and a day', whereby runaway serfs could claim freedom if they remained undisturbed in a town for this period; cf. Glanvill (Section II.17) 5.5, *si quis nativus quiete per unum annum et diem in aliqua villa privilegiata manserit ita quod in eorum communam scilicet gildam, tanquam civis receptus fuerit, eo ipso a villenagio liberatur,* and other works cited by S. Alsford (2011).

430 Fifteenth Century

brings by sea ought to be brought to the land, except salt; and herring should be sold on board the ship. If anyone has held land in burgage of a year and a day, justly and without challenge, he need not answer any claimant unless the claimant is outside the kingdom of England or unless he is a boy and is not of the age to plead. If a burgess has a son in his house and at his table, his son will have the same freedom as his father. If a villein (an unfree tenant) comes to live in the borough and remains as a burgess in the borough for a year and a day, he shall thereafter remain there altogether, unless there was a previous agreement between him and his lord for him to remain there for a fixed time. If anyone appeals against a burgess on any matter, he cannot force the burgess to trial by battle, but the burgess must defend himself by his oath, except in a charge of treason, against which he must defend himself by battle. Nor can a burgess offer battle against a villein unless he has first quit his burgage. No merchant except a burgess can buy wool or hides or other merchandise outside the town nor shall he buy them within the town except from burgesses. If a burgess incurs forfeitures he shall give 6 oras to the reeve. In the borough there is no merchet nor heriot nor bloodwite (i.e. fine for drawing blood) nor stengesdint (i.e. fine for striking someone else). Any burgess may have his own oven and handmill if he wishes, saving always the rights of the king's oven. If a woman commits an offence with reference to bread or ale, no one should get involved with it except the reeve. If she offends twice she shall be admonished by forfeiture. If she offends three times, she should be given a punishment. No one except a burgess may buy cloth for dyeing or make it or cut it. A burgess can give or sell his land as he wishes and go where he will, freely and with immunity, unless his claim is challenged.

Primary Sources and Related Texts

Stubbs, W. (1913) *Select charters and other illustrations of English constitutional history*, 9th ed., Oxford: 133–4.

Acts of the Parliaments of Scotland, ed. T. Thomson and C. Innes, RC, Edinburgh, 1814: 1.333–56 (*Leges quatuor burgorum*).

The Percy Cartulary, Surtees Society 117 (1909) 334–6.

BBC vol. 1 *passim*, where the document is divided up under different themes.

EHD 2.1040–1.

Further Reading

Alsford, S. (2011) 'Urban safe havens for the unfree in medieval England: a reconsideration', *Slavery and Abolition* 32.3: 363–75.

Johnson, C. (1925) 'The oldest version of the Customs of Newcastle upon Tyne', *Archaeologia Aeliana*, 4th ser. 1: 170.

Purdue, B. (2011) *Newcastle: the biography*, Chalford.

II.46 | Town Life and Trade 431

B: Sourcing Food for the King (excerpt: *Calendar of Patent Rolls*, p. 175)

Date: 16 January 1228.

TNA: C66/37 m. 6.

Work: This Patent Roll, documenting everyday royal business, contains a brief reference to a man and his wife whose work was of great importance to the king, though this person's status as a kind of royal officer was marginal and neglected: the couple was appointed to travel round Britain with horse and cart buying up necessities for the royal household. The king grants them a document of safe conduct to protect them on their lengthy business trip.

Linguistic points: *tranetarius* or rather *travetarius* gives English 'tranter', possibly derived from *transvectarius*, i.e. 'one who transports'; the word soon acquired a less reputable sense, applied to those who carried goods for sale without a licence.

TEXT II.46B

The king grants safe passage for the purchasing and delivery of his food
[1228] Willelmus Wygan, tranetarius domini regis de curia sua et Alicia uxor ejus habent literas de protectione in eundo per totam terram domini regis ad victualia et alias res venales emendas et ducendas ad curiam domini regis. et durant usque in duos annos a die Purificationis Beate Marie, anno etc. xij, teste rege apud Norhamton, xvj die Januarii.

Translation

William Wygan, the tranter (carrier) of the lord king from his court, and his wife Alice, have a letter of protection to travel throughout the whole land of the lord king to buy food and other items for sale and to bring them to the lord king's court. And it is valid for two years from the day of the Blessed Mary's Purification, in the twelfth year etc., with the king as witness at Northampton, on 16 January.

Primary Sources and Related Texts

Calendar of Patent Rolls (1225–32) 175.
Cf. *Calendar of Patent Rolls* (1232–47) 32–4 for similar documents.

432 Fifteenth Century

C: Records of Leicester: a Guild Meeting (excerpt: p. 105)

Date: January 1265.

Work: As a borough, Leicester was in many ways unusual, not least on account of the fact that the Guild of Merchants was granted a charter already before 1118 by Robert, first Earl of Leicester, the father of Waleran de Meulan (cf. Section II.44B). Its records cover the period 1196–1380, providing much material about trading regulations, monopolies etc., as well as many technical terms relating to various types of trade. The cloth industry flourished in Leicester: there are frequent references to the work of fullers and weavers and the import of woad. In 1260 the weavers had sworn not to weave at night and not to conceal any flaws in their work, but here in 1265 the Guild allows them to weave at night, but not to weave for those who live outside the city; it also sets the prices they can charge for their work, with russet cloth being more expensive.

Linguistic points: *gilda*, as an association of fee-paying members for mutual benefits of various kinds, occurs in BML first in Domesday, deriving from an English word: it later took on the more specific sense of a trade guild. *morgenspechium* ('morn-speech') derives from ME 'morgen speche' as a technical term for a guild business meeting held at regular intervals in connection with a feast. *tixere* is the alternative spelling for *texere*, common in documents from the Midlands. *visus* is here used in the sense of 'assessment', to be carried out by guild officers. *ponere in respectu(m)* is a legal phrase meaning 'to adjourn' a case. *vadiare*, the verb from *vadium*, has a range of meanings associated with offering a guarante, here with reference to the payment of a fine. *defectus* is used here both in the sense of a 'defect' and an 'insufficiency'.

TEXT II.46C

Guild rules regarding the weaving of cloth
[p. 105] A.D. mcclx quarto in pleno morespechio tento die S. Agnetis fuit provisum et concessum et pronunciatum quod textores qui volunt tixere in Leycestria bene possunt tixere tam per noctem quam per diem, ita tamen quod nullus defectus sit in opere suo; et capient ad quamlibet ulnam cuiuslibet generis panni obolum, exceptis omnibus russetis, et capient ad quamlibet ulnam russeti iii q^a; et non tixent aliquem pannum villarum campestrium dum possint habere sufficienter opus suum de hominibus Leycestrie et cum habuerint defectum operis sui de hominibus Leycestrie monstrabunt ipsum defectum ii hominibus de Gilda Leycestrie qui ad hoc erunt assignati et per visum illorum pro defectu pannorum

Leycestrie tixent pannum forinsecum. Rogerus de Kildisby textor pro defectu texture unius panni Marie le Stabler vadiavit misericordiam Gylde die Veneris proxima post octabas Epiphanie a.r.r. (i.e. anno regni regis) Henrici xlix et ponitur in respectu pro paupertate sed exigatur cum habeat unde possit inde satisfacere.

Translation: Records of Leicester

In the year 1264 in the full morning meeting held on St Agnes' Day it was arranged and granted and made known publicly that weavers who wish to weave in Leicester are able to do so both at night and by day, but in such a way that there should be no defect in their work; and they should receive a halfpenny for each ell of whatever kind of cloth, apart from all russets, and they should receive three farthings for each ell of russet cloth; and they should not weave any cloth for the villages in the countryside while they are able to get sufficient work from the people of Leicester, and when they have a lack of work from the people of Leicester they will demonstrate this lack to two men from the Leicester guild who will be assigned for this, and as a result of their assessment regarding the lack of cloth in Leicester, they will be allowed to weave cloth from outside (the city). Roger of Kildisby, weaver, for the defect in weaving one cloth for Mary le Stabler guaranteed the fine by offering surety to the guild, on the Friday next after the octave of Epiphany in the 49th year of the reign of King Henry. His case was adjourned on account of his poverty, but he should be forced to pay when he has the means to do so.

Primary Sources and Related Texts

The Records of the Borough of Leicester (1103–1835), ed. M. Bateson, 6 vols, London, 1899–1967, vol. 1.

Further Reading

A history of the county of Leicester, vol. 4: *The city of Leicester: social and economic history 1066–1509*, London, 1958. See also British History Online, www.british-history.ac.uk/.

Blair, J. and Ramsay, N. (ed.) (1991) *English medieval industries*, London.

Gross, C. (1890) *The gild merchant*, 2 vols, Oxford.

Lee, John S. (2018) *The medieval clothier*, Woodbridge.

434 Fifteenth Century

D: The King Settles the Price of Wine in London (excerpt: *Foedera* 2.268)

Date: 30 May 1315.

TNA: C54/132 m. 5.

Work: This writ from the king, recorded in the Close Rolls, imposes a restriction on the price of wine. It is one of numerous documents of a wide range of types, including the Close Rolls, dealing with questions of supply (largely imports), tolls, various kinds of wine, pricing and problems of fraud with regard to quantity and quality, from the wine for the king's table down to punishment of fraudulent vintners.

Linguistic points: *retallia* is the Latin form of AN 'retaille', the term for the practice of selling in small quantities rather than wholesale. CL *lagena* originally meant a flask but became applied to the contents and a unit of measure, like the equivalent *galo(na)* from the French 'galon/jalon'.[3] *forisfactura* ('forfeit'), like *forisfactum*, can refer to an offence, or (as here) the penalty for it; its earliest attestation in BML is in the Domesday Book.

TEXT II.46D

The price of wine in 1315
rex majori et vicecomitibus London' salutem. precipimus vobis, firmiter injungentes quod in civitate predicta et suburbio ejusdem, in locis ubi videritis expedire, sine dilacione qualibet, faciatis publice proclamari, quod omnes vinetarii et tabernarii vina ad retalliam in eisdem civitate et suburbio vendentes, lagenam vini pro tribus denariis ad plus decetero vendant, et quo nullus ipsorum sub gravi forisfactura nostra, plus quam tres denarios pro lagena vini exnunc presumat exigere vel capere quovis modo; et hoc nullo modo omittatis. teste rege apud Westm' xxx die Maii.

Translation: Close Roll for 1315

The king sends greetings to the mayor and sheriffs of London. We command you, resolutely enjoining that in the aforementioned city and its suburbs, in the places where you see that it is useful, without any delay, you should make a public announcement that all wine merchants and taverners selling wines by retail in this same city and suburbs should from now on sell a gallon of wine for 3d. at most, and

---

3   Cf. Matthew Paris, *Maj.* 5.594 *s.a.* 1256: *mensuras vini sive cervisiae quas lagenas vel galones appellamus.*

that none of them, on pain of a heavy fine from us, should presume to demand or accept in any way more than 3d. for a gallon of wine from now on; and you must by no means fail to do this. As witness, the king at Westminster, 30 May.

Primary Source and Related Texts

Foedera 2.268 (RC edition, 1816–69).
Calendar of Close Rolls (1313–18) 182.

Further Reading

Bolton, J. L. (1980) *The medieval English economy, 1150–1500*, London.
Davis, J. (2011) *Medieval market morality: life, law and ethics in the English marketplace 1200–1500*, Cambridge.
James, M. K. (1951) 'The fluctuations of the Anglo-Gascon wine trade in the fourteenth century', *Economic History Review* 4.2: 170–96.
Rogers, J. E. T. (1866) *A history of agriculture and prices in England (1259–1400)*, Oxford.

E: Imports and Exports: Customs Accounts

In 1303 King Edward I introduced new customs regulations, replacing those from 1275 and imposing an extra import duty on such goods as wool, leather and wax. According to the new regulations, foreign merchants had to pay the collectors at the port an ad valorem duty of 3d. in the pound on other goods.

The following excerpts are taken from the port records of the imports at the port of Sandwich in Kent (one of the original Cinque Ports, a confederation of five ports for military and trade purposes) and at King's Lynn in Norfolk. Each entry gives the amount of customs duty paid to the collectors by the merchants (including one woman from Bruges) for the specific cargo.

E(a): Imports at Sandwich (excerpts from *The early English customs system*, pp. 267–71)

Date: 1303.

TNA: E122/124/11.

Linguistic points: These port records are a good source of information about foreign trade, about ships, merchants and cargo. *sargia* came to denote woollen

436 Fifteenth Century

fabric (as in modern English 'serge') but may have originally applied to a kind of silk. *sandalum* is a spelling variant of *cendalum* (*OED s.v.* sendal), i.e. silk cloth, a form deriving from Arabic 'ṣandal'. *gingebrattum* developed from *zingiberatum* meaning 'preserved ginger'; in English usage it was originally corrupted to 'gingerbre(a)d', a word later applied to a kind of cake. It is uncertain whether *seffranne* ('saffron', from Arabic) and *zucare* (cf. Section II.48B), both common in medieval accounts, are ME or Latin; the -e termination could be a feminine genitive singular; 'banquers' ('bench-cover'), however, is definitely a vernacular form, probably ME derived from French. *brasillum* (or *bresill-*, from French 'bresil'), is 'brazil-wood dye', occurring in BML first in the mid-twelfth century (*Die Gesetze der Angelsachsen* 1.675), earlier than in surviving French texts; the dye was popular for silk. *costera* (here, 'seacoast') derives from AN 'costere', itself from CL *costa*.

TEXT II.46E(a)

A variety of imports coming through the port at Sandwich
[p. 267] particulae novae custumae receptae apud Sandwicum et in omnibus locis ab inde per costeram maris usque Winchelese a decimo die Februarii anno regni regis Edwardi xxxi usque v diem Maii proximo sequentem per manus Johannis Peny et sociorum suorum collectorum ibidem. (…)
[p. 269] De Katerina de Bregg pro lx soldatis ceparum, ix d. (…)
[p. 271] De Punchino dela Stryne pro xl libratis sargiarum, sandalli et tele tincte, x s. (…)
De Garcia de Castello Florentyno pro c vj libratis serici et sandalli, xxvj s. vj d.
De Betyno le Rous pro lxij libratis amigdolarum, allute et aliarum mercium xv s. vj d. (…)
De Valeriano le Chat' pro iiij^{xx} libratis serici, sandalli, tapetorum et *banquers*, xx s. (…)
De Martino de Barceles pro xxx libratis gingebratti, zucare, seffranne et aliarum specierum vij s. vj d. (…)
De Willelmo de Tornay pro xv libratis bresilii, iii s. ix d.

Translation: Customs Accounts

Items in the account of the new custom received at Sandwich and in all places from there along the seacoast as far as Winchelsea from 10 February in the 31st year of the reign of King Edward to the next 5 May, through the hands of John Peny and his fellow collectors there. (…)
From Katherine of Bruges for 60 shillings worth of onions, 9d. (…)
From Punchino dela Stryne for 40 pounds worth of serge woollen cloth, 'sendal' and dyed cloth, 10s. (…)

From Garcia de Castello, the Florentine, 26s. 6d. for 106 pounds worth of silken cloth and 'sendal'.
From Betyn le Rous 15s. 6d. for 62 pounds worth of almonds, tawed leather and other goods. (…)
From Valerian le Chat' for 80 pounds worth of silk cloth, 'sendal', carpets and furnishing materials, 20s. (…)
From Martin de Barceles 7s. 6d. for 30 pounds worth of 'gingerbread', sugar, saffron and other delicacies. (…)
From William of Tournai for 15 pounds worth of brazil dye, 3s. 9d.

E(b): Imports at King's Lynn (excerpts from *The early English customs system,* pp. 374–7)

Date: 1324–5.

TNA: E122/93/22.

Linguistic points: *dacra,* for a set or bundle of ten, derives ultimately from CL *decuria,* apparently passing into Germanic languages, and then into both French ('dacre') and English (*OED s.v.* dicker). *borda* (from OE 'bord', from Frankish) is found frequently from the twelfth century, coinciding with the growth of the construction industry; boards, i.e. planks, were imported particularly from the Eastern Baltic area, hence *estrensius.* In this excerpt the English word 'waye (wey)' is found as a unit of measure for salt, though it also occurs in a Latin form *waga,* with almost as many variant spellings as occurrences.

TEXT II.46E(b)

A variety of imports coming through the port at King's Lynn
[p. 374] rotulus particularum nove costume domini regis recepte apud Lennam per manus Johannis de Thornegg' et Willelmi de Whetacre collectorum eiusdem custume ibidem de pannis cera vinis ac aliis bonis et mercimoniis mercatorum extraneorum et alienigenarum ibidem adductis a festo Sancti Michaelis anno regni Regis Edwardi decimo octavo usque idem festum anno revoluto.
navis Hermanni Rode intravit iii die Octobris. idem H. pro xlviii quarteriis siliginis val. £vi [cust.] xviij d. (…) pro vj dacris pellium caprinarum val. xx s. [cust.] iij d. (…) pro xij barellis rosine val. xx s. [cust.] iij d. (…)
navis Petri Octen intravit vii die Octobris. idem P. pro c bordis estrens[iis] val. xij s. [cust.] ij d. idem Petrus pro uno dolio vini [cust.] ij s.
[p. 375] Alfridus Estrensius pro xxxj barellis calibis val. £lxij [cust.] xv s. vj d.
navis Willelmi filii Elone intravit vii die Octobris. idem W. pro l quarteriis ordei val. £vi [cust.] xviij d. (…) pro cepis et alleis val. lx s. [cust.] ix d. (…)

438 Fifteenth Century

[p. 376] navis Jacobi de la Watermilne intravit xii die Octobris. idem J. pro vii barellis sturgonum val. £xiiij, [cust.] iii s. vi d. (…)

[p. 377] navis Bartholomaei Babbard intravit v die Novembris. idem B. pro x *wayes* salis val c s. cust. xv d.

Translation: Customs Accounts

The roll with account details of the new custom of the lord king received at King's Lynn by the hands of John de Thornegg and William de Whetacre, collectors of this custom there, of cloth, wax, wines and other goods and merchandise of foreign and alien merchants brought there from the feast of St Michael in the 18th year of the reign of King Edward (II) until the same feast in the year just gone.

The ship of Herman Rode entered on 3 October. This same H. paid 18d. as a tariff on 48 quarters of grain, valued at £6, 6d. for 6 sets of 10 goatskins valued at 20s., 3d. for 12 barrels of resin valued at 20s. (…)

The ship of Peter Octen entered on 7 October. This same P. paid 2d. for 100 planks from the eastern Baltic valued at 12s. and 2s. as a tariff on a barrel of wine.

Alfred from the eastern Baltic paid 15s. 6d. for 31 barrels of iron valued at £62.

The ship of William son of Elon entered on 7 October. This same W. paid 18d. for 50 quarters of barley valued at £6, and 9d. for onions and garlic valued at 60s. (…)

The ship of Jacob de la Watermilne entered on 12 October. This same J. paid 3s. 6d. for 7 barrels of sturgeon valued at £14. (…)

The ship of Bartholomew Babbard entered on 7 November. This same B. paid 15d. for 10 weys of salt valued at 100s.

Primary Source

Gras, N. (1918) *The early English customs system*, Cambridge, MA.

Further Reading

Carus-Wilson, E. (1962) 'The medieval trade of the ports of the Wash', *Medieval Archaeology* 6: 182–201.

Cobb, H. S. (1973) 'Local port customs accounts prior to 1550' in *Prisca munimenta*, ed. F. Ranger, London.

Quinton, E. and Oldland, J. (2011) 'London merchants' cloth exports' in **Medieval clothing and textiles* (2005–).

http://lexissearch.arts.manchester.ac.uk.

Section II.47

Buildings: Construction and Reparation
A: Gervase of Canterbury, *The Destruction by Fire and the Rebuilding of Canterbury Cathedral in 1174* (*De combustione et reparatione Cantuariensis ecclesiae*) (excerpts: pp. 3–5, 19–21)
B: Fire Regulations in London after the Great Fire of Southwark, 1212 (excerpt: *Liber custumarum, RS* pp. 86–8)
C: Refurbishment and Repairs at Windsor Castle and at Westminster Abbey
D: Repairing the Clock on the Tower at Westminster Palace
E: Building a Merchant's House in the City of London: the Builder's Contract (excerpts from pp. 478–81)

A: Gervase of Canterbury, *The Destruction by Fire and the Rebuilding of Canterbury Cathedral in 1174* (*De combustione et reparatione Cantuariensis ecclesiae*) (excerpts: pp. 3–5, 19–21)

Date: c.1200.

This work is part of Gervase's *Chronicles*, found in BL MS Cotton Vespasian B.xix, Cambridge MS Trinity R.4.11 (James 644) and Cambridge University Library MS Ff.1.29.

Author: Gervase (died c.1210) was a monk at Christ Church, Canterbury whose life was powerfully affected by the murder of Thomas Becket and the fire that destroyed the cathedral, both of which changed Canterbury dramatically. Gervase's research regarding a dispute between Archbishop Baldwin (1185–90) and Christ Church Priory in Canterbury led him to start writing historical works, the most ambitious being the *Chronicles* and the *Gesta regum*, a political history of England. As a whole Gervase's work focuses on the monastery at Canterbury but also provides much information about Canterbury, following on from Eadmer and the biographers of Becket. Gervase's *Chronicles* also contains national and international events, though often from a local perspective, using letters and documents alongside oral sources and his own experiences. He also wrote a series of Lives of the Archbishops of Canterbury.

Work: Gervase provides a contemporary account of the destruction by fire of Canterbury Cathedral in 1174 and the first years of its rebuilding under William of

440 Fifteenth Century

Sens, until his accident in 1177. This account, often referred to as the *De combustione*, is actually part of his *Chronicles*. This section, with its brilliant description of the architecture, and of the dramatic movement of wind and flames, reveals his great love for the cathedral which he knew so intimately.

Linguistic points: In this passage one can see Gervase's predilection for antithetical wordplay, e.g. with *mirabile/miserabile* and *despicabilis/delectabilis*. As well as terms denoting building material, such as *tignum* and *asser*, there are a number of technical terms relating to church architecture, such as *caelum*, which Vitruvius had applied to the vault or ceiling (cf. *OED s.v.* ceil and ceiling for a possible connection with *caelum*) of a large building, and *ciborium*, which meant a 'cup' in CL (cf. Hor. *Odes* 2.7.21), but is here used of an arched vault, in which sense it is transformed into English as 'severy'. The phrase *sarta tecta* referred to roof repairs (from CL *sarcire*), but BML extends its sense to apply to the roof structure itself. *triforium* first occurs in this text in the sense of a 'gallery' in a church, though its precise sense is disputed. The word *pilarius* (*-are*), from which English derives 'pillar', is associated with OF 'piler', derived from Latin *pīla*: that Gervase writes *columpnae ... ecclesiae quae vulgo pilarii dicuntur* may mean that *pilarius* is a specific term for church columns, or it may point to an awareness of its vernacular association. Goscelin, about a century earlier, had written similarly, *columna quam vulgo pilare dicimus* (*Transl. Aug.* 412C).

TEXT II.47A

The fire at Canterbury Cathedral: the first outbreak
[p. 3] anno igitur gratiae Verbi Dei mclxxiiii, nonis Septembris, hora quasi nona, austro fere ultra humanam aestimationem furente, accensus est ignis ante portam ecclesiae extra muros atrii, quo tres domunculae semiustae sunt. quo cum cives concurrerent et praedictum incendium dissiparent, carbones et scintillae vento rapidissimo in altum delatae super ecclesiam depositae sunt, et vi furentis venti per juncturas plumbi intrusae, in tabulis ligneis semiputridis resederunt. sicque paulatim calore crescente, asseres putridi accenduntur. deinde tingni grossiores cum ligaturis suis, nemine vidente vel curam agente, succenduntur. caelum inferius egregie depictum, superius vero tabulae plumbeae, ignem interius accensum celaverunt. diripiuntur interim domunculae tres unde furor iste ascenderat, et jam tumultu [p. 4] populi sedato, ad sua quique redierunt.

The fire, unbeknown to anyone, spreads within: people's reactions and the material damage
[p. 4 cont.] sola Christi ecclesia nemine adhuc sciente quasi intestino premebatur incendio. tignis etenim et tignorum ligaturis ardentibus, flammaque usque in summa tecti fastigia elata, tabulae plumbeae tanto calori ulterius resistere non

II.47 | Building Construction and Reparation 441

valentes, paulatim liquescere coeperunt. ventus igitur furens, aditu liberiori reperto, flammas interiores in immensum furere coegit. et ecce, subito flammis paulisper apparentibus, clamatum est a plerisque in atrio ecclesiae, 'Vae, vae, ecclesia ardet!' accurrunt plurimi laici cum monachis, aquas hauriunt, secures vibrant, gradus ascendunt, ecclesiae Christi jam jamque periturae succurrere cupientes. pervenerunt igitur ad sarta tecta et ecce teter fumus et atrox flamma repleverant omnia. desperati igitur qui concurrerant, suae saluti providentes, redierunt. et ecce juncturis tignorum et pessulis igne dissolutis, ligna semiusta in chorum deorsum super monachorum sedilia corruerunt. sedilia igitur multa lignorum mole compacta succenduntur et sic undique mala multiplicata sunt. erat in hoc incendio mirabile, immo miserabile, videre spectaculum. chorus namque ille gloriosus, igne consumptus, se pejus consumebat. flammae enim ex tanta lignorum congerie multiplicatae, usque in cubitos quindecim in altum porrectae, parietes et maxime columpnas ecclesiae cremaverunt. accurrunt plurimi ad ornamenta ecclesiae: pallia et cortinas deiciunt, alii ut rapiant, alii ut eripiant. scrinia reliquiarum deorsum in pavimentum dejecta confracta sunt et reliquiae dispersae. veruntamen ne ab igne consumerentur, a fratribus collectae et repositae sunt. fuerunt autem quidam iniqua et diabolica cupiditate succensi qui res ecclesiae igni quidem subtraxerunt, sed absportare non timuerunt. hoc itaque modo domus Dei [p. 5] hactenus ut paradisus deliciarum delectabilis, jam tunc in sublimi trabe incendii cinere jacebat despicabilis, et quasi in solitudinem redacta, tempestatum aeriarum patebat injuriis. (…)

Translation: Gervase of Canterbury, The Fire at Canterbury Cathedral

And so in the year of grace of God's Word 1174, on the Nones of September (5 September), around the ninth hour, when the south wind was raging almost beyond human reckoning, a fire broke out in front of the gate of the church, outside the walls of the forecourt where three cottages were half burnt down. The citizens ran there and tried to put out the fire, but the coals and sparks were carried up high by a very strong wind and deposited on top of the church, and were driven by the force of the raging wind through the lead joints, settling on the half-rotten wooden beams. And so as the heat gradually increased, the rotten planks caught fire. Then the thicker beams with their braces started to burn, without anyone noticing or trying to prevent it. The vaulted ceiling was beautifully painted lower down, but further up the sheets of lead concealed the fire burning within. Meanwhile the three cottages from which the fire had moved upwards were being torn down; then the turmoil of the people subsided and everyone returned home.

Only the church of Christ was stricken by a blaze deep within, without anyone yet being aware. While the beams and the beam braces were burning, the flames were carried right up to the top of the roof; the sheets of lead could no longer withstand

442 Fifteenth Century

the great heat; the wind found a clearer path in and forced the flames inside to rage to immense heights. Look! suddenly flames were just visible and several people were shouting on the church forecourt, 'Oh no! the church is on fire!' Many lay people come running together with the monks; they draw water, they wield axes, they rush up the stairs, keen to save the church of Christ, which is on the point of destruction. And so they reached the roof, where everything is filled with thick smoke and fierce flames. Those who had gathered there gave up hope, and thinking of their own safety they went down again. Look now! the joints of the beams and the bolts have been loosened by the fire and the half-burnt timbers come crashing down into the choir onto the monks' stalls. And so the seats, fitted together with a great amount of wood, caught fire, and as a result the problems were multiplied on every side. The blaze produced a remarkable, no, rather a wretched sight. For that glorious choir, devoured by the fire, was devouring itself in an even more harmful manner. For the flames, fed by such a great pile of wood, reached a height of fifteen cubits and burned the walls and especially the columns of the church. Many people came running to the church's ornaments: they threw down the hangings and the curtains, some people to steal, others to save them. The reliquaries were thrown down from the high beam onto the pavement below and smashed, and the relics were scattered. They were collected by the brothers and put back to prevent them being consumed by the fire. But there were some people inflamed by a wicked and diabolical greed who were not afraid to carry off the church's possessions they had saved from the fire. And so God's house, which till now had been as delightful as a garden of delights, now lay in a dreadful state, more or less reduced to a desert waste and exposed to the damage of the elements. (…)

[*The cathedral lies in ruins for five years as discussions continue, with the advice of French and English building experts, as to whether to pull the whole thing down and start again or to build on what remained. Finally William of Sens is put in charge of the rebuilding. After a digression describing the Cathedral before this fire, Gervase resumes with his account of the rebuilding as William of Sens starts work.*]

Rebuilding starts

[p. 19] coepit, ut longe ante praedixi, novo operi necessaria praeparare et vetera destruere. in istis primus annus completus est. sequenti anno, id est post festum sancti Bertini, ante hiemem, quatuor pilarios erexit, id est, utrinque duos; peracta hieme duos apposuit, ut hinc et inde tres essent in ordine: super quos et murum exteriorem alarum, arcus et fornicem decenter composuit, id est tres claves utrimque. clavem pro toto pono ciborio, eo quod clavis in medio posita partes undecunque venientes claudere et confirmare videtur. in istis annus secundus completus est. anno tertio duos utrimque pilarios apposuit, quorum duos extremos in circuitu columpnis marmoreis decoravit et [p. 20] quia in eis chorus et cruces convenire debuerunt, principales esse constituit. in quibus appositis clavibus et fornice facta, a turre majore usque ad pilarios praedictos, id est

II.47 | Building Construction and Reparation 443

usque ad crucem, triforium inferius multis intexuit columpnis marmoreis. super quod triforium aliud quoque ex alia materia et fenestras superiores aptavit, deinde fornicis magnae tres claves, a turre scilicet usque ad cruces. quae omnia nobis et omnibus ea videntibus incomparabilia et laude dignissima videbantur. de hoc ergo tam glorioso principio hilares effecti et futurae consummationis bonam spem concipientes, consummationem operis ardentis animi desiderio accelerare curavimus. in istis igitur annus tertius completus est et quartus sumpsit initium. in cujus aestate a cruce incipiens, decem pilarios erexit, scilicet utrinque quinque. quorum duos primos marmoreis ornans columpnis contra alios duos principales fecit. super hos decem arcus et fornices posuit.

Disaster strikes again: William of Sens falls to the stone floor
peractis autem utrisque triforiis et superioribus fenestris, cum machinas ad fornicem magnam volvendam in anni quinti initio praeparasset, repente ruptis trabibus sub pedibus ejus et inter lapides et ligna simul cum ipso ruentibus, in terram corruit, a capitellis fornicis superioris, altitudine videlicet pedum quinquaginta. qui ex ictibus lignorum et lapidum acriter diverberatus, sibi et operi inutilis effectus est, nullusque alius praeter ipsum solum in aliquo laesus est. in solum magistrum vel Dei vindicta vel diaboli desaevit invidia. magister itaque sic laesus et sub cura doctorum ob spem salutis recuperandae aliquandiu lecto decumbens, spe fraudatus convalescere non potuit; veruntamen quia hiems instabat, et fornicem superiorem consummari oportebat, cuidam monacho industrio et ingenioso qui cementariis praefuit opus consummandum commendavit, unde multa invidia et exercitatio malitiae habita est, eo quod ipse, cum esset juvenis, potentioribus et ditioribus prudentior videretur. magister tamen in lecto recubans, quid prius, quid posterius fieri debuit ordinavit. factum est itaque ciborium [p. 21] inter quatuor pilarios principales; in cujus ciborii clavem videntur quodammodo chorus et cruces convenire. duo quoque ciboria hinc et inde ante hiemem facta sunt. pluviae autem fortiter insistentes plura fieri non permiserunt. in istis annus quartus completus est et quintus sumpsit initium. eodem anno, scilicet quarto, facta est eclipsis solis, idus Septembris, hora quasi sexta, ante casum magistri. sentiens itaque praefatus magister nulla se doctorum arte vel industria posse convalescere, operi renuntiavit et mari transito in Franciam ad sua remeavit. successit autem huic in curam operis alius quidam Willelmus nomine, Anglus natione, parvus quidem corpore sed in diversis operibus subtilis valde et probus.

Translation: Gervase of Canterbury, The Fire at Canterbury Cathedral

William of Sens began, as I mentioned much earlier, to prepare what was necessary for the new work and to clear away the old. This took up the first year. The following year, in other words after the feast of St Bertin but before the winter, he erected four

444 Fifteenth Century

columns, in other words two on each side; when winter had passed he added two, so that there should be three in a row on either side: upon these and on the outer wall of the aisles, he built impressive arches and a vault, that is three keystones on either side. By 'keystone' I mean the whole bay of the vaulted ceiling, because the central keystone seems to fasten together and strengthen the parts converging from both sides. This took up the second year. In the third year he added two pillars on either side, the last two of which he decorated with marble columns around them, and because here the choir and transepts were supposed to meet, he made them the principal ones. After adding keystones and making an arch from the greater tower as far as the aforementioned pillars, that is as far as the crossing, he created a triforium lower down with many marble columns. Above this triforium he fitted another one, too, from different materials, and upper windows, then three keystones of a huge arch, from the tower to the crossing. We and all who saw them considered these incomparable and most admirable. And so, gladdened by such a wonderful beginning and conceiving great hope of future achievement, we made an effort to accelerate the completion of the project, filled with a burning desire. This took up the third year and the beginning of the fourth. During the summer of this year, beginning with the crossing, he erected ten pillars, in other words five on each side. He decorated the first two of these with marble columns opposite the other two principal ones. On these ten he placed arches and vaults.

When both triforia and the upper windows were finished, and he had set up machines to construct the huge arch, at the beginning of the fifth year, suddenly the beams beneath his feet broke and collapsed with him, amid the stones and the pieces of wood: he fell to the ground from the capitals of the upper vault, from a height of 50 feet. He was badly bruised by the blows from the beams and the stones and was rendered useless to himself and to the project, but no one else apart from him suffered any injury. Only against the master builder did God's vengeance or the devil's jealousy rage. And so the master, injured in this way, lay in bed for some time under the care of doctors who hoped that he would be restored to health, but these hopes were dashed and he did not recover. However, because winter was at hand and it was necessary to complete the upper vault, he entrusted the completion of the task to an industrious and ingenious monk who was in charge of the stonemasons: this aroused a good deal of jealousy and a display of malice, because this man, despite his youth, seemed to be more clever than those more powerful and wealthy. But the master, lying in his bed, organised what needed to be done first and what later. And so the vault was made between the four principal pillars; the choir and transepts appear to meet in the keystone of this vault. Two vaults, one on either side, were also made before the onset of winter when heavy rains prevented any more work from being done. This took up the fourth year and the beginning of the fifth. In that same year, namely the fourth, there was an eclipse of the sun, on the Ides of September (13 September), around the sixth hour, before the master's fall. When Master William realised that he could not recover for all the doctors' skill and hard work, he gave up the task and crossed the sea to France, returning to his home. He was succeeded on this project by a man called William, an Englishman by birth, small of stature, to be sure, but very clever and reliable in many different tasks.

Primary Sources and Related Texts

De combustione et reparatione Cantuariensis ecclesiae, RS 73.1 (1879) 3–29.

Further Reading

Brooks, N. (1984) *The early history of the church at Canterbury*, Leicester.
Draper, P. (1997) 'Interpretations of the rebuilding of Canterbury Cathedral
   (1174–1186)', *Journal of the Society of Architectural Historians* 56: 184–203.
*Staunton (2017).
Willis, R. (1845) *The architectural history of Canterbury Cathedral*, repr.
   Cambridge, 2010.

B: Fire Regulations in London after the Great Fire of Southwark, 1212 (excerpt: *Liber custumarum, RS* pp. 86–8)

Following a great fire in London in 1135 in which St Paul's Cathedral was damaged, and another in 1189, fire regulations were introduced, but they failed to prevent the fire of 11 July 1212, in which, as Matthew Paris relates in his *Major Chronicles*, Southwark Cathedral burnt down, and the fire spread to the City of London across the wooden buildings on London Bridge (now built in stone), and a thousand people died. Already on 23 July the Mayor of London brought out a series of regulations to try and prevent a recurrence; the scribe, however, gives the date as 24 July, possibly distracted by the mention of the 14th year of King John's reign.

Work: The *Liber custumarum* is a collection of important London-related documents made by Andrew Horn, who started as a City fishmonger, and became a lawyer and then Chamberlain of the City of London from 1320–8; the *Liber* is now preserved in the London Metropolitan Archives (COL/CS/01/006), and also in BL MS Cotton Claudius D.ii.

Linguistic points: The verb *detorchiare* is only found here; more common is *torchiare*, deriving from the AN verb 'torcher', 'to wipe, or to rub down (a horse)'.

446 Fifteenth Century

plastrare ('to daub with plaster') occurs in BML earlier than it is attested in AN or ME. The Latin *visnetum* is formed from the AN 'visnet', deriving from CL *vicinus*, to mean 'neighbourhood'. For the etymology of *(de)torchiare* cf. *OED s.v.* torch v. 2. *crocus* is derived from ME 'crok' ('crook') and, as often in such cases, there is gender ambiguity; as there are no grammatical genders in ME to influence it, it is free to form as a masculine, feminine or neuter. It is noteworthy that the writer is aware that *mederi* is a deponent verb, and that it takes the dative. For *scotala*, see Section II.44C.

TEXT II.47B

The new building regulations and fire precautions
[p. 86] quaedam consideratio facta per consilium proborum virorum ad sedandam iram et pacificandam civitatem et contra incendium, cum Dei adjutorio, muniendam.

in primis consiliunt quod omnes scotallae defendantur, nisi de illis qui habuerint licentiam per commune consilium civitatis apud Gildhallam; praeter eos qui volunt aedificare de lapide, ut civitas sit secura; (...) et quod nullus pistor forniat vel braciator braciat de nocte neque de arundine vel stramine vel stipula nisi tantum de bosco. (...) item consuluerunt quod omnes coquinae[1] super Thamisiam dealbentur et plastrientur, intus et extra; et omnia intus claustra et diversoria deponantur omnino ita quod non remaneat nisi simpliciter domus et thalamus. [p. 87] quicunque aedificare voluerit, videat sicut se et sua diligit, quod non cooperiat de arundine nec de junco nec de aliquo modo straminis neque stipula; nisi sit de tegula vel cingula vel bordo vel si continget, de plumbo aut

l. extra estra detorchiato, infra civitatem vel Portsokne. item omnes domus quae usque nunc sunt coopertae arundine vel junco, qui possint plastriari, plastrientur infra octo dies. et qui infra terminum ita factae non fuerint, per Aldermannum et legales homines de visneto prosternantur. (...) omnes Aldermanni crocum aptum et cordam habeant. (...) [p. 88] bonum etiam dicunt esse, duntaxat, quod coram unaquaque domo plena cuva aquae adsit, sive lignea sit sive lapidea.

haec facta sunt autem anno regis Johannis xiiij, mense Julii, die Lunae, xxiiij die mensis apud Guihallam, Henrico filio Aylwini, tunc Majore, caeterisque ejusdem civitatis baronibus, ibidem tunc existentibus; civitati mederi volentes super infortunium ignis quod ibi evenerat in Translatione S. Benedicti, per decem dies antea, eodem anno et mense. qui ignis inconsolabiliter Pontem Londoniarum et quamplurima nobilium aedificia, cum innumerabilibus hominum mulierumque funeribus, usque ad nihilum destruxit.

---

1   Cf. *publica coquina* in Section II.15.

Translation: *Liber custumarum*

This decision has been made on the advice of reliable men in order to calm the anger and to pacify the city and with God's help to protect it against fire.

First of all they advise that all scot-ales should be banned except for people who have a licence from the common City council at the Guildhall; apart from those willing to build out of stone for the city's safety. (…) No baker should bake or brewer brew at night or with reeds or straw or stubble, but only with firewood. (…)

They also advised that all public kitchens along the Thames should be white-washed and plastered, inside and out; and all the walls and partitions inside should be taken down so that nothing remains apart from just the house and chamber. Anyone who wants to build should ensure, as he loves himself and his own, that he does not use reeds or rushes or any kind of straw or stubble as a roofing material; he should use tiles or shingle or planks or, if possible, lead, and with plaster on the outside, within the city limits or portsoken. Also all houses that have up till now been covered with reeds or rushes, if they can be plastered, should be so within eight days, while those that cannot be plastered within this period should be demolished by the alderman and the lawful men of the neighbourhood. (…) All the aldermen should have a suitable crook and cord. (…) They state that it is also advisable at least to have a tub, either of wood or stone, full of water in front of every house.

These regulations have been drawn up in the 14th year of King John, on Monday 24 (for 23) July, at the Guildhall, by the current mayor, Henry FitzAylwin, and the other barons of this city, also present, for they wish to bring healing to the city after the disastrous fire that occurred there on the Translation of St Benedict, ten days earlier, in the same month and year. This fire caused irreparable damage involving the total destruction of London Bridge and very many buildings of the nobles, together with the deaths of countless men and women.

Primary Sources and Related Texts

Munimenta Gildhallae Londoniensis: Liber custumarum, RS 12.2 (1860) 86–8.

RS 12.1: 319–32 for assize of building regulations in 1189, including measures to reduce fire-risk, especially (328–9) with reference to the fire in the time of King Stephen.

Further Reading

Carlin, M. and Crouch, D. (2013) *Lost letters of medieval life: English society, 1200–1250*, Philadelphia: 54–6.

448 Fifteenth Century

McEwan, J. (2019) 'Charity and the city: London Bridge, c.1176–1275' in *Medieval Londoners: essays to mark the eightieth birthday of Caroline M. Barron*, ed. E. New and C. Steer, London.

C: Refurbishment and Repairs at Windsor Castle and at Westminster Abbey

Accounts relating to building, from the period 1200–1500, which survive in abundance, fall into three main categories: royal, ecclesiastical and secular. They provide detailed information about materials and wages for many kinds of building projects, from cathedrals and castles to palaces and private houses. Those for castles, such as those built by Edward I throughout Wales, consist mainly of payments made to hundreds of stonemasons and mortar-makers.

C(a): Royal Building: Interior Decoration of the King's Chapel at Windsor

Date: 1248.

TNA: C54/61 m. 8.

Windsor Castle was built in the eleventh century as a fortification with a motte and bailey overlooking the Thames outside London. In the mid-thirteenth century Henry III decided to redesign it as a luxury residence. It is as part of that major project that this writ is sent to Godfrey de Liston, possibly the Warden of Windsor Forest, with regard to the materials needed for the scaffolding allowing the workmen to decorate the chapel with paintings. In the fourteenth century the castle was to become even more spectacular under Edward III, for whom Chaucer worked for a time as clerk of the king's works.

Linguistic points: *escaufacia* is a variant spelling of *scaffaldus*, another example of a word that appears in more variant spellings than one might think possible. It can mean both a 'scaffold' and a 'platform': this latter meaning might indicate that it is related to 'catafalque'. *cleia* is an alternative for LL *cleta* (deriving from Gaulish), meaning a 'hurdle': the form *cleia* derives from the French form 'cleie', but both forms are used in BML. Alder timber (*alnetum*) was often used for these.

TEXT II.47C(a)

The king bids Godfrey de Liston arrange the decoration of the chapel at Windsor
[1248] Mandatum est Godefrido de Liston quod faciat habere custodibus operacionum regis Windleshor' de alnetis et cleiis prout opus fuerit ad faciendum inde

II.47 | Building Construction and Reparation 449

escaufacia ad picturas quas rex injunxit Magistro Willelmo pictori faciendas in capella regis Windles'. Teste ut supra.

Translation: Close Roll

Godfrey de Liston is ordered to make available to the custodians of the king's works at Windsor what they need from the alder timber and hurdles, to make out of them a scaffold for the paintings which the king has enjoined Master William the painter to make in the king's chapel at Windsor. Witness, as above.

C(b): Royal Building: the Rebuilding of Westminster Abbey

Date: 1253–4.

TNA: E101/467/1.

Another of Henry III's major building projects was the rebuilding of Westminster Abbey, begun in 1245. This document dates from the first part of the project, with the building of the east end of the church. Here are recorded the wages of those supplying and working with stone, glass and lead for the windows, lime and sand for the mortar, and wooden boards and laths for the interiors. These entries are taken from a small roll, in the series of accounts of the Exchequer (KRAc), with sixteen lines of rather messy writing and many abbreviations.

Linguistic points: *cissor* (*scissor*) is not here a 'tailor' but that other important profession, a 'cutter' of stone. *albus* does not refer to the *cissor* but is a neuter substantive signifying '(a piece of) white stone'. *cubitor*, from *cubare*, is attested in CL but only as 'one who lies down', not, as here, 'one who lays (something) down', as in 'bricklayer'. *polisor* is associated more closely with French 'polisseur', derived from CL *politor*. *tascha* is a form of *taxa*, related to both 'tax' and 'task'. *lata* is taken from the ME form of OE 'lætt', given as a synonym for CL *asser* ('board') in Ælfric's Latin/OE glossary (cf. Section I.39A(b)). Note the surnames of the workmen, reflecting either their profession or their place of residence: *merinarius* derives from *maeremium* with the suffix *-arius*, i.e. 'one who deals in timber', while *calfonarius* is also a slight corruption, from *calcifurnarius* ('lime-burner'). Agnes bears her husband's surname, i.e. the masculine form, even though she is clearly involved in the lime-burning business in her own right. The surname Limeburner is still in use. The surname of the carpenter, Junur (i.e. Joiner), could be English or French; in either case it matches the use of the Latin verb *iungere* and also provides an early example of the vernacular noun in a Latin matrix.

450 Fifteenth Century

TEXT II.47C(b)

Workman's wages for Westminster Abbey
Ebdomada sexta [post Pascham] sine festo
[p. 256] In stipendiis xlj alborum cissorum xvj marmoriarorum, xxxv cubitorum, xxxiij carpentariorum, Petro [for Petri] pictoris, xv pollisorum, xviij fabrorum, xiij vitriariorum cum vj plumbatoribus, xix li. et xix d. In stipendiis cc et xiij minutorum operariorum cum custodibus et clericis et ij bigis diurnis, xiiij li. et j d. Summa totalis stipendiorum xxxiij li. et xx den.
Empciones: xlj cissoribus pro diversis taschiis france petre ad taschiam cisse iiij li. xvj sol. vj d. (…)
Ricardo Calfonario pro vij^c calcis, xxxv sol.; Agneti Calfonario pro cc calcis, x sol. Item Willelmo Porcario pro vj^c et lx caretatis sabulonis, xiij sol. ij d. ob. Ricardo de Estchepe pro ij duodenis craticularum, vj sol. (…) Ade Merinario pro bordis et lateis, xv sol. vij d. Jacobo Junur' pro panellis ad lectum domini Regis iungendis et pro tabulis ad scacarium et aliis tabulis de sape, lxvj sol. vj d.

Translation: Various Accounts of the Royal Exchequer

Sixth week after Easter, without a feast day.
For the wages of 46 cutters of white stone, 16 marble-masons, 35 stone-layers, 33 carpenters, Peter the painter, 15 polishers, 18 blacksmiths, 13 glaziers with 6 lead workers, £19 19d. For the wages of 213 labourers with keepers and clerks and two cartloads daily, £14 1d. The sum total of the wages, £33 20d.
Purchases: For 41 stone cutters for various tasks of free stone hewn per task, £4 16s. 6d. (…)
To Richard Limeburner for 700 (hundredweight) of lime, 35s.; to Agnes Limeburner for 200 (hundredweight) of lime, 10s. Also to William Swineherd for 660 cartloads of sand, 13s. 2½ d. To Richard of Eastcheap for 2 dozen hurdles, 6s. (…) To Adam the timber-merchant for planks and lathes, 15s. 7d. To Jacob the Joiner for joining panels for the lord king's bed and for wooden boards for chess and other pine boards, 66s. 6d.

Primary Sources

A: *Calendar of Close Rolls* (1247–51) 54.
B: Colvin, H. (ed.) (1971) *Building accounts of King Henry III*, Oxford.

II.47 | Building Construction and Reparation 451

D: **Repairing the Clock on the Tower at Westminster Palace**: a Woman Submits a Claim to the Exchequer for Expenses

Date: 1428.

These short accounts relating to an overhaul of the Westminster Palace clock in 1427 reveal an interesting interplay of languages, with code-switching between Latin and English (with the odd word in French), and different uses of these languages in different documents, i.e. more vernacular in the petition, more Latin in the formal record.

The Palace of Westminster may date back to the eleventh century, but the first clock tower seems to date from 1365–7, built at a cost of £246 16s. 8d. according to the Pipe Rolls (E372) for 1366–7. Repairs must have been necessary in 1427, and it is the cost of these repairs that is being sought from the royal Exchequer in these documents dating from 1428. After the Palace of Westminster was rebuilt following the devastating fire of 1834, a new clock was put into the clock tower now known as Big Ben and started working in 1859. This clock underwent a four-year restoration, completed in 2022.

The first document is E28/50 m. 2, now preserved among the Council and Privy Seal Records in the TNA, dating from February 1428. It is in the form of a petition, written on a small strip of parchment, from Agnes Dalavan, the wife of Geoffrey Dalavan, who was standing in for the custodian (John Lenham) of the King's clock at the Palace of Westminster. She is claiming 100s. 10d. which they had paid to Thomas Clockmaker for various repairs. A warrant for the issue of this money in July of the same year is recorded in the document referred to as E404/44 no. 181. Among the Exchequer accounts (E101/514/16 m. 2) is a fair copy of the petition, with the section that had been in English translated into Latin, as being a more formal version, though it is written on a small, thin roll with nothing but this short text in fine writing, with spelling variants. The translation is preceded by seven lines of Latin from the E28/50 document, i.e. *Particule compoti Agnis Dalavan uxoris Galfridi Dalavan* etc., including *pro reparacione, emendacione et salvam custodiam orelogii regis infra palacium suum Westm.* The details of the payment were then listed in the Foreign Accounts Roll of the Lord Treasurer's Remembrancer (E364/61 m. 25d).

Here the original and the Exchequer fair copy are given, together with an English translation of the fair copy.

Linguistic points: The Latin word (*h*)*orologium* is used to denote the whole machinery of the clock, for which the English word 'clok' is used, derived from Latin *clocca* (appearing in various spellings in medieval Latin), which had originally referred to a bell (cf. Section I.19B). From the twelfth century, with the rapid

452 Fifteenth Century

development of administration, CL *particula* becomes also a technical term within the language of accounting, for an item in an account. Also common in the language of accounting is the medieval formation *superplusagium*, as here, meaning the 'balance', i.e. the remaining amount owed. The French definite article *le* (also in the form *del* or *de la* for the genitive) occurs here, as occasionally from the fourteenth century, in front of some English nouns; elsewhere it is used in a Latin matrix in front of surnames and place names. Already from the twelfth century it is used in front of Latin nouns, particularly technical terms. Even the translation in the E101 document retains a number of English words, presumably for specific technical equipment. Among the English words, note 'tone' and 'tother'; the corresponding Latin *una ... altera* is helpful in interpreting the English as 'the one' and 'the other'. The term *regardum*, from which English derives 'reward', comes from the OF/AN 'regard/reward': while the Latin has the sense of 'forest inspection' from the twelfth century (cf. Section II.44C), and only extends to the sense 'remuneration' in the mid-thirteenth century, the French word has a broader range of meaning, covering 'look' (as in modern French), 'inspection' and 'remuneration'.

D(a): TNA: E28/50 m. 2 (Council and Privy Seal Records)

TEXT II.47D(a)

Agnes Dalavan submits an invoice
particule Agnetis Dalavan uxoris Galfridi Dalavan deputati Johannis Lenham custodis orelegii domini Regis infra palacium suum Westm' pro reparacione eiusdem orelegii, videlicet a festo sancti Michaelis anno regni Regis Henrici sexti post conquestum Anglie quarto usque idem festum proximum sequentem videlicet per unum annum integrum. in primis Thome Clokmaker *for makying of the saylle when it was brokyn*, viij s. Item *for amending of the sprying of the barell*, vj s. viij d. Item *for wire for the sto(ur)bill*, xij d. Item *for amendying of the Note and the spyndyll*, vij s. Item *to the sayd clokmaker for his rewarde for the sayd yere*, xiij s. iiij d. Item *for ij grete ropes, the tone pois lij lb. and the tother pois xlix lb.*, precii *le lb. j d. ob.* Summa xij s. vij d. ob. Item *for ij cordes of thred for the little pais*, ij s. Item *for bordes, lattes and mattes boght for to stoppe the wynde fro the sayd clok*, xxij d. Summa lij s. v d. ob.

  particule eciam eiusdem Agnetis pro reparacione eiusdem orelegii a festo sancti Michaelis anno regni Regis Henrici sexti post conquestum Anglie quinto usque idem festum proximum sequentem, videlicet per unum annum integrum. In primis pro reparacione del Extre, v s. Item *for iij lacches and ij pynnes of Irne*, iij s. Item *for amendying of iiij poleys of laton and iiij boltes and iiij clenches ther to that dragh the hamer*, iij s. iiij d. Item *for iij lenkes and i rynge and a bolt for the hamer*, ij s. Item *for amendyng of the lansyng of the orelege*, vj s. viij d. Item *for ij grete ropes, the tone pois lj lb. and the tother poys lij lb.*, precii lb. j d. ob. Summa xij s. x d. ob. Item *for cordes for the littel pays*, ij s. ij d. Item *to the said clokmaker for his rewarde for the said yere* xiij s. iiij d.

Summa xlviij s. iiij d. ob. Summa totalis pro duobus annis c s. x d.

D(b): TNA: E101/514/16 m. 2 (Various Accounts of the Royal Exchequer)

TEXT II.47D(b)

A Latin translation of the invoice, submitted to the Exchequer
eadem computat in denariis solutis Thome Clokmaker pro emendacione cuiusdam veli defracti Orelog(i)o predicto pertinentis, viij s. Item pro emendacione de *la Spryng del Barell* eidem Orelog(i)o pertinentis, vj s. viij d. Item pro *Wire* pro *le Stourbill*[2] xij d. Item pro emendacione *del Note* et fusi, vij s. Item pro ij magnis cordis quarum una pondere lij lb. et altera pondere xlix lb. emptis ad idem Orelogium, precii lb. j d. ob., xij s. vij d. ob. Item in ij cordis de filo empt' pro minore pondere eiusdem Orelogii, ij s. Item in *bordes, lathes* et *mattes* emptis pro obstupacione venti a predicto Orelogio, xxij d. Item pro emendacione *del Extre* eiusdem Orelogii, v s. Item pro iij *latches* et ij *pynnes* ferri emptis pro predicto Orelogio, iij s. Item pro emendacione iiij^{or} *Poleys* de *latoun*, iiij^{or} *boltes* cum iiij^{or} *clenches* pro tractacione mallii eiusdem Orelogii, iij s. iiij d. Item pro iij *lenkes* cum uno Anulo et j *bolt* emptis pro dicto mallio, ij s. Item pro emendacione de *lansyng* Orelogii predicti, vj s. viij d. Item pro ij magnis cordis ad deserviendum eidem Orelogii (?-io) quarum una lj lb. et altera lij lb. emptis, precii lb. j d. ob., xij s. x d. ob. Item pro corda empta pro minore pondere eiusdem Orelogii ij s ij d. Item solutis eidem *Clokmaker* pro regardo sibi facto ex convencione secum facta infra predictum tempus huius computi, xxvj s. viij d.
Summa expensarum c s. x d. Et habet superplusagium xxxiiij s. ij d.

Translation: E101/514/16 m. 2: English Translation of the Latin

The same accounts for the money paid to Thomas Clockmaker for mending a certain broken sail belonging to the same clock, 8s. Also for mending the spring of the barrel belonging to the same clock, 6s. 8d. Also for wire for the balance, 12d. Also

---

2   It is unclear what this word, whether *stobill* or *stourbill*, refers to: it could be related to OF 'estorbillon' ('whirlwind'), indicating a rotating part, or to ME 'stoppel' ('stopper') or ME 'stapel' for a 'wire ring' or 'staple': the word occurs also in a hawking context *s.v.* *stoppel* (*DMLBS*).

454 Fifteenth Century

for mending the cog and spindle, 7s. Also for 2 large cords, one of which weighs 52 pounds, and the other weighs 49 pounds, bought for the same clock, at the price of 1½ d. a pound, 12s. 7½ d. Also for 2 cords of thread bought for the lesser weight of the same clock, 2s. Also for boards, laths and matting bought for the blocking out of the wind from the said clock, 22d. Also for mending the axle-tree of the same clock, 5s. Also for 3 latches and pins of iron bought for the said clock, 3s. Also for mending the 4 pulleys of latten, 4 bolts with 4 clinch nails for the drawing of the hammer of the same clock, 3s. 4d. Also for 3 links with one ring and 1 bolt bought for the said hammer, 2s. Also for mending the lansing of the said clock, 6s. 8d. Also for 2 large cords bought for the use of the same clock, one of which weighs 51 pounds and the other 52 pounds, at the price of 1½ d. a pound, 12s. 10½ d. Also for a cord bought for the lesser weight of the same clock, 2s. 2d. Also 26s. 8d. paid to the same clockmaker as a remuneration made to him according to the agreement made with him during the said period of this account.

The total of the expenses, 100s. 10d. And there is 34s. 2d. still owing.

Primary Sources and Related Texts

Post, J. B. and Turner, A. J. (1973) 'An account for repairs to the Westminster Palace Clock', *Archaeological Journal* 130: 217–20.

Further Reading

Colvin, H. (1963) *The history of the king's works: the Middle Ages*, 3 vols, London.
Falk, S. (2020) *The light ages: a medieval journey of discovery*, London. On measuring time and building clocks.
Ingham, R. (2013) 'Language-mixing in medieval Latin documents: vernacular articles and nouns' in *Jefferson and Putter (2013).
North, J. (2005) *God's clockmaker: Richard of Wallingford and the invention of time*, London.

E: Building a Merchant's House in the City of London: the Builder's Contract (excerpts from pp. 478–81)

Date: 1405.

The contract is preserved as St Paul's MS no. 1717.

The following passage is taken from the building contract between the landlords, the Dean and Chapter of St Paul's Cathedral, and the builder, John Dobson. The

II.47 | Building Construction and Reparation 455

contract describes in detail a proposed set of buildings to be constructed, for letting purposes, around a courtyard comprising a merchant's residence above a shop and storage space. It would seem that there had already been a tenement, mentioned in 1277–8 in the Calendar of Wills in the Court of Hustings in London (1.29), on this site on the street called Bucklersbury in central London. Bucklersbury is mentioned in Shakespeare's *The Merry Wives of Windsor* (Act III, scene 3) as a street known for its herbalists. The timber for this building was being sourced from woodland around Hadleigh Castle in Essex in the same year that the young Duke Humfrey was installed in that castle by his father, King Henry IV (cf. Section II.36).

Linguistic points: This document contains some code-switching between the Latin matrix and the English vernacular (e.g. 'stage' for modern English 'storey', but cf. French 'étage'), but also integrated borrowings into Latin, such as *aleia*, *parlera* (*parlaria*) and *garita*. *manucapere* (cf. Section II.49A) is here employed with an infinitive used to mean 'to undertake to (do something)'. *gettare* is interesting, in that it preserves the phonetic variant of 'to jut', i.e. 'jet', as in the modern English 'jetty', though it ultimately derives from CL *jactare*. *assisa* (past participle of *assidere*, as a substantive) crops up often in medieval documents, first as an 'assessed payment', and then in connection with various regulations, concerning measures, quality and prices. When attached to a measurement, as here, it means 'standard'. The compound *attornare*, like its AN equivalent, 'aturner', is rich in senses, one of which is 'to appoint (a deputy)', often in a legal context, giving modern English 'attorney'. *shopa*, despite deriving from OE 'sc(e)oppa', only occurs in BML post-Conquest: it appears in a range of spellings, and with the suffix -*arius* produces a word for 'shopkeeper', but not, apparently, any word for 'shopping'. *mearemium* is one of many spelling variants for the ubiquitous word for timber, *maeremium*, following the AN/OF forms from LL *materiamen*. *costus* (*cust*-), which occurs in all three genders as well as a fourth-declension noun (as here), meaning costs or expenditure, derives from a sense of CL *constare*; *costus* was adopted widely into Germanic languages and French. With regard to the word 'estrichbord', cf. Section II.46E for the Latin equivalent, *bordus estrensius*.

TEXT II.47E

John Dobson agrees to rebuild the house on Bucklersbury in the City of London
[p. 478 Salzman] Hec indentura facta inter reverendos viros Decanum et Capitulum Sancti Pauli London' ex parte una et Johannem Dobson civem et carpentarium London' ex parte altera testatur quod predictus Johannes convenit et manucepit prefatis Decano et Capitulo bene competenter et sufficienter quantum ad carpentriam pertinet quedam domos et edificia subscripta eisdem Decano et Capitulo de novo facere, construere et edificare apud Bokeleresbury in parochia

456 Fifteenth Century

Sancte Sithe[3] [p. 479] London' super solum et in solo ubi certa vetera edificia ipsorum Decani et Capituli per ipsos ad suos custus proprios prosternenda et abinde amovenda modo stant et existunt. (...) In primis predictus Johannes cum gistis et bordis competenter et sufficienter teget et operiet tam quoddam celarium in dicto solo iuxta dictum tenementum quod Johannes Permounter predictus tenet ex parte occidentali, fiendum, contenturum in longitudine a dicto vico regio usque ad fundamenta dicti muri Willelmi Walderne quadraginta et quinque pedes assise et in latitudine decem pedes assise quam quoddam alium celarium in parte posteriori dicti soli (...) ac eciam quendam puteum vocatum Cave ad orientalem finem dicti maioris celarii fiendum et pro latrina deserviturum, contenturum in longitudine sexdecim pedes assise et in latitudine decem pedes assise. preterea dictus Johannes Dobson faciet construet et edificabit bene competenter et sufficienter de carpentria super solum et fundamenta predicta iuxta vicum regium predictum versus boriam (bore-) unam magnam shopam cum quadam domo ex parte orientali predicte shope vocanda *Sotelhous* cum quadam porta et aleia ex parte orientali dicte shope servitura pro ingressu et introitu ad quasdam domos retro dictam shopam et *Sotelhous* edificandas. (...) super quasquidem shopam [p. 480] Sotelhous et aleiam predictus Johannes Dobson construet et edificabit duo *stages* quorum unum videlicet primum gettabit tam supra vicum regium versus boriam quam versus partem australem et aliud gettabit solomodo versus vicum regium cum uno garito supra dicta duo *stages*. (...) primum *stage* habebit duas fenestras versus vicum regium competentes et honestas vocatas *Bay Wyndowes*, unam videlicet pro una camera et alteram pro una parlera ibidem fiendis (...). insuper dictus Johannes Dobson super solum predictum retro dictam Shopam et *Sotelhous* videlicet super magnum celarium construet et faciet unum *Warehous* altitudinis novem pedum assise et supra dictum *Warehous* unam aulam competentem et honestam cum uno *Upright roof* contenturam in longitudine triginta et tres pedes assise et in latitudine viginti pedes assise, cuius aule postes et muri erunt altitudinis *de le Flore* usque ad *le Reson*[4] sexdecim pedum assise; (...) et ad finem orientalem dicte aule fiet unum *Oryell* cum gradu pro introitu ad eandem aulam quodquidem *oryell* reddet lumen pro panetria et botilleria ibidem fiendis (...) et eciam fiet ad dictam finem orientalem aule predicte una coquina continens in longitudine sexdecim pedes assise et in latitu-

---

3 The reference here to St Sitha seems to be to St Osyth, an obscure Anglo-Saxon saint, to whom the twelfth-century church of St Benet Sherehog (destroyed in the Fire of London of 1666) was dedicated and who gave her name to a village in Essex; however, confusion is caused (in, for example, the interpretation of nearby 'Sise Lane') by the fact that this church had, by the fourteenth century, a chapel of St Zita of Lucca, a thirteenth-century saint who became popular in London, perhaps as the result of Italian merchants in the City: cf. C. M. Barron (2017) 'The travelling saint: Zita of Lucca and England' in *Medieval London: collected papers of Caroline M. Barron*, ed. J. Rosenthal and M. Carlin, Kalamazoo: 193–212, esp. 198).

4 This is a variant spelling of ME 'rasen': a beam supporting the roof timbers ; cf. *OED s.v.* raising (plate).

dine quindecim pedes assise simul cum uno stabulo et [p. 481] cum *colehous*, *wodehous* et latrina communi subtus dicta panetria botilleria et coquina (…)

The Dean and Chapter of St Paul's will source the timber for the house in the forest of Hadleigh in Essex
ad que omnia et singula edificia et opera predicta prefatus Decanus et Capitulum invenient et deliberabunt predicto Johanni Dobson vel suis in hac parte attornatis boscum competentem et sufficientem pro omnimodo mearemio (maerem-) dictis edificiis et operibus pertinente et indigente inde faciendo de et in Bosco ipsorum Decani et Capituli stante et crescente in parochia de Hadlee in comitatu Essex. (…) et eciam predictus Decanus et Capitulum Estrichbord clavos et omnia alia necessaria tam ferrea quam lignea dictis operibus indigencia ad custus suos proprios Johanni Dobson invenient et deliberabunt ita quod idem Johannes nichil aliud inveniet eisdem operibus nisi solomodo [p. 482] omne opus manuale quantum ad carpentriam et ad prostracionem cecacionem (sec-) aptaturam facturam et sarraturam mearemii et tabularum predictarum ac edificacionem levacionem et construccionem domorum et edificiorum predictorum cum suis apparatibus predictis pertinet et incumbit. (…)

Dat' sexto die Septembris Anno regni regis Henrici quarti post conquestum sexto.

Translation: Building Contract of 1405

This indenture made between the reverend men, the Dean and Chapter of St Paul's in London on the one hand and John Dobson, citizen and carpenter of London on the other, witnesses to the fact that the said John agrees with the said Dean and Chapter and undertakes, with competent and proper carpentry, to restore, construct and build the houses and buildings detailed below for this same Dean and Chapter at Bucklersbury in the parish of St Sitha in London on and in the plot where certain old buildings of the Dean and Chapter now stand, which must be knocked down by them at their own expense and removed from there. (…) Firstly the said John will competently and properly cover and roof with boards and planks both a storeroom on the said plot next to the tenement which John Permounter holds on the west side: this storeroom is to be made to comprise 45 standard feet in length from the royal highway to the foundations of the wall of William Walderne and 10 standard feet in breadth, as well as another cellar in the rear part of this plot (…) and also a pit called a Cave needs to be made on the eastern boundary of the larger cellar and to serve as a privy, comprising 16 standard feet in length and 10 standard feet in breadth. In addition, John Dobson will make, construct and build with competent and proper carpentry on the plot and foundations next to the royal highway a large north-facing shop with a building to be called the 'sotelhous' on the east side of this shop, with a gate and alley on the east side of this shop to serve as an entrance to some buildings to be constructed behind the shop and the 'sotelhous' (…) Above the

458 Fifteenth Century

shop, 'sotelhous' and alley, John Dobson will construct and build two storeys, one of which, namely the first, will jut out both above the royal highway and towards the south side and the other will only jut out over the royal highway with a loft above these two storeys. (...) The first storey will have two suitable and handsome windows known as 'bay windows' facing the royal highway, one window for one chamber and the other for a parlour to be made there (...) In addition John Dobson on this plot behind the shop and 'sotelhous', namely above the large cellar, will construct and make one warehouse 9 standard feet high and above this warehouse a suitable and handsome hall with an upright roof comprising 33 standard feet in height and 20 standard feet in breadth, and the posts and walls of this hall will be 16 standard feet from the floor to the roof beam. (...) and at the east end of this hall an oriel should be made with a step as an entrance to this hall: this oriel will provide light for the pantry and buttery which are to be constructed there (...) and also construct at this east end of the hall a kitchen 16 standard feet long and 15 feet wide together with a stable, with coalhouse, woodhouse and a shared latrine under the pantry, buttery and kitchen. (...)

For each and every one of these buildings and works, the Dean and Chapter will find and deliver to John Dobson or his men who have been appointed in this role a sufficient quantity of good-quality woodland for all the timber needed for these buildings and works and necessary for completing them, from and in the wood of the Dean and Chapter, standing and growing in the parish of Hadleigh in the county of Essex. (...) And also the Dean and Chapter will find and deliver to John Dobson the planks from the eastern Baltic, nails and everything else necessary, both of iron and wood, needed for these works, at their own expense, so that John will not have to find anything else for these works apart from all manual labour relating and appertaining to carpentry and for the felling, cutting, fitting, preparing and sawing of timber and boards and for the building, raising and construction of these houses and buildings with their fittings. (...)

Dated 6 September in the sixth year of the reign of King Henry IV after the Conquest.

Primary Source

Salzman, L. F. (1952) *Building in England, down to 1540: a documentary history*, Oxford: 478–82.

Further Reading

Pantin, W. A. (1962) 'Medieval English town-house plans', *Medieval Archaeology* 6: 202–39, esp. 223–5 with ground plan.

Schofield, J. (1991) 'The construction of medieval and Tudor houses in London', *Construction History* 7: 3–28.

Section II.48

Royal and Ecclesiastical Accounts
A: Liberate Roll Payments for the King's Bear at the Tower of London (excerpts)
B: Countess Eleanor's Accounts for the de Montfort Household (excerpts)
C: Accounts of Everyday Expenditure at the Priory of Durham (excerpts: pp. 536, 539, 581)
D: Royal Household Expenditure: the Wardrobe Book of William de Norwell (excerpts: from f. 1 and f. 90)
E: An Account Entry from the Scottish Exchequer Rolls (excerpt: 2.38)

As seen in the building accounts included in the previous section, accounts often provide a rich source of linguistic knowledge, relating as they do to contemporary, everyday life in a way that literary works often do not. In many cases accounts provide evidence of code-switching between languages, mainly between Latin, English and French, revealing an easy multilingualism among those who wrote them. Accounts can also reflect major events experienced by those whose daily lives are being recorded in such mundane detail, as for example in the accounts of Eleanor, Countess of Leicester, whose plan to flee across southern England after the escape of the future King Edward I from the de Montforts' custody is indicated by the unusual bulk purchase of 84 horseshoes and 2,000 nails on 8 July 1265. The repercussions of the battle of Evesham can similarly be found among the documents known as *Inquisitions Miscellaneous* (CalIMisc, TNA: C145), where property is changing hands between the royal supporters and those on the de Montfort side (e.g. vol. 1, no. 700).

Further Reading

Woolgar, C. (ed.) (1992–3) *Household accounts from medieval England*, 2 vols, Oxford. Records of social and economic history.

Wright, L. (2013) 'Mixed-language accounts as sources for linguistic analysis' in *Jefferson and Putter (2013).

460 Fifteenth Century

A: Liberate Roll Payments for the King's Bear at the Tower of London (excerpts)

Date: 1252.

TNA: C62/28 m. 4 and C62/29 m. 15.

Work: The Liberate Rolls provide a record of the writs authorising royal administrators to make payments or provision of equipment on behalf of the king. They were created as a separate series in 1226, distinct from the Close Rolls. 'Liberate' is the plural imperative of the CL verb *liberare*: the original sense of setting free was extended, by means of different senses of 'to deliver', to mean 'to hand over', and in the context of these writs, 'to pay'. Here the writ relates to the delivery, as a present from King Haakon IV of Norway, of a polar bear to add to King Henry III's growing menagerie at the Tower of London. In 1255 the king of France gave Henry an elephant, which Matthew Paris depicted in Cambridge MS CCC 16, f. 4r, and whose brief life in England can also be traced in various records. In the nineteenth century the animals then in this menagerie were moved to Regent's Park for the founding of London Zoo.

Linguistic points: *musellum* (French 'musel') is here used not in the usual sense of the 'muzzle' of an animal but as the only instance of a 'guard for an animal's muzzle'.

TEXT II.48A

Money granted for the upkeep of the polar bear and his keeper
[13 September 1252] vicecomitibus Londin' salutem. precipimus vobis quod cuidam urso nostro albo quem mittimus usque Turrim nostram Londin' ibidem custodiendum et custodi ipsius singulis diebus quamdiu fuerint ibidem habere faciatis quatuor denar' ad sustentacionem suam.

To the sheriffs of London, greetings. We order you to arrange for our white bear which we are sending to our tower in London to be kept there and for his keeper to have each day, for as long as they are there, 4 pence for their upkeep.

A muzzle, a chain and a long rope are granted so that the polar bear can fish in the Thames
[30 October 1252] custodi albi ursi nostri qui nuper missus fuit nobis de Norvag' et est in turri nostra Lond', habere facias unum musell' et unam cathenam ferream ad tenendum ursum illum ex aqua et unam longam et fortem cordam ad tenendum eundem ursum piscantem in aqua Thamis'.

To the sheriffs of London, greetings. Let the keeper of the king's white bear which was recently sent to him from Norway and is now in our tower in London have a muzzle and an iron chain to hold that bear (when it is) out of the water and a long and strong rope to hold this same bear when it is fishing in the Thames.

Primary Source

Calendar of Liberate Rolls 4.70 and 84.

Further Reading

Borg, A. (1978) 'The royal menagerie' in *The Tower of London: its buildings and institutions*, ed. J. Charlton, London.

Lewis, M. (2016) *Henry III: the son of Magna Carta*, Stroud.

B: Countess Eleanor's Accounts for the de Montfort Household (excerpts)

This household account roll, comprising thirteen membranes sewn together at the top, remained at Montargis in France, where Eleanor died in 1275, until it was acquired by the British Library in 1831.

Date: 1265.

This roll is now referred to as BL MS Add. 8877.

Eleanor,[1] born in about 1215, was a daughter of King John and younger sister of King Henry III. At the age of 9 she was married to William Marshal Junior (one of the enforcers of the Magna Carta, and son of the William Marshal who helped to depose the chancellor William de Longchamp in 1191 (see Section II.20) and was later regent of England), but she was widowed by the age of 16. Although she then vowed not to marry again, in 1238 she married the ambitious baron Simon de Montfort, thereby becoming Countess of Leicester. From this period date a number of letters from Adam Marsh, the Franciscan theologian who acted as her spiritual adviser; Eleanor's letters to Adam which he mentions are unfortunately lost. Eleanor and her husband rebelled against Henry III in the late 1250s. The

---

1 This Eleanor should not be confused with three other powerful women of that name at this period: Eleanor of Aquitaine, wife of Henry II, Eleanor of Provence, wife of Henry III, or Eleanor of Castile, wife of Edward I.

462 Fifteenth Century

year 1265 finds her at first at a financial and political highpoint after her husband's victory at the battle of Lewes in 1264, after which King Henry was temporarily in their power, but then at her lowest point, when her husband and eldest son were killed at the battle of Evesham in August 1265. She was then forced to go into exile in France, where she died in 1275 at the Dominican convent of Montargis.

Work: This household roll, a working document covering expenses in Eleanor's household between 19 February and 29 August 1265, is the only surviving set of accounts for the households of either Eleanor or Simon de Montfort, as well as being one of the earliest sets of private accounts in Britain, but with parallels in Continental examples of the period. Samples are given here from the three types of accounts found on these membranes: the 'diet accounts', i.e. daily accounts mainly of food and drink, and feed for animals, set out in a rather formulaic manner; secondly, the lists of special allowances of additional items; and thirdly, the record, made on the dorse of each membrane, of items from the so-called wardrobe, i.e. from the department that controlled valuable items in the countess' possession, whether wax, spices and exotic foods, or clothes and jewels, together with information about payments for messengers and other servants. The items listed in these three types of accounts provide much lexical interest, especially in the areas of foodstuffs and cloth.

The excerpts show not only items used by Eleanor but also payments and gifts for members of her family: for her brothers, King Henry III and Richard, Earl of Cornwall (referred to here as king of Germany, a title he held from 1257), both in custody at the time following their defeat at the battle of Lewes in 1264, and for her youngest child, her daughter Eleanor.[2] A particular point of interest is the predominance of fish in the diet: while herring was in general the most common item on the menu, when the countess flees to the coast of Kent, she has a much more varied diet of locally caught fish. Among the special allowances, mention is made of deliveries of royal fish, namely sturgeon and whale, to King Henry III at Wallingford Castle: if whales were washed onto the coast, their meat was reserved by law for the use of the king.

Linguistic points: *marescalcia*, from *marescalcus* (already in Frankish Latin and the *Lex Salica*), is derived from a Germanic word ('marahscalc') meaning 'one who looks after horses', and here the word relates to the horses' stables. It also came to be applied to a high-ranking steward or officer: from these English

---

2   Young Eleanor, aged about 12, was exiled to France with her mother, but after the countess' death, young Eleanor was married to Llewellyn ap Gruffudd, the last Welsh-born Prince of Wales: she died giving birth to a daughter, Gwenllian, who at the age of 1, after Llewellyn's death, was banished by Edward I to Sempringham Priory in Lincolnshire, where she lived till her death in 1337 (cf. Section II.14 for life in another double monastery founded by Gilbert of Sempringham).

II.48 | Royal and Ecclesiastical Accounts 463

derives the word 'marshal'. The word for 'sugar', *succarum* (with multiple spellings in BML), derives from Arabic. For *pochia* ('bag', *s.v. poca* in *DMLBS*), compare the form *powchia* in Section II.34A. *fraellus* is derived from the AN form 'frael' (English 'frail'), a rush basket for transporting fruit. The vernacular words for different types of fish could have been given in their cognate Latin forms, *brema*, *darsus* and *plaicia*, but here they are given in forms which are quite ambiguous, as is not uncommon in the Anglo-Norman and English of the period, given the orthographical fluidity: *bremes* (originally a Germanic word) and *dartes* (probably from Gaulish) could be AN or ME, while *playz* is more likely to be an AN spelling.

TEXT II.48B(a)

Diet account for 22 July 1265, at Dover Castle, from the tenth membrane (no. 463)
Die Mercurii sequenti, pro comitissa et predictis; panis, j quarterium et j busellus. vinum album, dimidium sextarium. vinum rubeum, vj sextaria dimidium. cervisia, xxxvj [galone], xviij d. *Coquina:* piscis, de Heithe, iv s. *Bremes* et *dartes*, ij s. vi. d. *Soles*, xij d. *Playz*, vij d. Crevicie et capre marinae, v d. ob. In v^c ovorum, ij s. iij d. ob. *Mostarde*, iij d. In color' ad coquinam, vj d. In fabis [et] pisis, iv d. ob. In lacte j d. ob. *Mareschalcia:* fenum pro xvj equis. Avena, j quarterium. Summa xiij s. vij d.

Translation: Household Roll of Eleanor

On the Wednesday following, for the countess and the others mentioned: (flour for) bread, 1 quarter and one bushel; white wine, half a sester; red wine, six and a half sesters; ale, 36 gallons, 18d. Kitchen: fish from Hythe (Kent), 4s. Bream and dace, 2s. 6d., Sole, 12d., Plaice, 7d. Crayfish and goatfish, 5½ d. For 500 eggs, 2s. 3½ d. Mustard 3d. For dye, for the kitchen, 6d. For beans and peas, 4½ d. For milk, 1½ d. Stables: Hay for 16 horses; oats, 1 quarter. Total: 13s. 7d.

TEXT II.48B(b)

Special allowances made from Odiham Castle until Palm Sunday, 29 March 1265, from the second membrane (no. 79)
Allocationes facte domino Guillielmo de Wortham pro rebus missis ad regem Alem' et comitissam, usque Diem Palmarum.
pro ij lib. zingiberi et ij lib. piperis, iiij s. pro xx lib. Amygdalorum, iiij s. pro j quart' croci, ij s. vj d. pro pochiis, ij d. pro ij caldariis ad opus domini Almarici, xxiij s. ob. pro xviij saccis, viij s. vj d. pro j vanno vij d. pro j barillo sturjoni qui dimissus fuit Walingef' ad opus regis xxxj s. pro baleyna vj s. j d. dimissa ibidem, ad opus ejusdem. item pro c et dimid. cent. lib. amygdalorum xlij s. pro c lib. risae

xiiij s. pro x lib. piperis viij s. iiij d. pro vj lib. canellae, v s. pro vj lib. galingalium
ix s. pro j lib. croci x s. pro dimid. lib. gariofili v s. pro x lib. cimini xx d. pro saccis
xij d. portagium iij ob. pro x lib. zingiberi xv s. pro x lib. zucari x s. item pro saccis
ij d. pro j fraello racemorum xij s. pro cc de balena xxxiiij s. de ista speceria missa
domino regi Al[emannie], xx lib. amygdalorum vj s., v lib. risae, ix d., ij lib. piperis, xx d., ij lib. canellae xx d., dimid. lib. galingalium ix d., j lib. zingiberi xviij d.,
ij lib. Zucari ij s., et xx peciae de balena. Summa xij li. vij s. ij d.

Translation: Household Roll of Eleanor

*Allowances made to Lord William de Wortham for things sent to the king of Germa-
ny and the countess, until Palm Sunday.*
*For 2 lbs of ginger and 2 lbs of pepper, 4s. For 20 lbs of almonds, 4s. For 1 quarter of
saffron, 2s. 6d. For bags, 2d. For 2 hot-water pots for the use of Lord Amaury, 23s.
½ d. For 18 sacks, 8s. 6d. For 1 winnowing fan, 7d. For 1 barrel of sturgeon which was
sent to Wallingford for the king's use, 31s. For whale, 6s. 1d., sent to the same place,
for the use of the same. Also for 150 lbs of almonds, 42s. For 100 lbs of rice, 14s. For
10 lbs of pepper, 8s. 4d. For 6 lbs of cinnamon, 5s. For 6 lbs of galingale, 9s. For 1 lb
saffron, 10s. For half a pound of cloves, 5s. For 10 lbs of cumin, 20d. For sacks, 12d.
Transport costs, 1½ d. For 10 lbs of ginger, 15s. For 10 lbs of sugar, 10s. Also for sacks,
2d. For 1 rush basket of raisins, 12s. For 200 (pieces) of whale meat, 34s. Out of these
spices there were sent to the lord king of Germany 20 lbs of almonds, 6s., 5 lbs of rice,
9d., 2 lbs of pepper, 20d., 2 lbs of cinnamon, 20d., ½ lb of galingale, 9d., 1 lb of ginger,
18d., 2 lbs of sugar, 2s. and 20 pieces of whale meat. Total £12 7s. 2d.*

TEXT II.48B(c)

*Two entries from the wardrobe accounts relating to the young Eleanor's breviary,
from the dorse of the first membrane (no. 46) and the third membrane (no. 139)*
in xx duodenis parchameni abhortivi emptis Lond' per fratrem G. Bozun ad por-
tiforium Domiselle Alianore ad Purificationem, x s. (…) eadem die soluti per
manus ejusdem, apud Oxon', pro scriptura Breviarii Domiselle A. de Monteforti,
per visum fratris G. Boyon, xiiij s.

Translation: Household Roll of Eleanor

*For 20 dozen (sheets) of uterine vellum bought in London by brother G. Bozun for
Damsel Eleanor's portable breviary at the Purification (2 February), 10s. (…) On
the same day (9 May) paid by the hand of the same, at Oxford, for the writing of the
breviary of Damsel Eleanor de Montfort, under supervision of brother G. Boyon, 14s.*

Primary Sources

Wilkinson, L. (ed.) (2020) *The household roll of Eleanor de Montfort, Countess of Leicester and Pembroke, 1265 (British Library, Additional MS 8877)*, Woodbridge.

Lawrence, C. H. (ed.) (2006–10) *The Letters of Adam Marsh*, 2 vols, OMT, Oxford.

Johnstone, H. (1922) 'The wardrobe and household of Henry, son of Edward I', *Bulletin of the John Rylands Library* 7: 384–420.

Further Reading

Crawford, A. (ed.) (2002) *Letters of medieval women*, Stroud.

Earenfight, T. (ed.) (2018) *Royal and elite households in medieval and early modern Europe: more than just a castle*, Leiden.

Labarge, M. W. (1965) *Mistress, maids and men: baronial life in the thirteenth century*, repr. London, 2003.

Wilkinson, L. (2018) 'The great household in wartime: Eleanor de Montfort and her familia' in *The elite household in England, 1100–1550: Proceedings of the 2016 Harlaxton Symposium*, ed. C. Woolgar, Donington.

Medieval clothing and textiles (2005–).

C: Accounts of Everyday Expenditure at the Priory of Durham (excerpts: pp. 536, 539, 581)

Date: fourteenth century.

Work: The account rolls of the bursars of Durham Priory, covering the period 1278–1580, are a treasure trove of Latin and English vocabulary relating to every aspect of medieval life, from vegetable seeds to coal mines, from kitchen utensils to copies of Donatus and rodent operatives brought in to deal with black rats operating in the bursar's office, all seen through the lens of (often high) expenditure. Even in these rolls the reader has glimpses of the wider world, with travel to Holy Island and mention of the threat of attacks from Scotland. Excerpts from these fill three volumes of the Surtees Society, but many lie unedited. Unfortunately, their condition is sometimes poor: as the rolls themselves record, by the 1430s many were already *consumpti ... partim per pluviam, partim per ratones et mures* ('ravaged ... partly by rain, partly by rats and mice').

Linguistic points: ME 'winden' ('to haul or hoist') gives a range of related words in BML formed with various CL suffixes, with *wyndatio* here, as the act of hauling

466 Fifteenth Century

water. *sincatio* is similarly formed from ME 'sincen' (OE 'sincan'), to mean the sinking of a shaft for a mine or well, as is clear from its use on p. 585: *in sinctatione* (sic) *unius putei apud Heworth cum piks, bukets et cordis factis pro eodem, 6 li. 6s. 6d. ob. stangnum* is a variant spelling of the CL word for 'tin', *stagnum* (*stannum*). These excerpts also include some vernacular words, such as 'soudur' ('solder'), an alloy of tin used to join bits of metal. Another is 'kirn', which is the earliest example of the northern dialect word for 'churn' in written sources, showing how BML texts often preserve vernacular words before they appear in vernacular written sources, as well as regional forms. Note the spelling *ciphus* for *scyphus* ('cup'): this CL word, adopted from the Greek, provided many spelling problems to writers of BML, as is clear from the entry in *DMLBS*.

TEXT II.48C

Everyday expenses at Durham Priory
[p. 536] (1338–9) mulieribus portantibus aquam pro bracina et pistrina et coquina in septimana post festum Purificacionis eo quod pipa fuit gelidata, 6s. In aqua wyndanda de fonte tracticio in claustro ad idem, et pro opere circa pipam, 16d.
[p. 539] (1340–1) et cuidam deferenti literas Prioris usque Insulam Sacram in vigilia Nat. Sci Johannis, 12d. et cuidam eunti Mukelingswyk ad premuniend' Instaurarium ibidem de elongando instaurum per metum invasionis Scottorum (…)
[p. 581] (1374) Comp. fr'is Hugonis de Hawyk a festo Pen., 1374, usque f'm Circumcis. D'ni ejusdem anni. (…)
Exp(ensae) nec(essariae). In reparacione unius ciphi dat' refectorio per d'num Ric'm de Bikerton, 34s. In uno *kirn* empt. pro le Nethirdeyhous, 8d. In sale de Bayon empt. apud Novum Castrum pro priore et celer. cum cariacione, 56s. 10d. In sale albo empt. de Joh'e fil. Agn., 43s. In una corda empt. ad trahenda ligna ad stangnum molendini, 11d. In sincacione unius putei apud Nethirheworth, et in instrumentis empt. pro eodem, 46s. 8d. In stangno emp. pro *soudur*, 6s. ob. In expen. d'ni Roberti de Claxton versus Lond. ad Ep'm Dunelm. pro liter. petend. eligendi priorem, 106s. 8d. In exp. Stephani del Kiln versus Oxon. cum literis ad citand. confratres ad eleccionem, 8s. 1d. In exp. Ade Cariageman versus Lethom pro eadem causa, 3s. In exp. factis circa adduccionem magistrorum Joh'is de Norton et Hugonis de Fletham venient. ad eleccionem una cum conduccione equorum pro eisdem, 42s. 4d. Item cuidam occidenti ratones in scaccario et stabulo bursar', 12d. Summa omn. exp., etc. 1010 li. 19s. 4d. ob. q^{a}r.

Translation: Account Rolls of the Priory of Durham

(1338–9) *For the women carrying water for the brewery and bakery and kitchen in the week after the feast of the Purification because the pipe had frozen, 6s. For*

II.48 | Royal and Ecclesiastical Accounts   467

drawing water from the draw-well in the cloister for the same and for work on the pipe, 16d.

(1340–1) For someone carrying the Prior's letter to Holy Island on the eve of the Nativity of St John, 12d., and for someone going to Mukelingswyk to warn the stockman there to remove the stock because of fear of an invasion by the Scots (…)

(1374) The account of Brother Hugh de Hawyk from the feast of Pentecost 1374 to the feast of the Circumcision of the Lord of the same year. (…)

Necessary expenses: for the repair of one cup given to the refectory by Lord Richard de Bikerton, 34s. For one kirn bought for the Nethirdeyhous, 8d. For Bayonne salt bought in Newcastle for the prior and cellarer with transport, 56s. 10d. For white salt bought from John son of Agnes, 43s. For one rope bought to pull logs to the millpond, 11d. For the sinking of one pit at Nethirheworth and for the tools bought for it, 46s. 8d. For tin bought for solder, 6s. ½ d. For the expenses of Lord Robert of Claxton on his journey to London to the Bishop of Durham to ask for a letter to elect a prior, 106s. 8d. For expenses for Stephen del Kiln on his journey to Oxfordshire with a letter to summon the brothers to the election, 8s. 1d. For the expenses of Adam Cariageman on his journey to Lytham for the same reason, 3s. For expenses made for the bringing of masters John de Norton and Hugh de Fletham when they came to the election, together with the hiring of horses for them, 42s. 4d. Also for someone to kill the rats in the exchequer and the bursar's stable, 12d. Total of all expenses, £1,010 19s. 4¾ d.

Primary Sources

Extracts from the account rolls of the Abbey of Durham, Surtees Society 99, 100, 103 (with continuous pagination) (1898–1901).

Further Reading

Dobie, A. (2008) 'An analysis of the bursars' accounts at Durham Cathedral Priory', *Accounting Historians Journal* 35.2: 181–208.

D: Royal Household Expenditure: the Wardrobe Book of William de Norwell (excerpts: from f. 1 and f. 90)

Date: 1338–40.

TNA: E36/203.

Work: This excerpt is taken from the records of the Wardrobe department, which dealt with the finances of the royal household, within the Exchequer. William de

468 Fifteenth Century

Northwell (Norwell) (1311–52) was controller of this department from 1338–40. These records are some of the many documents, of various kinds, that mention William de la Pole (d. 1366), who has been called the 'greatest businessman of his time', having learnt the merchant's trade (*mercandizandi scientia*) at Ravenser Odd (according to a history of the period, *Chronicle of Meaux* 3.48), a market town on the Yorkshire coast washed away by the storms of 1356–62 and replaced by Kingston upon Hull, of which de la Pole became the first mayor. He was much involved in the export of wool, an area of business with which Chaucer was engaged during the 1370s when he worked as controller of export customs for wool at the port of London. As often happens, this account tells the reader more than might be expected: those trading and travelling could also be involved in secret business on behalf of the members of the royal family, as in the reference to Francesco Forcetti. This was a Florentine here working as the minder of someone calling himself William the Welshman who claims to be Edward II, who had supposedly died in 1327, but was now, in September 1338, apparently arranging to meet his son, Edward III, in Koblenz.[3] Mention here is made of Sluys in Flanders, the site of a naval battle between the English and the French two years later (1340): this document is written in the context of the beginning of the Hundred Years War (cf. Section II.41B).

The passage from the Wardrobe Book given here is preceded by a writ from Edward III in 1339 relating to the excerpt. The writ mentions both William de Norwell and William de la Pole and gives permission to William de Norwell to transport wool to Antwerp without paying customs.

Linguistic points: Firstly, it is necessary to think beyond the usual connotations of the word 'wardrobe' when encountering *garderoba* (*ward-*): although it could mean a small-scale place for hanging clothes, and indeed, a toilet, it was most often used in the sense of an official storeroom, and then an administrative department dealing with items of value and the royal finances. *senescalcus*, like *marescalcus* (cf. Section II.48B for *marescalcia*), is a Germanic import, also meaning some kind of officer in a household, from which English derives 'seneschal' (cf. *Fleta* 2.72 for a description of this post). *batellus* (and the related *batellarius*) is related to English 'boat' (a word with a complex etymology) and the other Germanic forms of the word for a small vessel, but BML derives the word via the French form 'batel'. *flota* ('fleet') appears in BML in the thirteenth century (e.g. *RL* 1.302 in a letter to Ralph Neville), apparently deriving its form from French 'flote', though the word also occurs in Germanic languages, as in OE 'fleot' ('boat'). *rescussus* is an intriguing word, occurring in BML from the late twelfth century: it, too, comes from a French form deriving from the prefix

---

3 For the unresolved mystery of whether Edward II in fact remained alive after his alleged death in 1327, see e.g. J. R. S. Phillips (2010) *Edward II*, New Haven, CT and Kathryn Warner (2017) *Long live the King: the mysterious fate of Edward II*, Stroud.

re- and CL *excutere*, 'to shake'; and yet it almost exclusively has the sense 'rescue', often in legal documents, with the implication of an illegal recovery of something impounded or someone arrested.

Close Roll (*Calendar of Close Rolls* (1339–41) 323) 13 Edw. III part 3 m. 2:

29 December 1339

To the collectors of customs in the port of Boston. Order to permit William de North-well, keeper of the Wardrobe, to load what remains of 100 sacks of wool in that port and take them to the staple at Antwerp in ships not ordained for the king's service, without paying the custom and subsidy, in accordance with the king's grant and a previous order, as he paid 2 marks a sack for the custom and subsidy to William de la Pole in parts beyond the sea and the king pardoned him the residue. The king has learned that the collectors have not hitherto cared to execute the order.

TEXT II.48D

Wool exports from England to the Continent and various items of the king's business
[f. 1] Liber de particulis compoti Willelmi de Northwell custodis garderobe regis Edwardi Tercii post conquestum (…) inter xi diem Julii anno regni sui xii° et xxviii diem Maii anno regni sui xiiii°. (…)
[f. 90] (1338) Magistro Roberto de Chikewell clerico misso de Andewarpia usque Gaunt in negociis regis secretis eundo, morando et redeundo per 20 dies percipienti per diem 2s. per manus proprias pro expensis suis apud Andewarpiam, xxii die Augusti, 40s. Potterwille de Brelle misso per comitem Derbeie et dominum Johannem Darcy senescallum ad premuniendum flotam regis Anglie de galeis Francie existentibus in le Swyn ex convencione per manus proprias ibidem secundo die Octobris, 10 li. Johanni de Padbury pro tot denariis per ipsum solutis pro 1 batello conducto pro sagittariis regis missis usque Ernemuth per aquam pro rescussu faciendo de navibus regis (videlicet *Cristofre*, *Cokedward* et aliis navibus ibidem postea per galeas regis Francie captis) per manus proprias apud Andewarpiam, eodem die, 43s. Domino Reginaldo de Cobham pro conductione quarundam navium per ipsum conductarum pro consimili rescussu faciendo (…) ibidem, iiij die Octobris, 31s. Claisio de Brucelles pro 1 dextrario ab eo empto ad opus regis per preceptum ipsius regis per manus domini Johannis de Molyns recipientis denarios in garderoba ibidem, v die Octobris, 162 li. 9s. (qui dextrarius liberatur dicto Johanni Brocaz qui inde respondet infra inter prestita). Willelmo de la Pole pro tot denariis per ipsum solutis 2 batellariis conductis cum batellis suis ad certificandum naves Anglie oneratas de lanis venientes versus Lesclus de capcione

470 Fifteenth Century

navium regis apud Middelburgh per manus proprias ibidem, eodem die, 21 li. 12s. (…) Domino regi ad ludendum in camera sua apud Dest per manus Guidonis Brian, xv die Octobris, 61 li. 17s. 6d. Domino Ricardo de Monchensy militi misso per regem et consilium suum usque partes Flandrie tam pro dampnis, homicidiis et aliis transgressionibus diversis de eisdem partibus per flotam regis Anglie redeundo versus Angliam perpetratis emendandis quam pro pace et concordia inter ipsum regem et gentes Flandrie reformanda pro expensis suis percipienti 10s. pro se et 3 scutiferis suis per manus proprias eodem die videlicet per 42 dies (mensibus Septembris et Octobris anno xii), 21 li. Francekino Forcet pro denariis per ipsum receptis pro expensis Willelmi Galeys in custodia sua existentis quia nominavit se regem Anglie patrem regis nunc videlicet per tres septimanas mense Decembris dicto anno xii° per manus proprias ibidem xviij die Octobris, 13s. 6d. etc.

Translation: The Wardrobe Book

[f. 1] *A book regarding the items in the account of William of Northwell, the keeper of the Wardrobe of King Edward, the third after the Conquest (…) between 11 July in the twelfth year of his reign and 28 May in the fourteenth year of his reign. (…) [f. 90] To Robert de Chikewell, clerk, sent from Antwerp to Ghent on secret business for the king, for going, staying and returning over a period of 20 days, receiving 2s. a day by his own hands for his expenses at Antwerp, 22 August, 40s. To Potterwille de Brelle sent by the Earl of Derby and Lord John Darcy, the seneschal, to warn the fleet of the king of England about the galleys of France which are in the (river) Zwyn by agreement by his own hands there on 2 October, £10. To John de Padbury for as much money paid by him for the hire of 1 boat for the king's archers sent to Yarmouth by sea to carry out the rescue of the king's ships (namely the Christopher, Cokedward and other ships captured there afterwards by the galleys of the king of France) by his own hands at Antwerp on the same day, 43s. To Lord Reginald de Cobham for the hire of certain ships hired by him for carrying out a similar rescue (…) there on 4 October, 31s. To Claisio of Brussels for 1 warhorse bought from him for the use of the king at the command of the king by the hands of Lord John de Molyns receiving money in the wardrobe there on 5 October, £162 9s. (this warhorse was delivered to John Brocaz who answers for it below among the prests). To William de la Pole for as much money paid by him for 2 ships hired with their boats to certify the ships of England laden with wool coming to L'Escluse (i.e. Sluis in Flanders) from the capture of the king's ships at Middelburg by his own hands there on the same day £21 12s. (…) To the lord king for games in his chamber at Diest by the hands of Guy Brian on 15 October, £61 17s. 6d. To Lord Richard de Monchensy, knight, sent by the king and his council to Flanders both to pay for the losses, murders and various other crimes perpetrated by the fleet of the king of England on their journey back to England from those regions, and also to restore peace and harmony between the king and the people of Flanders, receiving for his expenses 10s. for himself and for 3 shield-bearers by his own hands on the same day, namely for 42 days (in the months of September and October in the twelfth year), £21. To Francesco Forcetti for the money received through him for the expenses of William the Welshman who is in his custody because he called himself king of England and father of the present king, namely for 3 weeks in the month of December in this twelfth year by his own hands there, on 18 October, 13s. 6d.*

Primary Source and Related Texts

The Wardrobe Book of William de Norwell, 12 July 1338–27 May 1340, ed. M. Lyon, B. Lyon and H. Lucas, Brussels, 1983.

Foedera 2.705 (RC edition, 1816–69) for the year 1327, for rules about belonging to a staple, i.e. one of the towns in England or on the Continent (in these texts, Antwerp) through which wool exports had by law to pass during a predetermined period. The BML *stapula* (in the form *estapula*) occurs in a text of 1314, whereas the same term in AN ('estaple') does not occur until 1338, and in English not until 1423. The BML term therefore helps to demonstrate that there existed a regulated market at least as early as the beginning of the fourteenth century.

EHD 4.1032–3 for a 1337 exchequer account, including places to which de la Pole exported wool (from TNA: E101/457/8).

Further Reading

Brush, K. (1984) 'The *Recepta jocalium* in the Wardrobe Book of William de Norwell', *JMH* 10.4: 249–70.

Cushing, G. (2011) *Edward III and the war at sea*, Woodbridge.

Fryde, E. B. (1988) *William de la Pole, merchant and king's banker*, London.

Lloyd, T. H. (1977) *The English wool trade in the Middle Ages*, Cambridge.

Rose, S. (2013) *England's medieval navy 1066–1509: ships, men, warfare*, Barnsley.

E: An Account Entry from the Scottish Exchequer Rolls (excerpt: 2.38)

Date: 1360.

National Records of Scotland E38–44.

The medieval contents of the Scottish archives are unfortunately less numerous than they would have been had not many been lost when sent to London during

472 Fifteenth Century

the War of Independence under Edward I in the early fourteenth century, and again by Oliver Cromwell during the English Civil War in the seventeenth century: when they were finally returned to Scotland under Charles II, one of the two ships carrying them, the *Elizabeth of Bruntisland*, sank, taking a large number of documents to the bottom of the sea. Among the surviving national records of Scotland are the Exchequer Rolls of the kings of Scotland: few survive before the reign of Robert the Bruce in the early fourteenth century, but from 1327 they provide the largest body of medieval accounting material to survive in Scotland. They record the revenue coming to the king from rents, fines, wardships etc., whether in coin or in kind.

King David II (1324–71) of Scotland, the son of Robert the Bruce, was captured after the battle of Neville's Cross, just outside Durham, in 1346[4] and spent the next eleven years in comfortable captivity in England, including for a time at Odiham Castle in Hampshire, which had belonged to Eleanor, Countess of Leicester, a century earlier (cf. Section II.48B). David was released at the end of 1357 after the Treaty of Berwick agreed on a ransom of 10,000 marks to be paid to England every year for ten years. He levied this ransom by heavy taxation, while apparently negotiating with Edward III whether the debt could be written off if David named Edward or one of his sons as the heir to the throne of Scotland. In the following account entry the income will go to pay the ransom sum in the third year.

Linguistic points: This brief account contains many of the typical linguistic features of Scottish accounting methods of this period, namely the so-called 'charge' and 'discharge' account, as indicated by *receptae* and *expensae*, 'receipts' and 'expenses'. *redemptio* here has the sense of 'ransom', the payment for the release of a captive, referring to the ransom for David II. The CL *onerare* undergoes a semantic extension to mean 'to hold accountable', here as often in accounts used reflexively (cf. Section II.45D). *firma*, i.e. 'farm', in the sense of fixed rent, occurs already in the Domesday Book. *et sic eque* indicates that the books balance and nothing is still owed.

TEXT II.48E

Accounts regarding the levying of the ransom for King David II
Compotum Henrici Ker, domini Patricii de Gelchestane, capellani, et Ade Wardlaw, collectorum tercie contribucionis, pro redempcione regis ordinate, infra vicecomitatum de Roxburgh, redditum apud Perth, xxij° die Aprilis, anno supradicto, coram auditoribus predictis, de omnibus receptis suis et expensis de tota

---

4 For a rhetorical description of this battle, see the *Chronicle of Lanercost*, pp. 344–51, a work that is also a source for a description of the battle of Bannockburn (see Section II.41A).

II.48 | Royal and Ecclesiastical Accounts   473

contribucione predicta. iidem onerant se de iiij^{xx} xix li. xj s. et v d. receptis de omnibus bladis, bonis, catallis, firmis, redditibus et artificibus dicti vicecomitatus. Summa recepte patet.

Expense eorundem. In primis, allocantur computantibus pro collecta dicta contribucionis, v li. Et in liberacione facta camerario super compotum, iiij^{xx} xiiij li. xj s. et v d. de quibus respondit. Summa expense iiij^{xx} xix li. xj s. et v d. Et sic eque.

Translation: Exchequer Rolls of Scotland

The account of Henry Ker, Lord Patrick de Gelchestane, chaplain, and Adam Wardlaw, collectors of the subsidy of a third, decided upon for the king's ransom, within the sheriff's district of Roxburgh, presented at Perth, 22 April, in the above year, before the aforementioned auditors, regarding all their receipts and expenses from this whole subsidy. These same men take responsibility for £99 11s. 5d. received from all the crops, goods, possessions, fixed rents, returns and craftsmen of the said sheriff's district. The total of the amount received is shown.

The expenses of the same. Firstly £5 are allocated to those who account for the said collection of the contribution. And in the payment made to the Chamberlain on the account, £94 11s. and 5d. for which he is accountable. The total of the expenses is £99 11s. and 5d. And so it is in balance.

Primary Sources

Rotuli scaccarii regum Scotorum (The Exchequer Rolls of Scotland, 1264–1600), Edinburgh, 1878–1908.
Knighton's Chronicle (1337–1396), ed. G. Martin, OMT, Oxford, 1995: 92.

Further Reading

Dobie, A. (2012) 'Accounting in medieval Scotland to 1500', *Scottish Business and Industrial History* 27: 3–28.

Section II.49

In the Courts
The following passages are taken from some of the many types of documents that record legal disputes (tried in the king's courts, in local ones, or in those dealing with a special interest), crimes and punishments.
A: Two Entries from the Curia Regis Rolls: Alice Takes on the Bishop of Lincoln in a Property Dispute; Flemish Merchants Take Two Jewish Men to Court on a Charge of Assault and Robbery (excerpts for 1225 and 1230)
B: Ecclesiastical Suit Rolls: Litigation with Reference to Sex and Marriage (excerpts from pp. 96–102)
C: Gaol Delivery Rolls (excerpt: Channel Islands Assize Rolls, pp. 177–8)
D: The Assize of Bread (*Assisa panis*) at the Guildhall (excerpt: pp. 415–19)

A: Two Entries from the Curia Regis Rolls: Alice Takes on the Bishop of Lincoln in a Property Dispute; Flemish Merchants Take Two Jewish Men to Court on a Charge of Assault and Robbery (excerpts for 1225 and 1230)

TNA: KB 26.

A(a): Curia Regis Rolls (excerpt: 12 no. 705)

Date: 1225.

TNA: KB26/88 m.1d.

This excerpt records the case of a widow from Chiselhampton outside Oxford taking the Bishop of Lincoln, Hugh of Wells (d. 1235, not to be confused with St Hugh of Lincoln (d. 1200), to court in an attempt to receive the two pieces of land her husband gave her on her marriage, but the bishop argues that she was not properly married in the eyes of the church. He apparently is aware that the woman was only this man's mistress while he was healthy, and if they were married at home during his final illness, the bishop claims that it does not count, even if the man put a ring on Alice's finger. The case presents some complexity. Alice is well informed, and her account of the situation is convincing: the final ruling is more of a shock than a surprise. Oxfordshire was at the time part of Lincoln diocese.

Linguistic points: *suinetagium* is a spelling variant of *soignantagium*, from the AN form (suign-) of OF 'soignantage', meaning 'protection', i.e. 'concubinage', as in modern French 'soigner', 'to look after'.[1] The phrase *in misericordia* occurs repeatedly at the end of court cases, meaning that the person is liable to a fine. For *attornatum* as a 'proxy', cf. Section II.47E. *affidavit* is familiar as the name of a written statement made on oath, but here it has the sense 'to affiance', i.e. 'to pledge to marry'. The phrases *itinerans de loco in locum* and *sanus et itinerans* occur in legal texts as a formula implying that someone has recovered enough from illness or injury to be unaffected, when their physical condition affects the outcome of the trial, as here.[2]

TEXT II.49A(a)

Alice v. Bishop Hugh of Lincoln

(1225) Oxon.: Alicia que fuit uxor Jacobi de Cardunvill' petit versus H. Lincolniensem episcopum terciam partem duarum carucatarum terre cum pertinenciis in Chiselhamton' et terciam partem x virgatarum terre cum pertinenciis in Middelton' ut dotem suam, unde predictus Jacobus eam dotavit die quo eam desponsavit. et episcopus per attornatum suum venit et dicit quod non intelligit quod debeat inde dotem habere, quia ipsa nunquam fuit desponsata in facie ecclesie; set bene potest esse quod ipse affidavit eam in egritudine sua unde obiit et in domo sua. set bene scit quod dum ipse fuit sanus et itinerans, semper tenuit eam in suinetagio ut amicam suam; et petit judicium si pro tali fide data debeat ei dotem facere. et Alicia dicit quod revera fuit desponsata eidem Jacobo in domo sua in egritudine sua, ita quod ipse inposuit ei anulum digito; et postea convaluit et fuit itinerans de loco in locum; et dicit quod desponsalia denunciata fuerunt ad tres vicinas ecclesias per tres Dominicas antequam eam desponsavit; et eam predicto modo in domo sua desponsavit in crastino sancti Georgii; et obiit postea in die Nativitatis sancti Johannis Baptiste. et petit judicium similiter si debeat dotem habere vel non. et quia ipsa cognoscit quod non fuit desponsata ad hostium ecclesie nec ibi dotata, consideratum est quod episcopus inde sit quietus; et Alicia in misericordia; et nullum inde dotem habeat, eo quod fidem quam inde Jacobus dedit fecit pro salute anime sue et pro periculo mortis.

---

1 Cf. *soignanta* (concubine) in *CurR* 1.100 (sp. *sunianta*) from 1199.

2 Cf. F. Maitland (ed.) (1884) *Pleas of the Crown for the county of Gloucester (1221)*, London, nos. 21 and 99.

476 Fifteenth Century

Translation: Curia Regis Rolls

(1225) Alice who was the wife of Jacob de Cardunvill makes a claim against H(ugh) the Bishop of Lincoln for a third part of two carucates of land with appurtenances in Chiselhampton and a third part of 10 virgates of land with appurtenances in Milton as her dower, which the said Jacob gave her as a dower on the day when he married her. The bishop, by means of his attorney, comes and says that he does not recognise that she should have a dower from this, because she was never married in the eyes of the Church; but it may well be that he pledged to marry her during the illness from which he died and in his house. But the bishop knows well that while Jacob was healthy and travelling around, he always kept her as his mistress; and the bishop seeks judgement as to whether he should give her a dower for such a betrothal. Alice says that she did indeed marry this Jacob in her house during his illness in such a way that he placed a ring on her finger; and afterwards he recovered and travelled around from place to place; and she says that the marriage was announced in three neighbouring churches on three Sundays before he married her; and he married her in the manner mentioned on the day after St George's Day; and he died later on the day of the Nativity of St John the Baptist. She seeks judgement similarly as to whether she should have the dower or not. And because Alice acknowledges that she was not married at the door of the church and not given a dower there, it has been decided that the bishop is quit of this; and Alice is liable to a fine; and she should not have a dower because the troth that Jacob gave her, he did for the salvation of his soul and when he was in danger of death.

A(b): Curia Regis Rolls (excerpt: 14 no. 1027)

Date: 1230.

TNA: KB26/107 m.32.

The following excerpt from the Curia Regis Rolls tells of an encounter between two Flemish merchants and three Jews in London who get into a dispute about the payment for a goblet, leading to a brawl. A court case ensues to establish the truth of what happened, and the result is that two of the Jews go into exile. The episode sheds light on a part of Jewish society in thirteenth-century England which is less evident in the documents of the time.

Linguistic points: *transitum facere* means 'to pass through', possibly with some sense of 'to cut through, take a short cut' (cf. Section II.49B). *felonia* is much used in BML, but its etymology is unclear: Latin and Romance, Germanic and Celtic origins have been suggested. *cifus* is a common spelling of CL *sciphus* from Greek, presumably giving some indication of how it was pronounced (cf. Section II.12

for the spelling *ciphus*). There appears to be confusion about the word *murra*, which does not occur in BML until the late thirteenth century; it is related to the adjective *murrinus*, which is attested earlier in BML. *murra* may be regarded as a synonym of *masera*, i.e. a 'cup of maple wood', by confusion with CL *murra* (not to be confused with a spelling variant of *myrrha* ('myrrh')), which seems to mean a kind of decorative glassware, often used for goblets. *falsonarius* (AN 'fausener') is attested in the *Laws of Henry I* (cf. Section II.10B), where the forger is accorded a brutal punishment. *gurlus* is related to 'girdle' (OE 'gyrdel'), but based on the AN form 'gurle', meaning a 'money-belt' or 'purse'. *uthesium* or *hutesium* derives from ME 'uthes', surviving in modern English in the reduced form 'hue (and cry)', the phrase used of the outcry raised to start the pursuit of a criminal when a crime is committed. *manucapere* (attested in CL as a past participle) bursts forth suddenly in BML from the late twelfth century, as a useful word in a number of legal contexts (cf. Section II.47E). The phrase *ponere in respectum* is legal jargon for 'to adjourn'. *defendere* often means 'to deny', as here: the Jews are denying the charge of breach of the peace. Note the use of the pluperfect subjunctive after *quod* in reported speech.

TEXT II.49A(b)

Two Flemish merchants v. two Jews of Northampton
London: Hugo de Erdeburg mercator Flandr' queritur de Deodato de Norhamt' Judeo et Bonefey de Bed' filio Joscei et Jacobo de Norhamt' quod ipse die Martis proxima ante festum sancti Andree circa horam vespertinam simul cum Boydino Flandrensi socio suo transitum fecisset per Judaismum in redeundo de domo Stephani de Bomine, cui reddidisse debuit denarios pro j sacco lane, et idem Deodatus tulisset in manu sua unum cifum de murra ad vendendum, tandem convenit inter eos quod cifum haberet pro xij denariis; et intravit in domum illius Judei ad solvendum denarios illos et eos reddidisset eidem Judeo. ipse Judeus calumniavit denarios illos esse falsos et dicebat ipsum esse falsonarium; et ipsi (sic) ei respondit ei (sic) quod denarii illi erant boni, et si boni non essent, libenter daret ei alios. et cum extraxisset quemdam gurlum in quo fuerunt xj marce et xl denarii, quo gurlo viso ipse Deodatus statim cepit eum per gulam; et Bonefey cepit denarios illos et cum toto gurlo et posuit illos in sinum suum. et Jacobus de Norhamt' cepit pollicem suum in ore suo, ita quod eum fere abcidit cum dentibus suis. et Deodatus eum strangulasset nisi ei succureretur ad clamorem predicti Boydini socii sui, ad cujus clamorem venerunt Galfridus le Especer et Willelmus de Norf' et Ascerus Clericus et alii tam Christiani quam Judei plusquam centum, inter quos fuit Hugo serviens de Judaismo et Petrus serviens de recepta, qui testantur quod invenerunt denarios sparsos per herbarium; et Hugo dicit quod invenit sanguinem effusum circa plenam pugnatam. et quando illi supervenerunt, fugerunt

478 Fifteenth Century

ipsi Judei et asportaverunt omnes denarios preter lxiiij solidos et iiij denarios qui inventi fuerunt in herbario et qui postea traditi fuerunt constabulario ad custodiendum. et quod hoc fecerunt nequiter etc. et Deodatus et alii Judei veniunt et defendunt pacem domini regis infractam et feloniam et roberiam et quicquid est contra pacem domini regis et totum; et inde ponunt se super veredictum Judeorum et Christianorum. et dicunt quod revera ita convenit inter eos de cipho illo emendo pro xij denariis et quod duxerunt eundem Hugonem per mediam domum usque ad in curiam ubi solvere debuit denarios. et quia invenerunt denarios illos falsos, retinuerunt eundem Hugonem et miserunt propter Galfridum le Spicer servientem domini regis per filium ipsius Deodati.

et Galfridus, requisitus si venisset ad mandatum ipsorum, dicit quod non, sed ad clamorem et uthesium. et recognitum est per visnetum proximum quod isti Judei venerunt ad clamorem, scilicet Benedictus le Evesk', Elia filius ejus, Jacobus frater ejus Pictaviensis, filius Benedicti, Vyves frater Aron, Abraham filius Murielle Aron Pinche, qui venerunt coram justiciariis. et Josceus Presbiter secundum consuetudinem et morem legis sue, assumptis secum x Judeis, excommunicavit omnes istos qui veritatem celarent vel falsum dicerent. postea veniunt Judei in communi et offerunt domino regi lx marcas argenti quod judicium ponatur in respectum usque ad adventum domini regis apud Lond' (...) et tota communa Judeorum hoc manucapit. et Deodatus et Bonenfaunt custodiantur; et Jacobus sit sub plegiis. postea offerunt c marcas per sic quod ipsi duo possint abjurare regnum.[3]

Translation: Curia Regis Rolls

London: Hugo de Erdeburg, a merchant from Flanders, accuses Deodatus, a Jew of Northampton, and Bonefey of Bedford, the son of Josce, and Jacob of Northampton, on the grounds that on the Tuesday just before the feast of St Andrew, around evening, he was passing through the Jewish quarter together with Boydin his colleague from Flanders on their way back from Lord Stephen de Bomine, to whom he had had to give money for a sack of wool, and this Deodatus was carrying in his hand a goblet of (?)maple wood to sell, and at last they agreed that he (Hugo) could have the goblet for 12d.; and he went into this Jew's house to pay the money and when he had given it to this Jew, the Jew claimed that the money was counterfeit and said that he was a counterfeiter; and he replied that the money was genuine and if it was not genuine, he would willingly give him some other money. And when he had pulled out a purse in which there were 11 marks and 40 pence, when Deodatus saw the purse he immediately took him by the throat and Bonefey took the money and the whole purse and put them in his pocket. And Jacob of Northampton put Hugo's

---

3   Cf. *Fleta* 1.29 on the correct procedure for abjuring the realm.

thumb in his mouth and almost bit it off. And Deodatus would have strangled him if help had not been forthcoming as the result of the shouts of Boydin his colleague, at whose shouts Geoffrey the spice-dealer and William of Norfolk and Ascer the clerk and more than 100 others, both Jews and Christians, including Hugh the sergeant of the Jewish quarter and Peter, sergeant of the Receipt, who testify that they found the money scattered around the garden. And Hugh says that he found blood spilled all over the whole handful. And when they arrived, the Jews fled and took with them all the money except 64s. and 4d. which were found in the garden and which were afterwards handed over to the constable for safekeeping. And that they did this wickedly etc. Deodatus and the other Jews come and deny that the lord king's peace has been broken, and deny felony and robbery and whatever is against the lord king's peace and everything; and they agree to accept the verdict of the Jews and Christians. And they say that in truth they did agree about buying the goblet for 12d. and that they led Hugh through the middle of the house right into the hall where he was supposed to pay the money. But because they found the money was counterfeit, they detained Hugh and sent Deodatus' son for Geoffrey the spice-dealer, the king's sergeant.

Geoffrey, questioned as to whether he had come at their request, said that he had not, but at the hue and cry. And it was acknowledged by the next neighbourhood jury that these Jews came at the cry, namely Benedict l'Evesk, Elia his son, Elia's brother Jacob of Poitiers, son of Benedict, Vyves, Aaron's brother, Abraham son of Muriella, and Aaron Pinche, who came before the justices. And Josce the Priest, according to the custom and ways of his law, brought with him ten Jews and excommunicated any who concealed the truth or told lies. Afterwards the Jews came as a group and offered the lord king 60 marks of silver to adjourn the verdict until the arrival of the lord king in London. (…) The whole community of the Jews guarantee this payment. Deodatus and Bonenfaunt should be kept in custody; and Jacob should be released on bail. Afterwards the Jewish community offers 100 marks to allow these two (Jews) to go into exile.

Primary Source

*Curia Regis Rolls.

Further Reading

Walker, S. S. (1993) 'Litigation as personal quest: suing for dower in the royal courts, circa 1272–1350' in *Walker (1993).

Lipman, V. (1962) 'The anatomy of medieval Anglo-Jewry', *Transactions of the Jewish Historical Society of England* 21: 64–77.

480 Fifteenth Century

B: Ecclesiastical Suit Rolls: Litigation with Reference to Sex and Marriage (excerpts from pp. 96–102)

Date: 1269–71.

Canterbury Cathedral Archives: CCA DCc/ES Rolls.

The Ecclesiastical Suit Rolls are the earliest surviving church court records, going back to 1200, and mostly dealing with tithes, disputes over presentations to churches, and marriages. These rolls record an interesting practice within canon law known as *abjuratio sub poena nubendi*. It meant that a man and woman caught in fornication could be taken to court and made to contract a conditional marriage, each party stating, 'If I know you carnally from now on, you will be my lawful wife/husband.'[4] If they then had sex, they were automatically married. This was an attempt to stop people living together without being married and to enforce marriage rather than casual relationships. The problems with this 'solution' were that there were difficulties of proof and of enforcement. It was gradually abandoned because using marriage as a punishment was not consistent with the principle of consent in Christian marriage. The two passages below (relating to one case) record the witness statements of ordinary people containing information about everyday life, no doubt in translation into Latin from the vernacular.

In the case of Johanna de Clapton against Richard de Bosco, the trial took place first in the consistory court at Salisbury, where Johanna states that Richard had abjured further intercourse *sub pena nubendi*; however, he later had sex with her, and she asks the court to rule that as a result he is her husband, presumably because she wishes to claim certain conjugal rights. Richard admits the abjuration but denies that he had sex with her and presents other impediments to their marriage. Witnesses are called, including a husband and wife apparently supporting opposing sides. It would seem that Richard later appealed to the court at Canterbury, where the original sentence was upheld and Richard adjudged to be the husband of Johanna.

Linguistic points: One might note the rather unwieldy way of referring to a past date, common in legal texts, complicated by the fact that *proximus* in time phrases can mean both 'immediately preceding' and 'immediately following'. *crofta*, from OE 'croft', referring to a small piece of land on which a house was built, is another example of a word borrowed from the vernacular that can be found as

---

4 Cf. *Statutes of Salisbury* (1238–44) [53] in *Councils and Synods* (1964): *promitto tibi quod si te de cetero carnaliter cognovero, te tamqam in uxorem meam legitimam … consentio* ('I promise you that if in future I have sex with you, I will acknowledge you as my legitimate wife').

masculine, feminine or neuter. *cervisia* has a transferred sense as an 'ale', i.e. a social gathering at which ale-drinking occurs, and here it seems to be used as a synonym for *taberna*: *cervisia* is a not uncommon word in the records of court cases. *requirere* occurs frequently in the sense of 'to question' in a legal context, as in Section II.39 in the past participle form *requisitus*. *bluettus* ('blue') is a different spelling of *blodius* (cf. Section II.35). For *in victu et vestitu* one may note that the similar phrase *pro victu et vestitu* occurs frequently in wills. *sicut* here is used in a temporal sense, i.e. 'just at the moment when', as not infrequently in similar legal contexts, as if it were the English 'just as'. The rare word *mireleve*, i.e. AN 'mirelevé', was formed from *medium relevium* to mean 'mid-afternoon': cf. *inter horam que vocatus* (?l. *vocatur*) *Gallice 'mireleve' et horam vespertinam* (p. 104) for an awareness of its linguistic provenance.

TEXT II.49B(a)

Alicia, called on behalf of Johanna, is interrogated
[p. 98] Alicia uxor Nicholai de Clopton iurata et diligenter examinata dicit quod a die natalis Domini proximo preterito fuit unus annus elapsus in tres septimanas transitum fecit per croftum Ricardi Byssewode contra horam cubandi ubi vidit Ricardum de quo agitur et [p. 99] Johannam de qua agitur carnaliter commiscentes. requisita qualiter hoc vidit cum nox esset, dicit quod per lumen stellarum et per nivem. requisita an habebat colloquium cum eis, dicit quod non. requisita qualiter scit quod ipsi fuerunt cum non haberet colloquium cum eis, dicit scit quia scit. requisita quo die fuit dies natalis Domini eo anno, dicit quod die martis ut credit. requisita qua de causa fecit ibi transitum circa illam horam, dicit quod venit de le Karferd de cervisia. requisita qualiter scit quod carnaliter commiscuerunt, dicit quod vidit virum jacentem supra mulierem. requisita versus quam partem versa fuerunt capita eorum vel pedes, dicit quod nescit nec versus quam partem jacuerunt pedes ipsorum. requisita si alii hoc viderunt una cum ea, dicit quod sic, Johanna filia Alicie Helte et nullus alius. requisita ob quam causam venit ibi dicta Johanna, dicit quod venit una secum de taberna. requisita utrum luna lucebat eo tempore, dicit quod non, sed clarum erat tempus et minute stelle lucebant. (…)

Translation: Ecclesiastical Suit Rolls

Alice the wife of Nicholas of Clopton, under oath and carefully examined, says that from last Christmas Day one year has passed in three weeks since she was passing through the croft of Richard Byssewode around bedtime when she saw Richard, the man concerned, having sex with Johanna, the woman concerned. When asked how

482 Fifteenth Century

she saw this when it was night, she says that she did so by the light of the stars and the snow. Asked whether she had a conversation with them, she said no. Asked how she knows that it was them when she did not converse with them, she says that she knows because she knows. Asked on what day Christmas Day was that year, she says that she thinks it was a Tuesday. Questioned as to why she was passing at that hour, she says that she came from le Karferd from the drinking session. Questioned as to how she knew they were having sex, she says that she saw the man lying on the woman. Asked in which direction their heads and feet were turned, she says she does not know, nor where their feet were lying. Asked if others saw this with her, she says that yes, Johanna daughter of Alice Helte did and no one else. Asked why this Johanna came there, she says that she came with her from the pub. Asked whether the moon was shining at that time, she says that it was not, but the weather was clear and the tiny stars were shining. (…)

Richard had claimed in his defence that he could not be regarded as Johanna's husband because he had sex with a relative of Johanna named Matilda, this being an accepted impediment to marriage. A witness, namely the husband of the previous witness, is interrogated on behalf of Richard:

TEXT II.49B(b)

Nicholas, called on behalf of Richard, is interrogated

[p. 101] Nicholaus piscator de Clopton iuratus et diligenter examinatus, requisitus utrum Ricardus de Clopton cognoverit Matillidam Aldred carnaliter, dicit quod sic. requisitus qualiter hoc scit, dicit quod vidit ipsos carnaliter commiscentes sicut fuit versus domum Osmundi le Tanerius et dicit quod vidit dictum Ricardum jacentem inter crura Matilde prenominate, braccis predicti R. depositis, vestibus etiam mulieris levatis usque ad zonam; dicit etiam quod vidit membrum viri in membro mulieris et fecit cum ipsa sicut vir facit cum muliere. requisitus quando ipsum carnaliter cognoverit, dicit quod proxima die dominica ante pentecosten proximo venturam erunt decem anni elapsi. requisitus qualiter recolit quod tantum tempus est elapsum, dicit per hoc quod retulit patri suo quando venit de cervisia quod vidit ipsos carnaliter commiscentes et pater suus computavit annos. requisitus ubi eam carnaliter cognovit, dicit quod in crofto Rogeri Byssewode in parte occidentali crofti cito post horam qua (?l. que) vocatur 'mireleve' et dicit quod vir induebatur russeto et mulier supertunica de blueto et tunica rubea; dicit quod croftum non fuit tunc seminatum et quod tempus fuit clarum sole lucente, et dicit quod post illud factum vir fuit versus occidentem, mulier vero versus orientem. dicit etiam quod predictus R. suscitavit puellum ex dicta M., puerum masculum quem pro suo tenuit. requisitus qualiter hoc scit, dicit quia ministravit sibi neccessaria tanquam filio suo in victu et vestitu, et puer fuit nutritus aliquando in domo patris predicti R. et aliquando cum matre sua Matillida. requisitus utrum esset instructus vel conductus ad perhibendum testimonium, dicit quod non. requisitus de fama sui contestis, dicit quod est bone fame.

Translation: Ecclesiastical Suit Rolls

Nicholas, a fisherman from Clopton, on oath and carefully examined, questioned as to whether Richard of Clopton had sex with Matilda Aldred, says yes. Asked how he knows this, he says that he saw them having sex just as he was on his way to the house of Osmund the tanner and he says he saw this Richard lying between the legs of this Matilda, with Richard's trousers pulled down and the woman's clothes pulled up as far as the belt; he says, too, that he saw the man's member in the woman's member and he was doing with her what a man does with a woman. Questioned as to when Richard had sex with her, Nicholas says that it was on the Sunday just before Pentecost, and at the next Pentecost it will be ten years ago. Asked how he remembers how much time has elapsed, he says that he does so because he told his father when he came from the drinking session that he saw them having sex, and his father reckoned the years. Asked where Richard had sex with her, Nicholas says that it was in the croft of Roger Byssewode, in the west part of the croft soon after the hour which is called 'mireleve' (mid-afternoon) and he says that the man was wearing russet cloth and the woman had a blue overtunic and a red tunic; he says that the croft was not sown at the time and that the weather was clear and the sun was shining, and he says that after this was done the man went off to the west and the woman to the east. He says also that this R. raised the child born of this Matilda, a boy child whom he regarded as his own. Asked how he knows this, Nicholas says that Richard gave the boy the clothes and food he needed as if he were his own son and the child was sometimes brought up in the home of his father, this man R., and sometimes with his mother Matilda. Questioned as to whether he was instructed and brought along to give testimony, Nicholas says that he was not. Asked about the reputation of his fellow witness, he says that he is a person of good reputation.

Primary Sources and Related Texts

Select cases from the ecclesiastical courts of the province of Canterbury c.1200–1301, Selden Society 95 (1981) 96–102.

Further Reading

Helmholz, R. (1974) *Marriage litigation in medieval England*, Cambridge.
Karras, R. (1992) 'The Latin vocabulary of illicit sex in English ecclesiastical court records', *JML* 2: 1–17.

484 Fifteenth Century

C: Gaol Delivery Rolls (excerpt: Channel Islands Assize Rolls, pp. 177–8)

Date: 1309.

TNA: JUST 1/1161 m. 20d.

Work: This Gaol Delivery Roll is for the parish of Peter-in-the-Wood, Guernsey, one of the Channel Islands: it lists the names of prisoners, the charge for which they have been imprisoned to await trial, and then the verdict once they are brought to trial before the itinerant judges sent from London. This was part of the process whereby a gaol was cleared (which is an early sense of the verb 'to deliver' (*OED s.v.* deliver v. 1, sense 2c), deriving from the LL *deliberare*) of prisoners by bringing them to trial and either condemning or (as with the prisoners listed below) acquitting them. Gaol Delivery Rolls (which exist for the years 1271–1486) are usually found in the National Archives series JUST 3, but here it is actually an Assize Roll (JUST 1) that contains gaol delivery information. The abbreviations in the printed text have here been expanded.

Linguistic points: The text is formulaic, as in many legal documents. With regard to spelling, c and t are interchangeable, as is clear from *furcum* for *furtum* and *lutrum* for *lucrum*. *rectatus* is a form of *rettare*, which is (confusingly) a spelling that occurs in four different BML verbs: this is the *rettare* deriving from CL *reputare* by way of AN 'ret(t)er', meaning 'to accuse'. 'To ret' in this sense is one of the many words unable to transition from ME to modern English. *dedicere* ('to deny or refuse') is a useful word that first appears in BML in about 1200, mostly in legal texts; it does not appear in CL, though *dedicare* ('to dedicate') of course does. *garba* is a LL word deriving from a Germanic word meaning a 'sheaf',[5] which passes into modern French 'gerbe' but leaves only a light linguistic footprint on English (cf. *OED s.v.* garb n. 1). *burgiare* is associated with AN 'burgier', meaning 'to burgle', while *accabliare*, 'to knock over', is associated with OF 'achaabler'. *malecredere* occurs frequently in the records of court cases, applied to a person who is suspected of wrongdoing. *defendere* develops a long list of mainly legal senses: here it means 'to deny', for which *dedicere* is here a synonym. The odd phrase *ponere se super patriam* is another legal usage, meaning 'to submit one's case to a jury'. *wreccum* derives, via a French form, from an Old Norse word, and means

---

5 *garba* appears as a gloss on the CL *manipulus* in the Reichenau Glossary, compiled in northern France in the eighth century: W. Klein (ed.) (1968–72) *Die Reichenauer Glossen*, 2 vols, Munich. This is a fascinating series of Latin words, often of Gallo-Romance and Frankish origin, explaining the Latin of Jerome's translation of the Bible. Many of the glosses are in forms that survive in French, Italian and Spanish.

anything washed up on shore (as here) or the right of the king to claim this, or the duty of others to hand it over. Note the Channel Island variation on *abjurare regnum*, for which cf. Section II.49A(b). The repeated *etc.* after *defendit totum* probably stands for the phrase *de verbo in verbum*, meaning 'categorically' in the context of the defendant's denial.

TEXT II.49C

A list of prisoners, their supposed crimes and the outcome of their trial
[p. 177] Johannes de la Mare rectatus quod furatus fuit garbas et alia bona Roberti de Gorrys venit et defendit totum etc. et de bono et malo ponit se super patriam. et Radulphus Ledevin rectatus de eo quod furatus supertunicam suam propriam inponendo maliciose furtum illud Stephano le Jovene fideli homini ut sic faciet ipsum suspendi, venit et dedicit totum etc. et de bono et malo ponit se super patriam. et Johannes Adam rectatus quod burgiavit domum Radulphi Adam et inde furatus pannos et alia bona ipsius Radulphi venit et dedicit totum etc. et de bono et malo ponit se super patriam. et Radulphus Adam et Robertus Adam rectati quod ipsi ceperunt predictum Johannem Adam in domo ipsius Radulphi furantem bona ibidem et quod ipsum tenuerunt per totam noctem et postea promiserunt abire. veniunt et dedicunt totum etc. et de bono et malo ponunt se super patriam. et Johannes Payen rectatus de eo quod est communis latro de multonibus, garbis et de j quadrigata wrecci venit et defendit totum etc. et de bono et malo ponit se super patriam. [p. 178] (…) et Ricardus Marche rectatus quod receptavit Guillermum Renouf postquam abjuravit insulas et quod furatus fuit unum monile argenteum de Johanne de Kemyno venit et defendit totum etc. et de bono et malo ponit se super patriam. et Oliverus Belassegium rectatus de furto j porci et de aliis latrociniis venit et defendit totum etc. et de bono et malo ponit se super patriam. et Ricardus le Rey et Guillermus frater ejus rectati quod sunt conspiratores et falsi testes communiter pro lutro (i.e. lucro) habendo et eciam quod sunt latrones de filo quod eis venit ad opus textrinum veniunt et defendunt totum etc. et de bono et malo ponunt se super patriam. juratores dicunt super sacramentum suum quod praedicti Johannes, Radulphus (a further ten names of the jury members are given) (…) non sunt inde culpabiles nec de aliis malefactis malecreditur. ideo sint quieti.

Guillermus filius Symonis May et Guillermus Durel rectati de eo quod robbiaverunt filiam Canse de una supertunica, j lintheamine, j pecia tele linee et lana et aliis bonis suis veniunt et defendunt totum etc. et de bono et malo ponunt se super patriam. juratores dicunt super sacramentum suum quod predicti Guillermus et Guillermus non sunt inde culpabiles. ideo quieti sint. Jordan Thoroude rectatus de eo quod verberavit Helenam uxorem Guillermi Restaud et eam acabliavit ad terram propter quod eadem Helena cito postea obiit, venit et defendit omnem feloniam et totum etc. et de bono et malo ponit se super patriam. juratores dicunt per sacramentum suum quod predictus Jordanes in nullo est inde culpabilis. ideo sit quietus.

Translation: Gaol Delivery Rolls

Johannes de la Mare, accused of stealing sheaves and other things belonging to Robert de Gorrys, comes and denies everything etc. and for good and ill he submits his case to the jury. And Ralph Ledevin, accused of stealing his (own) overtunic, maliciously blaming the theft on Stephen le Jovene, a trustworthy man, so that he would thus get him hanged, comes and denies everything etc. and for good and ill he submits his case to the jury. And John Adam, accused of burgling the home of Ralph Adam and stealing from there cloths and other things belonging to Ralph, comes and denies everything etc. and for good and ill he submits his case to the jury. And Ralph Adam and Robert Adam are accused of catching this John Adam in Ralph's home stealing goods there and of holding him all night, and of afterwards promising to go away. They come and deny everything etc. and for good and ill submit their case to the jury. And John Payen, accused of being a common thief of sheep, sheaves and one wagonload of wrecked goods, comes and denies everything and for good and ill he submits his case to the jury. (…) And Richard Marche, accused of harbouring William Renouf after he abjured the islands and of stealing a silver necklace from John de Kemyno, comes and denies everything etc. and for good and ill he submits his case to the jury. And Oliver Belassegium, accused of the theft of one pig and of other thefts, comes and denies everything etc. and for good and ill he submits his case to the jury. And Richard le Rey and his brother William, accused of being conspirators and false witnesses jointly to make a profit and also because they are thieves of thread which came to them for the purpose of weaving, come and deny everything etc. and for good and ill they submit their case to the jury. The jurors say on oath that John, Ralph etc. are not guilty of these things and are not suspected of the other crimes. And so they are cleared.

William, son of Simon May, and William Durel, accused of robbing the daughter of Canse of an overtunic, one linen cloth, a piece of linen cloth and wool and other things belonging to her, come and deny everything and for good and ill they submit their case to the jury. The jurors say on oath that William and William are not guilty of these things. And so they are cleared. Jordan Thoroude, accused of beating Helena the wife of William Restaud and knocking her to the ground, as a result of which Helena died soon after, comes and denies all felony and everything etc. and for good and ill he submits his case to the jury. The jurors say on oath that Jordan is in no way guilty of this. And so he is cleared.

Primary Sources and Related Texts

Rolls of the Assizes held in the Channel Islands (1309), Société jersiaise 18, 1903: 177–8.

Further Reading

Lemprière, R. (1974) *The history of the Channel Islands*, repr. London, 1980.

D: The Assize of Bread (*Assisa panis*) at the Guildhall (excerpt: pp. 415–19)

This text is one of several documenting the investigation by the mayor, six aldermen and a sheriff of London into fraudulent activity by certain bakers, including women. The comedy of the elaborate description of their ingenious trick – and its punishment – is at odds with the serious and legalistic manner in which it is recounted. There had been attempts to impose standards for the weight and price of bread from Anglo-Saxon times, and in the mid-thirteenth century a statute, *Assisa panis et cervisiae*, was published. Criticism of fraudulent bakers and brewers is found in various English literary texts of the time: indeed, see also Section II.46A for municipal regulations regarding women selling ale and bread in Newcastle in the early twelfth century.

Date: 1320s.

The surviving documents relating to the series of Assizes of Bread held in London are preserved in the London Metropolitan Archives.

Linguistic points: Here *assisa* (cf. Section II.47E) signifies the regulations governing the quality and price of bread. *piloria* ('pillory'), as a device for punishment, first surfaces in BML around 1190: like *pilarius* ('pillar'), it derives ultimately from CL *pīla*, while the other word for 'pillory', *collistrigium*, is a neologism attested from the late thirteenth century and based on CL *collum* and *stringere*. *wikettum*, a small gate, occurs first around the same time, clearly associated with the AN form 'wiket' (rather than the Old, and modern, French form, 'guichet'). *claviger* here has the sense of 'mace-bearer', from the CL for 'one who bears a club' (like Hercules), rather than that of 'bearer of keys', often used in an ecclesiastical sense. The appearance of the vernacular *coppewebbe* is interesting, this being the earliest evidence for the word 'cobweb', from the OE word for a spider. The other

488   Fifteenth Century

vernacular word here is *moldingborde*, added to specify the kind of table in question, i.e. a baker's kneading board.

TEXT II.49D

[p. 415] Johannes de Strode, pistor, habuit judicium piloriae die Veneris proxima post Festum Sancti Dunstani anno regni Regis Edwardi, filii regis Edwardi xvi°, eo quod panis predicti Johannis erat nullius generis bladi sed collectio domus in qua bultavit quando domus erat mundata; et omnis putredo et spuria posita et pistata ita quod in fractione panis nihil substantiae panis apparebat, sed fila de *coppewebbes*. per quod adjudicatum fuit (...) [p. 416] quod haberet judicium piloriae. (...) congregatio facta (...) apud Gyhaldam die Jovis in ebdomada Pentecostes, videlicet iiij^to die Junii, anno Domini mcccxxvii et regni regis Edwardi tertii, post conquestum, primo. Johannes Brid, pistor, attachiatus fuit ad respondendum super quibusdam falsitate, malitia et deceptione per ipsum factis ad nocumentum communis populi; secundum quod datum fuit intelligi majori, aldermannis et vicecomitibus civitatis, videlicet quod idem Johannes, pro singulari commodo sibi ipsi falso et malitiose adquirendo, quoddam foramen super quamdam tabulam suam, quae vocatur *moldingborde*, ad pistrinam pertinentem, prudenter artificioseque fieri fecit, ad modum muscipulae in qua mures capiuntur, cum quodam wyketto caute proviso ad foramen illud obturandum et aperiendum. et cum vicini sui et alii qui ad furnum suum panem solebant furniare, veniebant cum pasto suo vel materia ad panem inde faciendum apta, dictus Johannes illud pastum sive illam materiam super dictam tabulam vocatam *moldingborde*, ut praedictum est, et ultra foramen praenotatum, ponebat, ad panes exinde ad furniendum praeparandos; et cum ille pastus, sive materia, sic positus esset super tabulam praedictam, habuit idem Johannes quemdam de familia sua, ad hoc assignatum, [p. 417] sedentem occulte sub eadem tabula; qui quidem famulus suus, sub illo foramine sedens, illudque caute aperiens, particulatim et minutatim de pasto praedicto subtiliter extraxit, magnas quantitates de hujusmodi pasto frequenter colligendo, falso, nequiter et malitiose, ad magnum damnum omnium vicinorum et proximorum suorum ac aliorum, cum tali pasto furniando ad se venientium, et in scandalum et dedecus totius Civitatis, et praecipue Majoris et Ballivorum ad assisas Civitatis custodiendas assignatorum. quod quidem foramen, in tabula sua praedicta inventum, fuit prudenter operatum; et similiter, magna quantitas de hujusmodi pasto sub foramine praedicto et per illud foramen extracta, erat inventa et per Willelmum de Hertynte, clavigerum, et Thomam de Morle, clerici Ricardi de Rothinge, unius Vicecomitum Civitatis praedictae, juratos, qui materiam praedictam sive pastum sic in loco praedicto suspecto invenerunt, hic in curia erat portata. (...) [p. 419] et habito

?l. spurca
or spurcitia

consilio et tractatu inter Majorem et Aldermannos ad judicium super falsitate, malitia et deceptione praedictis formandum. (…) concordatum est et ordinatum quod omnes illi de praedictis pistoribus sub quorum tabulis cum foraminibus pastum inventum fuit, ponantur super collistrigium cum quadam quantitate illius pasti pendente circa collum suum; (…) et quod morentur super collistrigium quousque Vesperae apud Sanctum Paulum Londoniarum percantentur.

Translation: *Munimenta Gildhallae Londoniensis*

John de Strode, baker, was sentenced to the pillory on the Friday just after the feast of St Dunstan in the sixteenth year of the reign of King Edward, the son of King Edward, because John's bread was not made of any kind of wheat but was made of what was collected up in the place where he sifted when that place was cleaned, and all the mouldy and dirty bits collected there were put in the bread and baked, so that when the bread was torn apart it did not look like bread at all but strands of cobwebs. As a result it was judged (…) that he should be sentenced to the pillory. (…) A meeting took place (…) at the Guildhall on the Thursday in the week of Pentecost, namely 4 June, in the year of the Lord 1327 and the first year of King Edward the third after the Conquest. John Bird, baker, was bound by pledge to answer to certain things he had done falsely, maliciously and deceitfully to the harm of the common people; according to what was given to the mayor, aldermen and sheriffs of the city to understand, namely that this John, in order to gain special benefits for himself falsely and maliciously, had cleverly and skilfully made a narrow hole in one of his tables which is called a moulding-board, used for baking, cunningly fitted with a wicket to open and shut the hole in the manner of a mouse trap in which mice are caught. And when his neighbours and others who used to bake their bread in his oven came with their dough or the ingredients for making bread, this John put the dough or those ingredients on the said table called a moulding-board, as was mentioned, on top of the hole, to prepare the bread for baking. And when that dough or the ingredients had been placed on the table, John arranged for one of his servants, whom he had assigned to this task, to sit hidden under the table; this servant, sitting under the hole and opening it cautiously, delicately pulled out small bits of the dough, bit by bit, often collecting large quantities of this kind of dough, dishonestly, wickedly and maliciously, to the great loss of all his neighbours and friends and others who came to him to bake their dough, and thus causing the whole city scandal and dishonour, and particularly the mayor and the bailiffs assigned to protect the City regulations. This hole, found in his table, was deliberately operated; and likewise a great quantity of dough extracted underneath this hole, through this hole, was discovered and was carried here to the court by William de Hertynte, mace-bearer, and Thomas de Morle, jurors of the clerk Richard de Rothinge, sheriff

490 Fifteenth Century

of this city, who found this matter or dough in the place under suspicion. (…) and after consideration and a discussion between the mayor and aldermen regarding the formulation of the sentence for this dishonesty, malice and deceit, (…) it was agreed and decided that all those bakers under whose tables dough and holes were found, should be put in the pillory with a quantity of that dough hanging round their neck (…) and that they should remain in the pillory until the chanting of Vespers at St Paul's in London was finished.

Primary Source

Munimenta Gildhallae Londoniensis: excerpts from the *Assisa panis*, RS 12.3 (1862) appendix 1, 411–29.

Further Reading

Davis, J. (2004), 'Baking for the common good: a reassessment of the Assize of Bread in medieval England', *Economic History Review* 57.3: 465–502.

Kernan, S. Peters (2014) 'From the bakehouse to the courthouse: bakers, baking and the Assize of Bread in late medieval England', *Food and History* 12.2: 139–78.

Section II.50

Safeguarding, Accidents and Death
A: The Bishops' Safeguarding Advice for Mothers and Babies: Statutes of Church Councils of the Thirteenth Century
B: Reports of Accidental Deaths in Various Sources: a Miracle Associated with Thomas Becket; Assize Rolls; Curia Regis Rolls; Coroners' Rolls

Many medieval texts make the reader aware of the precariousness of life in the Middle Ages, from the frequent accidents involving, for example, people falling from scaffolding during the building of the thousands of churches erected at this period, or suffering mishaps while out travelling or in domestic situations, to the effects of natural forces such as floods and pandemics. Here the focus is on some of the less dramatic but nevertheless tragic incidents recorded, including attempts to prevent such accidents, and the miraculous outcome of some.

A: The Bishops' Safeguarding Advice for Mothers and Babies: Statutes of Church Councils of the Thirteenth Century

Date: thirteenth century.

The admonitions regarding certain domestic dangers are recorded in the statutes of various diocesan councils, among the regulations approved by the bishops and clergy as necessary for the Church. The bishops remind the congregation that in an emergency, the mother and/or father of a child may baptise it, as long as they say the baptismal phrase properly, whether in Latin, French or English. The bishops evince some compassion for the sufferings of their flock, as is shown by Grosseteste's reference to the practice of allowing a baby to sleep beside the care-giver, *inde fiat eisdem mortis occasio unde putatur vite tenere prestari confotio* ('and thus cause the death of those whose tender life they intended to protect'). In the case of a Caesarean section being performed if the mother dies in childbirth, the statute says that the mother's mouth must be kept open: an additional phrase in the Statutes of Exeter (1225–37) [23], *ut puer in utero clausus aerem attrahere possit*, shows that this was so that the foetus in the womb could breathe. It is clear from visitation documents (cf. Section II.30) that each church was expected to hold a copy of the statutes of the church synods.

492 Fifteenth Century

Linguistic points: The phrase *prima tabula post naufragium* relates figuratively to the Church's theory of penance, where a *tabula* is a plank providing safety after the shipwreck of sin, and this image is applied to the sacraments (here, baptism). *confotio*, formed from CL *confovere*, occurs only in this one passage.

TEXT II.50A

Advice to pregnant mothers; preparation for emergency baptism of child and confession of mother
Statutes of Canterbury (1213–14) [59]
commoneat sacerdos quilibet mulieres pregnantes parrochie sue ut, cum tempus partus sui sibi instare intelligunt, sibi provideant quod aquam promtam habeant et paratam, et hoc propter imminens pueri periculum. et loquantur cum sacerdote de confessione, ne subito preoccupate non possint cum voluerint habere copiam sacerdotis.[1]

Translation: Statutes of Ecclesiastical Councils

Canterbury 1213–14
Each priest should warn pregnant women in his parish that when they understand that the birth is imminent, they should make sure they have water ready and at hand, because of the imminent danger to the child. And they should talk to the priest about confession in case they are suddenly caught unprepared and are unable to get access to the priest when they want it.

Emergency baptism for infants; Caesarean sections when the mother has died
Statutes of Salisbury (1217–19) [20, 28]
[20] cum baptismus ianua sit omnium sacramentorum et prima tabula post naufragium, quam sit necessarium patet ex verbis Domini dicentis: nisi quis renatus John 3:5 fuerit ex aqua et spiritu sancto non intrabit in regnum Dei. (…) cum ergo tanta sit virtus et efficacia huius sacramenti et cum ab ipso Domino sit institutum et eius sanguine rubricatum, precipimus quod cum honore et reverentia magna celebretur hoc sacramentum et magna cautela, maxime in distinctione et prolatione verborum, in quibus tota vis consistit sacramenti et salus puerorum. hec autem

---

1 With reference to women's confessions, cf. 42, *Confessiones autem mulierum audiantur in propatulo quantum ad visum hominum, non quantum ad auditum,* i.e. they should be visible when they are confessing (perhaps to protect them against abuse) but not audible.

II.50 | Safeguarding, Accidents and Death 493

est forma: Ego baptizo te in nomine Patris et Filii et Spiritus Sancti;[2] et in romano vel anglico sub eadem forma. doceat sacerdos frequenter laicos debere pueros baptizare in necessitate, patrem etiam et matrem sine preiudicio matrimonii. (…) [28] si mulier mortua fuerit in partu et de hoc bene constiterit, scindatur si infans credatur vivere, ore tamen mulieris aperto.

Translation: Statutes of Ecclesiastical Councils

Salisbury 1217–19
Since baptism is the door to all the sacraments and the first plank after shipwreck, it is clear from the Lord's words how necessary it is when he says, 'unless someone is reborn of water and the Holy Spirit he will not enter into the kingdom of God.' (…) Since, then, the power and efficacy of this sacrament is so great and since it was instituted by the Lord himself and authenticated by the shedding of his blood, we order that this sacrament be celebrated with honour and great reverence and with great care, especially in the distinct articulation and pronunciation of the words in which the whole force of the sacrament and the salvation of the children consists. This is the form of words: 'I baptise you in the name of the Father and of the Son and of the Holy Spirit' [in Latin] and in French and in English in the same form. The priest must frequently instruct the lay people that they ought to baptise their children in an emergency, the father and also the mother in an emergency, without the need for them to be married. (…) If the woman dies in childbirth and this has been properly ascertained, they should cut her open if the baby is believed to be alive, but the woman's mouth must be open.

The care of babies and toddlers; the dangers of co-sleeping
Statutes of Salisbury (1217–19) [29]
femine commoneantur ut pueros suos caute alant et iuxta se de nocte non collocent teneros ne opprimantur; solos in domibus ubi ignis fuerit vel solos iuxta aquam sine custode non relinquant; et hoc eis omni die dominica dicatur.

Mandates of Robert Grosseteste (1235–6) pp. 204–5
faciatis quoque in singulis ecclesiis frequenti predicatione commoneri ne matres vel nutrices parvulos suos in lectis suis iuxta se collocent ne forte eosdem, ut frequenter contigit, incaute suffocent et inde fiat eisdem mortis occasio unde putatur vite tenere prestari confotio.

---

2 In 746, Pope Zacharias, shocked at the standard of Latin he saw even among the clergy, wrote to Boniface (*Ep.* 68) of a priest in Germany *qui Latinam linguam penitus ignorabat et dum baptizaret, nesciens Latini eloquii infringens linguam diceret, 'Baptizo te in nomine patria et filia et spiritus sancti'*, thereby getting into theological as well as linguistic difficulties with regard to God's gender.

494 Fifteenth Century

Statutes of Coventry (1224–37) [21–2]
[21] Item districte precipiatur ut nulla mulier ponat puerum suum in lecto secum, nisi sit ad minus trium annorum vel circiter. [22] item si ponatur in cunabulo, ita fulciatur cunabulum ut non possit volvi et ita puer cadat super faciem suam.[3]

Translation: Statutes of Ecclesiastical Councils

Salisbury 1217–19
Women should be warned to take care in feeding their babies and should not place them next to themselves at night, in case the babies be suffocated; and they should not leave the children alone at home where there is a fire or alone next to any water without someone to watch them; and they should be reminded of this every Sunday.

Grosseteste 1235–6
You should also arrange to make frequent announcements in each church, warning that mothers or nurses must not place their little ones next to them in their beds in case by chance, as often happens, they should suffocate them out of carelessness and thus cause the death of those whose tender life they intended to protect.

Coventry 1224–37
Also it should be strictly commanded that no mother should put her child in her bed with her unless it is at least three years old or thereabouts. Also if the baby is placed in a cradle, the cradle should be propped up in such a way that it cannot overturn and thus cause the baby to fall on its face.

A warning of the dangers of domestic drunkenness from a tract on the seven mortal sins
Statutes of Coventry (1224–37) pp. 214, 220
quidam tractatus de vij criminalibus (peccatis): (…) et multotiens videmus ebrios se in aquis submergere et interfici et alios interficere, ignem in propriis domibus incendere et seipsos cum propriis pueris comburere. tota etiam die videmus patres et matres karissimos filios suos suffocare. Quid plura? 'miseros facit populos

Prov. 14:34 istud peccatum et maledictos' Unde Ysaias: 've qui consurgitis mane ad sectandam ebrietatem'. ecce maledictio sequitur: 'propterea captivus ductus est populus

Isa. 5:11, 13 meus'. ecce miseria. credo quod ex ebrietate proveniunt guerre, fames, et pestilentie, quia ubi plus regnat ebrietas, plus accidunt.[4]

---

3 Cf. *Mir. Hen. VI* 4.142, where a baby is accidentally hanged from its suspended cradle.

4 Cf. Boniface's *Aenigma* on drunkenness in Section I.7D.

Translation: Statutes of Ecclesiastical Councils

Coventry 1224–37
A treatise on the seven mortal sins. (...) We often see drunken people drown in water and get killed and kill others, or set fire to their own homes and burn themselves and their own children. For every day we see fathers and mothers suffocate their own children. What more need I say? This sin makes people wretched and accursed. And so Isaiah writes: 'Woe to you who rise in the morning to go in search of inebriation.' A curse follows. 'That is why my people have been led captive.' What wretchedness! I believe that drunkenness is the cause of wars, hunger, pestilence, because these occur more where drunkenness is more widespread.

Primary Sources and Related Texts

Councils and Synods (1964) part 1.
William de Pagula, *Oculus sacerdotis* (part 2), a hitherto unpublished handbook for priests from the early fourteenth century.

Further Reading

Blumenfeld-Kosinski, R. (2019) *Not of woman born: representations of Caesarean birth in medieval and Renaissance culture*, Ithaca, NY.
Green, M. (2013) 'Caring for gendered bodies' in *The Oxford handbook of women and gender* (2013).
Shahar, S. (1990) *Childhood in the Middle Ages*, London.

B: Reports of Accidental Deaths in Various Sources: a Miracle Associated with Thomas Becket; Assize Rolls; Curia Regis Rolls; Coroners' Rolls

Although these passages come from different literary and documentary sources, many of them will have involved the work of the coroner, in whose rolls the deaths were recorded. The role of the *coronator* or *coronarius* came to the fore at the end of the twelfth century as part of the development of legal administration under royal authority. At first the coroner was a county keeper of the pleas of the Crown,[5] but one of their roles was to hold inquests on dead bodies to establish the cause of death, and this became the primary sense of the word. Miracle accounts are a

---

5   Cf. R. Howden, *Chronica* 3.264.

496 Fifteenth Century

rather different source for records of accidental deaths, given that, unlike coroners' reports, miracle accounts usually have a happy ending. The later medieval period saw an increase in the number of miracle accounts associated with a particular saint, rather than just embedded in a hagiographical narrative: this is accounted for by the Church's requirement that miracles whose veracity has been ascertained were needed if the person in question was officially to qualify as a saint. These miracle accounts often, as here, provided vivid details about the lives of ordinary people, including women and children, who are less visible in certain types of text.

Primary Sources

Miracle accounts, from saints' Lives, and collections of miracles.
Curia Regis Rolls (TNA: KB 26).
Assize Rolls (TNA: JUST 1).
Coroners' Rolls (TNA: JUST 2).

B(a): Benedict of Peterborough, A Miracle Associated with Thomas Becket

Date: c.1174.

This work is preserved in several MSS, including those at Lambeth Palace (MS 135), London and Trinity College (MS B.14.37), Cambridge.

Author: Benedict (c.1135–93) was one of the eyewitnesses of Becket's murder in 1170; part of his account of the murder survives (cf. Section II.16B). The miracles he recorded occurred in the early 1170s, after he was appointed in 1171 to welcome sick visitors to Becket's tomb, to record miracles and where possible to check their authenticity, often by interviewing those involved, presumably in the vernacular, and recording their statements in Latin. When Benedict became Abbot of Peterborough in 1177 – where he played an important part in cultural and political life – he was replaced by William of Canterbury, whose miracle accounts are more literary and characterised by a number of rare technical terms, mostly medical and legal, that he adopts from Greek into Latin. Here Benedict adds the detail that he visited the home of the child to check on the veracity of the story; for this, cf. Ælred of Rievaulx in Section II.14, who visits Watton for the same purpose.

Linguistic points: *paropsis* is a CL word, derived from Greek, which is not uncommon in BML, perhaps picked up from a reading of Juvenal's *Satires*. *complicare* ('to fold back, or bend') is an interesting usage here: not only is it unusually applied to the opening of eyelids as if they were a kind of roller blind over the eye, but the form *complicuit* displays knowledge of the irregular perfect form. *decoquere* is a rather shocking word to find in this context, as it is usually applied

II.50 | Safeguarding, Accidents and Death 497

to more extreme conditions, e.g. 'to bake (bread)' or 'to execute by boiling'. The phrase *veritatem eliquare* applies figuratively the action of discovering something valuable by straining or melting, as perhaps in panning for gold.

TEXT II.50B(a)

The miracle of the drowned child

[4.63, p. 227] in balneo parvuli duo sedebant, alter annorum circiter trium, alter anni dimidii. sperans amborum mater quia minoris curam major esset habiturus, ad aream ventilandam exivit; et surrexit major ludere, minor autem in balneo submersus est. summam hordei mater ventilaverat quum sibi parapsidem praecepit afferri; currens puella ut afferret, triste nuntium [p. 228] reportavit, submersum videlicet infantulum. expalluit mater mox ut audivit, et infantem de balneo arripiens extra domum in via projecit. clamante et ejulante illa accurrunt mulieres vicinae; nam fere quicquid sexus erat virilis vel piscari perrexerat vel metere. suspendunt pedibus infantem et ad vitam revocare casso conatu contendunt. ait ergo quidam ex convicaneis, qui a Jerosolimis redierat, 'Utquid laboratis frustra? inferte infantem; diu est quod spiritum exhalavit.' tunc una ex viduis, 'Nonne sumus hic viduae quinque? flexis novies genibus beatum Thomam martyrem invocemus, et in ejus nomine novies orationem Dominicam repetamus, si forte exaudiat'; et factum est ita, et non surrexit puer. et ait una ex illis ad matrem ejus, 'Currens affer filum et infantem metire, ejusdem longitudinis candelam martyri promittens.'⁶ quod ut factum est, exivit continuo ab ore mortui sanguis et aqua, et post pusillum cilia puer complicuit et in ejulatus erupit. nomen parvuli Gillebertus, matris Wulviva, patris Radulfus, Brithwini filius de Serris.⁷ ipse vicum de Serris adii, ut veritatem diligentius eliquarem, et cognovi ex eorum testimonio qui affuerant, quia revera suscitavit eum martyr a mortuis et reddidit eum matri suae. erat autem ab hora tertia usque ad horam sextam in balneo decoctus; sexta vero extractus, usque ad decimam vel undecimam sine spiraculo vitae jacuit, donec tandem, ut praedictum est, resuscitatus revixit. audet adhuc forsitan obtrectatorum aliquis obviare, et anni dimidii infantem asserere dimidio die absque aura vitali vivere potuisse; qui enim incredulus est, infideliter et agit et loquitur.

---

6 This is a reference to the custom of measuring the sick or dead person and making a votive candle of the same length to present at the saint's shrine, in the hope of a cure.

7 Sarre is a village in Kent situated some 9 miles from Canterbury, at the point where the old road from the Isle of Thanet crosses the Wantsum channel, for which see Section I.3 and Bede, *HE* 1.25 (Section I.17). Ralph of Sarre, the baby's father, was a supporter of Becket when the latter went into exile and may be the writer of a letter to Becket (*Ep.* 33) in 1164; the letter incidentally mentions Rainald of Dassel, the imperial chancellor and patron of the Archpoet.

498 Fifteenth Century

Translation: Benedict of Peterborough

Two little children were sitting in a bath, the one about three years old, the other one and a half years. Their mother, hoping that the older one would look after the younger, went to winnow the threshing floor; and the older child got up to play, but the younger one was drowned in the bath. The mother had winnowed the top layer of barley when she instructed that a dish should be brought to her; the little girl came running to bring it and gave her the dreadful news, namely that the baby was drowned. As soon as she heard this the mother turned pale and snatching the baby from the bath she threw it down on the road outside the house. Hearing her cries and wailing, the women neighbours came running (for almost all the men had gone off to fish or reap). They held the baby upside down by its feet and tried in vain to bring it back to life. One of the neighbours, who had returned from Jerusalem, said, 'Why are you wasting your efforts? Bring the child in; it is a long time since it breathed its last.' Then one of the widows said, 'Are we not five widows here? Let's bend the knee nine times and call on the blessed Thomas Martyr, and let's repeat the Lord's Prayer nine times in his name, in the hope that he will hear us.' And so they did this, but the boy did not come back to life. And one of the women said to his mother, 'Run and bring thread and measure the child, promising the martyr a candle the same length as the child.' When this was done, blood and water immediately poured out of the dead child's mouth and after a little while the boy rolled up his eyelids and started to wail. The little one's name was Gilbert, his mother's Wulviva, his father's Ralph, son of Brithwin of Sarre. I myself went to Sarre to strain out the truth more carefully, and I found out from the testimony of those who had been there, that the martyr had indeed brought him back from the dead and returned him to his mother. For from the third hour to the sixth he was stewing in the hot bath; at the sixth hour he was pulled out, and he lay without the breath of life until the tenth or eleventh hour, until at last, as has been stated, he revived and came back to life. It is still possible that some critic will perhaps dare to contradict this and claim that a child of one and a half years could have lived for half a day without vital breath; but anyone who is incredulous acts and speaks without faith.

Primary Sources and Related Texts

Benedict of Peterborough, *Miracles of St Thomas*, RS 67.2 (1876).
William of Canterbury, *Miracles of St Thomas*, RS 67.1 (1875).
For a child's drowning reported in a Coroner's Roll, see e.g. *Select cases from the Coroners' Rolls 1265–1413*, Selden Society 9 (1896) 7; in a Curia Regis Roll, see e.g. *CurR* 13 no. 2272.

Further Reading

Koopmans, R. (2011) *Wonderful to relate: miracle stories and miracle collecting in High Medieval England*, Philadelphia.

Krötzl, C. and Katajala-Peltomaa, S. (ed.) (2018) *Miracles in medieval canonization processes: structures, functions and methodologies*, Turnhout.

White, C. (2017) 'Latin in ecclesiastical contexts' in *Ashdowne and White (2017).

B(b): Assize Rolls (excerpt)

Date: 1219.

TNA: JUST 1/1053 m. 1.

Assize Rolls were the records of itinerant justices, who travelled round the country, hearing court proceedings and making decisions. Here a woman's death, ruled as accidental, is recorded in the sparsest possible terms, and yet these few words almost read like a short story.

Linguistic points: The intriguing verb *accoillare* occurs only here. Although it appears in a text from Yorkshire, it is associated with AN 'acoillir', which was to become modern French 'accueillir'. The AN word has a wide range of meanings, such as 'to gather, welcome, attack' etc. Here it is used in the sense of 'to seize', for which cf. *Bedfordshire Historical Record Society* 41 (1961) no. 165 for the similar case of Emma of Hatch, begging bread from door to door, who dies, 'seized' by cold, near Beeston (TNA: JUST 2/3 m. 9).

TEXT II.50B(b)

Agnes dies of cold in the woods: a verdict of misadventure
[184] Agnes filia Reginaldi de Waleton inventa fuit in bosco de Hou.[8] Adam filius suus invenit eam. Nullus malecreditur quia accoillata fuit frigore. Judicium: infortunium.

---

8   Haw Park Wood is a piece of ancient woodland outside Wakefield, Yorkshire.

500 Fifteenth Century

Translation: Assize Roll

Agnes, daughter of Reginald de Waleton, was found in Haw (Park) Wood. Adam, her son, found her. No one is suspected of a crime, because she was seized by cold. Verdict: accidental death.

Primary Sources and Related Texts

Rolls of justices in eyre for Yorkshire (1218–9), Selden Society 56 (1937) 184.
Court Rolls of the manor of Wakefield (1274–1331), Yorkshire Archaeological
Society, record series, 1902–45: vols 29, 36, 57, 78, 109.

Further Reading

Brereton, G. (1942) 'Cueillir, accueillir: essai d'explication sémantique', *Medium Aevum* 11: 85–9.

B(c): Curia Regis Rolls (excerpt: 16 no. 101)

Date: 1237.

TNA: KB 26/117 m.6d.

The Curia Regis Rolls are a series of government documents containing the records of a range of legal cases brought before the Court of Common Pleas and the King's Bench, or the so-called Justices in Eyre (Justices Itinerant). The cases involve people from all strata of society, with the highest and lowest sometimes encountering each other in court or, as here, with the highest involving themselves in the lives of the lowest. It is true that the Curia Regis Rolls do not normally record accidents, but usually injuries that are recorded are the result of criminal assault, which is the category into which this episode might have fallen, were it not for the fact that a verdict of misadventure was recorded: the mother's recourse to corporal punishment causes her daughter's death, but the mother did not intend this outcome. The Archbishop of York (Walter de Grey) intervenes on her behalf, arguing that she is not guilty of a crime.

Linguistic points: CL *infortunium* becomes the technical legal term for 'misadventure' when the coroner decides on the cause of death: sometimes it is contrasted, as here, with *felonia*, elsewhere with *stultitia*. *fugere* with *ad*, in the sense of 'to seek sanctuary by fleeing to (a place)', is unusual – indeed, non-existent – in CL, where it is the flight from a place that is stressed.

TEXT II.50B(c)

A mother punishes her daughter for stealing apples: a verdict of misadventure
Juliana de Fencot fugit ad ecclesiam de Kyrkeby Fletam (i.e. Kirkby Fleetham, Yorks.) pro morte filie sue. Et super hoc venit archiepiscopus Eboracensis et supplicavit domino regi pro ea, eo quod filia ipsius obit per infortunium et non per feloniam, ut idem archiepiscopus dicit. Et super hoc commissa est eadem mulier custodie ejusdem archiepiscopi, ita quod, si dominus rex nolit ei facere gratiam suam, quod ipsa remittitur ad eandem ecclesiam in eo statu in quo prius fuit. et postea inquisitum est per patriam quod predicta filia ipsius Julianae non occidebatur per feloniam set, quia eadem filia sua ceperat poma in gardino cujusdam vicini sui, causa castigationis posuit capud ipsius inter tibias suas quamdiu ipsam verberaret, ita quod ibi extincta fuit per infortunium et non per feloniam.

Translation: Curia Regis Roll

Juliana of Fencot sought sanctuary at the church of Kirkby Fleetham as the result of the death of her daughter. And in connection with this matter the Archbishop of York came and interceded with the lord king on her behalf on the grounds that this woman's daughter died by accident and not as the result of felony, as this archbishop says. And on this account this same woman has been entrusted to the custody of the archbishop, so that if the lord king refuses to grant her a pardon, she should be sent back to the same church with the same status as she had previously. And afterwards it was discovered by the jury that the aforesaid daughter of this Juliana did not die as the result of felony but, because this girl had taken apples in the garden of one of the neighbours, the mother put her daughter's head between her knees while she beat the girl to punish her, with the result that she died there by misadventure and not as the result of felony.

Primary Source

*Curia Regis Rolls.

Further Reading

Kamali, E. Papp (2019) *Felony and the guilty mind in medieval England*, Cambridge.

B(d): Coroners' Rolls (excerpts)

The Coroners' Rolls recorded, in Latin or French, the inquests into all sudden and unnatural deaths to decide on the cause of death. Many records were presented to

502 Fifteenth Century

the Court of the King's Bench, where they are preserved in the National Archives series JUST 1 and JUST 2 for the medieval period, but others were stored in other series, such as those for the Justices in Eyre. For the period 1228–1426 there are about 260 rolls.

Date: 1270.

TNA: JUST 2/46 m. 3.

Linguistic points: The Coroners' Rolls are a good source of unusual vocabulary, mostly based on the vernaculars. *hamellus* ('hamlet') is the Latin form of *hamel*, a form that occurs in both AN and ME; however, it was the alternative diminutive (Latin *hamelettus*) that passed into modern English, attested from the mid-fourteenth century (cf. Section II.43A). *bracina* is the Latin form of the French 'bracin' (related to modern French 'brasserie'). *cuva* and *tubba* are both words for vessels used in brewing, the former (cf. Section II.47B) associated with AN 'cuve', but ultimately developing from Latin *cupa*, while the latter is of Germanic origin, with a particular vogue in the fourteenth century (cf. Section II.36, where it is used in a royal household), though the English form, 'tub', survives down to the present day. Although Middle and modern English have the form 'grout', the Latin, appearing in the early twelfth century, sticks to the form *grutum*, which has more in common with the OE 'grut'. The verb *scaturizare* appears as two separate words in BML: the first, as here, means 'to scald', probably related to *cauterizare*, while the second ('to bubble up or exude') is a compound of CL *scaturire* and the suffix *-izare*, derived from Greek. BML has the synonym *escaldare*, which also occurs in the Coroners' Rolls. *tinellus* (AN 'tinel') is a pole intended for carrying the tub of grout, but the records reveal that it was often used as a weapon. *appreciare* is a LL word, meaning 'to value'. Here it is used in connection with the custom of the 'deodand' (*deodandus* being a term evident from the mid-thirteenth century) whereby the objects involved in the death were given a monetary value; this sum was supposed to be given to the church as an offering for the soul of the dead person but was then forfeited to the king to be used for 'charitable' purposes: the practice was only officially abolished in 1846.

TEXT II.50B(d)

A girl is scalded in the brewhouse: accidental death and the ensuing inquest
(2 October 1270) [p. 14] contigit in villa de Etone in uno hamello qui vocatur Stapelho in bracina domine Juliane de Bello Campo die Jovis prox' post festum Sancti Michaelis anno l°iiij° circa horam nonam quod Amicia [p. 15] Belamy,

filia Roberti Belamy, et Isabella Bonchevaler portaverunt inter se unam cuvam plenam de gruto et deberent versare grutum in quodam plumbo bulliente ita quod Amicia Belamy titubavit cum pedibus et cecidit in dicto plumbo bulliente et cuva super eam. dicta Sibilia (i.e. Isabella) Bonchevaler statim saltavit ad eam et abstraxit eam a dicto plumbo et clamavit, et famuli domus venerunt et invenerunt eam scaturizatam fere ad mortem. dicta Amicia habuit jura sua ecclesiastica et die Veneris prox' sequente obiit circa horam primam. predicta Sibilia que erat cum ea invenit plegios Gervasium de Seltone et Robertum le Moine de Stapelho.

Inquisicio facta coram R. de Goldingtone coronatore per iiij vill' propinquiores, Etone, Wybaudstone, Chalvesterne, Colmmorthe, que dicunt per sacramentum suum quod nichil sciunt nisi ut predictum est. plumbum apreciatur xij d. et cuva apreciatur ij d., tinellus apreciatur ad obolum, et liberantur vill' de Etone.

Translation: Coroner's Roll

It happened in the village of Eaton (Socon) in a hamlet called Staploe in the brewhouse of Lady Juliana de Beauchamp on the Thursday just after the feast of St Michael in the 54th year (of the reign of King Henry III) around the ninth hour that Amicia Belamy, the daughter of Robert Belamy, and Isabella Bonchevaler were carrying between them a tub full of grout and they were supposed to tip the grout into a frothing lead vessel and Amicia Belamy tripped and fell into the boiling lead vessel and the tub (fell) on top of her. Sibilia Bonchevaler immediately leapt forward towards her and pulled her from the lead vessel and shouted, and the servants of the house came and found her scalded almost to death. Amicia had the last rites, and on the Friday immediately following she died around the first hour. This Sibilia who was with her found as pledges Gervase de Shelton and Robert le Moine of Staploe.

An inquest was held before the coroner R. de Goldington, with representatives from the four nearest villages, Eaton, Wyboston, Chawston and Colmworth, who say on their oath that they know nothing other than what has been said. The lead vessel is valued at 12d. and the tub at 2d., the pole used to carry the tub is valued at a halfpenny, and these are handed over to the village of Eaton.

Primary Sources and Related Texts

Select cases from the Coroners' Rolls A.D. 1265–1413, Selden Society 9 (1896) 14–15.
Bedfordshire Coroners' Rolls, ed. R. Hunnisett, *Bedfordshire Historical Record Society* 41 (1961) no. 35.

Calendar of Coroners' Rolls of the City of London (1300–78), ed. R. R. Sharpe, London, 1913.

Further Reading

Hunnisett, R. (1959) 'The medieval Coroners' Rolls', *American Journal of Legal History* 3.2: 95–124.

Select Bibliography for Volume II

Specific bibliographical information relating to the selected passages is given under 'Further Reading' in each Section in this volume. See also the Bibliography in Volume I.

Primary Sources

The primary sources for these writings are mostly manuscripts or administrative documents. For further information about medieval Latin sources:

Carpenter, D. (2020) *Henry III: the rise to power and personal rule, 1207–58*, New Haven, CT, 717–24, for a list of unprinted and printed primary sources.

Guide to the contents of the Public Record Office, vol. 1 (1963), London.

The National Archives website, www.nationalarchives.gov.uk.

The Oxford companion to local and family history (2008), ed. D. Hey, Oxford.

Sharpe, R. (1997) *A handlist of the Latin writers of Great Britain and Ireland before 1540*, Turnhout.

A Selection of Administrative Records in the National Archives Referred to in This Volume

Assize Rolls TNA: JUST 1

Chancery: Inquisitions post mortem TNA: C137; 138; 139

Chancery Miscellanea TNA: C47

Close Rolls TNA: C54

Coroners' Rolls TNA: JUST 2

Curia Regis Rolls TNA: KB 26

Exchequer: Accounts of customs officials TNA: E122

Exchequer: King's remembrancer, accounts various TNA: E101

Exchequer: Treasury of the receipt TNA E23 etc.

Fine Rolls TNA: C60

Gaol Delivery Rolls TNA: JUST 3

Ministers' and Receivers' Accounts TNA: SC6

Patent Rolls TNA: C66

Pedes finium (Feet of fines or Final concords) TNA CP25/1 etc.

Pipe Rolls TNA: E372

Special collections: ancient correspondence of the Chancery and Exchequer: TNA: SC1/6

For examples of vernacular-based Latin, refer in particular to the TNA class numbers E101, SC6 and JUST 1.

506 Select Bibliography

Printed Administrative and Historical Sources Used in This Volume

Calendar of the Close Rolls preserved in the Public Record Office (1272–)
Calendar of the Fine Rolls of the reign of Henry III, vols 1–, 2007–. Also available
   at https://finerollshenry3.org.uk.
Calendar of Inquisitions Miscellaneous (1219–)
Calendar of Inquisitions post mortem
Calendar of the Liberate Rolls (1226–1272)
Calendar of the Patent Rolls (1232–)
Close Rolls of the reign of Henry III (1227–72), 14 vols
Councils and Synods with other documents relating to the English Church, vol. 2
   in 2 parts: *1205–1313*, ed. F. Powicke and C. Cheney, Oxford, 1964.
Curia Regis Rolls of the reigns of Richard I, John and Henry III (in Latin)
Die Gesetze der Angelsachsen, 3 vols, ed. F. Liebermann, Halle, 1898–1916.
Foedera, Conventiones, Litterae etc., ed. T. Rymer, RC, 3rd ed., London, 1816.
Patent Rolls of the reign of Henry III, 6 vols (in Latin)
Recueil des Actes des ducs de Normandie de 911 à 1066, ed. M. Fauroux, Caen,
   1961.
Rotuli de oblatibus et finibus in Turri Londoniensi asservati
Rotuli Hundredorum (Hundred Rolls)
Rotuli litterarum clausarum (Close Rolls, 1204–27), 2 vols, ed. T. D. Hardy, RC,
   London, 1833–4.
Rotuli scaccarii regum Scotorum (The Exchequer Rolls of Scotland, 1264–1600),
   Edinburgh, 1878–1908.
Royal and other historical letters illustrating the reign of Henry III, ed. W. Shirley,
   RS 27.1–2 (1862–6).
The Rolls Series (*RS*) – a series of 99 titles, some of them multi-volume, begun
   in 1847, to publish historical texts, mostly from the period post-1066. Also
   available online: Cambridge Library Collection – Rolls.

Reference Works

The agrarian history of England and Wales, vol. 2: *1042–1350* (1988), ed.
   H. Hallam; vol. 3: *1348–1500* (1991), ed. E. Miller, Cambridge.
The Cambridge economic history of Europe, vol. 2 (1987): *Trade and industry in
   the Middle Ages*, ed. M. Postan and E. Miller, 2nd ed., Cambridge.
The Cambridge history of literary criticism, vol. 2 (2005), ed. A. Minnis and
   I. Johnson, Cambridge.
Encyclopaedia of dress and textiles of the British Isles c.450–1450 (2012), ed.
   G. Owen-Crocker, E. Coatsworth and M. Hayward, Leiden.
English historical documents, vol. 2: *1042–1189* (1981), ed. D. C. Douglas and
   G. Greenaway; vol 3: *1189–1327* (1996), ed. H. Rothwell; vol. 4: *1327–1485*
   (1979), ed. A. R. Myers; vol 5: *1485–1558* (1979), ed. C. Williams. London.

A handbook of dates (rev. ed. 2000), ed. C. R. Cheney and M. Jones, Cambridge.

The handbook of historical sociolinguistics (2012), ed. J. Hernández Campoy and J. Conde Silvestre, Chichester.

Medieval clothing and textiles (2005–), ed. R. Netherton and G. Owen-Crocker, Woodbridge.

Medieval dress and textiles in Britain: a multilingual sourcebook (2014), ed. L. Sylvester, M. Chambers and G. Owen-Crocker, Woodbridge.

Medieval Latin: an introduction and bibliographical guide (1996), ed. F. Mantello and A. G. Rigg, Washington, DC.

The new Cambridge medieval history (1995–2005), 7 vols covering the period c.500–1500, Cambridge.

The new Oxford history of England, vol. 1: *1075–1225* (2000), ed. R. Bartlett; vol. 2: *1225–1360* (2005), ed. M. Prestwich; vol. 3: *1360–1461* (2005), ed. G. Harriss, Oxford. Vol. 1, 695–703 includes brief accounts of Latin records of Church and state; cf. 703–4 for English and Anglo-Norman writing.

The Oxford dictionary of national biography (2004), ed. H. C. G. Matthew and B. Harrison. 60 vols, Oxford. Also www.oxforddnb.com.

The Oxford dictionary of the Middle Ages (2010), ed. R. Bjork, Oxford.

The Oxford guide to the Romance languages (2016), ed. A. Ledgeway and M. Maiden, Oxford.

The Oxford handbook of Neo-Latin (2015), ed. S. Knight and S. Tilg, Oxford.

The Oxford handbook of women and gender in medieval Europe (2013), ed. J. Bennett and R. Karras, Oxford.

The Oxford history of classical reception in English literature, vol. 1: *800–1558* (2016), ed. R. Copeland, Oxford.

The Oxford history of the laws of England, vol. 2: *871–1216* (2004), ed. J. Hudson. Oxford.

Secondary Sources of General Interest

Adams, J. N. (2003) *Bilingualism and the Latin language*, Cambridge.

—— (2007) *The regional diversification of Latin 220 BC–600 AD*, Cambridge.

—— (2013) *Social variation and the Latin language*, Cambridge.

—— (2016) *An anthology of informal Latin, 200 BC–AD 900: fifty texts with translations and linguistic commentary*, Cambridge.

Ashdowne, R. and White, C. (ed.) (2017) *Latin in medieval Britain*, Oxford.

Bailey, M. (2013) *The English manor, c.1200–c.1500*, Manchester.

Bates, D., D'Angelo, E. and Van Houts, E. (ed.) (2018) *People, texts and artefacts: cultural transmission in the medieval Norman worlds*, London.

Bourgain, P. (2005) *Le latin médiéval*, Turnhout.

Clackson, J. (ed.) (2011) *A companion to the Latin language*, Chichester.

Clanchy, M. T. (1993) *From memory to written record: England, 1066–1307*, 2nd ed., Oxford (4th ed. 2014).

508 Select Bibliography

Dickey, E. and Chahoud, A. (ed.) (2010) *Colloquial and literary Latin*, Cambridge.

Fontaine, J. (1970) 'Le latin médiéval et la langue des chartes', *Vivarium* 8: 81–98.

Garnett, G. (2007) *Conquered England: kingship, succession and tenure, 1066–1166*, Oxford.

Garrison, M., Orban, A. and Mostert, M. (ed.) (2013) *Spoken and written language: relations between Latin and the vernacular languages in the earlier Middle Ages*, Turnhout.

Gransden, A., *Historical writing in England*, vol. 1: *c.550–c.1307* (1974); vol. 2: *1307 to the early sixteenth century* (1982), London.

Houghton, L. and Manuwald, G. (ed.) (2012) *Neo-Latin poetry in the British Isles*, London.

Ingham, R. (ed.) (2010) *The Anglo-Norman language and its contexts*, Woodbridge.

—— (2012) *The transmission of Anglo-Norman: language history and language acquisition*, Amsterdam.

Jefferson, J. and Putter, A. (ed.) (2013) *Multilingualism in medieval Britain, c.1066–1520: sources and analysis*, Turnhout.

Lapidge, M. (ed.) (2003) *The cult of St. Swithun*, Winchester Studies 4.2, Oxford.

Morgan, N. and Thomson, R. M. (2008) 'Language and literacy' in *The Cambridge history of the book in Britain*, vol. 2: *1100–1400*, Cambridge.

Orme, N. (1976) *English schools in the Middle Ages*, London.

—— (2021) *Going to church in the Middle Ages*, New Haven CT/London.

Rigg, A. G. (1992) *A history of Anglo-Latin literature 1066–1422*, Cambridge.

Rosenthal, J. T. (ed.) (2012) *Understanding medieval primary sources: using historical sources to discover medieval Europe*, London.

Seiler, A., Benati, C. and Pons-Sanz, S. (ed.) (2023) *Medieval glossaries from north-western Europe: tradition and innovation*, Turnhout.

Short, I. (1980) 'On bilingualism in Anglo-Norman England', *Romance Philology* 33.4: 467–79.

Staunton, M. (2017) *The historians of Angevin England*, Oxford.

Stotz, P. (1996–2004) *Handbuch zur lateinischen Sprache des Mittelalters*, 5 vols, Munich.

Trotter, D. (ed.) (2000) *Multilingualism in later medieval Britain*, Cambridge.

Tyler, E. (ed.) (2011) *Conceptualizing multilingualism in England, c.800–1250*, Turnhout.

—— (2017) *England in Europe: English royal women and literary patronage, c.1000–c.1150*, Toronto.

Van Houts, E. (2000) *The Normans in Europe*, Manchester.

Vincent, N. (ed.) (2009) *Records, administration and aristocratic society in the Anglo-Norman realm*, Woodbridge.

Walker, S. S. (ed.) (1993) *Wife and widow in medieval England*, Ann Arbor, MI.

Some Online Resources

Anglo-Norman (includes online Anglo-Norman dictionary), https://anglo-norman.net.

Brepolis databases: source collections, Latin dictionaries and the Cross Database searchtool, via www.brepolis.net.

DEEDS (Documents of Early England Data Set), University of Toronto, https://deeds.library.utoronto.ca/charters/.

Dictionary of Old French (*Dictionnaire de l'ancienne langue francaise*, ed. F. Godefroy), http://micmap.org/dicfro/search/dictionnaire-godefroy/.

Domesday Book, www.domesdaybook.net, Hull Domesday project.

Internet History Sourcebooks Project, Fordham University (includes some British Latin authors), https://sourcebooks.fordham.edu.

Henry III Fine Rolls Project, www.finerollshenry3.org.uk. See especially the article 'The language of making fine': Fine of the month for June 2007.

The Medieval Academy of America: Medieval Digital Resources, http://mdr-maa.org.

Monumenta Germaniae Historica, http://clt.brepolis.net/eMGH.

The National Archives, www.nationalarchives.gov.uk/latin.

Oxford dictionary of national biography (2004) online (www.oxforddnb.com)

The Oxford English dictionary, www.oed.com.

Oxford Scholarly Editions Online, www.oxfordscholarlyeditions.com.

Patrologia Latina database, http://proquest.com/patrologialatina; http://documentacatholicaomnia.eu.

SCRIPTA, database of Norman documents from the tenth–thirteenth centuries, www.unicaen.fr/scripta/.

Vetus Latina database, via www.brepolis.net.

York's Archbishops Registers database, http://archbishopsregisters.york.ac.uk.

General Index

See also the Index to Passages Cited for specific references to authors.

For information on vocabulary and interlinguistic borrowing, grammar and style of British Medieval Latin, see the Introduction, and the Linguistic Points paragraph in each section.

Abelard 242
 and Heloise 48, 151
Adam Marsh 276, 461
Adam of Balsham 267, 272
Adam of Dryburgh 335
Adam of Murimuth 357
Aldhelm 96
Alexander Neckam 6, 131, 267, 273–6,
 319, 336
Alfred of Shareshill 235, 277, 280
allegory 179, 285, 336, 340
Amesbury Priory 404–6
Anglo-Norman, *see* languages
Anglo-Saxon Chronicle 20, 37, 56, 70, 112,
 229
Apuleius 300, 336
Arabic (*see also s.v.* translation) 12, 26,
 236, 243, 278
 derived from Arabic 289, 436, 463
 loan translation from 16
 the Qur'an 243
Aramaic 277
Aristotle 235, 277, 280
Arthur, Celtic leader 134–5, 137–8, 296
Asser, 127
Augustine of Canterbury 6, 76, 143
Augustine of Hippo 18, 49, 86, 91, 281,
 283, 300, 335, 336, 338
autograph (MS in author's hand) 8–9,
 40, 95, 228, 241, 374, 411
Avicenna 304

Ælred of Rievaulx 8, 150–63, 335
Æthelstan, king 295–7
Æthelwold, Bishop of Winchester 68

babies 42, 97, 158–9, 301, 354, 491–4
bakers 418, 446, 488
Basil the Great 180, 282

battle
 of Agincourt 360–74
 of Badon Hill 135, 137
 of Bannockburn 357–60
 of Bosworth Field 374–7
 of Brunanburh 284
bears, polar 460–1
Bede 8, 37, 56, 58, 127, 134, 152, 221, 384
Benedict of Peterborough 142, 179,
 496–9
Bernard of Chartres 131
Bethlehem 102–3
Beverley, Yorks. 284, 296
Bible, *see* Scriptures
Black Death, the 382, 388, 420
Boccaccio 135
Boethius 235–6, 277, 280
borrowings, linguistic 4, 10, 13–16, 23, 27,
 61, 204, 210, 309, 421, 455
Bracton, compiler of laws 191, 417
brewers 62, 318, 390, 446, 487
 breweries 466
British Celtic, *see* languages
Byrhtferth of Ramsey 127

Canon of Bridlington 357
Caradoc of Llancarfan 134
Catullus, poet 121
Chanson de Roland 21, 37, 38, 248
charters 44–7, 61, 247, 408
Chaucer, Geoffrey 4, 18, 135, 304, 319,
 448, 468
childbirth *see* pregnancy
children 6–7, 25, 51, 96–7, 143, 167,
 169–70, 197, 274, 286, 344, 346, 354,
 492–4, 495, 497–8, 501
Cicero 13, 236, 274
Cistercians 136, 204–6, 335
Constantinus Africanus 304

Indices 511

Cotton Library fire 228
cross-dressing 214–15, 310–11

Dante 13, 295
dialect 2, 3, 4, 10, 21, 229, 232, 277–8, 344, 366
Dionysius the Areopagite 282
Distichs of Cato 274, 336
Donatus 274, 465
dower (for women) 117, 193, 249, 252, 259, 348
drama, church 169, 285
drunkenness 116, 122, 358, *494–5*
Dunstan, Archbishop of Canterbury 68, 95

Eadmer of Canterbury 8
Eclogues of Theodulus 274
education 6–7, 18–19, 95–9, 131, 146, 150, 173, 219, 224, 235, 267–83
    BML as taught language (L2) 6, 15, 23, 24, 27
    spectrum of educational levels 24–6
embroidery 33, 290
Ennius 129
epic literary language or style 29, 79, 115, 120, 151
Euclid 235
Eusebius of Caesarea 180, 186, 279
Eustochium, friend of Jerome 103

fish and fishing 21, 29, 64, 122, 166, 168, 214, 250, 268, 272, 390, 399, 427, 460, 462–3, 482, 497
Florence of Worcester 127
foreign languages, attitude to 51, 76, 278
Frithegod 7

Gaimar 33
Galen 304
Geoffrey le Baker 358
Gerald of Wales 7, 12, 198, 203, 228, 346
Gerard of Cremona 280
Gervase of Tilbury 57, 346
Gesta Edwardi de Carnarvan 357
Gesta Romanorum 135, 344
ghosts 344–6
Gildas 43, 135, 242, 374
glass 286, 290, 449
glossary 9, 16, 248, 257, 366, 378, 409, 484
    of Ælfric of Eynsham 267, 268, 449

glosses 13, 56, 107, 257, 262, 268, 318, 366
    Latin glossed by English or French 107, 225, 269, 274, 319, 361, 425
Goscelin of Canterbury 15, 48–54, 68, 74, 151, 440
Greek, *see* languages
Gregory I ('the Great') 335, 358
Gregory of Nazianzus 48
Guy of Amiens 33

Hadleigh, Essex 260, 327, 457
Hebrew, *see* languages
Hengist 136
Henry of Huntingdon 56–7, 130–3, 134, 298, 394
Herbert of Bosham 173
    Liber melorum 179
heresy 300, 352–6
Herman the German 280
Hippocrates 238
History of the Britons 298
Horace 75, 111, 164, 198, 204, 229, 274, 336
Hubert Walter 190, 219
Humfrey, Duke of Gloucester 327, 367, 371
humour 29, 131, 209, 219, 268, 340

Ilias Latina 360
Inquisitions post mortem 55, 347–51
interpreter 3, 26, 61, 137, 244, 281
Ireland 2, 219, 225, 299–300
Isidore of Seville 129, 273, 340, 342, 393

Jack Straw 312, 314
Jerome 13, 103, 219
    Against Jovinianus 8, 203
    as translator of Greek Septuagint 86, 281
Jerusalem
Jews 197, 198–200, 383, 476–8
Josephus 282
Johannes de Sacrobosco 340
John Ball 312, 316
John Chrysostom 282
John de Trokelowe 357
John of Beverley 284–8, 297
John of Damascus 282
John of Ford 335
John of Salisbury 7, 95, 173, 203
John of Worcester 113
Julius Caesar 56, 74
Juvenal 26, 198, 204, 274, 336, 496

512   Indices

languages (vernacular)
*for specific examples of mutual linguistic
influence between Latin and the
vernacular languages, see Linguistic
Points in each section*
Anglo-Norman (AN)   2, 3, 4, 10, 19, 27,
58, 191, 242, 463
in Latin text   225, 328
knowledge of   20
written texts in AN quoted or
referred to   20, 38, 263, 357, 417
British Celtic/Welsh   4, 204, 220
knowledge of   219, 330
mentioned or cited in Latin text   221
Cornish   13, 21, 285
Dutch (Middle)   318, 352
Frankish   10, 13, 14, 21, 121, 204, 210,
271, 382, 393, 437, 462, 484
French (including Old and Norman
French)   10, 12, 19, 21, 34, 41, 60,
61, 210, 229, 232, 248, 267–8, 273,
424–5
in Latin text   225
see also Anglo-Norman *s.v.* languages
Gaelic   15
Gaulish (as ancient language of
Gaul)   10, 278, 398, 410, 448, 463
Gothic   10, 13
Greek
in BML text   12, 120
knowledge of   277
*for words derived from Greek see
Linguistic Points in each section*
see also translation
Hebrew   86, 273, 277–8, 336
Irish   13, 304
Middle English (ME)   13, 19, 20, 143,
214, 261, 262, 264, 289, 299
in Latin text   107, 316, 319, 320, 328,
341–2, 353–4, 362–3, 385, 414–15,
421–2, 429, 436, 438, 452–3, 456,
463, 466, 488
written texts in ME quoted or
referred to   135, 143, 264, 299
Norse (Old)   3, 60–1, 142, 344, 484
Old English (OE)   10, 64, 106, 269, 421,
477, 487
in Latin text   35, 45, 46, 58, 59, 107–9
written texts in OE quoted or referred
to   33, 56, 62, 428
Spanish   12, 277, 484

Livy   274
loanwords, *see* borrowings
Lollards   352, 436
London   165–70, 199
St Paul's   44, 165, 289
Tower of London   84, 166, 212
Westminster Abbey   449–50
Lord's Prayer, the   262–3, 353, 358, 497
Lorenzo Valla   17
Lucan   75, 129, 336, 360
Lydgate, John   299

Macrobius   236
Magna Carta   173, 247–51, 252, 256, 323,
392, 397
Manuscripts referred to:
Bern, Burgerbibliothek 568   134
Bruges, Openbare Bibliotheek 546
267
Cambridge, Corpus Christi College 16
241, 460
Cambridge, Corpus Christi College 26
241
Cambridge, Corpus Christi College 111
100
Cambridge, Corpus Christi College 139
126, 150
Cambridge, Corpus Christi College 184
243
Cambridge, Corpus Christi College 339
197
Cambridge, Corpus Christi College 341
8
Cambridge, Corpus Christi College 371
95
Cambridge, Corpus Christi College 452
113
Cambridge, Corpus Christi College 455
336
Cambridge, Gonville and Caius College
385/605   267, 273
Cambridge, Trinity College
B.14.37   496
Cambridge, Trinity College R.4.11
(James 644)   439
Cambridge, University Library
Dd.11.78   78
Cambridge, University Library Ff.1.29
439
Canterbury, Cathedral Archives: CCA
DCc/ES Rolls   480

Indices 513

Durham University Library MS Cosin
V.ii.6   127
Gotha, Forschungsbibliothek MS
1.81   74, 142
London, British Library
Additional 8877   461
Additional Ch. 24712   397
Arundel 12   366
Arundel 27   179
Arundel 60   20
Cotton Claudius D.ii   445
Cotton Claudius D.vii   357
Cotton Claudius E.iii   309, 366
Cotton Claudius E.iv   241
Cotton Domitian A.viii   130
Cotton Domitian A.xiii   197
Cotton Julius B.viii   416
Cotton Julius D.v   276
Cotton Julius E.iv   361, 364
Cotton Nero D.vi   416
Cotton Nero E.i (part 2)   142
Cotton Tiberius B.xiii   220
Cotton Tiberius C.vii   309
Cotton Titus A.ix   113
Cotton Vespasian B.xix   439
Cotton Vespasian E.x   179
Cotton Vitellius C.xii   179
Cotton Vitellius D.xv   228
Harley 641   299
Harley 1005   228
Lansdowne 398   164, 179
Royal 13.C.viii   378
Royal 13.E.ix   312
Royal 14.C.vii   100, 241, 242
Royal 15.C.vii   70
Sloane 1776   361
Sloane 3103   48
London, Corporation of London Record
Office MS Cust. 6   164
London, Lambeth Palace Library
135   496
London, Lambeth Palace Library
236   223
London, Metropolitan Archives
CLC/313/L/F/002/MS25516
289
London, Metropolitan Archives COL/
CS/01/006   445
London, St Paul's MS no. 1717
454
London, Westminster Diocesan
Archives, MS B.2   352

Oxford, Bodleian Library
Additional A.44   204, 209
Ashmole 833   394
Auct. F.2.14   70
Auct. F.3.10   237
Bodley 40   78
Bodley 462   312
Bodley 649   340
Bodley 791   285
Bodley 851   203
Digby 23   21, 37
Digby 235   276
Douce 287   164, 179
Hatton 26   261
Laud 636   20
Marshall 75   164
Oxford, Magdalen College 172   8, 37
Oxford, Trinity College 7   344
Paris, Archives nationales MS J516.B.40
(part 1) and J516.A.29 (part 2)   330
Paris, MS BN lat. 5506   40
Vatican, MS 4086   276
Vatican, MS Reg. lat. 703B   40
York Minster Library MS L2/1   129
Marius Victorinus   277
marriage   252–3
Martial   274
Matilda, empress, daughter of Henry
I   24, 112, 173–8, 395
Matilda, wife of Henry I   112, 115, 117
measures (of land, wine etc.)   21, 250, 455
Michael Scot   280
misunderstanding (linguistic)   6, 16
Modus componendi brevia   191
multilingualism   4, 19–21, 23, 27, 219, 245,
340, 459
music   48, 179, 312
Muslims   241–2, *see also* Saracens

Nativity of Christ   102–3, 262, 265
neo-Latin   22, 25, 30
neologisms   12–13, 16, 17, 27, 37, 58, 204,
238, 268, 305, 310, 487
Nigel of Canterbury   135, 209
Northern Annals   127

Orderic Vitalis   33
orthography   9, 96, 331
Osbern of Canterbury   48
Osbern of Gloucester   219, 273
Oswald, Archbishop of York   95
Ovid   26, 79, 203, 204, 229, 267, 274, 312

514 Indices

parchment 8, 85, 254, 404, 420, 451, 464
Paul the Deacon 56
Paula, friend of Jerome 103
Peregrinatio Aetheriae 105
Persius 129, 164, 360
Peter Comestor 262
Peter of Blois 24, 26, 209, 228
Peterborough Chronicle 13, 20, 112
Petronius 274
pilgrimage 44, 100, 168, 213, 220
Plato 236
Plautus 8
Pliny the younger 221
Pompeius Trogus 274
pregnancy and childbirth 155, 158, 239, 354, 492–3

Quintilian 120
Quintus Curtius 274

Ralph de Coggeshall 346, 356
Ralph Higden 309
reeves 62, 64, 408, 416–18, 420, 428–9
regional words in BML 21, 204, 466
Renwein, daughter of Hengist 136
Richard Ledrede, bishop 299
Robert Grosseteste, bishop 276, 280, 340
Robert of Cricklade 142
Robert of Ketton 235, 244
Roger of Wendover 241
Rome 6, 22, 51, 75, 103, 203, 219, 225, 330, 366

Sallust 129, 274
Saracens 102, 243, 383
satire 197, 203 (*see also* humour)
Scotland 21, 114, 295, 319, 357, 385, 427, 471–3
  the language of 21, 344
  the people of 358–9, 382
Scriptures/Bible 41, 75, 86, 120, 131, 144, 146, 151, 180, 210, 220, 222, 224, 229, 261, 279, 284, 336
Seneca the elder 274
Seneca the younger 236, 274, 336
Septuagint 86, 280–1
servitude 64, 316
Severn, river 15, 137, 250
sex 154, 236, 238, 289, 300, 480–3
Sidonius Apollinaris 274

sociolinguistic study of Latin 23–4
sociolinguistic terms
  calque (loan translation) 16, 45, 58, 106, 281, 305, 344, 407
  code-switching 14, 16, 26–8, 340, 407, 451, 455, 459
  diachronic and synchronic analysis 23
  diglossia 26
  semantic extension 60
Solinus 274
sorcery, *see* witchcraft
spelling, *see* orthography
spoken Latin 7, 21–2, 23, 120
  direct speech in Latin text 96–7, 101, 121, 137–8, 144, 147–8, 160, 180–2, 185–6, 198–200, 221–2, 230–1, 232–3, 236, 244–5, 345, 353–4, 497
  reported direct speech in Latin text 481–3
sport
  football 350, 378–81
  skating 170
Statius 274, 360
Stephen, king 121
Suetonius 274
Symmachus 274

Textus Roffensis 83
Thames, river 147, 166, 250, 446
Theodore, Archbishop of Canterbury 262, 303
Thomas Grey, *Scalachronica* 358
tournament 310–11
translation 8, 26, 61, 278–9
  between Latin and Anglo-Norman 20, 261–4
  between Latin and Arabic 235, 244, 277, 304, 385
  between Latin and Middle English 262, 347, 352, 451
  between Latin and Old English 20, 106
  from Greek 235, 277
typology 284, 285

Venantius Fortunatus 71
verse 394
  elegiac couplets 365
  hexameter 52, 80–1, 120, 134, 272
  trochaic line of fifteen syllables 71–2
Vikings 3, 55, 108

Vindolanda tablets 11
Virgil 75, 111, 136, 164, 204, 229, 360
virginity 157
vision 158, 160, 380
Vortigern 136

Wace 20, 33, 38, 120, 135
wages 385–6, 388–90, 448, 449, 450
Waleran of Meulan 134, 394–7
Wales 134, 137, 330–2
  the Welsh, 63–4, 134, 199, 205, 219
Walter Bower 358
Walter of Guisborough 309
Walter of Henley 408, 417
Walter Map 7, 198, 219, 228, 346
Wilfrid, Bishop of York 95
William de Longchamp, chancellor 3, 16,
  57, 197, 209–18
William Fitzstephen 164–72, 184–8
William of Canterbury 179, 496, 498
William of Jumièges 33, 40
William of Malmesbury 8, 11, 33, 113, 134,
  346
William of Newburgh 134, 346
William of Poitiers 33, 37, 41
William of Sens, architect 442–3
William Shakespeare 135, 364, 366, 369,
  374, 455
William the Welshman (Edward II) 468
wills 318–24

Wilton, convent of 48–54, 151
Winchester 55, 72, 198–200
wine 34, 116, 121, 136, 168, 250, 270,
  404–5, 434–5, 437, 463
witchcraft 289, 299–303
women
  alongside men 42, 63, 101, 114, 116–17,
    121–3, 127–8, 285, 389, 446
  and property rights in marriage 193,
    248–9, 252–3, 259–60, 348
  as feudal tenants 414
  as mistresses 344–5
  as wives/mothers/daughters 51, 136,
    144, 156, 176, 265, 300, 344, 349,
    482, 491–4, 497, 501
  as writers of wills 319, 321
  baking 429
  brewing 62, 429, 501–4
  dancing 170
  having sex 154, 236, 238
  in court 299–303, 352–6, 474–6, 480–3,
    501
  monastic 24, 48–53, 143–8, 150–63, 289
  of unspecified status 214–15, 236,
    238–9, 289, 349, 481–3, 485, 499
  royal 24, 51–2, 113–27, 174–8, 405,
    461–5
  working independently or for others
    64, 69, 71, 271, 389, 418, 429, 431,
    436, 450, 451–2, 466, 487, 502–3

Index of Passages Cited

Bible

Old Testament

Genesis
1:27 88
22 287
35:19 337

Exodus
9:12 212
17:16 176

Leviticus
16 198

2 Samuel
15:31 212

Job
3:24 87
14:2 337

Psalms
1:4 132
5:9 290
7:13–14 175
13:1 89
22:6 144
26:8 87
31:9 157
37:5 88
44:11–12 51
50:3 50
50:13 87
50:19 50
52:1 89
65:19–20 102
67:5 75
68:16 88
75:12–13 175
76:11 132
77:25 87

101:7 50
101:20–1 50
106:3 212
111:9 204
113:9 205
114:9 290
126:2 87
146:11 161
149:8 338

Proverbs
14:34 494
28:1 181

Ecclesiastes
5:12 338

Canticum Canticorum
2:12 337
6:9 75

Sapientia
4:3 281
6:9 175

Isaiah
5:4 154
5:11, 13 494
9:5 132
11:15 337
40:7 337
42:20 221

Hosea
7:11 154

Jonah
3:8 212

Malachi
4:2 75

1 Maccabees
3:60 156

Indices 517

New Testament

Matthew
5   **95**
6:6   **87**
7:20   **337**
10:16   **182**
16:19   **161, 230**
19:6   **338**
25   **337**

Luke
1:78   **75**
2:7   **262**
2:20   **161**
7:41–3   **224**
11:16   **340**
12:48   **221**
18:13   **185**
19:3–4   **286**
23:31   **212**

John
1:13   **337**
3:5   **492**
18:8   **181**
18:40   **224**
19:34   **182**

Acts
2:2   **225**
5:14   **143**
5:20   **158**
10:15   **161**
26:24   **230**

Romans
5:20   **158**
10:2   **157**
13:1–2   **75**
13:12   **153**

1 Corinthians
7:27   **338**

2 Corinthians
1:3   **175, 212**
4:4   **212**
11:29   **175**

1 Timothy
6:16   **87**

Hebrews
7:3   **337**
10:38   **341**
13:16   **176**

2 Peter
1:19   **75**

1 John
4:18   **79**

Revelation
2:28   **75**
20:13   **313**

Latin Writings

Abelard
Historia calamitatum 59   **242**

Adam of Eynsham
Life of St Hugh 5.8   **3**

Adomnán of Iona
The Holy Places 1.1   **105, 311**

Aegidius Romanus (Giles of Rome)
3.3.20   **362**

Alcuin
Letter 16   **142**

Aldhelm
On Virginity (prose) 19   **96**

Alexander of Neckam
The Priest at the Altar 8   **131**

Anonymous
Miracles of John of Beverley
(A) 296–7   **295**

Anonymous (of Whitby)
Life of Gregory the Great
9   **358**
20   **354**

Anselm of Canterbury
Monologion, preface   **25**

518 Indices

Arnulf of Lisieux
Epitaph **175**

Augustine of Hippo
Confessions 1.1 **49**
De civitate Dei 15.23 **300**
De doctrina Christiana
    2.11.16 **283**
    2.12.18 **280**
    4.10.24 **19**
Enarration on Psalm 149 **338**

Ælred of Rievaulx
Life of St Ninian, preface **8**

Bede
Commentary on Luke, PL 92.394D **221**
Commentary on Mark, PL 92. 155B **221**
Historia Ecclesiastica
    1.1 **242**
    1.14 **384**
    1.23 **76**
    1.25 **497**
    3.7 **74**
    4.24(22) **62**
    5.2–6 **284**
    5.3 **152**

Benedict of Peterborough
Miracles of Thomas Becket 96–101 **142**

Boethius
De topicis differentiis 1184a15 **232**

Boniface
Letter 75 **142**
Aenigma on drunkenness **494**

Book of St Gilbert 3 **6**

Catullus, Poem 4 **121**

Chronicle of Lanercost 344–51 **472**

Chronicle of Meaux
3.45 **29**
3.48 **468**
3.69 **311**

Cicero
Philippics 3.9.22 **25**

Domesday Book
f.40c **55**
f.50a **35, 55**
f.63c **121**

Eadmer
Historia novorum
    122 **112**
    276 **113**
    288–9 **114**
Life of Archbishop Anselm
    2.58 **15**
    1.19 **91**
Vita Oswaldi 37 **155**

Fleta
1.29 **478**
1.45 **45**
2.72 **468**
2.76 **409**
2.89 **408**

Geoffrey le Baker
Chronicon 7 **358**

Geoffrey of Monmouth
History of the Kings of Britain
    22 **171**
    44 **171**
    100 **38**
    107 **300**
Vita Merlini 1529 **134**

Gerald of Wales
De gestis Giraldi 1.119 **223**
De principis instructione p. 602 **101**
Descriptio Kambriae 1.9–10 **205**
Expugnatio Hibernica
    introduction **25**
    1.40 **26**
Gemma Ecclesiastica 2.36 **9**
Itinerarium Kambriae 1.2 **3**
Life of Archbishop Geoffrey
    2.9 **16**
    2.12 **210**
Speculum Ecclesiae
    2.23–4 **210**
    3.13 **136**
    3.14 **203**
    3.20 **204, 206**

Indices 519

Gervase of Canterbury
Chronica
  1 prol. **111**
  1.349 **209**
  1.504–8 **210**
Combust. 6 **15**
Gesta regum 2.60 **5**

Gervase of Tilbury
Otia imperialia
  1.17 **300**
  2.17 **171**

Gesta Edwardi de Carnarvan (i.e. Edward
    II) by a canon of Bridlington
    (46) **357**

Gesta Monasterii Sancti Albani
1.236–42 **241**
2.113 **22, 227**

Gildas
The Destruction of Britain 3 **43, 242**

Glanvill
5.5 **429**
6.1 **193**
7.1 **193**
7.5–6 **323**

Goscelin of Canterbury
Life of Edith **79**
Translation of Augustine of Canterbury
  412C **440**

Gregory I ('the Great', Pope)
Homily 1.6 on Ezechiel **336**
Regula pastoralis 3.22 **221**

Henry of Avranches
Life of St Birinus 364–6 **114**

Henry of Huntingdon
Historia Anglorum
  1.5 **45**
  6.17 **56**
  6.39 **392**
  7.32 **131**
  7.43 **56**

Historia Brittonum
37 **135**
41 **169**
56 **140**

Horace
Epistle
  1.7.65 **271**
  1.18.29 **338**
  1.18.82 **167**
Epode 7.1 **185**
Odes
  1.1.1 **245**
  1.4.5 **170**
  1.37.2 **170**
  2.7.21 **440**
  4.2.10 **167**
Satire 1.2.1–2 **199**

Hugeburc of Heidenheim
Life of Willibald 4 **243**

Isidore of Seville
Etymologiae
  12.2.5 **342**
  17.2.4 **393**
  19.23.4 **121**

Jerome
Against Jovinianus, preface **8**
Letter 46 **103**
Letter 57 **279**
Letter 107 **99**
Preface to Eusebius' *Chronicon* **279**
On Hebrew Names, PL 23.783 **337**

Joannes de Sacrobosco
Sphaera mundi 2 **341**

John Amundesham (i.e. Amersham)
Annales 1.126–7 **29**

John de Trokelowe
Annals 84–6 **357**

John Major
History 1.2 **15**

John of Garland
Dictionarius 9 **310**

520 Indices

John of Salisbury
Letter 272 **242**
Polycraticus 689A **192**

Juvenal
Satire
  3 **198**
  8.1–3 **337**
  8.20 **337**
  10.22 **338**

Lanfranc
Letter 1 **76**
Letter 19 **167**

Leges Henrici Primi, proem 2 **112**

Leo the Great
Sermon 82 **75**

Life of St Frideswide (A) 4 **12**

Lucan
Pharsalia 1.8 **185**

Magna Carta
7–8 **323**

Matthew Paris
Chronica majora
  1.272 **242**
  2.380–2 **210**
  3.306 **25**
  4.274 **242**
  5.709 **15**
  5.594 **434**

Miracles of John of Beverley, see
  Anonymous

Nigel of Canterbury
Speculum stultorum
  1521 **135**
  2141–8 **206**

Orderic Vitalis
An Ecclesiastical History
  2.256 **3**
  3.234 **224**
  5.20 **15**

6.458 **210**
6.550 **40**

Ovid
Fasti 1.493–4 **199**
Heroides 9.31 **230**
Metamorphoses 1.104 **274**

Paula and Eustochium
Letter to Marcella (Ep. 46 in Jerome's letter
  collection) **103**

Persius
Satire
  3.86–7 **167**
  5.58 **165**

Peter of Blois
Letter 14 **208**
Letter 66 **24**
Letter 87 **209**
Sermon 65 **26**

Petrus Comestor
Historia scholastica, PL 198.1540A **262**

Phaedrus
Fabulae 1.2 **230**

Plato
Gorgias 464d (from Latin paraphrase in
  Quintilian, *Inst.* 2.15) **168**

Plautus
Pseudolus 25 **8**

Pliny the elder
Natural History 7.17 **236**

Pliny the younger
Letters 1.3, 1.9 **221**

Polydore Vergil
English History 22.7–9 **369**

Prosper of Aquitaine
Poem, *PL* 51.614B **52**

Quintilian
Institutes 9.3.1 **121**

Ralph Diceto
Ymagines historiarum 2.97–101 **210**

Ralph Higden
Polychronicon 2.156–62 **5**

Ralph of Coggeshall
Chronicon Anglicanum 121–5 **356**

Reginald of Durham
Life and Miracles of Godric, Hermit of Finchale 79.170 **220**

Richard FitzNigel
Dialogue of the Exchequer
  1.10 **107**
  1.11 **108**
  2.24 **253**

Richard of Devizes
Chronicle 48–54 **210**

Robert Grosseteste
Dicta 137 **341**
Hexaemeron, proem **283**
Letter 8 **24**

Roger Bacon
CSPhil 479 **9**
Opus maius part 5 **307**
Opus tertium
  10 **6, 277**
  28 **277**

Roger of Howden
Gesta Ricardi 2.214 **209**
Chronica
  3.148 **209**
  3.264 **495**

Statius
Thebaid 9.300 **117**

Terence
Eunuch 732 **206**
Phormio 454 **230**

Tertullian
Against Marcion 2.19 **417**

Theodore of Canterbury
Laterculus Malalianus 14 **262**
Penitential 1.xv.4 **303**

Thomas Becket
Correspondence
  Letter 40 (to Empress Matilda) **24, 175–6**
  Letter 41 (from the Prior of Mont-Rouen) **175**
  Letter 49 (from Empress Matilda) **177–8**

Thomas Brinton
Sermon 99 **313**

Thomas Elmham
Historia monasterii S. Augustini Cantuariensis 209 **353**

Thomas Walsingham
Chronicon Angliae 26 **311**
Major Chronicles
  1.838 **310**
  2.666–72 **364**
  2.672–82 **369**
Ypodigma Neustriae
  459–62 **364**
  463–8 **369**

Turgot
Life of St Margaret of Scotland, preface **112**

Ulpian
Digest 1.4.1 **192**

Virgil
Aeneid
  1.702 **168**
  2.428 **116**
  5.205–6, 207–9 **117**
Eclogues
  3.92–3 **274**
Georgics
  1.1 **166**
  2.517 **166**
  3.13 **268**

522 Indices

Walter Map
De nugis curialium
  1.10 **25**
  1.25 **204**
  2.20–1 **205**
  4.3 **203**
  7.9 **204**

William Fitzstephen
Life of St Thomas 39 **58**

William of Canterbury
Miracles of Thomas Becket 5.30 **6, 18**

William of Malmesbury
Gesta pontificum
  1.15 **7**
  4.146 **100**
  4.153 **15**
  4.178 **142**
Gesta regum
  1 prefatory epistle **174**
  1.7 **140**
  2.122 **61**
  2.204 **303**
  3 pref. **3**
  3.245 **11, 34, 37**
  3.249 **43**
  3.257 **310**
  4 pref. **37**
  4.310 **37**
  4.342 **48**
  4.373 **37**
  5.438 **174**

William of Newburgh
Historia rerum Anglicarum
  preface **134–5**
  4.17 **210**

William of Poitiers
Gesta Guillelmi 2.42 **33**

Willibald of Mainz
Life of Boniface
  4 **120, 243**
  6 **22**

Wulfstan Cantor
Life of Aethelwold 34 **284**

Zacharias (Pope)
Letter to Boniface 68 **493**

Old and Middle English Writings

Alfred the Great
Prologue to OE translation of Gregory the Great's *Pastoral Rule* **4**

Anglo-Saxon Chronicle
s.a. 855 **70**
s.a. 1066 **33**
s.a. 1120 (*The Peterborough Chronicle*) **112**

Chaucer, Geoffrey
Prologue to the Canterbury Tales 434 **304**
The Friar's Tale 82 **319**
The Miller's Tale 3449 **143**

Gower, John
Vox clamantis
  Book 1 **317**
  5.577–8 **388**

Langland, William
Piers Plowman, C-text, passus 5, line 46 **290**

Lydgate
Troy Book **299**

Speculum vitae 61–78 **4**

Printed by Integrated Books International,
United States of America